BOOKS BY CHARLES ADDAMS

Creature Comforts (1981)

Favorite Haunts (1976)

My Crowd (1970)

The Groaning Board (1964)

Black Maria (1960)

Nightcrawlers (1957)

Homebodies (1954)

Monster Rally (1950)

Addams and Evil (1947)

Drawn and Quartered (1942)

THE
WORLD
OF
CHARLES
ADDAMS

THE
WORLD
OF

Chas Addams

Introduction by Wilfrid Sheed

ALFRED A. KNOPF · NEW YORK 1993

This Is a Borzoi Book Published by Alfred A. Knopf, Inc.

 Published in the United States by Alfred A. Knopf, Inc., New York, and simultaneously in Canada by Random House of Canada Limited, Toronto. Distributed by Random House, Inc., New York.

Library of Congress Cataloging-in-Publication Data
Addams, Charles, [date]
The world of Charles Addams / Charles Addams ; introduction by Wilfrid Sheed.
p. cm.
ISBN 0-394-58822-3
ISBN 0-679-74813-X (pbk.)
1. American wit and humor, Pictorial. I. Title.
NC1429.A25A4 1991
741.5'973—dc20 90-53166 CIP

Manufactured in the United States of America
Published October 31, 1991
First Paperback Edition, November 1993

With thanks to Barbara Nicholls for her help in the preparation of this book.
Tee Addams

This is Charlie's book—selections from his work of sixty years. The first drawing, the skater, was printed in *The New Yorker* when he was twenty-one years old; the last few appeared in 1990 after his death. With a few minor exceptions, I've put everything into chronological order. I hope that the drawings in this book are the ones that he too would have chosen.

Tee Addams
July 1991

Introduction

Charles Addams is one of a small handful of Americans—most of the others being jazz musicians—that you have to go abroad to appreciate fully. Virtually alone among the brilliant cartoonists from the *New Yorker* stable, and all our other stables, Addams travels beautifully—and not just to England, like Thurber and Arno, but to the Bermuda Triangle and the heart of the rain forest and to wherever headhunters are gathered together.

In other words, Addams speaks squarely to the inhuman condition, the Caliban or goat beneath the skin in all of God's children: and he doesn't just speak, he haunts. Nobody ever forgets an Addams cartoon, as I learned yet again when I leafed through this splendid collection and found myself not only saluting old friends but remembering exactly where and when I met them. Once you've encountered that stark line and that mordant wit in any of its manifestations, be it in the form of wayward ski tracks or inappropriate boiling oil, you have, for better or worse, a companion for life.

So what manner of strange man was this and how did he get that way? One might as well begin with the legend, if only because so many people believed it implicitly. I myself first heard and believed it at Oxford, which shows how widespread it was; you may have heard it in Borneo (I always imagined that Addams was big in Borneo).

The story in brief went that every year or so, Charles Addams would grow weary of tap dancing around the brink of insanity and slip over the edge for a breather, finally submitting a cartoon so bloodcurdling that he had to be put in restraints. There, naturally enough, Addams slept like a baby, to awaken each time like an ogre refreshed and resume his mad dance.

Nothing could have made the Charlie I knew happier than such stories, and anything he could do to confirm them was lovingly supplied. Since his motto in art as in life might have been "the less said the better," he let his somewhat unusual paraphernalia do most of the talking for him, and visitors to his apartment soon found themselves awash in, not to say silenced by, an embalming table here and a headsman's axe there and everywhere bats and skulls and other cheery bric-a-brac that his ghoulish fans had sent in (one shuddered to imagine what kind of fans this man attracted). And over this feast of necrophilia presided the host himself, a tall, laconic man with a head he might have drawn himself and a voice straight out of *Casket and Sunnyside,* the mortician's manual—a dry chuckle of a voice perfect for pitching funeral plots and layaway plans to newlyweds and small children on the way home from school.

In other words, Charles Addams was a consummate craftsman, or magician, who understood that it's not a bad idea to keep the illusion going between tricks if it helps the tricks to work better. Just as the greatest comedians give the impression of having recently escaped from lunatic asylums, it suited Charlie very well to be taken for a madman: he knew that the jig was up if anybody thought he was just kidding.

Nevertheless, students of that rather special art form, the Charles Addams interview, may note a recurrent phenomenon: in every case, the interviewer seems to start out with high hopes that the legend will prove true and that Addams will turn out to be every bit as weird as his drawings (if he doesn't, there's no story); and each time, the interview founders about halfway on the rock of Charlie's manifest sanity and profound good nature.

Although Addams never failed to oblige with his stock routine about choosing his dog because it hated children and marrying his third wife, the delightful Tee, in a pet cemetery, there really wasn't that much to it—maybe about ten minutes' worth—and it was manifestly just a gag. Charlie's doleful remark that he was simply "a normal all-American boy" was a nice piece of dramatic irony, because for all its considerable truth, there was no way anyone was ever going to believe it.

It didn't matter, of course, whether he was normal or not. The strangeness we had sensed all the way from England didn't really come from the imaginary life that the world had decided to bestow on him as a sort of tribute, but from the drawings themselves, in which he was decidedly not kidding, or winking at the audience, or pulling his punches. Groucho Marx once said that the difference between a professional comedian and an amateur was that if the script called for an old lady to crash down the hill and into a wall in her wheelchair, the professional insisted on using a real old lady. And this is what caused the sharp intake of breath with an Addams cartoon: this guy really means it, doesn't he— he is using a real old lady. And artistically speaking, he certainly was. In a period when Disney and lesser functionaries had domesticated evil and almost rendered it cute, Addams went all the way with his ideas, crashing them into the wall and leaving them there bleeding: there are no happy endings or jolly signatures—no evidence, indeed, that this thing was drawn by a human.

In the roped-off area that we have agreed to call "real life," an old lady probably couldn't have been in safer, kinder hands than Charlie's. But as anyone who's ever seen a movie biography knows, there is nothing harder to convey than the artistic talent and discipline it takes to break through the walls of reality and establish your own version. It is, therefore, much easier to imagine Charles Addams eating babies than to watch his hand doodling and turning a line this way and that, combining disparate things like "dwarfs and airplanes" (his examples) and, as he put it, "mauling clichés," until he sees what he wants—and then going after it with the glee of a bird dog and the skill of a lifetime, not to say the killer instinct of a man who once had to live on the thirty-five dollars *The New Yorker* used to pay for each cartoon it accepted. (That magazine's tradition of keeping its geniuses hungry was maintained right to the end of his career, and Charlie was *never* sure of acceptance.)

In one of the extremely rare interviews that lasted long enough for Charlie to take off his armor and get comfortable, he admitted that he had rather stumbled into the Gruesome by accident: it certainly wasn't what he had in mind when he started out as a child in Westfield, New Jersey, that least Transylvanian of states, scrawling pictures of his real passion—knights in armor and the castles they hung out in. His favorite author was Sir Arthur Conan Doyle, but not on account of Sherlock Holmes, with his corpses in the fog, but on the strength of the sunlit pages of *The White Company,* a novel of chivalry in which nobody pours boiling oil on anyone, except maybe Saracens, who don't count.

One probably shouldn't go too far in demythologizing Charles Addams. He *did* like to kill time in the local cemetery, where he tried to imagine what the people in the graves looked like, and he *was* caught trespassing once in the nearby Victorian house that would later be the home of the Addams Family (it's nice to think of the eight-year-old Charlie solemnly inspecting the house for its future tenants).

But what's really interesting about the graves is that young Charlie also suffered from claustrophobia, this being the closest he ever came to a neurosis. So imagining the inside of coffins presumably wasn't all fun. (Indeed, he built himself a tree house at a time when his friends were building underground hideouts.) And what's interesting about the Addams house is that it was only a few years older than he was—almost a contemporary, in fact.

Just as Charlie's ghost (which I wouldn't want to get on the wrong side of) should be spared any further revisionism, it should even more fiercely be spared the clumsy gropings of psycho-biography. But it would be equally cheating Addams to deny a dark side to his comic obsessions. Baudelaire once said that genius is the capacity to recall one's childhood at will, and this is the bell that Charles Addams's work strikes so universally, especially with the children he pretended to hate (but who loved him more than any grownup in the world). In line and in thought, Charlie returns to his childhood again and again—but in triumph now, looking it square in the eye and going it one better. If you thought that was scary, take a look at this. Insofar as Charles Addams has any message at all (and he resisted the possibility firmly), it would have to be that there is *nothing* in this world or the next too horrible to laugh at. And in case you're wondering, it might be worth adding that no one ever faced the prospect of his own death and whatever else more serenely, or died more peacefully, than Charlie himself.

The age of the Addams house may be even more revealing than the cemetery, because it may help to explain something quite cryptic that Charlie once said when he was asked what he wanted to be remembered for: "That I left a record of my times," he said in his inscrutable way. And the reader can only wonder what planet Addams was living on that experiences such times as these.

But if you look closely at the details and backgrounds in Addams's work, you will see what a punctilious draftsman he was and how much of his own inner and outer world he managed to convey on the sly and in the interstices, beginning with an America in which Addams houses were a dime a dozen and ending—for good, one imagines—with Noah's animals boarding a spaceship. As his great colleague Saul Steinberg once remarked of Charlie's drawings, "The modern architecture was drawn seriously and intelligently for the first time in a cartoon; it's never been done before." So a house didn't have to be old to catch Charlie's eye. He was in love with the sheer thingness of things, and Tee Addams remembers some hours he once spent in an aquarium studying the differences between saltwater and freshwater fish, for a drawing in which it really didn't matter. But just standing next to Charlie, one felt that his benign but piercing gaze was studying everything in this way and that the whole world was his studio.

At his best, which was for an incredibly high percentage of the time, Charlie's inner and outer worlds ran together into one, as when he fantasized in conversation about emptying one of his very best crossbows into the first mugger who intruded on his apartment—the old world redressing the balance of the new. But although he tended to his armor collection lovingly, oiling it regularly as if he might need it at any moment, he maintained an equal and opposite love affair with the great American automobile, the faster the better. Born as he was in 1912, he practically grew up with this curious invention, and he always made sure to surround himself with as many of his particular sweethearts, the cars of the twenties, as he could squeeze onto the estate—but always leaving room for one hellacious speedster, a Ferrari or a Bugatti, with which he would race anybody on any surface. So it seems like a mark of favor in high places that he should have died peacefully at the wheel of his Audi 4000, just before starting it and revving it home from New York to Bridgehampton: a still life with auto, his final composition.

One of the great pleasures of this chronological collection is that it allows us to trace Charlie's steps back from that last moment to his beginnings as an art student, when he was still sending in anonymous-looking illustrations to *The New Yorker* and hoping for the best. From these tentative beginnings, we can watch his line firming up and the wit starting to flow as his genius gradually asserts and defines itself, carrying Charlie along with it, no doubt wondering where all this is leading and what the hell he's going to do

next. Even when the Addams Family puts in its first shy appearance, there is no reason to suppose he ever expected to use it again, let alone knew that he'd created an American classic, a Halloween version of Norman Rockwell and Grant Wood, only somehow happier and better adjusted, which would someday develop its own unearthly life as a TV show and lead millions of people back to his drawings to find out where it all came from.

The real adventures of such a life occur at the drawing board, and the best possible biography of Charles Addams is the one you're just about to look at, if you've waited this long. Inquirers looking for anything deeper are likely to fall back baffled by the serene monomania of a pure artist. The schools Charlie went to were all art schools, or quickly became so (he began drawing in kindergarten), and the only job he ever admitted to might have been chosen expressly to dress up the Addams dossier: the job required him to touch up the photos of corpses for a detective magazine in order to make them look more palatable. "I was definitely working against the grain," I can almost hear him saying in his best friendly-undertaker voice.

Once he had hit his stride, outside events really had to hammer to get his attention on his daily rounds "to and from the barn," as Flannery O'Connor once described the creative life. World War II did so fairly spectacularly by enlisting him to help make instructional films about syphilis and such for the U.S. Army Signal Corps, thus drawing a line between his early scatter-gun brilliance and the Addams Era, when you had only to mention his name to start people laughing. Strangely. Charlie had clearly used his early retirement to regroup and he came out of it firing on all cylinders, in full control and possession of his talent.

And there he stayed, with only two other events adding the smallest ripples to the lava-like flow raining down from Addams onto the public—namely, the arrival and the departure of William Shawn as editor of *The New Yorker*. Shawn was by most accounts a great and lovable editor, but he was also a bit of a fussbudget and he didn't like jokes about death (or "for some reason spaceships," said Charlie quizzically), and he didn't want any part of the Addams Family after it had appeared on dreaded television in 1964 and gone

commercial on him. Charlie, it goes without saying, didn't strictly need *The New Yorker* by that time—he could have drawn for any magazine he liked—but it was his home, his graveyard of choice, and asking him to move would have been like transferring the Addams Family to a split-level. So he soldiered on at the old stand, accepting the occasional rejection with good-natured groans and contributing some of his best and most ingenious work during the Shawn years.

And artistically speaking, he was, as usual, right. The effect of an Addams cartoon exploding from the ominously quiet pages of *The New Yorker* could not be duplicated anywhere else, not even the *National Geographic.* But it's a pleasure to report that he finally outstayed Shawn's fuddy-duddy qualms and was shouted to an Indian summer of morbidity by the current editor, Robert Gottlieb, who agreed that in his particular hands the more death the merrier. Charlie had always struck me as one of the happiest men I knew anyhow, but this was a splendid extra gift for his last years, allowing him to end his career on the upbeat and leave his audience laughing: and he celebrated as usual by showering his friends with *jeux d'esprit,* funny drawings of a kind that kids pass back and forth under their desks until the teacher asks why the whole class is laughing. And there is Charlie, looking around innocently, the eternal indestructible imp who hasn't learned to behave himself properly in seventy years.

In case you're wondering, Charlie did get off some snappy one-liners, unadorned by pictures, in that early American Gothic voice of his, but on reflection I decided not to use them. If Charlie really wanted to amuse you he drew you a cartoon, and if the cartoon needed a caption, he felt it had failed in some way, even if the caption was brilliant. And since this instinct was at the very heart of his aesthetic, of his integrity, I'll honor it here.

We may want Harpo Marx to say something but it's really better if he doesn't. And it's really better just to look at Charlie's drawings without any further talk, except to add this: if you *only* had the drawings to go on, you couldn't imagine calling him Charlie; but if you ever met him, you couldn't imagine calling him anything else. And if I had all day, I couldn't describe him better than that.

Wilfrid Sheed

THE
WORLD
OF
CHARLES
ADDAMS

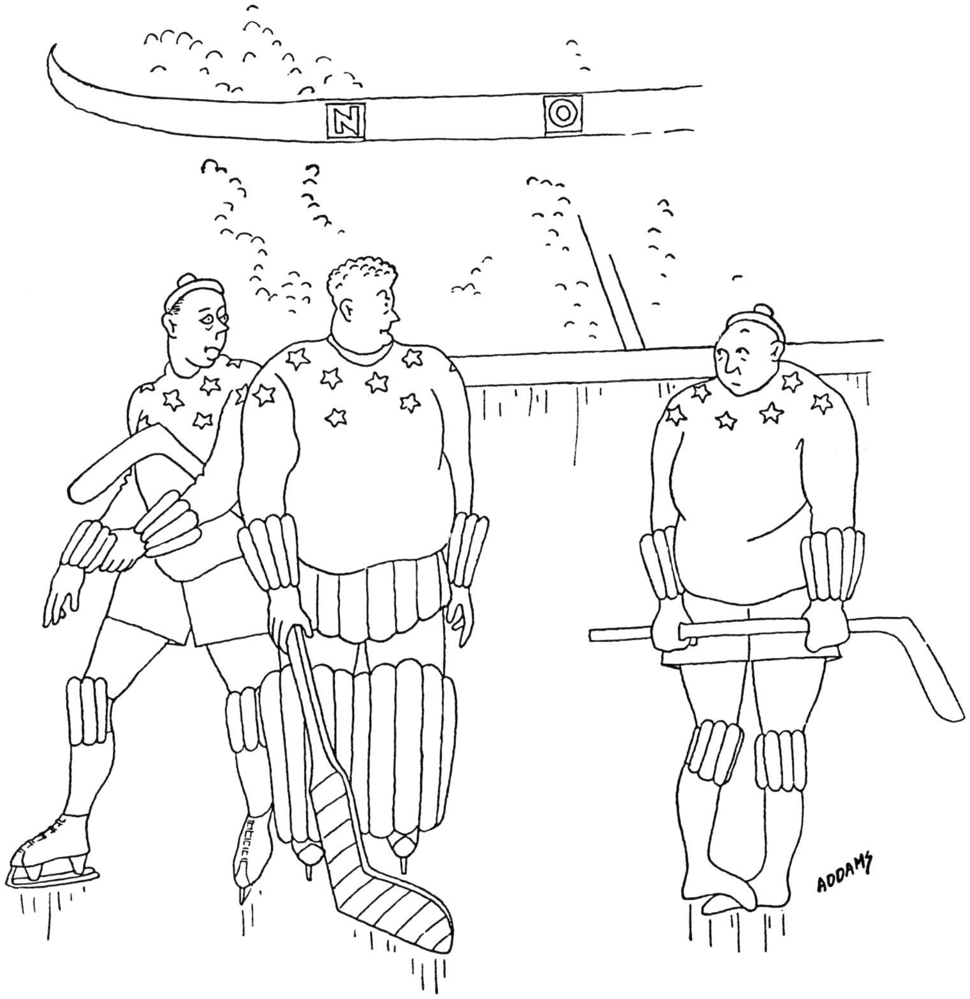
N
O
ADDAMS

"I forgot my skates."

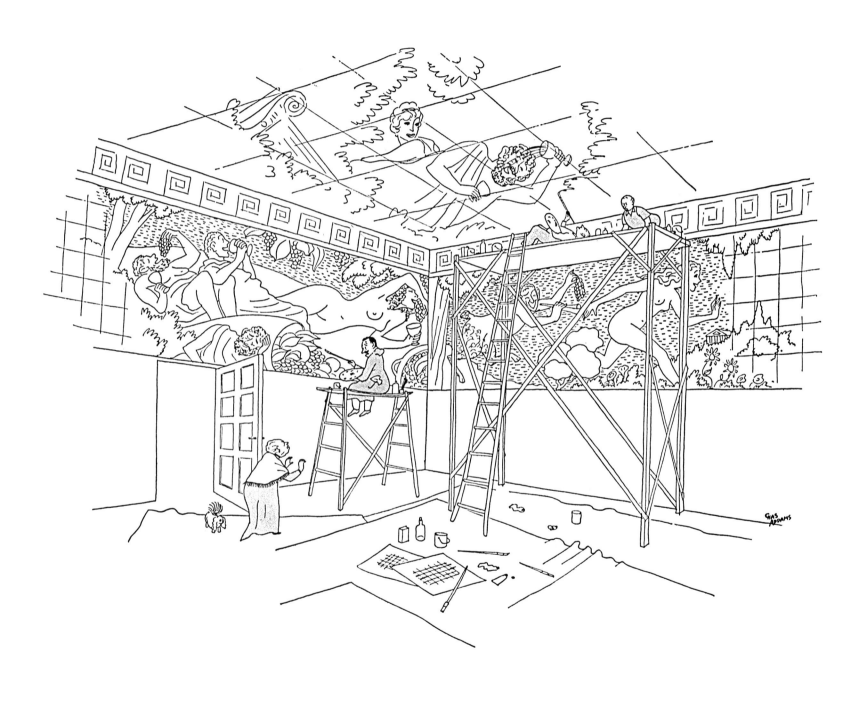

"No, no, no! I just wanted the room tinted a light buff."

"Meow"

"Let's have a pillow fight."

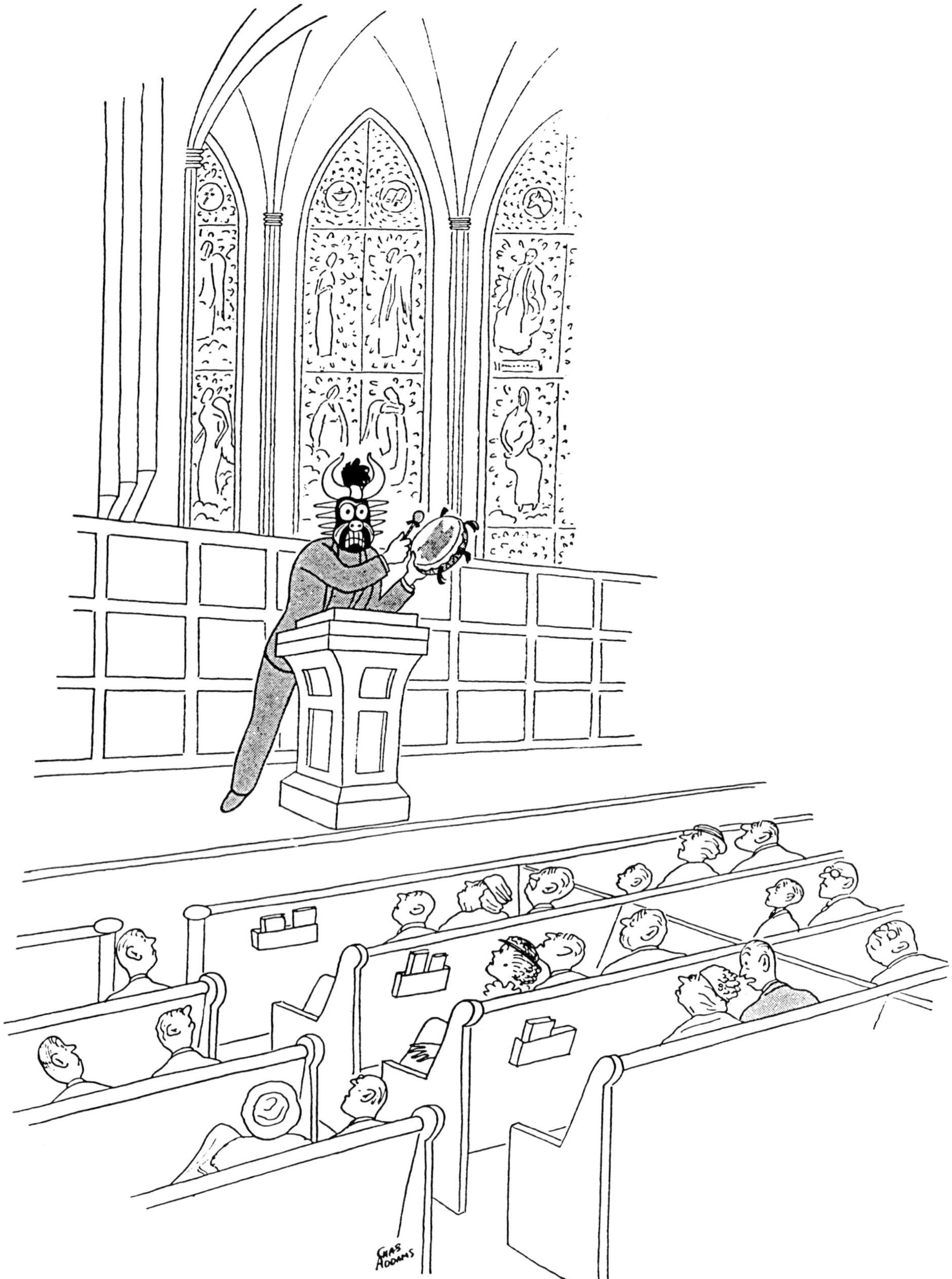
CHAS ADDAMS

"Dr. Carberry has been showing much more originality in his sermons lately, hasn't he?"

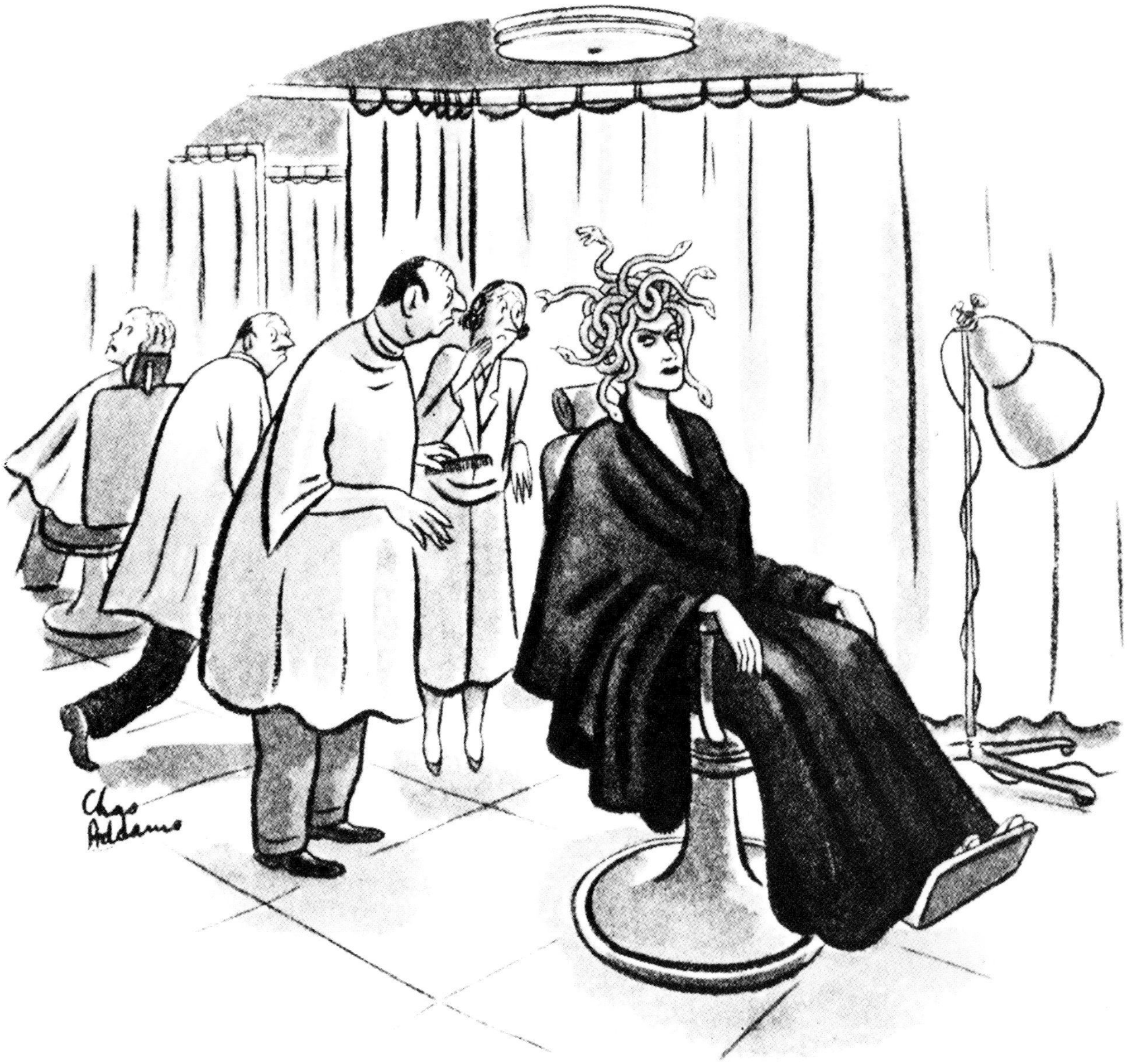
Chas Addams

"Psst! Brother Sebastian has done his room over again."

"Pombo learn things fast, eh, doctor?"

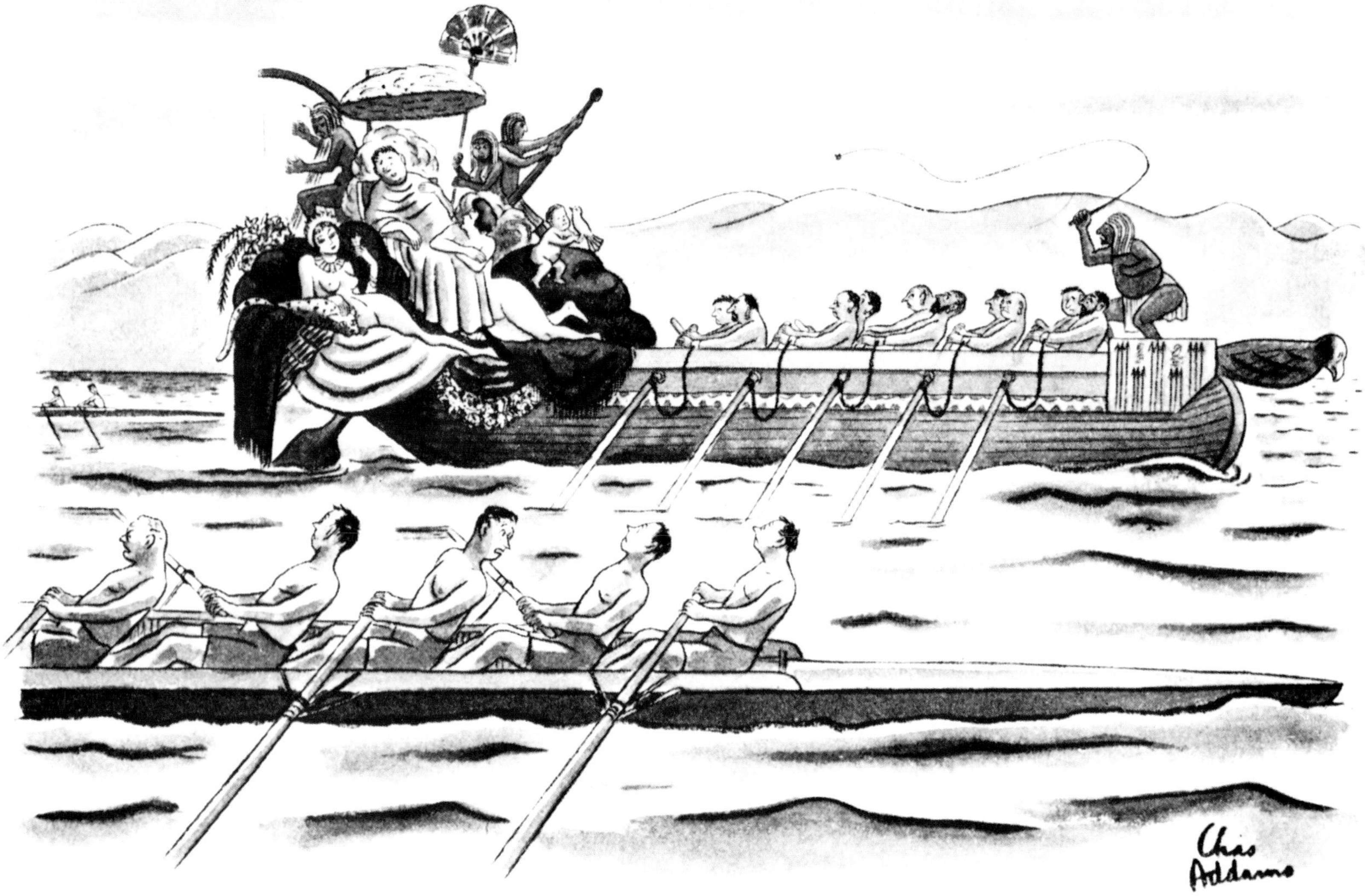
Chas Addams

"I imagine it's the University of Southern California."

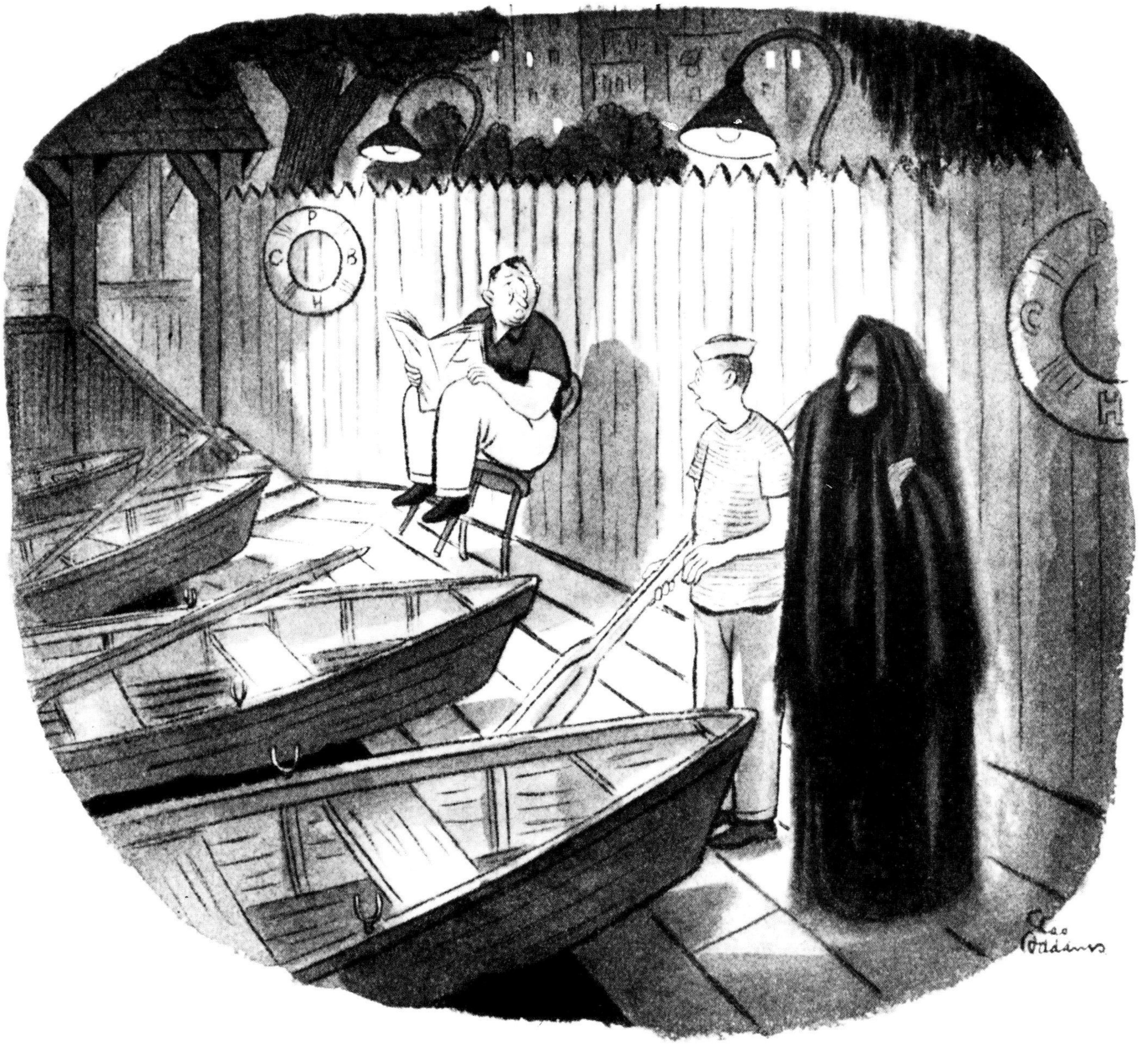
P C B H

"Say, Donovan, do we have one with muffled oars?"

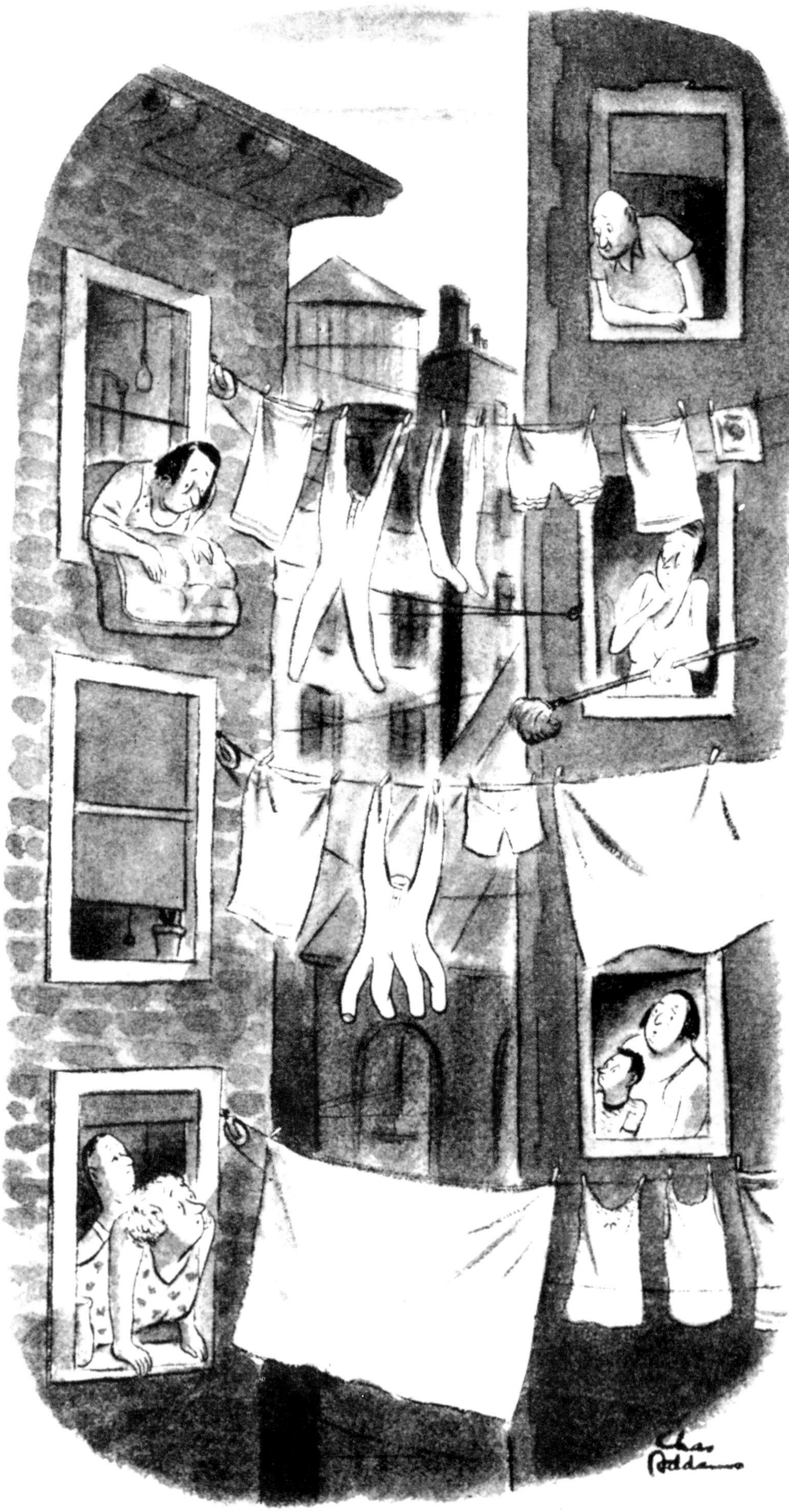
Chas Addams

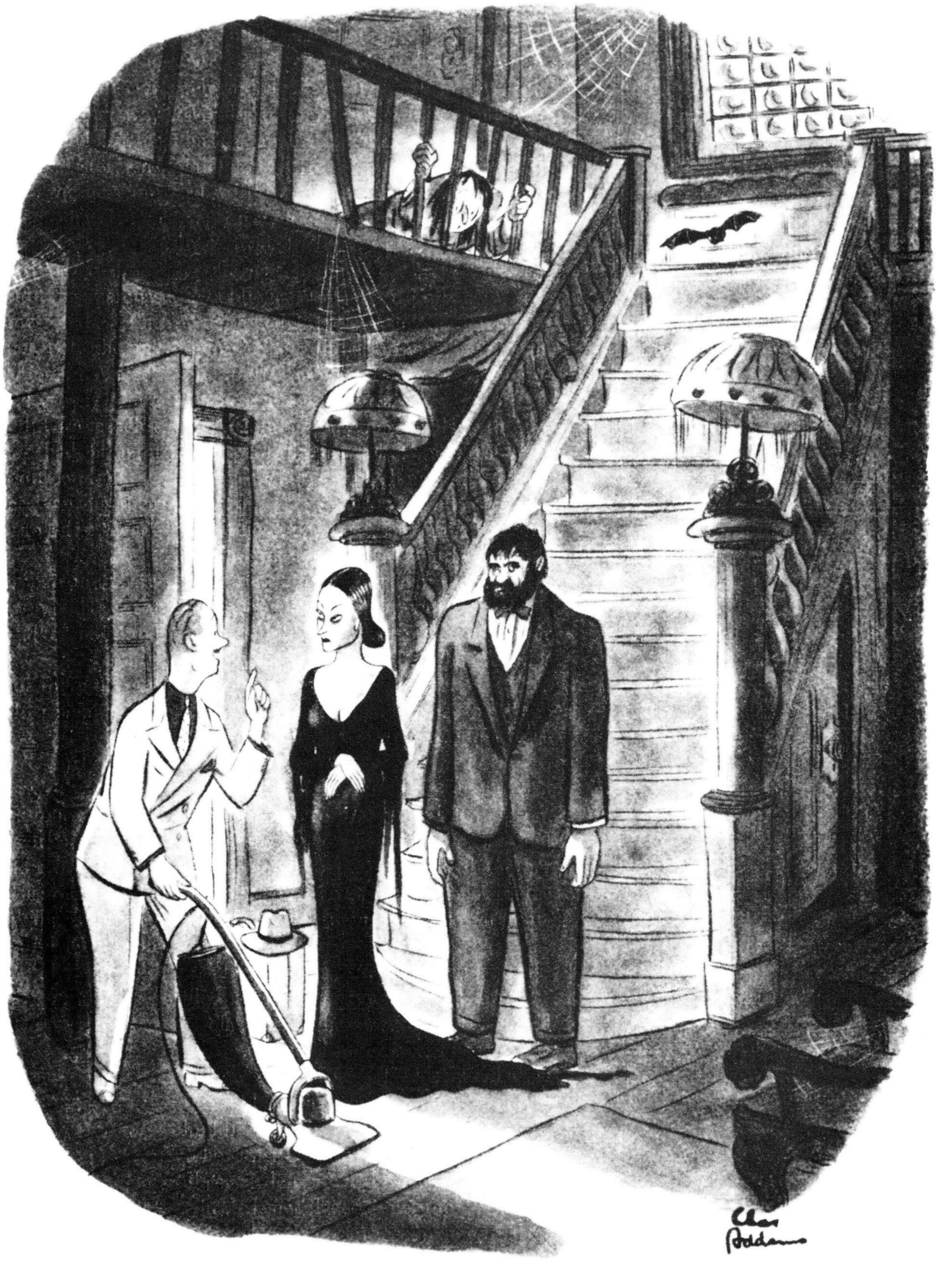
Chas Addams

"Vibrationless, noiseless, and a great time and back saver.
No well-appointed home should be without it."

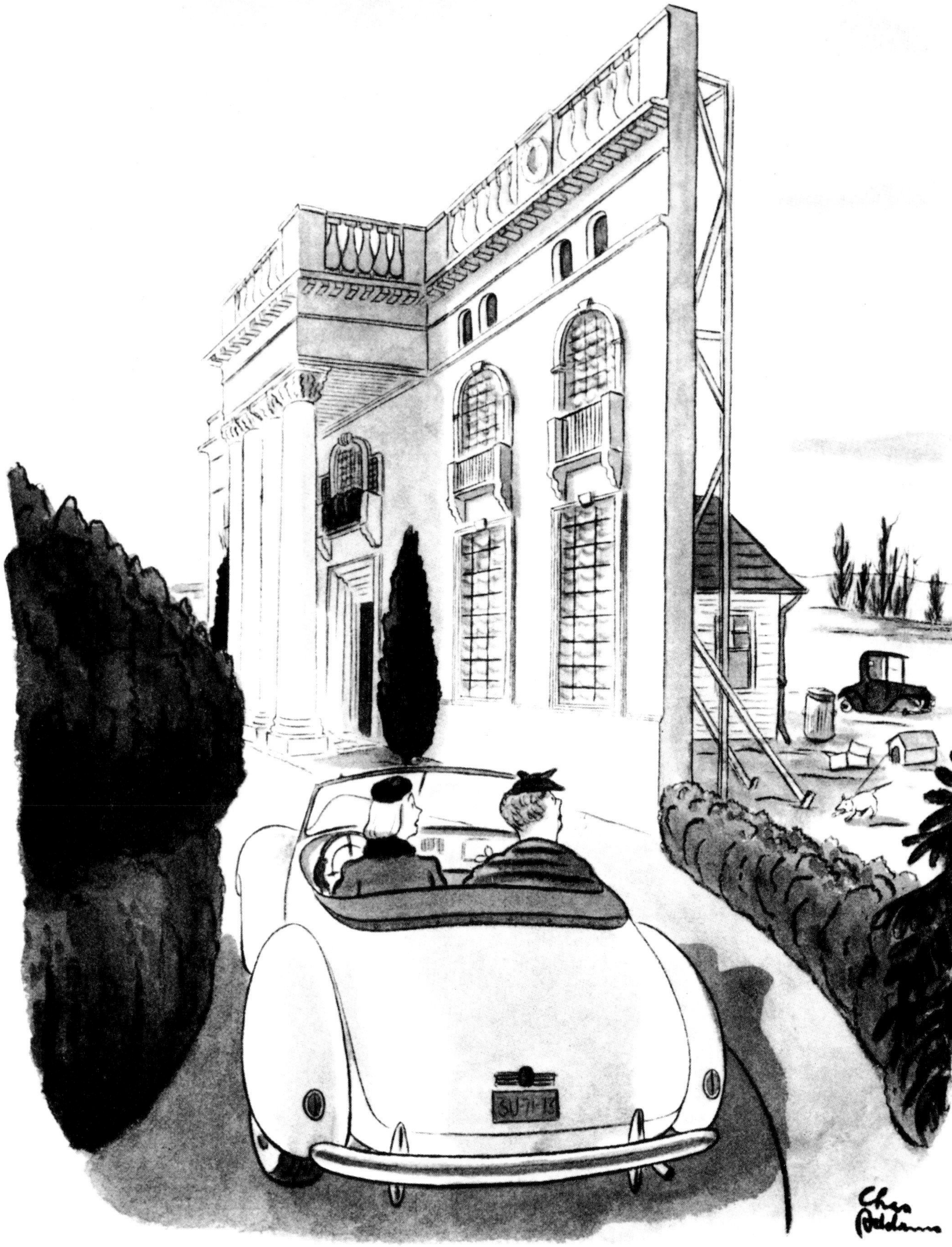

"I have the impression that they're not very substantial people."

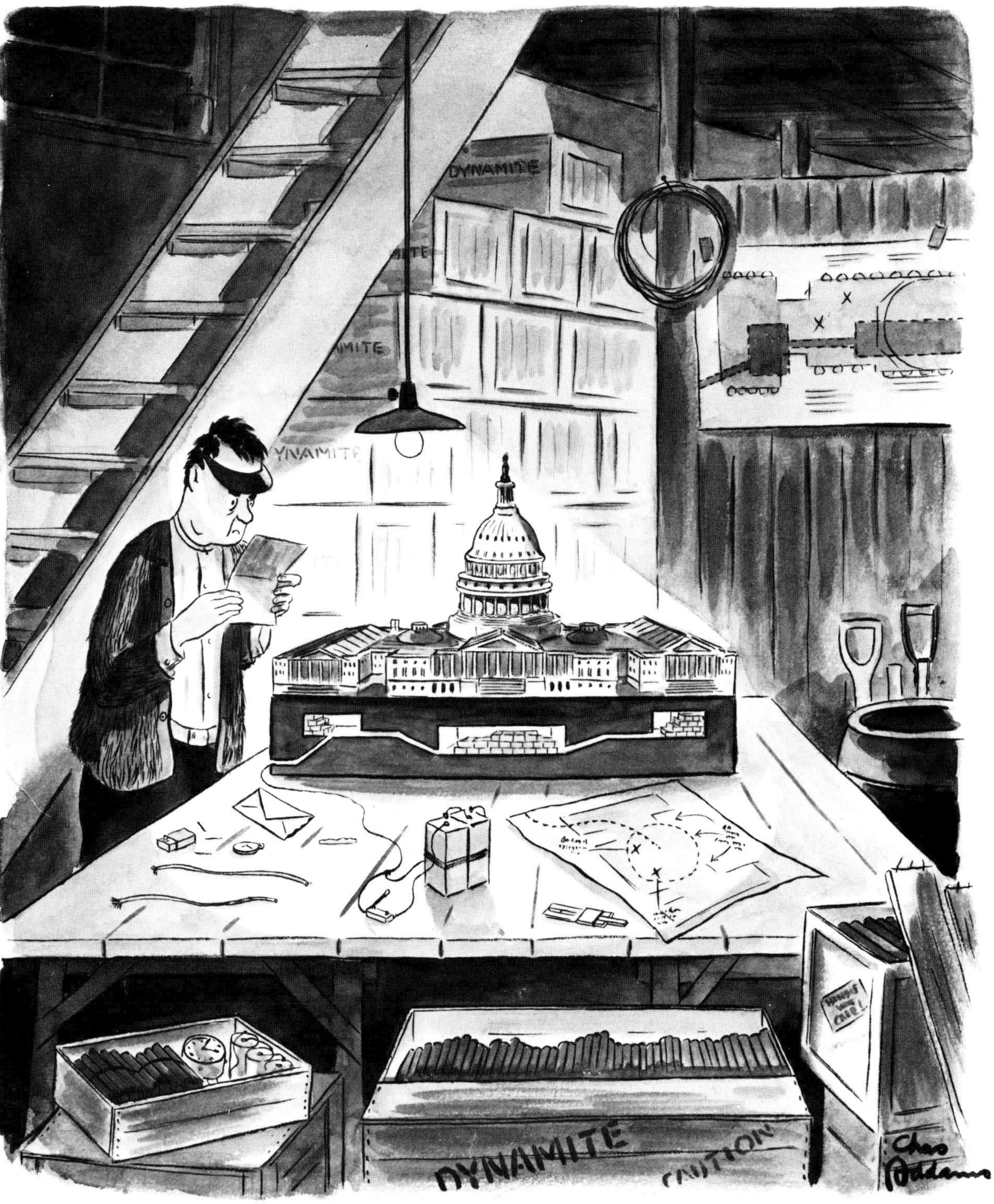
DYNAMITE
DYNAMITE
CAUTION
Chas Addams

"Dear Fellow Alumnus:
Your face was among the missing at our annual reunion last June. Won't you help us to keep 'tabs' on members of the class of '17 by telling us what you are doing now? . . ."

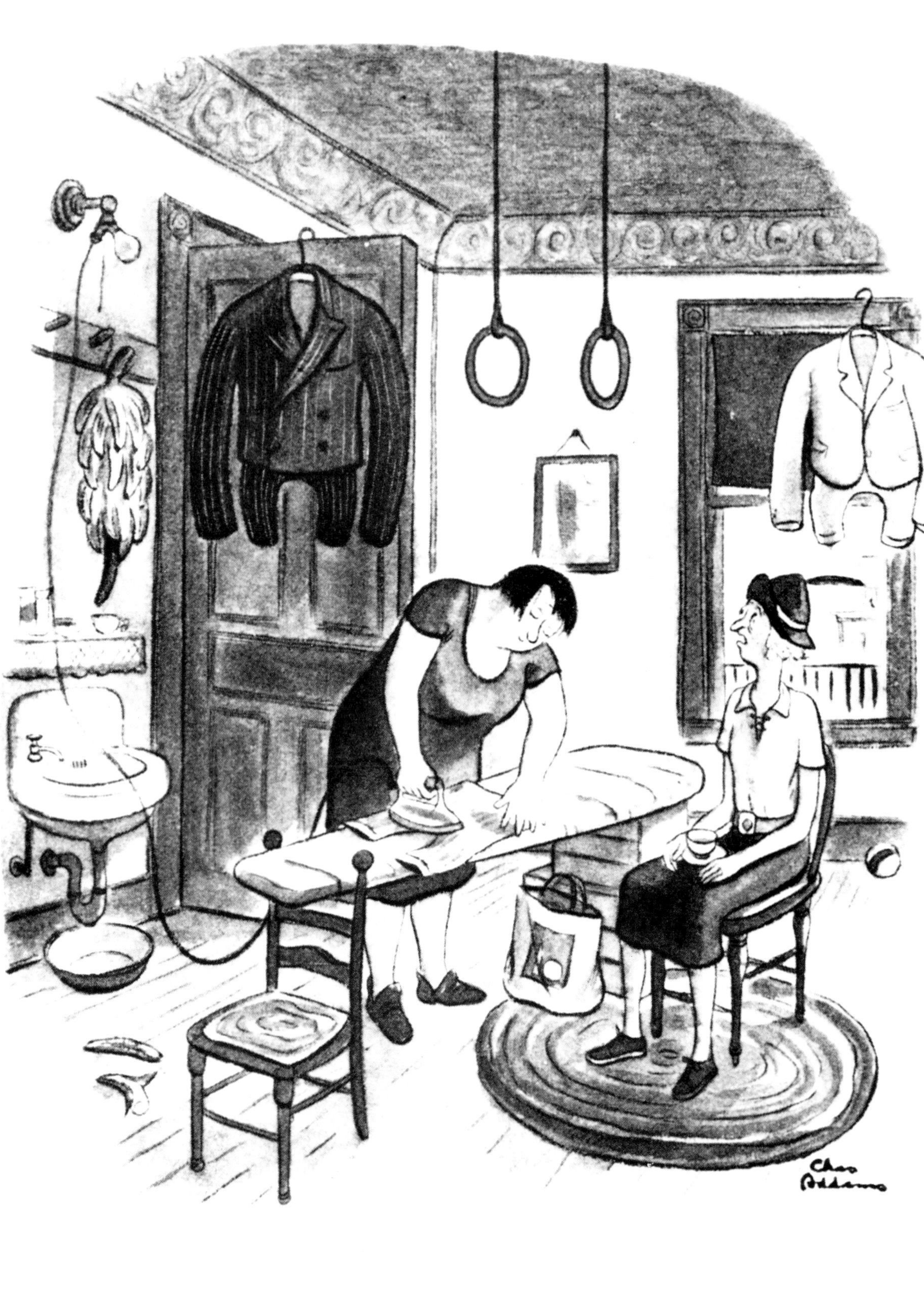
Chas Addams

"Tell me more about your husband, Mrs. Briggs."

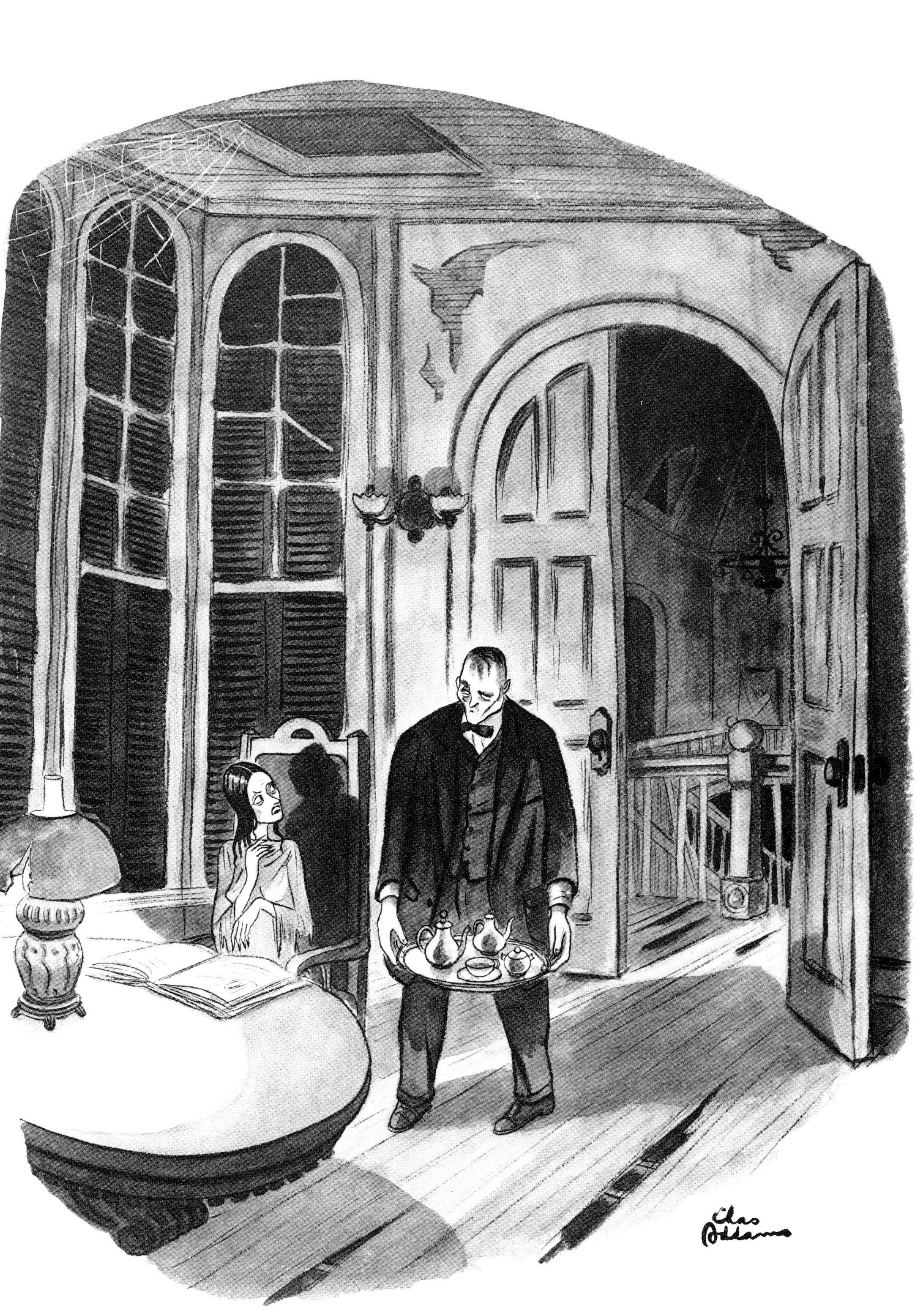
Chas Addams

"Oh, it's you! For a moment you gave me quite a start."

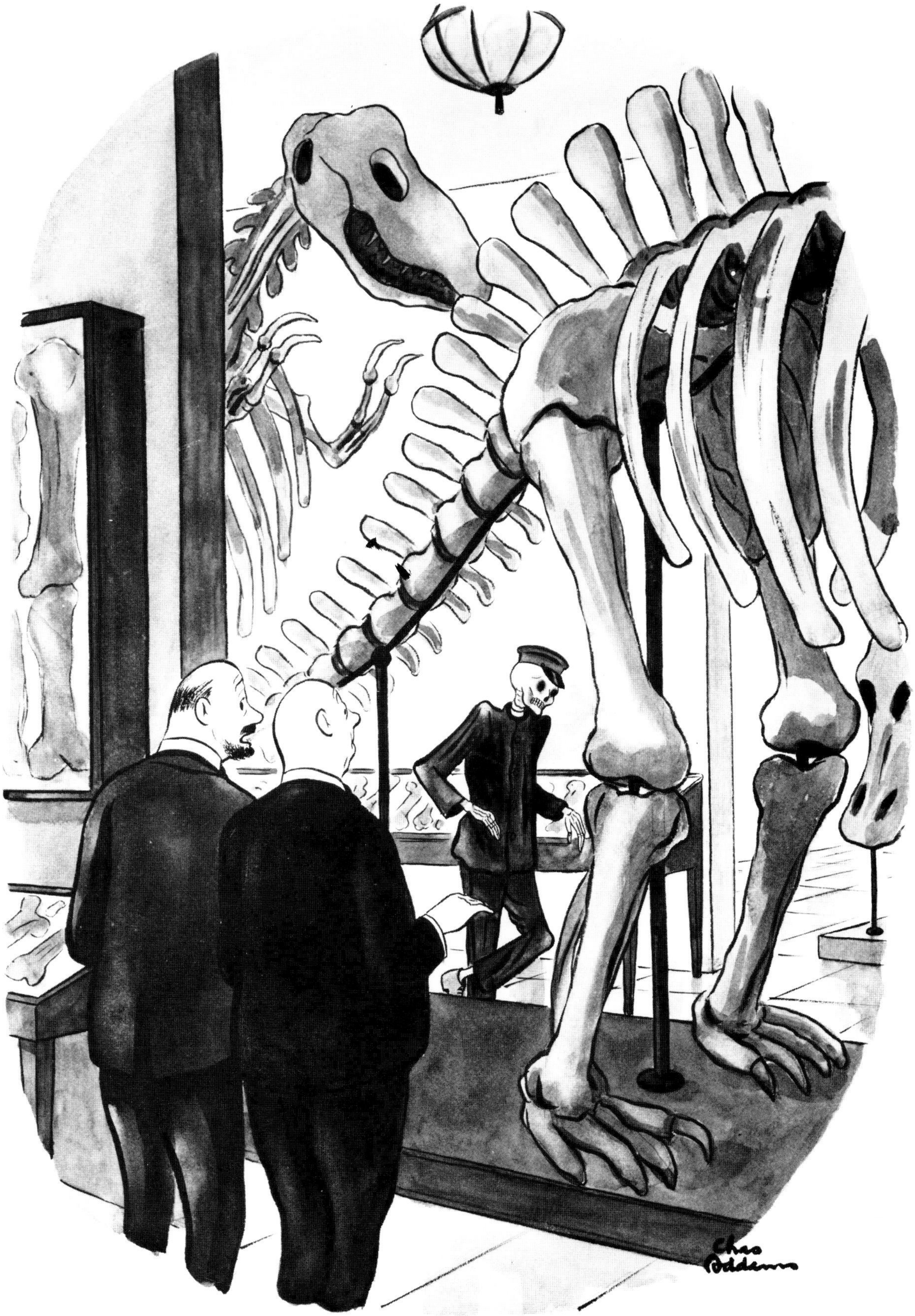
Chas Addams

"Perhaps Comstock needs a vacation."

"You certainly have a peculiar sense of humor."

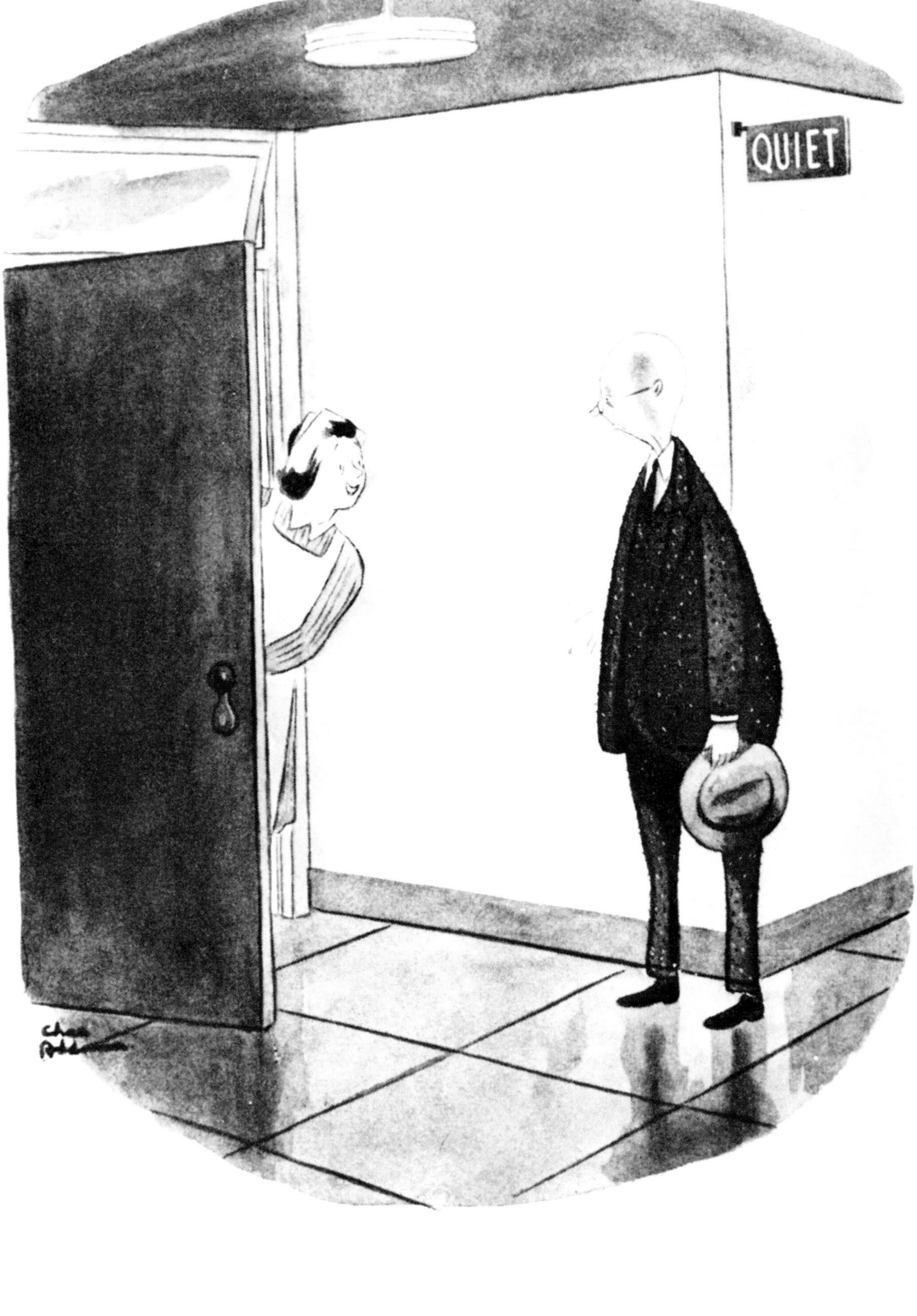
QUIET

"Congratulations! It's a baby."

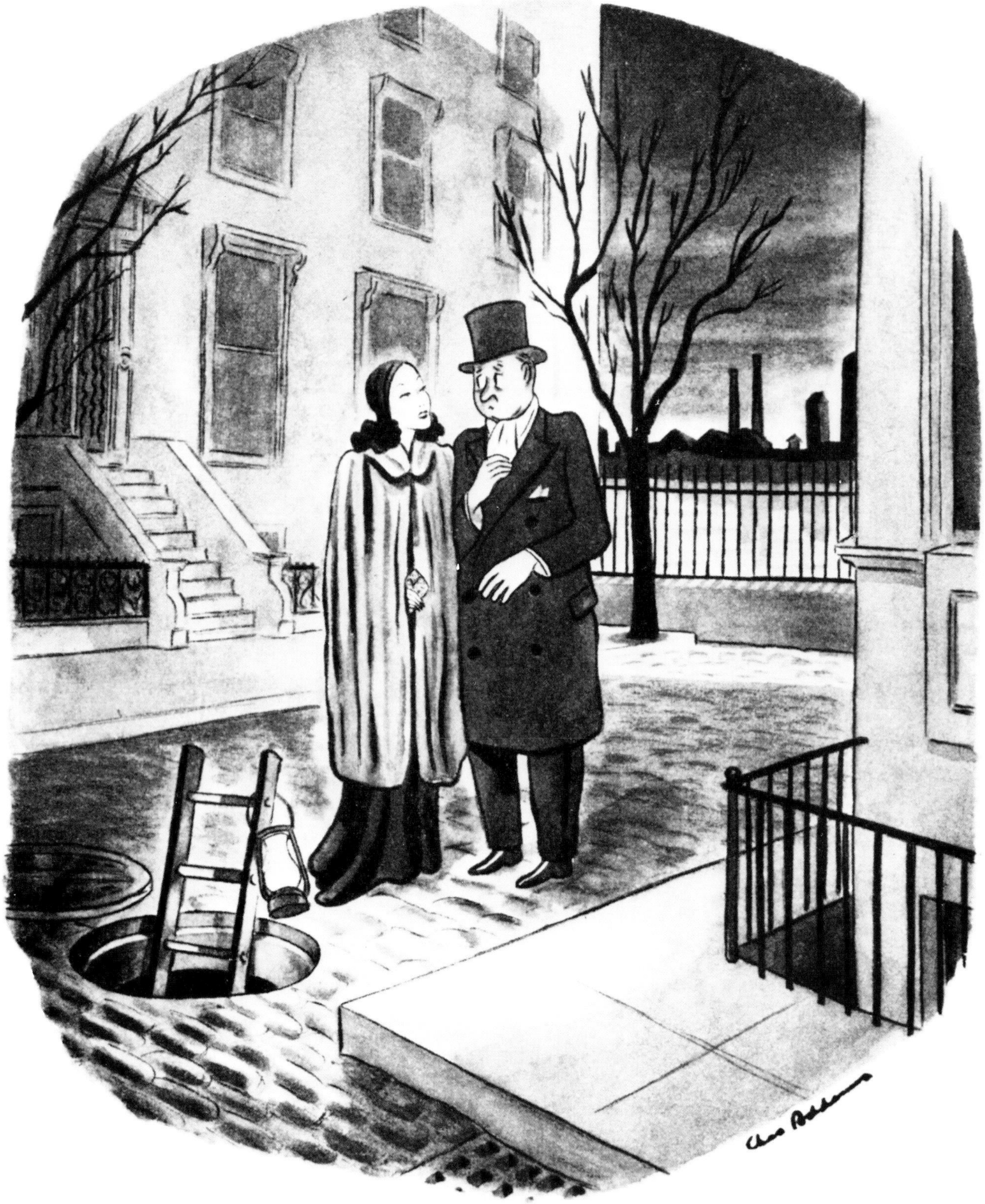

"Well, here's where I say good night."

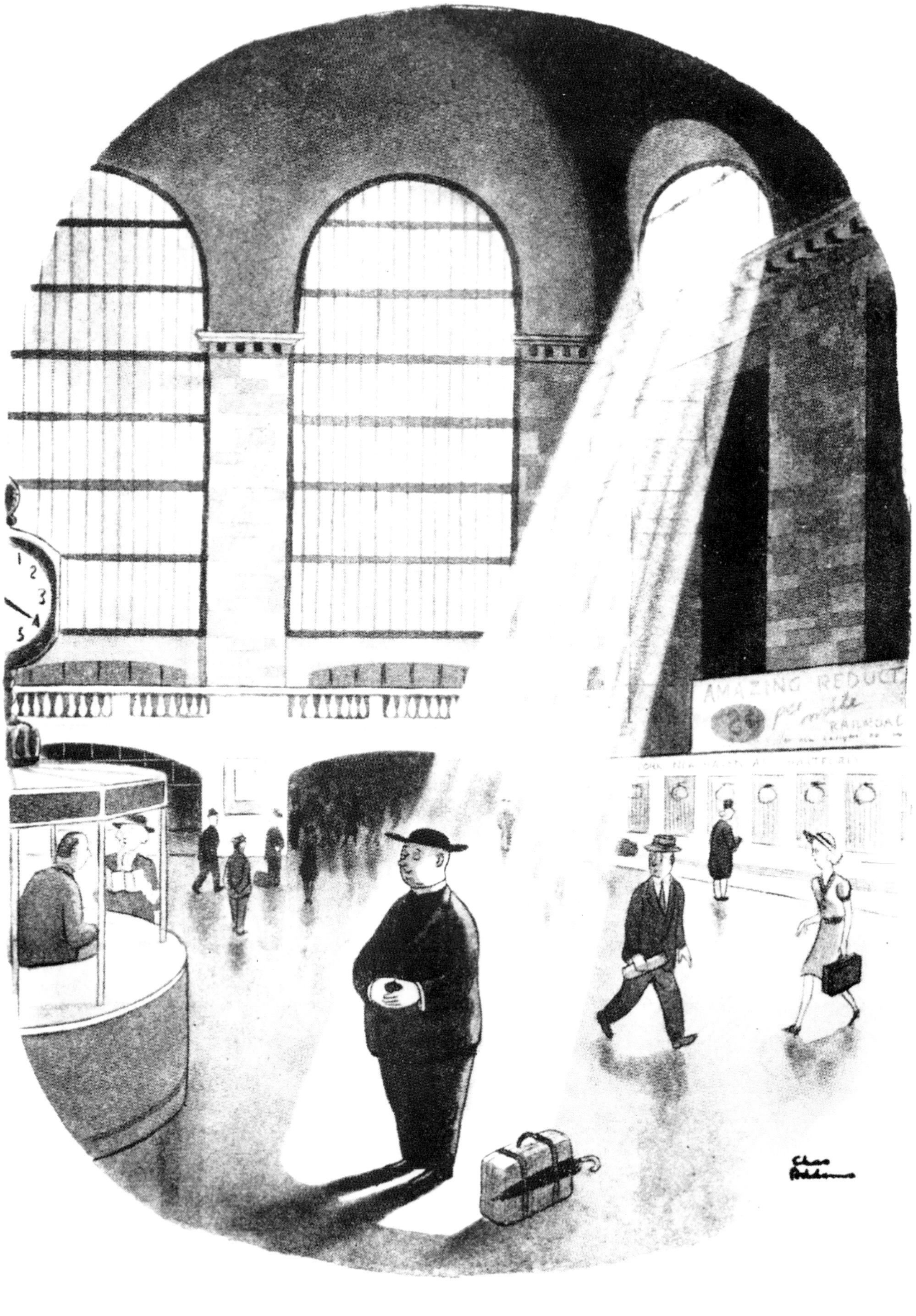
AMAZING REDUCT
Chas Addams

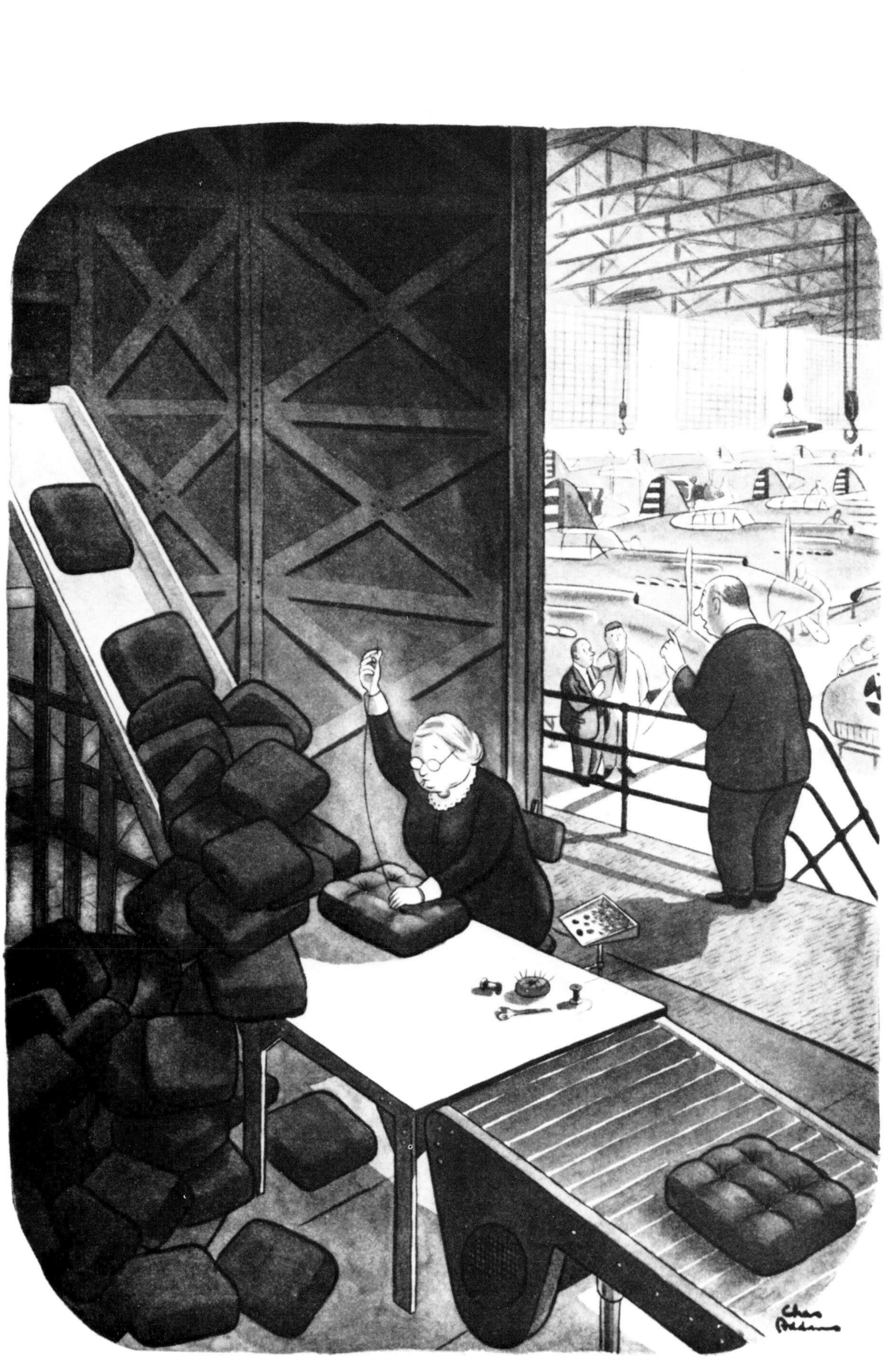

"Can you step up here just a moment, Mr. Hodgins? I think I've found your bottleneck."

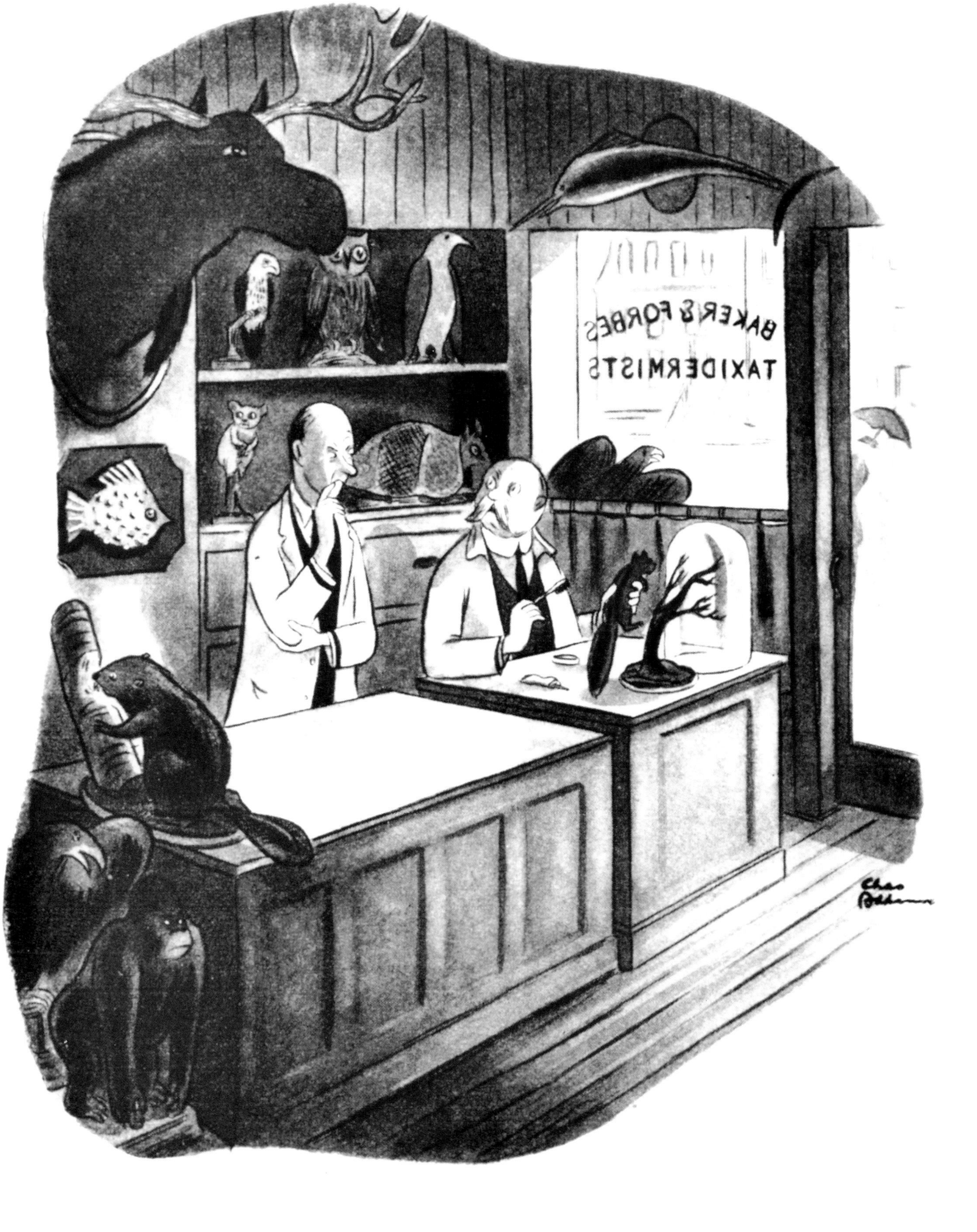
BAKER & FORBES
TAXIDERMISTS

"Damnation, Forbes, stop looking at me like that."

"Why, there's Carver now."

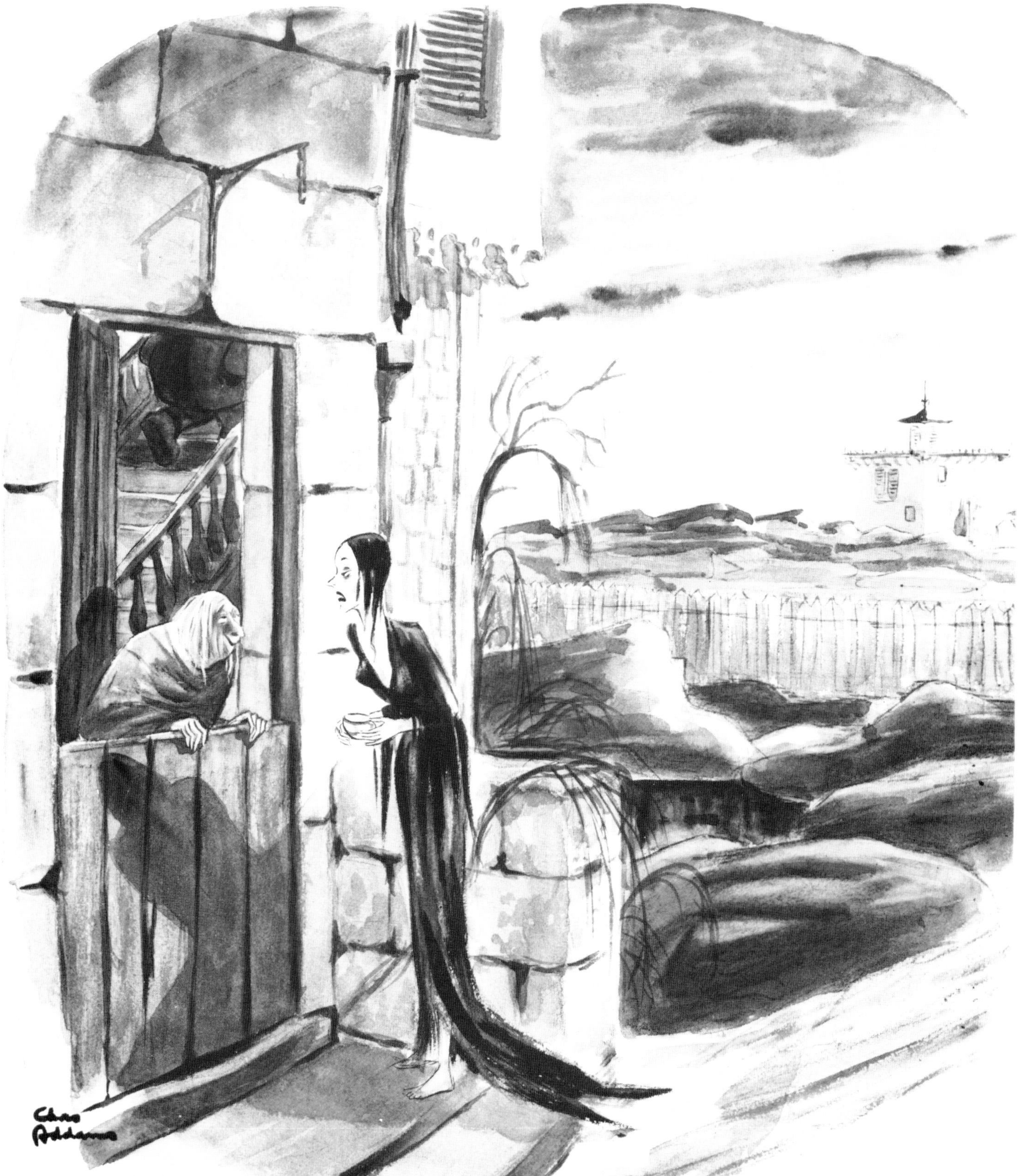
Chas Addams

"May I borrow a cup of cyanide?"

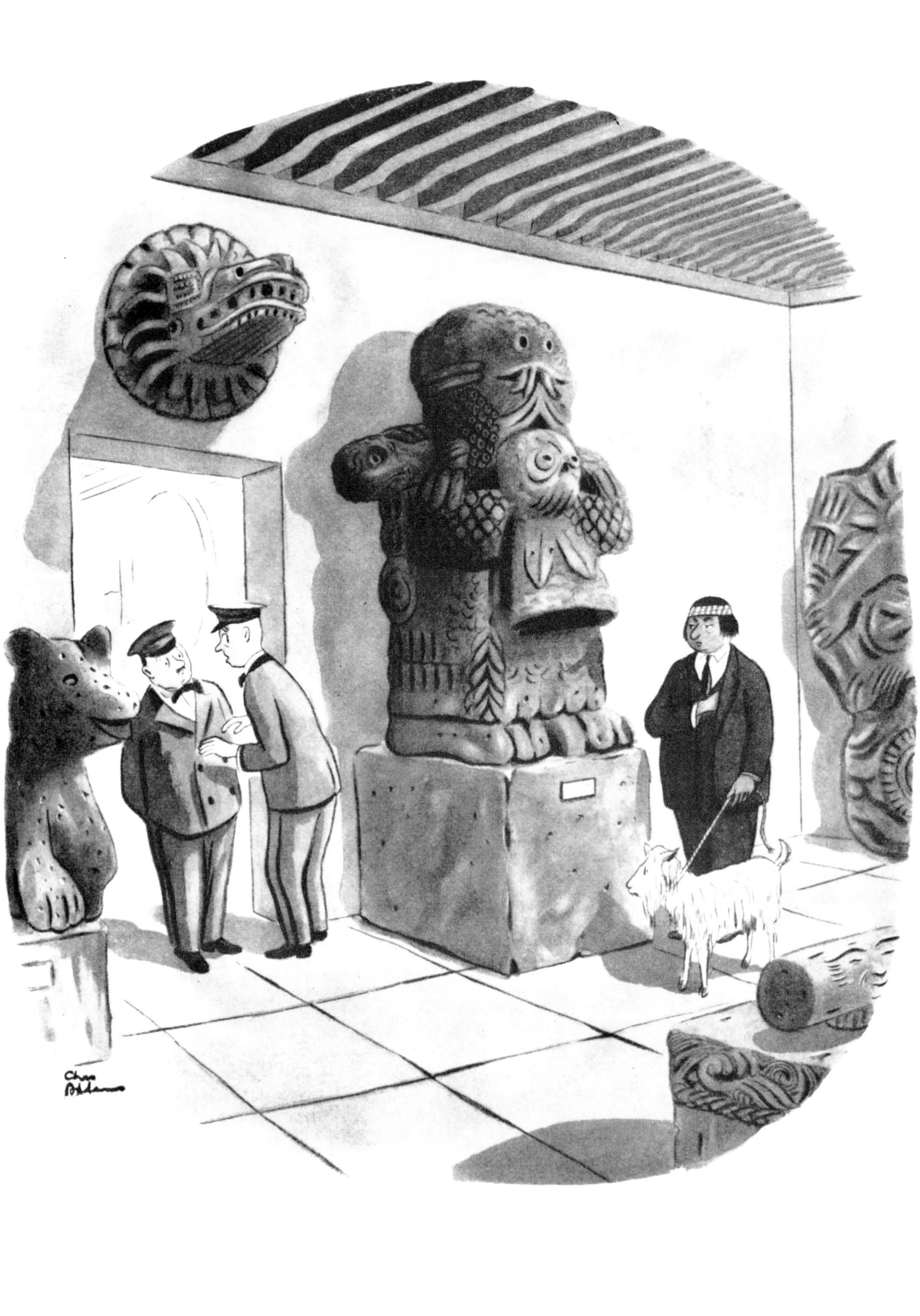

"He wants to know if he may make a small sacrifice in front of it."

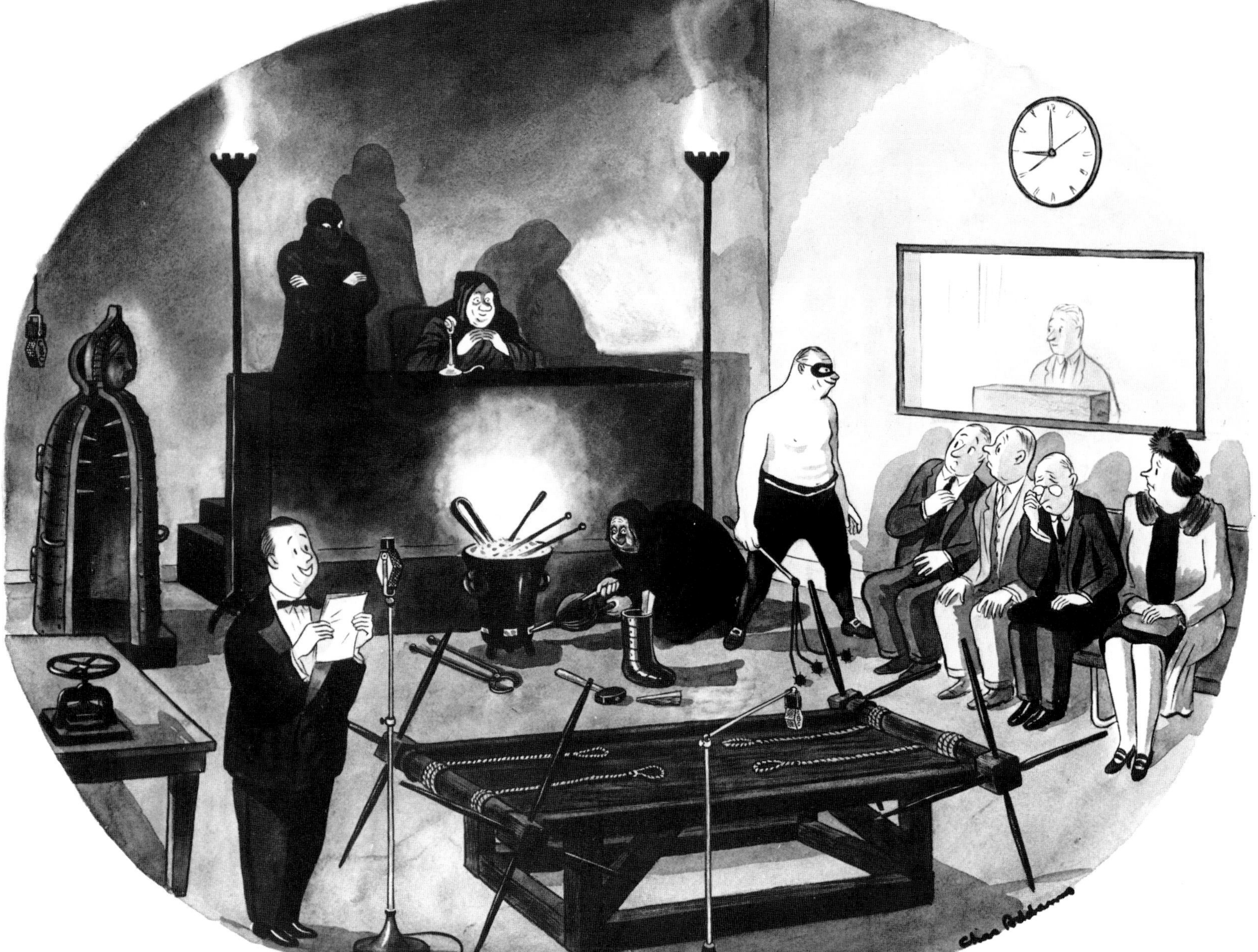

"The makers of Sun-Glo Toilet Soap bring you an entirely different type of quiz program."

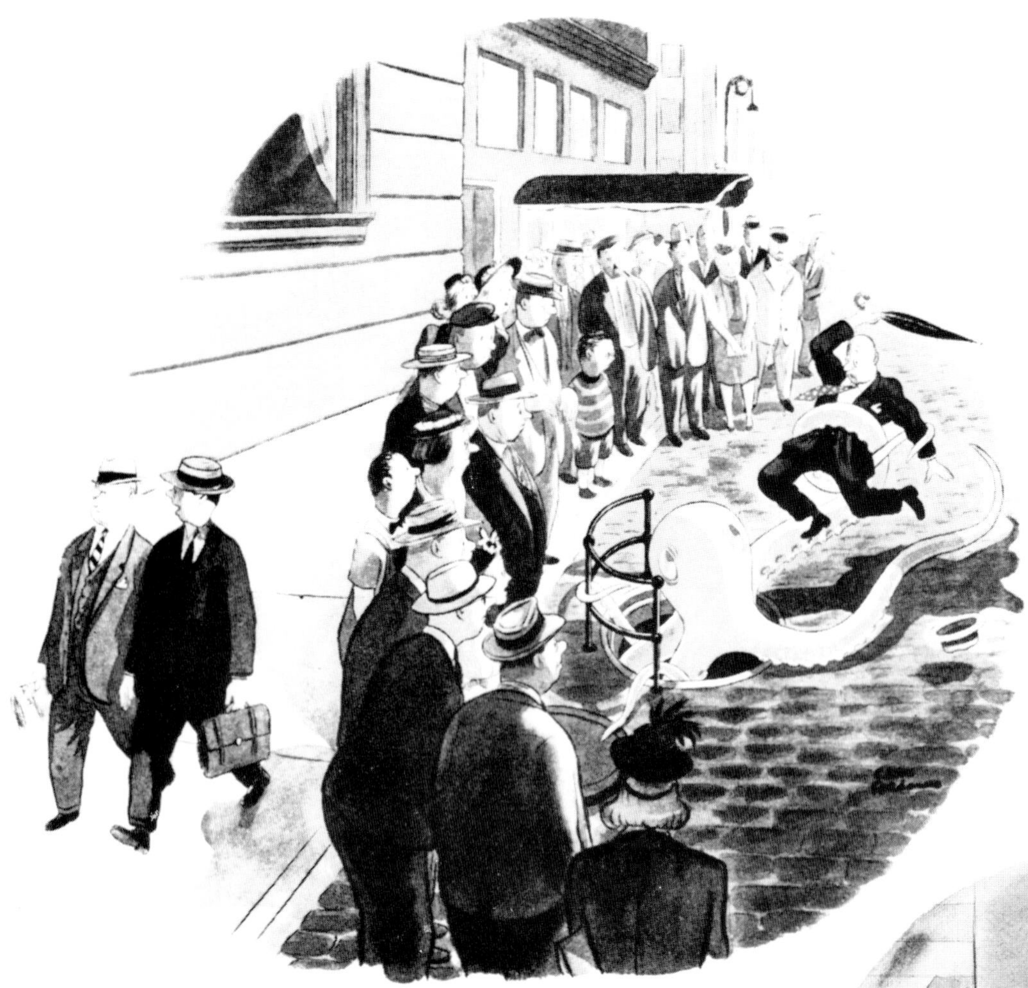

"It doesn't take much to collect a crowd in New York."

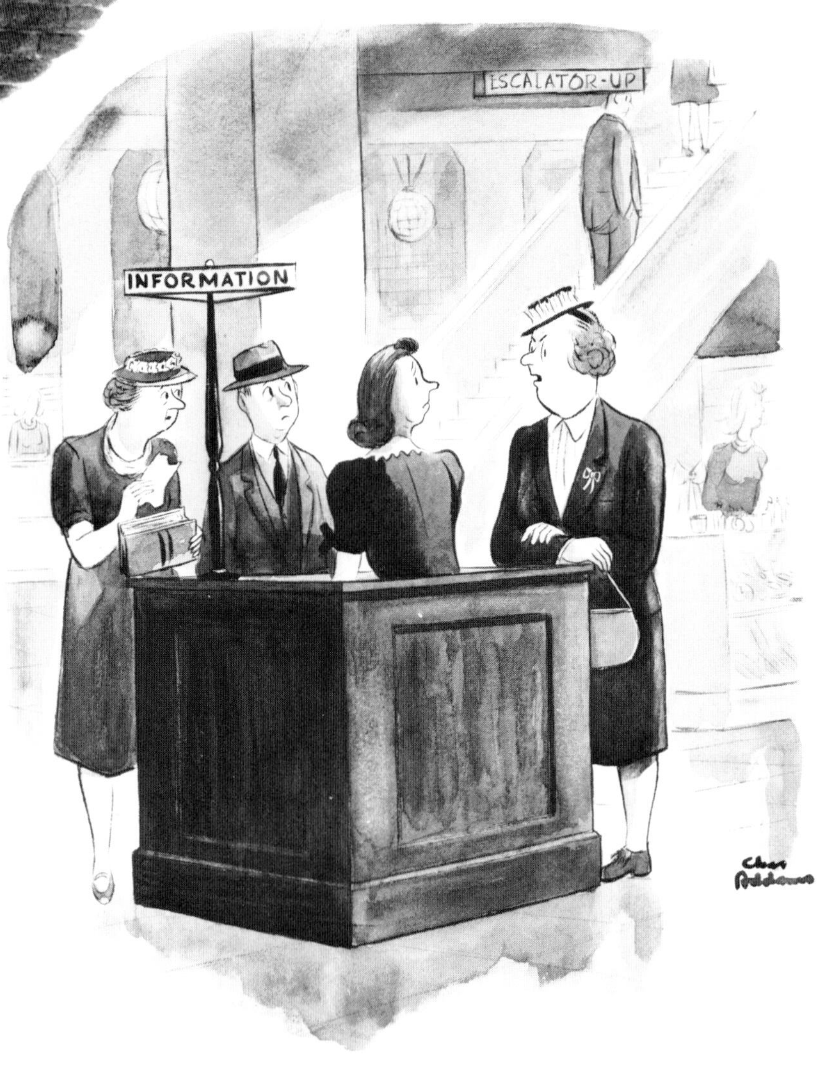
ESCALATOR-UP
INFORMATION

"Blunt instruments?"

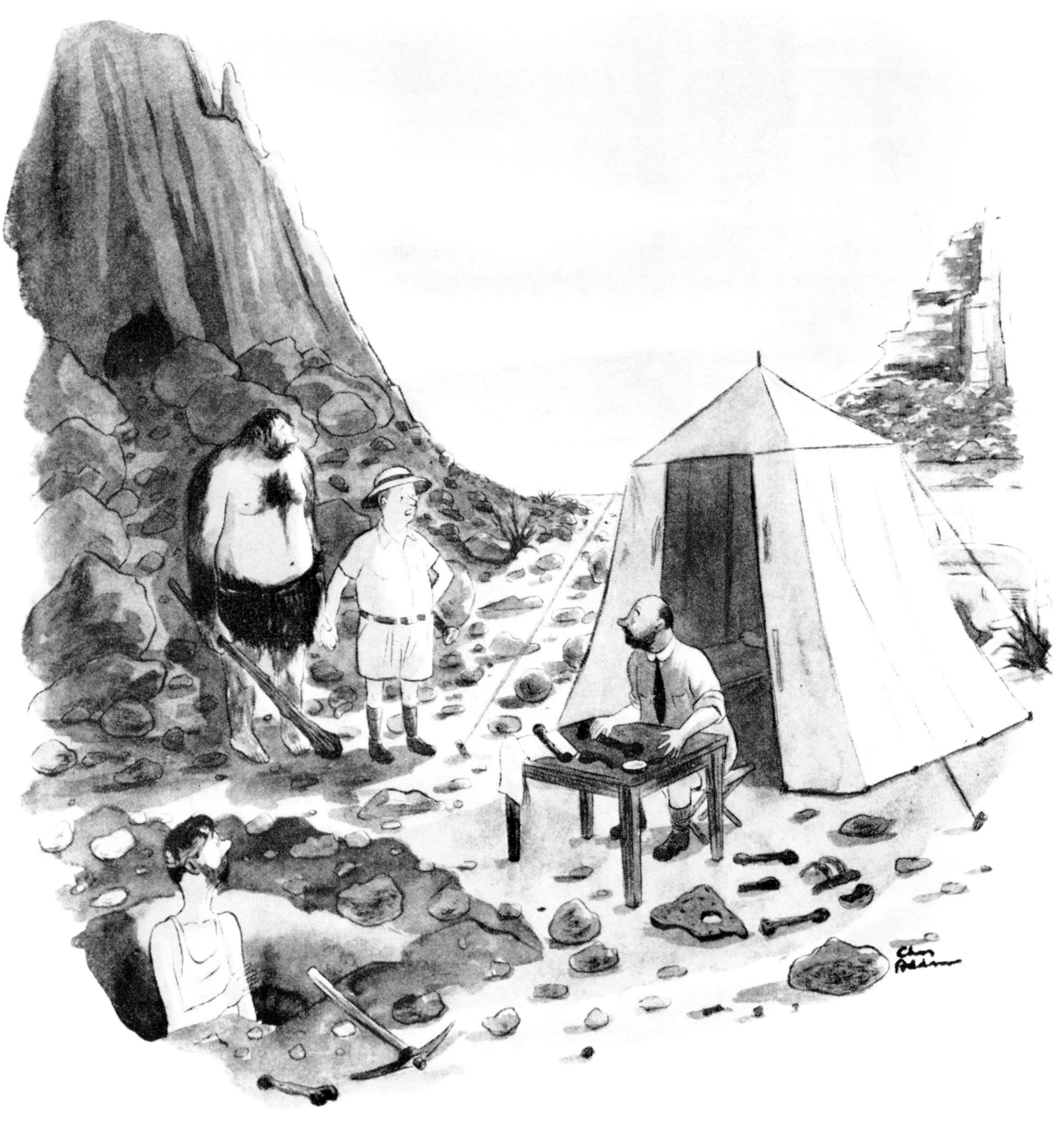

". . . or are we only interested in fossils?"

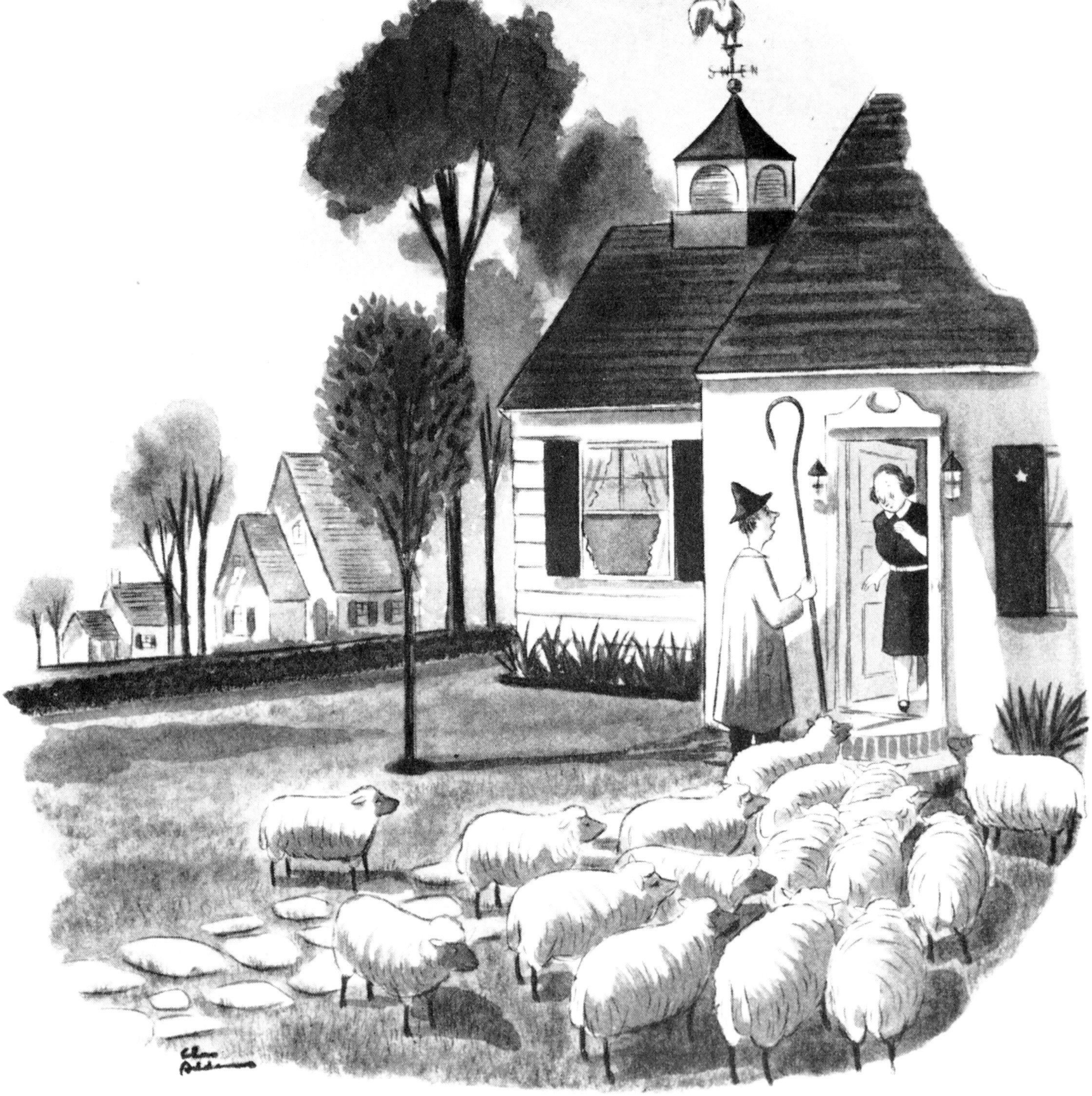

"Crop thy lawn, lady?"

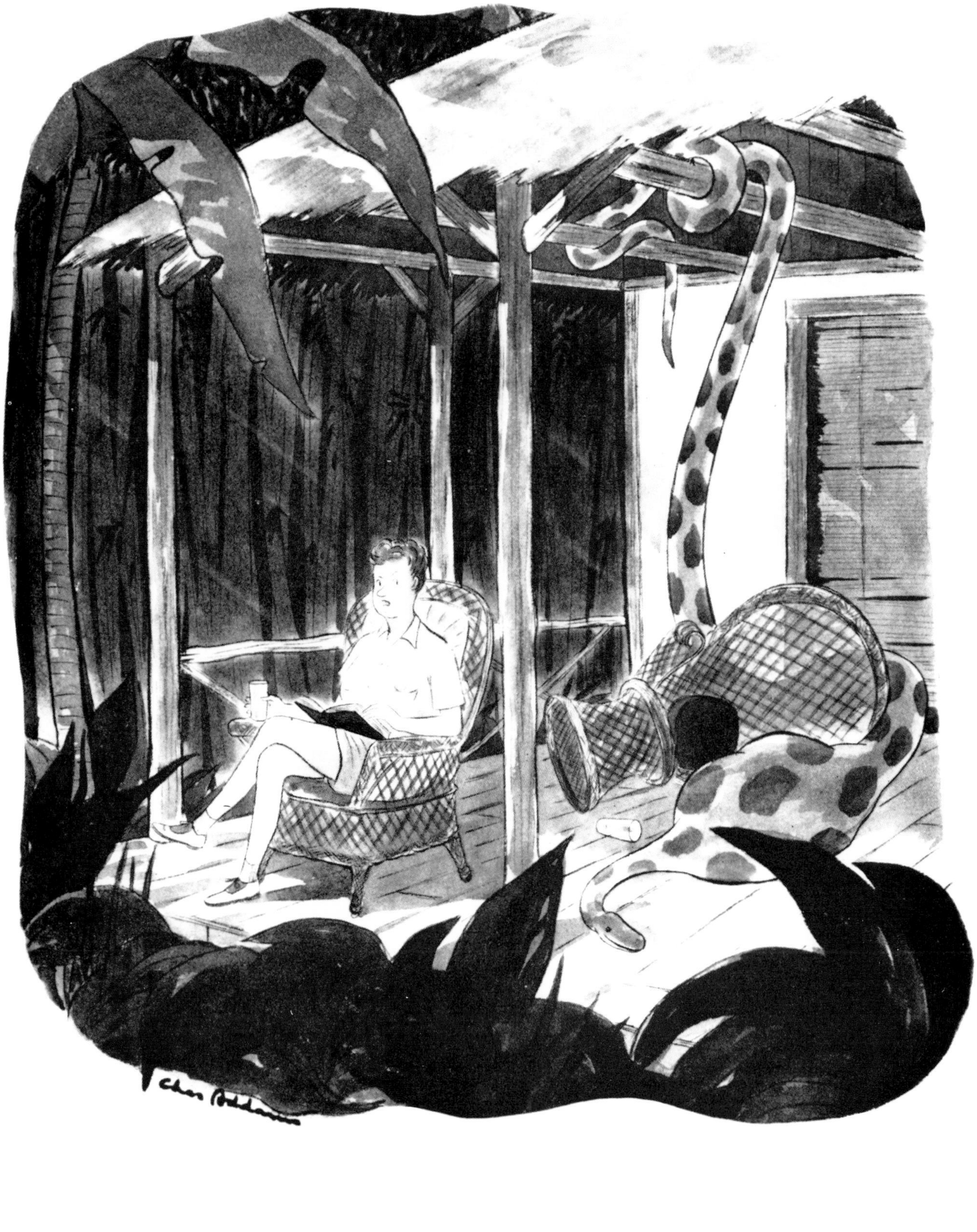

"Oh, speak up, George! Stop mumbling!"

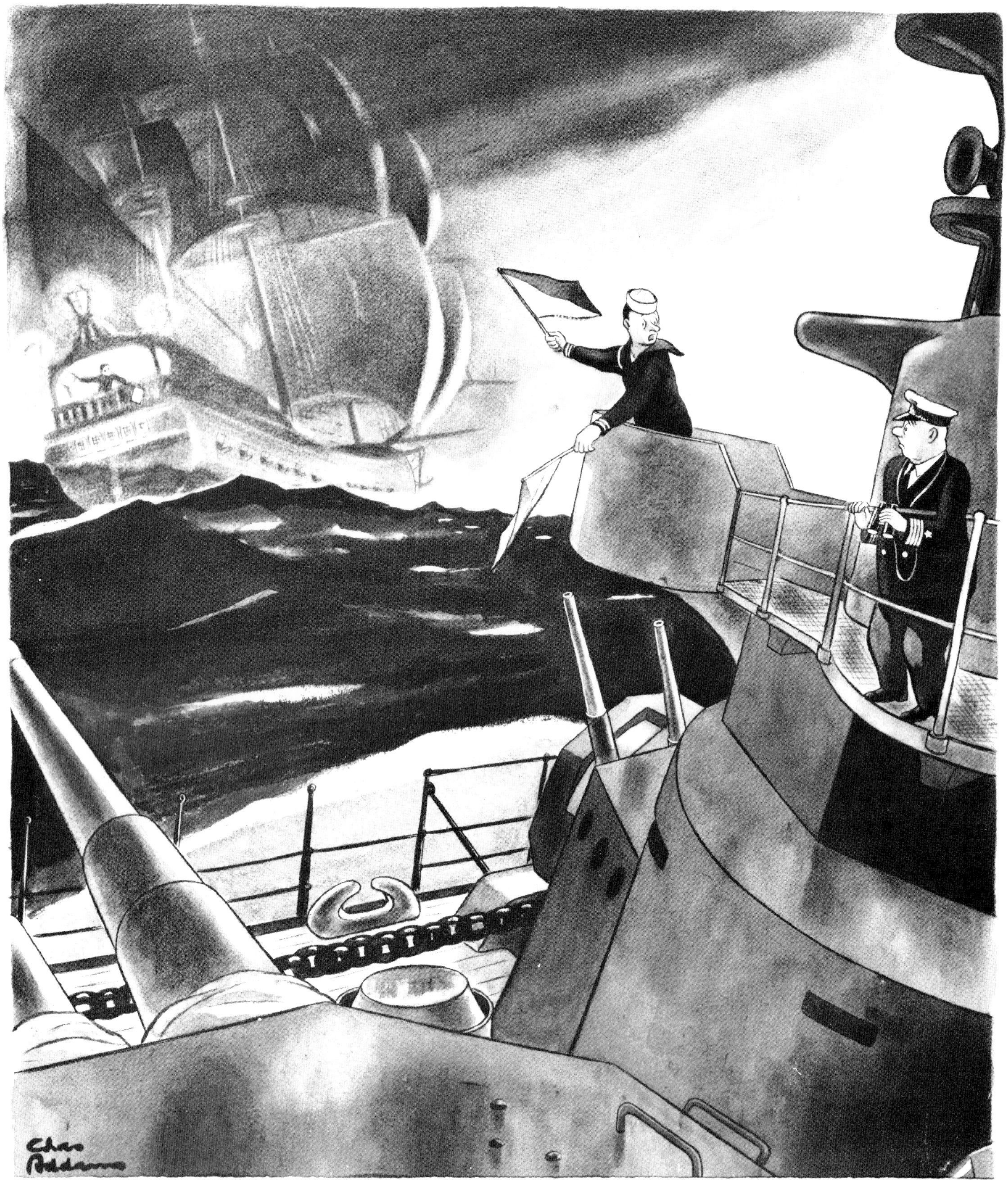
Chas Addams

"Dutch registry, sir. Says he can't stop—sailing under a curse."

"You have the wrong cell, Chaplain. He's just serving a short term for a traffic violation."

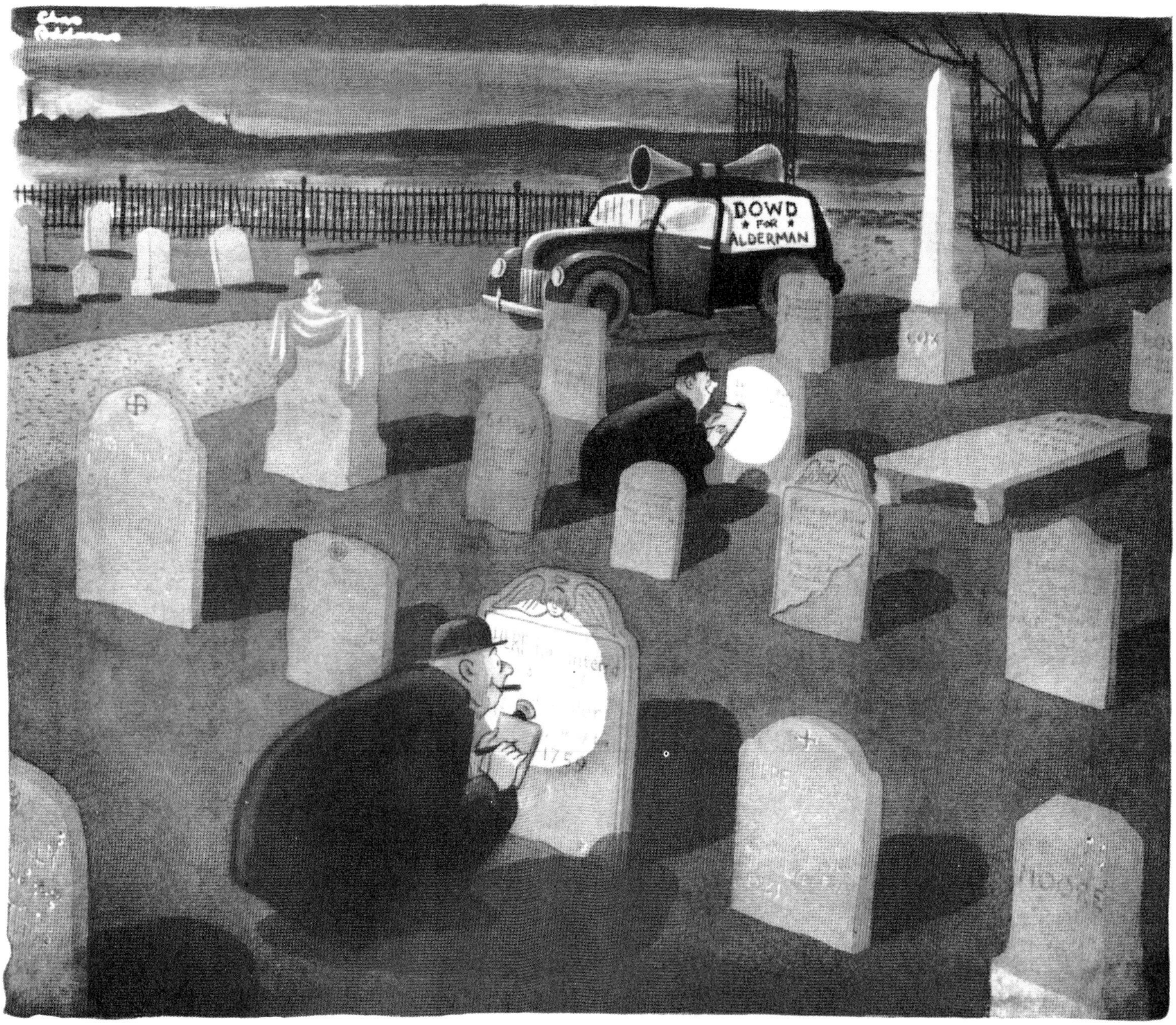
DOWD
FOR
ALDERMAN
COX
MOORE

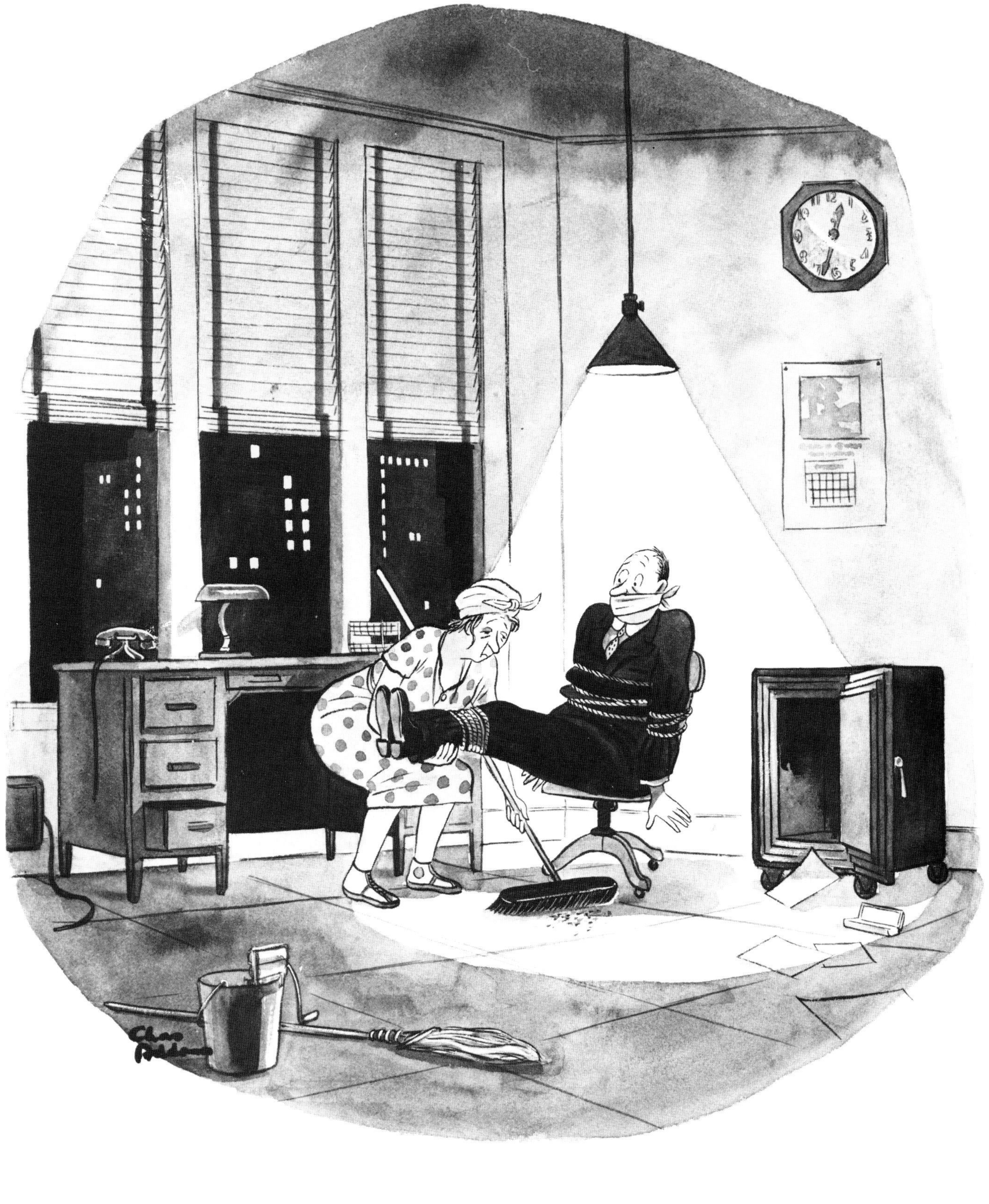
Chas Addams

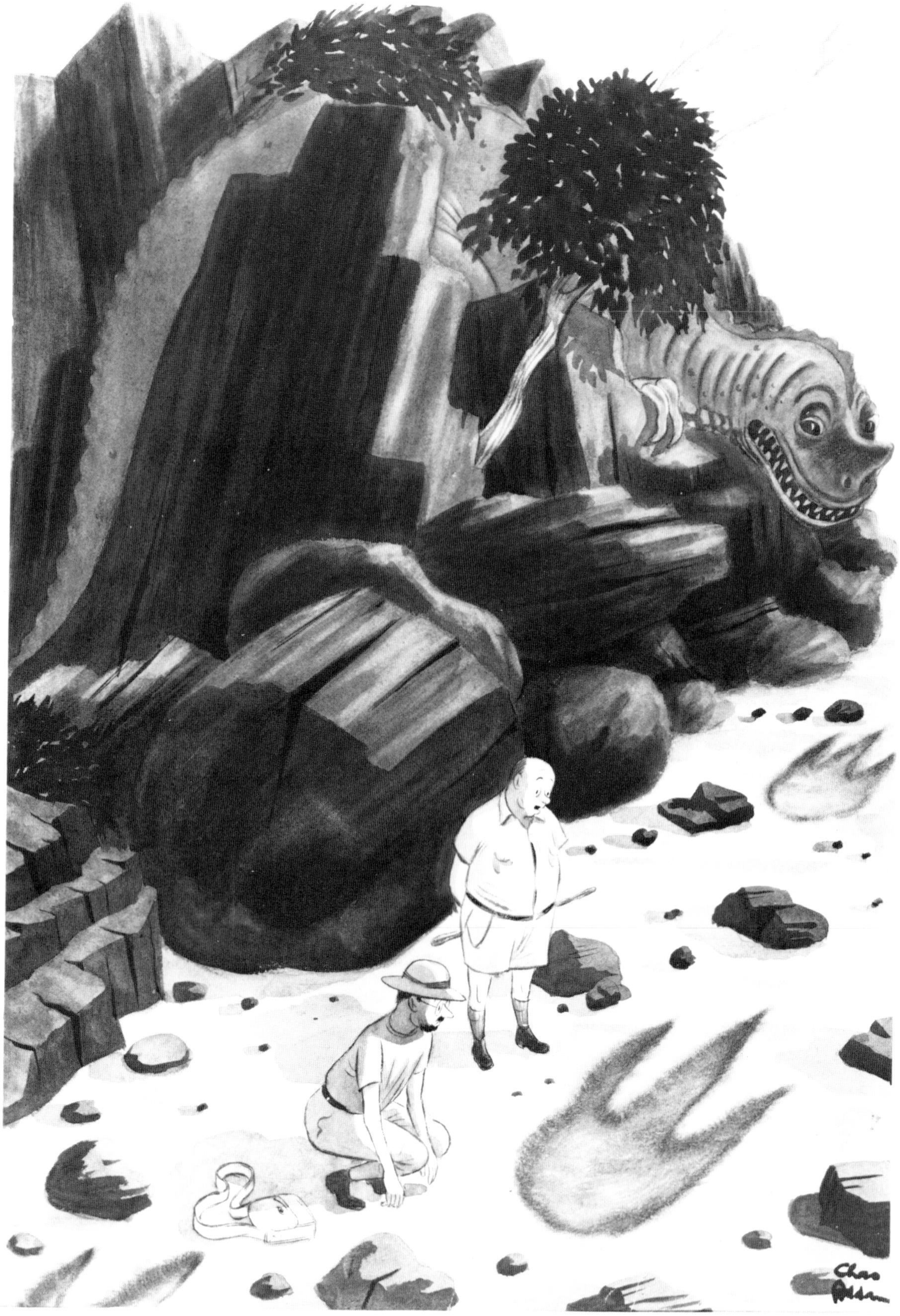

"Imagine it, Barclay. Here we stand gazing down at tracks made ten million years ago."

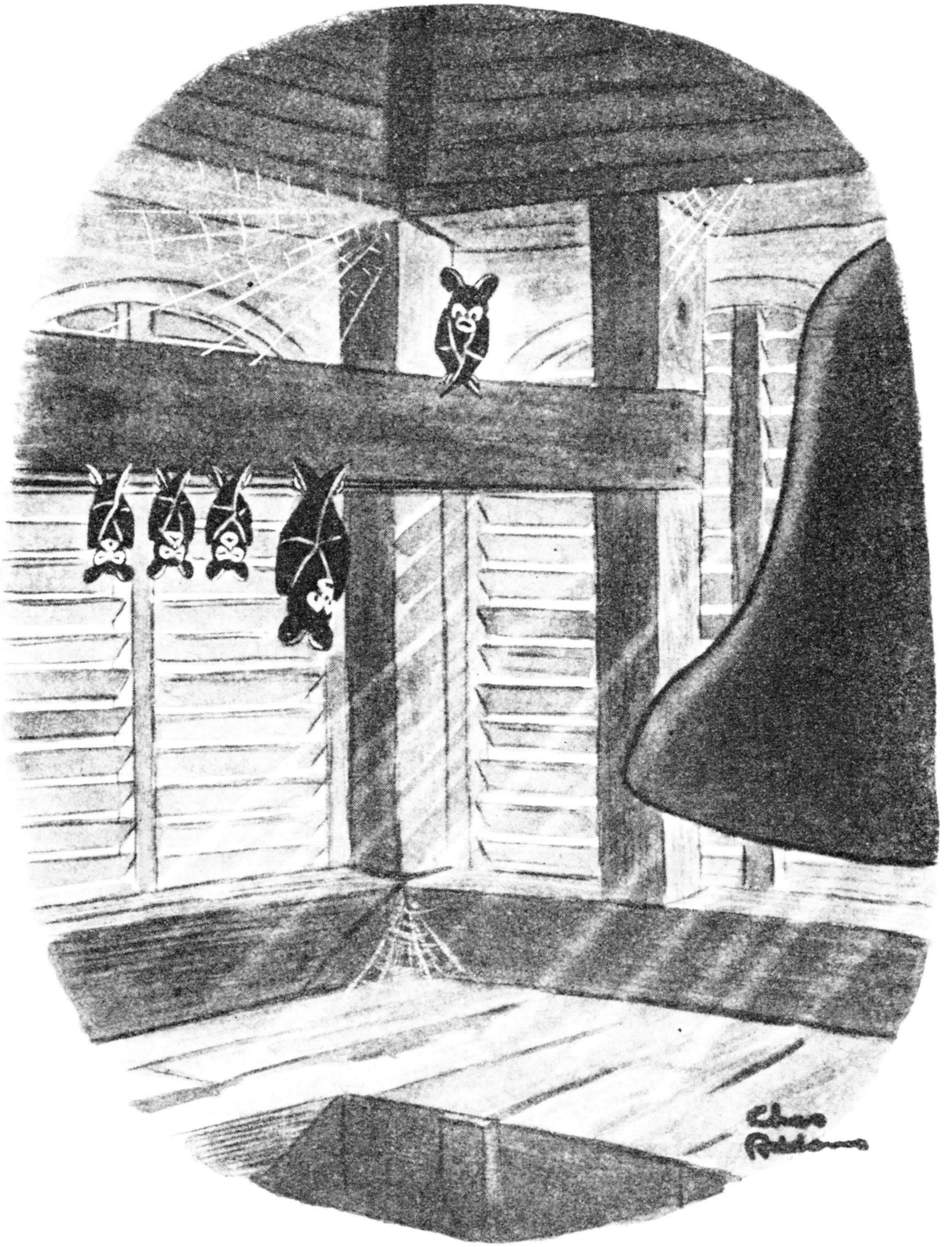

"I tell you, Mama, the blood keeps going to my head."

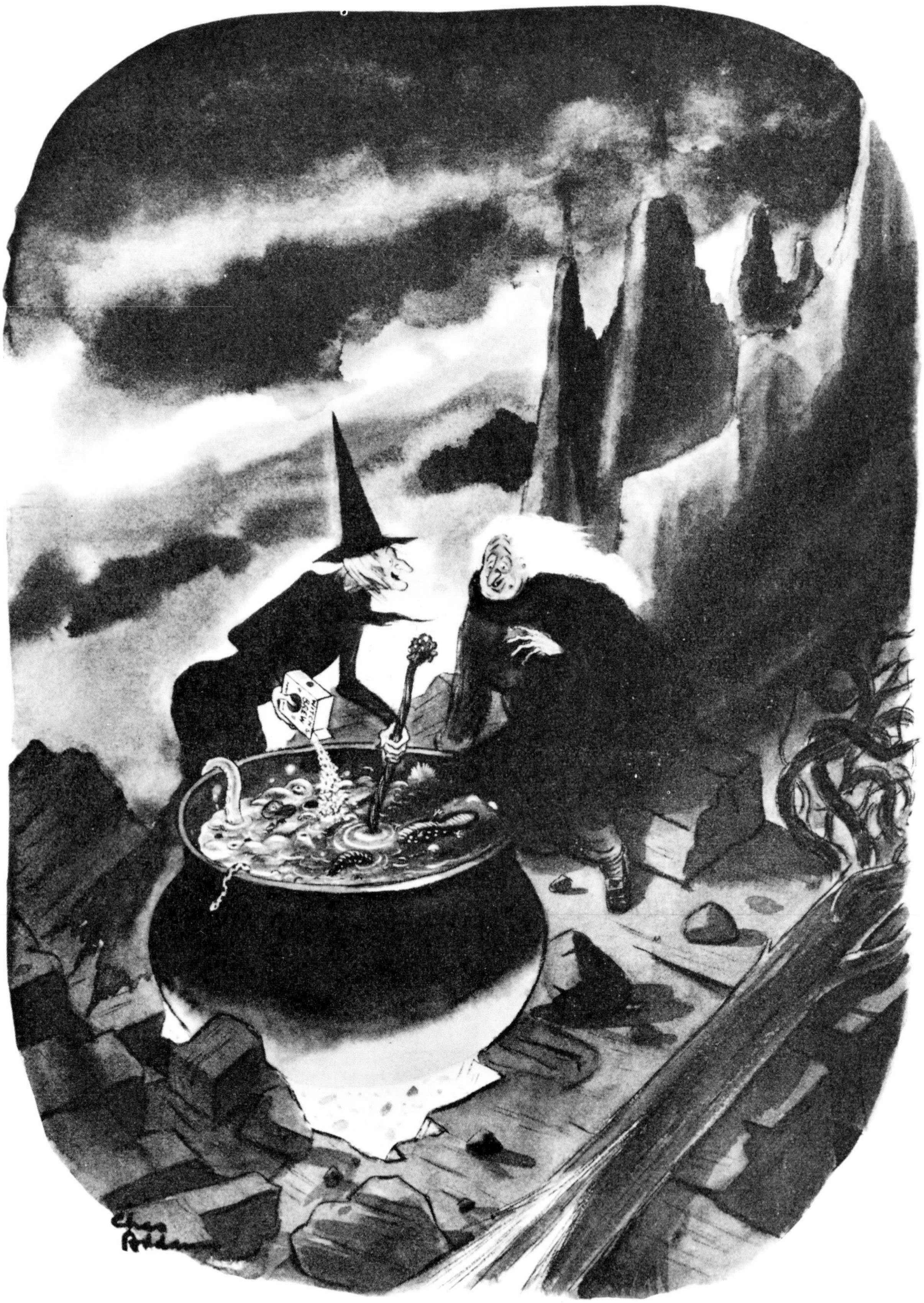

"It's marvelous! All you do is add water."

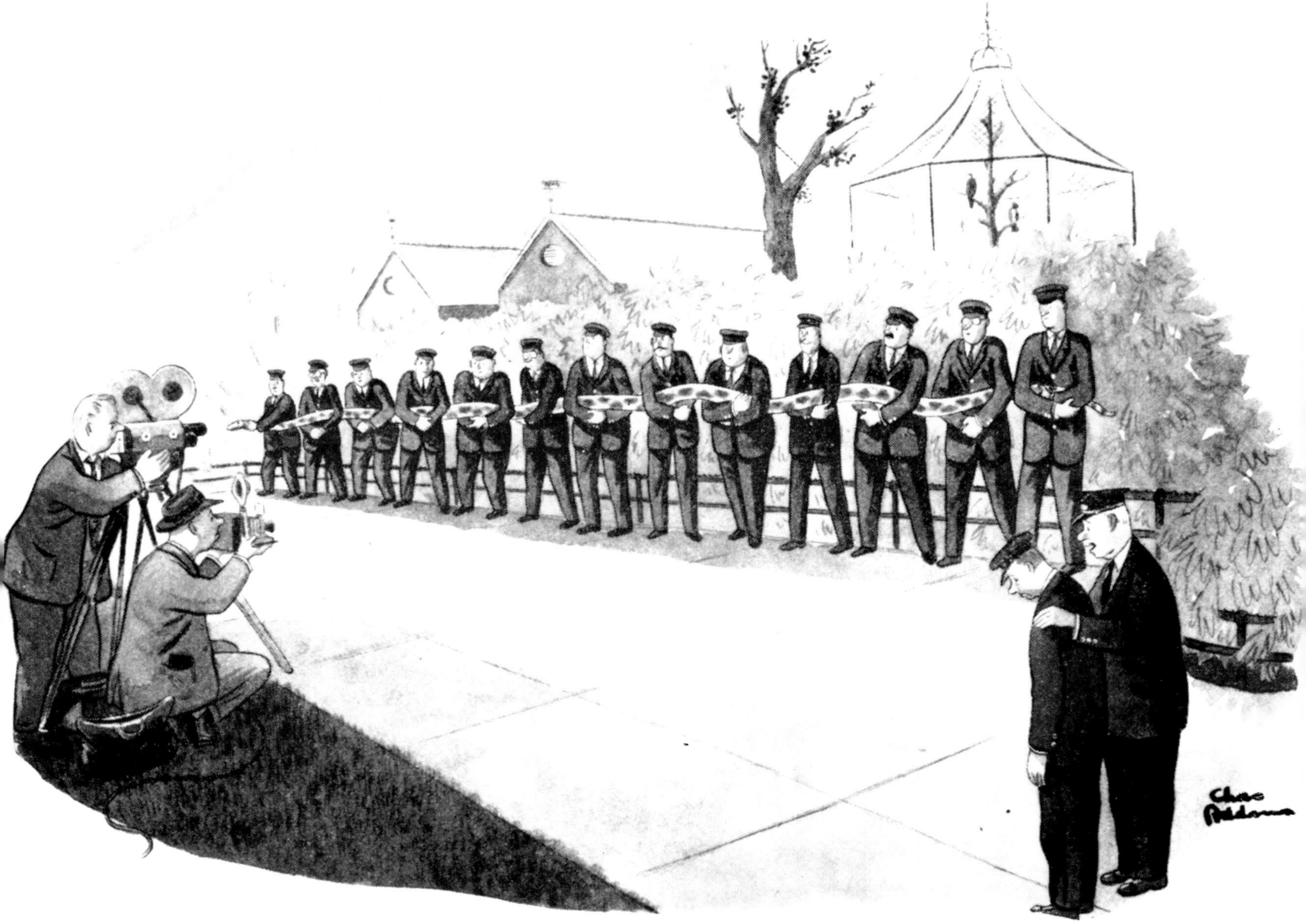
Chas Addams

"Don't feel badly, Nelson. With normal growth, you'll be in there next year."

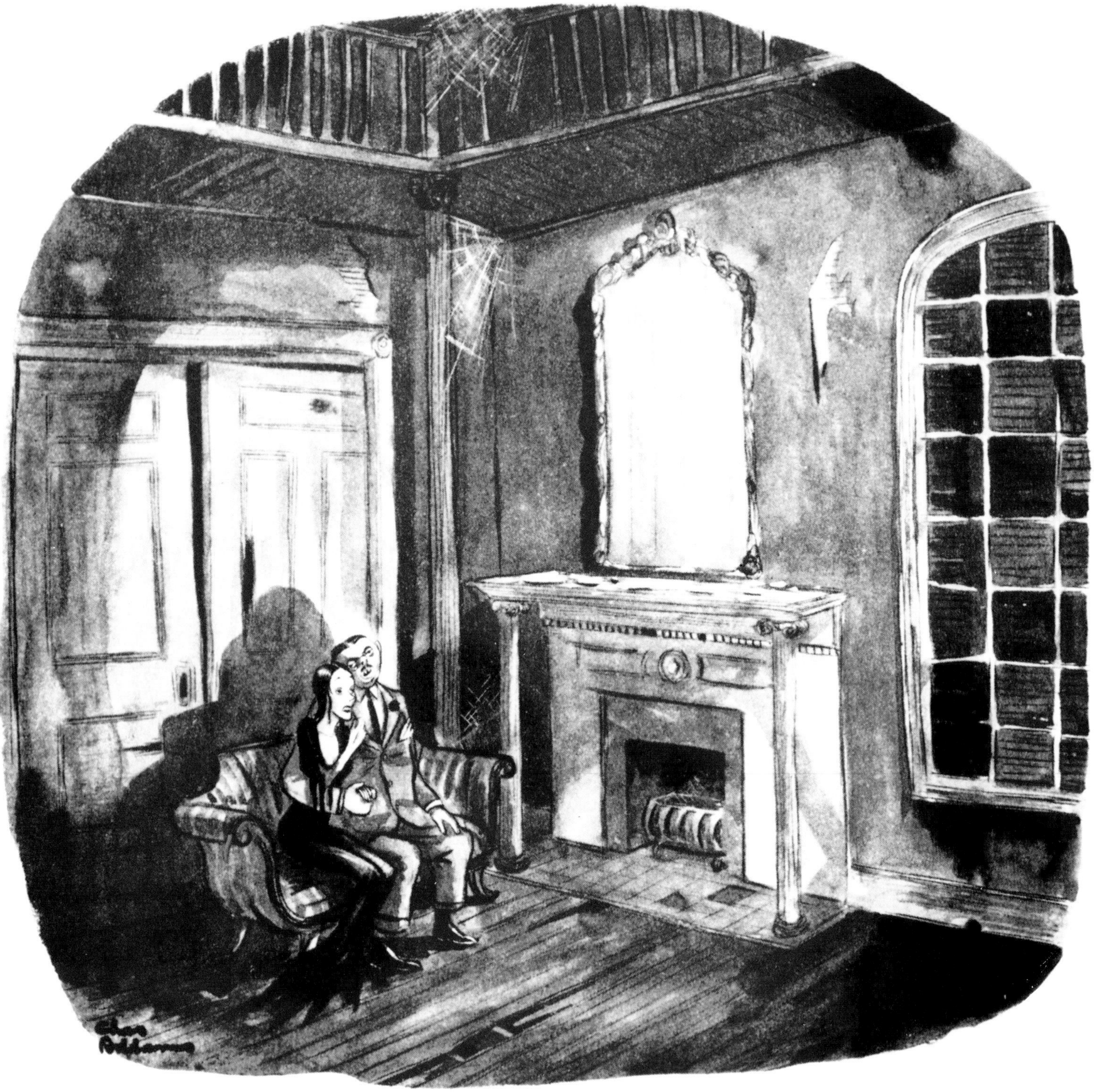

"Are you unhappy, darling?"
"Oh, yes, yes! Completely."

"Any children?"

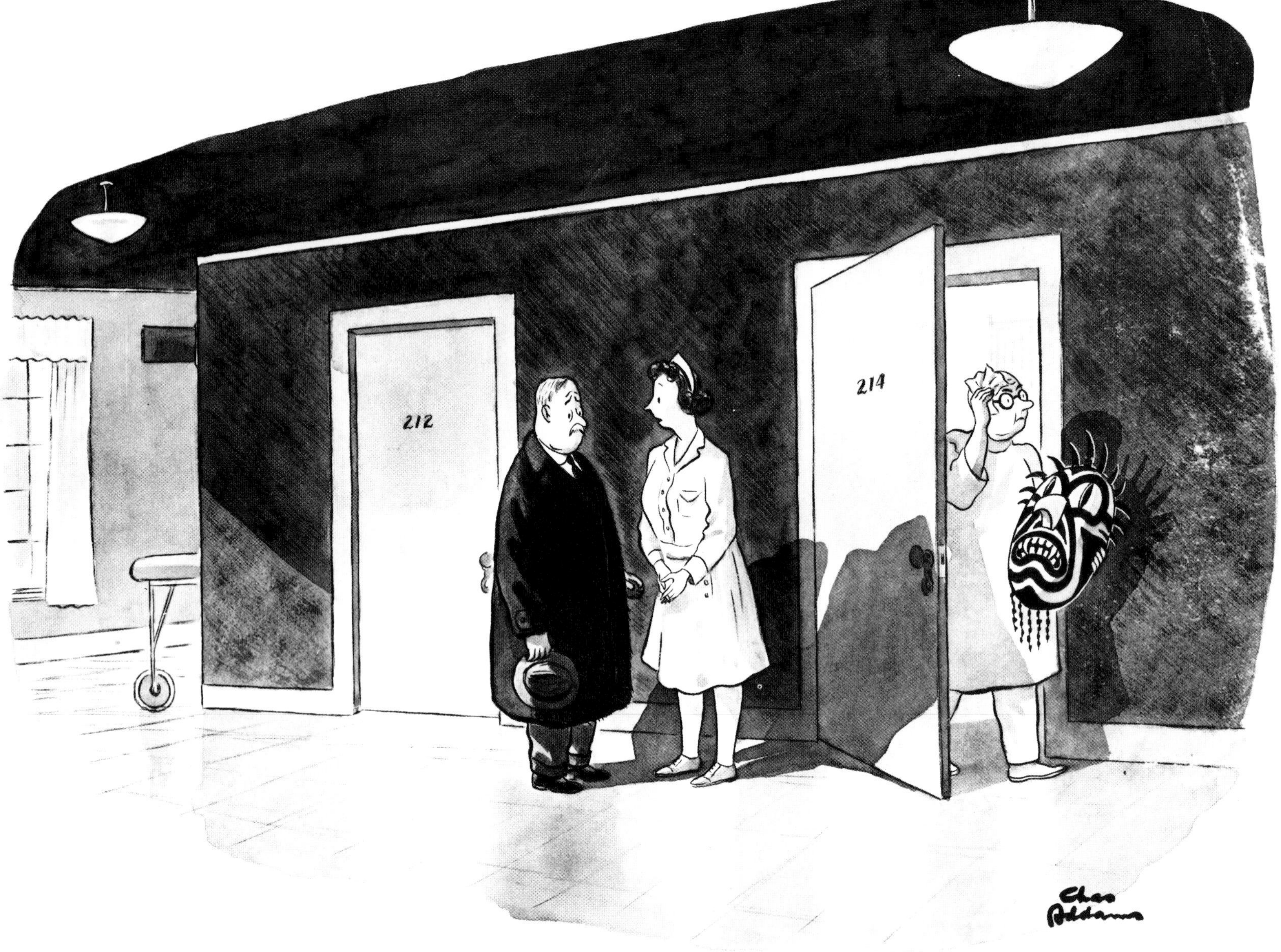
212
214
Chas Addams

"You must try not to worry. Dr. Perry is doing everything humanly possible."

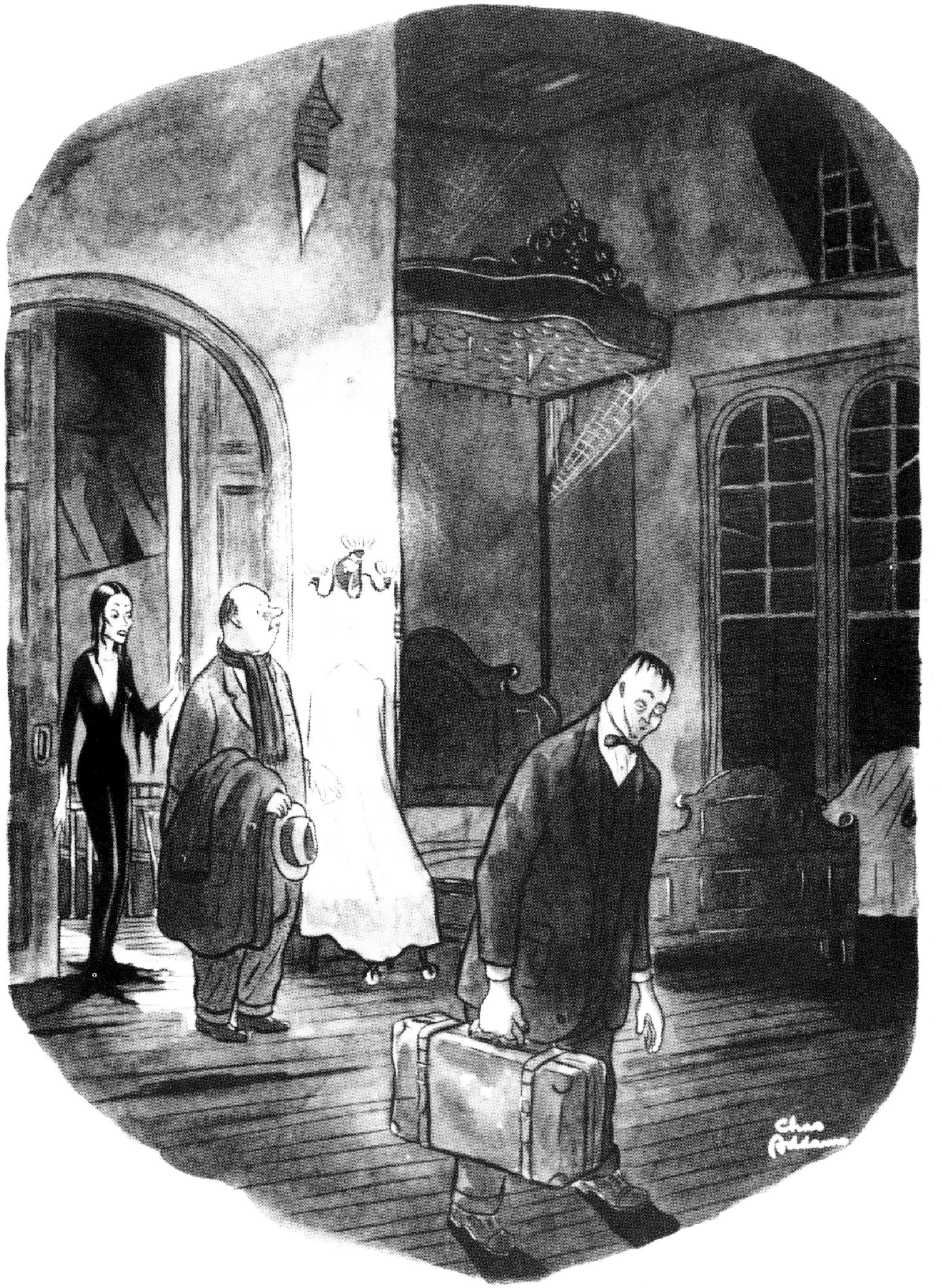
Chas Addams

"This is your room. If you should need anything, just scream."

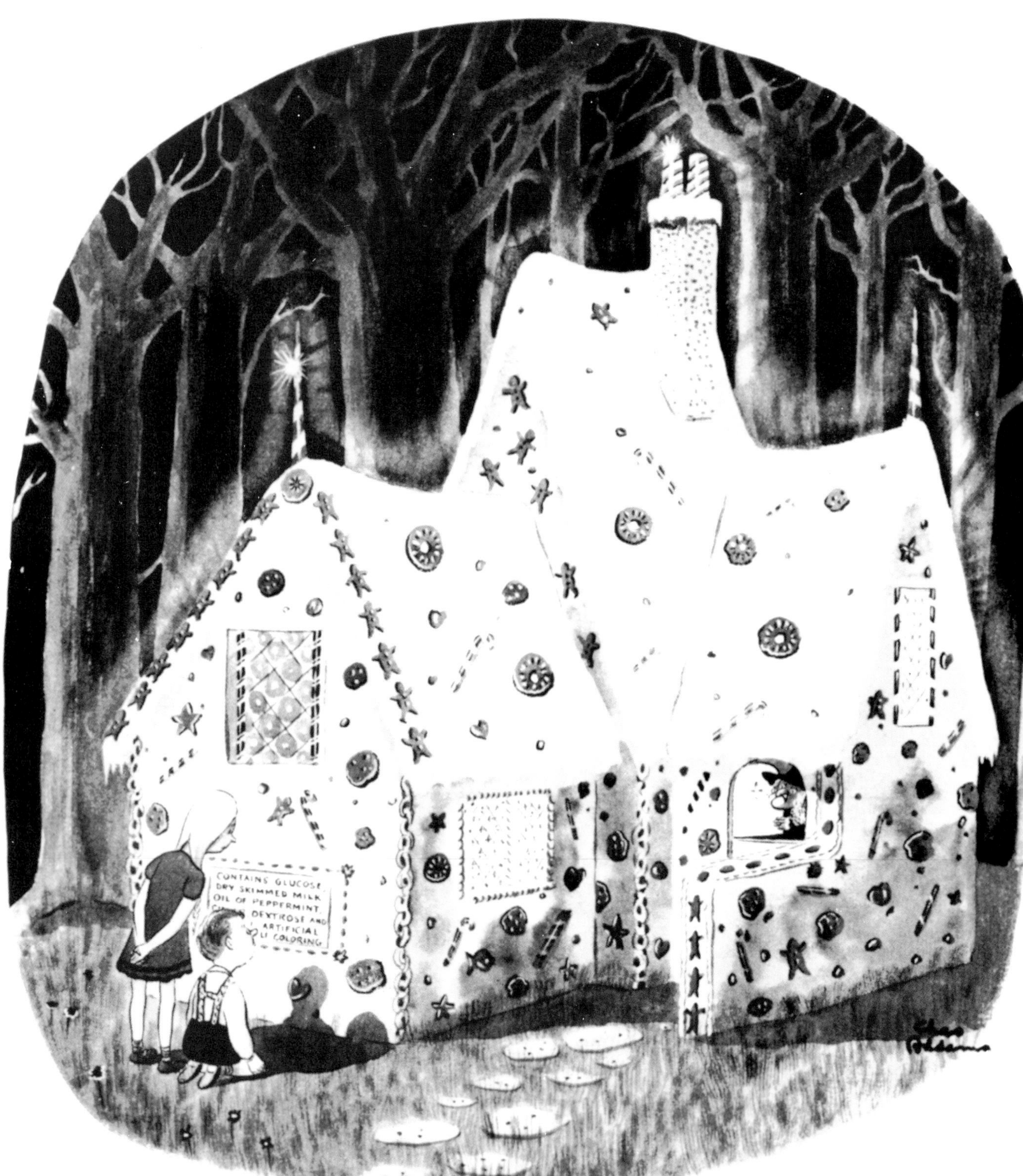
CONTAINS GLUCOSE
DRY SKIMMED MILK
OIL OF PEPPERMINT,
DEXTROSE AND
ARTIFICIAL
COLORING
Chas Addams

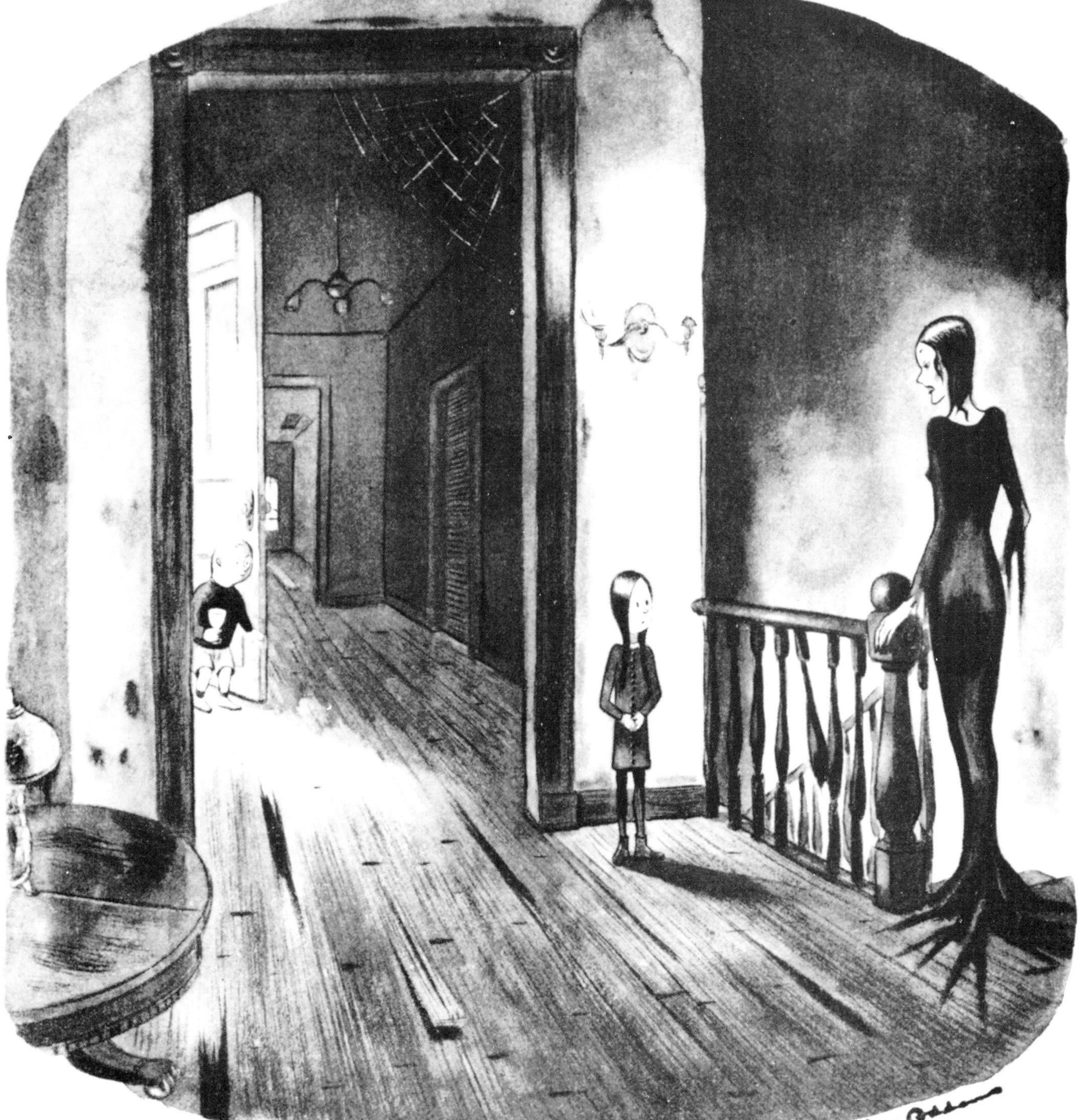

"Well, don't come whining to me. Go tell him you'll poison him right back."

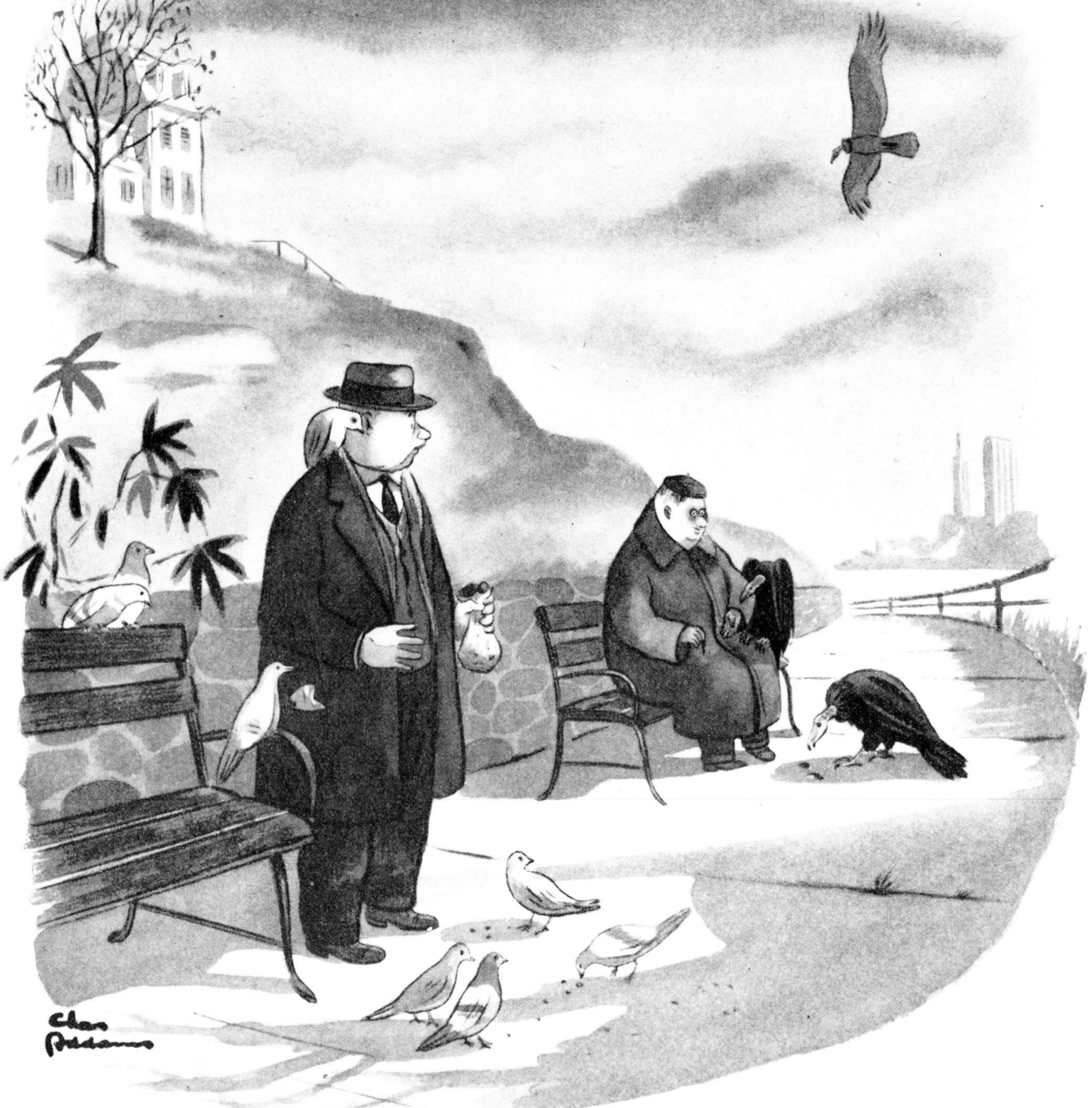
Chas Addams

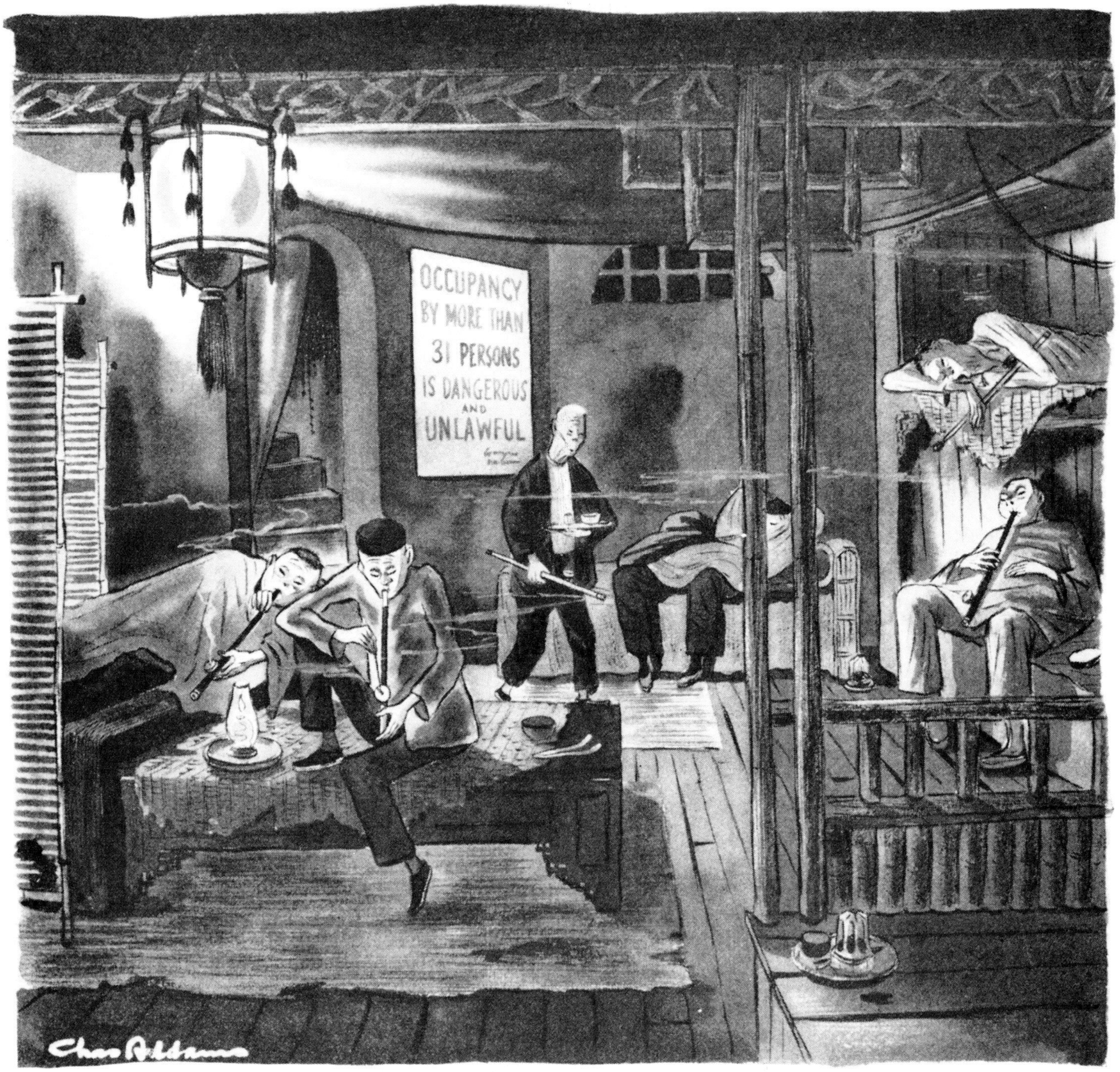
OCCUPANCY
BY MORE THAN
31 PERSONS
IS DANGEROUS
AND
UNLAWFUL
Chas Addams

"Miss Osborne poses for subway posters."

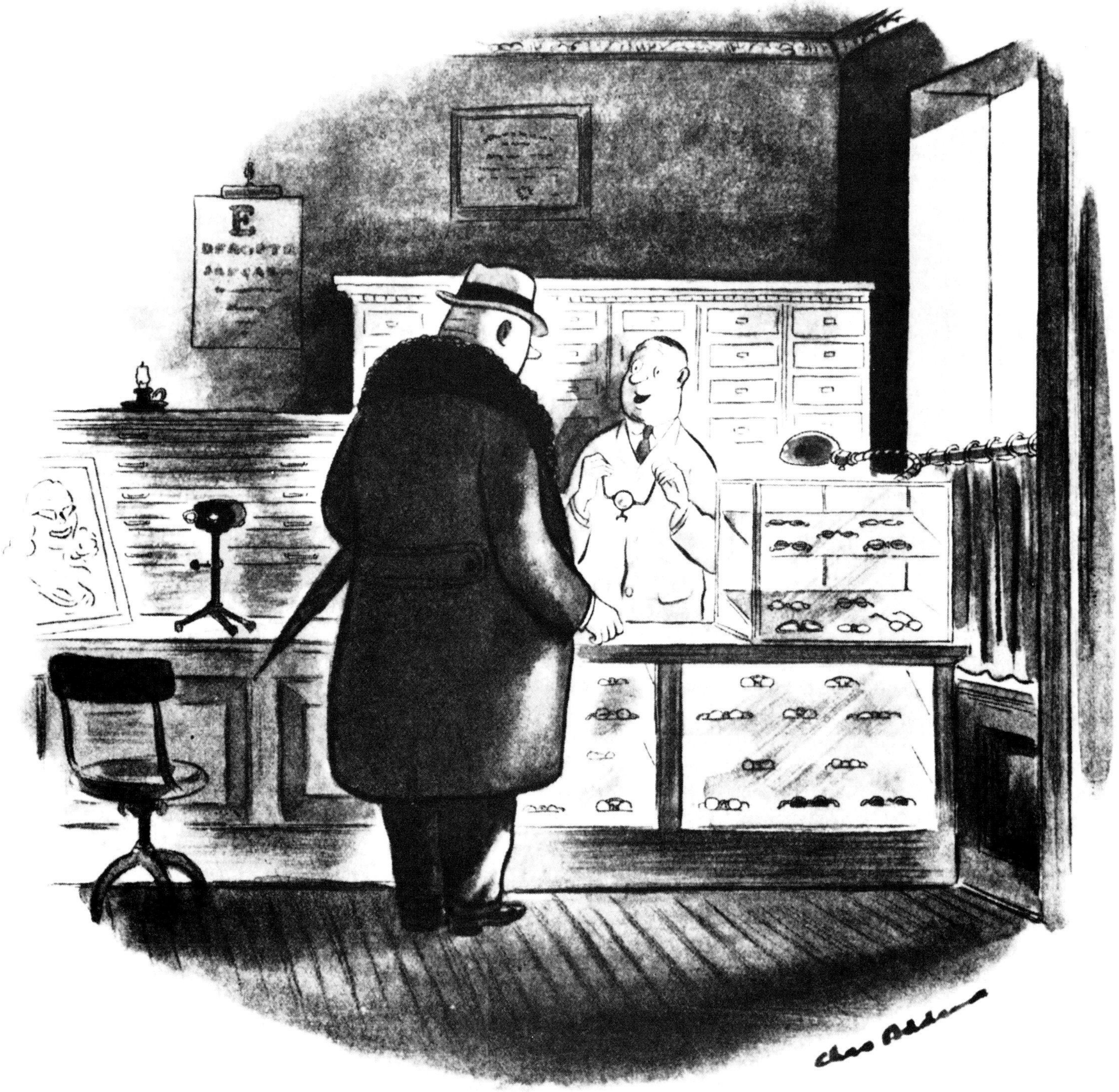
Chas Addams

"Now, let's just slip it on and see how it fits."

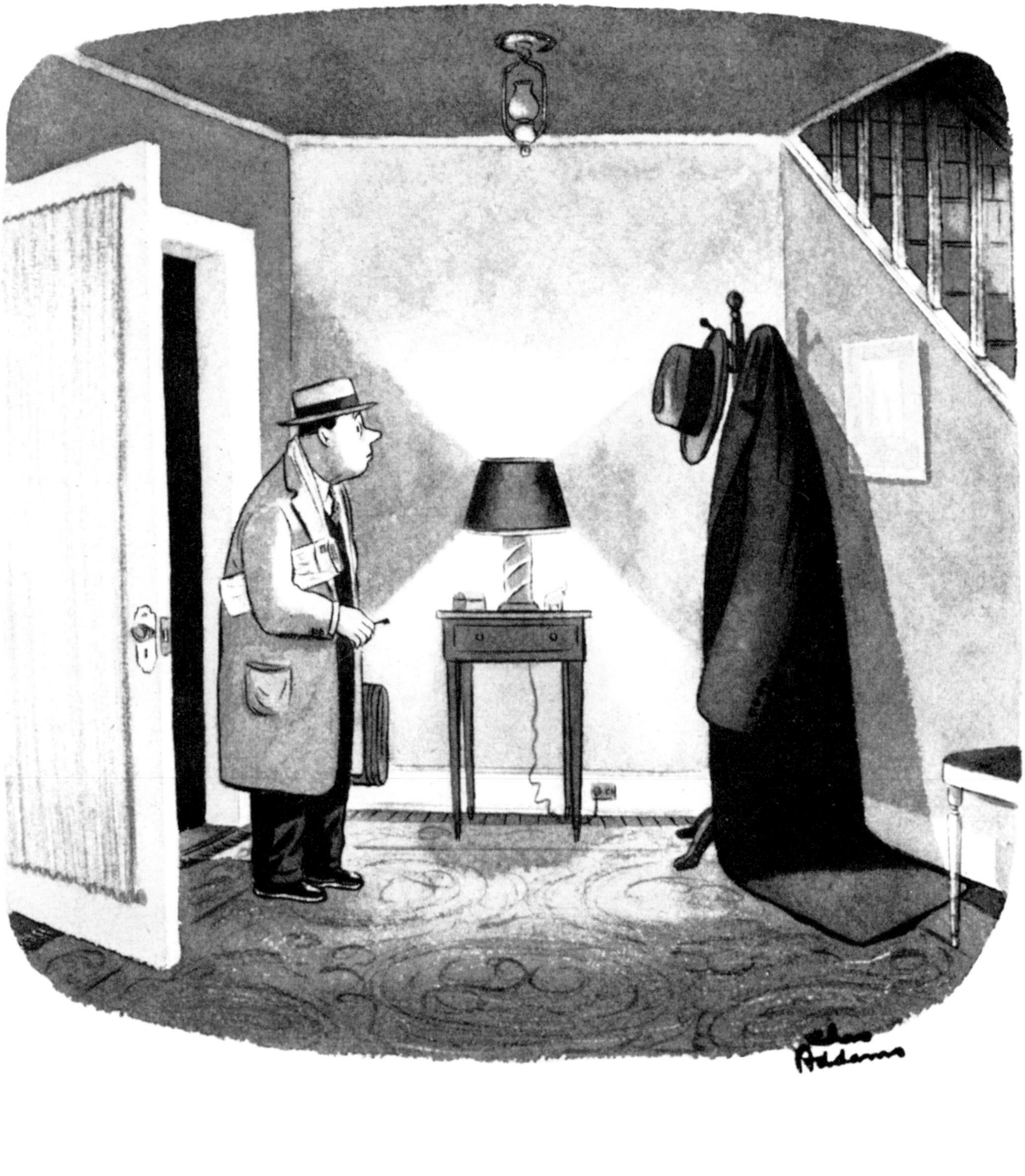
Chas Addams

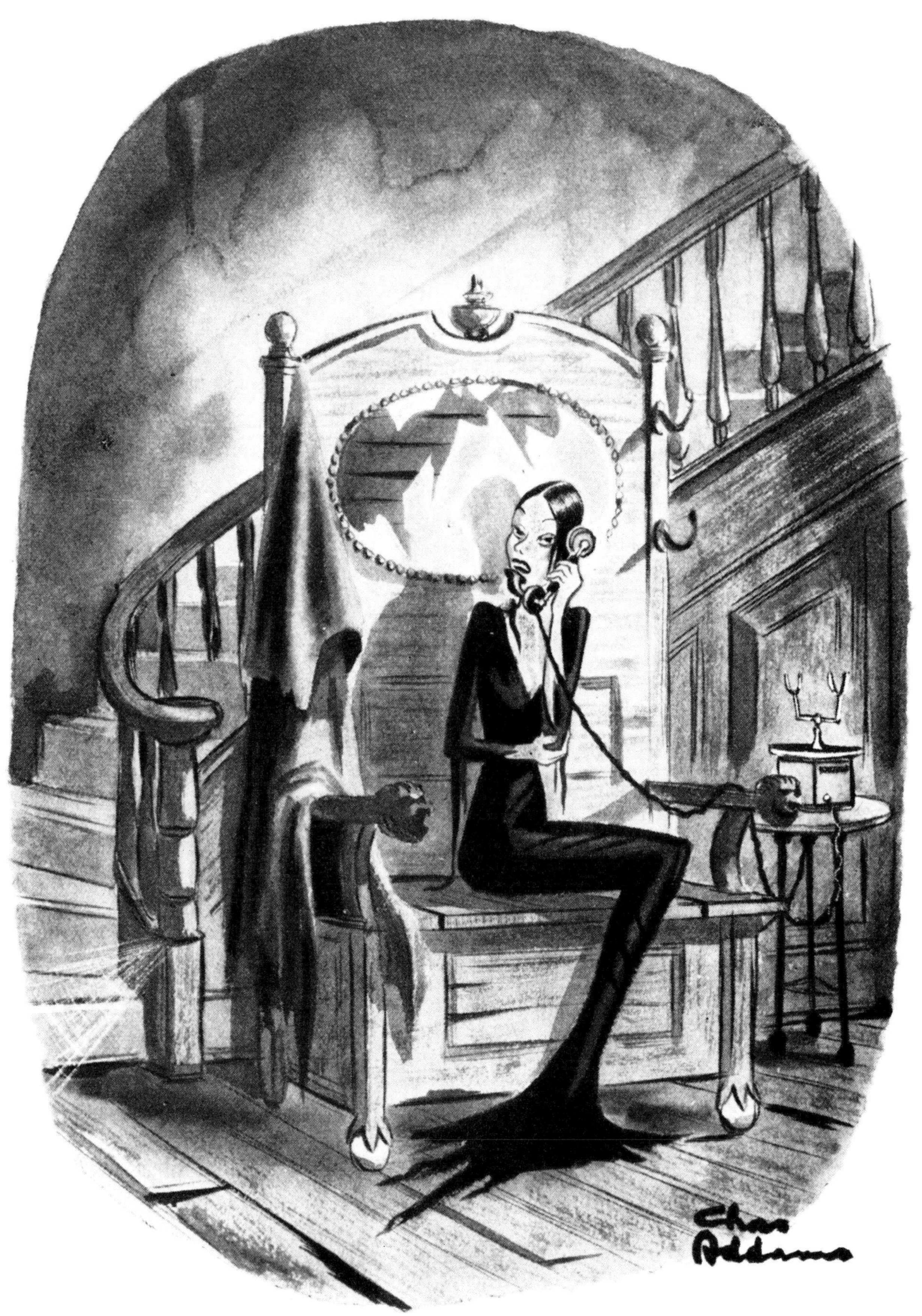
Chas Addams

"Oh, I couldn't make it Friday—I've so many things to do. It's the thirteenth, you know."

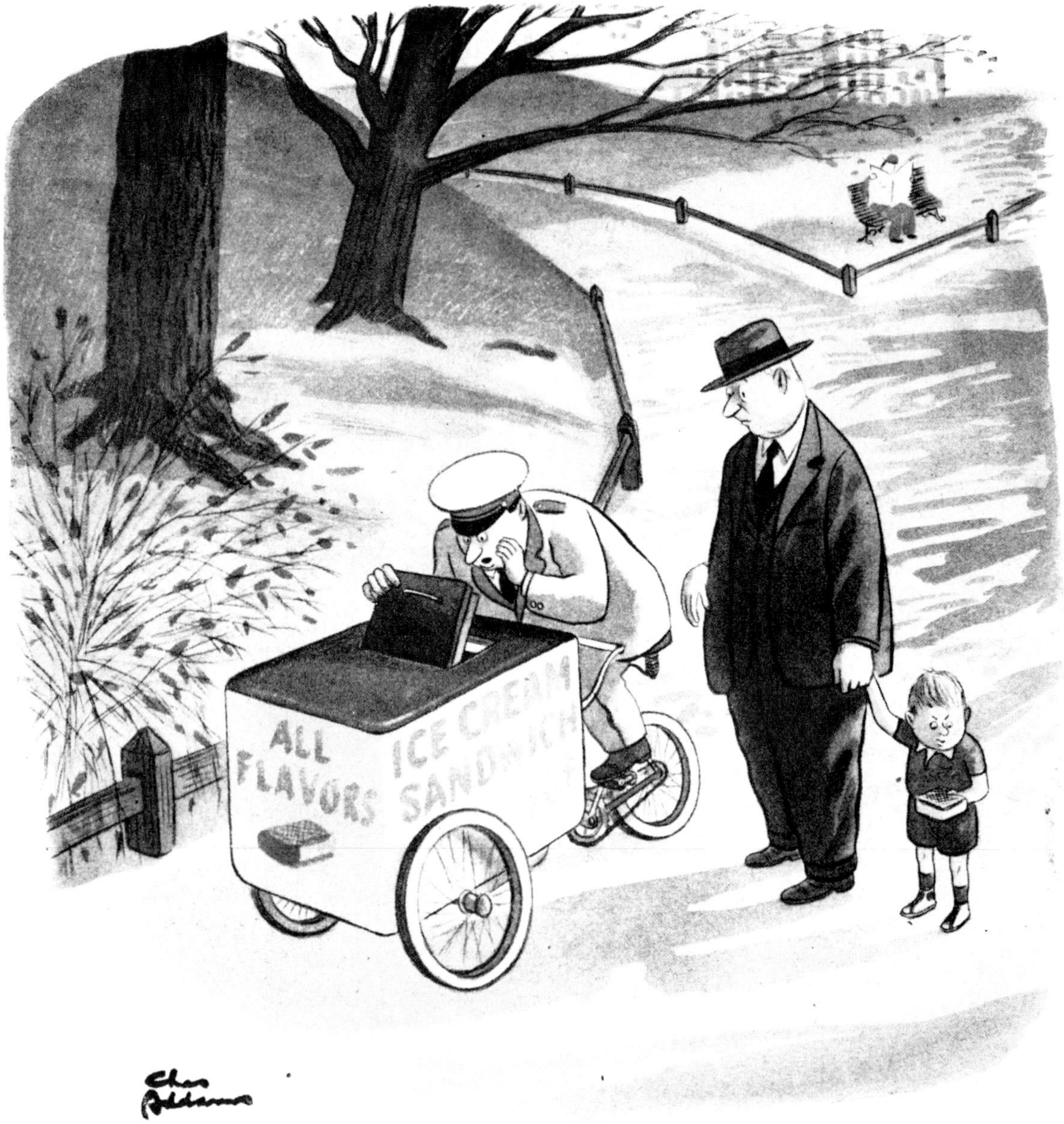
ALL
FLAVORS
ICE CREAM
SANDWICH

"Another vanilla, Benny."

"This little piggy went to market, this little piggy stayed home,
This little piggy had roast beef, this little piggy had none,
This little piggy went wee wee wee all the way home,
And this little piggy . . ."

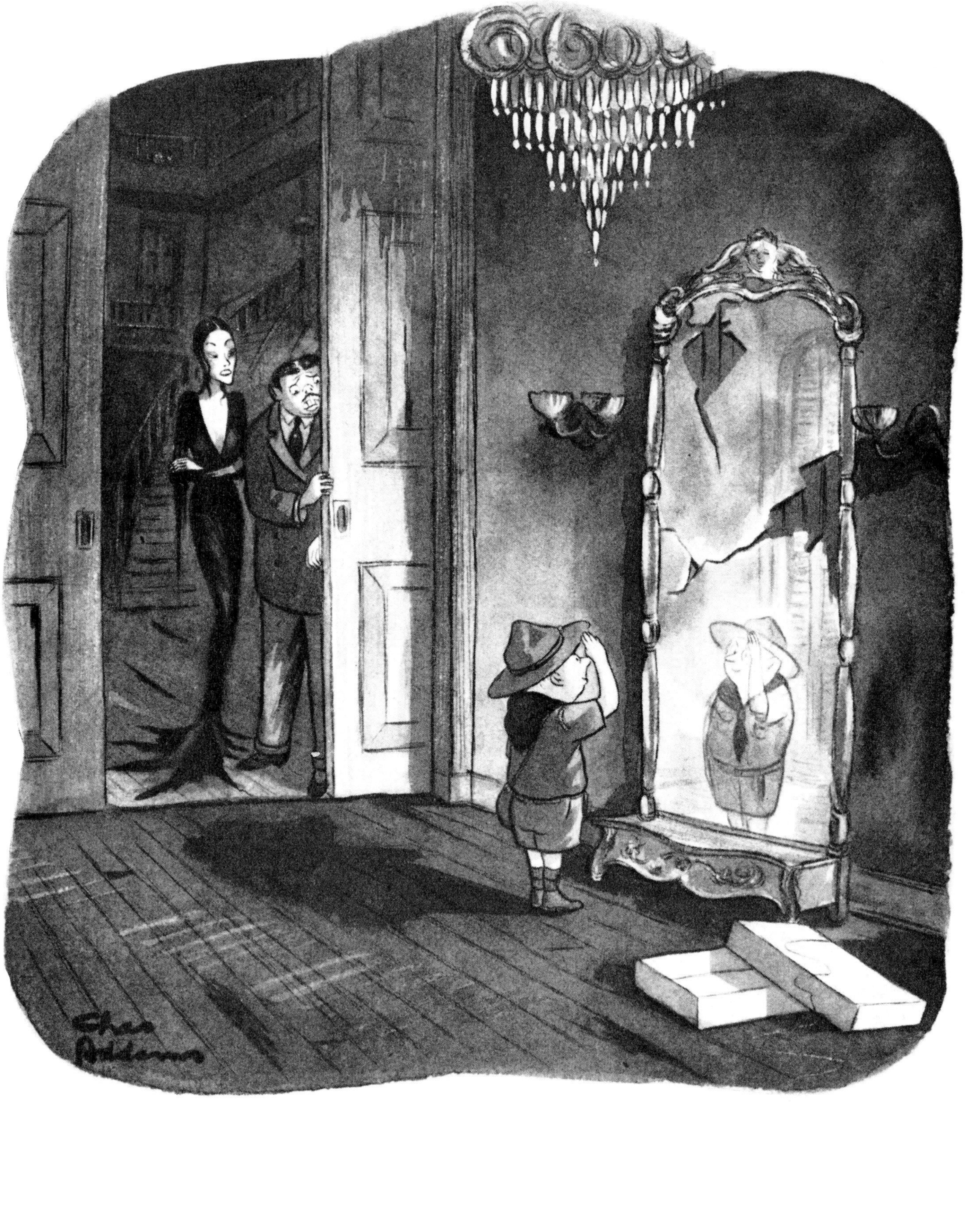
Chas Addams

"Well, he certainly doesn't take after my *side of the family."*

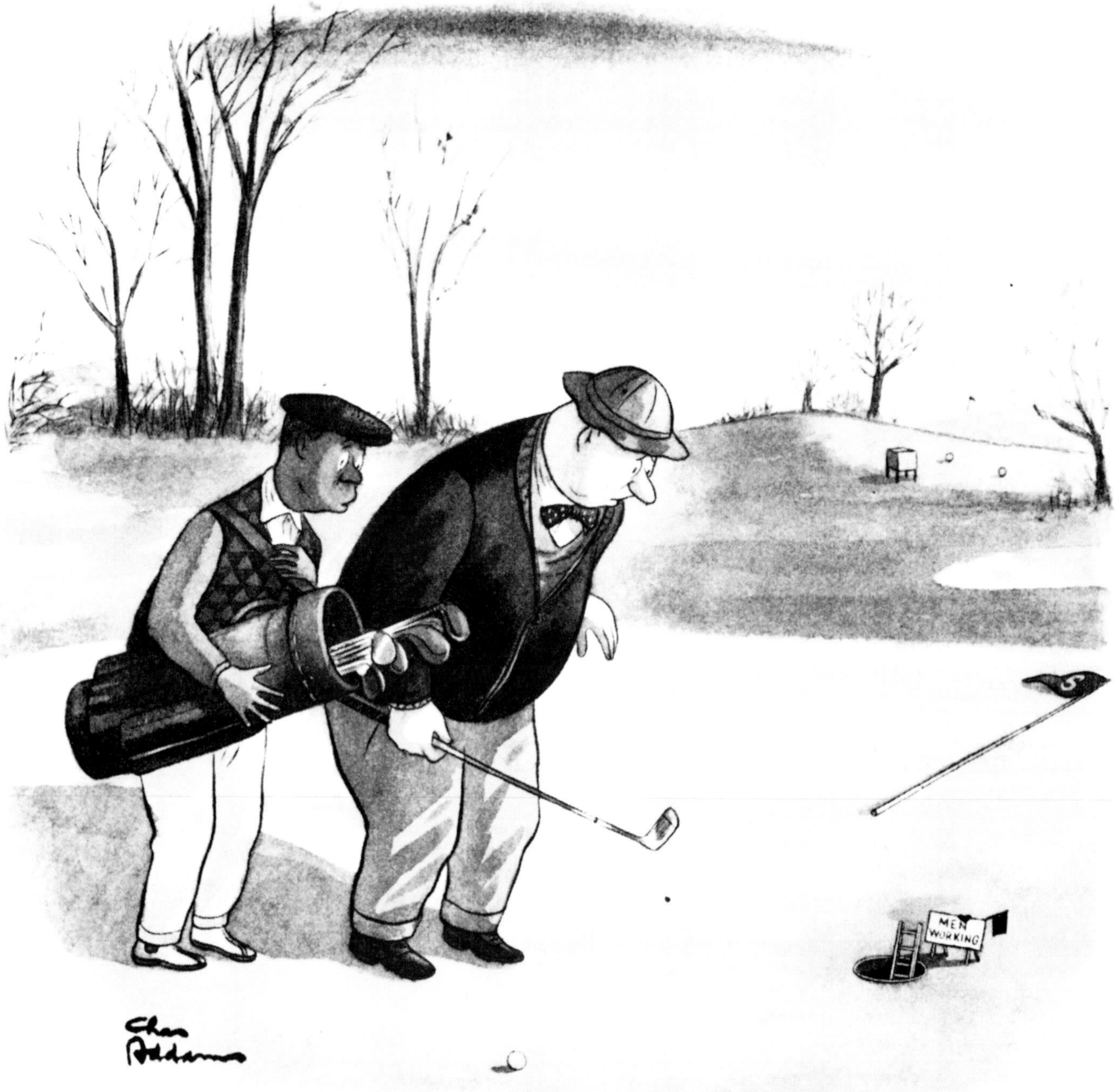
MEN WORKING
Chas Addams

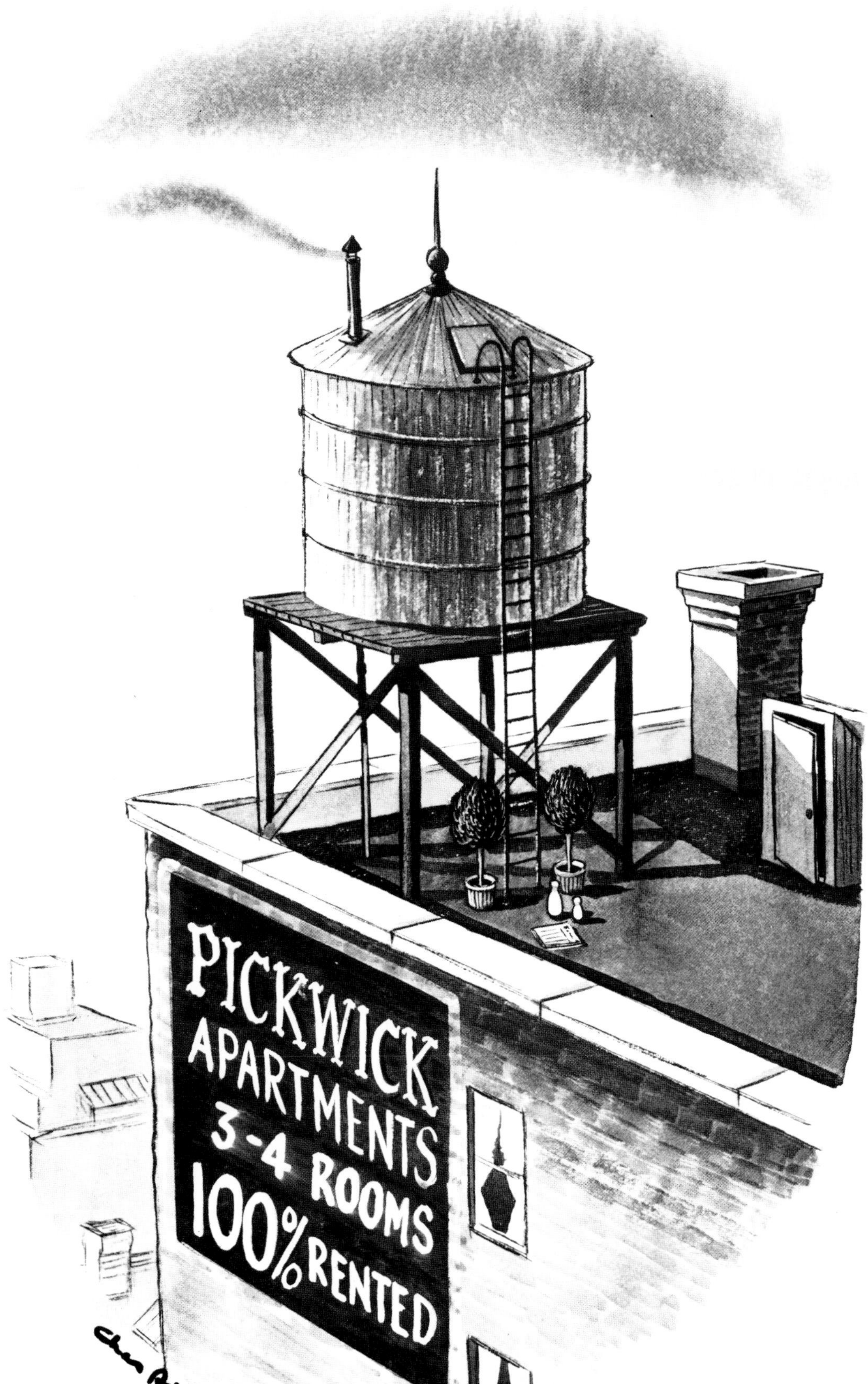
PICKWICK
APARTMENTS
3-4 ROOMS
100% RENTED

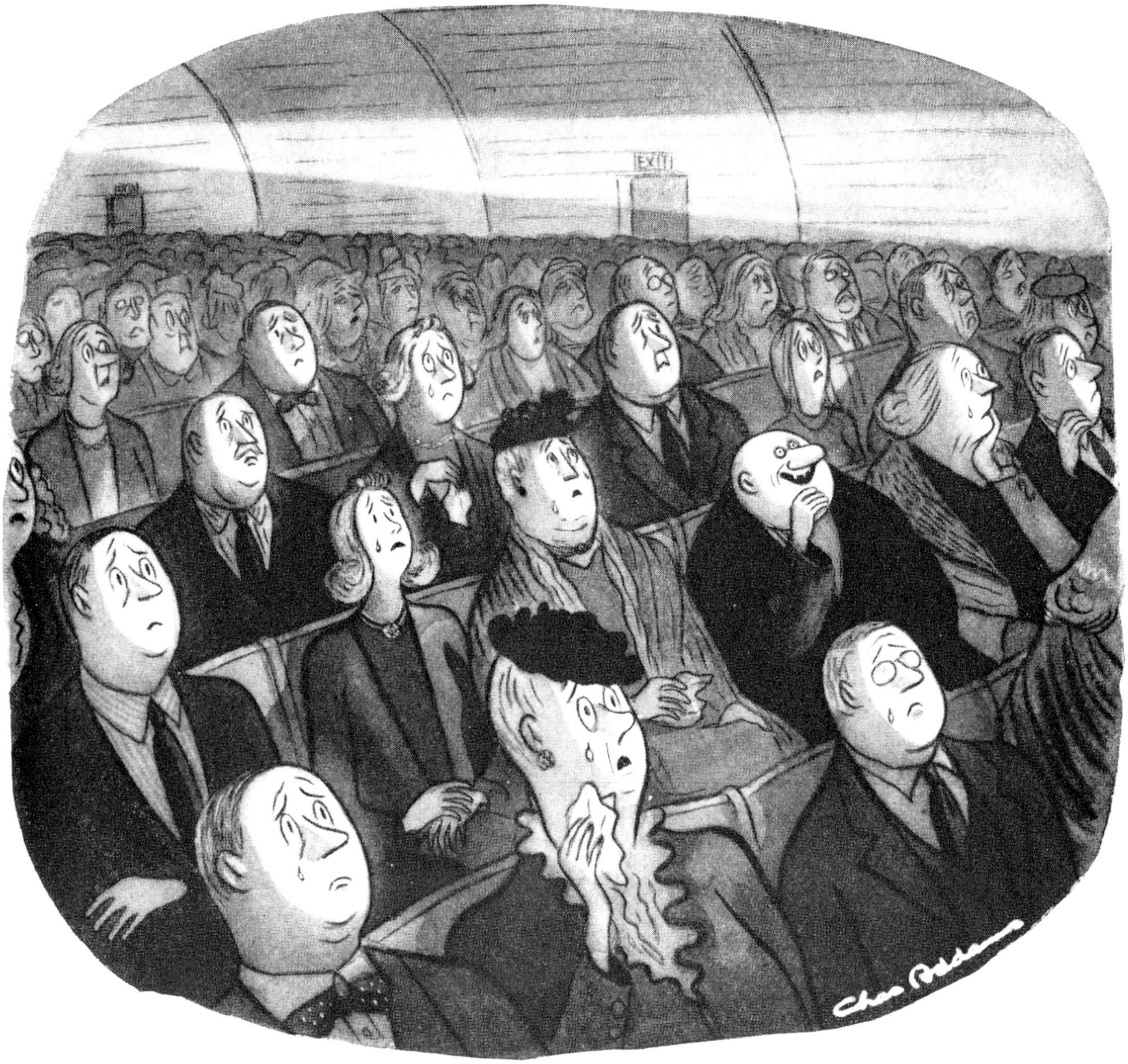
EXIT
Chas Addams

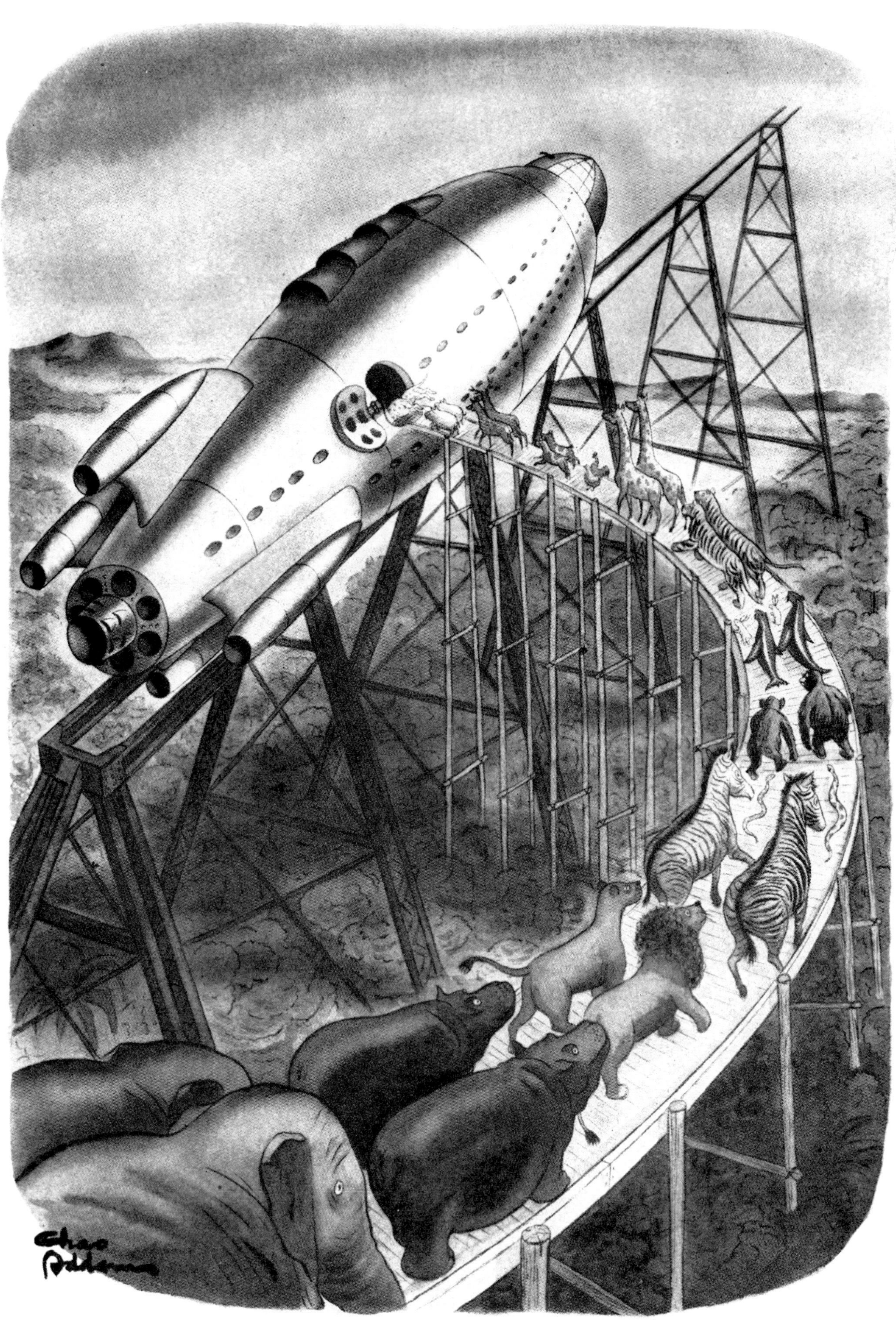
Chas Addams

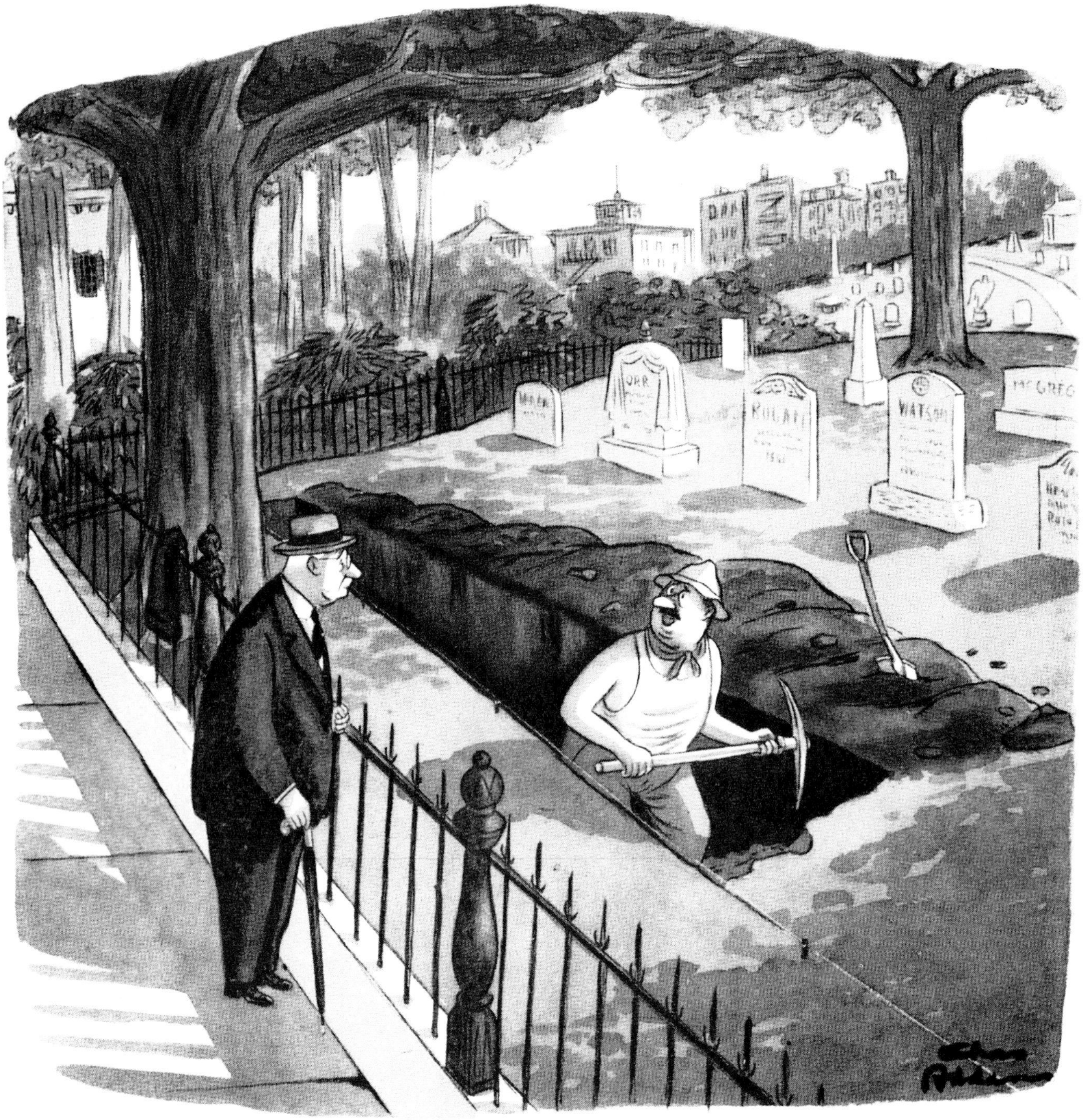
ORR
WATSON

"Oh, my goodness, no! Just a water main."

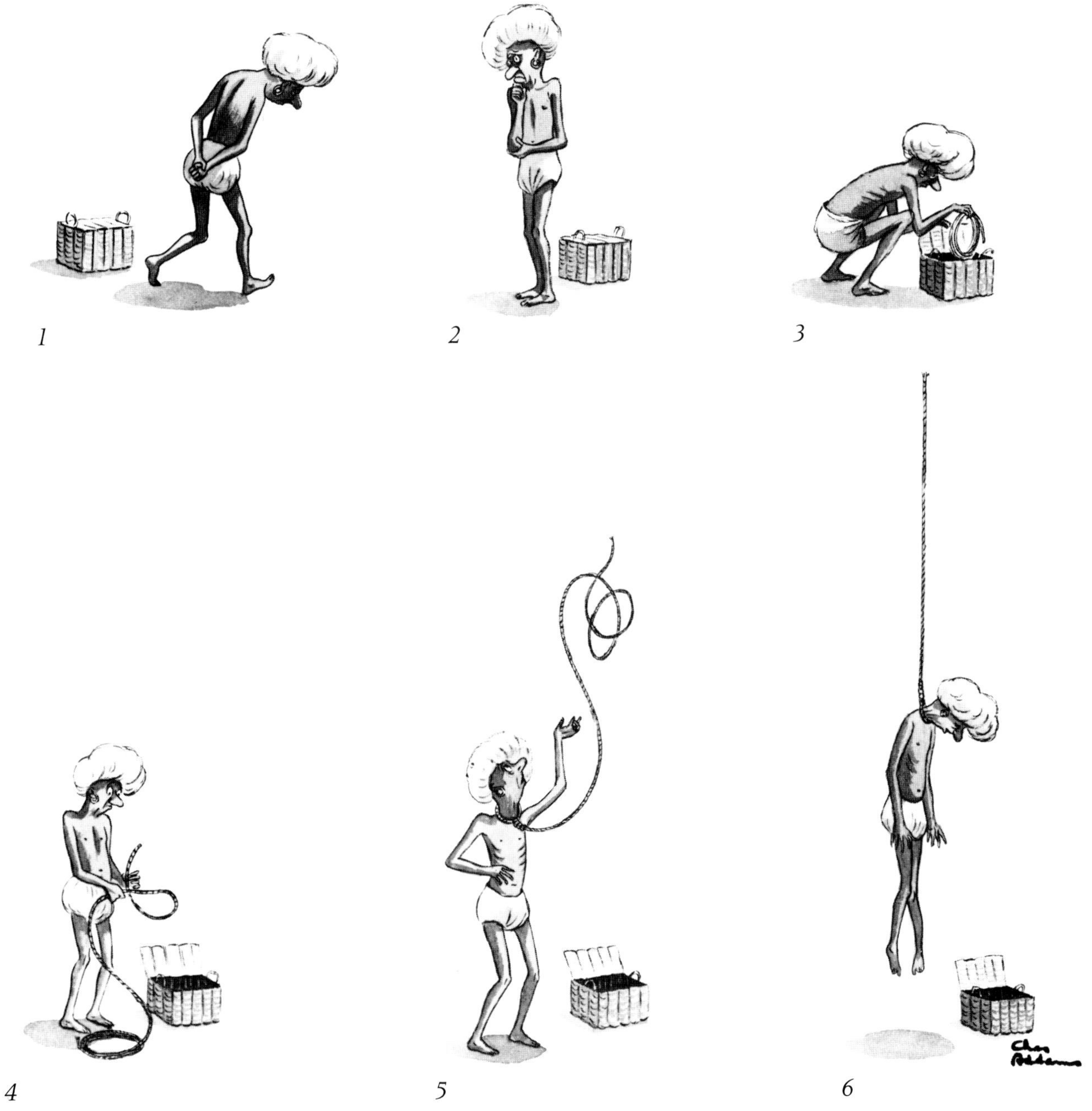
1
2
3
4
5
6
Chas Addams

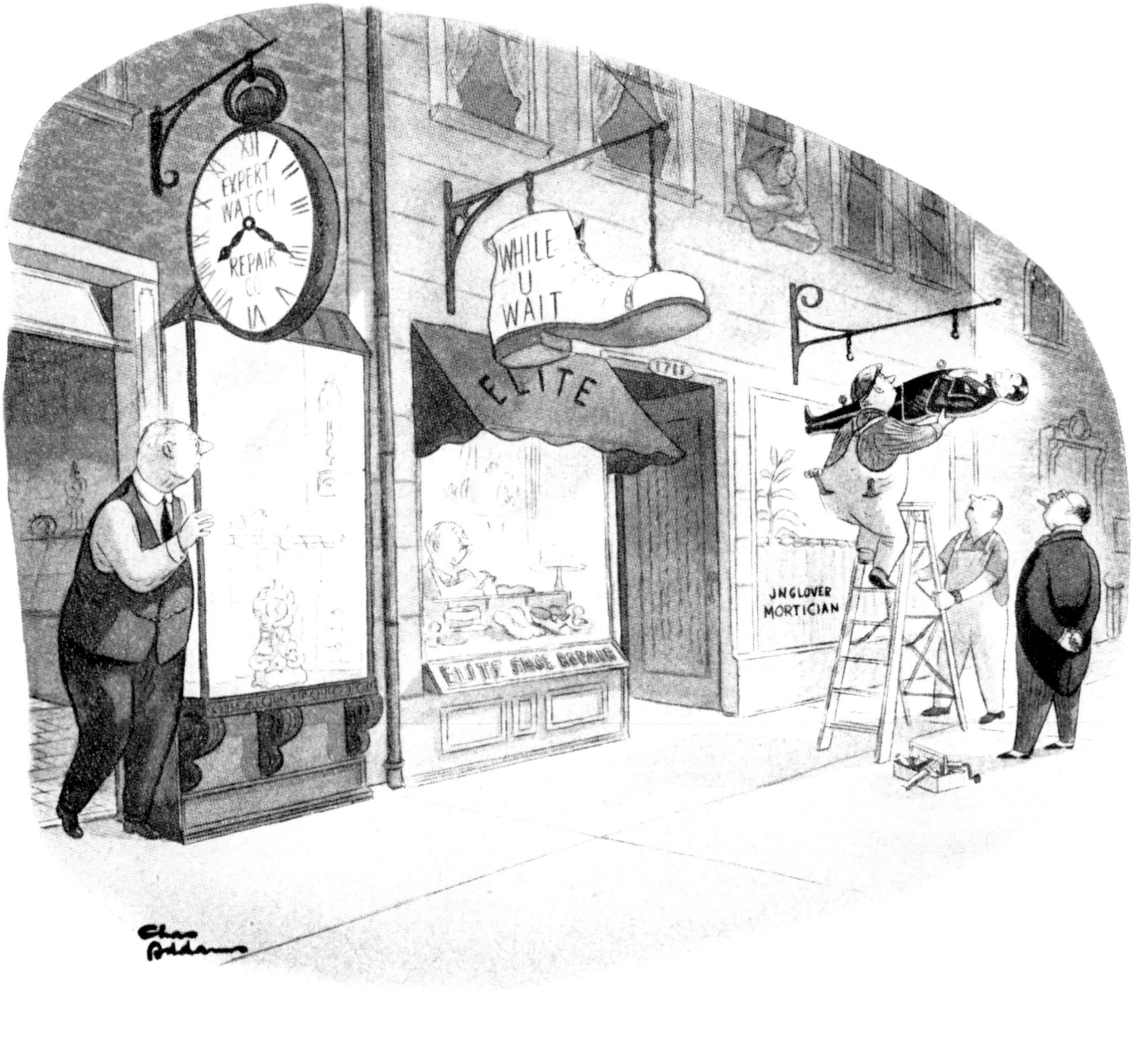
EXPERT
WATCH
REPAIR
CO
WHILE
U
WAIT
ELITE
ELITE SHOE REPAIR
JN GLOVER
MORTICIAN
Chas Addams

67

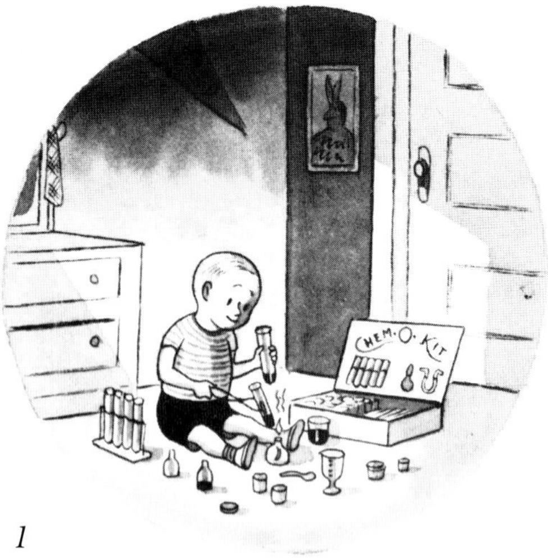
CHEM·O·KIT

1

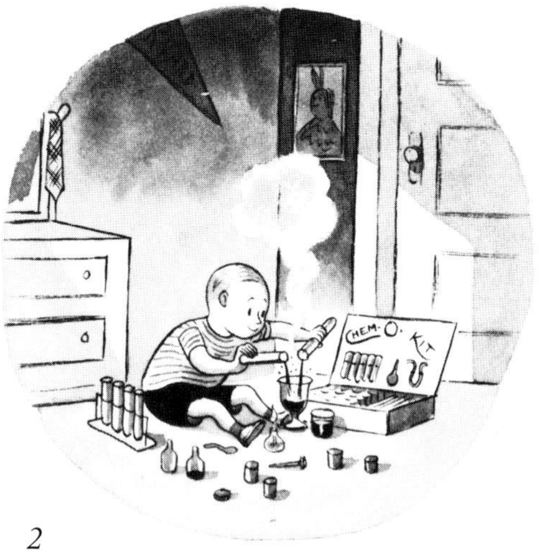
CHEM·O·KIT

2

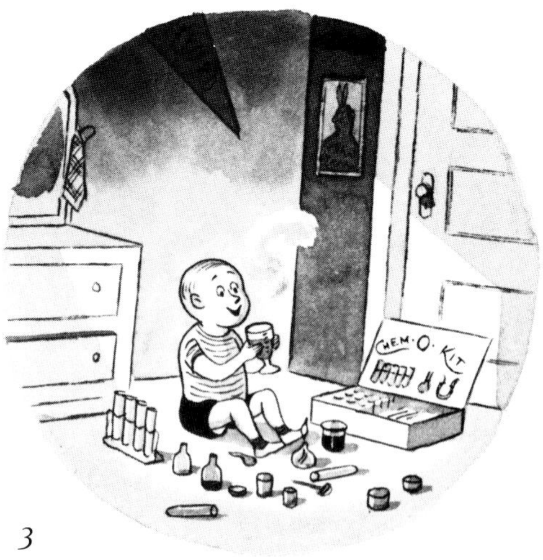
CHEM·O·KIT

3

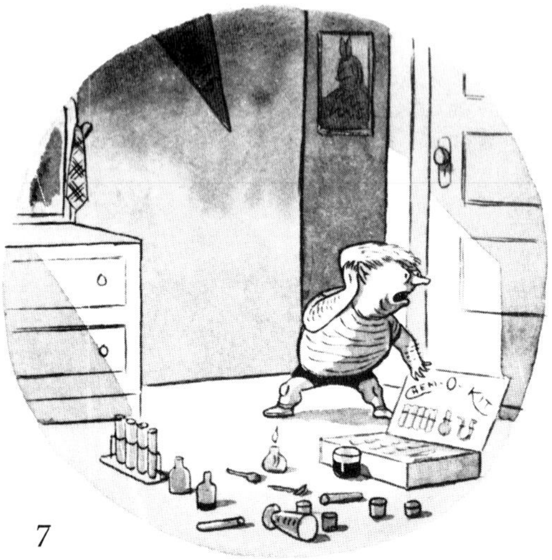

7

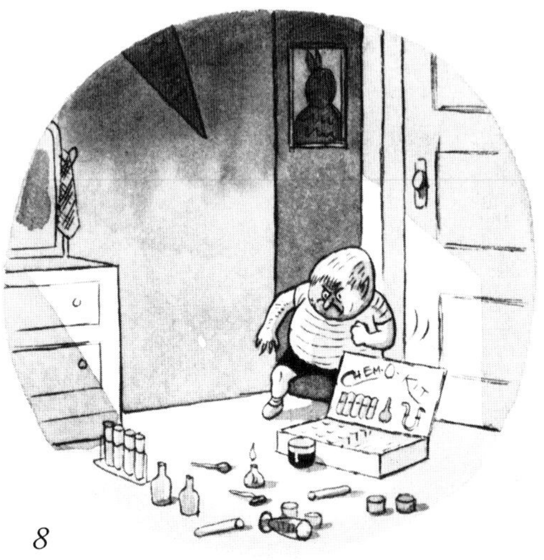

8

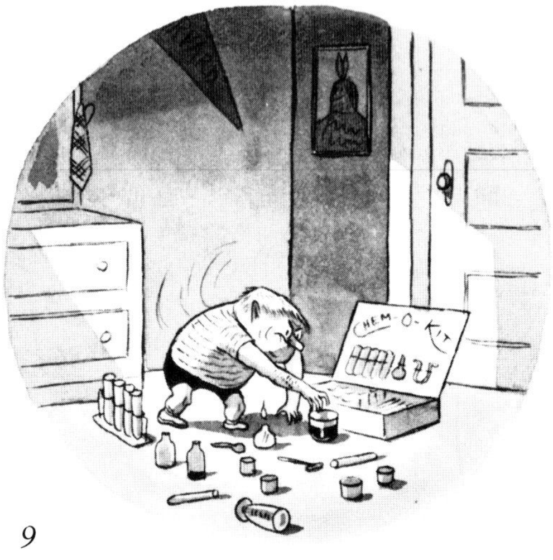
CHEM·O·KIT

9

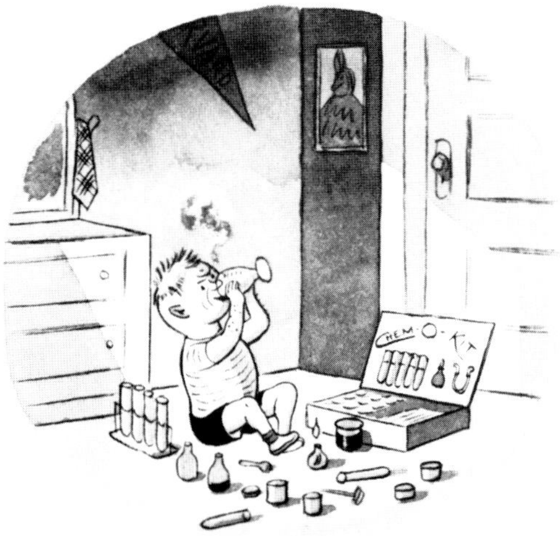
CHEM-O-KIT

4

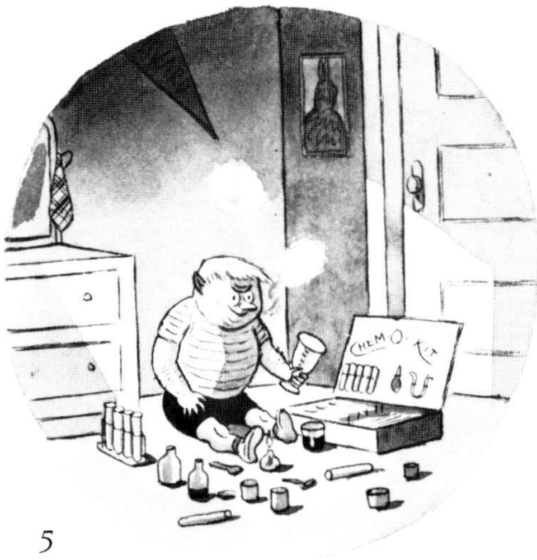
CHEM-O-KIT

5

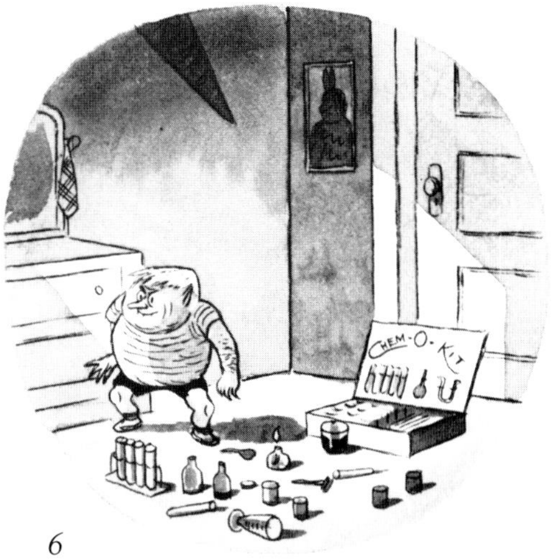
CHEM-O-KIT

6

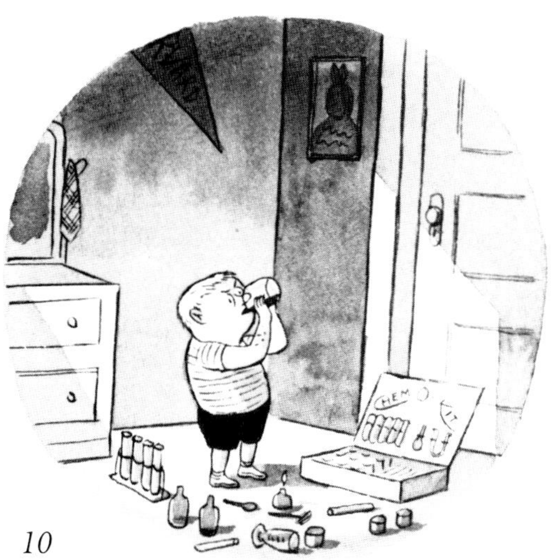
CHEM-O-KIT

10

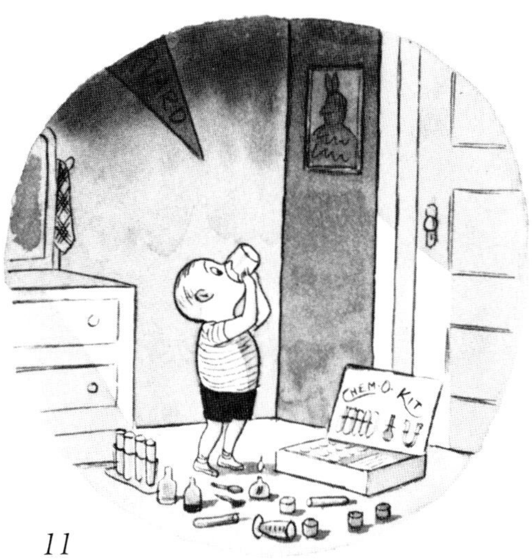
CHEM-O-KIT

11

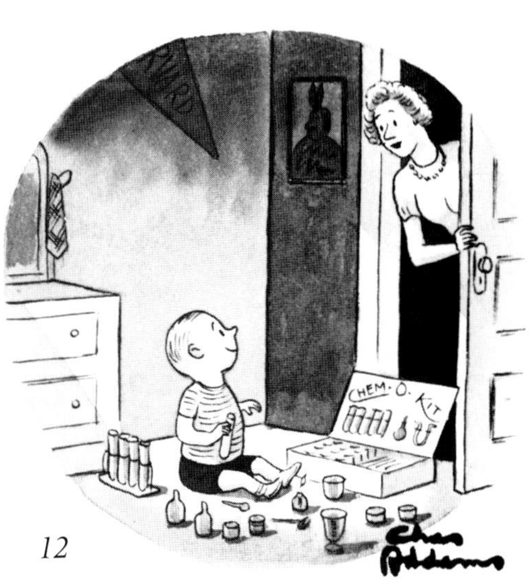
CHEM-O-KIT

12

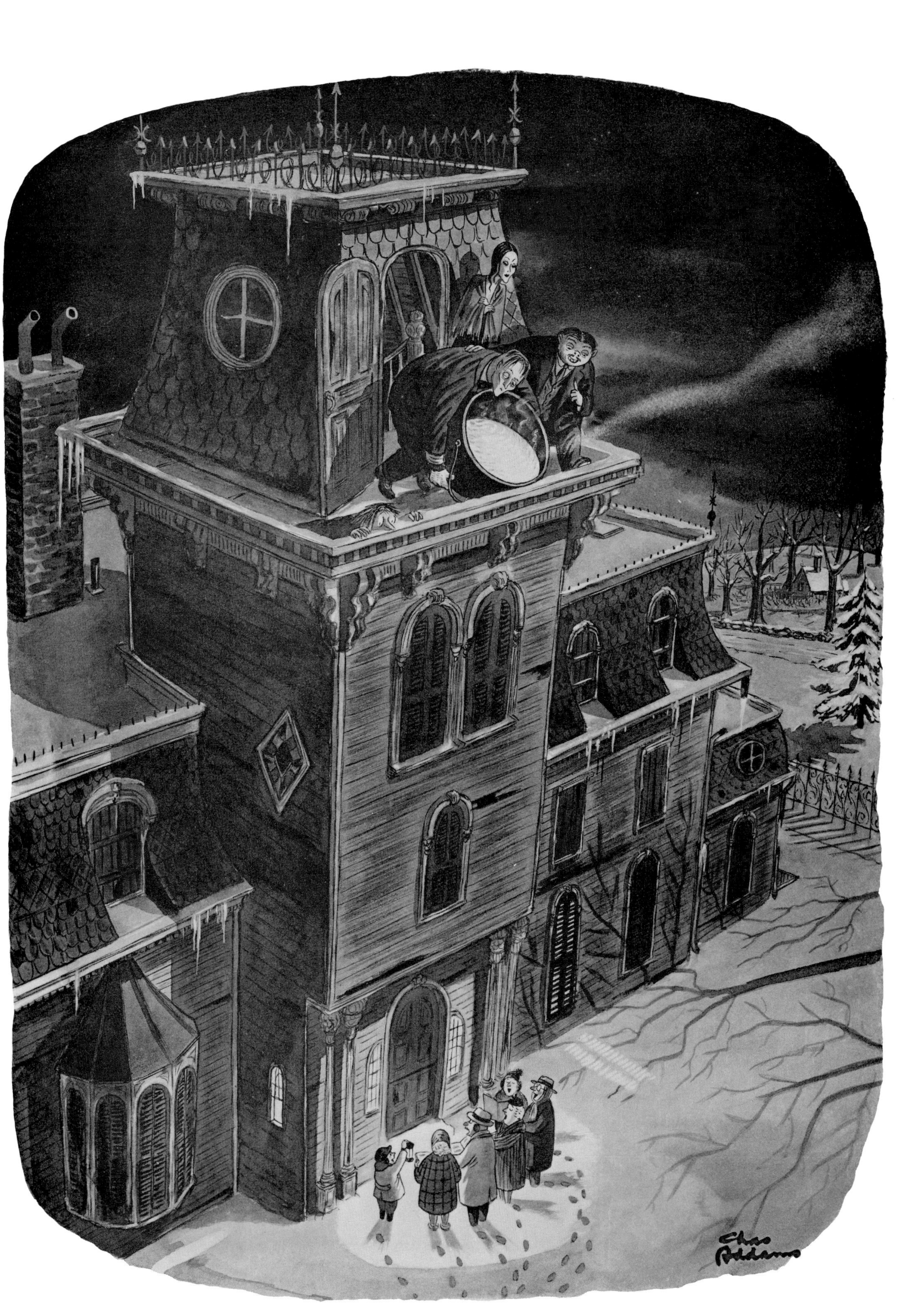
Chas Addams

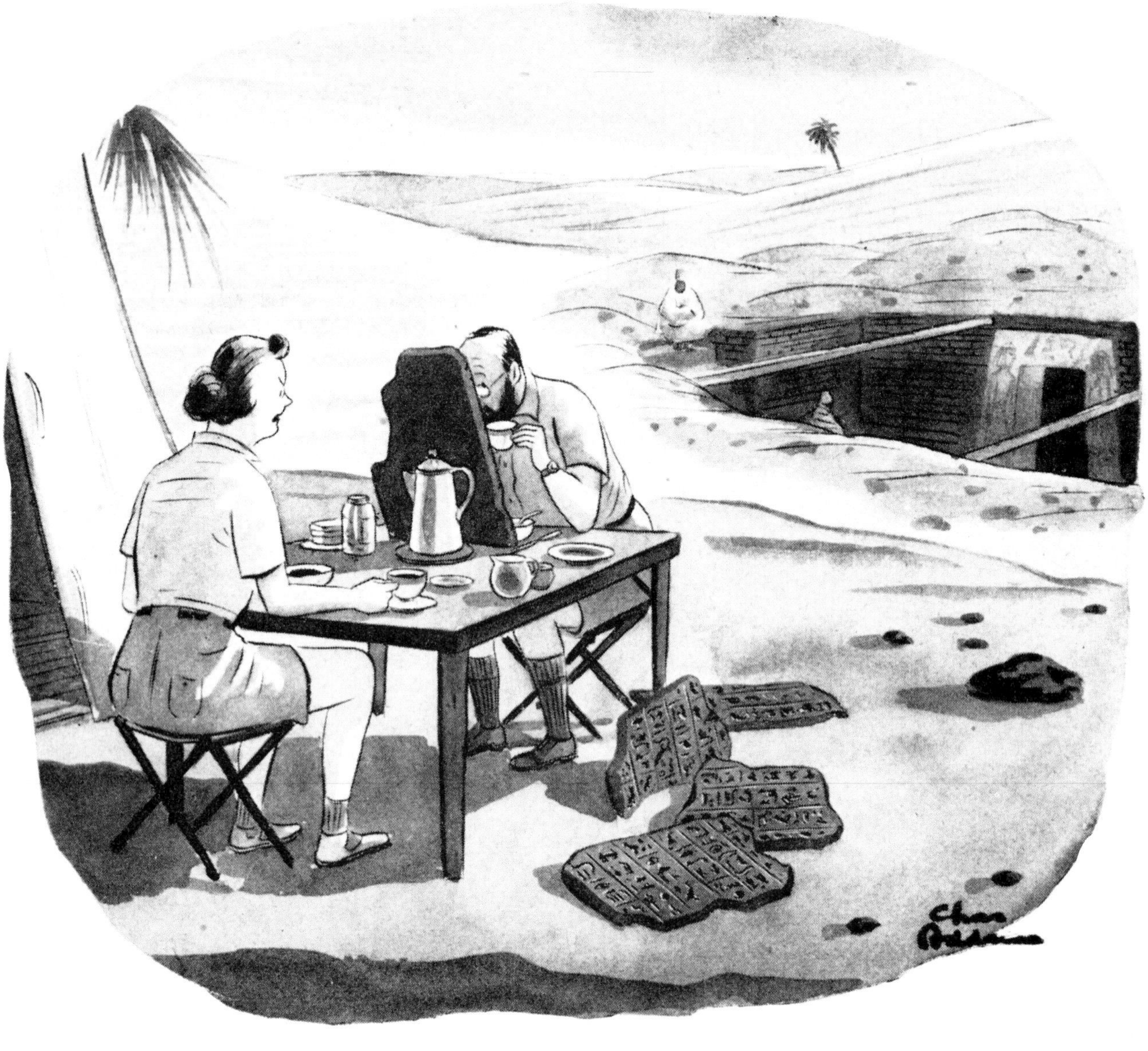
Chas Addams

"It's the children, darling, back from camp."

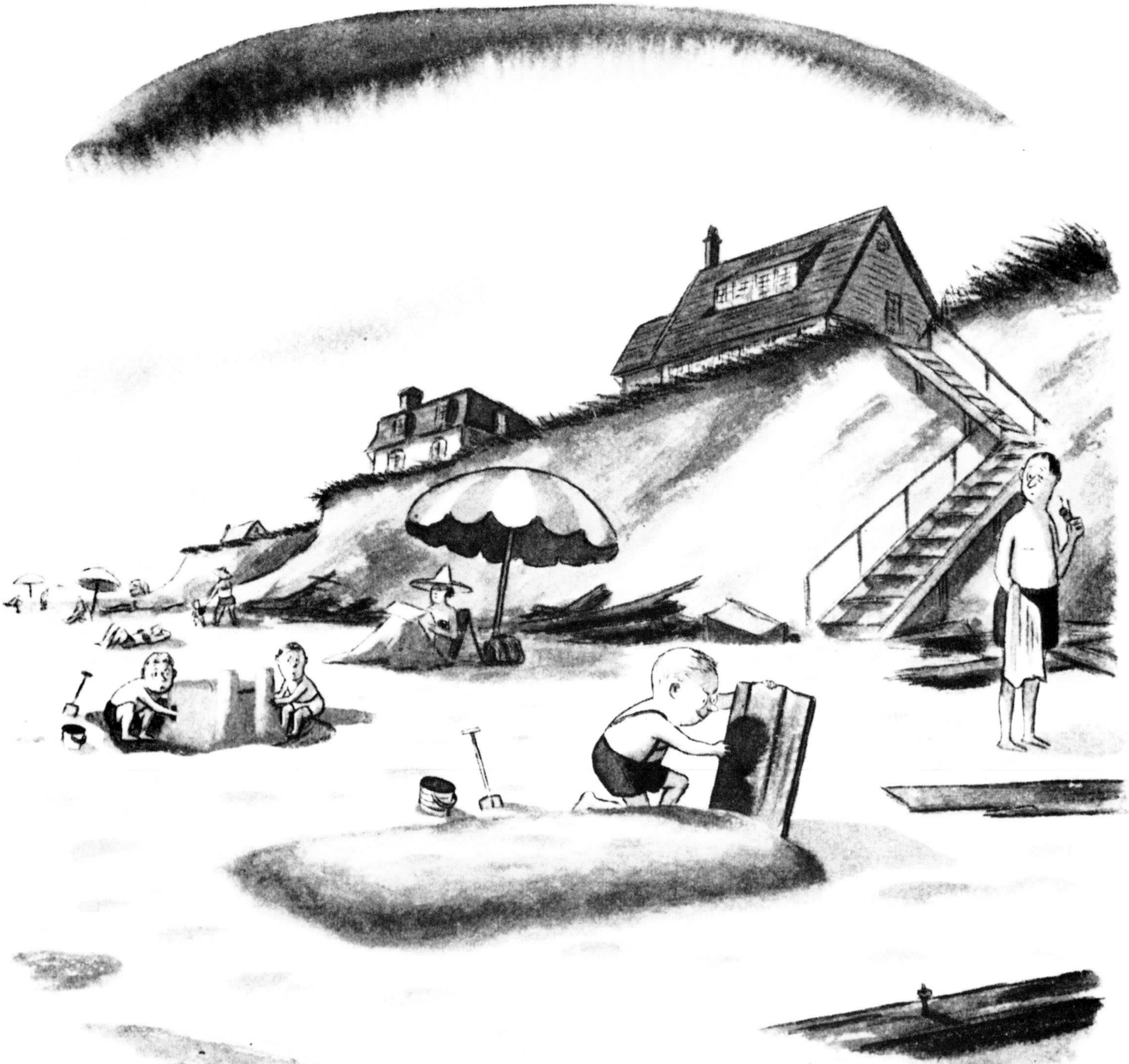
Chas Addams

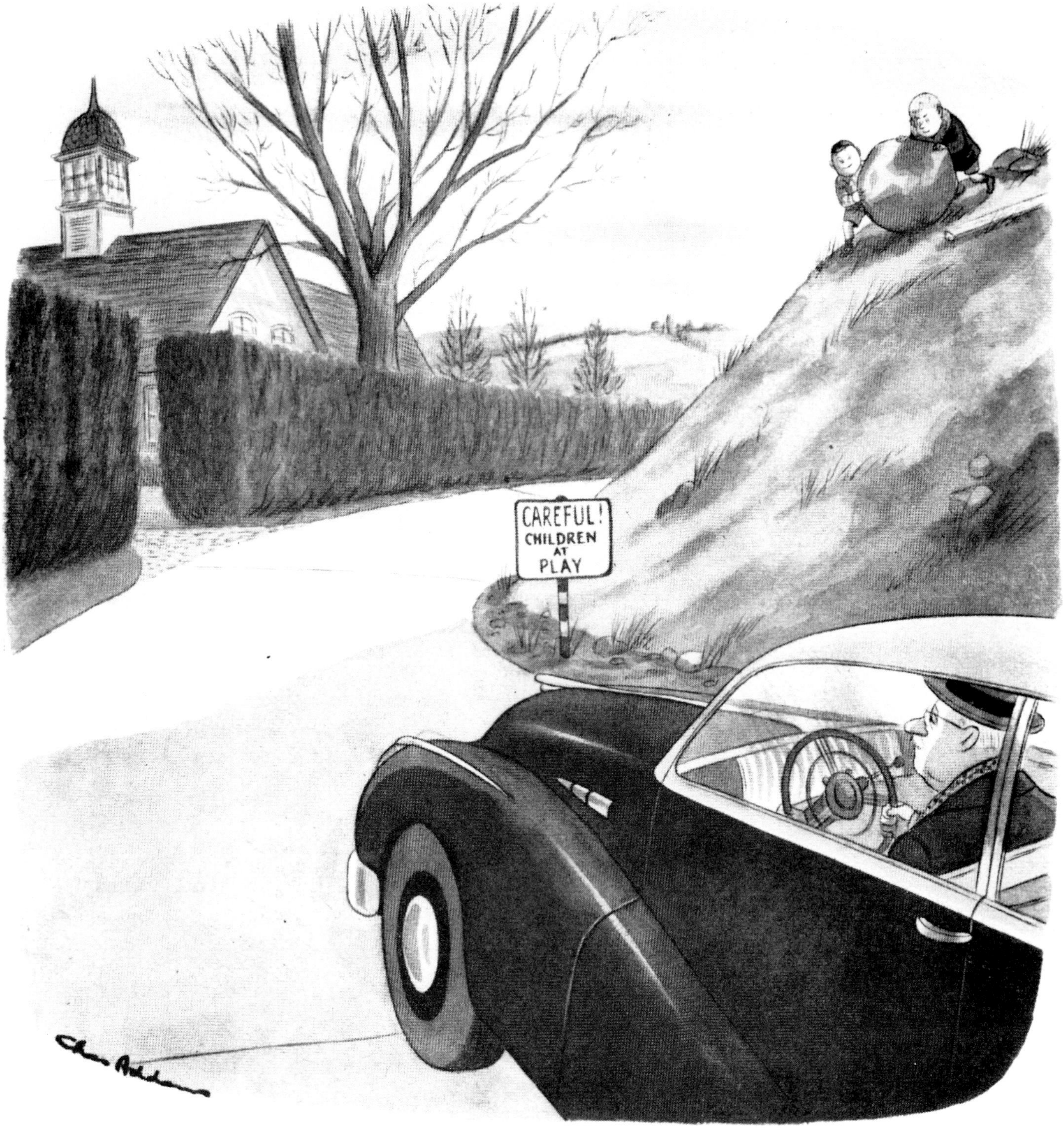
CAREFUL!
CHILDREN
AT
PLAY

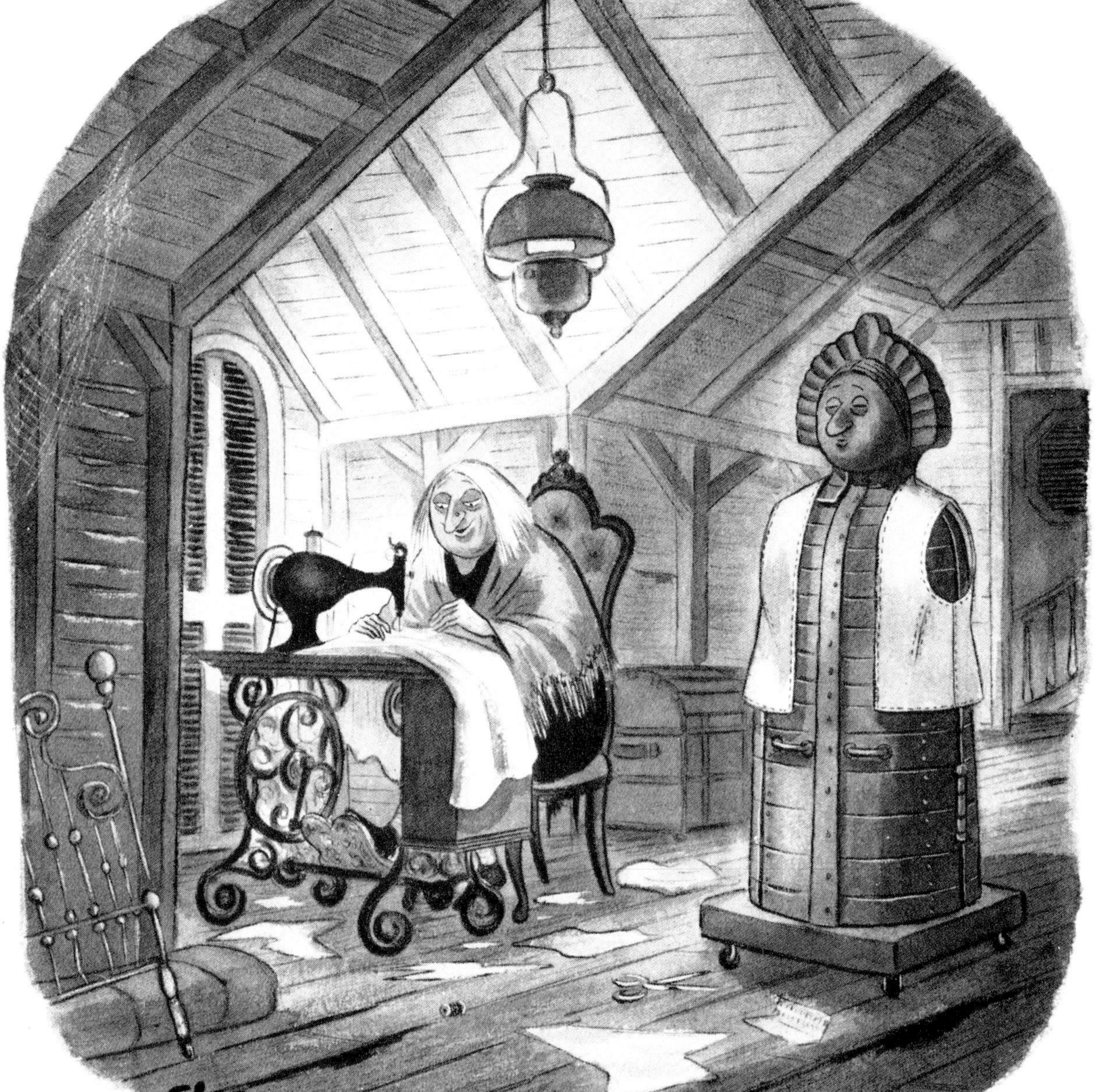
Chas Addams

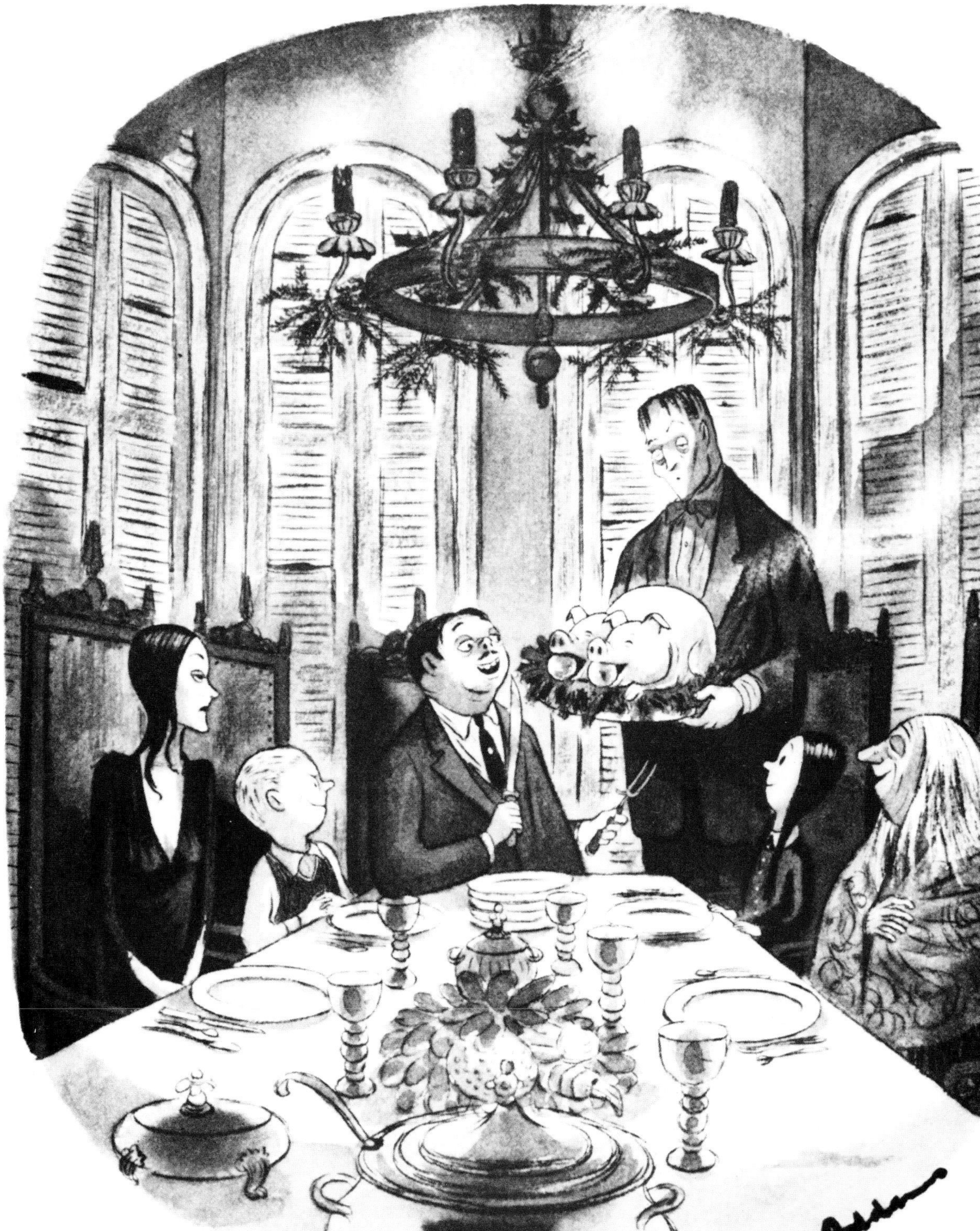
Chas Addams

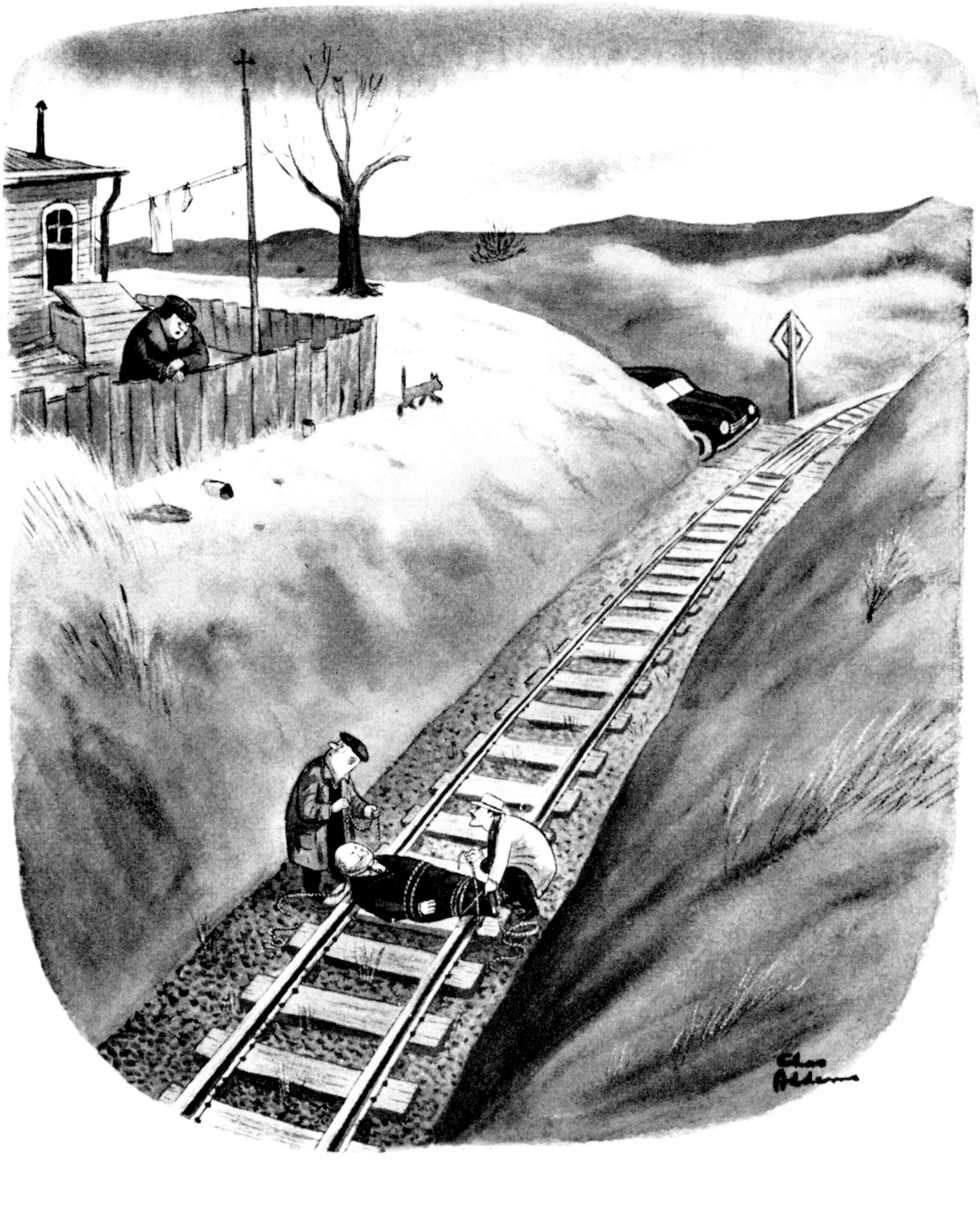

"It may be none of my business, but there hasn't been a train over that line in eight years."

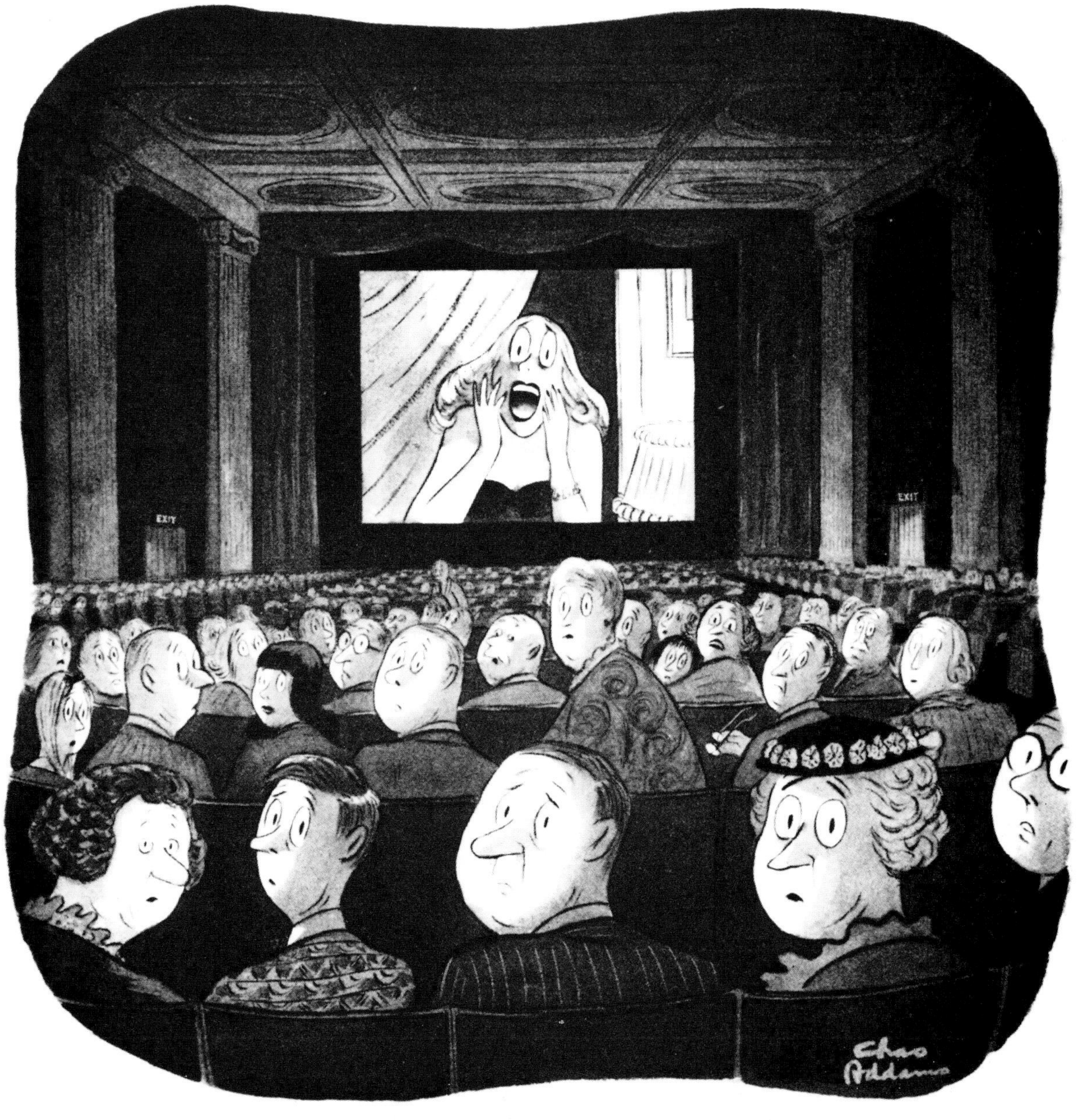
EXIT
Chas Addams

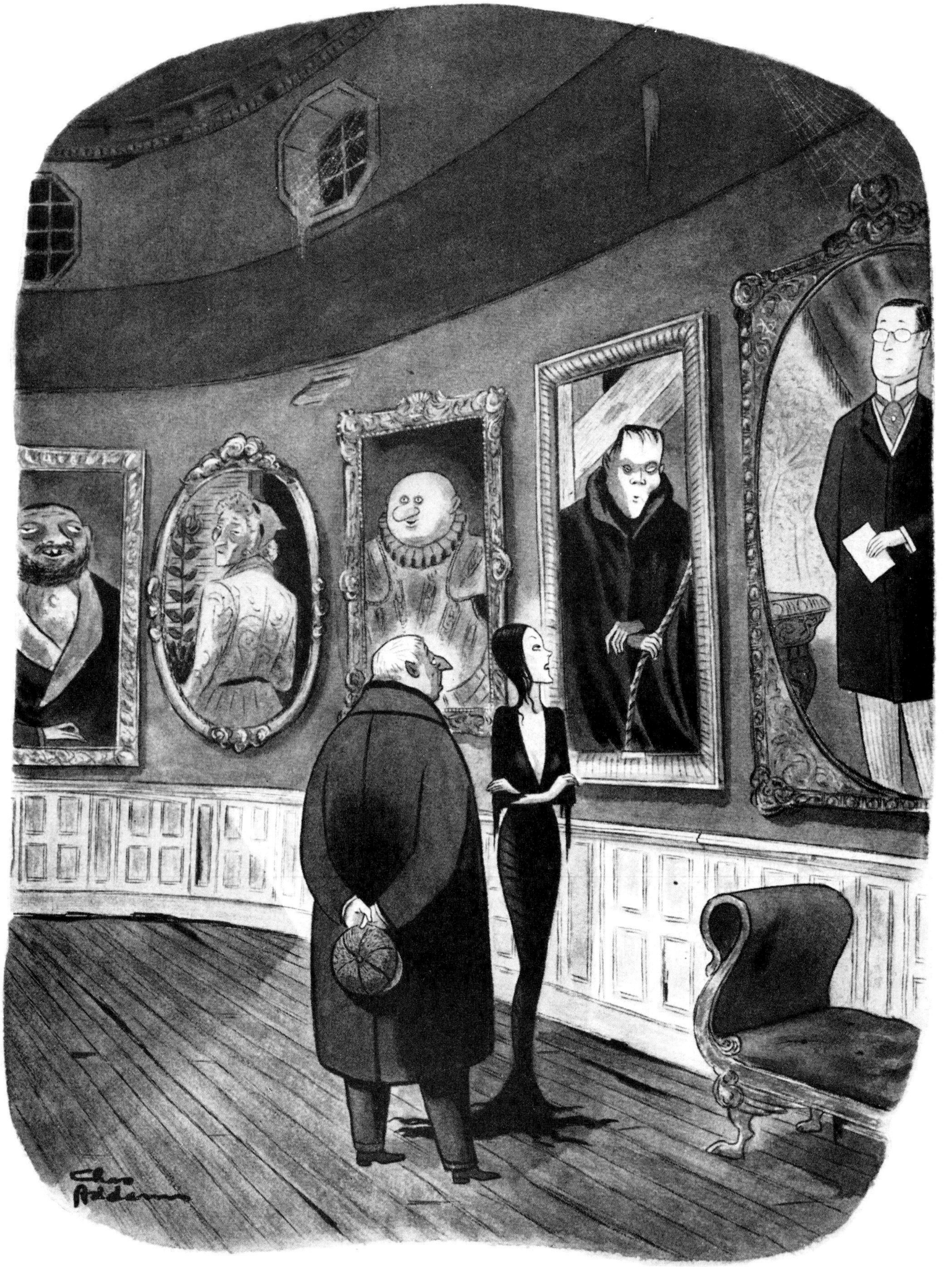

"This is Uncle Zander. Grandfather always called him the black sheep."

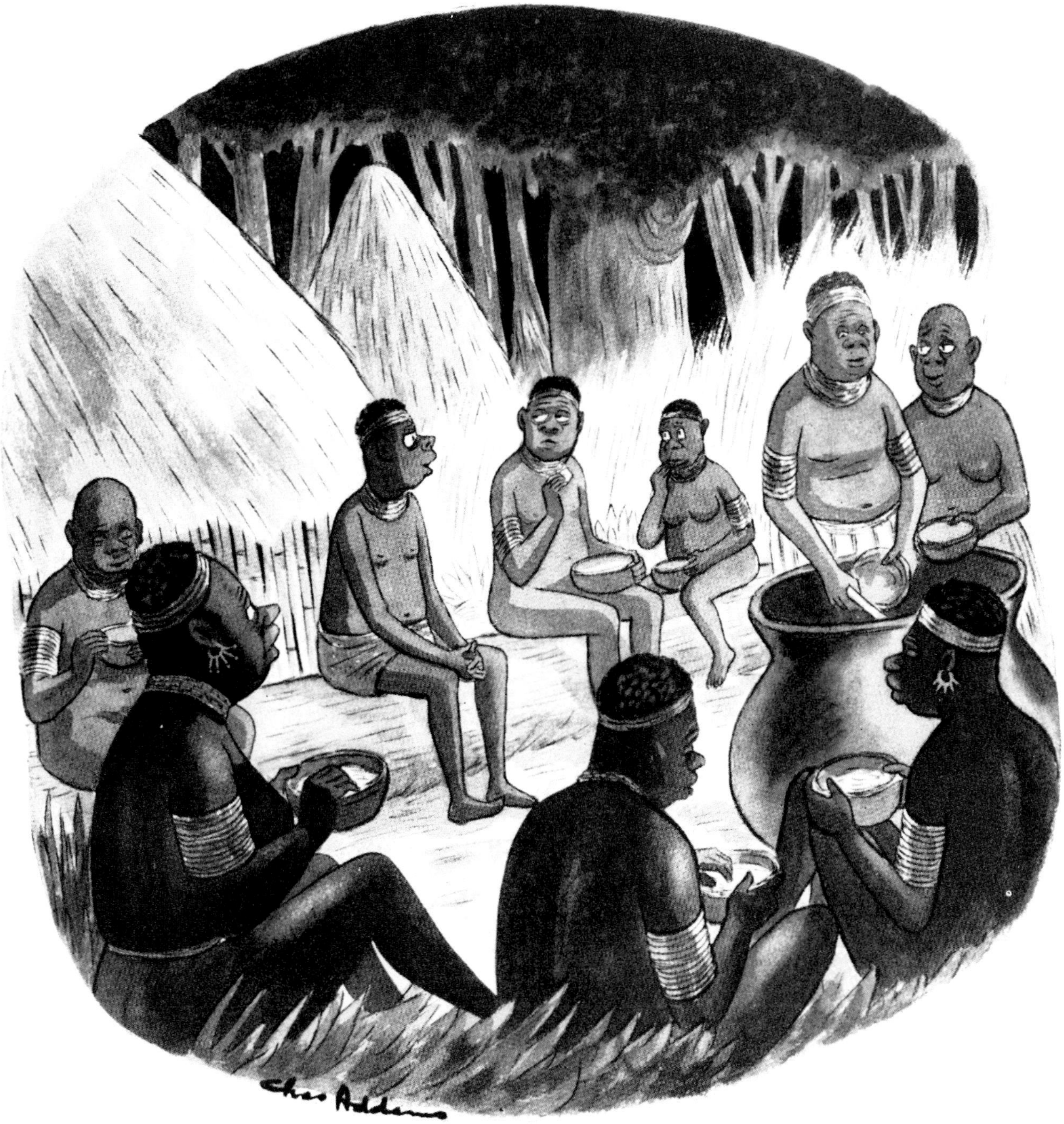
Chas Addams

"Oh, I like missionary, all right, but missionary doesn't like me."

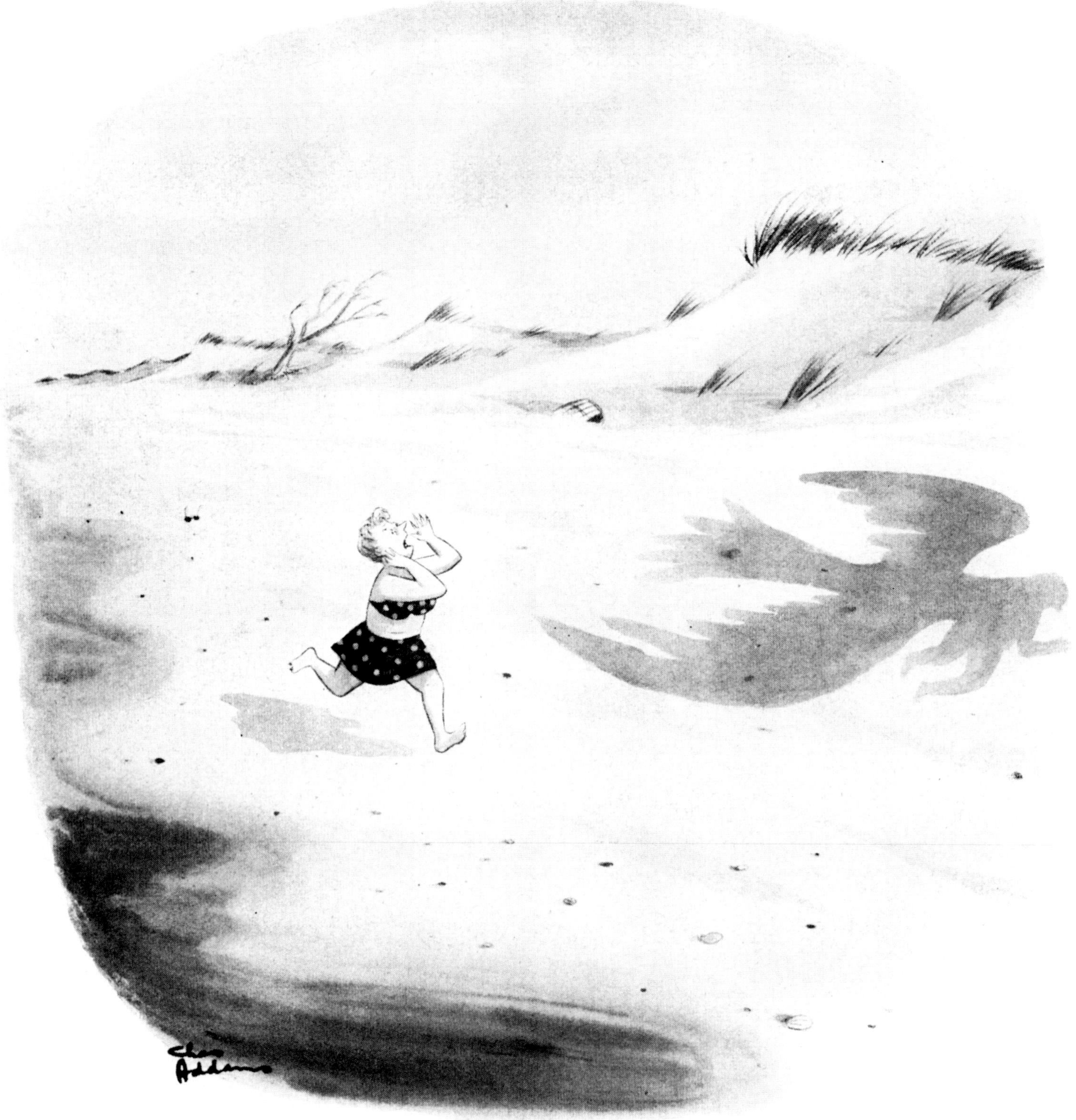

"George! George! Drop the keys!"

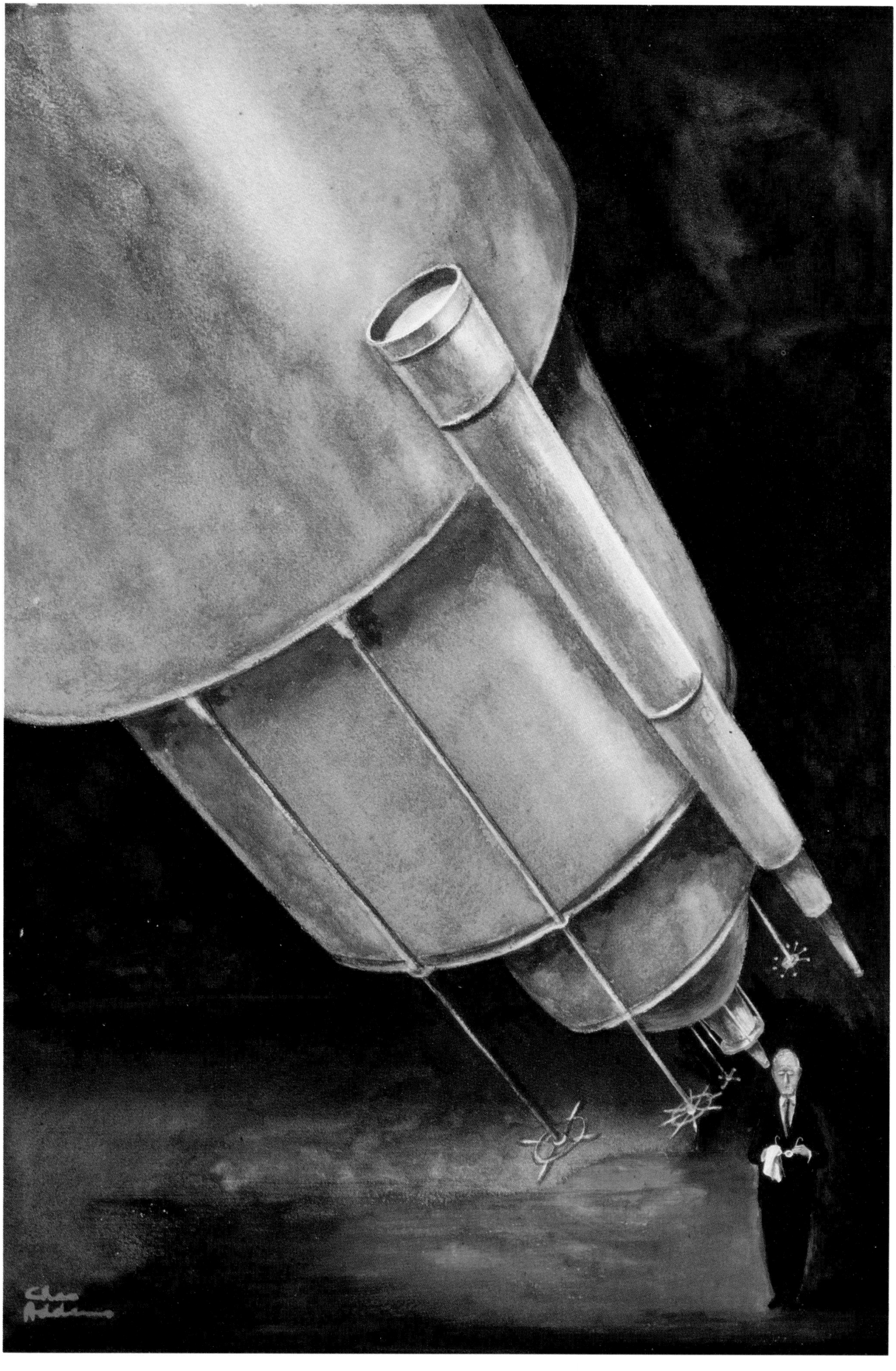
Chas Addams

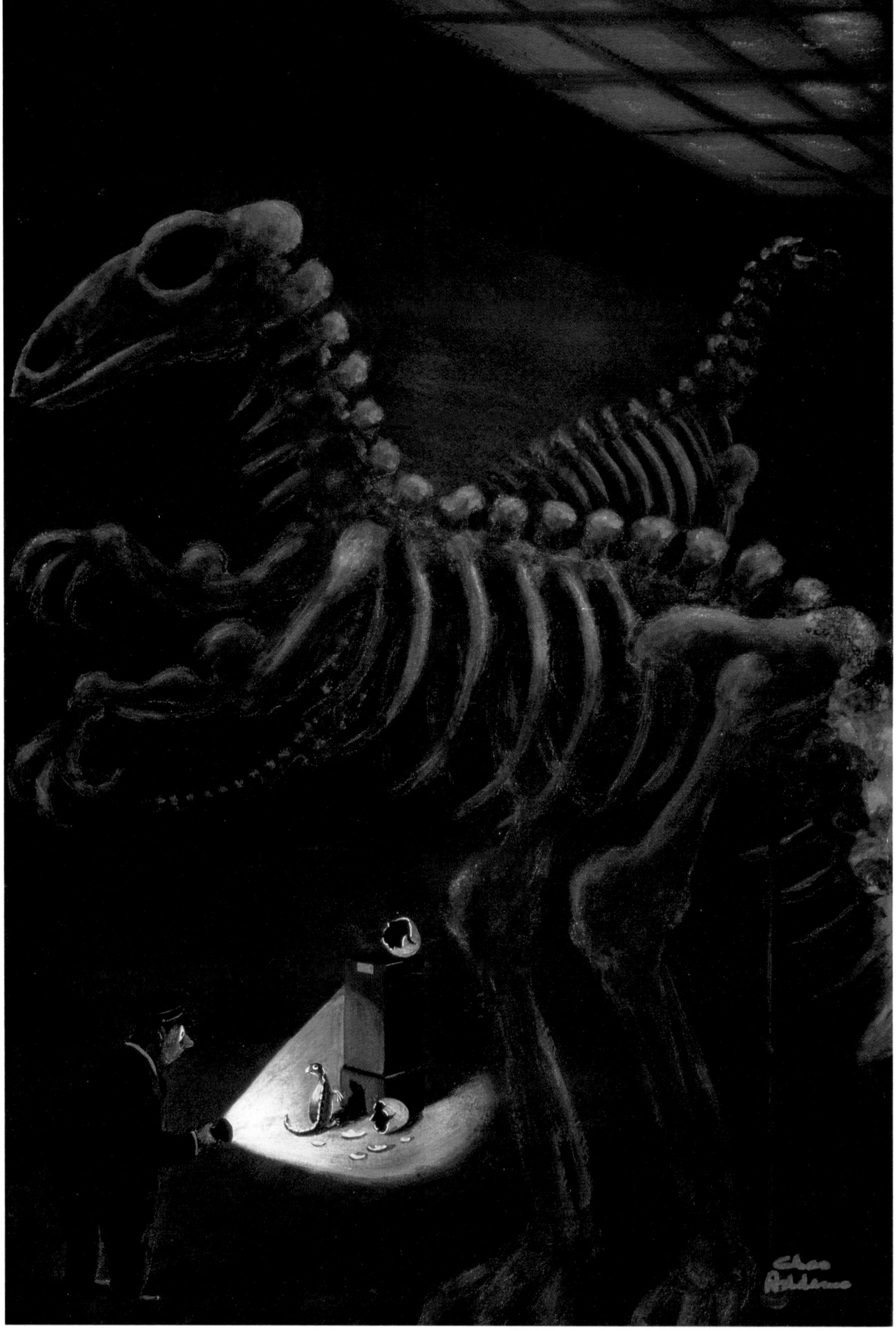
Chas
Addams

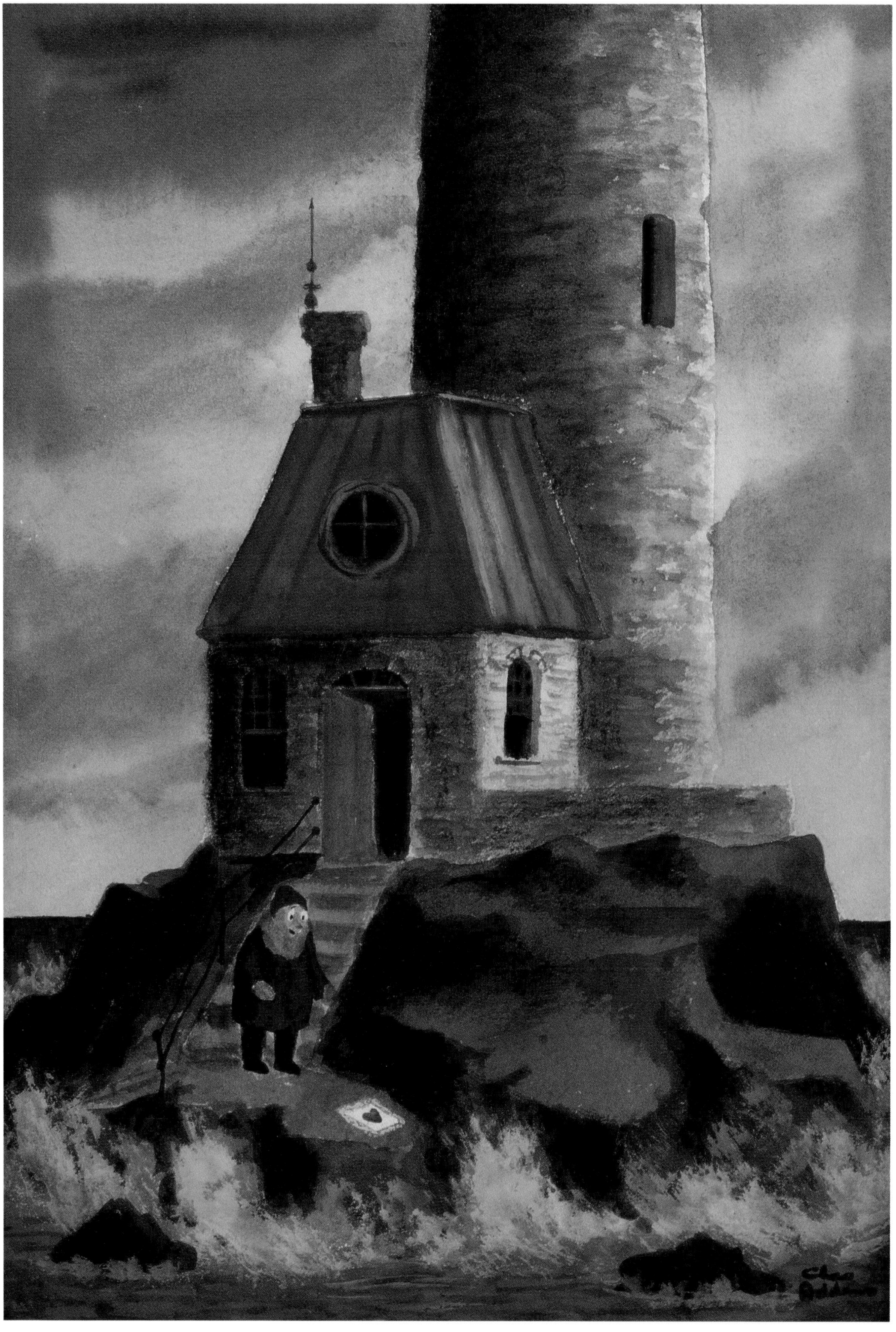

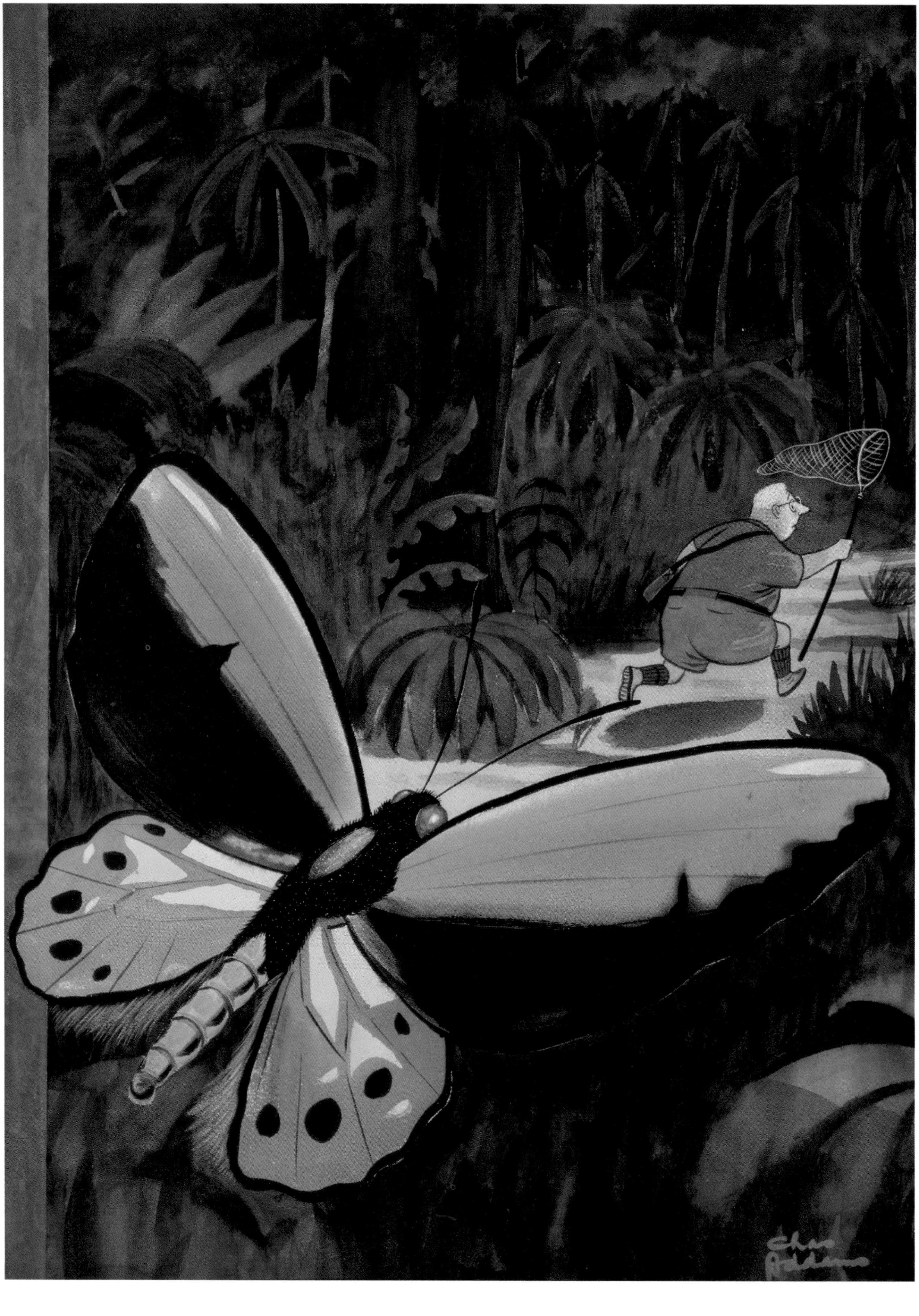
Chas Addams

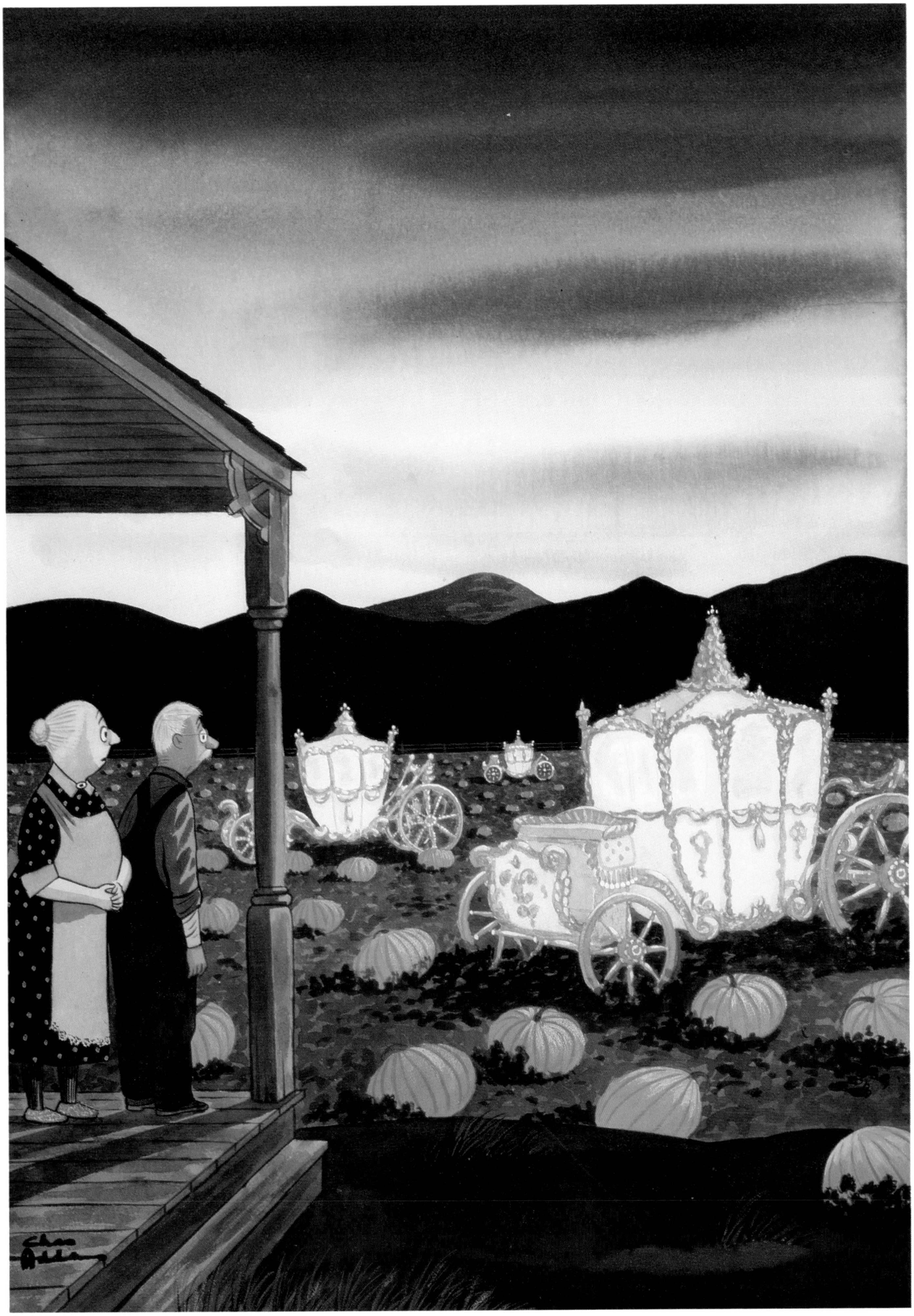
Chas Addams

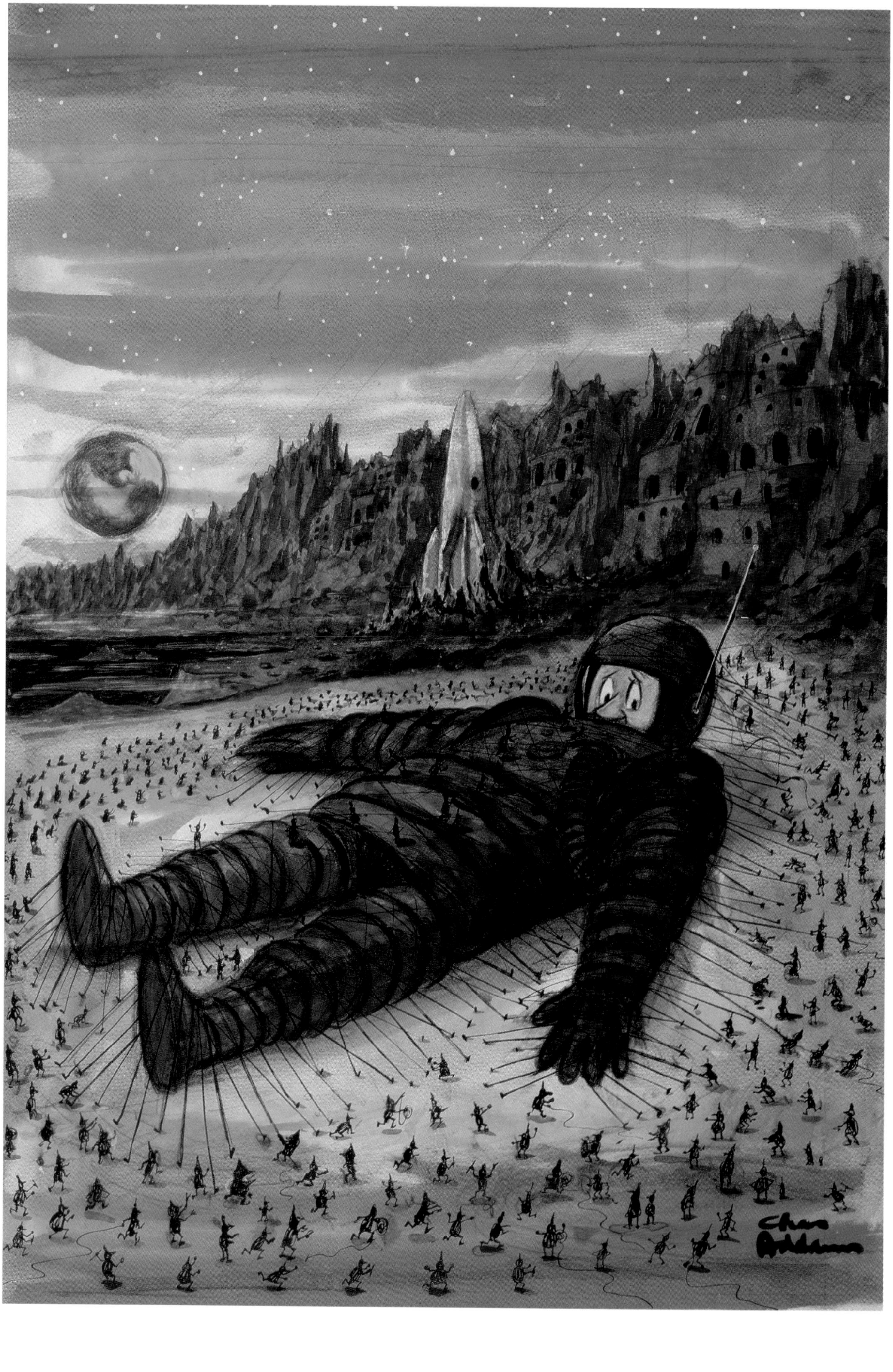
Chas Addams

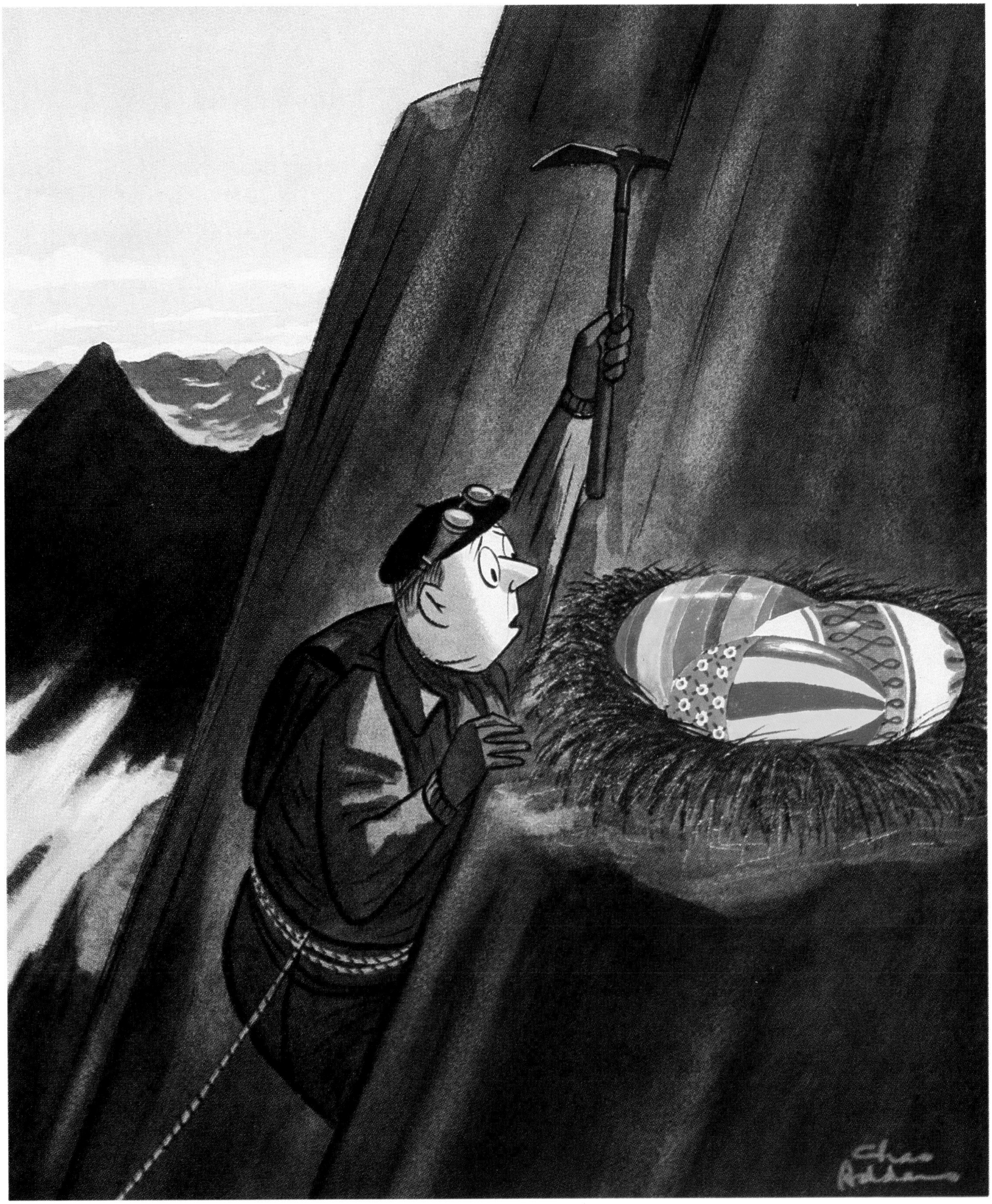
Chas Addams

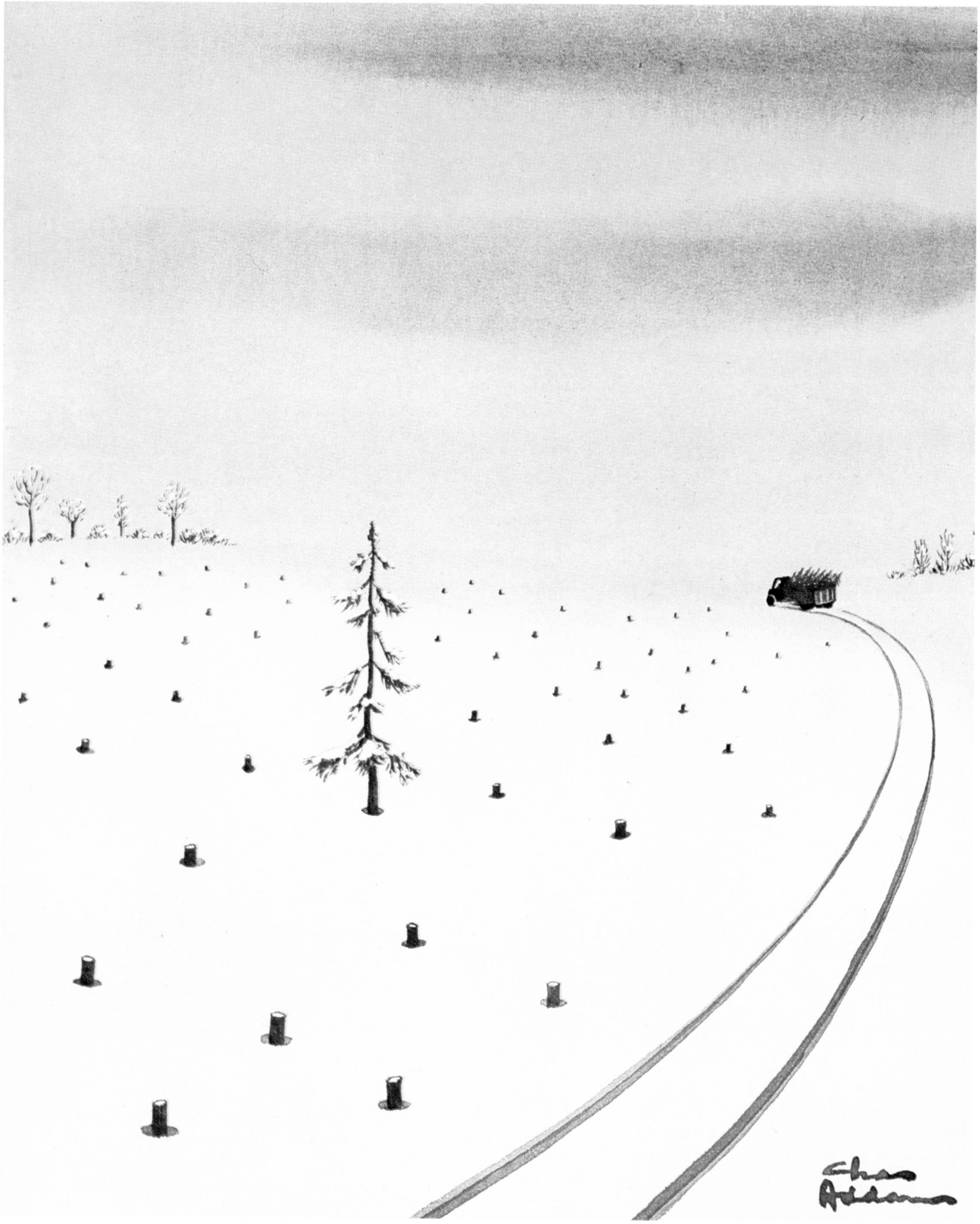
Chas Addams

*"You know, sometimes I can't help wondering if
Mr. Lawrence really did go to Chicago."*

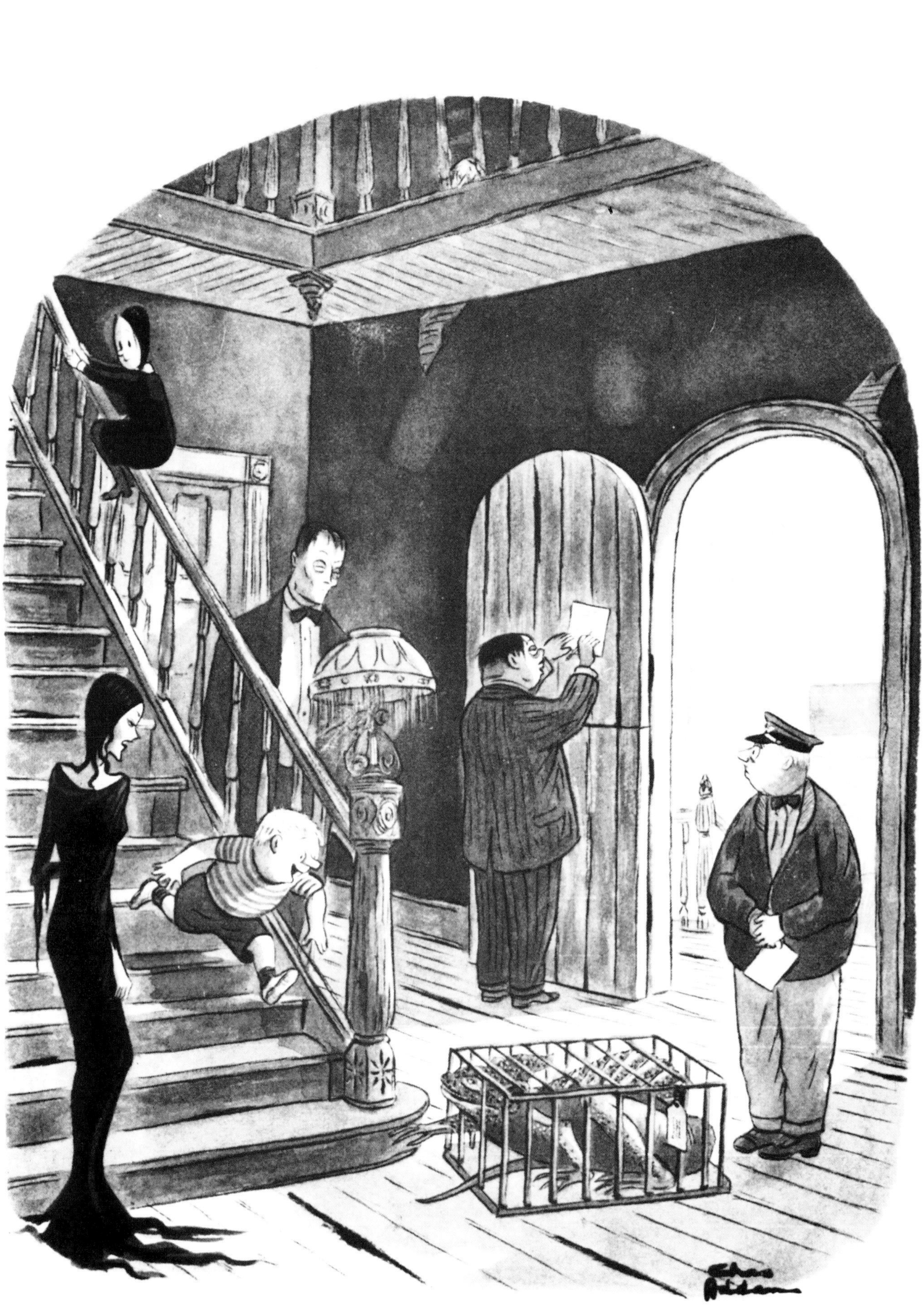

"Now, remember, you can have him as long as you feed him and take good care of him. When you don't, back he goes."

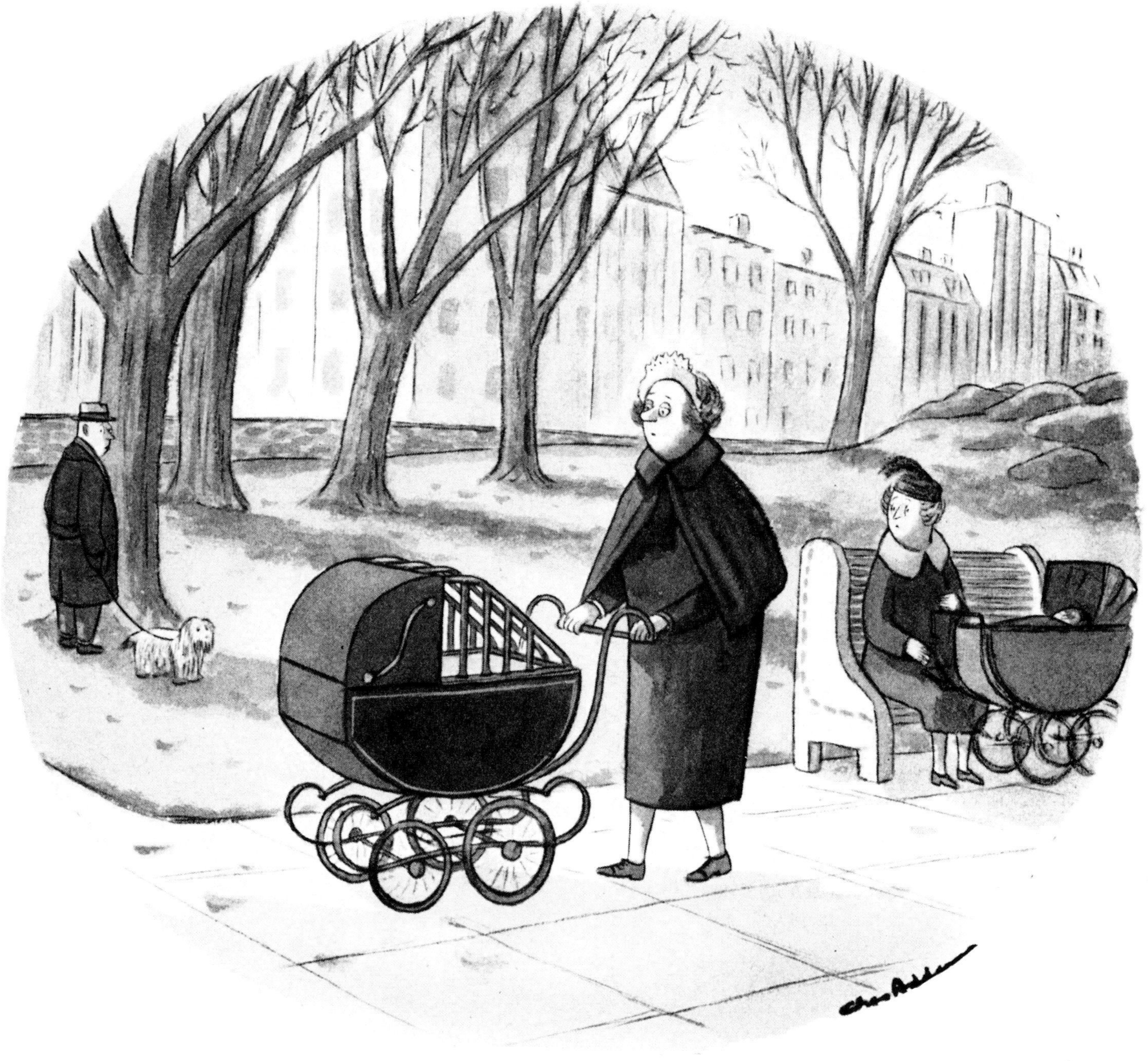

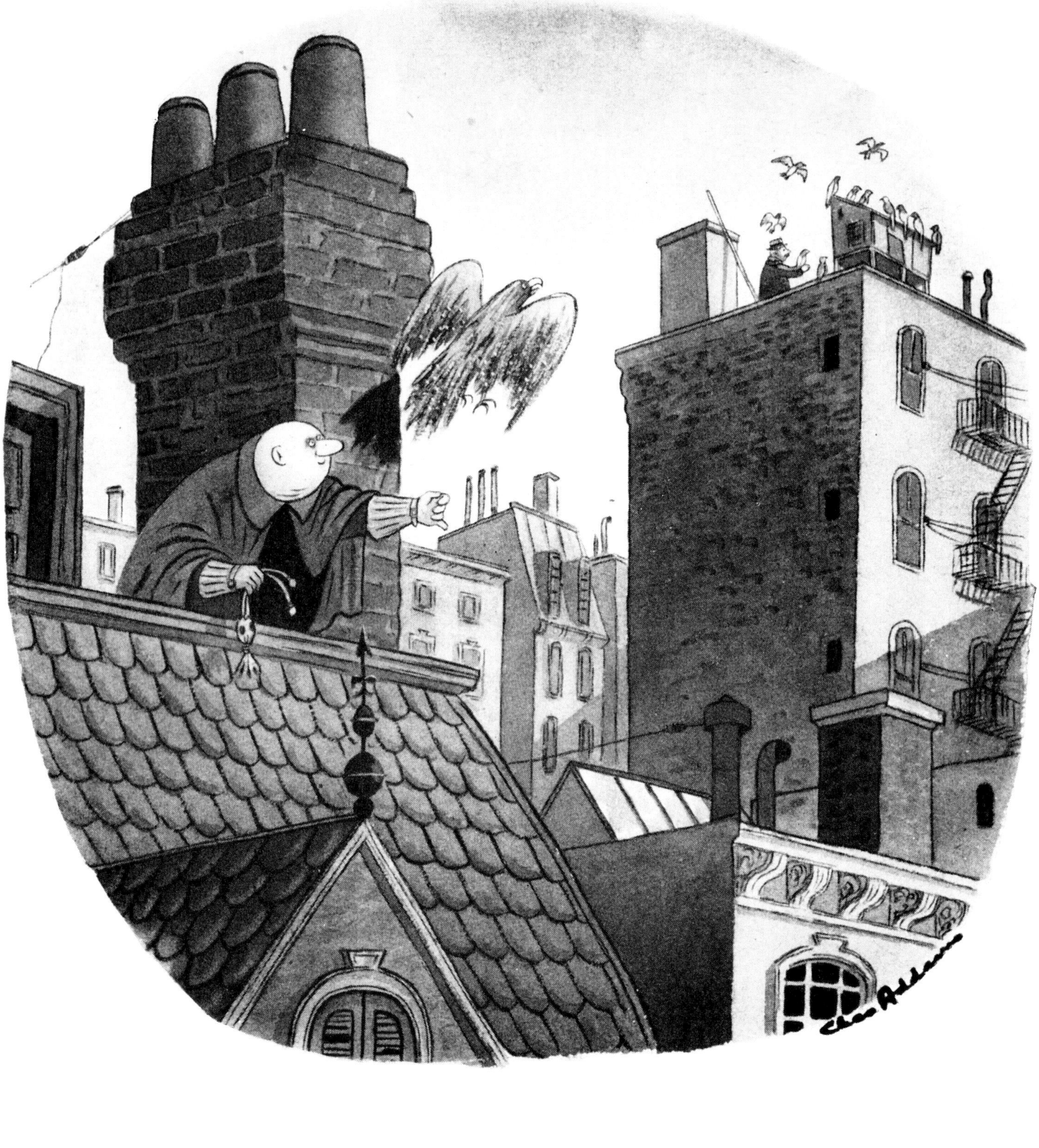

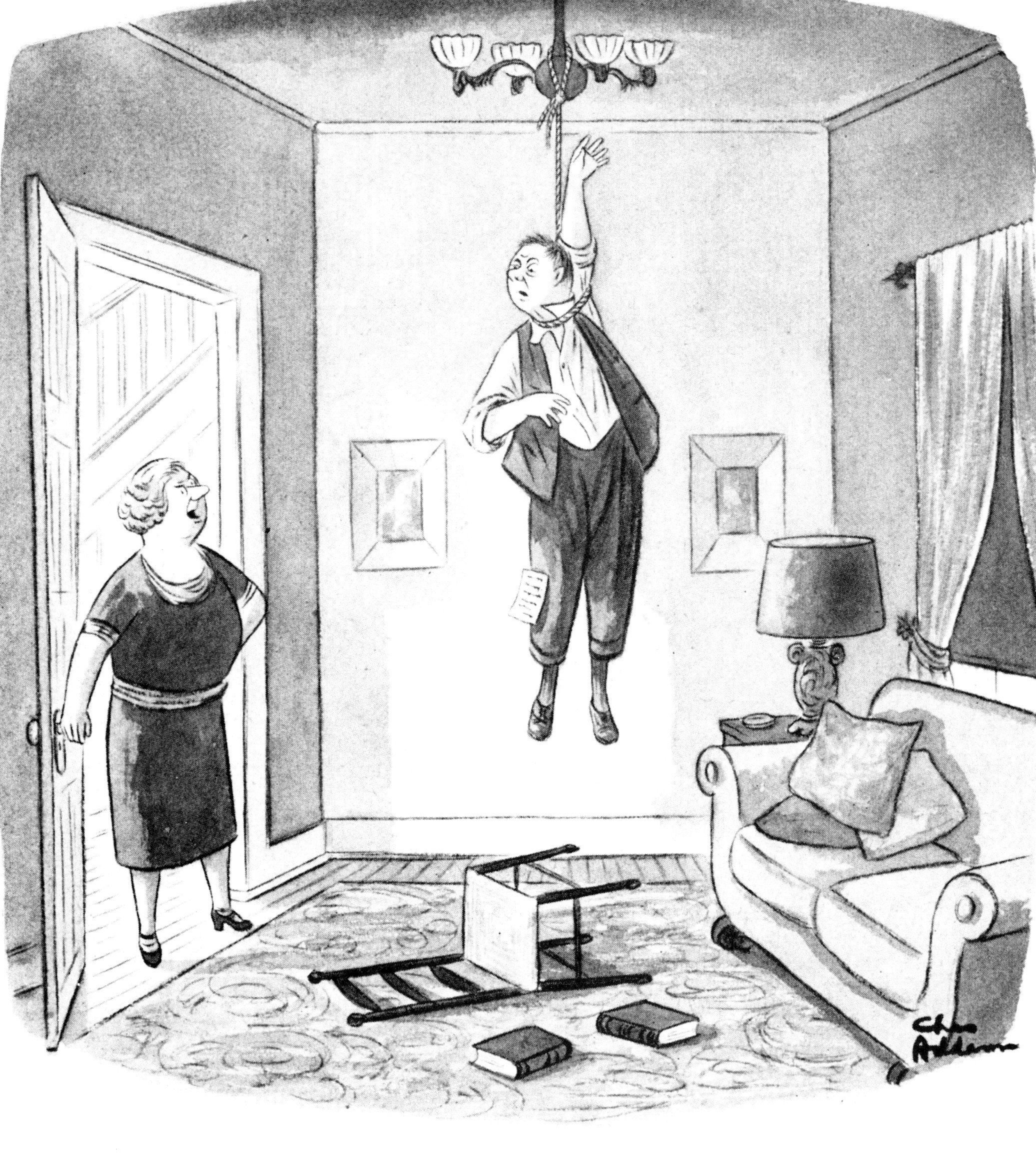
Chas Addams

"For heaven's sake, can't you do anything right?"

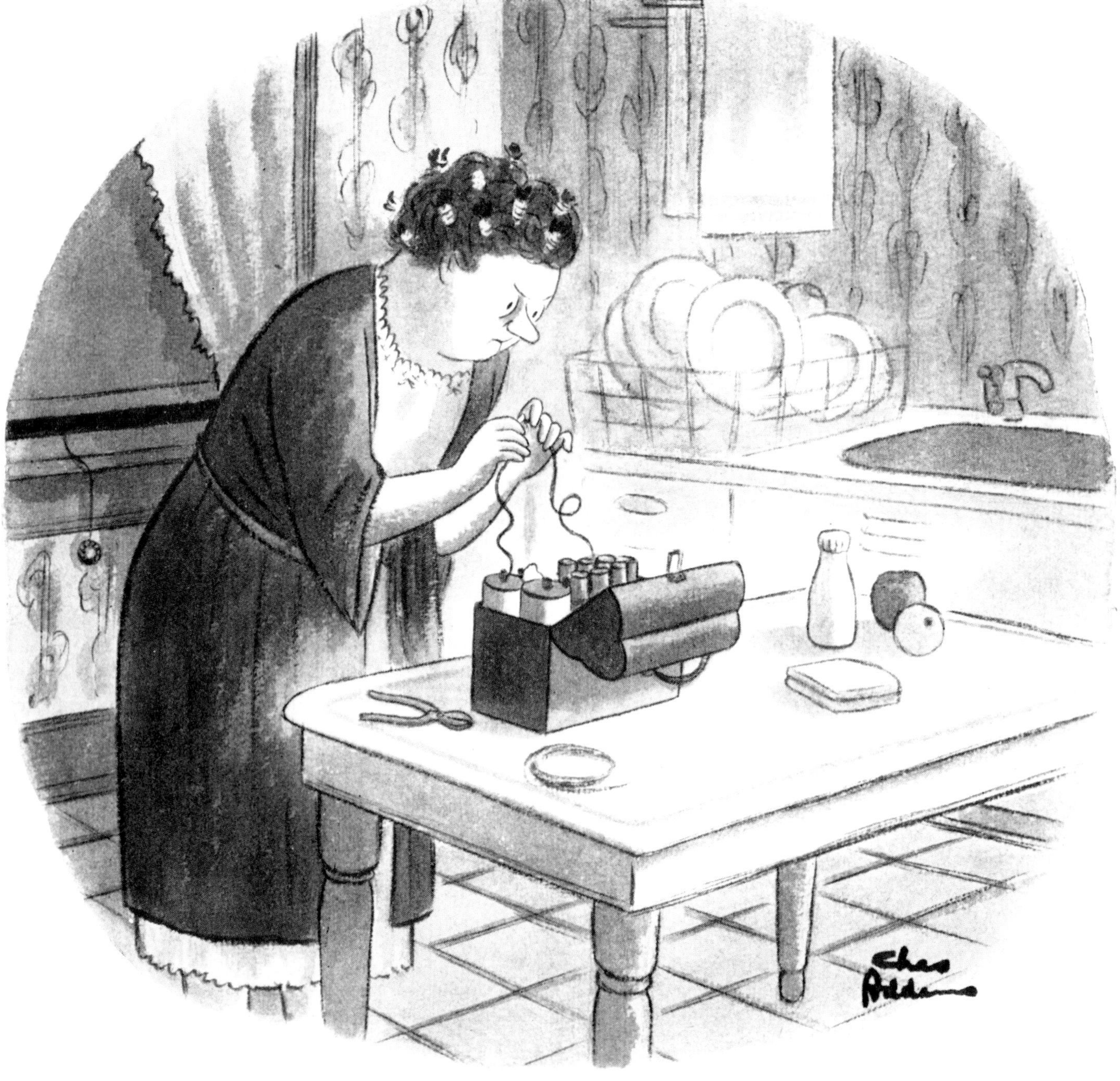
Chas Addams

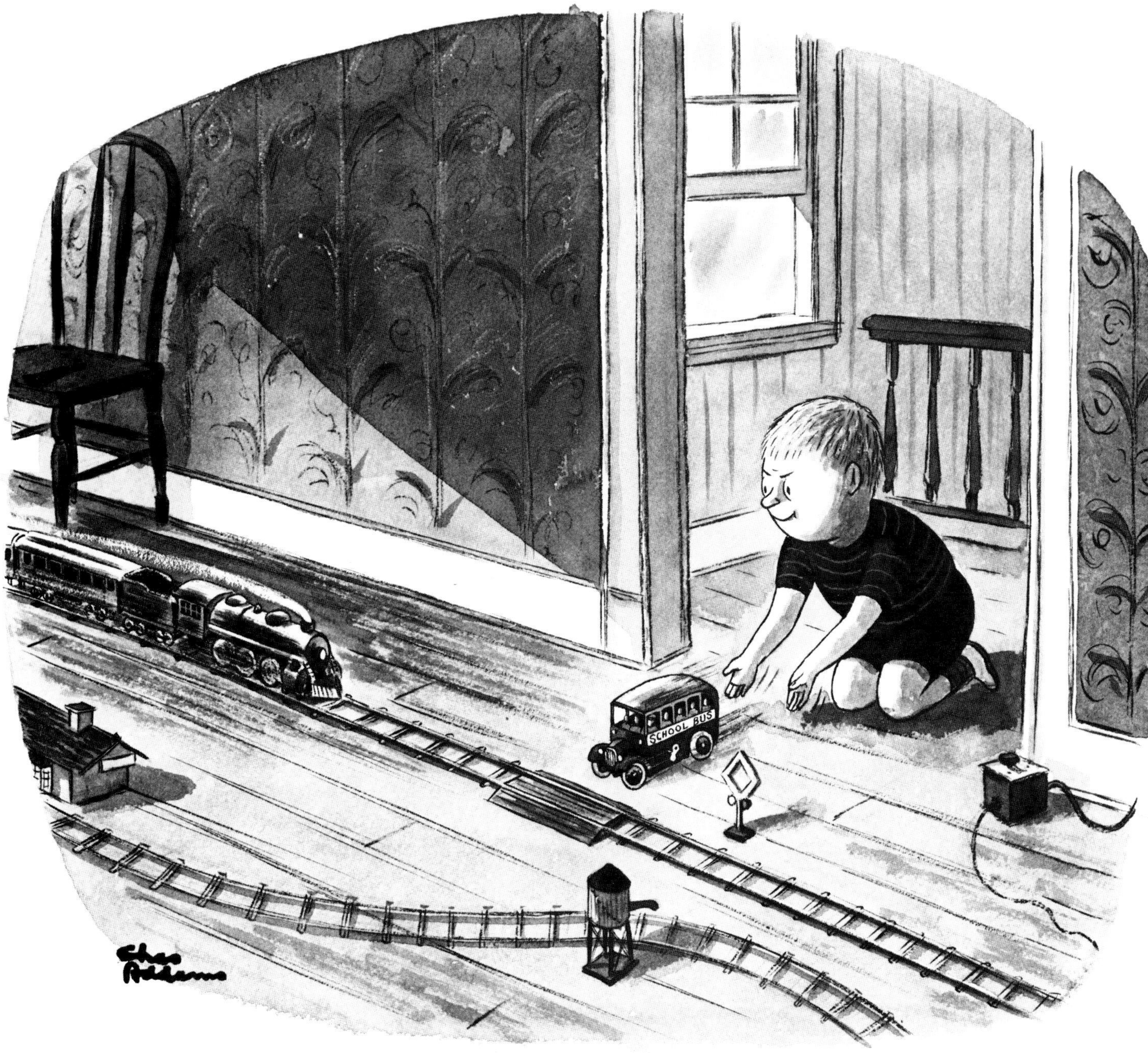
SCHOOL BUS
Chas Addams

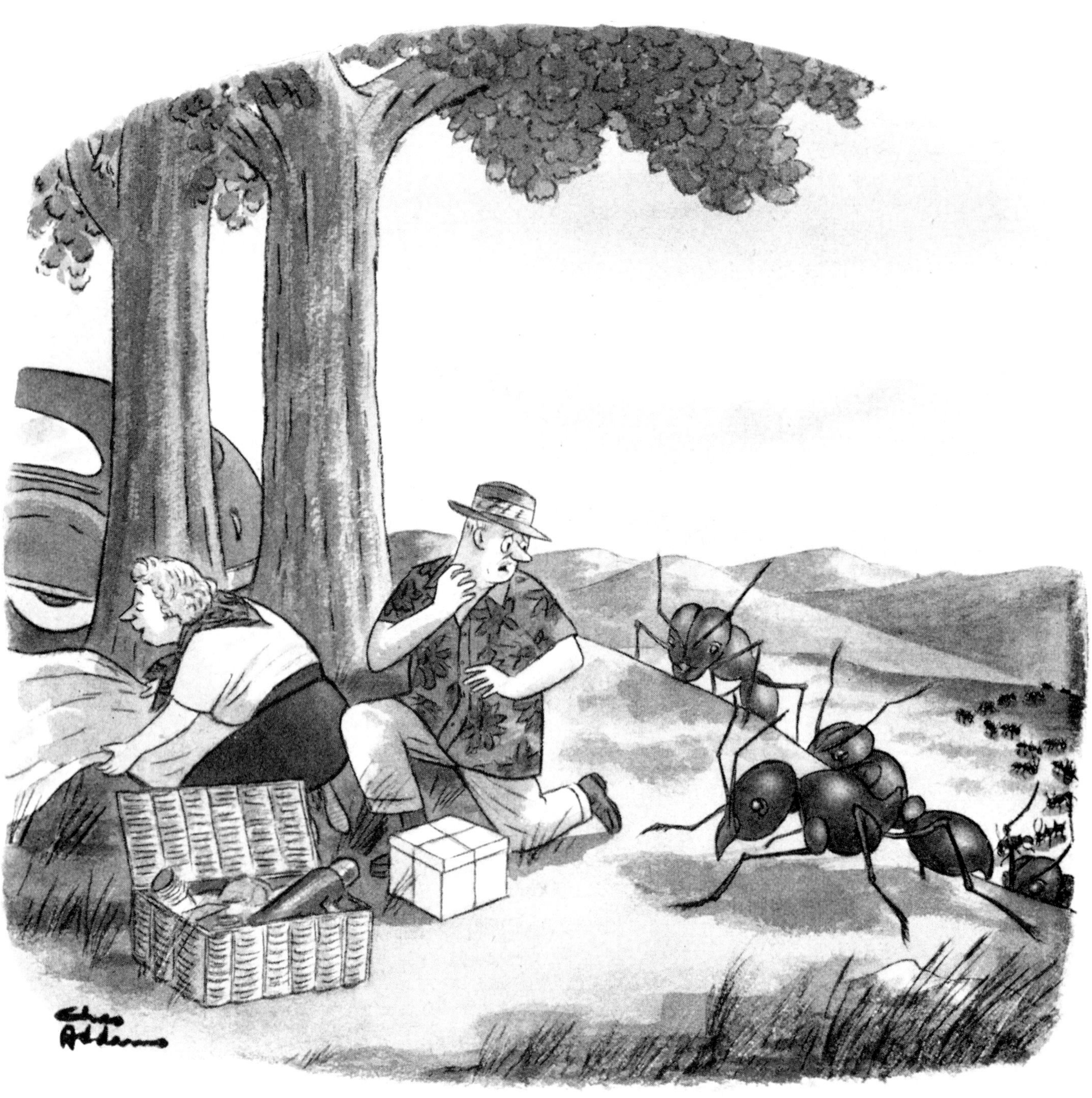

"Goodness, Murray, it wouldn't be a picnic without ants."

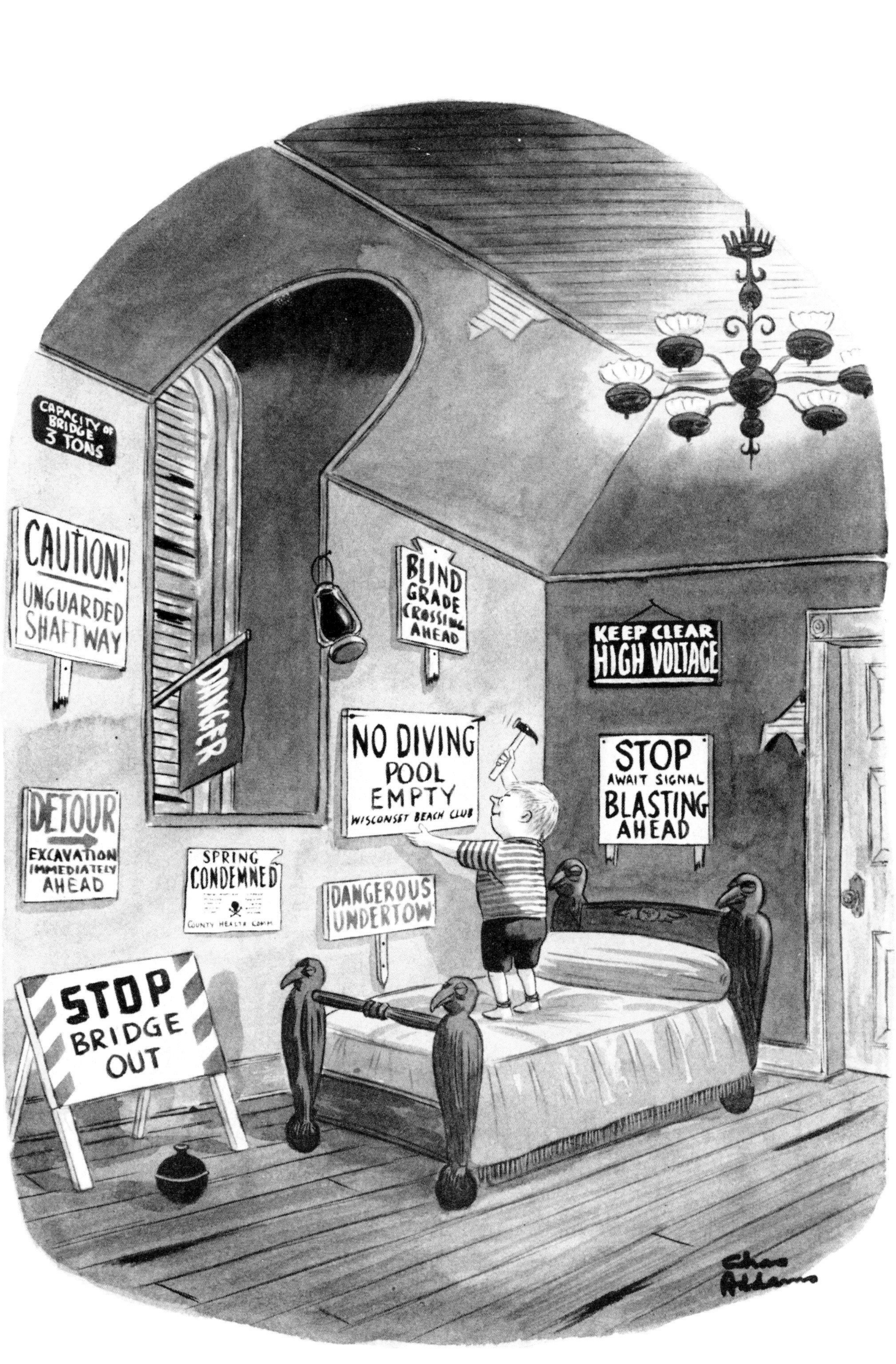
CAPACITY OF BRIDGE 3 TONS
CAUTION! UNGUARDED SHAFTWAY
DANGER
BLIND GRADE CROSSING AHEAD
KEEP CLEAR HIGH VOLTAGE
NO DIVING POOL EMPTY WISCONSET BEACH CLUB
STOP AWAIT SIGNAL BLASTING AHEAD
DETOUR EXCAVATION IMMEDIATELY AHEAD
SPRING CONDEMNED
COUNTY HEALTH COMM
DANGEROUS UNDERTOW
STOP BRIDGE OUT
Chas Addams

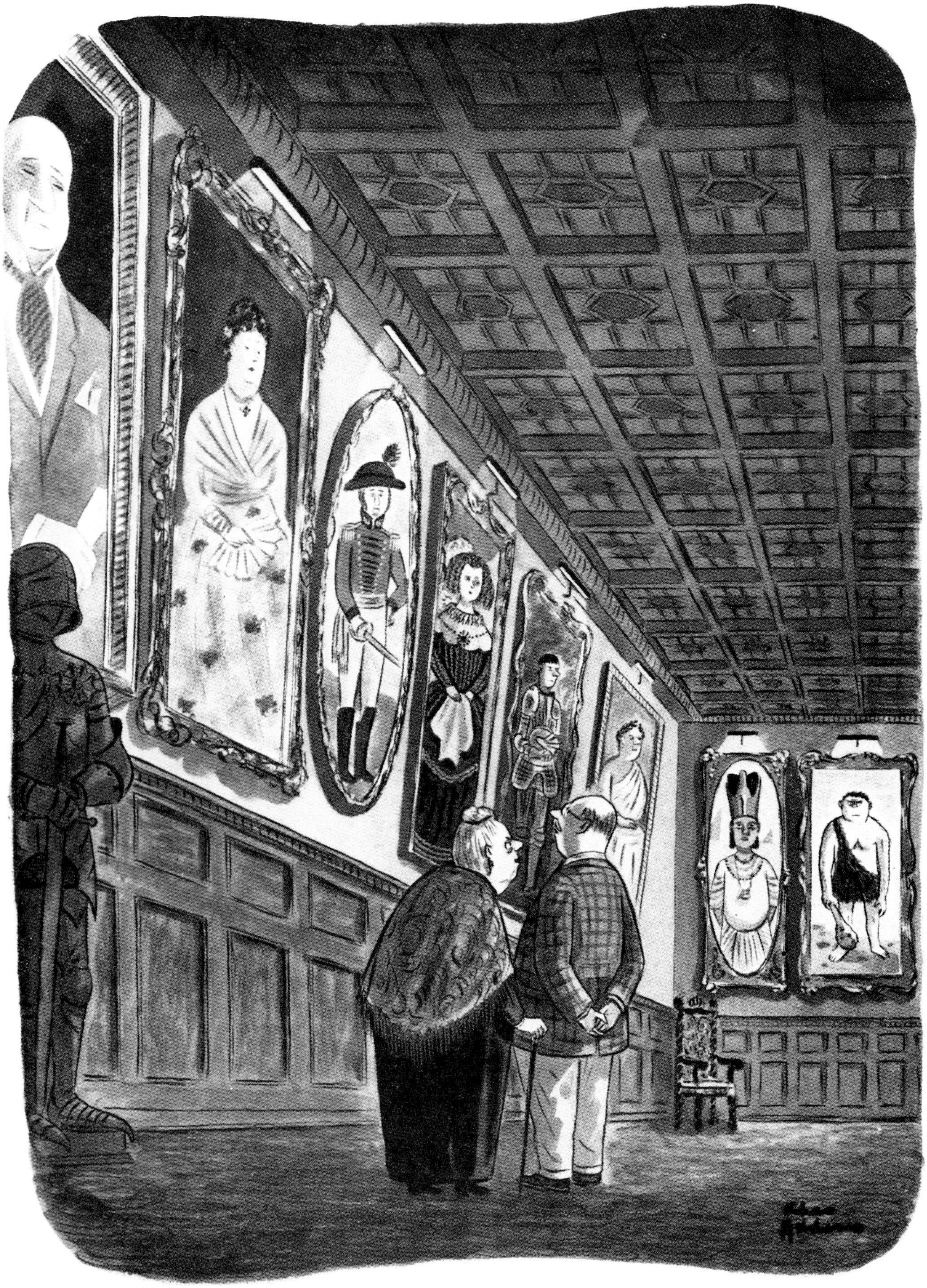

"Ours is a very old family."

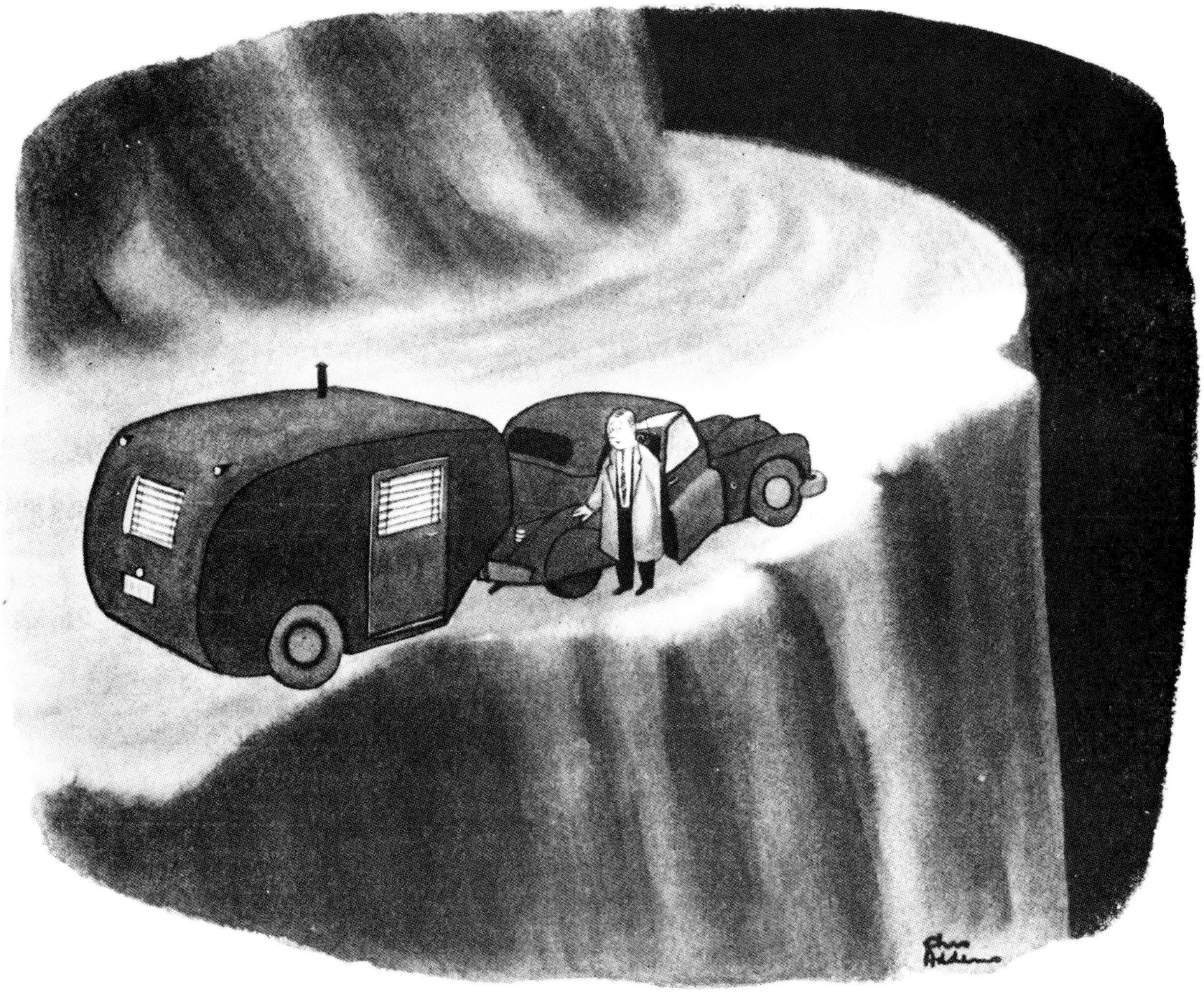
Chas Addams

"Oh, darling, can you step out for a moment?"

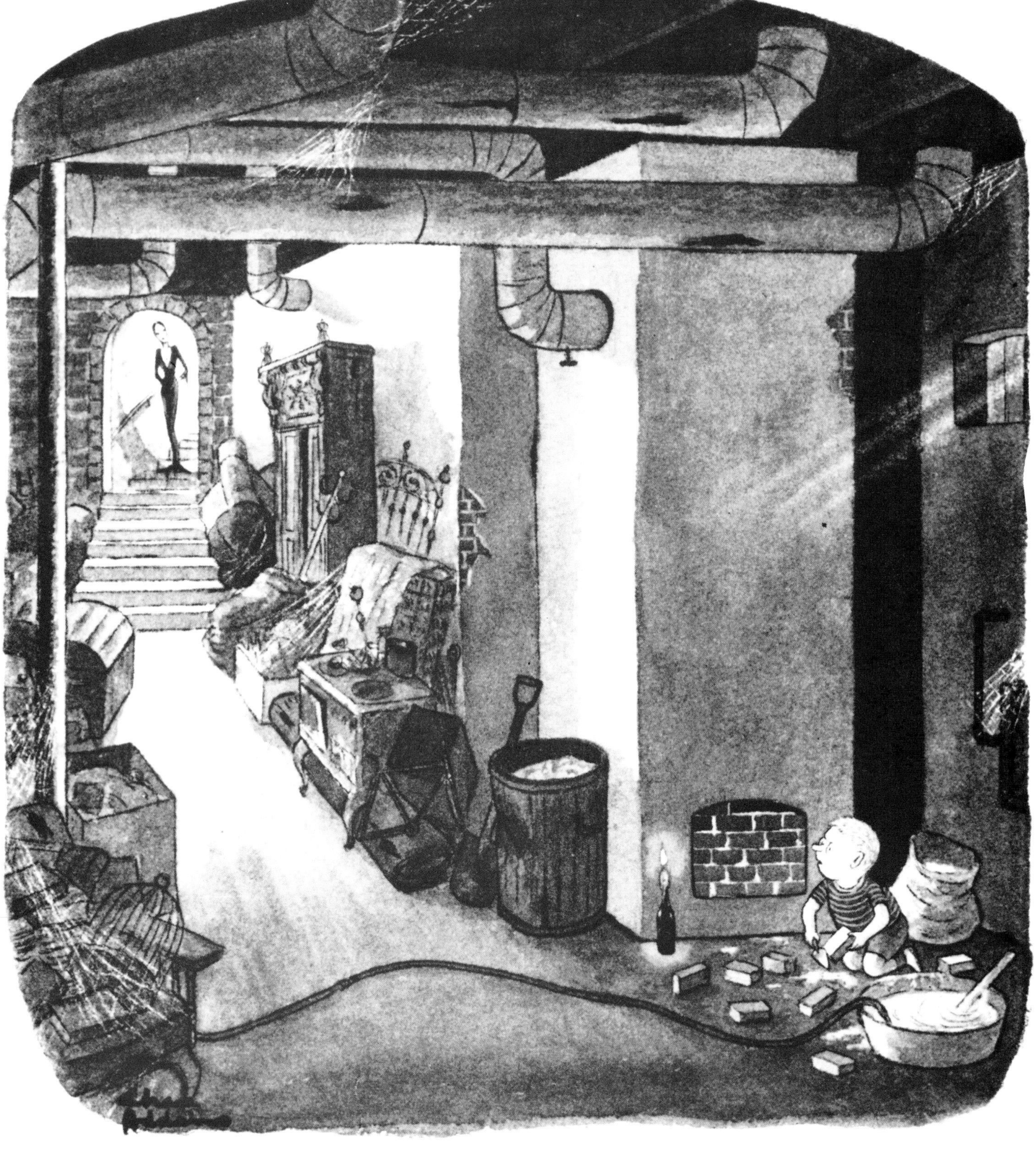

"Come along, children—time for your nap."

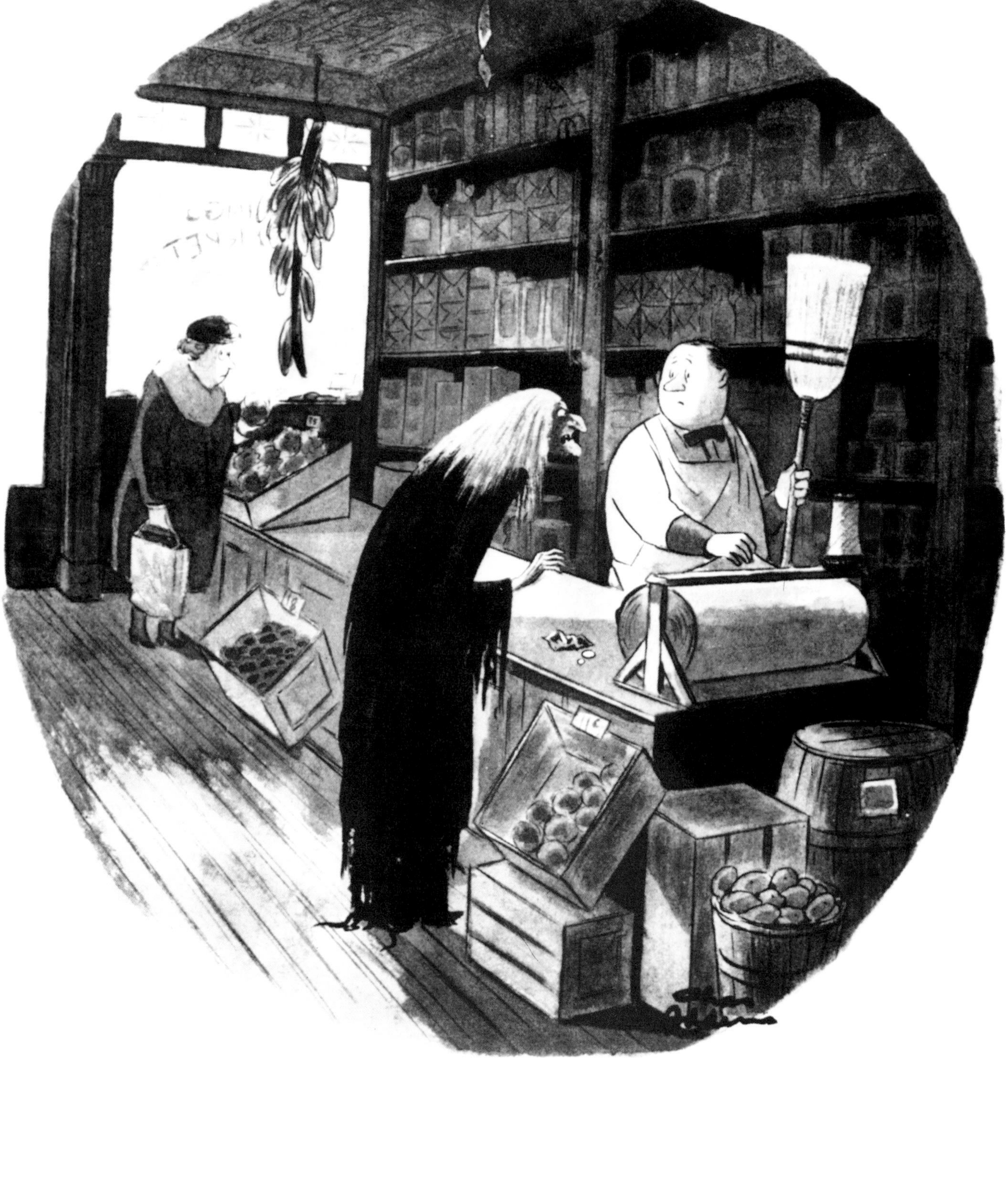

"You needn't wrap it. I'll ride it home."

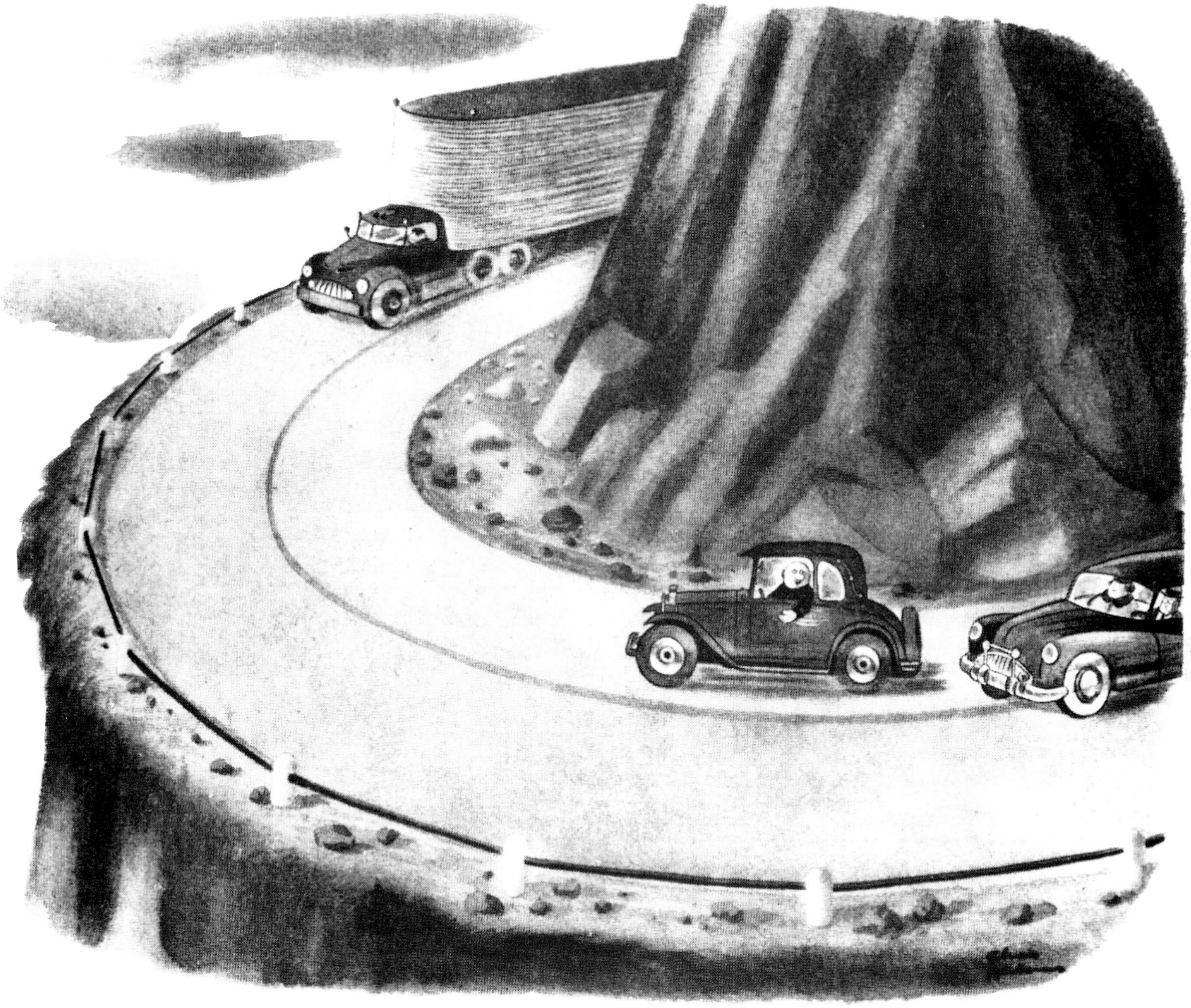

"Do you, Oliver Jordan III, take this woman to be your lawful wedded wife?"

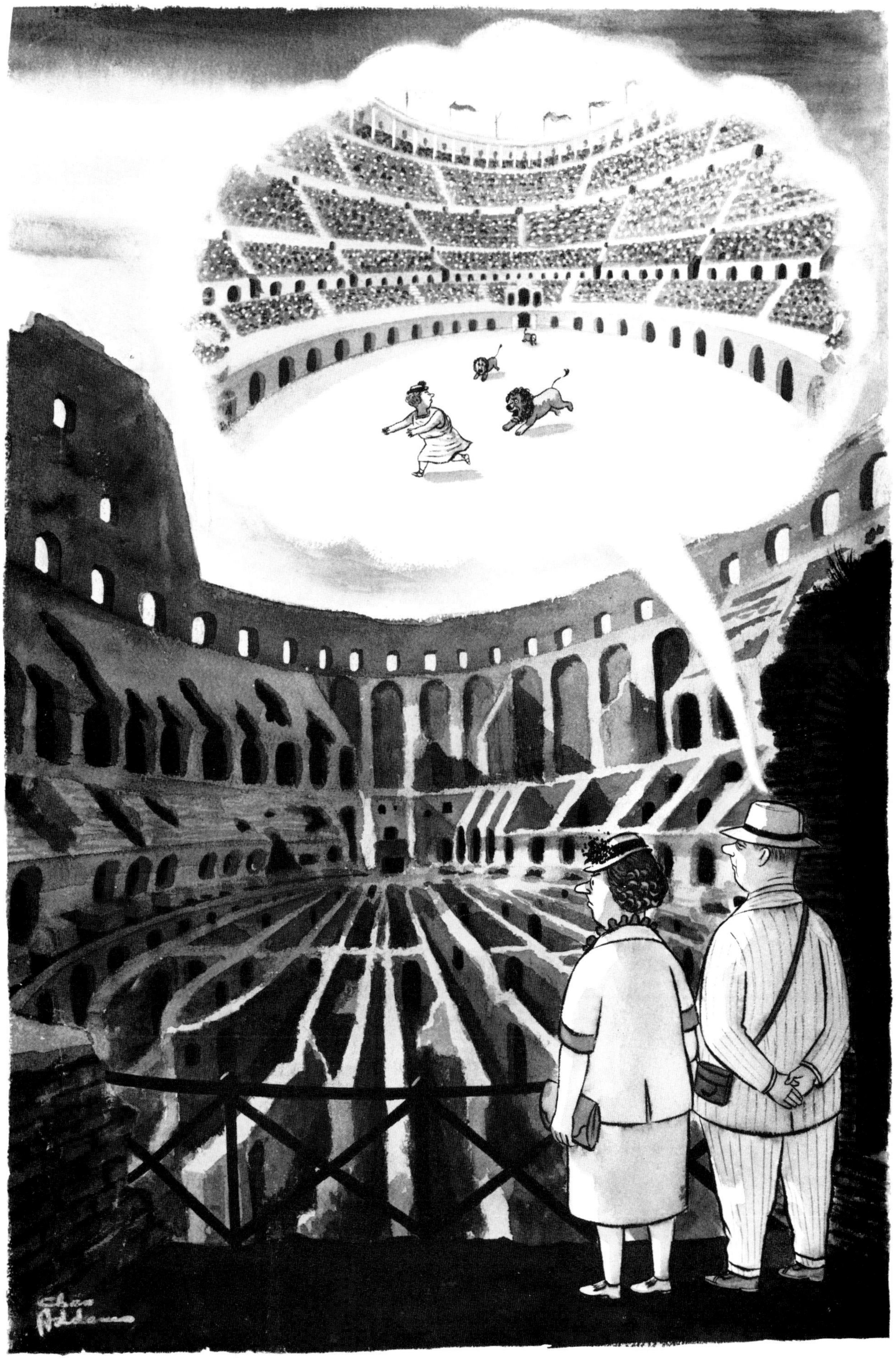
Chas Addams

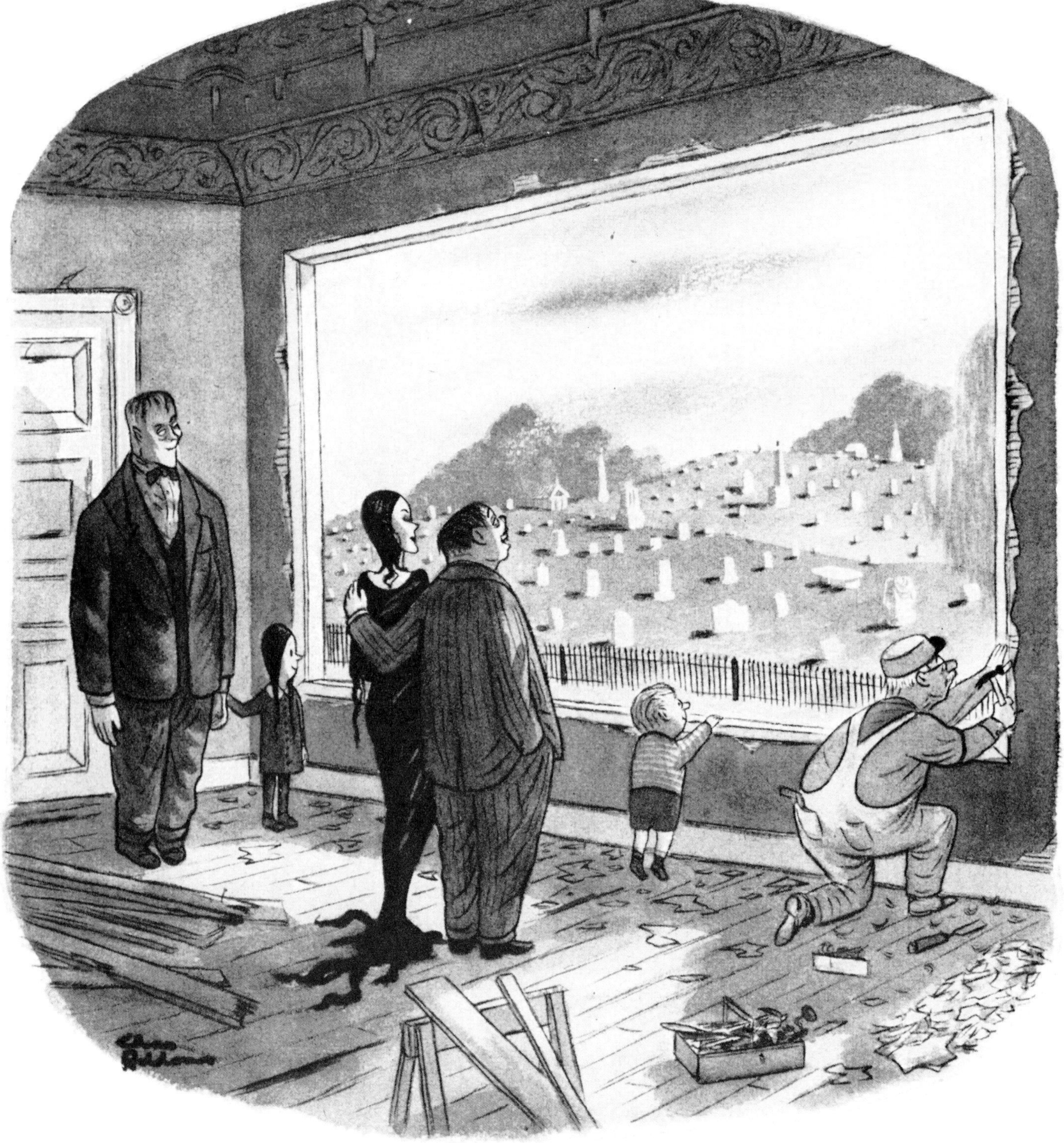

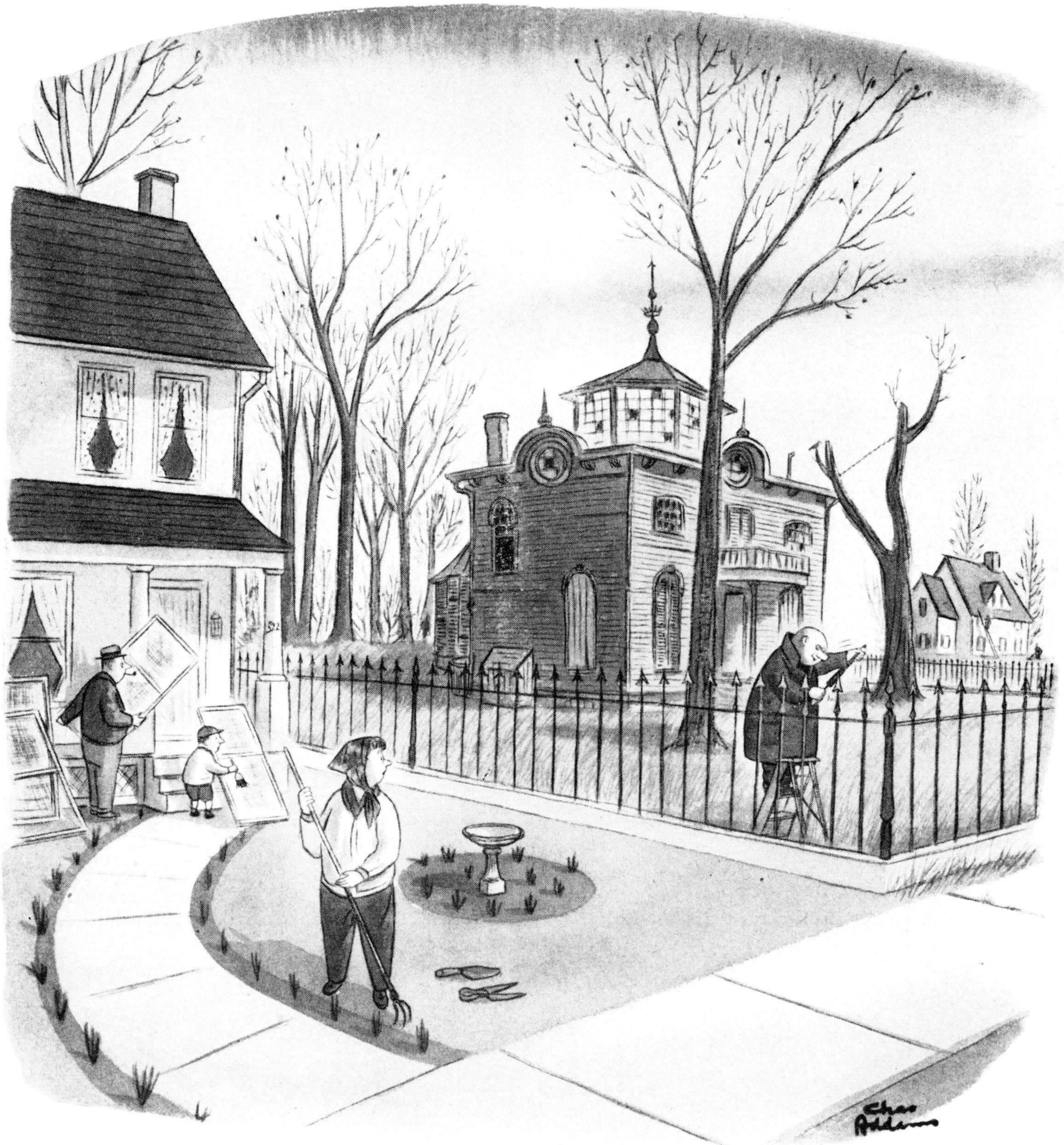
Chas
Addams

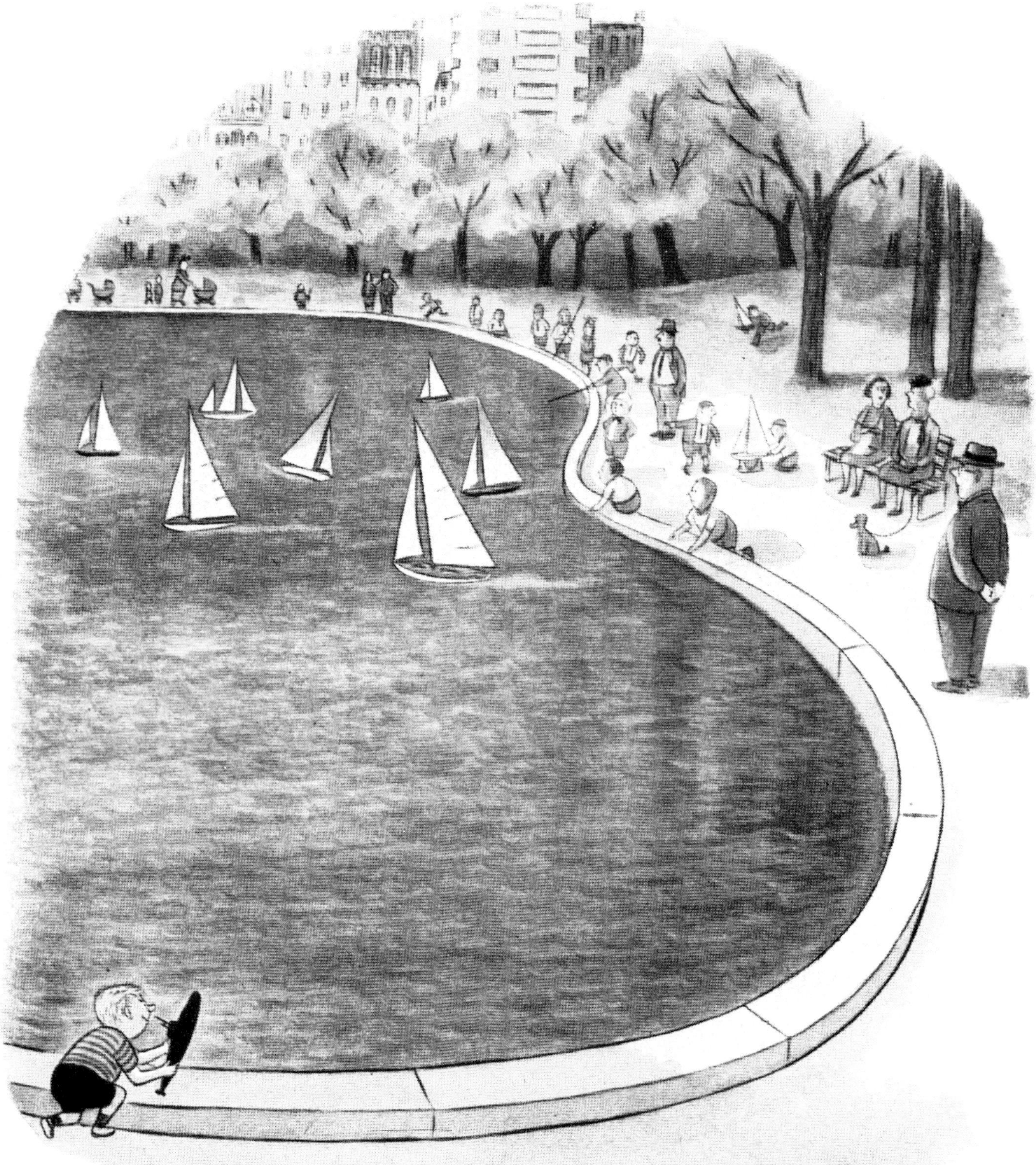
Chas Addams

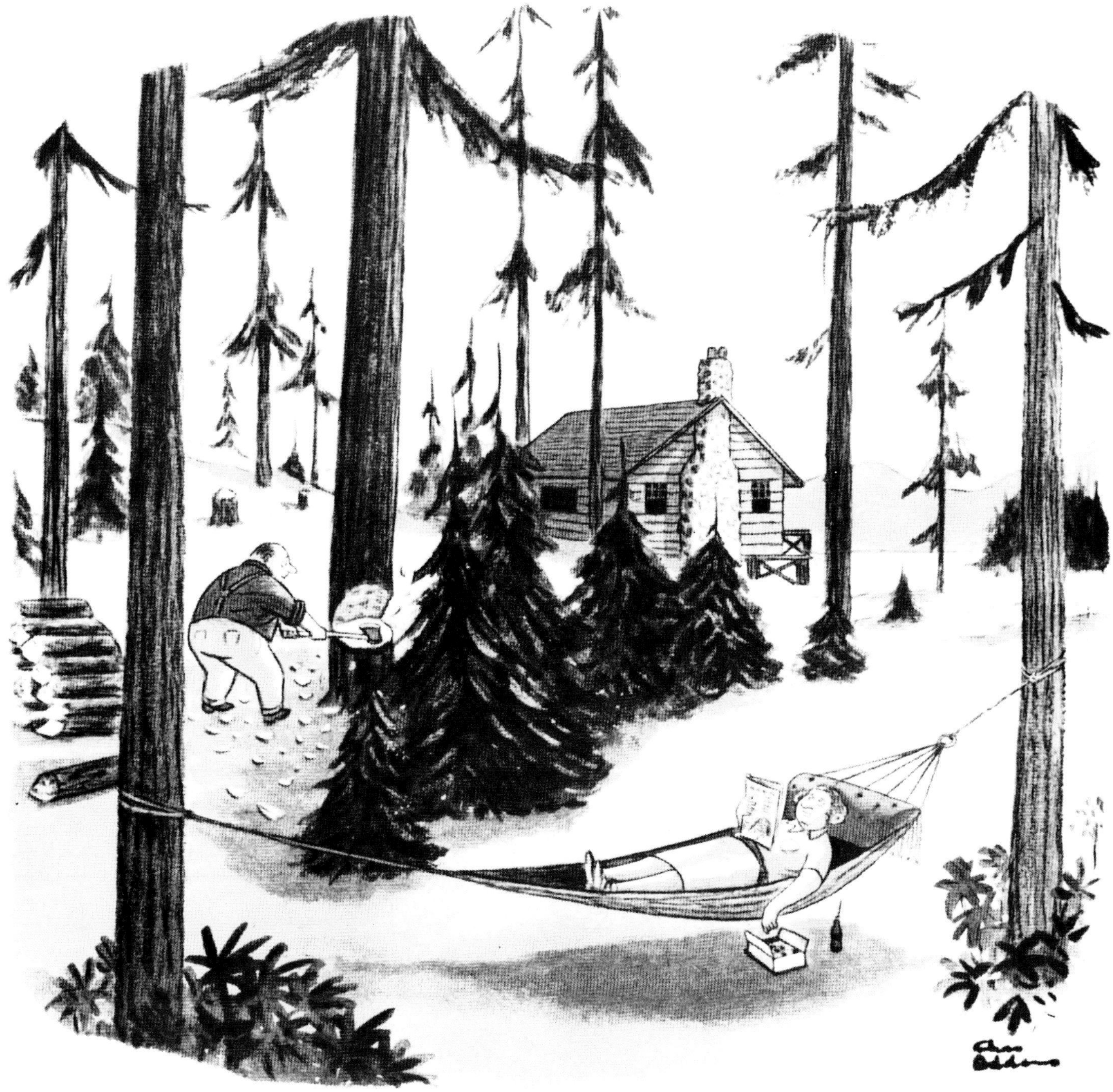

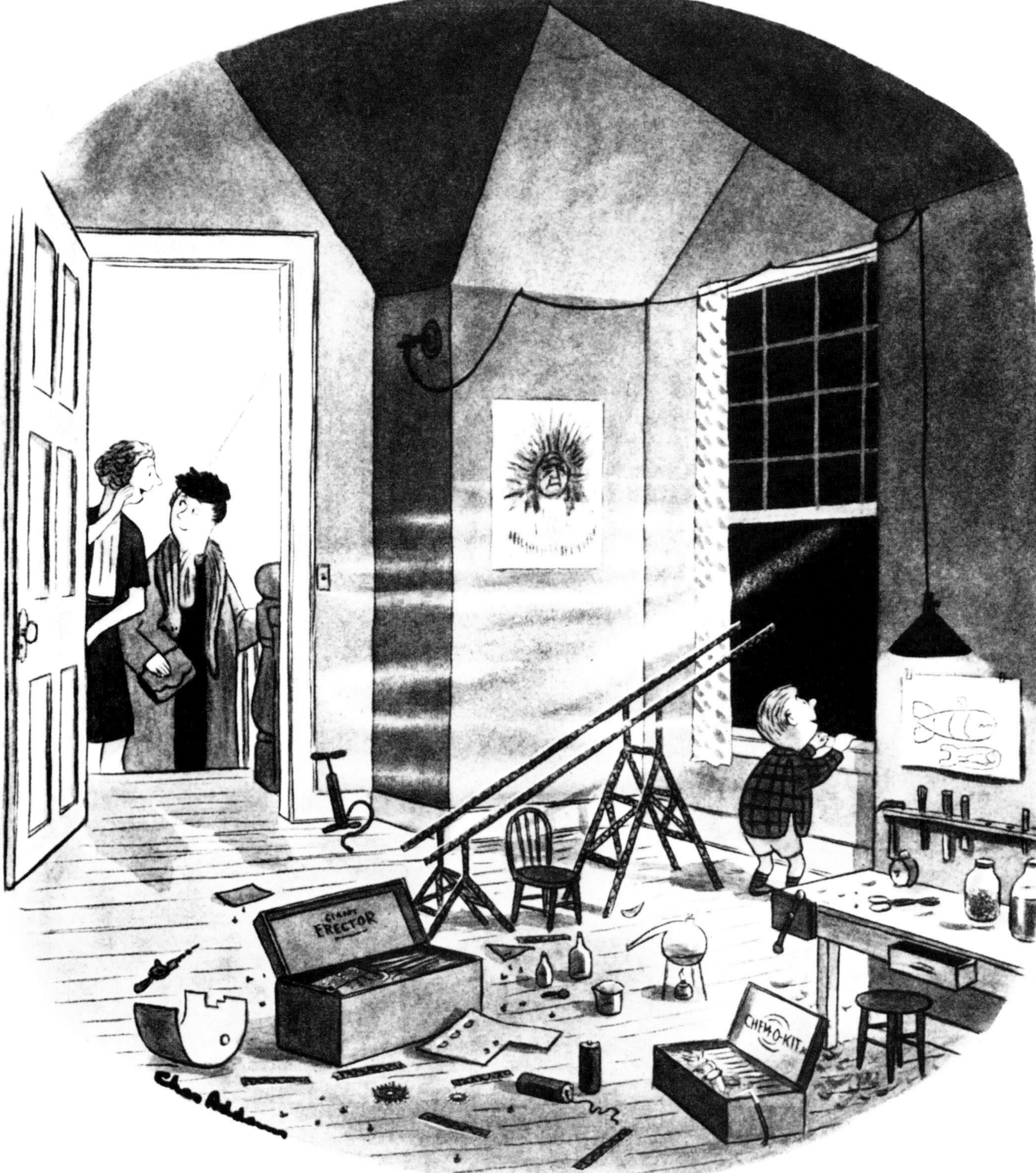
ERECTOR
CHEM-O-KIT

"It's priceless. Normie's building a rocket to shoot Pamela to the moon."

"Mr. Mitchell! You <u>know</u> you don't have kitchen privileges."

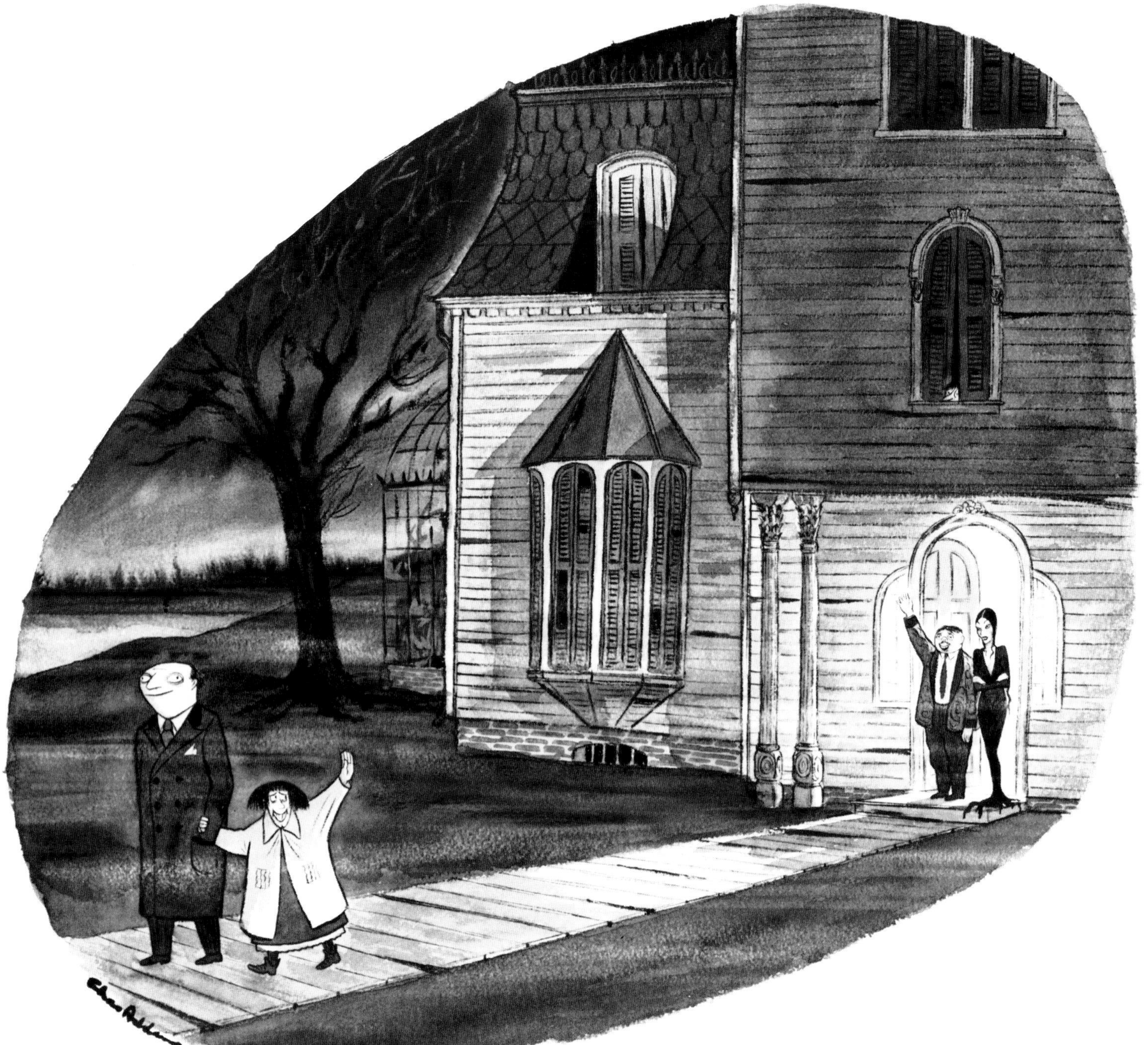

"I like them. They wear well."

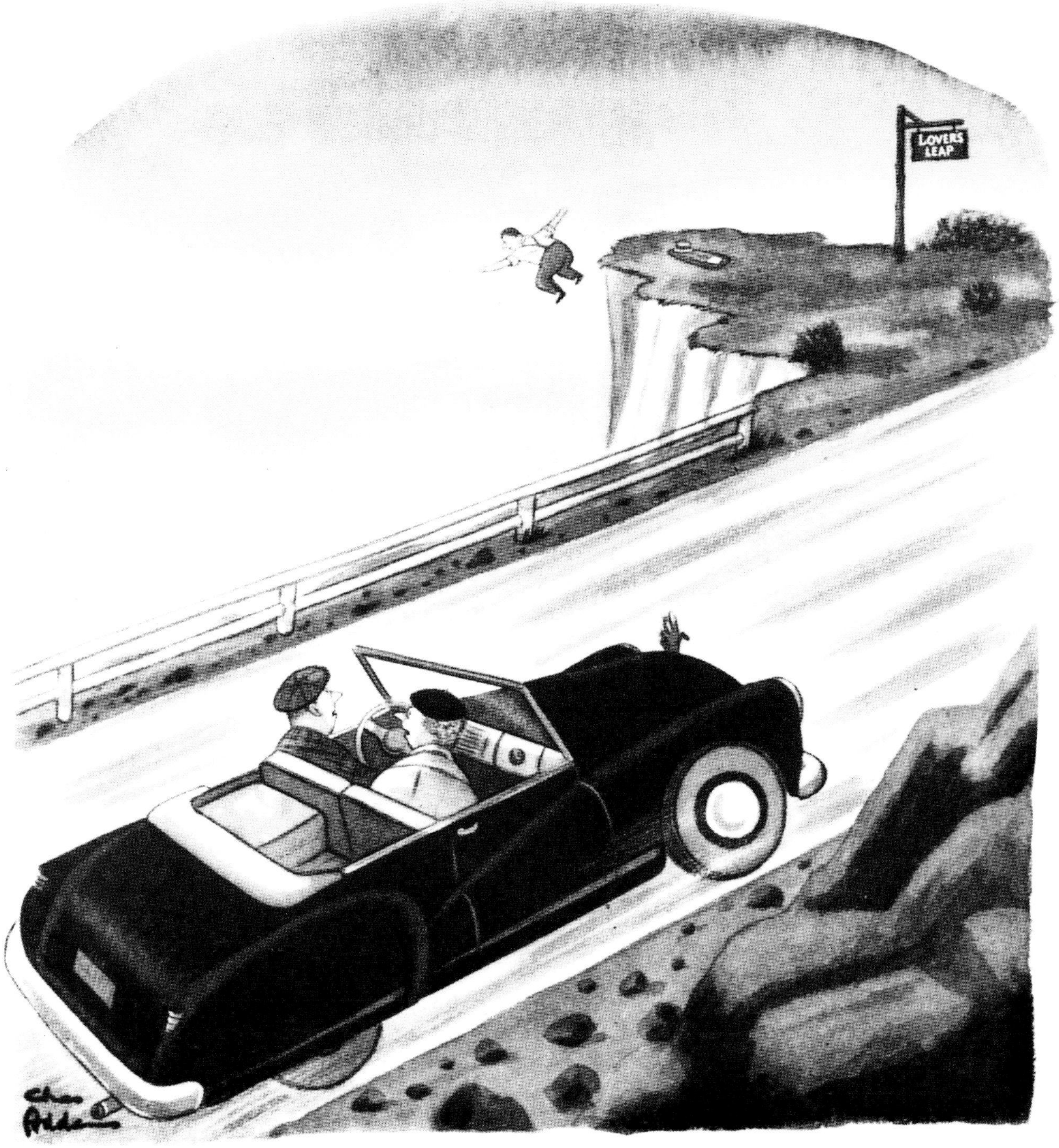
LOVER'S
LEAP

"You've never felt that way about me."

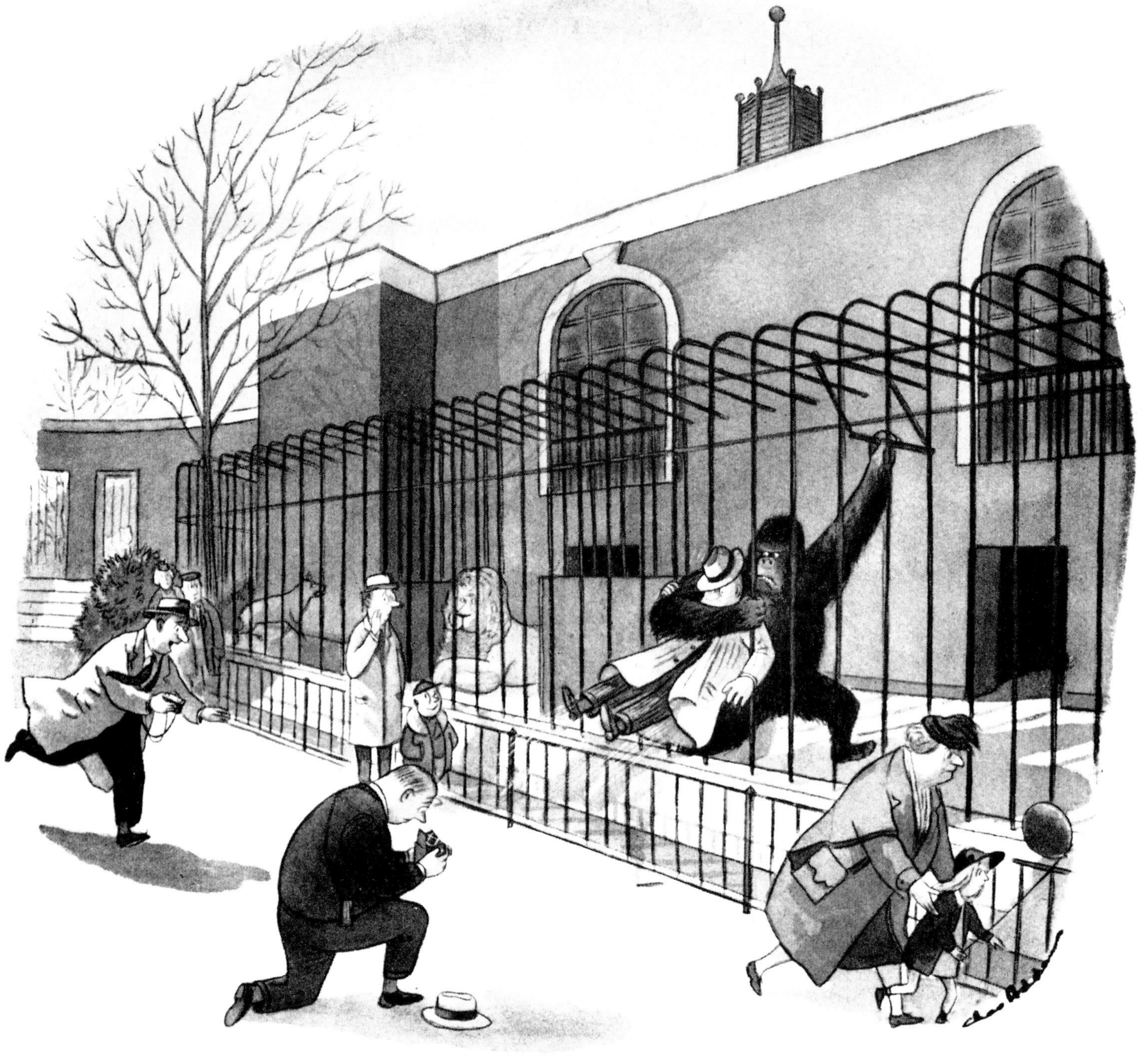

"What light you giving it?"

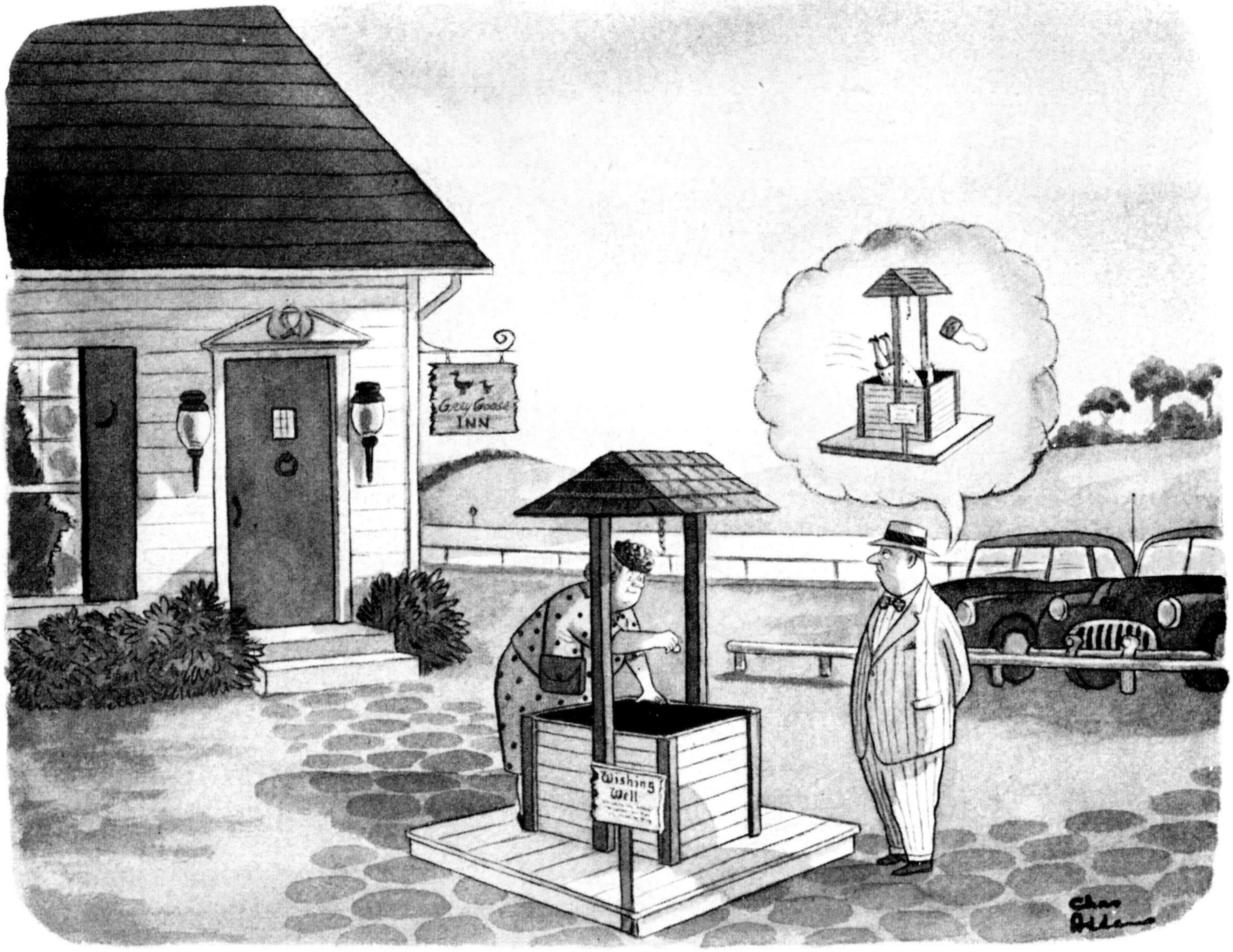
Grey Goose
INN
Wishing
Well
Chas
Addams

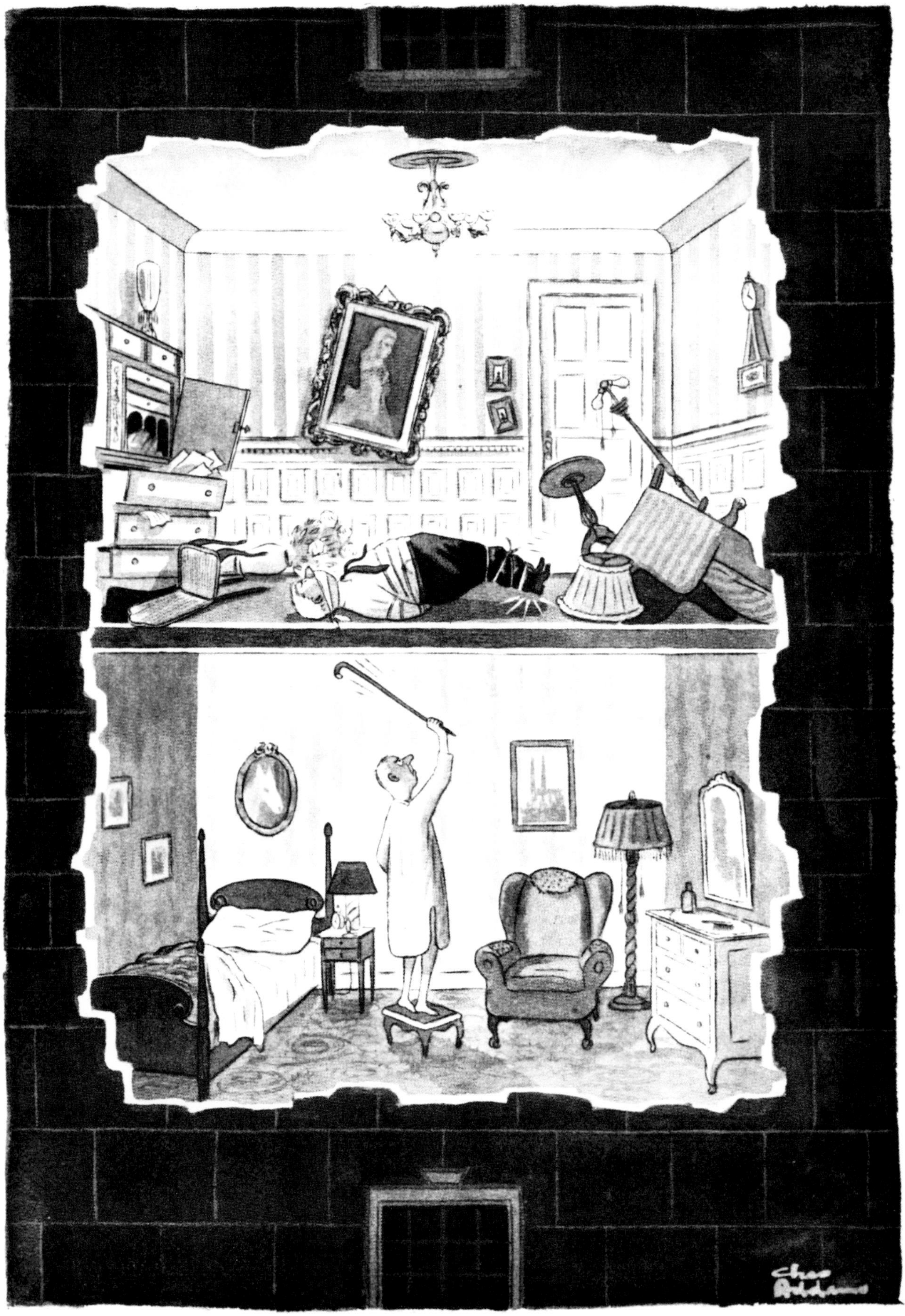
Chas Addams

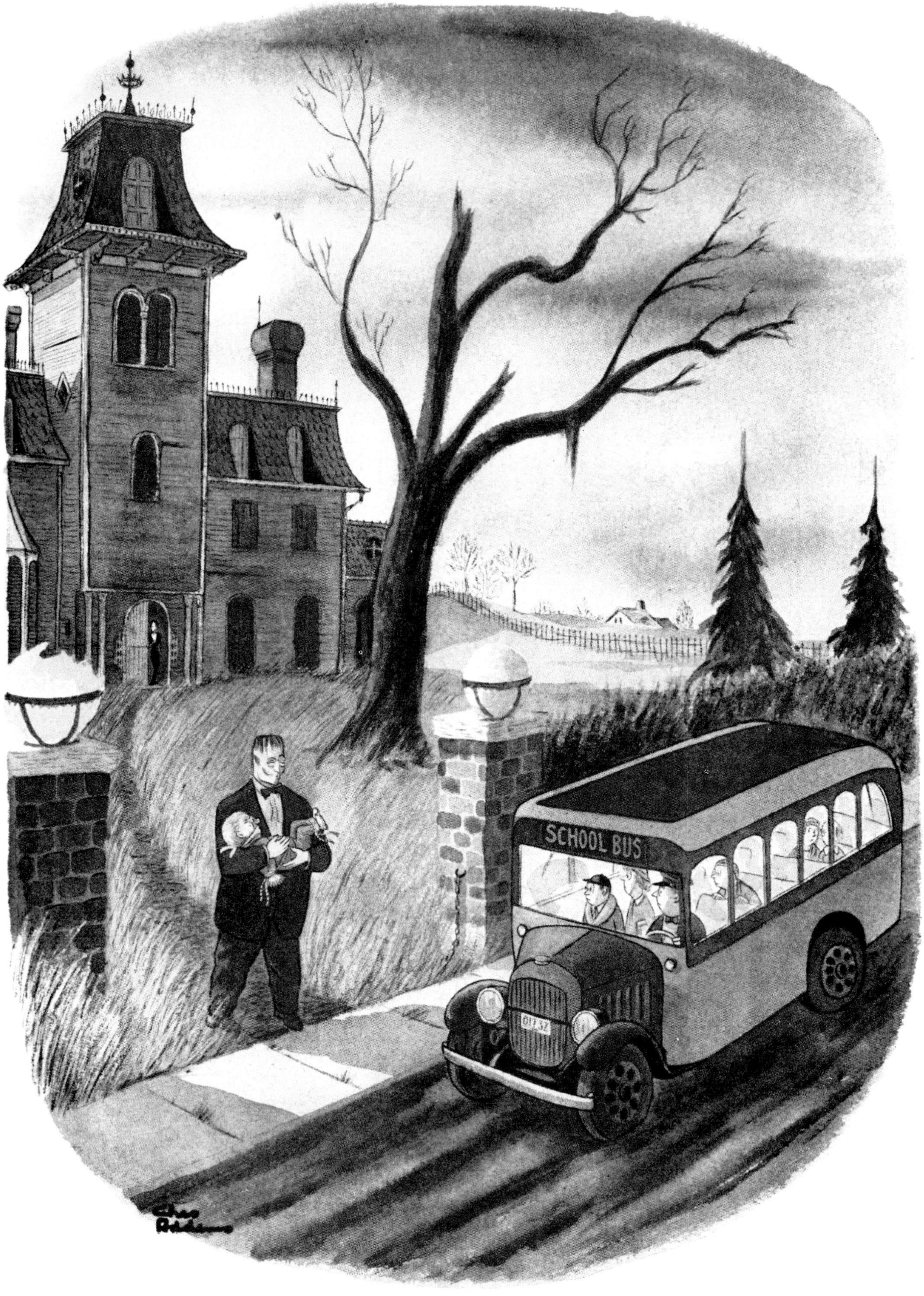
SCHOOL BUS
Chas Addams

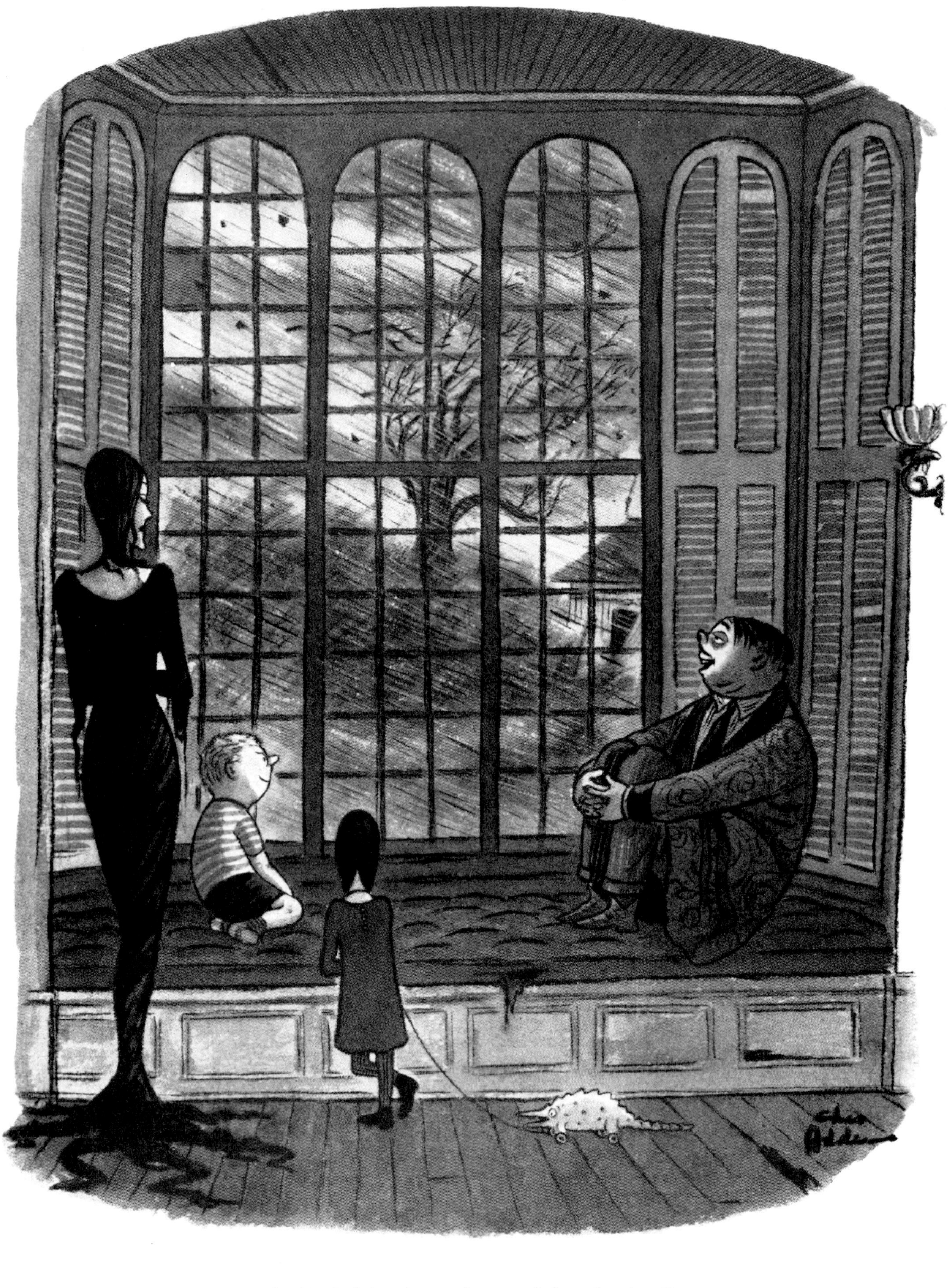

"Just the kind of day that makes you feel good to be alive!"

"Nothing much, Agnes. What's new with you?"

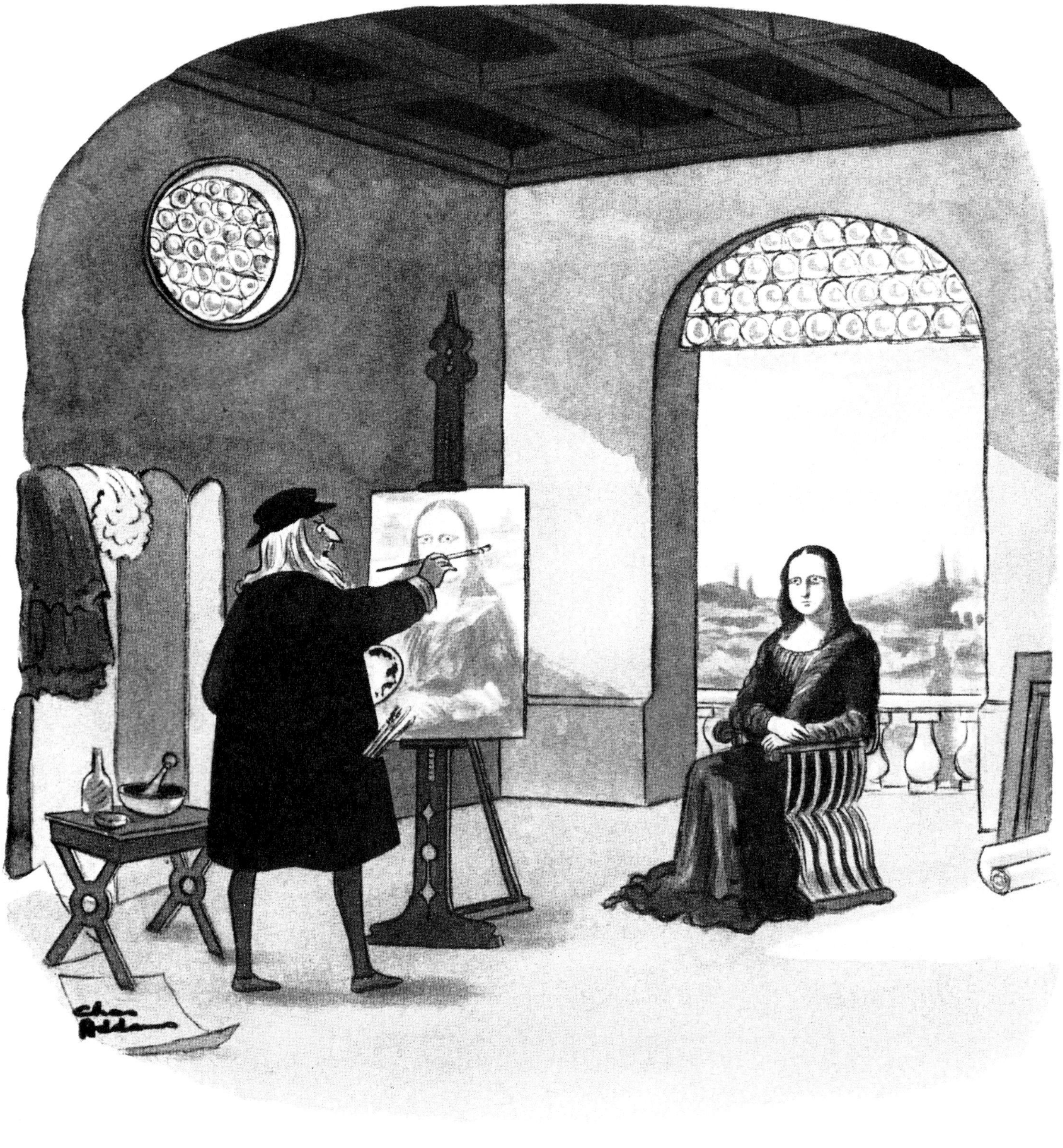
Chas Addams

"All right, now, a little smile."

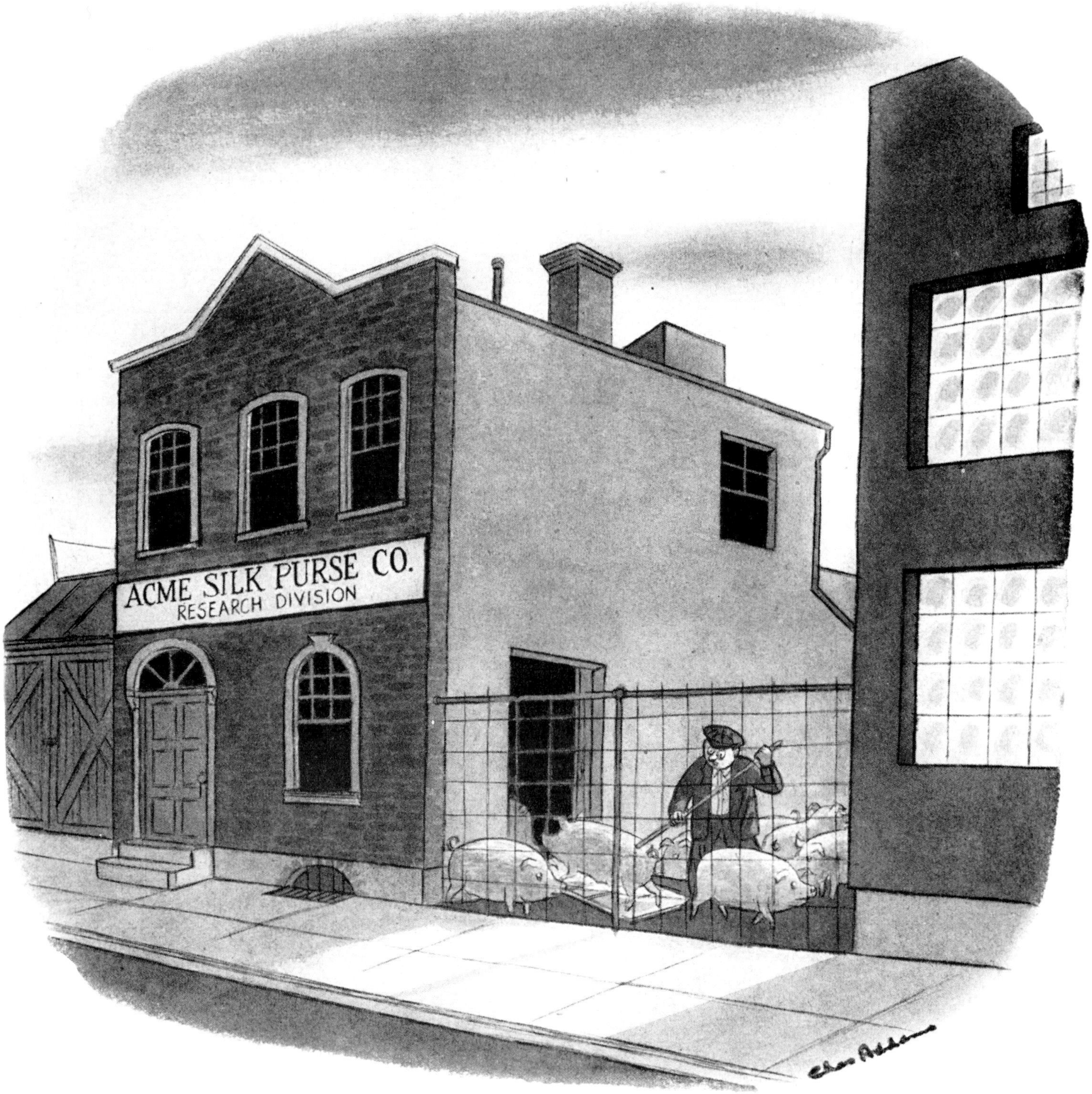
ACME SILK PURSE CO.
RESEARCH DIVISION
Chas Addams

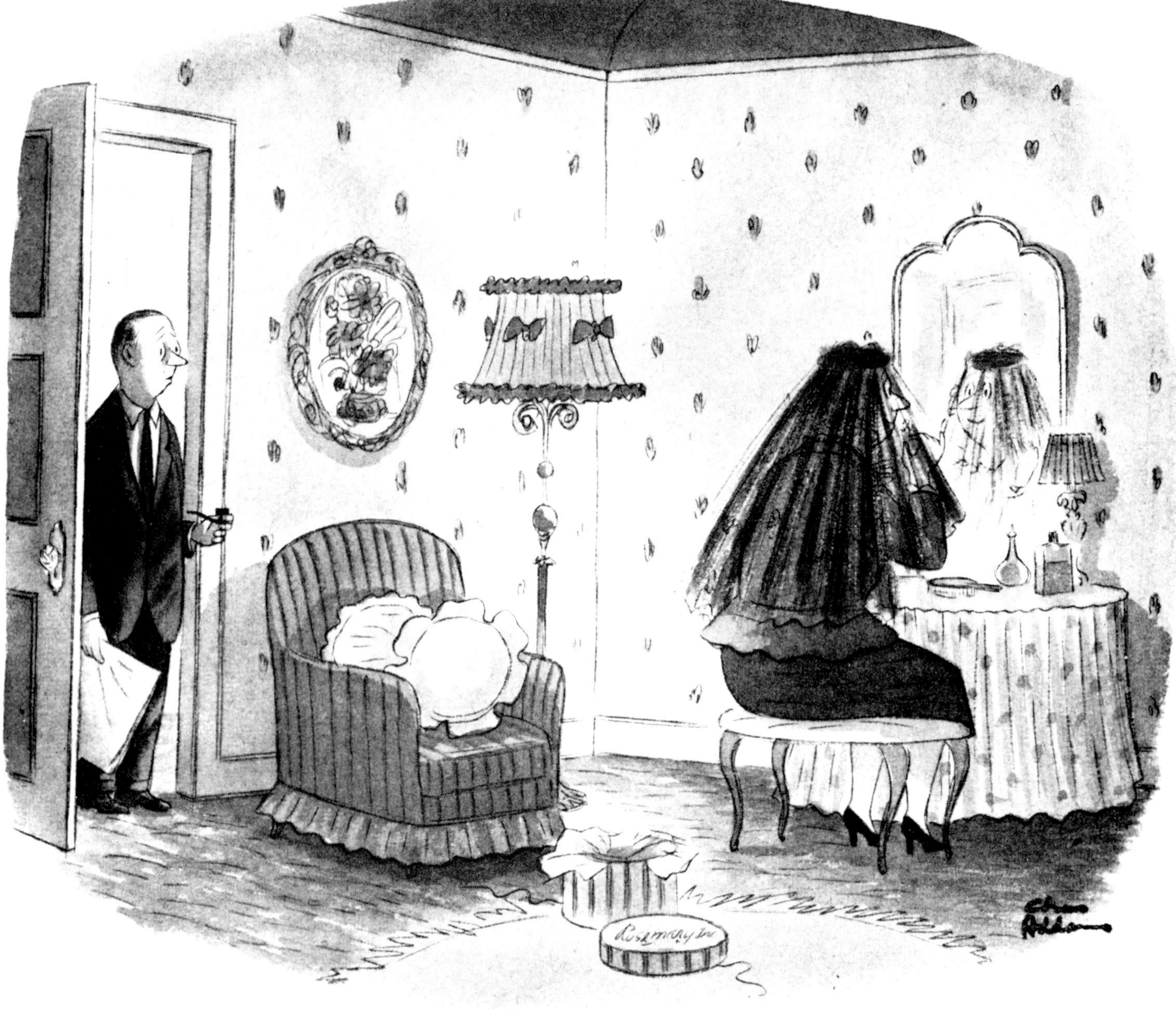
Chas Addams

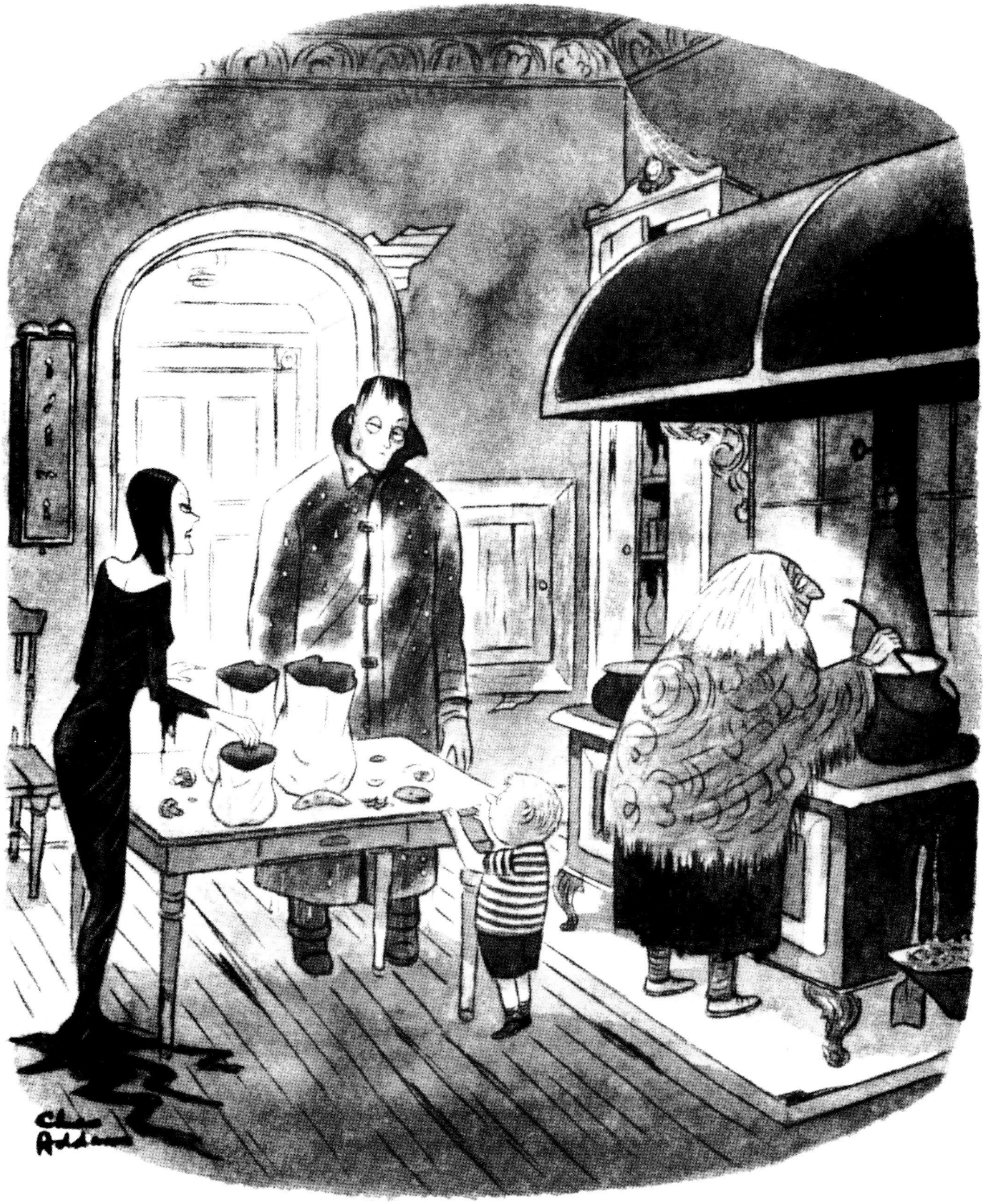

"You forgot the eye of newt."

118

"I'm sorry, sonny. We've run out of candy."

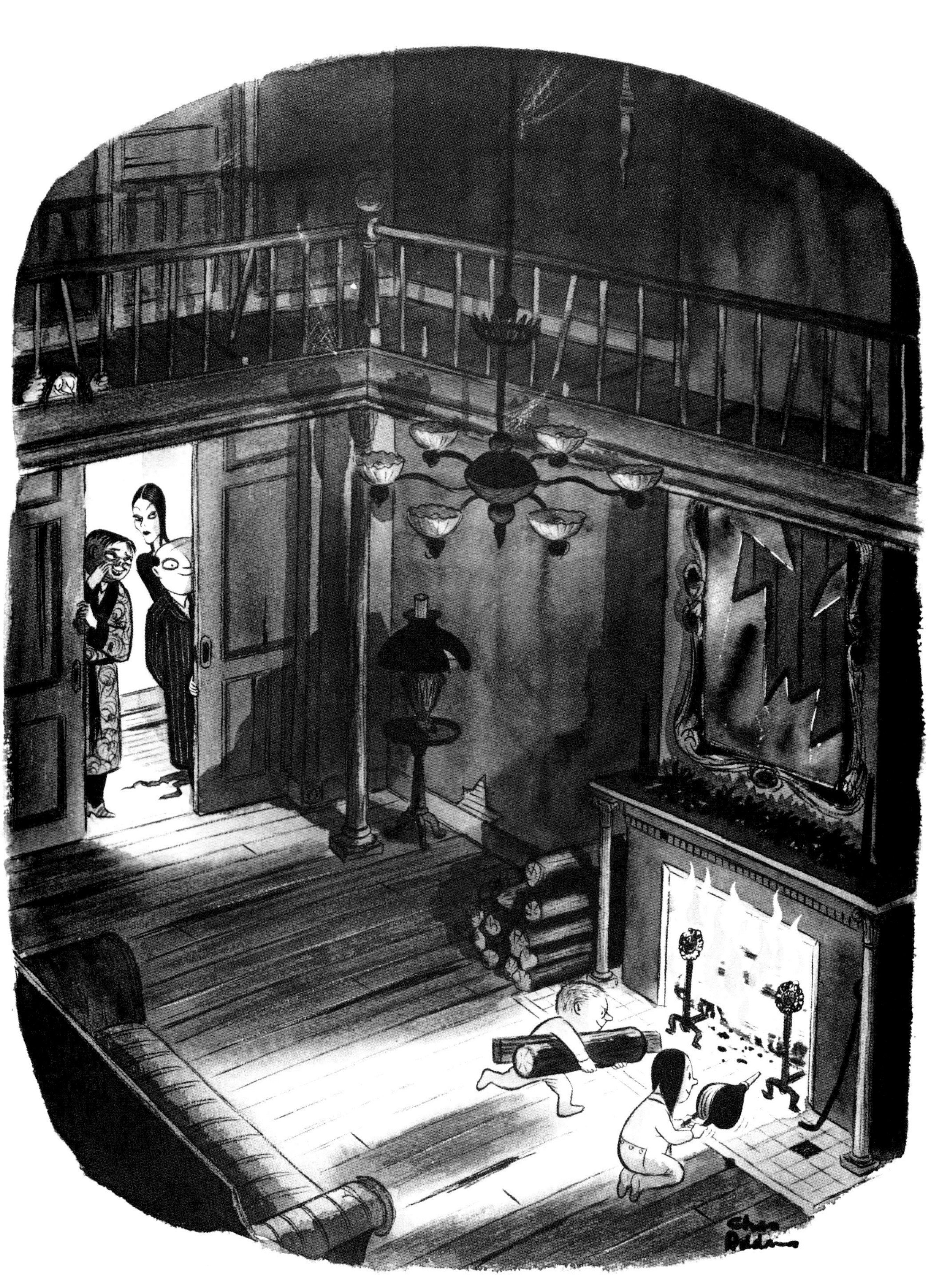

"The little dears! They still believe in Santa Claus."

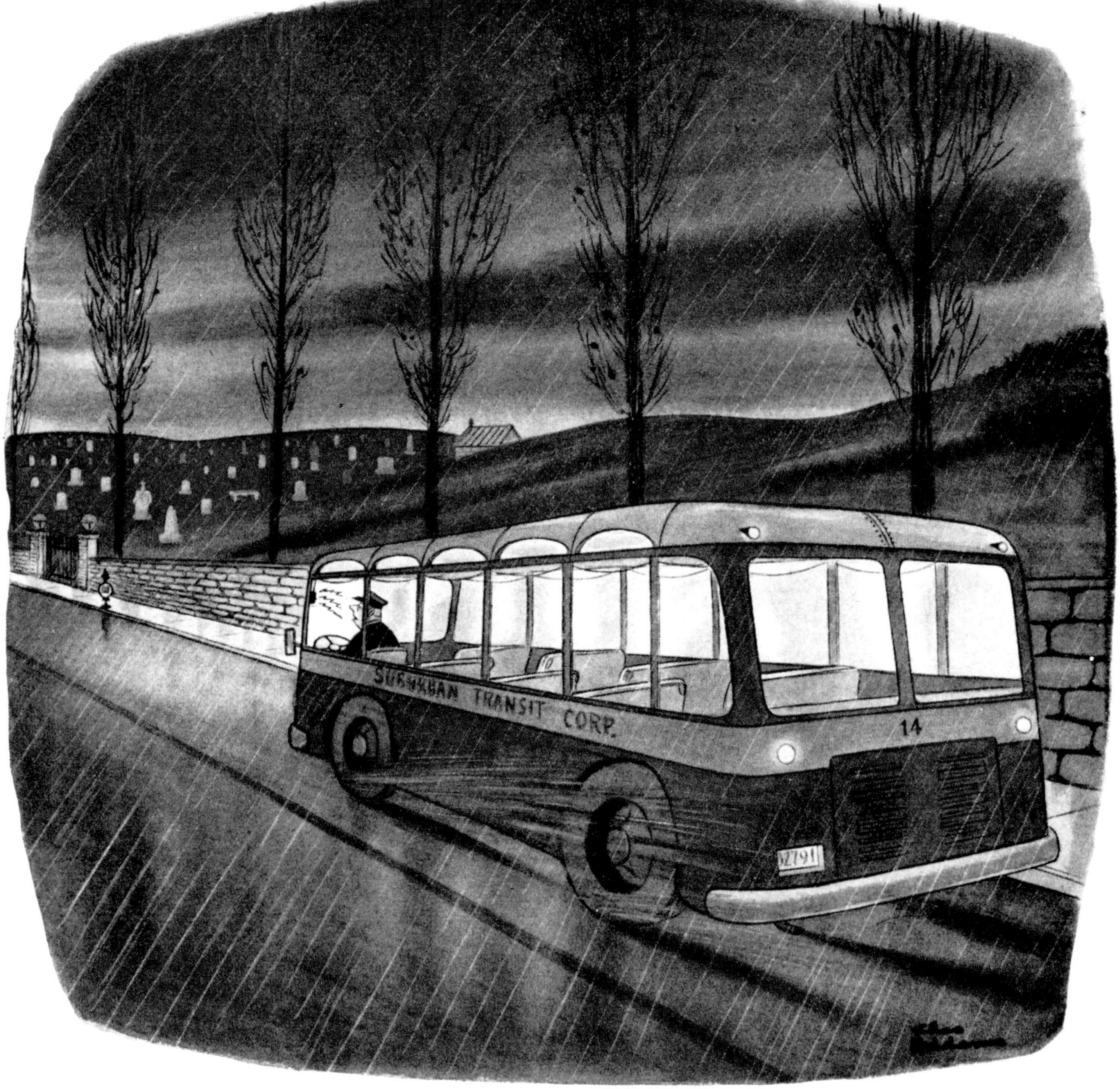
SUBURBAN TRANSIT CORP.
14

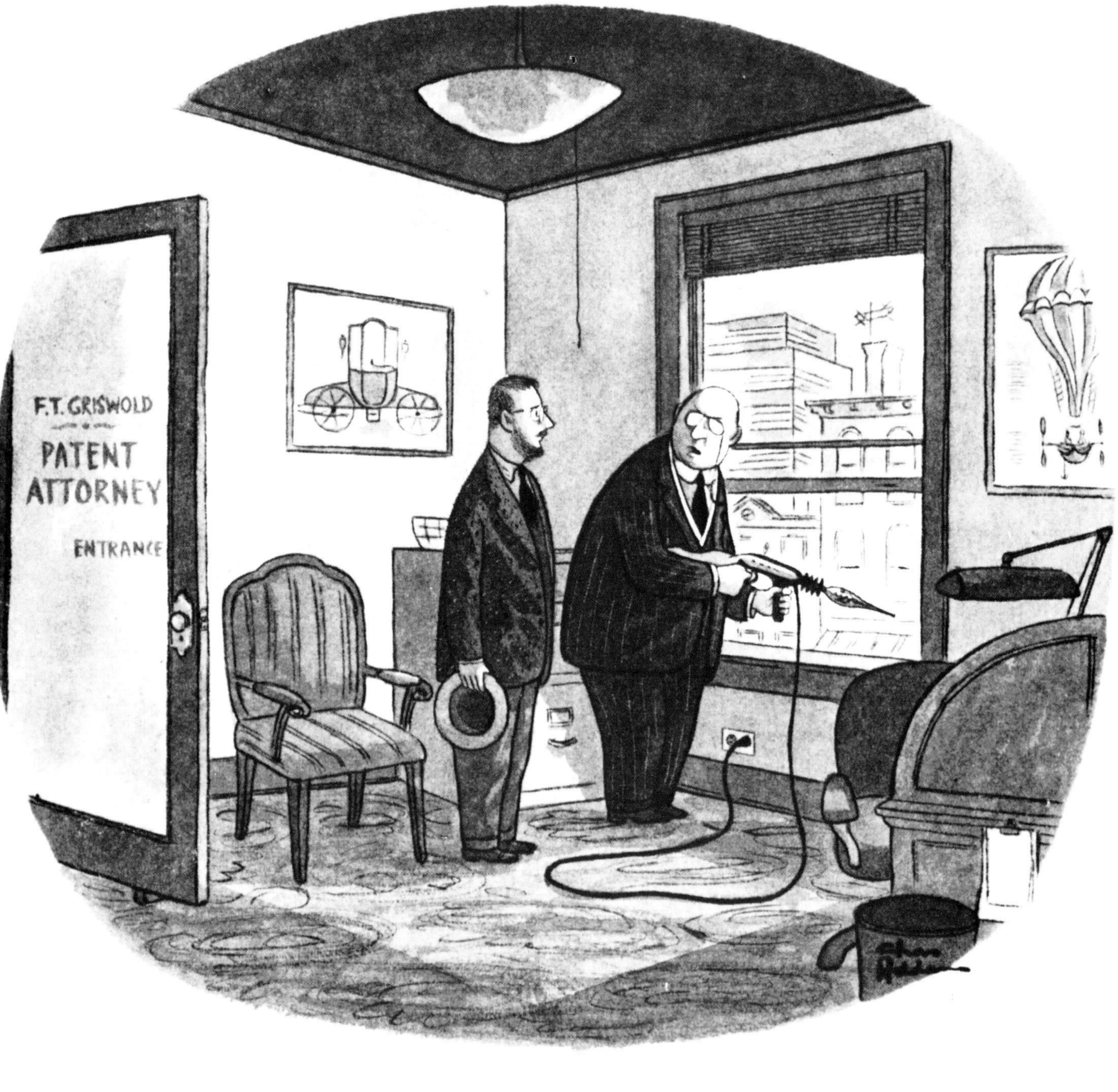
F.T. GRISWOLD
PATENT
ATTORNEY
ENTRANCE

"Death ray, fiddlesticks! Why it doesn't even slow them up."

"I give up, Robert. What does have two horns, one eye, and creeps?"

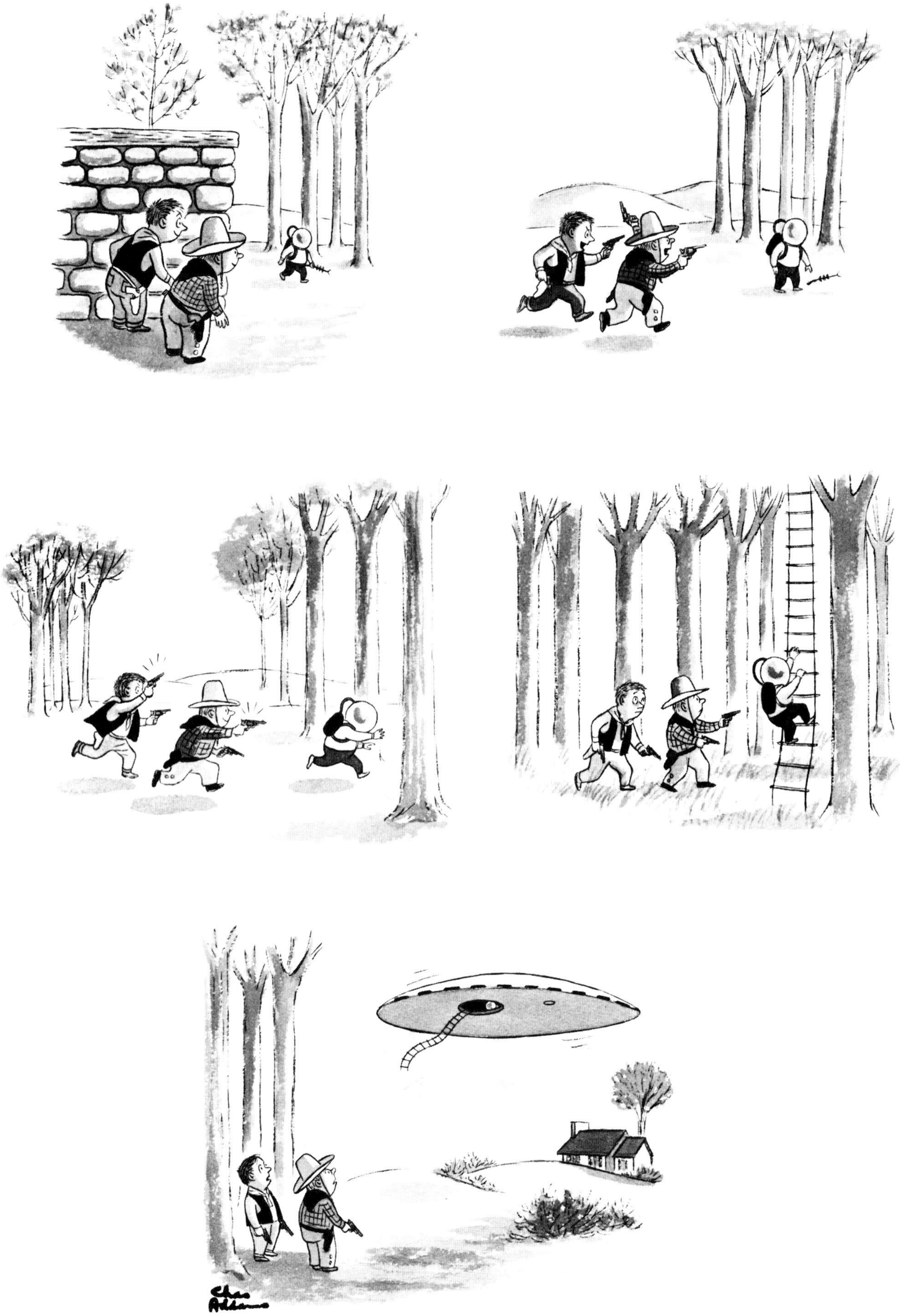
Chas Addams

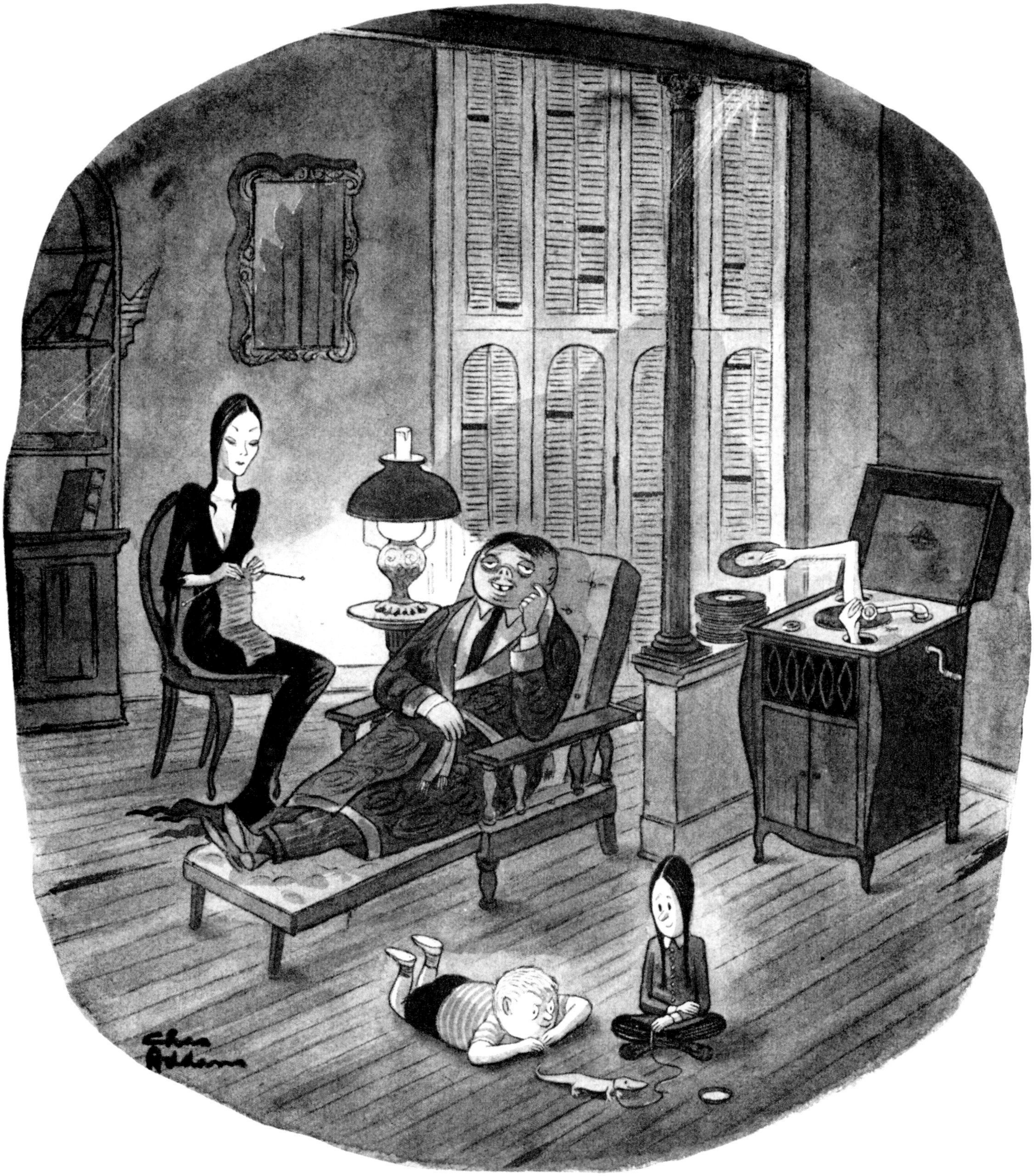
Chas Addams

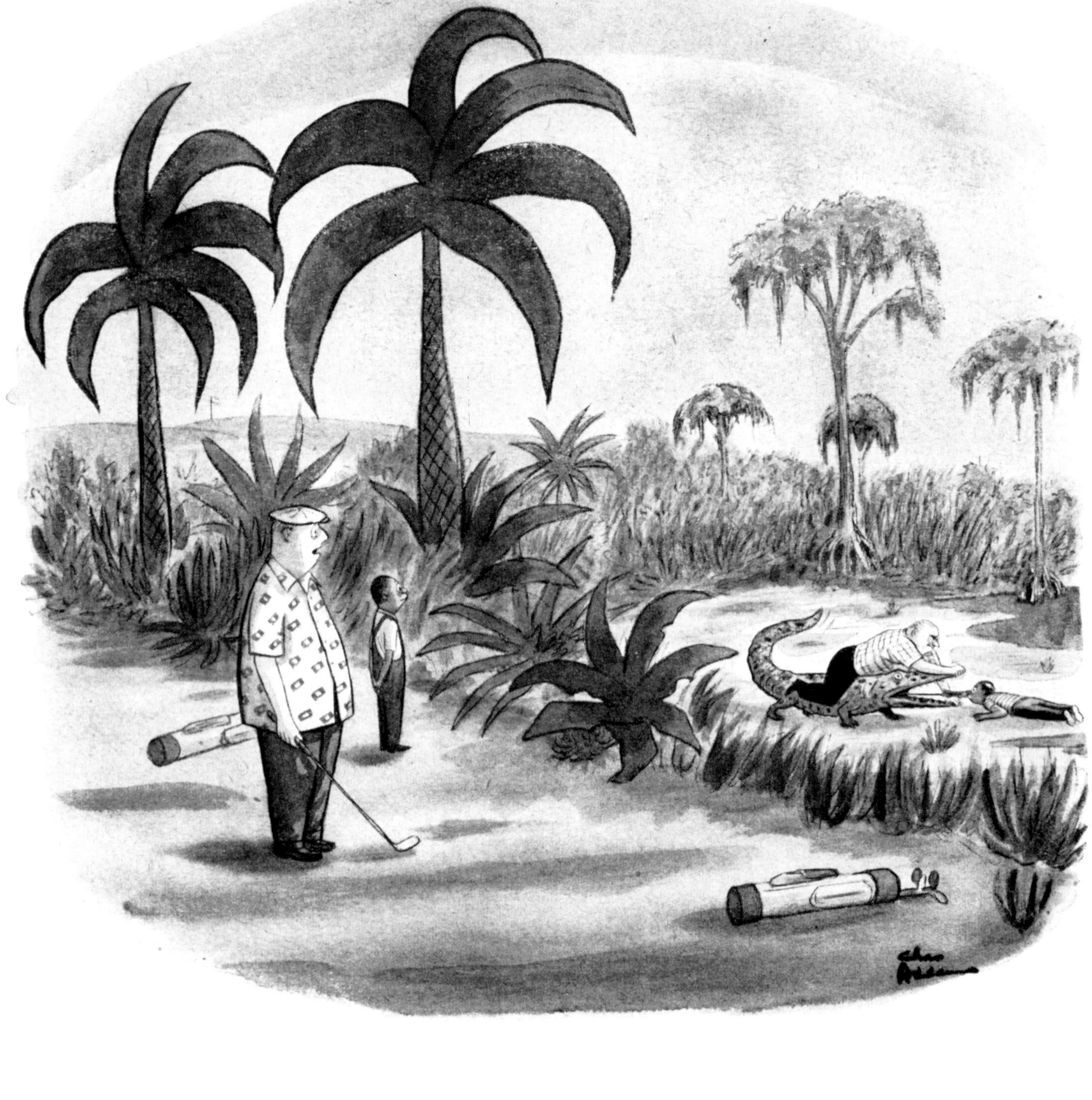

"Oh, for goodness' sake, forget it, Beasley. Play another one."

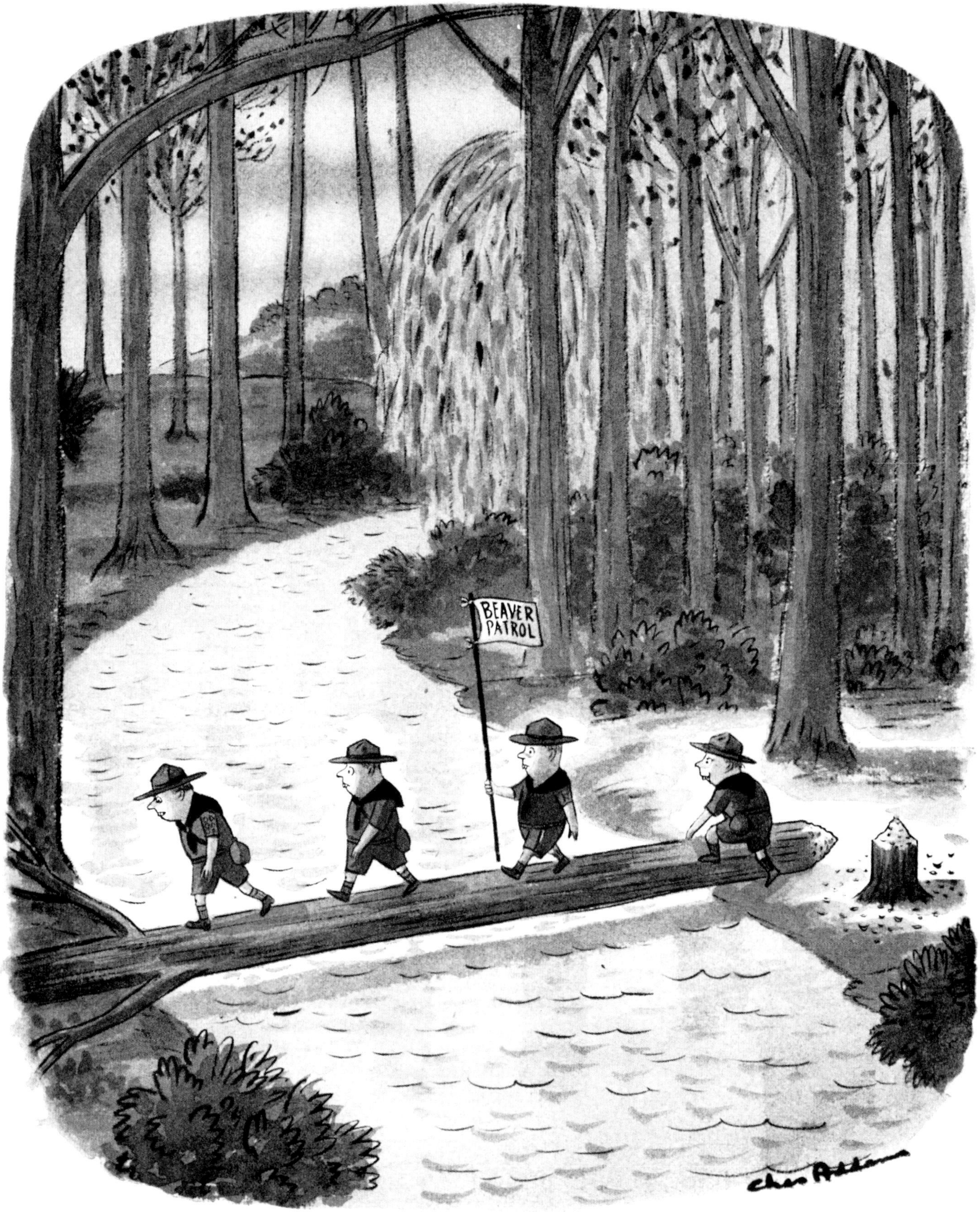
BEAVER
PATROL

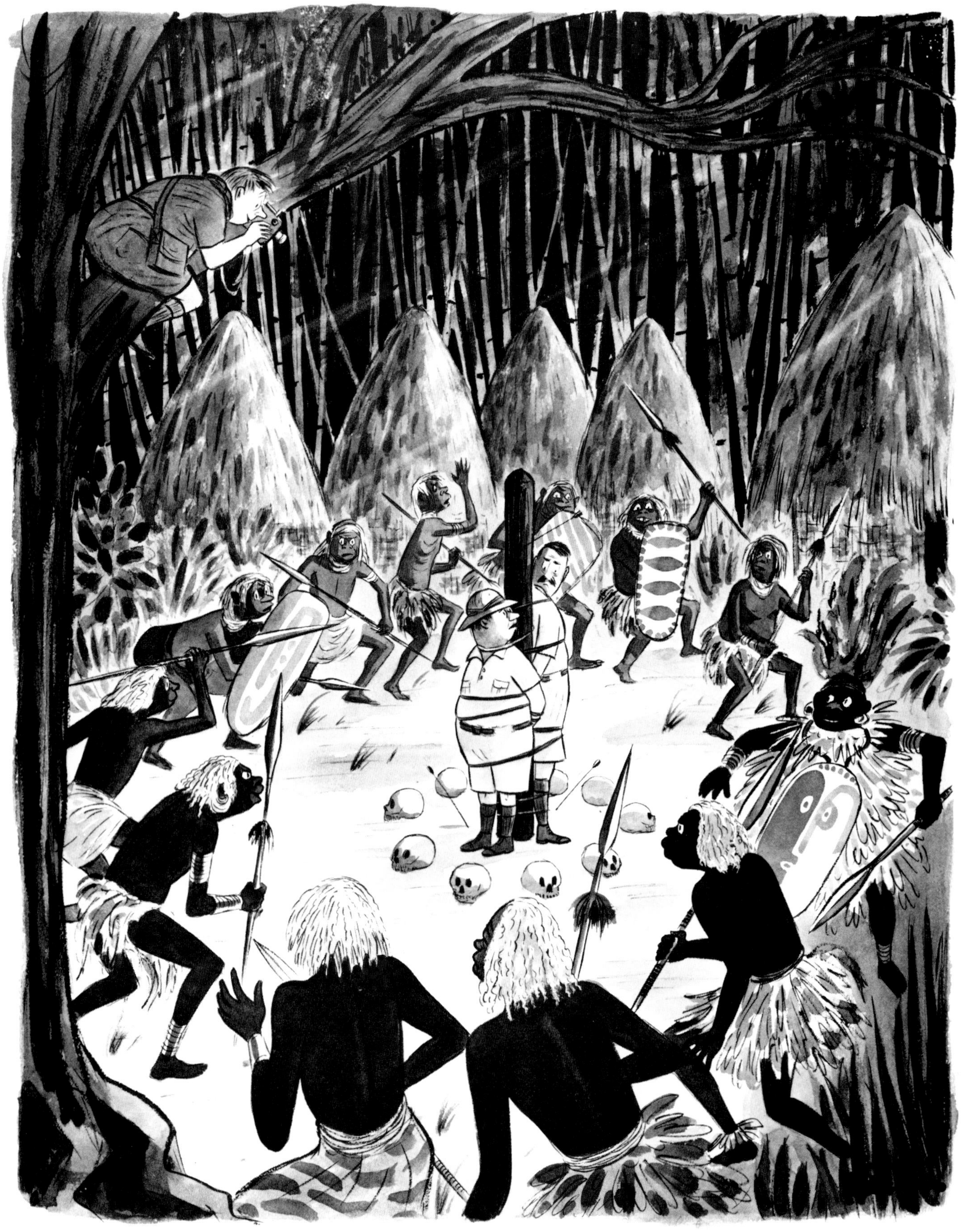

"Wouldn't you know that at a time like this Haley would be off somewhere photographing some damn ritual?"

"Mom, can I have the broom tonight?"

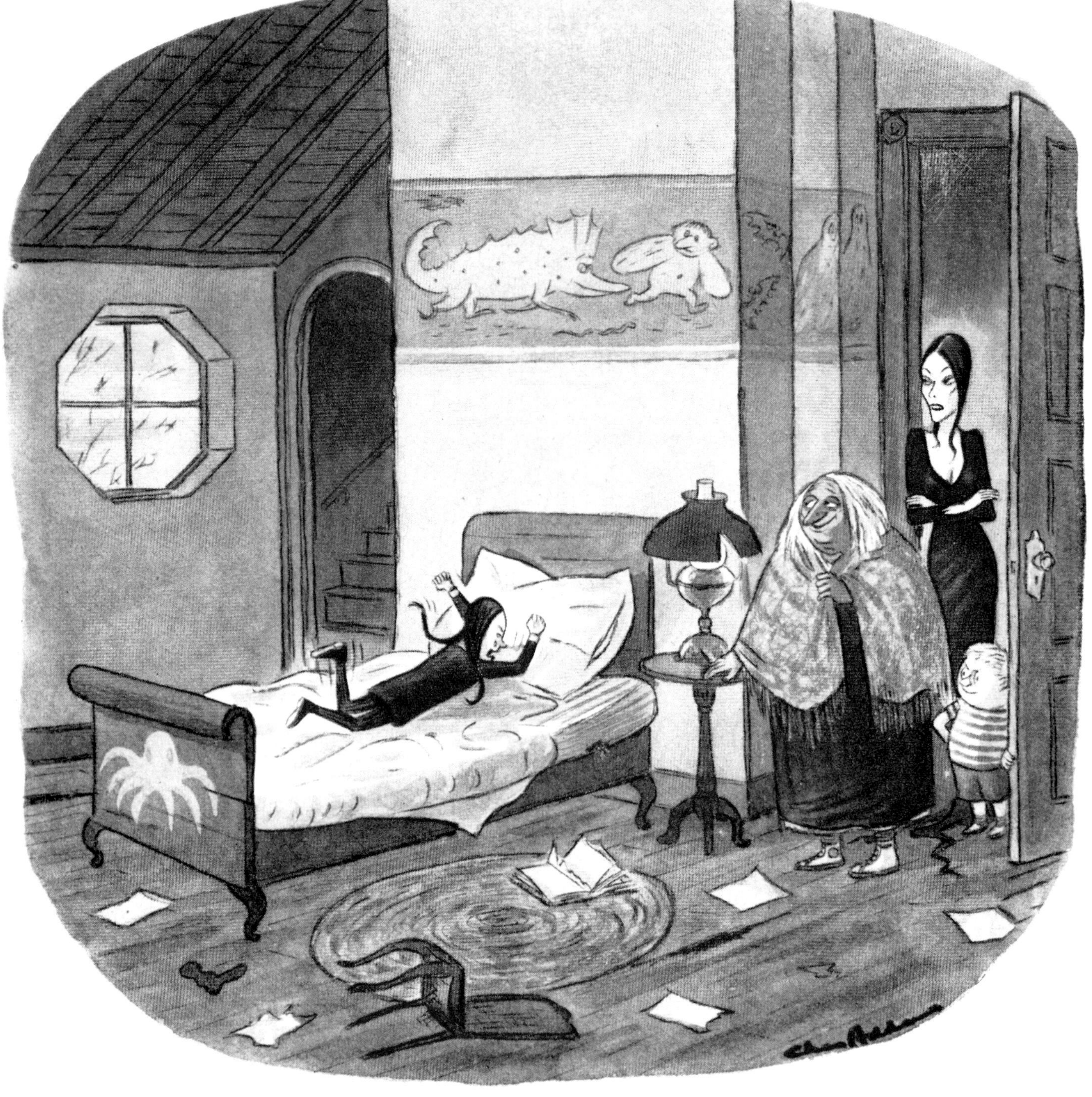

"Oh, she's furious because they put her on the honor roll at school."

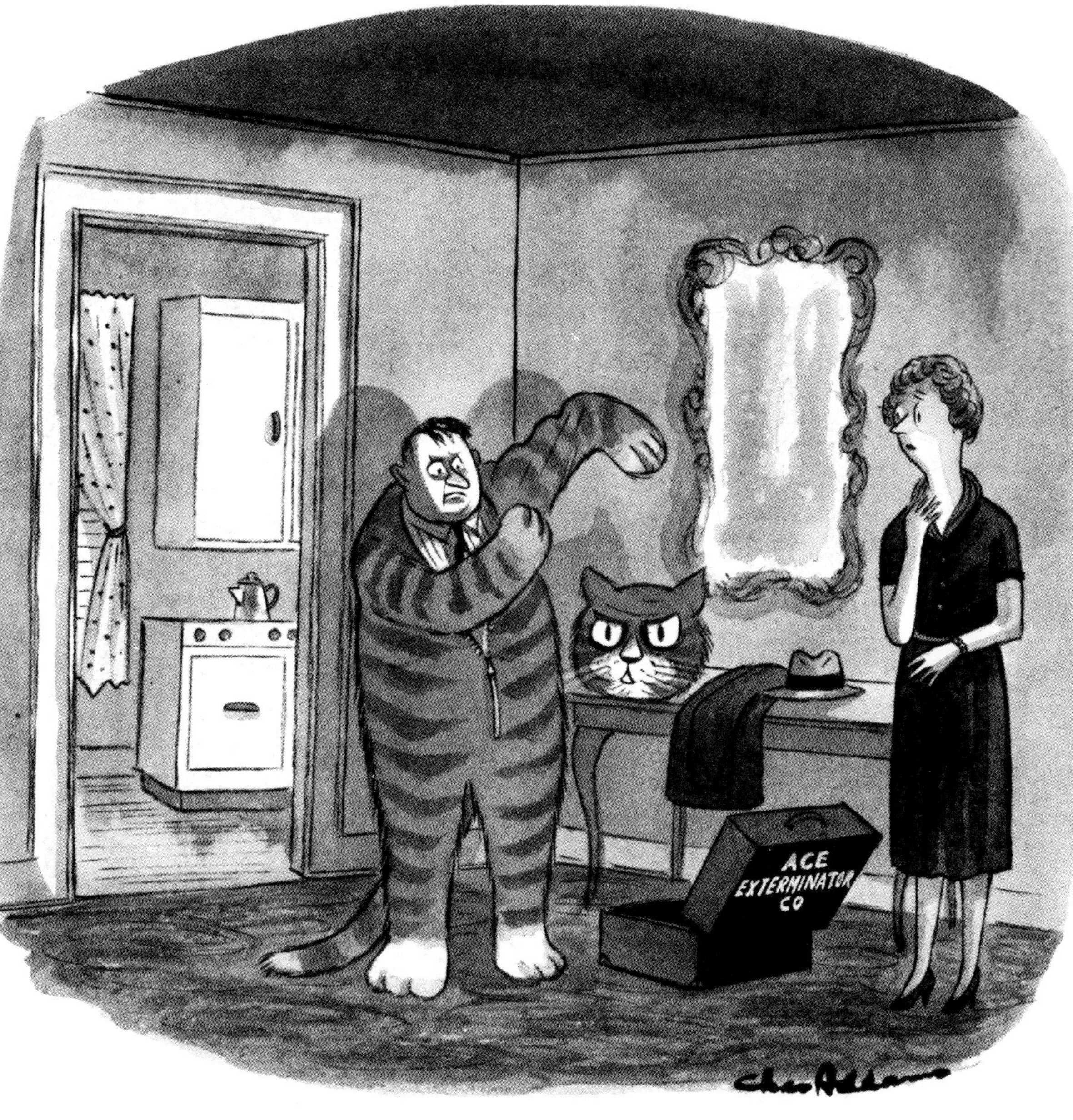
ACE
EXTERMINATOR
CO

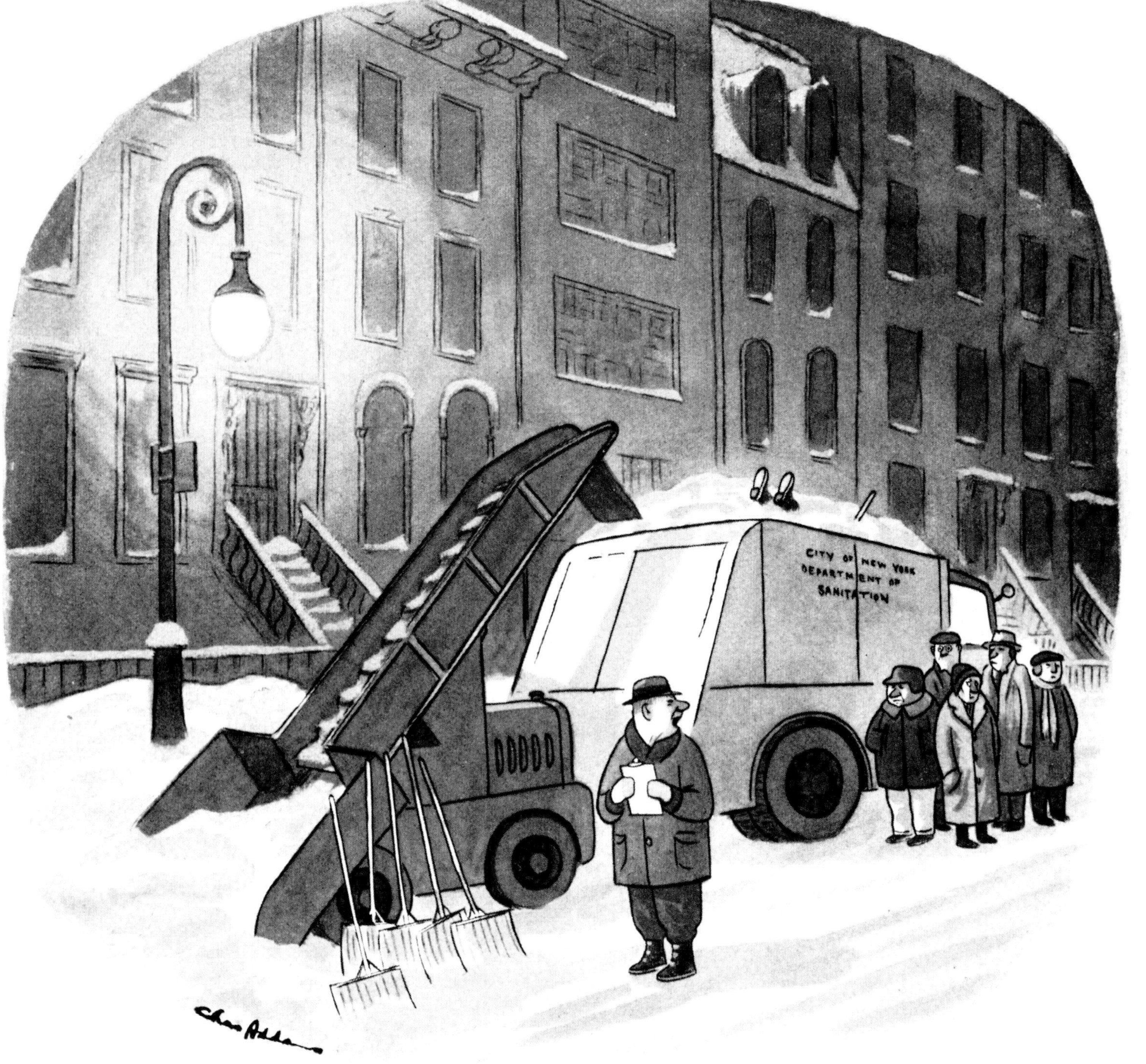
CITY OF NEW YORK
DEPARTMENT OF
SANITATION

"Just a minute, you guys—we're missing one shovel."

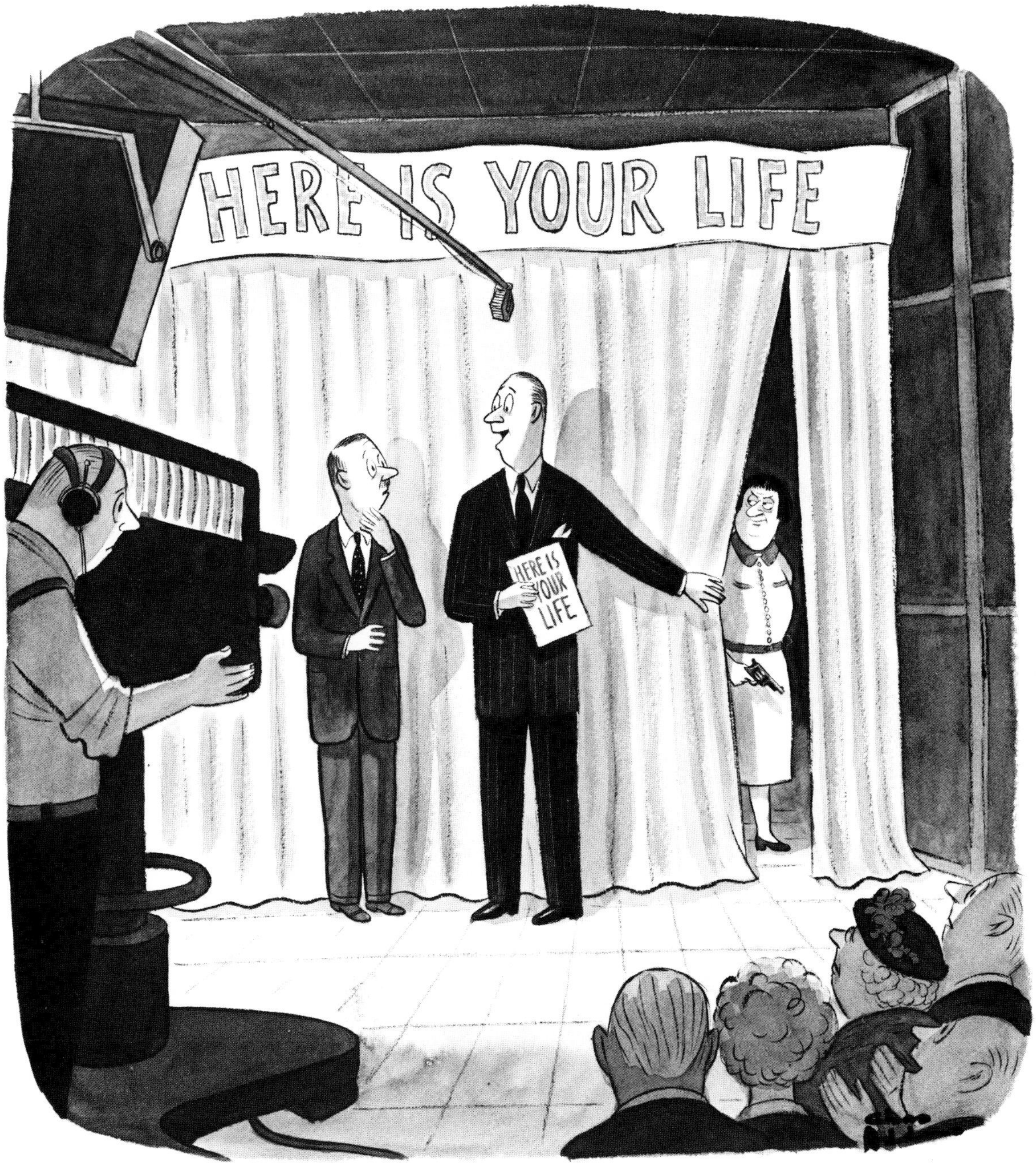
HERE IS YOUR LIFE
HERE IS YOUR LIFE

". . . and now, George Pembrook, here is the wife you haven't seen in eighteen years!"

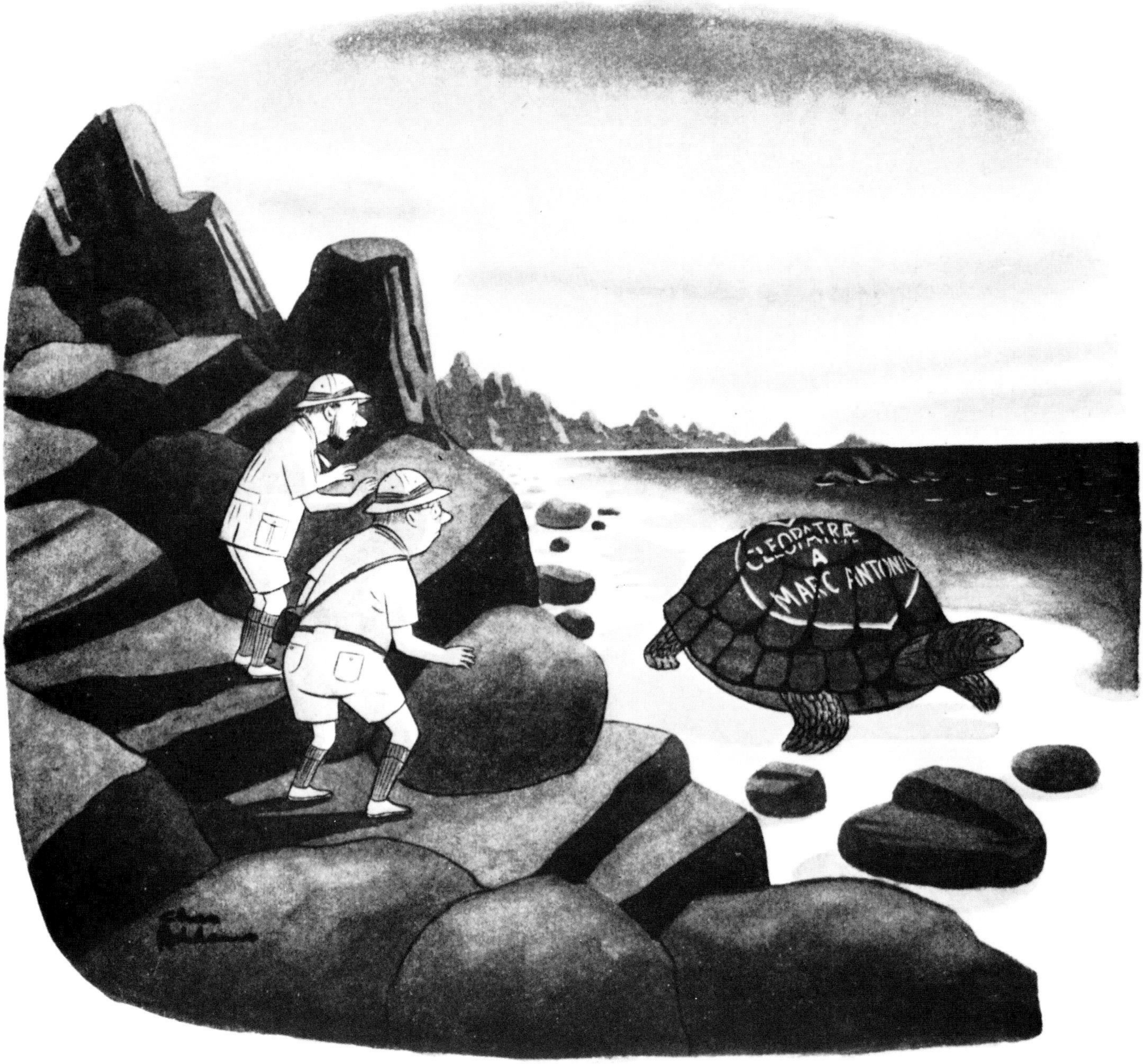
CLEOPATRE
A
MARC ANTONIO

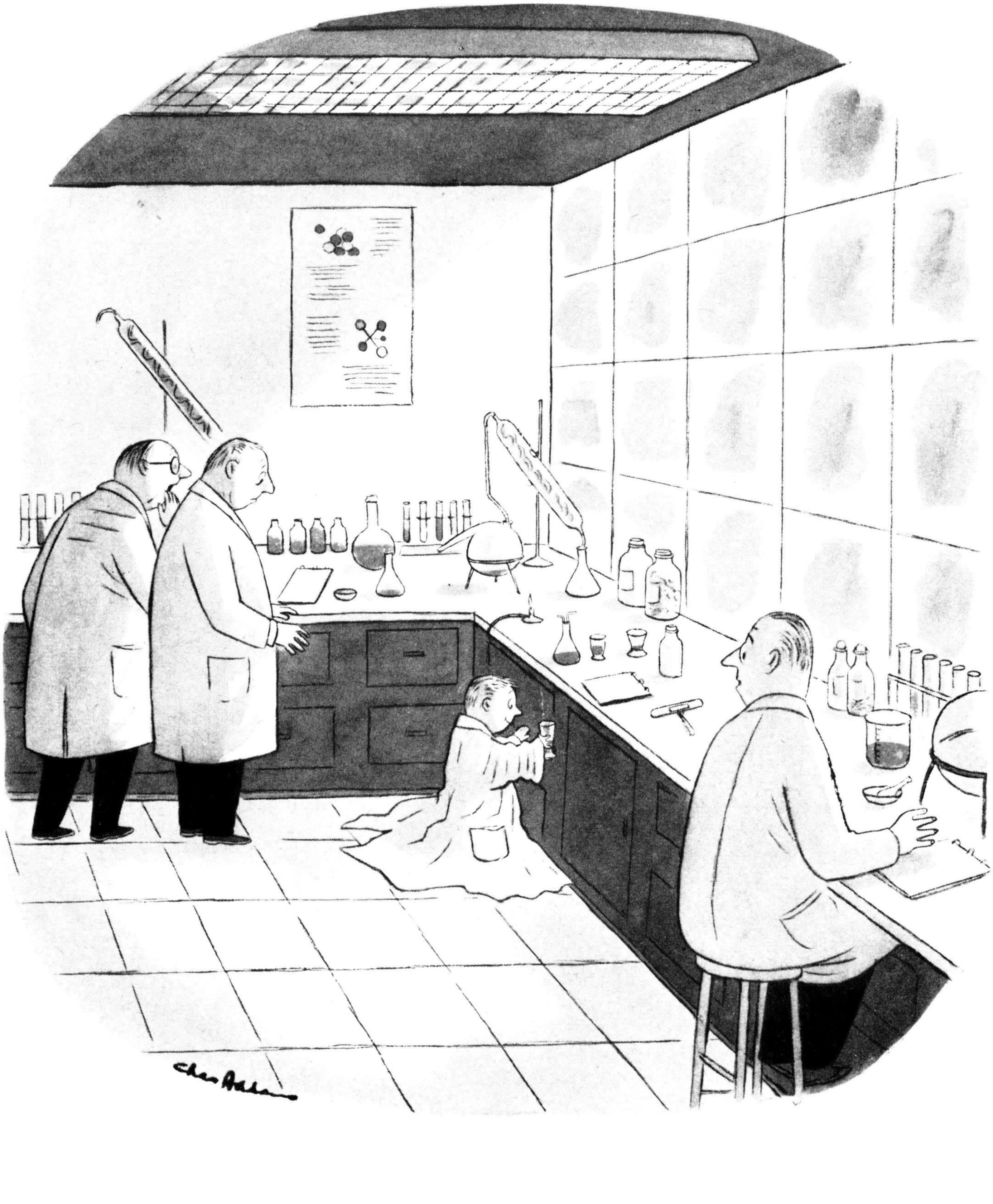

"Looks like Wesselman's hit on something interesting."

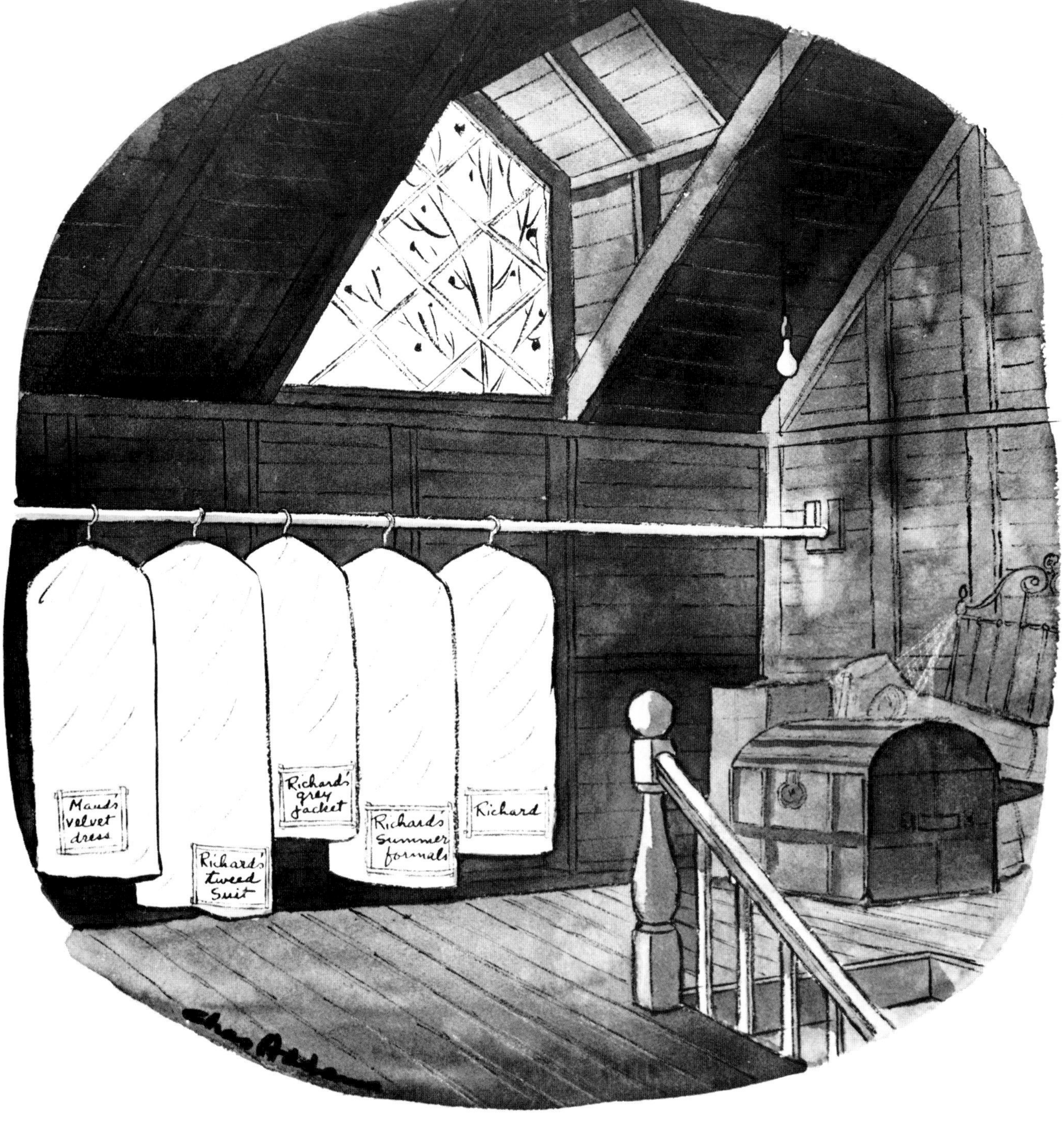
Maud's velvet dress
Richard's tweed Suit
Richard's gray jacket
Richard's Summer formals
Richard

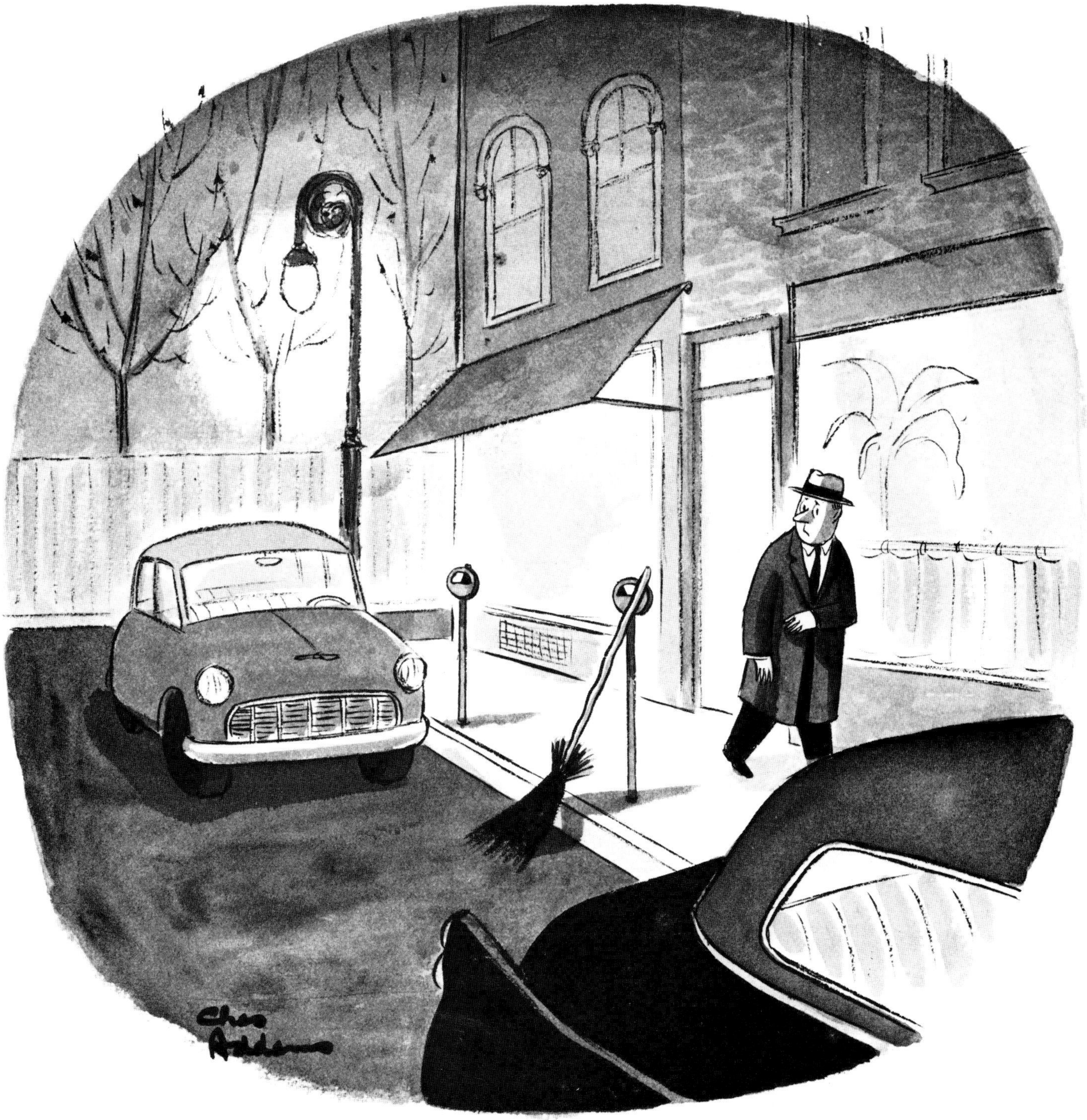
Chas Addams

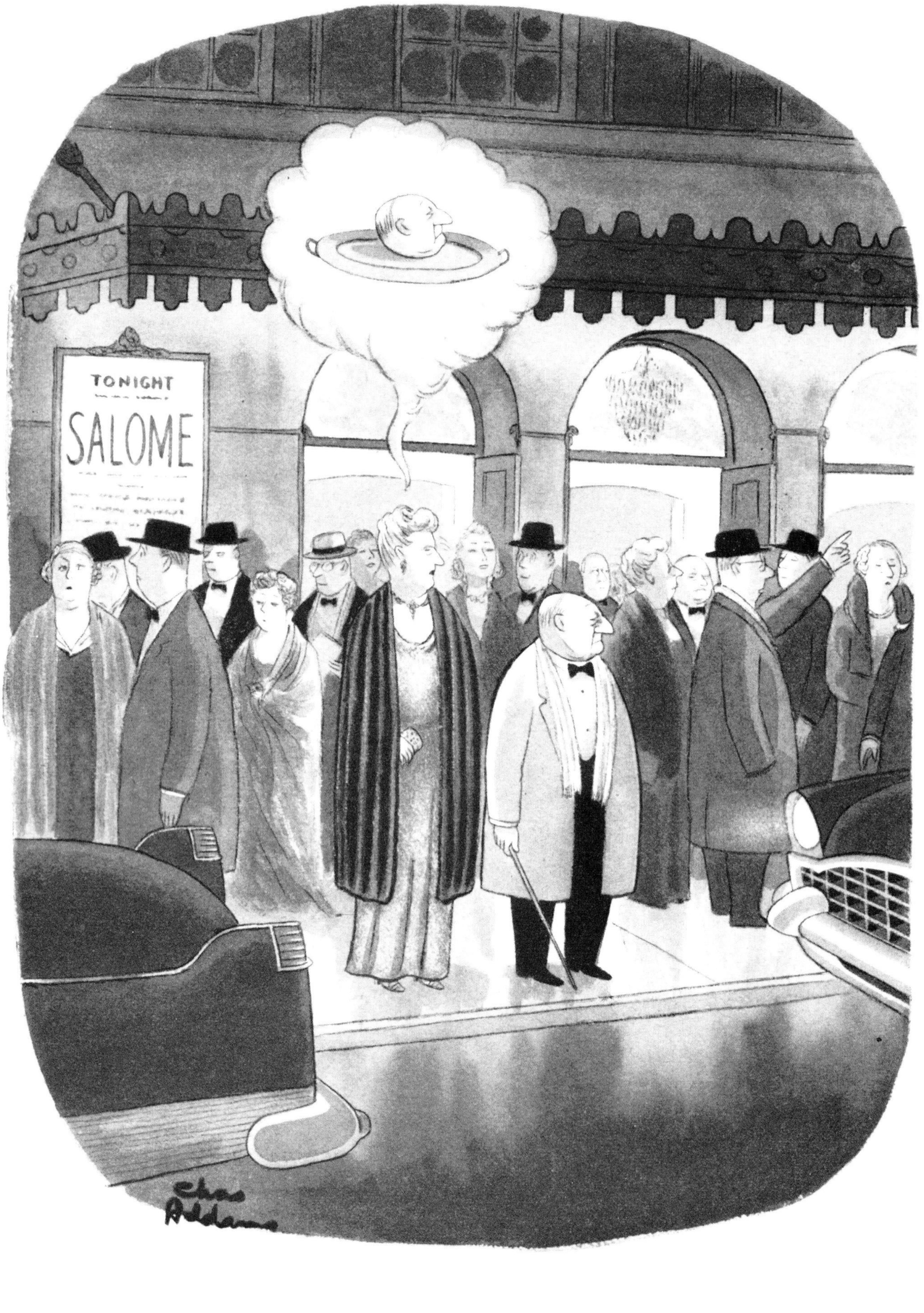
TONIGHT
SALOME
Chas Addams

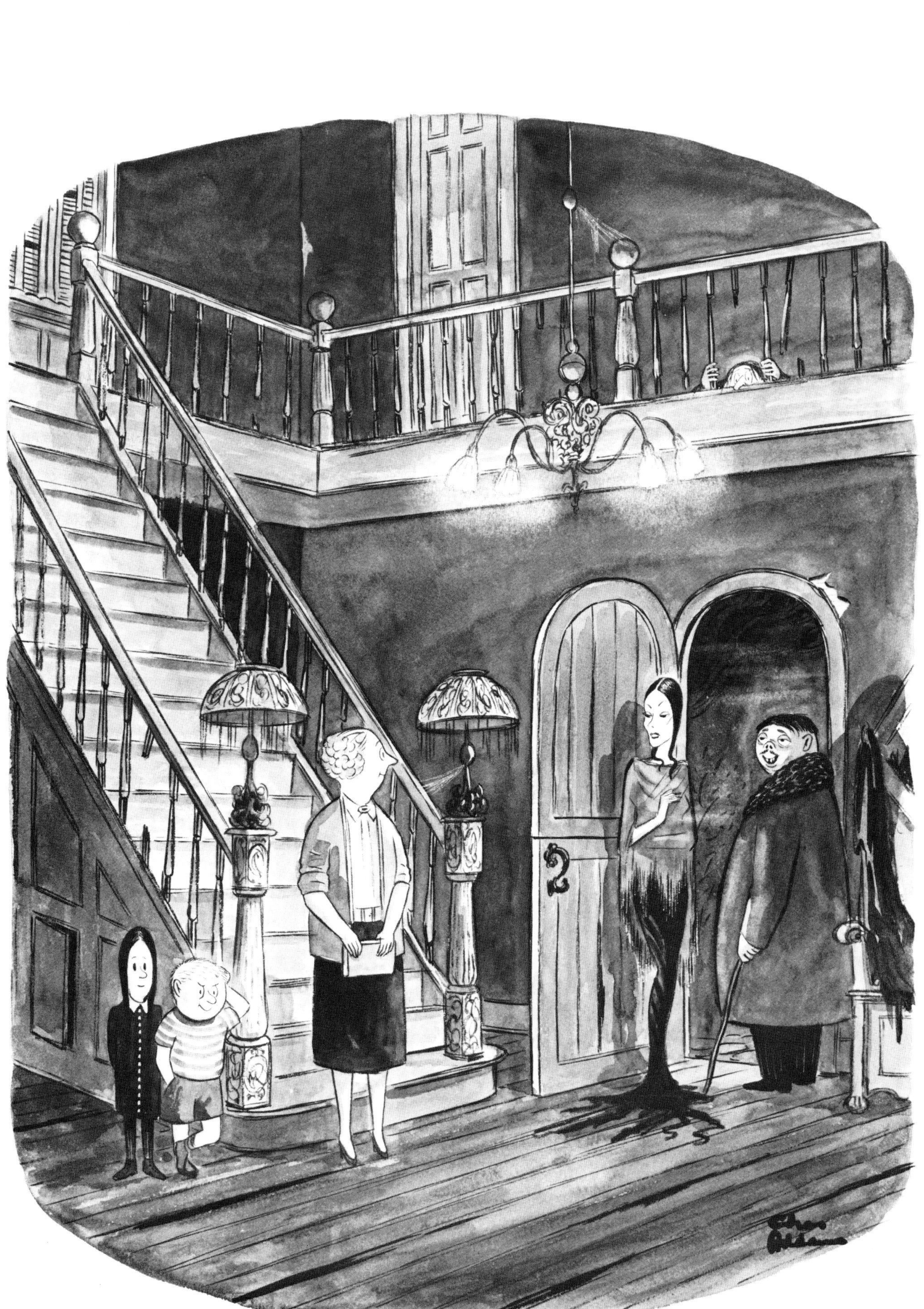

"We won't be late, Miss Weems. Get the children to bed around eight, and keep your back to the wall at all times."

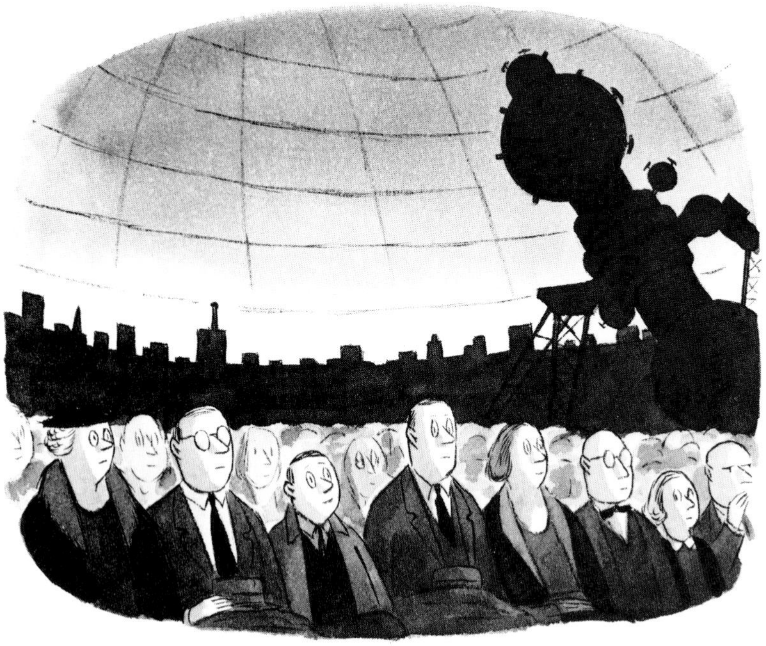

1

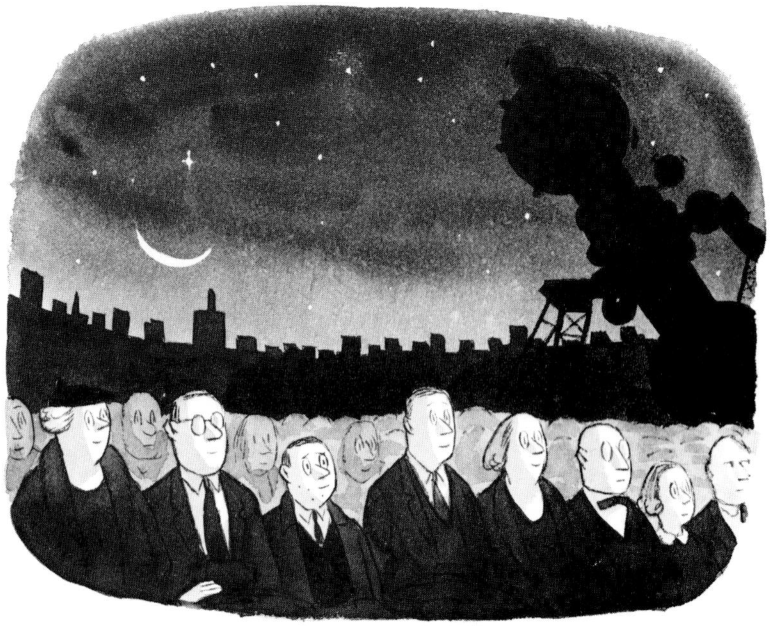

2

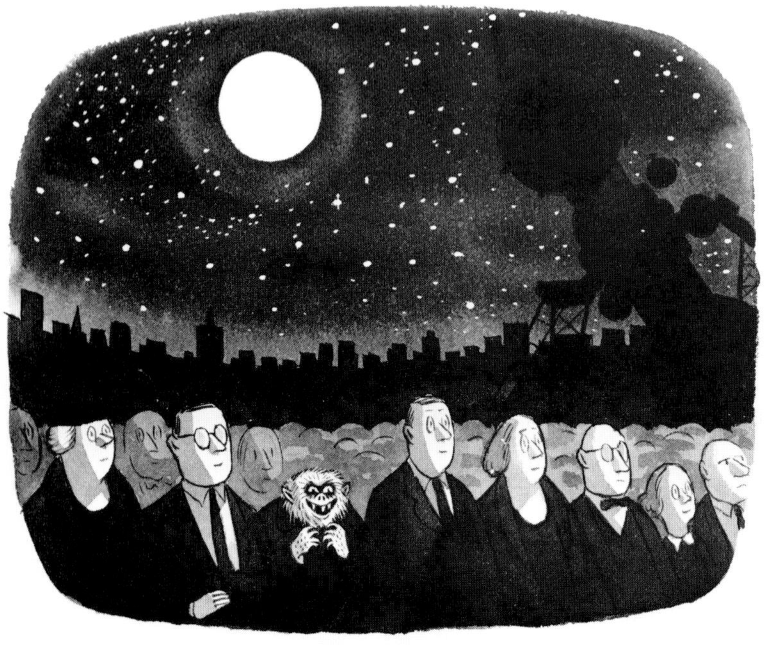

5

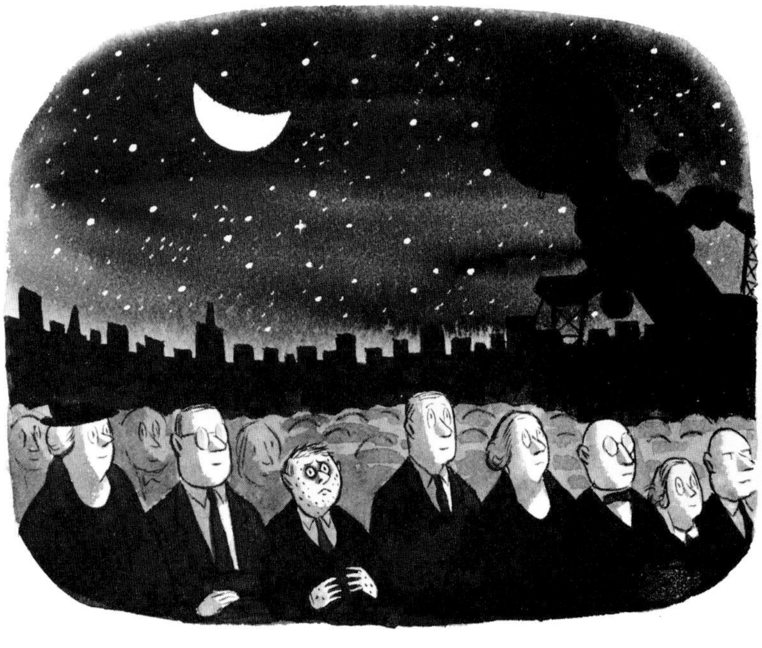

6

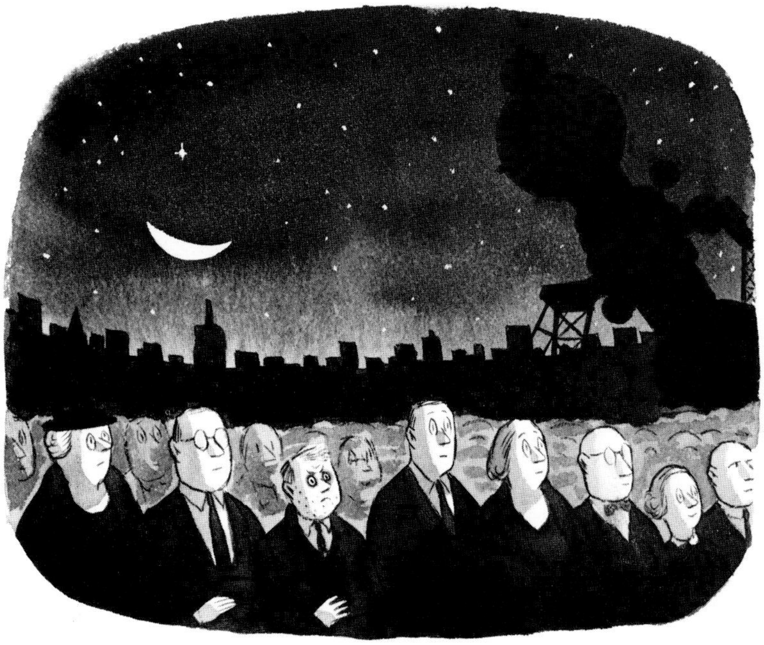

3

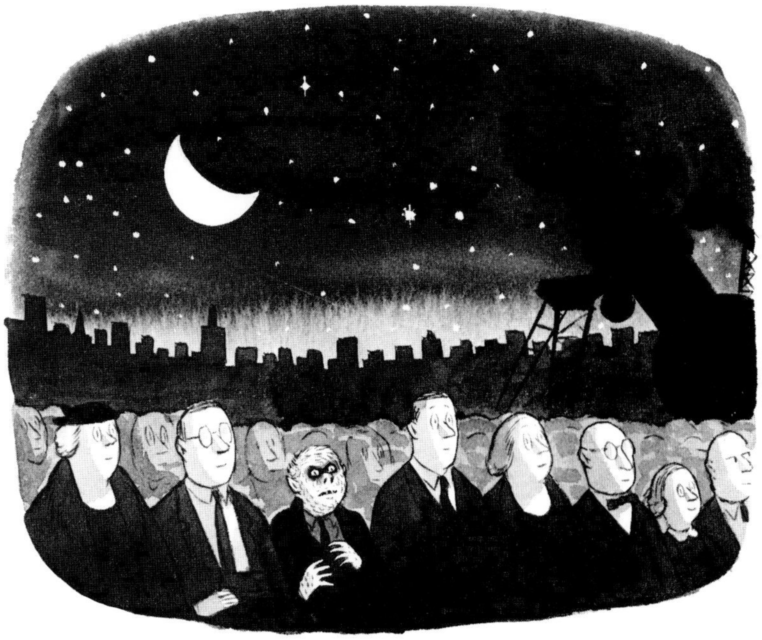

4

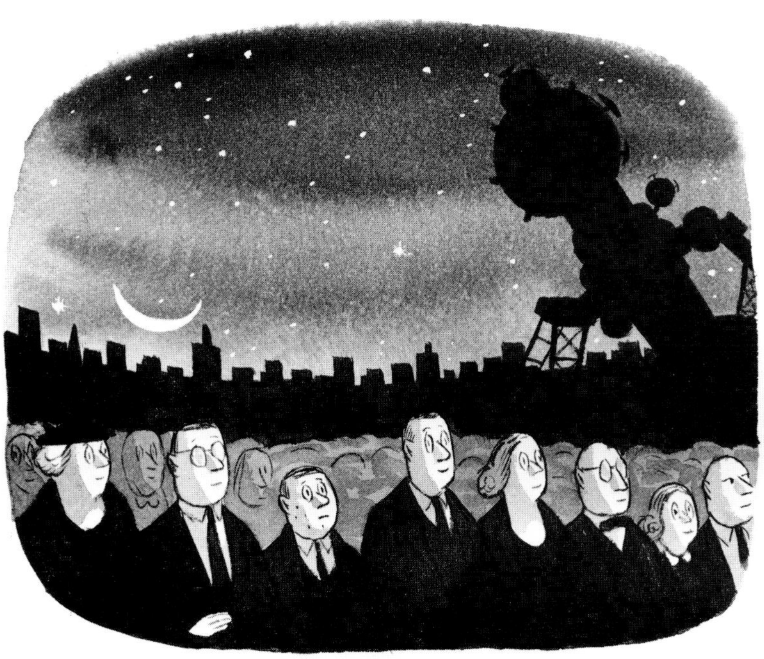

7

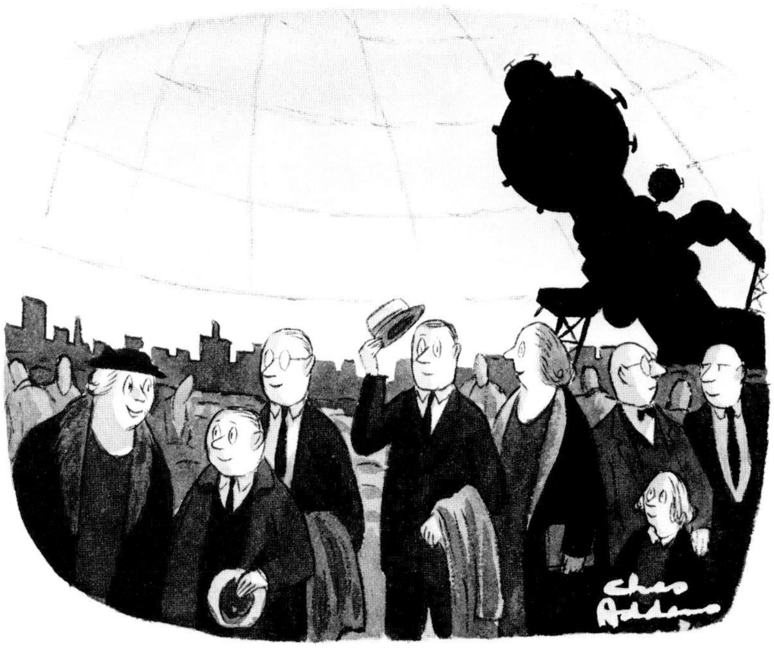
Chas Addams

8

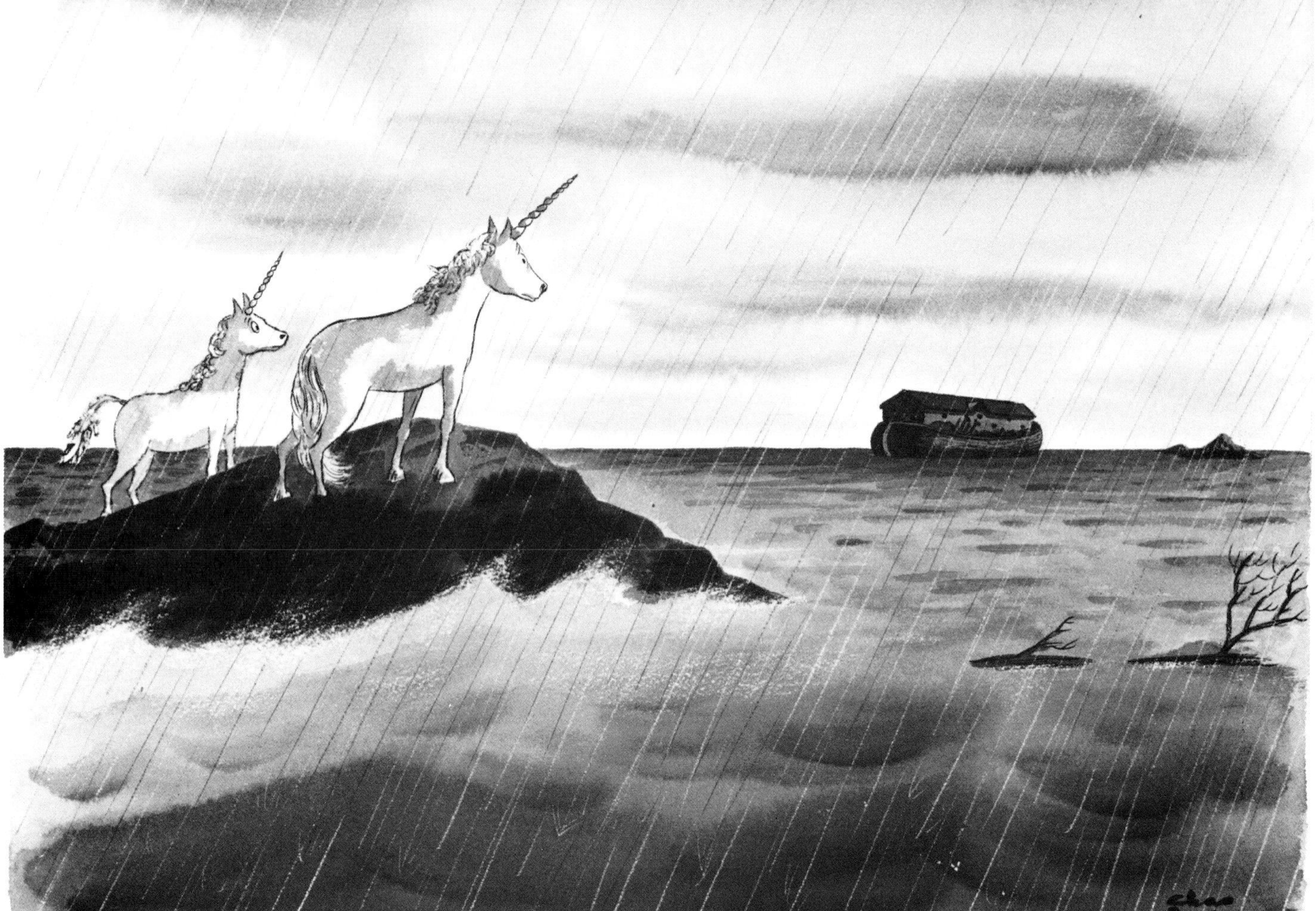
Chas Addams

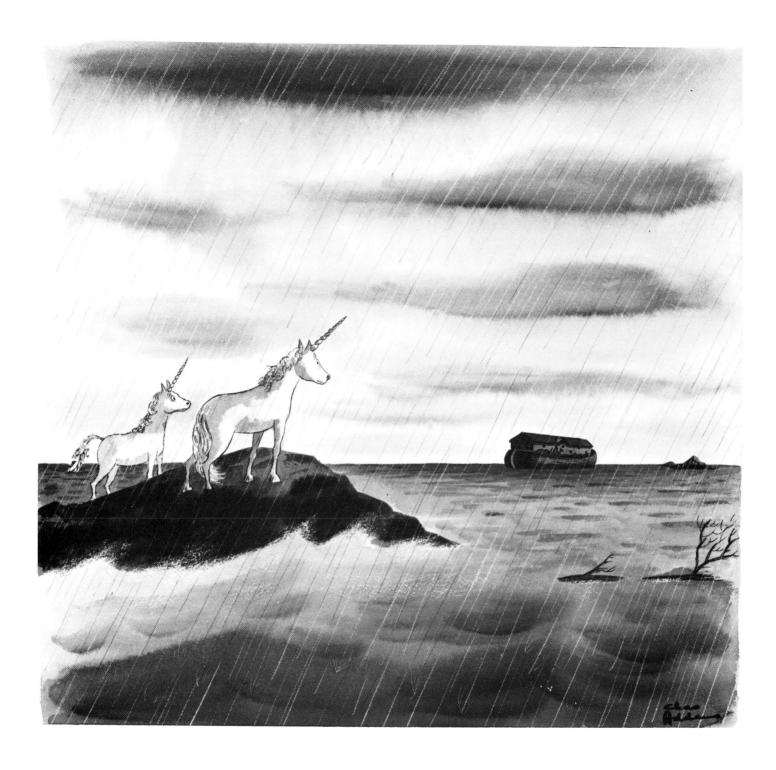

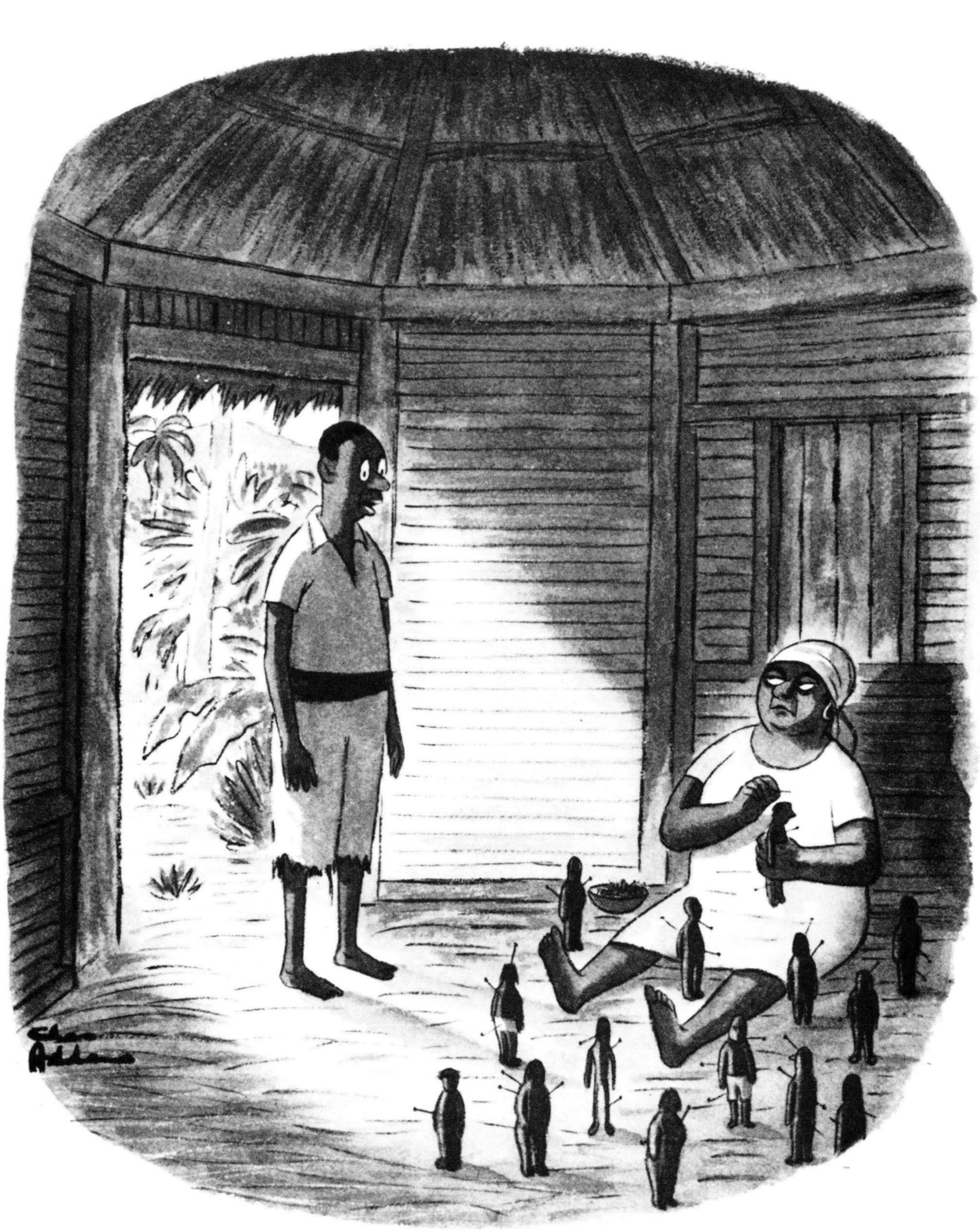
Chas Addams

"Can't you get along with anybody?"

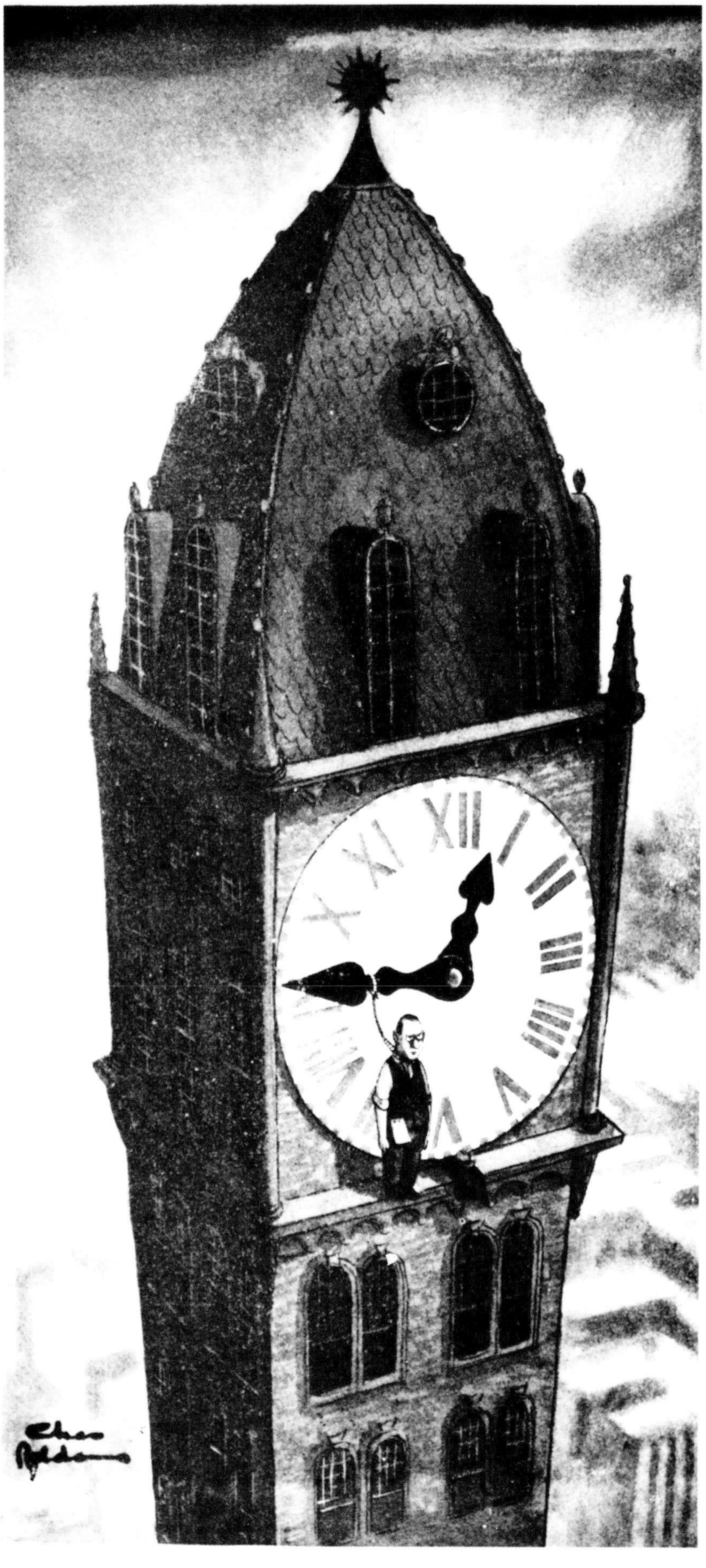
Chas Addams

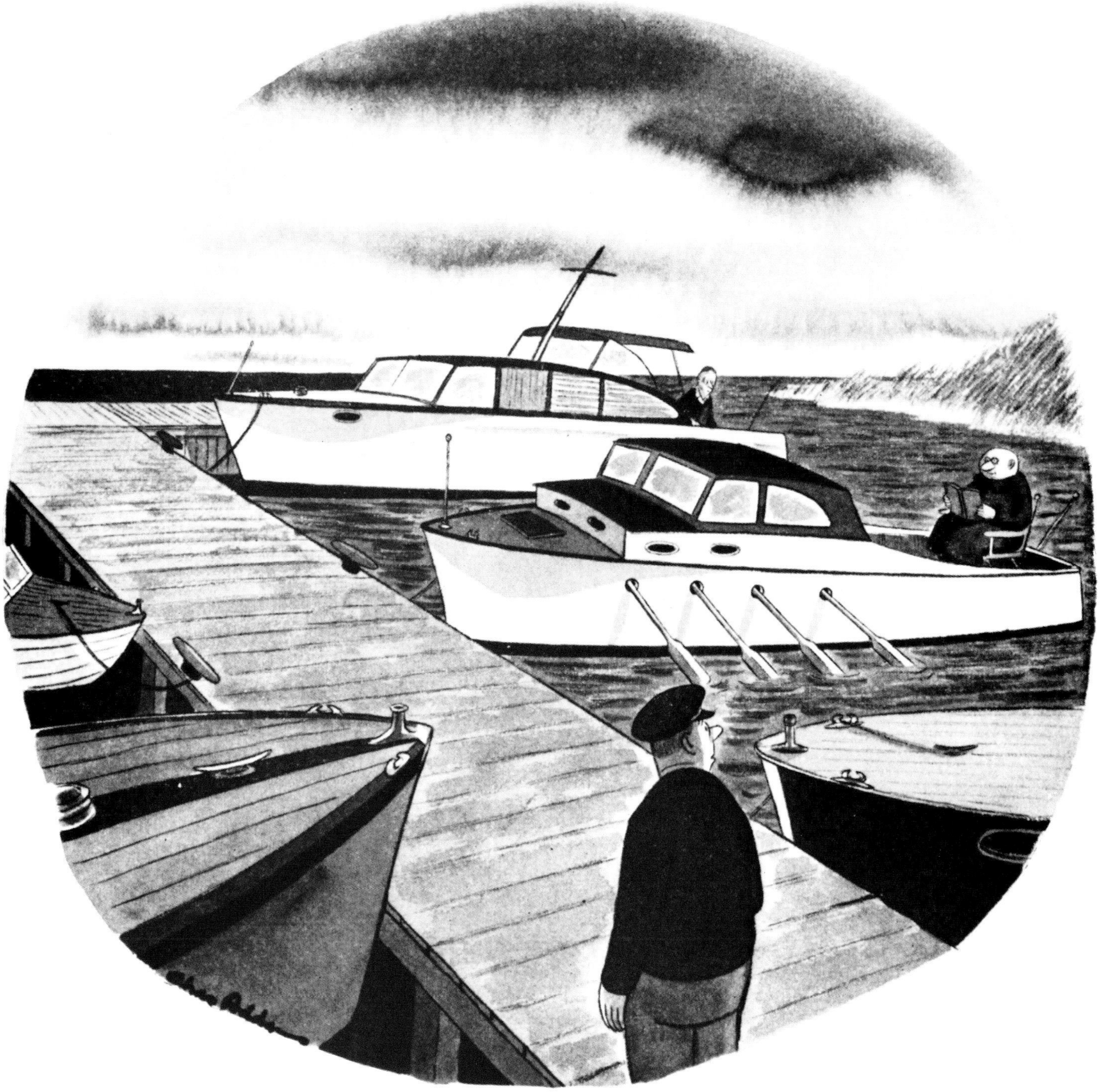

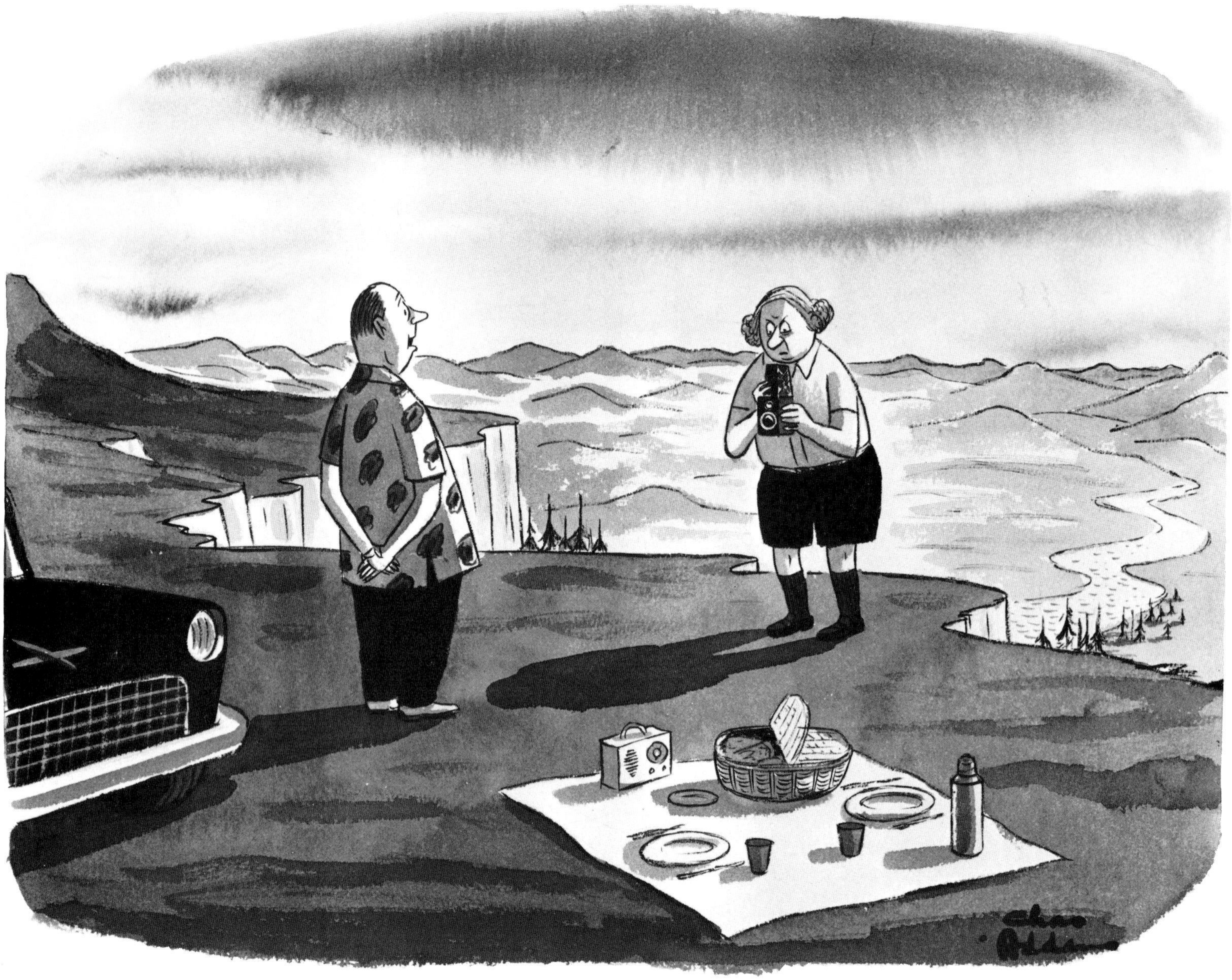

"Just back up a little, dear, so you won't cut my head off."

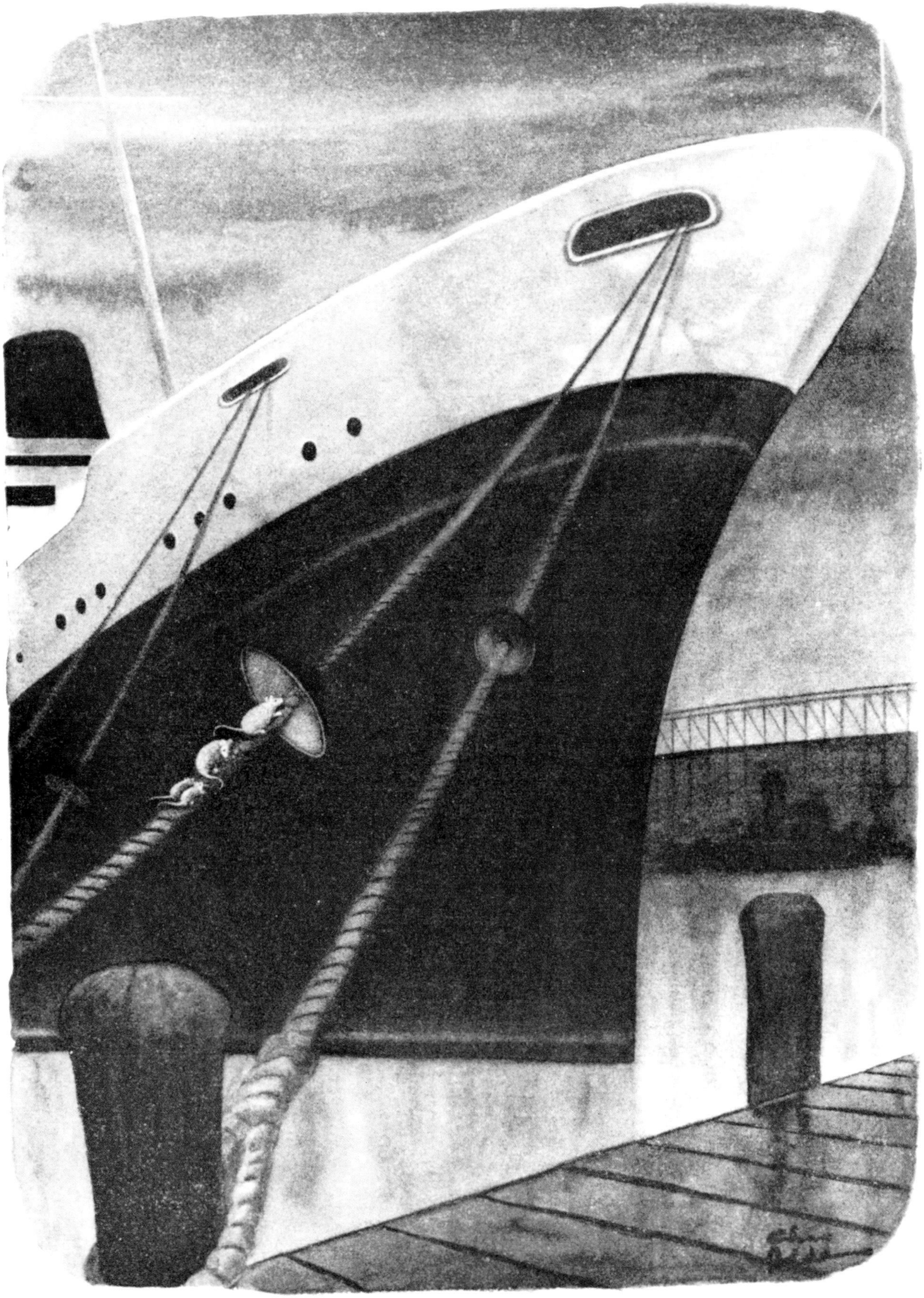

"For goodness' sake, stop that chattering and let your father think."

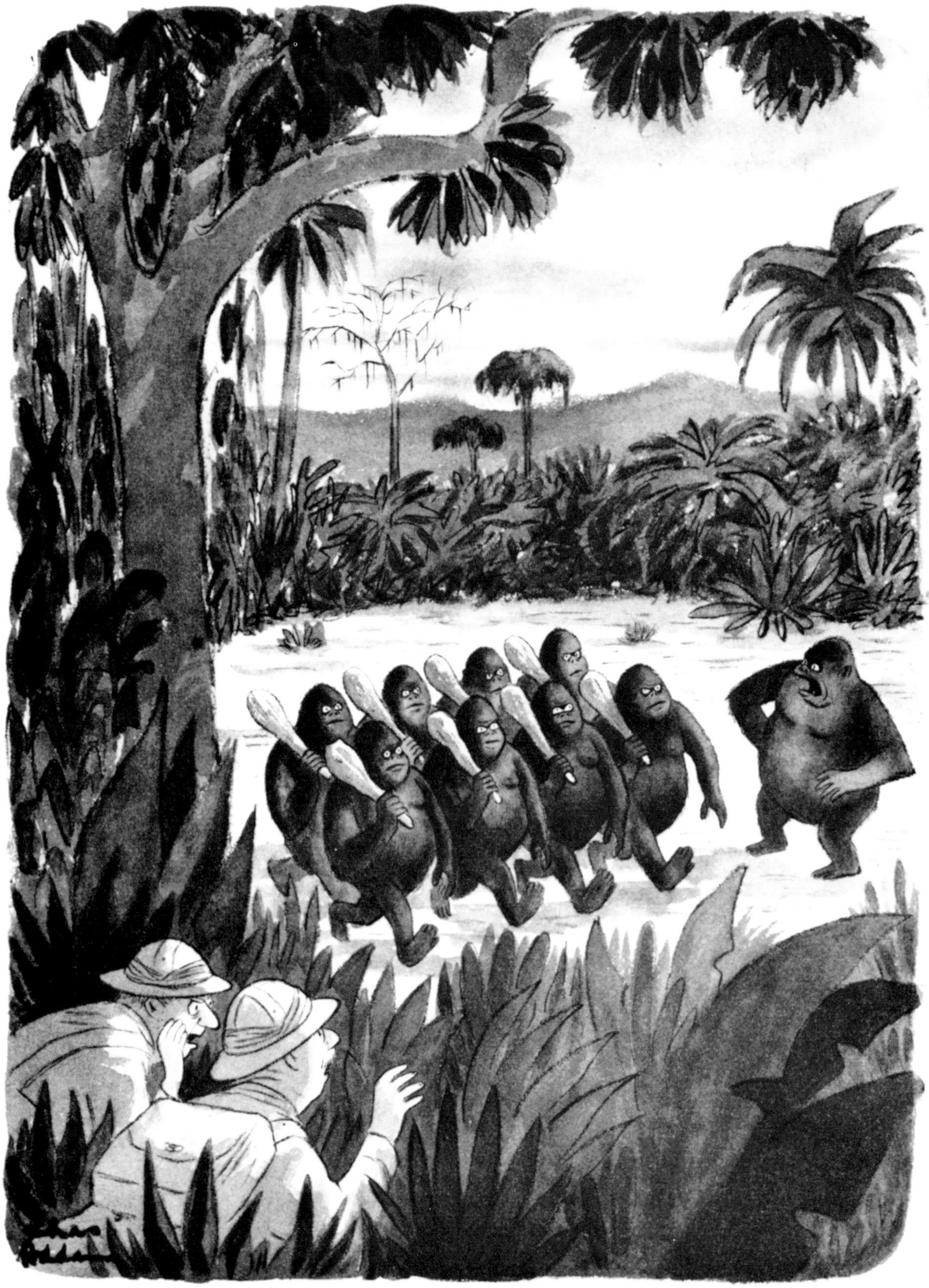

"Well, Kendrick, still think I'm just an alarmist?"

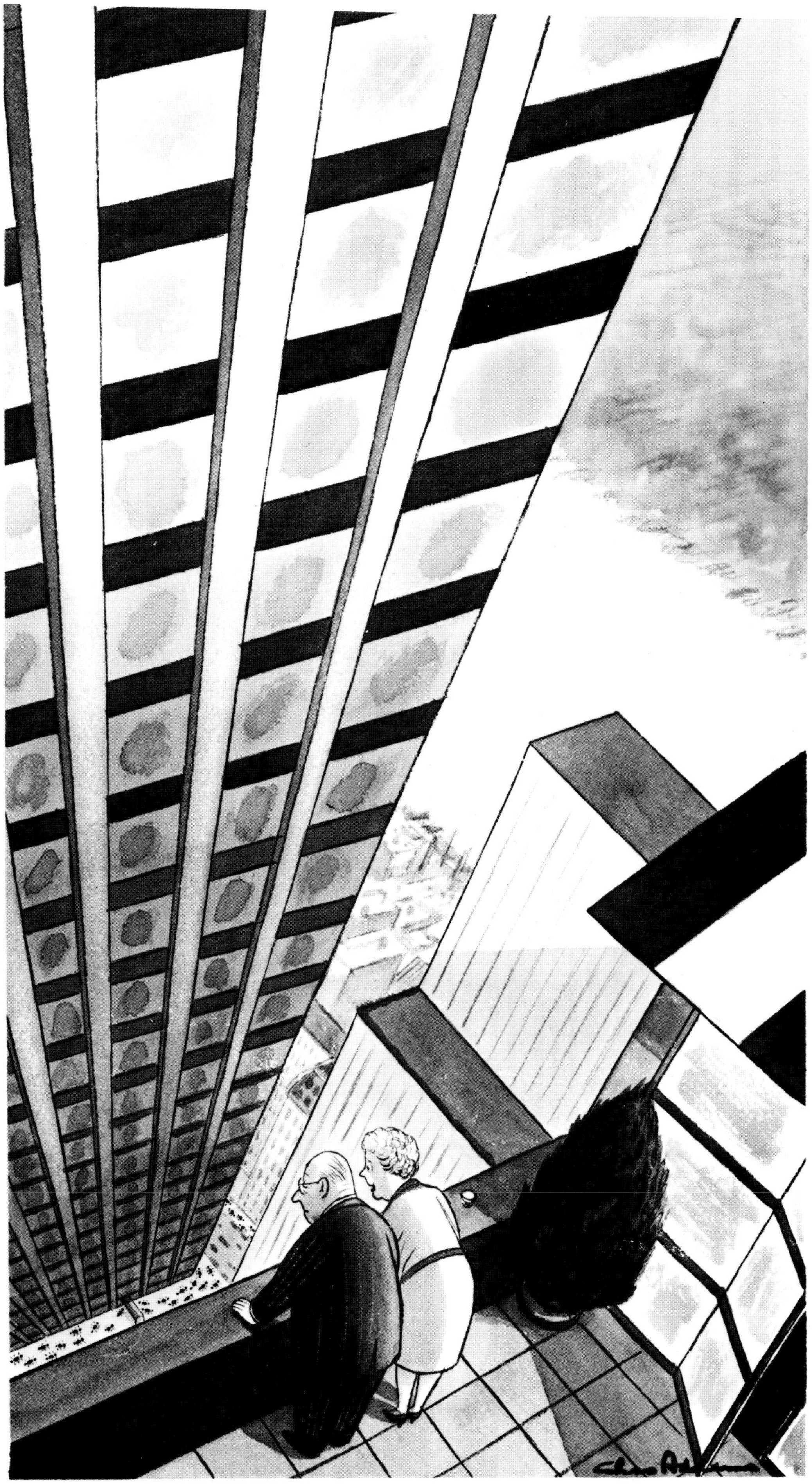

"You're right. That's exactly what they look like."

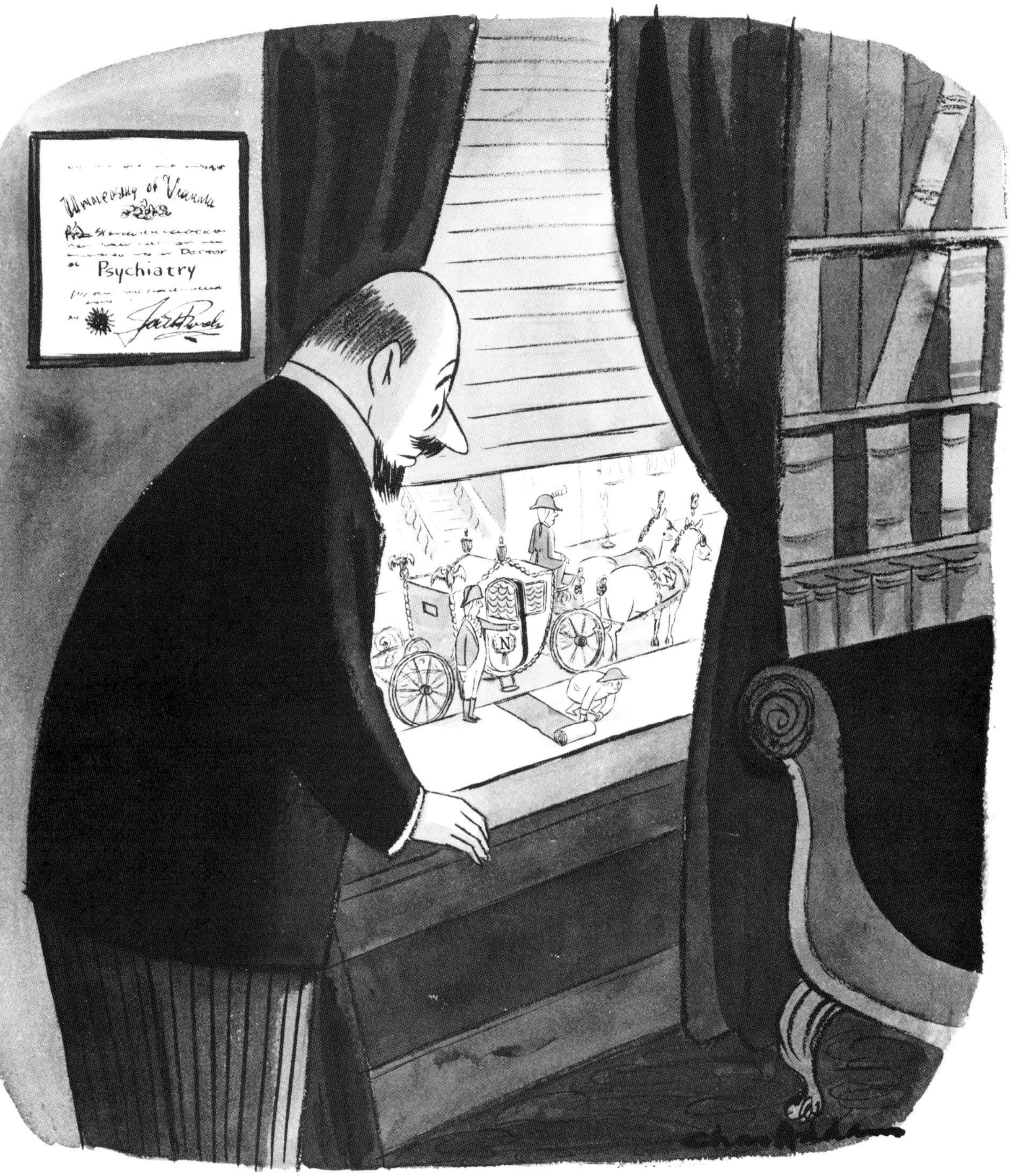
Psychiatry

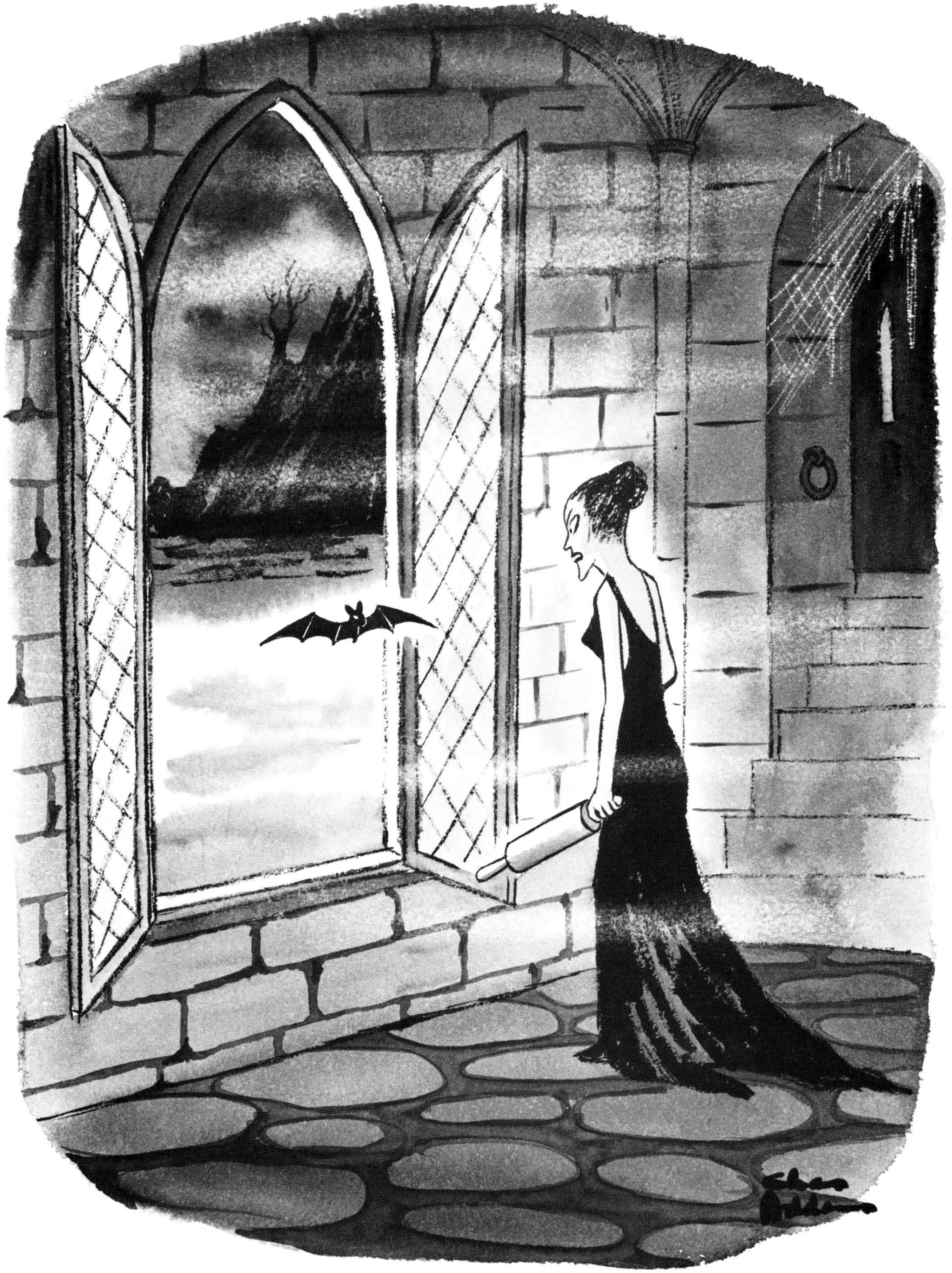

"Where have you been until this hour of the morning?"

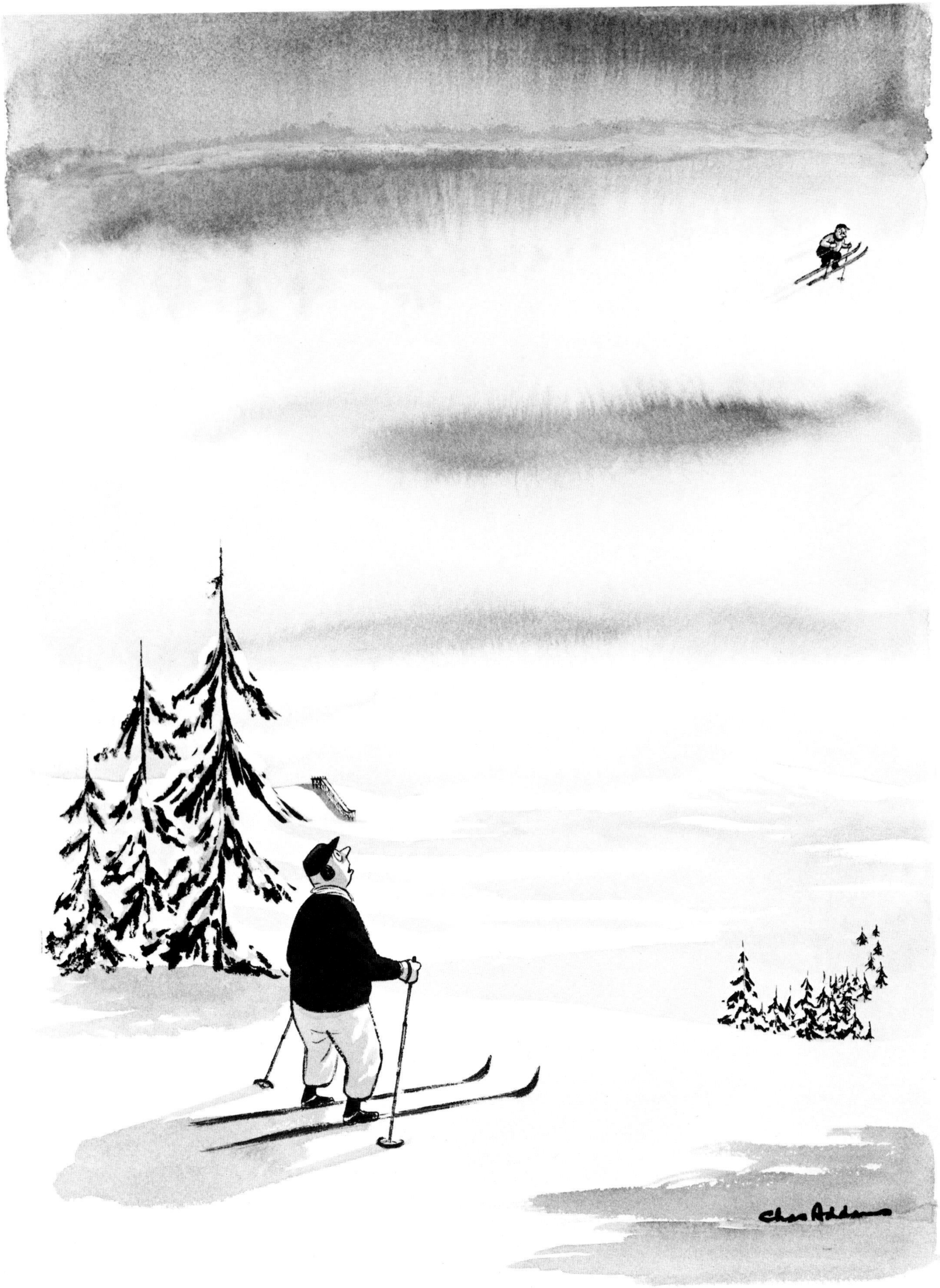
Chas Addams

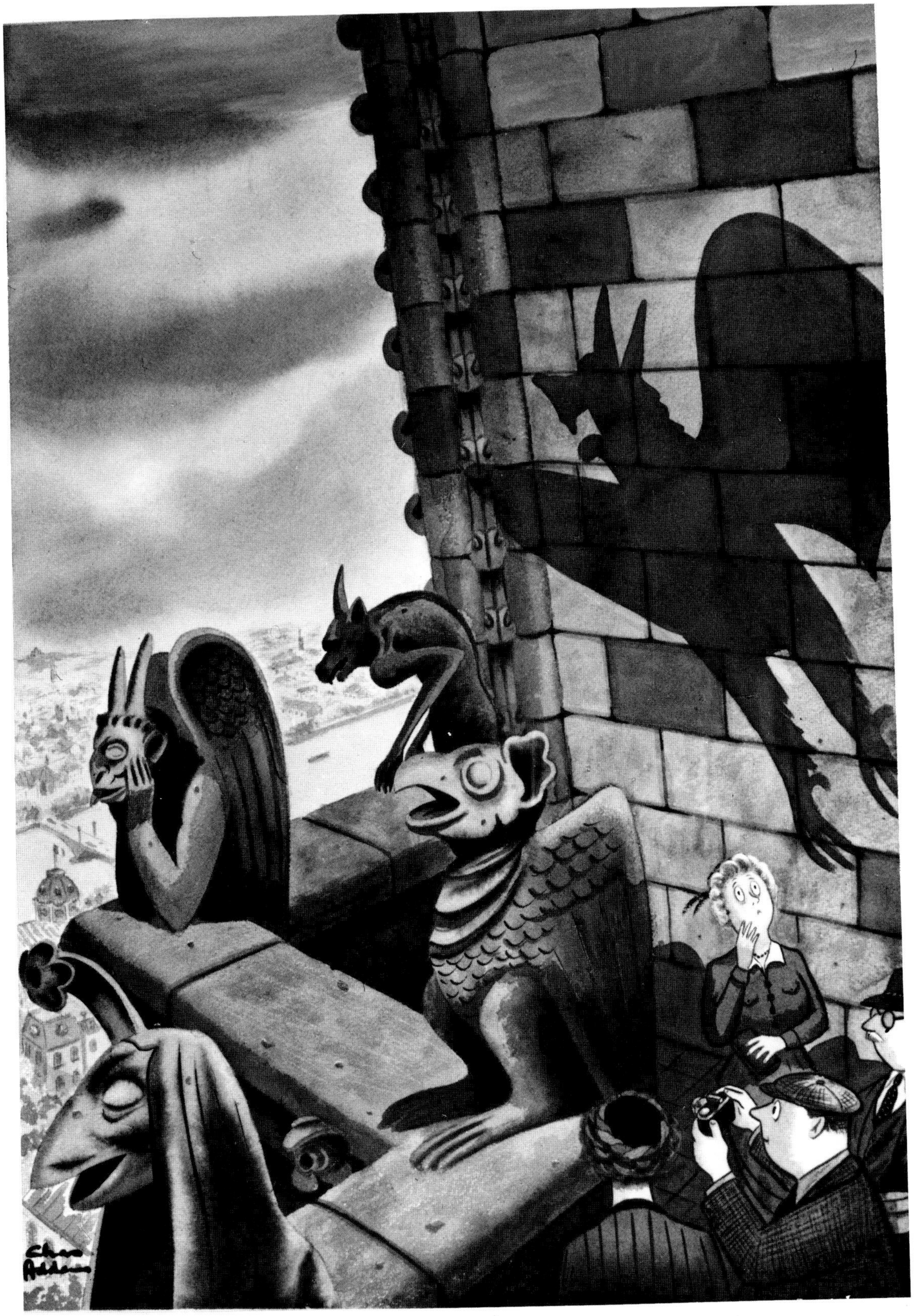
Chas Addams

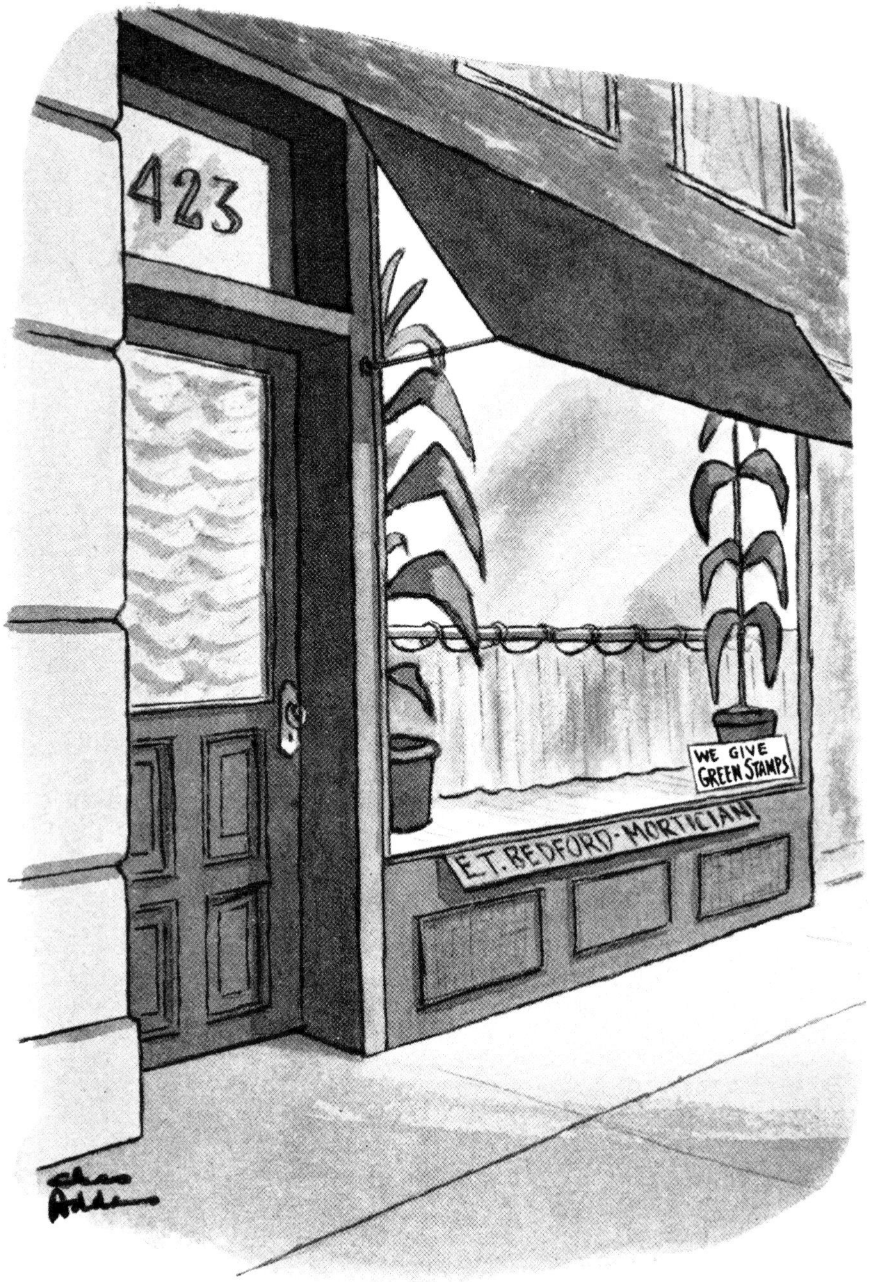
423
WE GIVE
GREEN STAMPS
E.T. BEDFORD - MORTICIAN

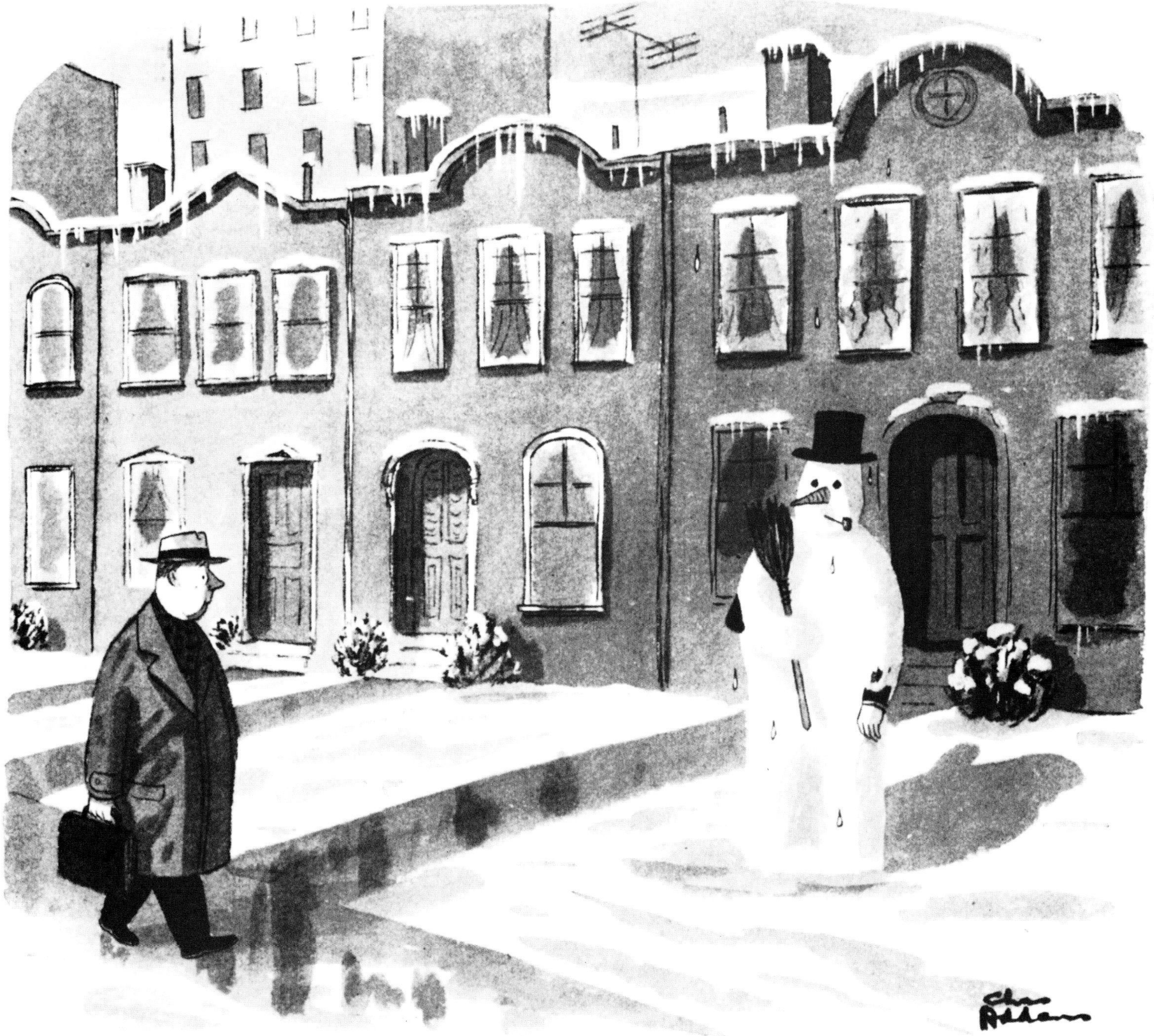

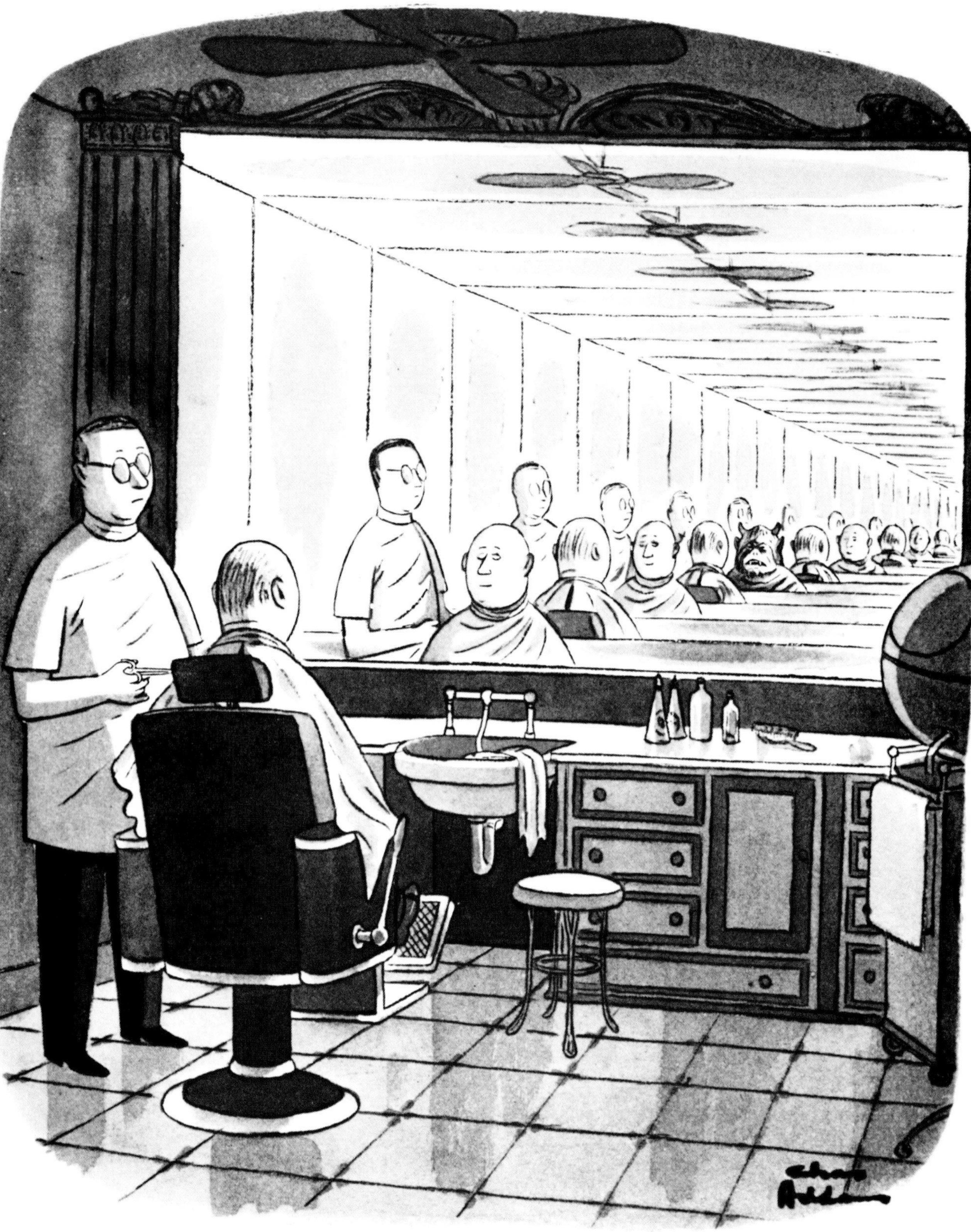
Chas Addams

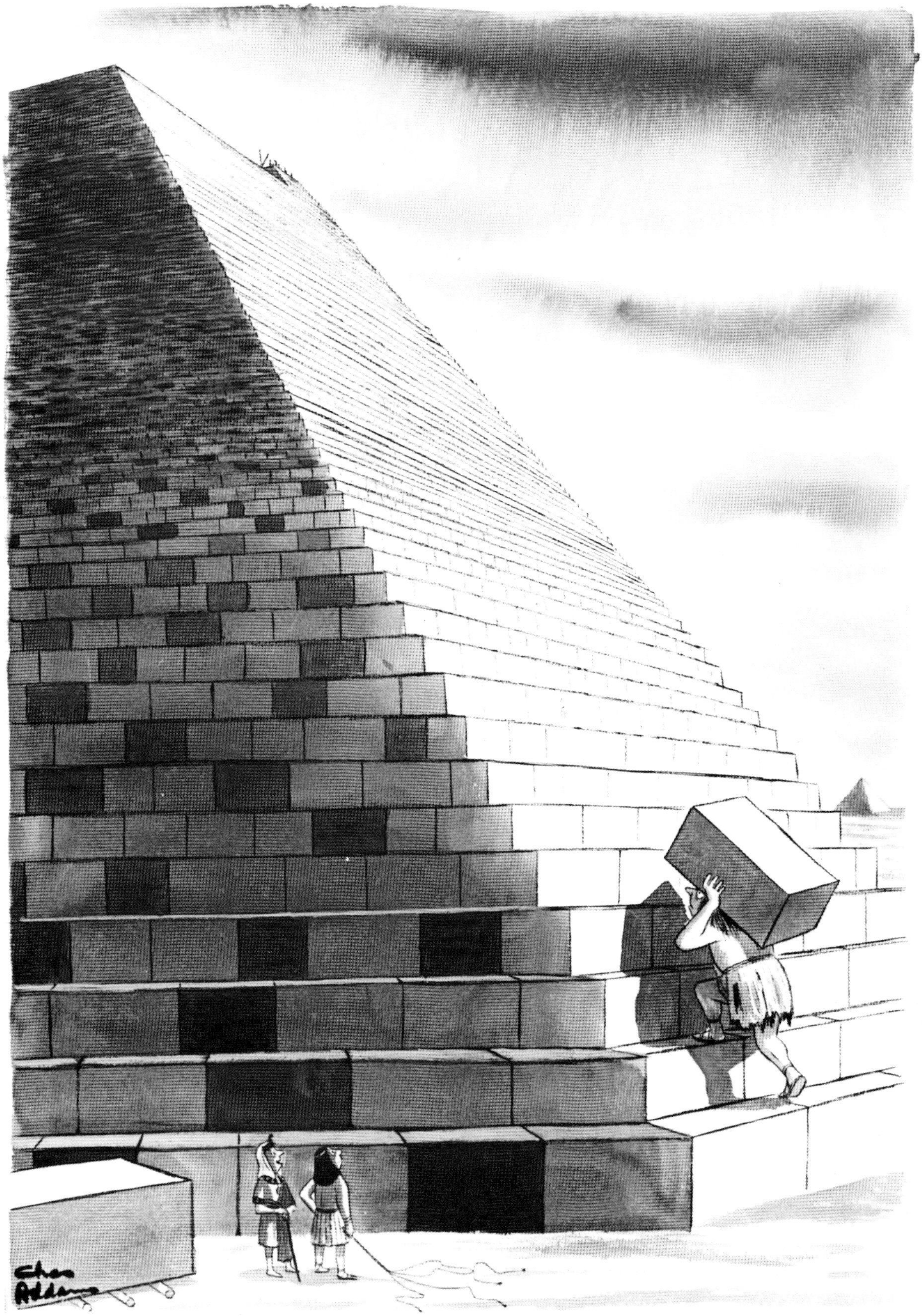
Chas Addams

"We could never have done it without him."

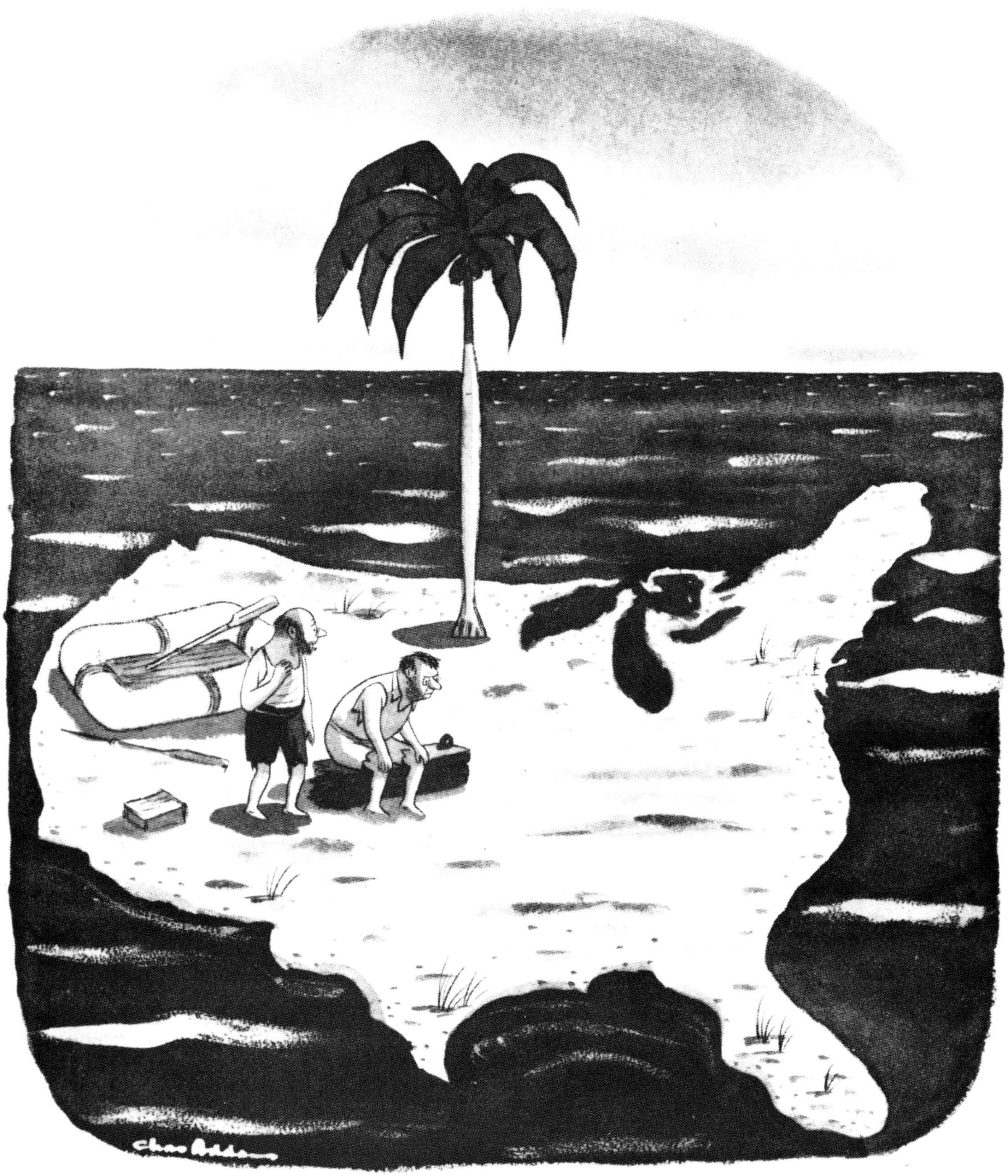
Chas Addams

"By George, you're right! I thought there was something familiar about it."

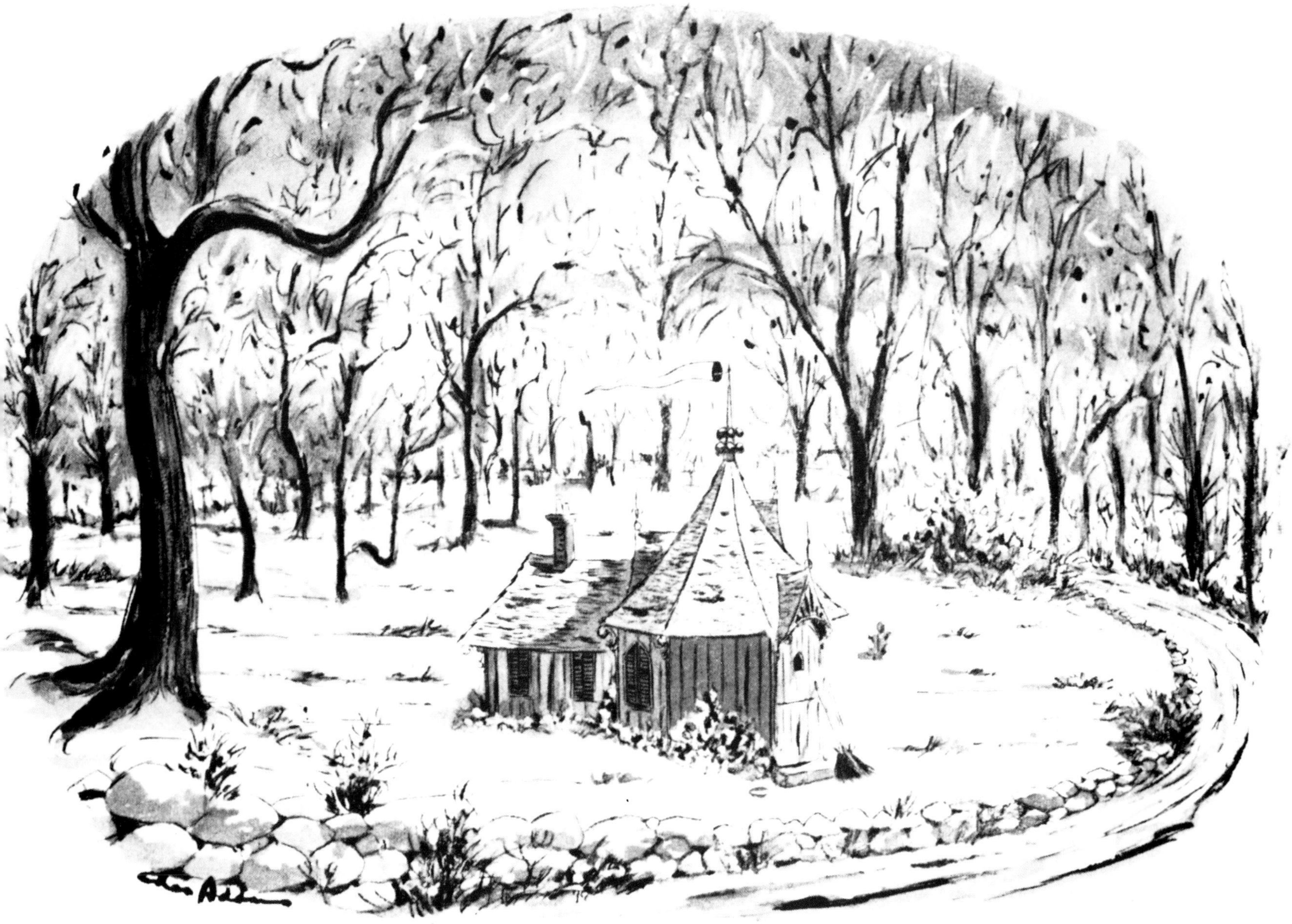

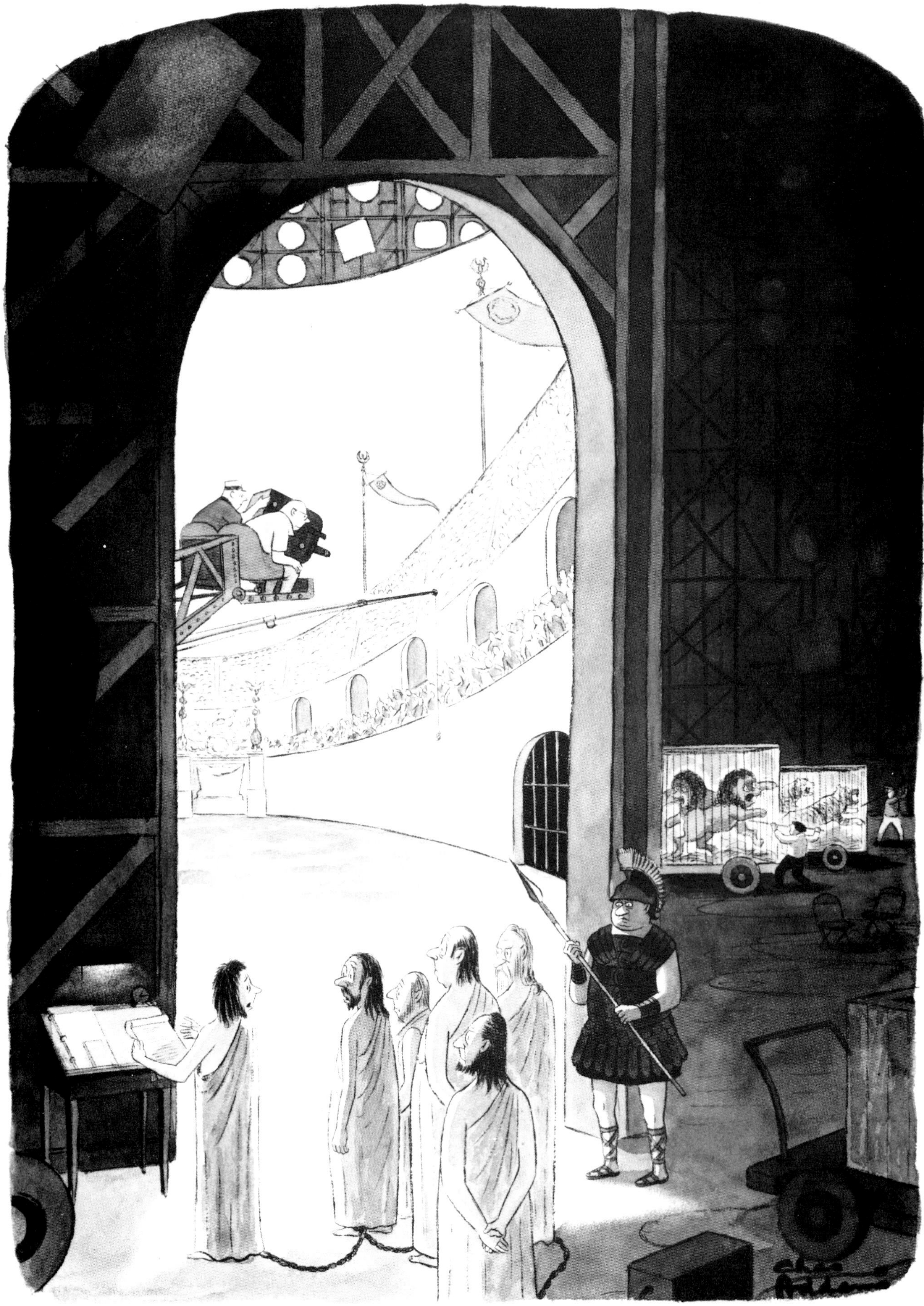

"Holy smoke! Have you guys seen this script?"

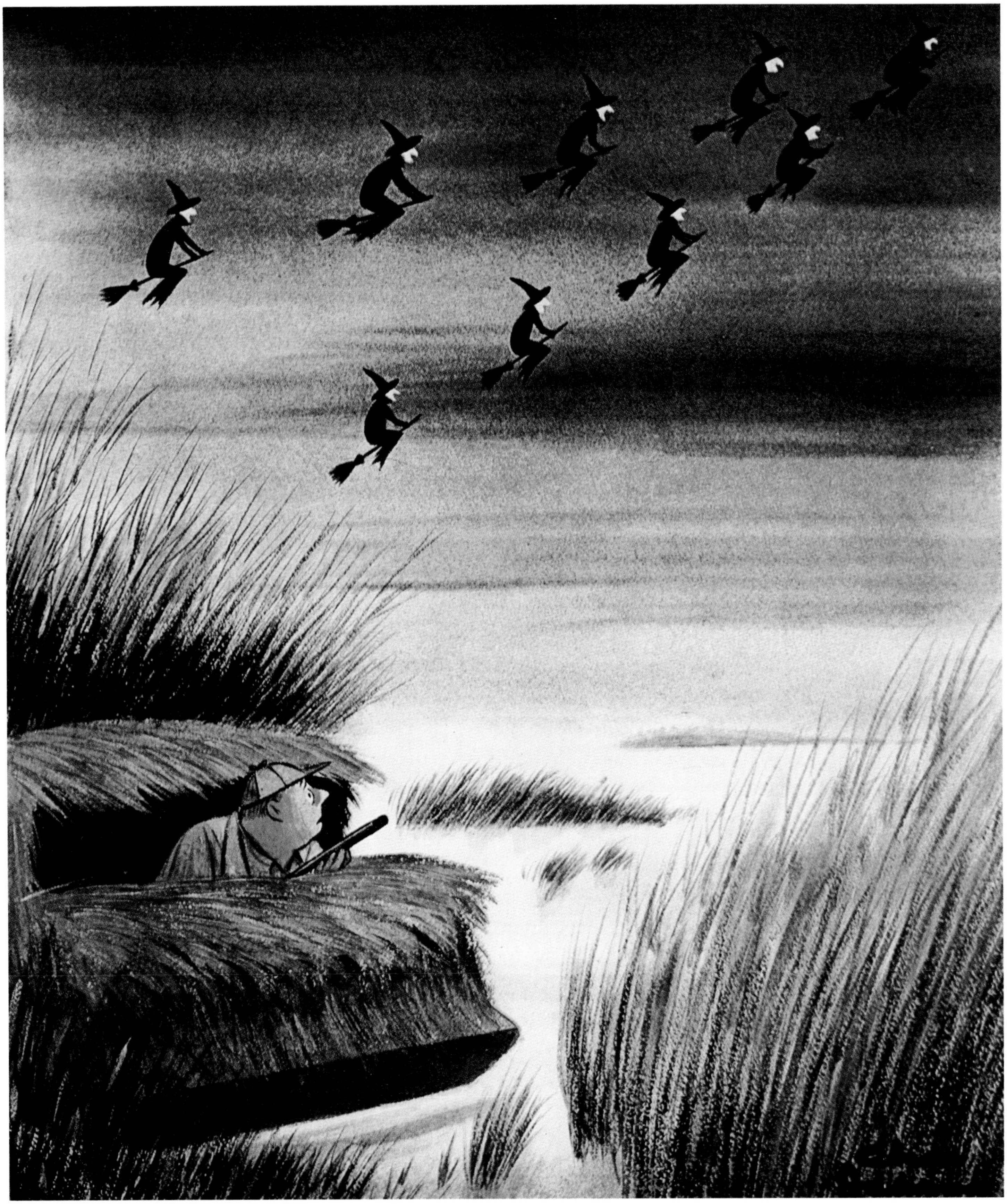

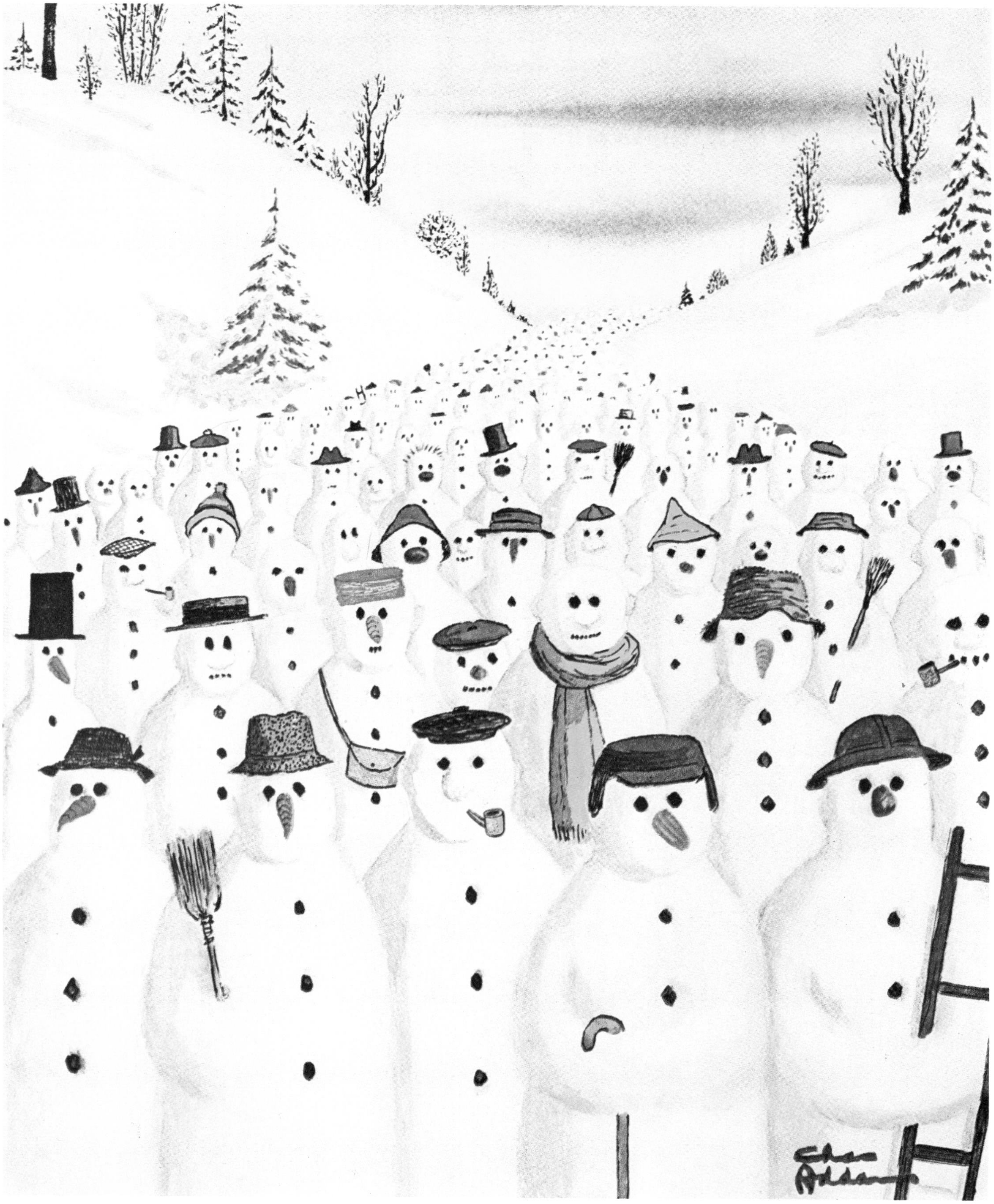
Chas Addams

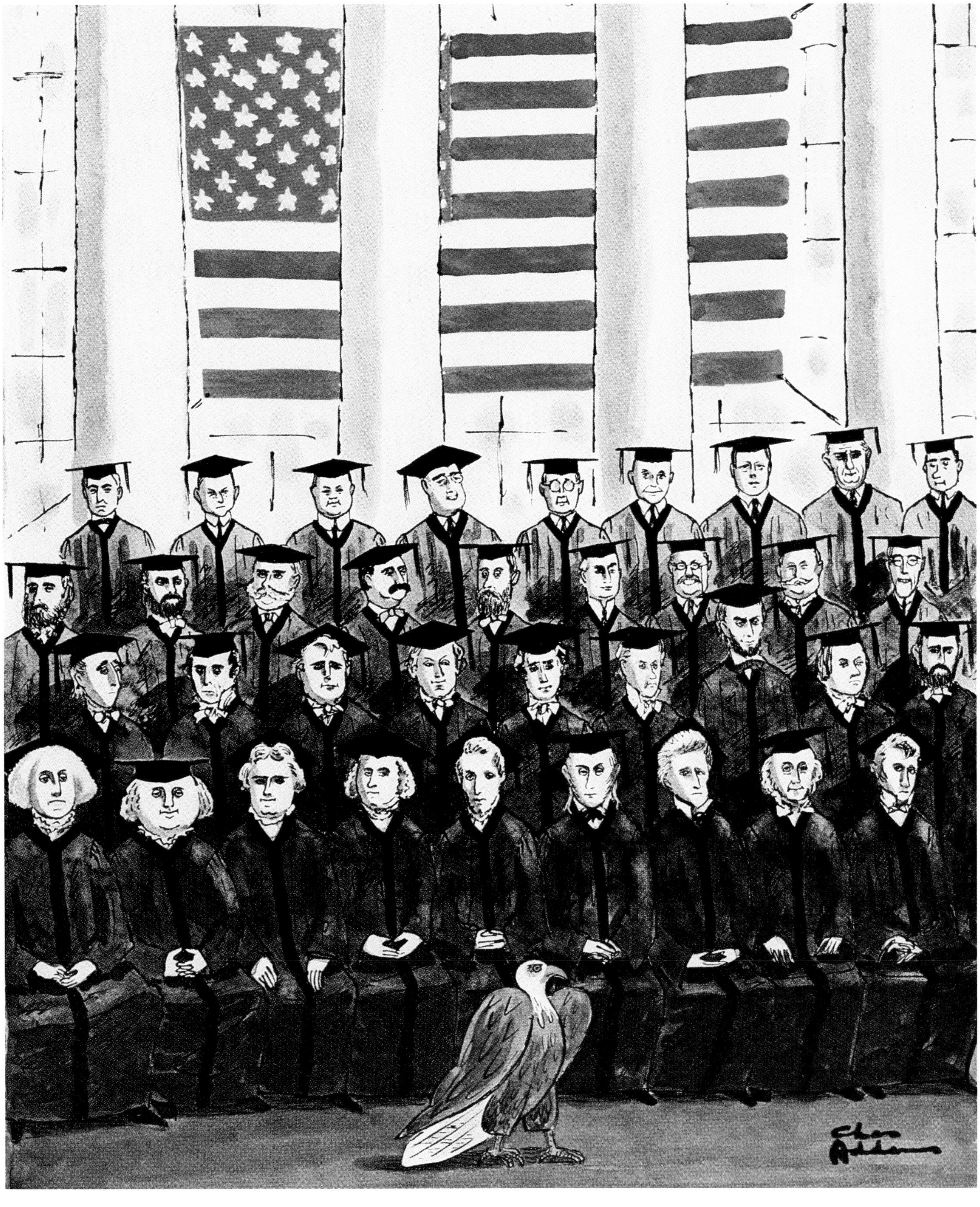
Chas Addams

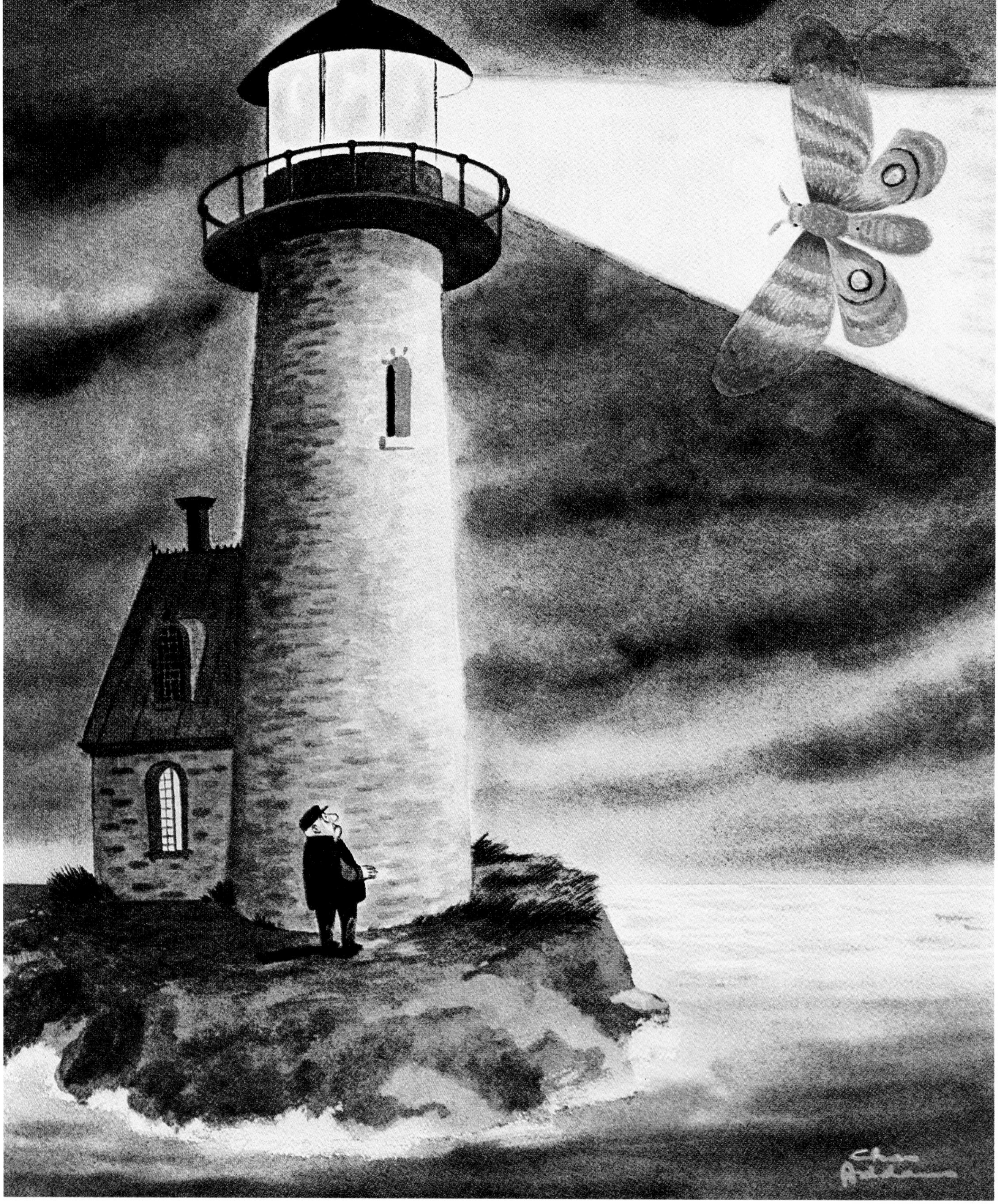

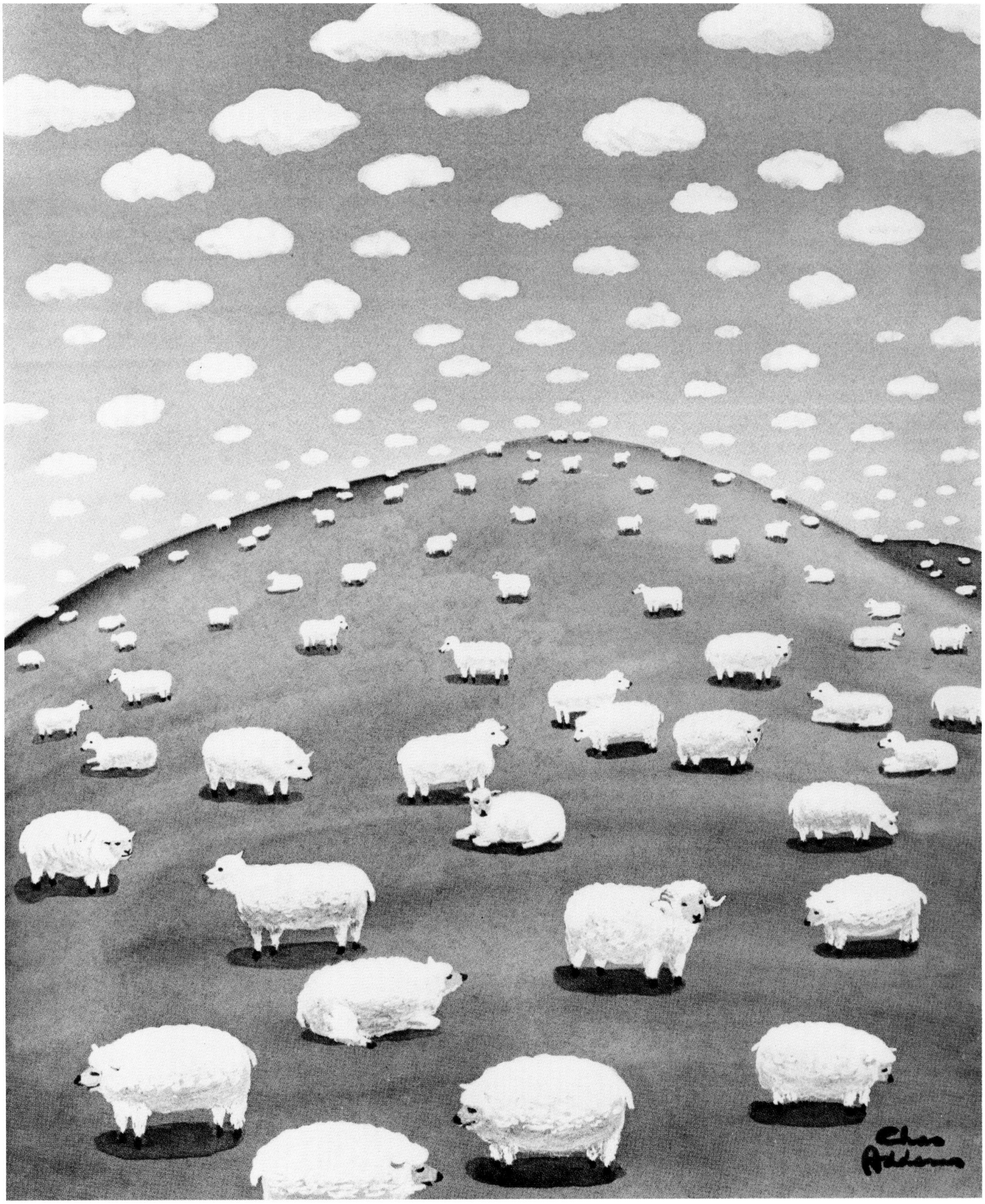
Chas Addams

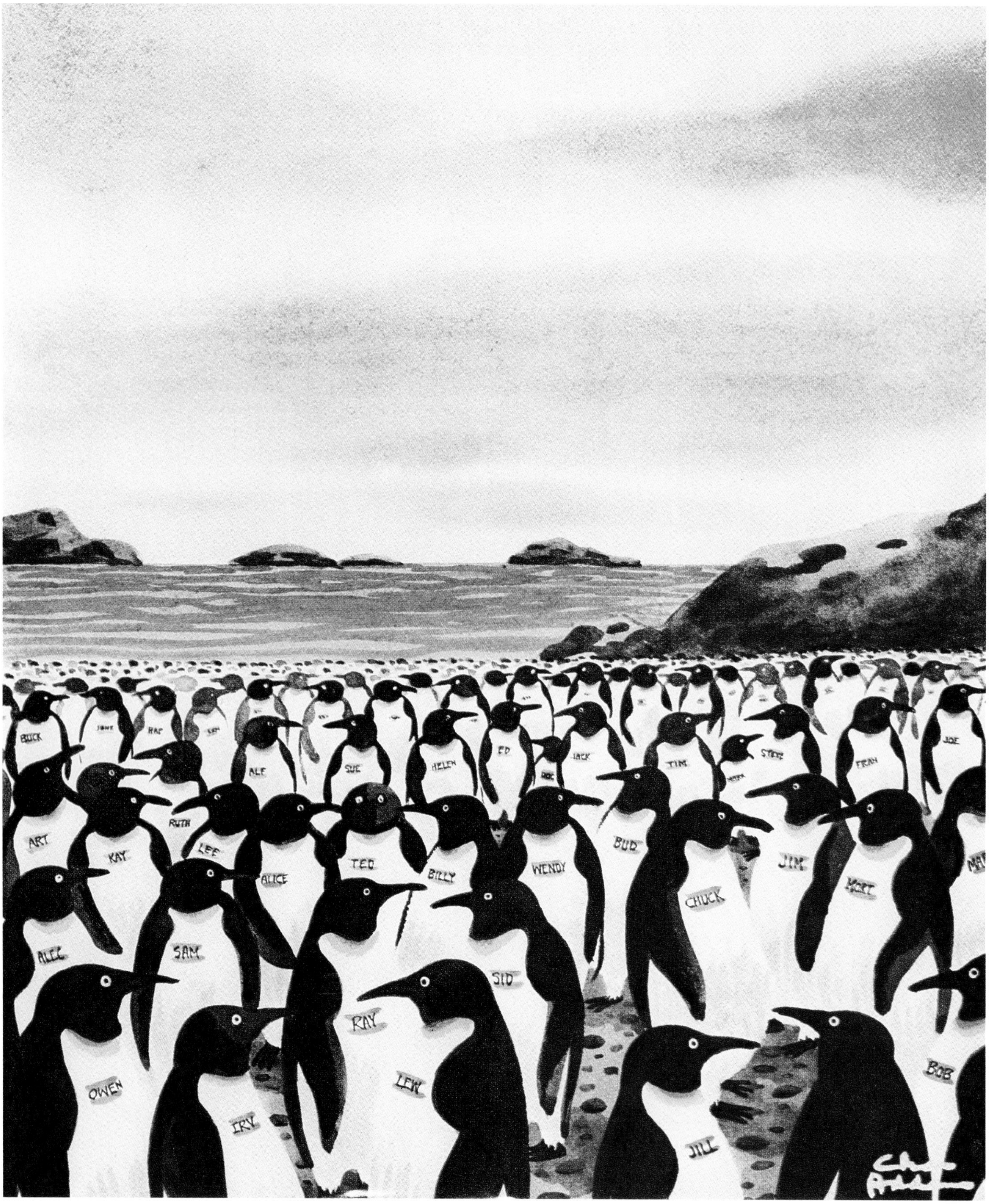
BUCK
ALF
SUE
HELEN
ED
JACK
TIM
STEVE
FRAN
JOE
ART
RUTH
KAY
LEE
ALICE
TED
BILLY
WENDY
BUD
JIM
MORT
CHUCK
ALEC
SAM
SID
RAY
OWEN
LEW
IRV
JILL
BOB

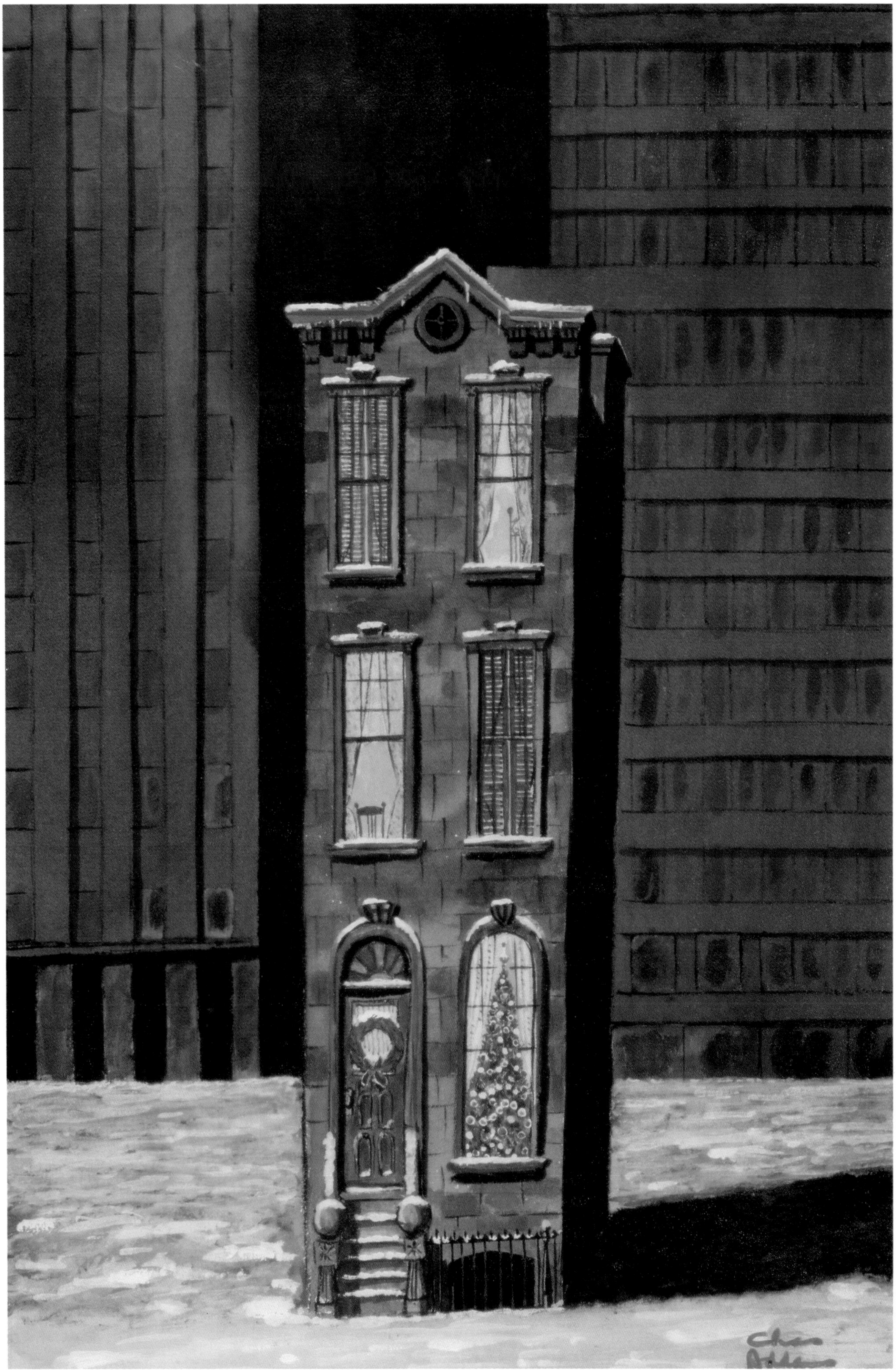
Chas Addams

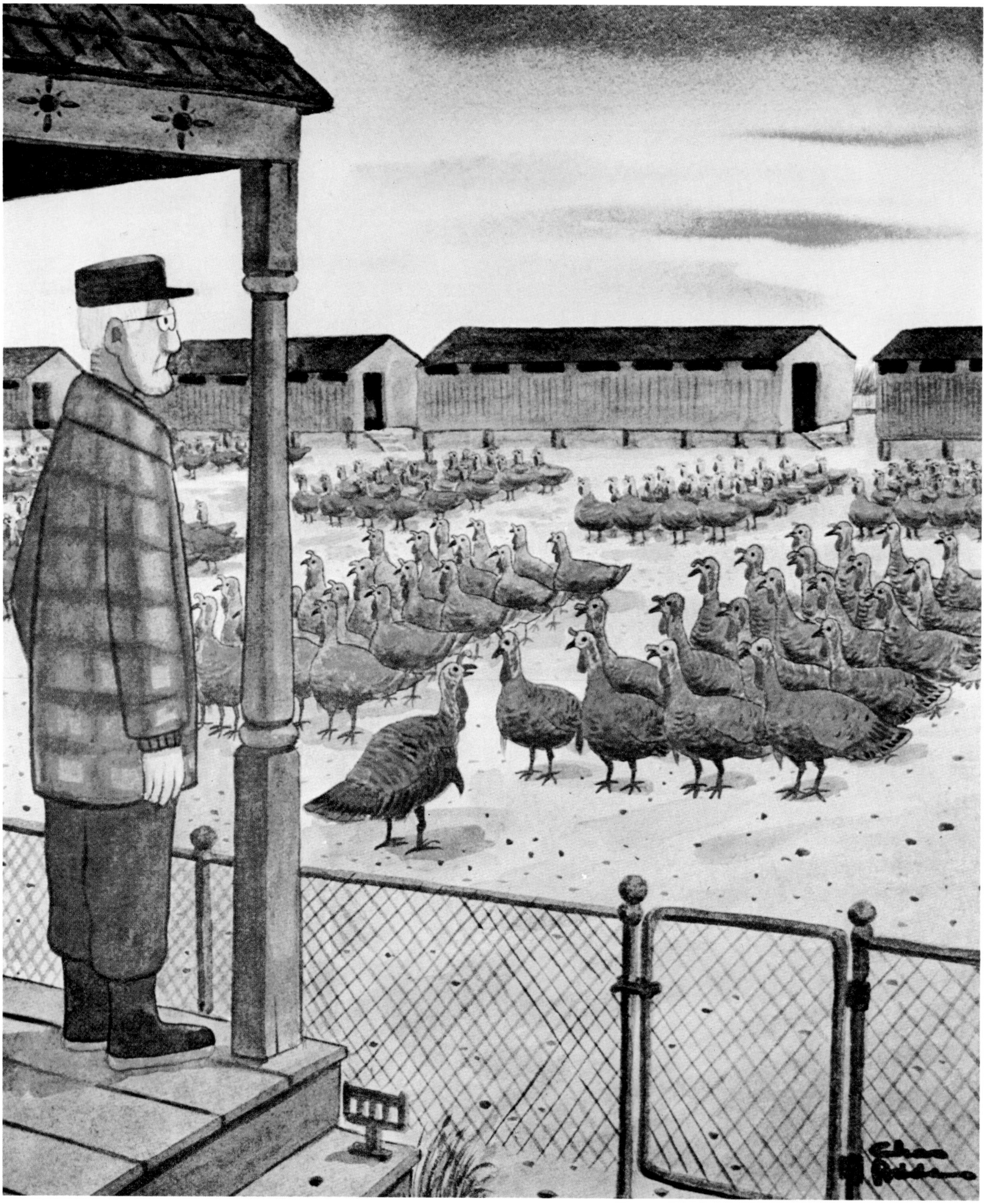

"You're right. It is still wet."

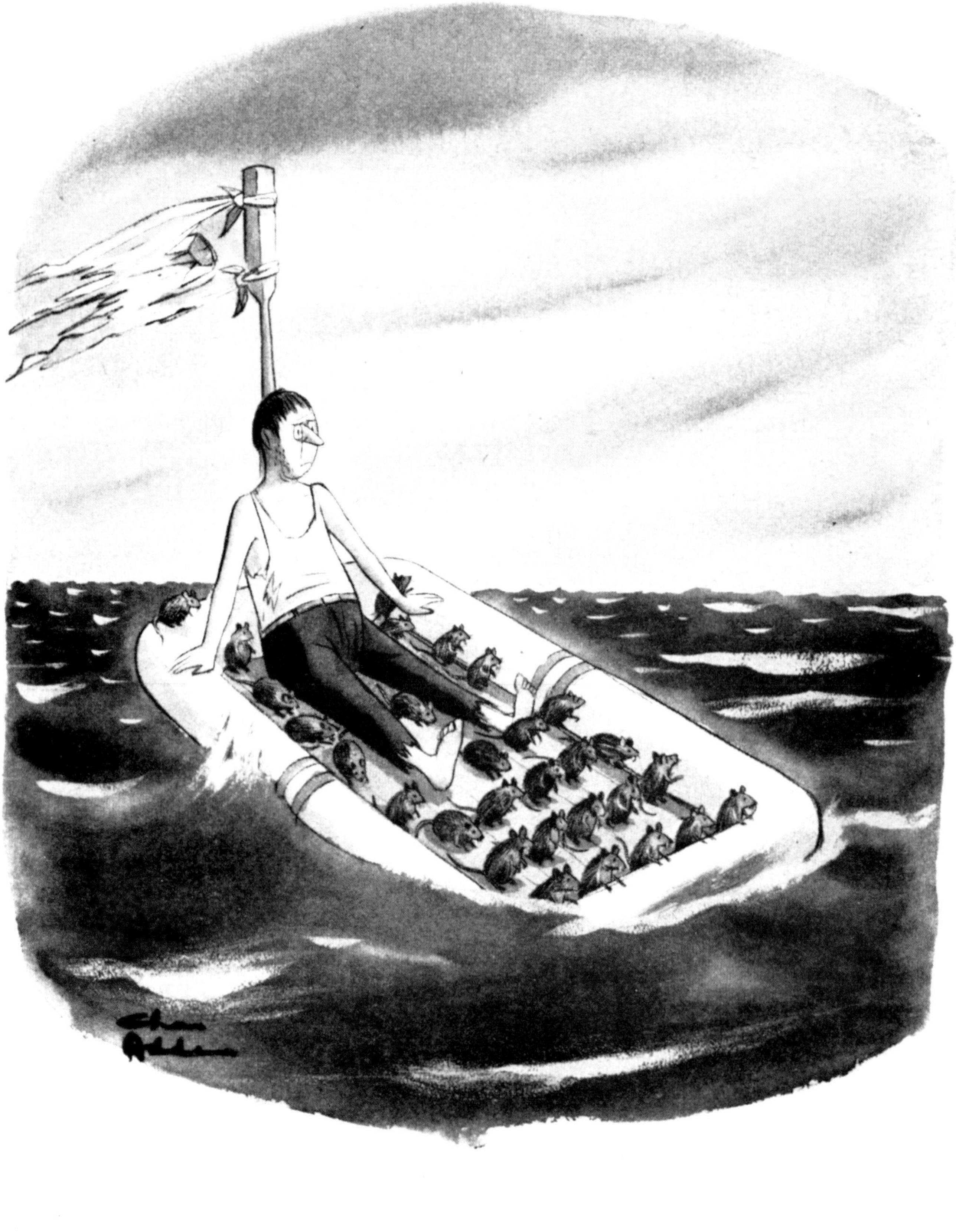

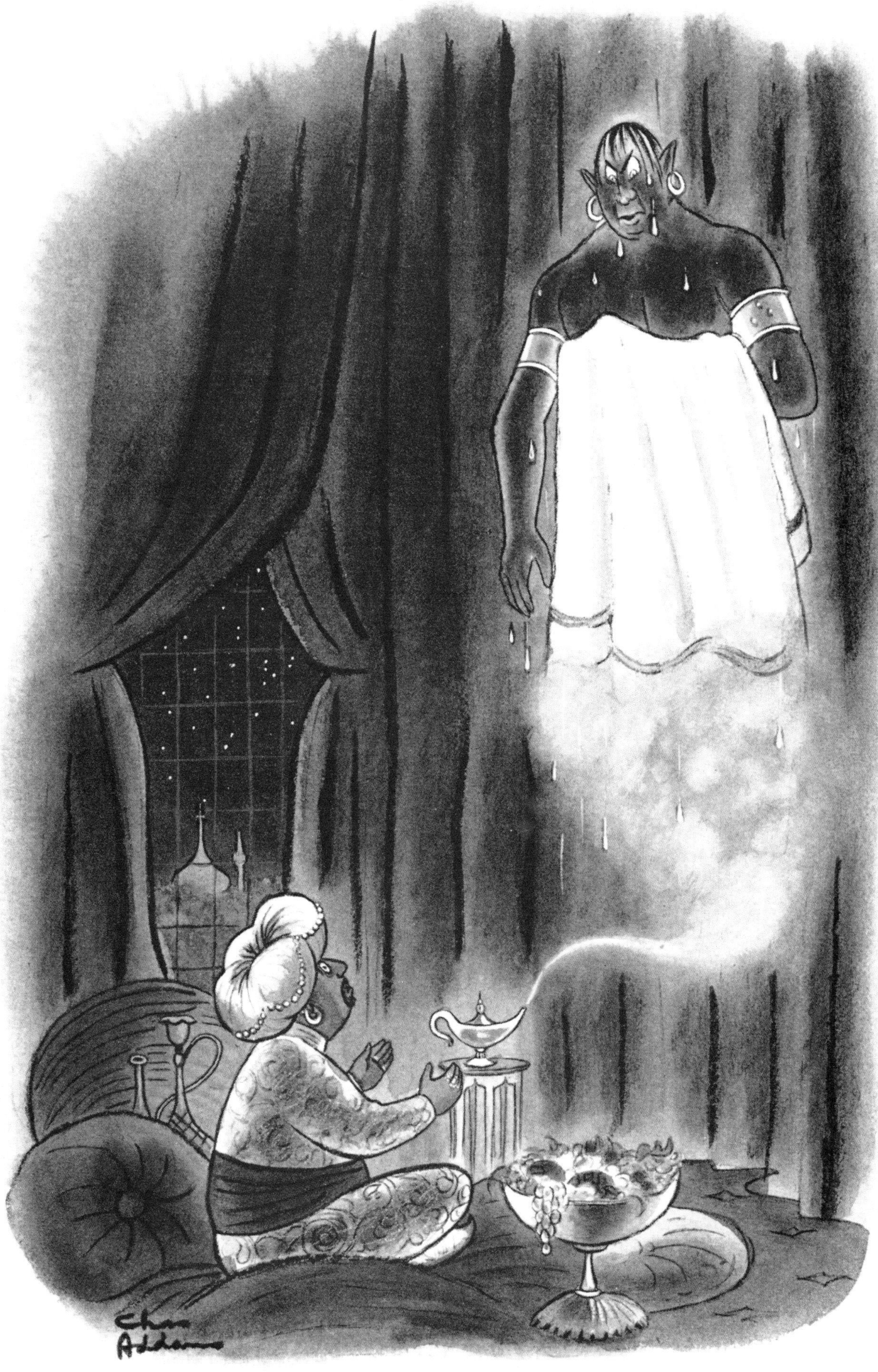
Chas Addams

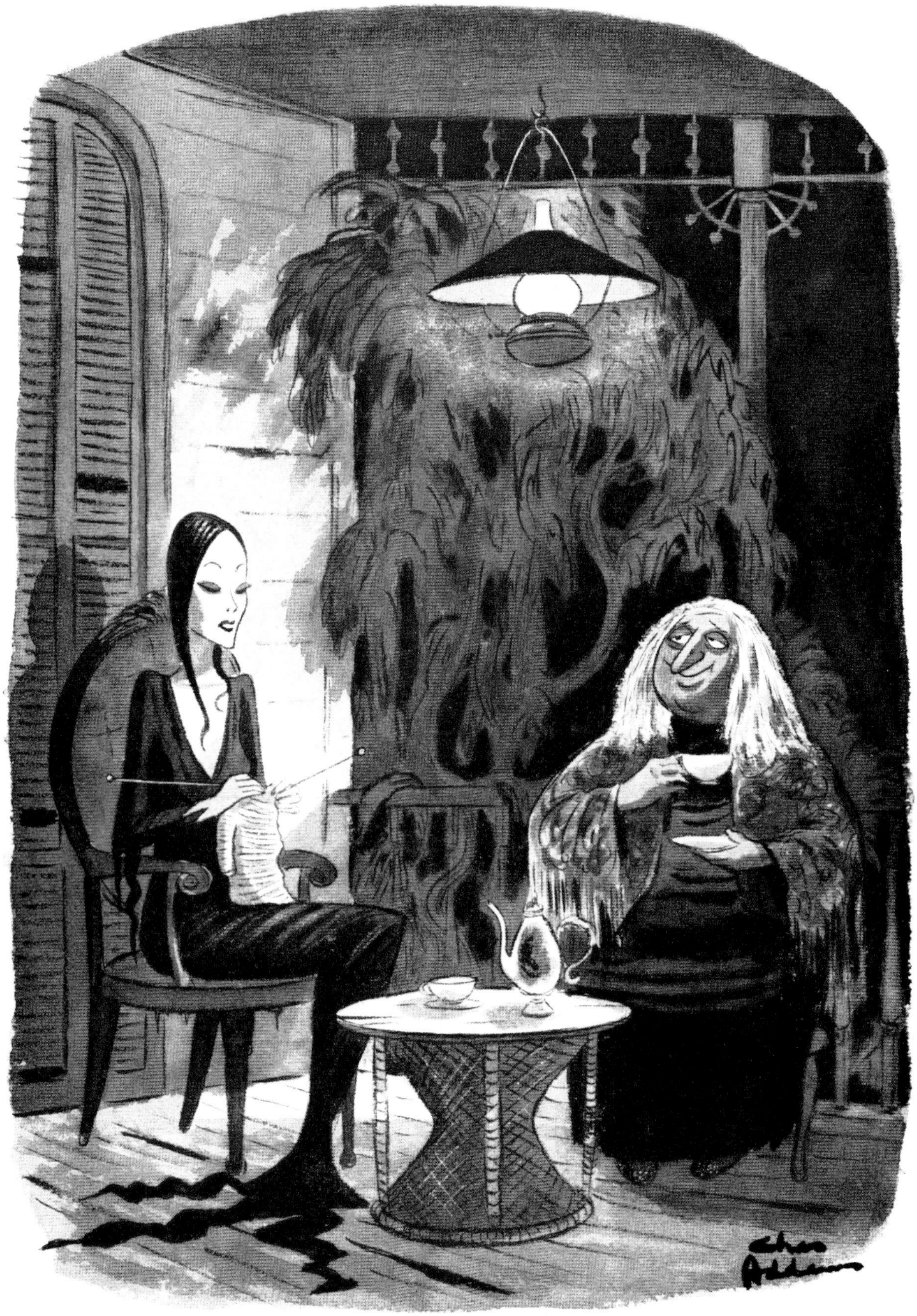

". . . and if it's a boy, we're going to give him a Biblical name, like Cain or Ananias."

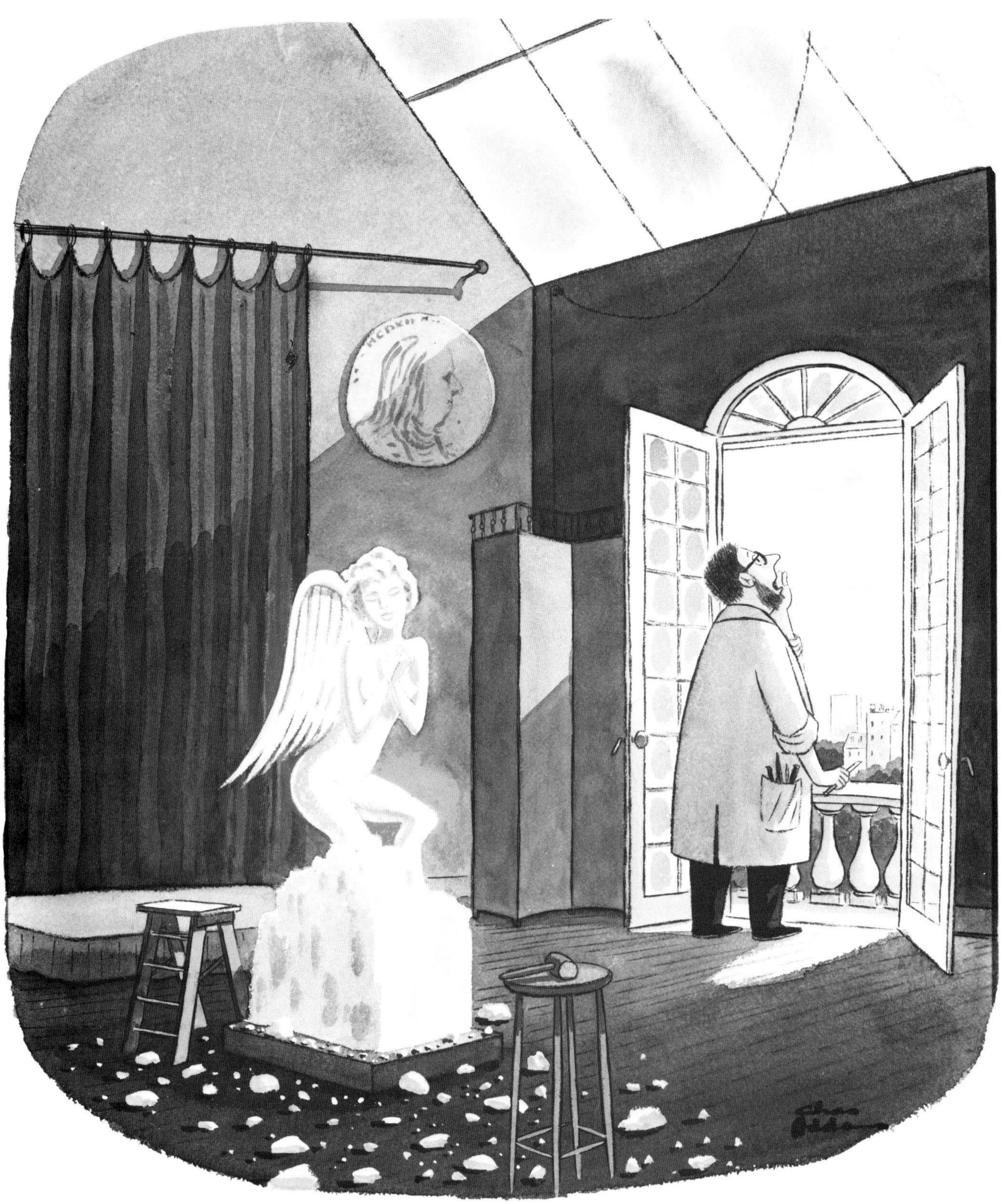

"Same time next Monday, then, Miss Grant?"

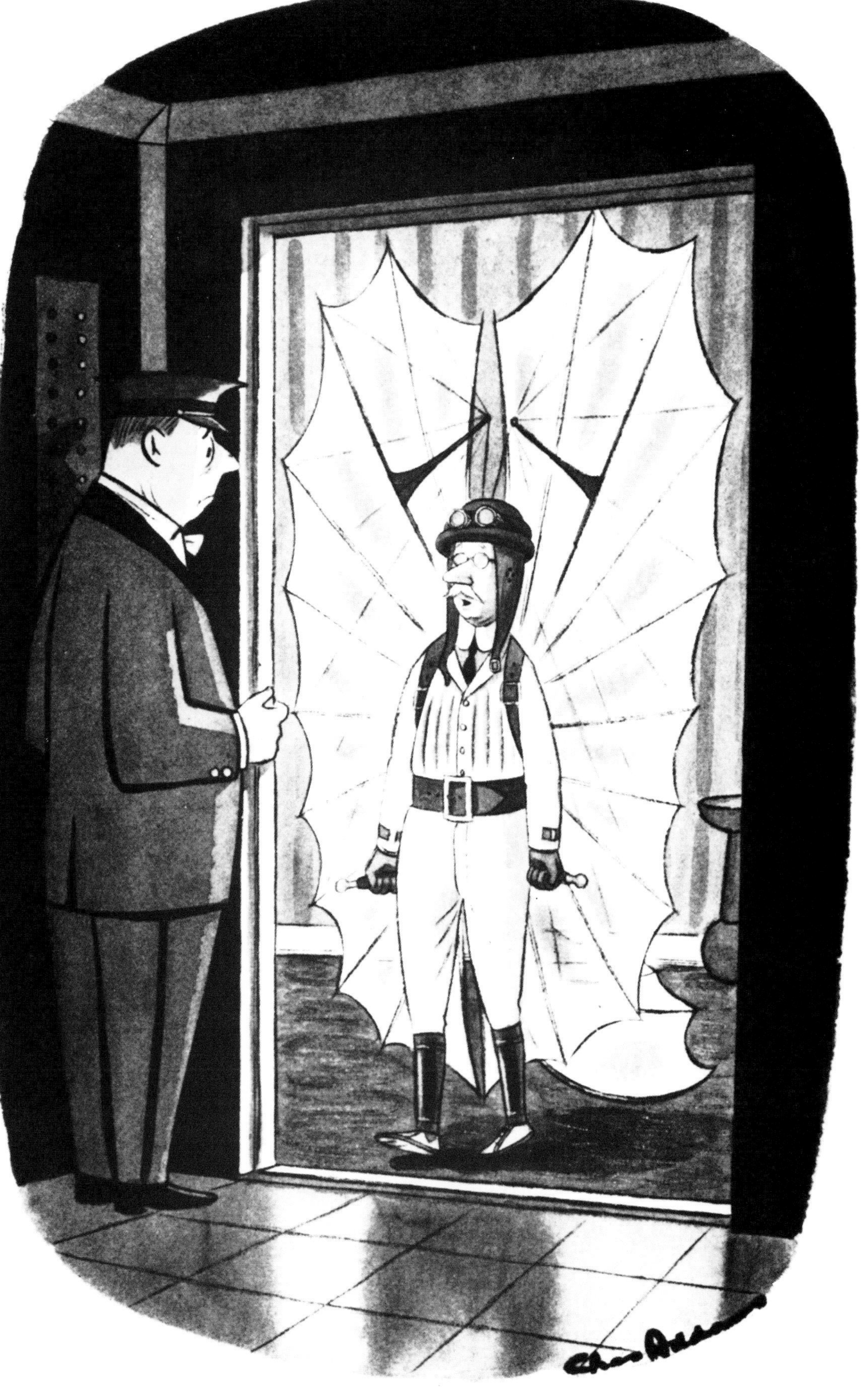

"The roof, please."

"You'll never get me up in one of those things."

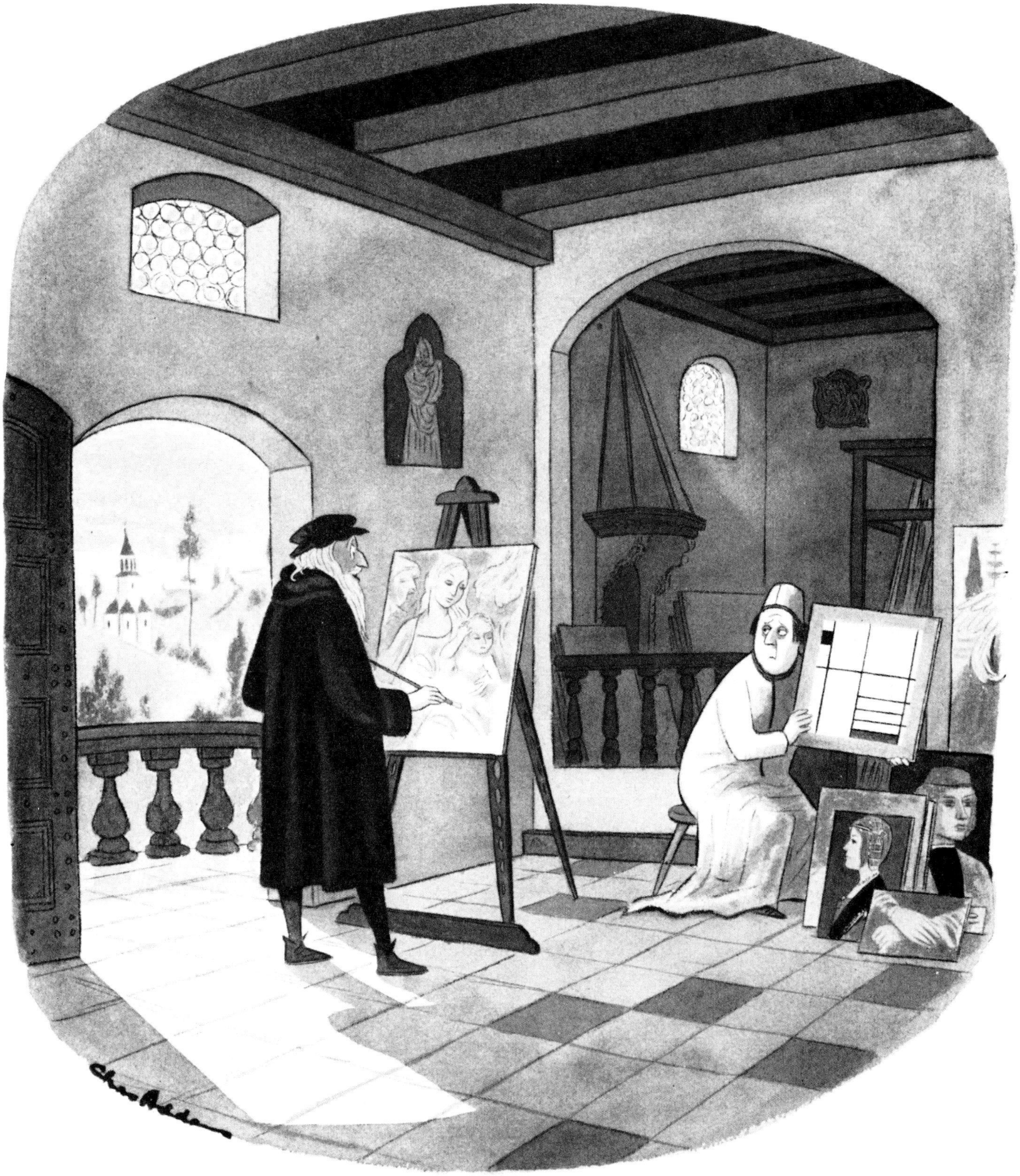

"That? Oh, that's nothing. Just something I was fooling around with."

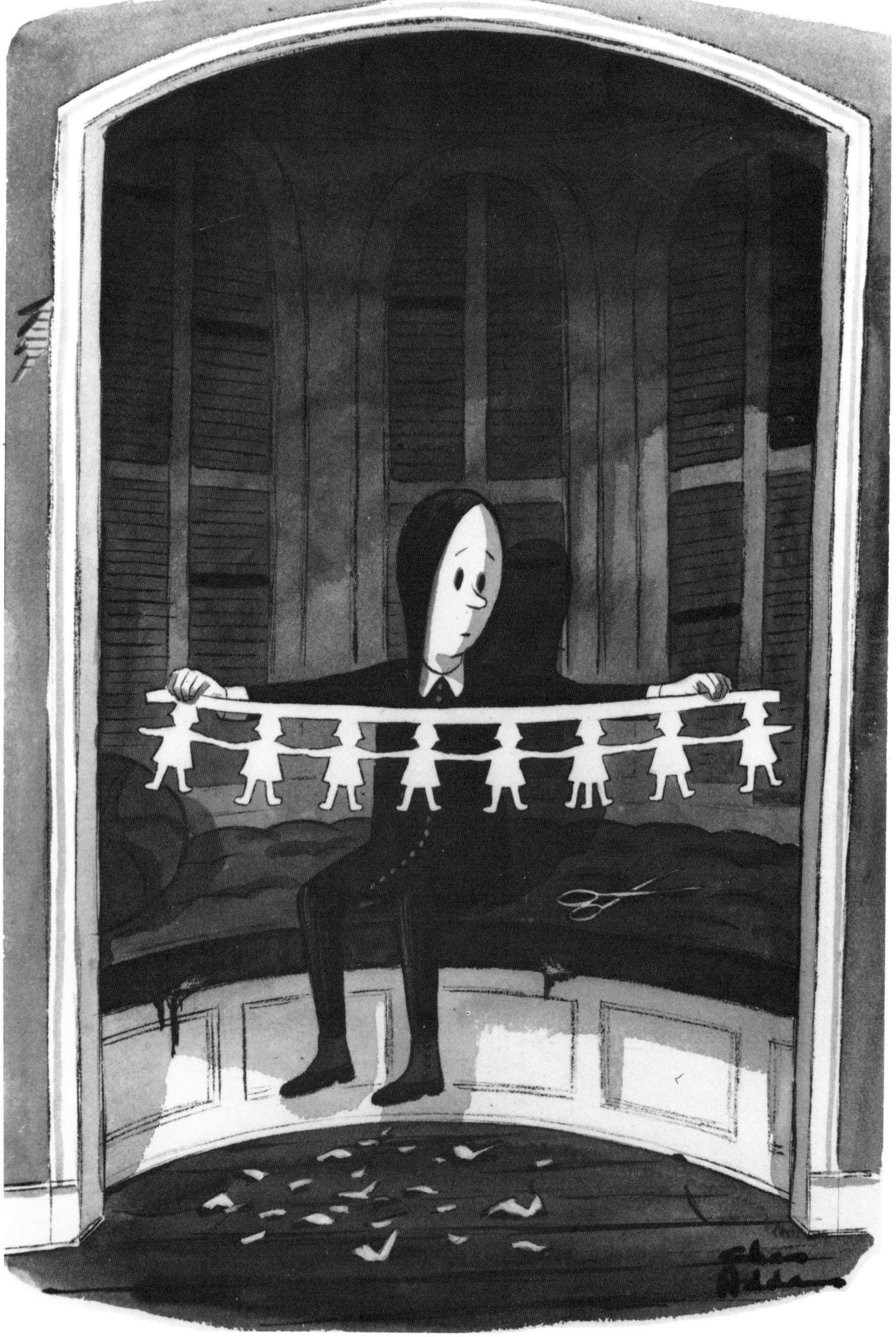
Chas Addams

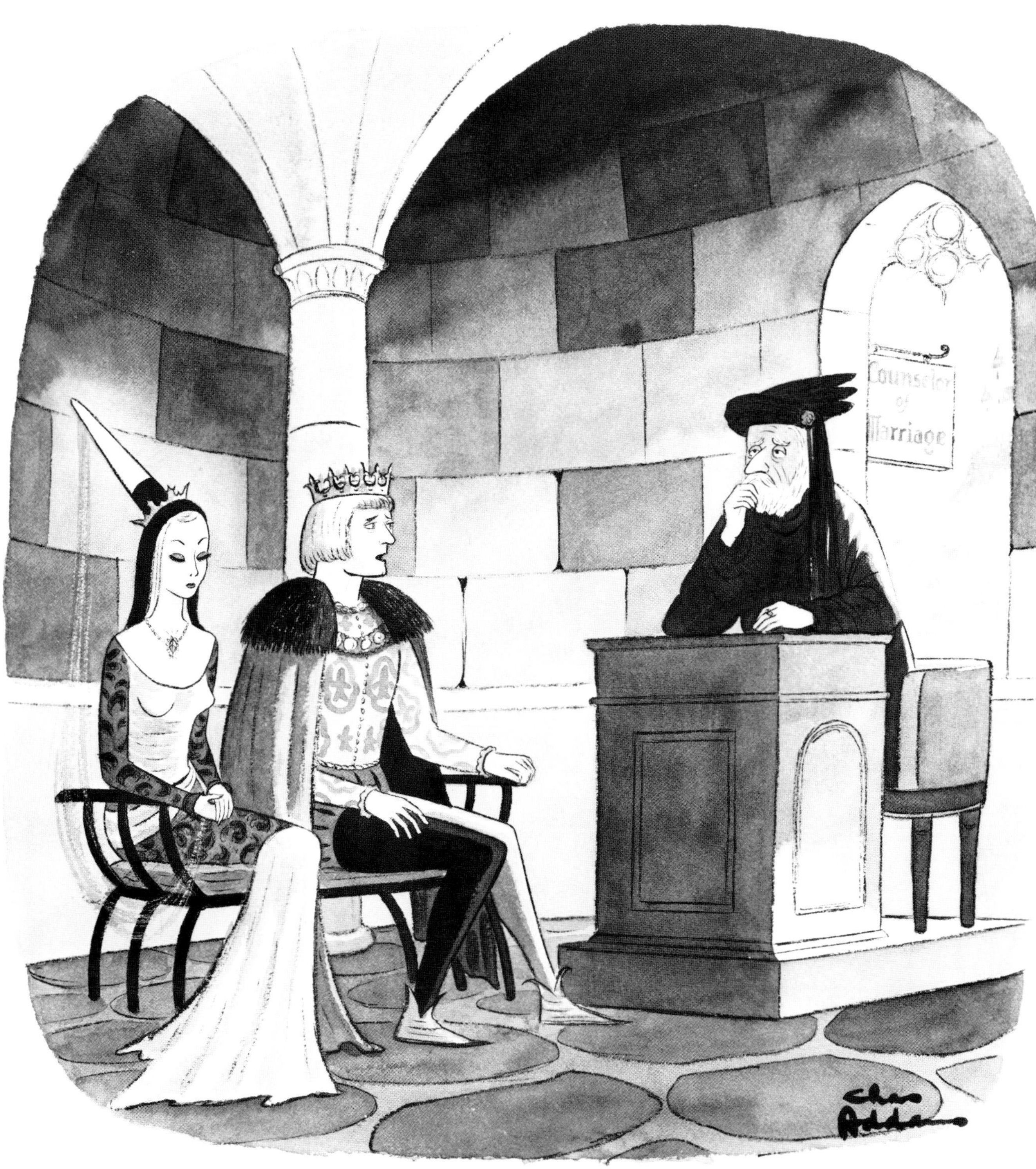
Counselor
of
Marriage

"We're not living happily ever after."

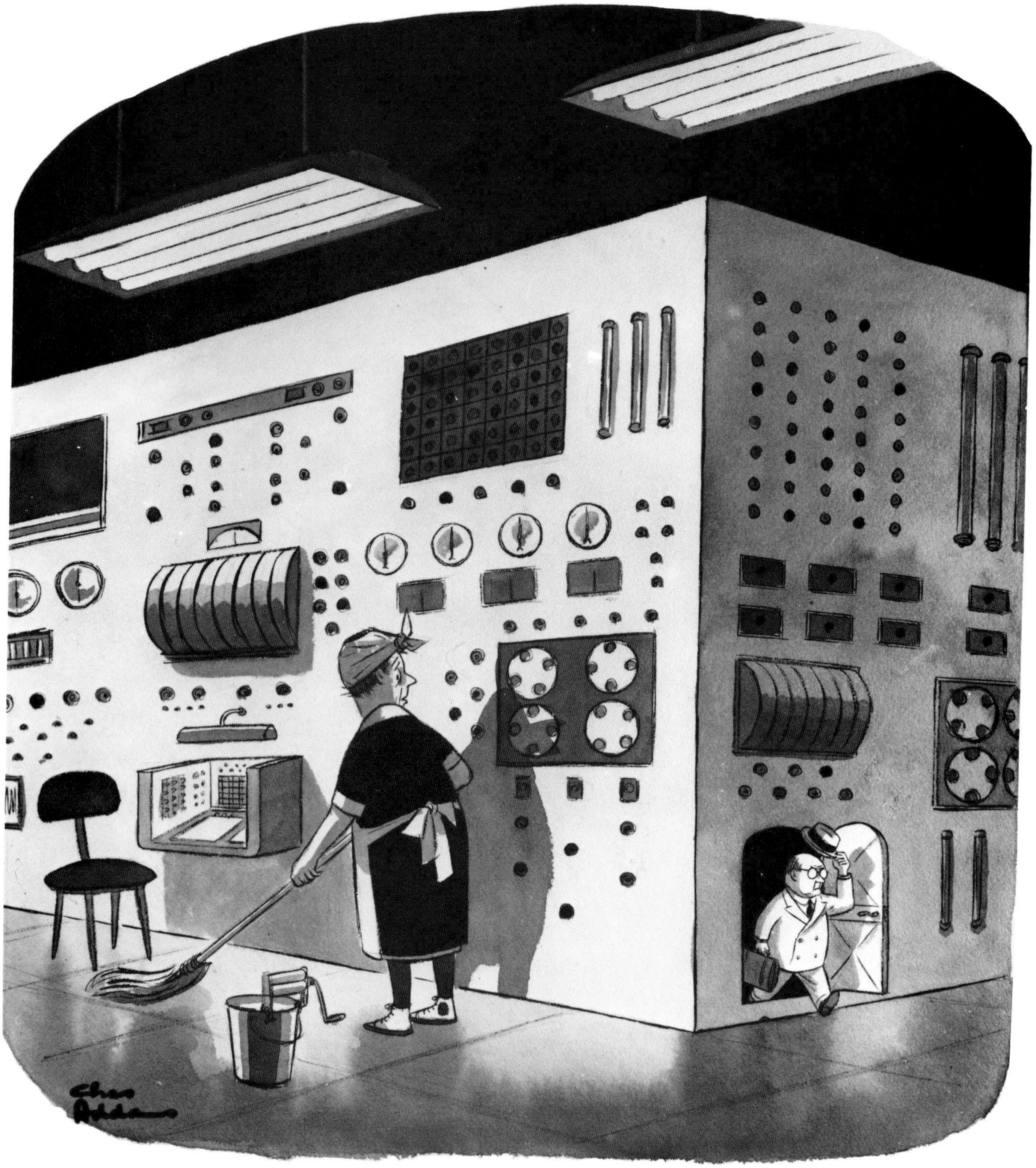
Chas Addams

"Grandmother! You're not cheating!"

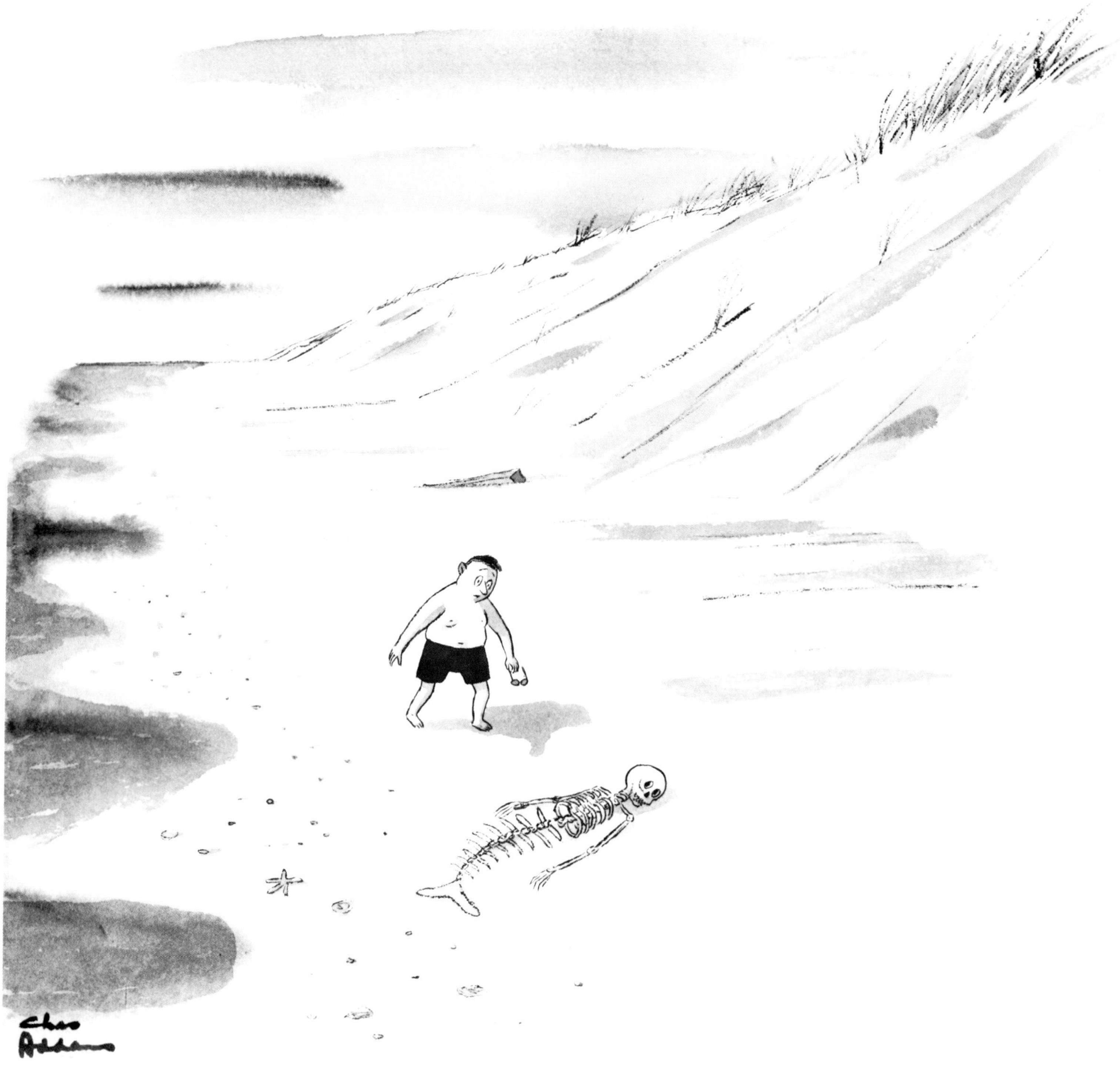
Chas Addams

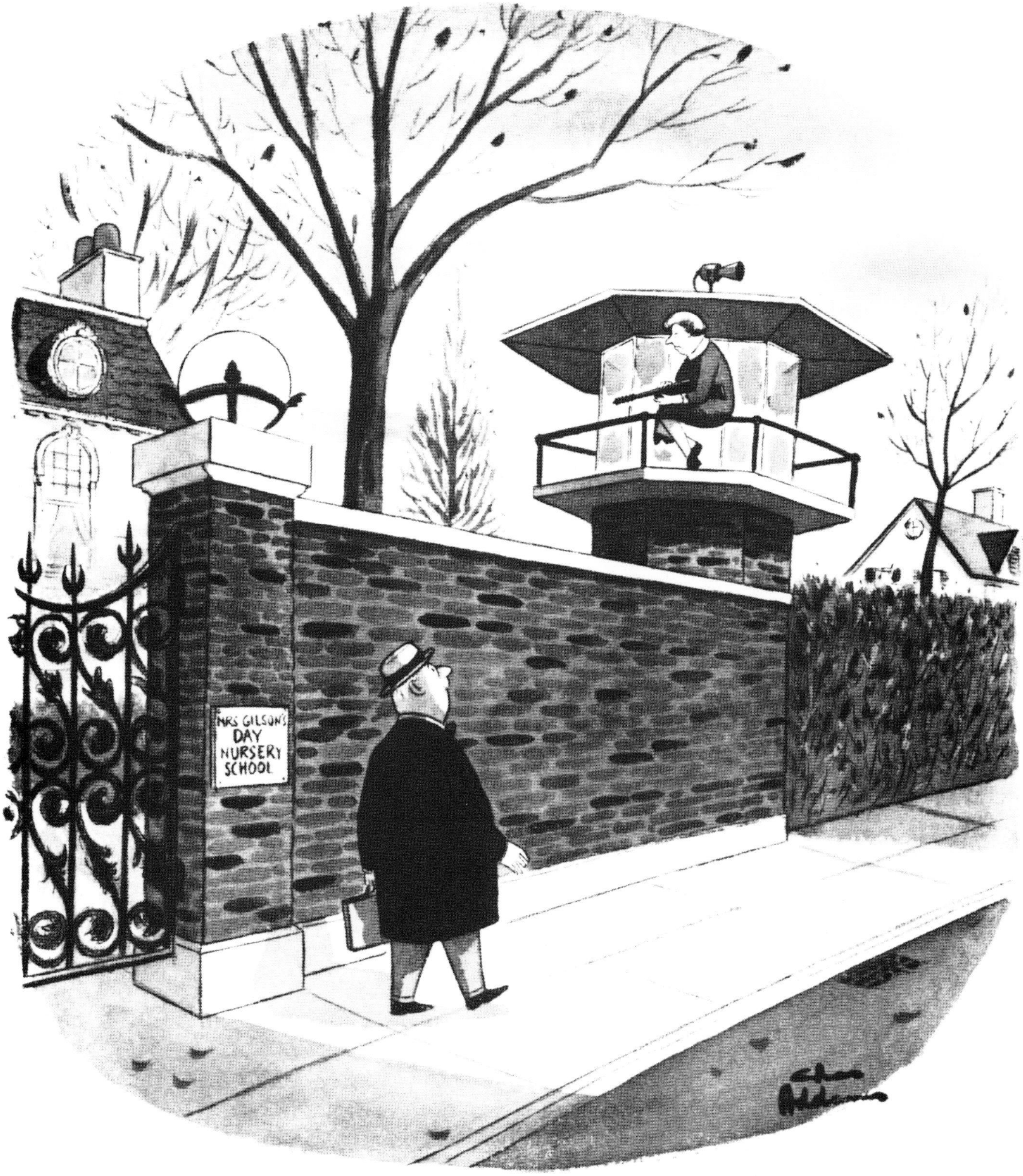
MRS GILSON'S
DAY
NURSERY
SCHOOL
Chas Addams

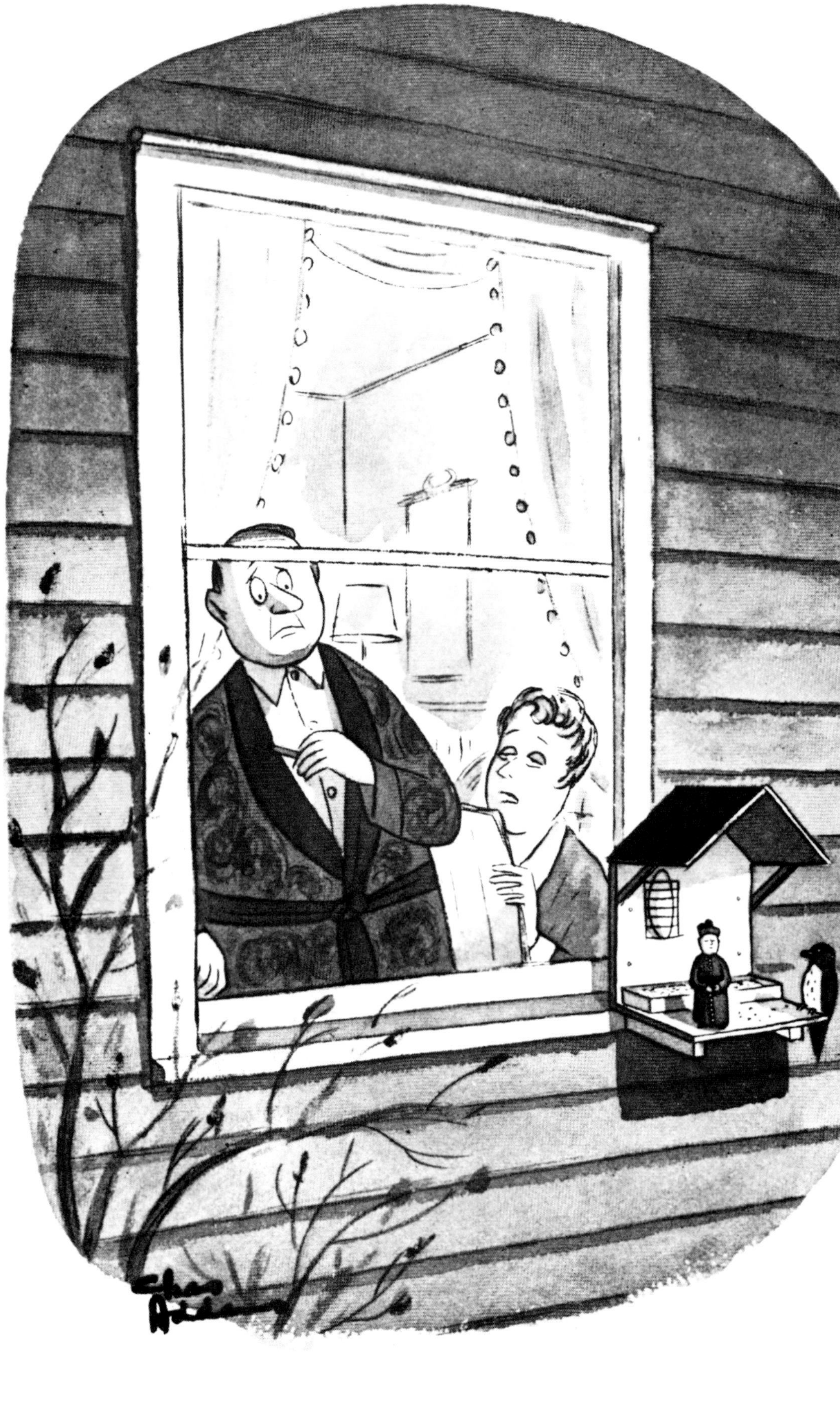

"What's so amazing about a cardinal in the bird feeder?"

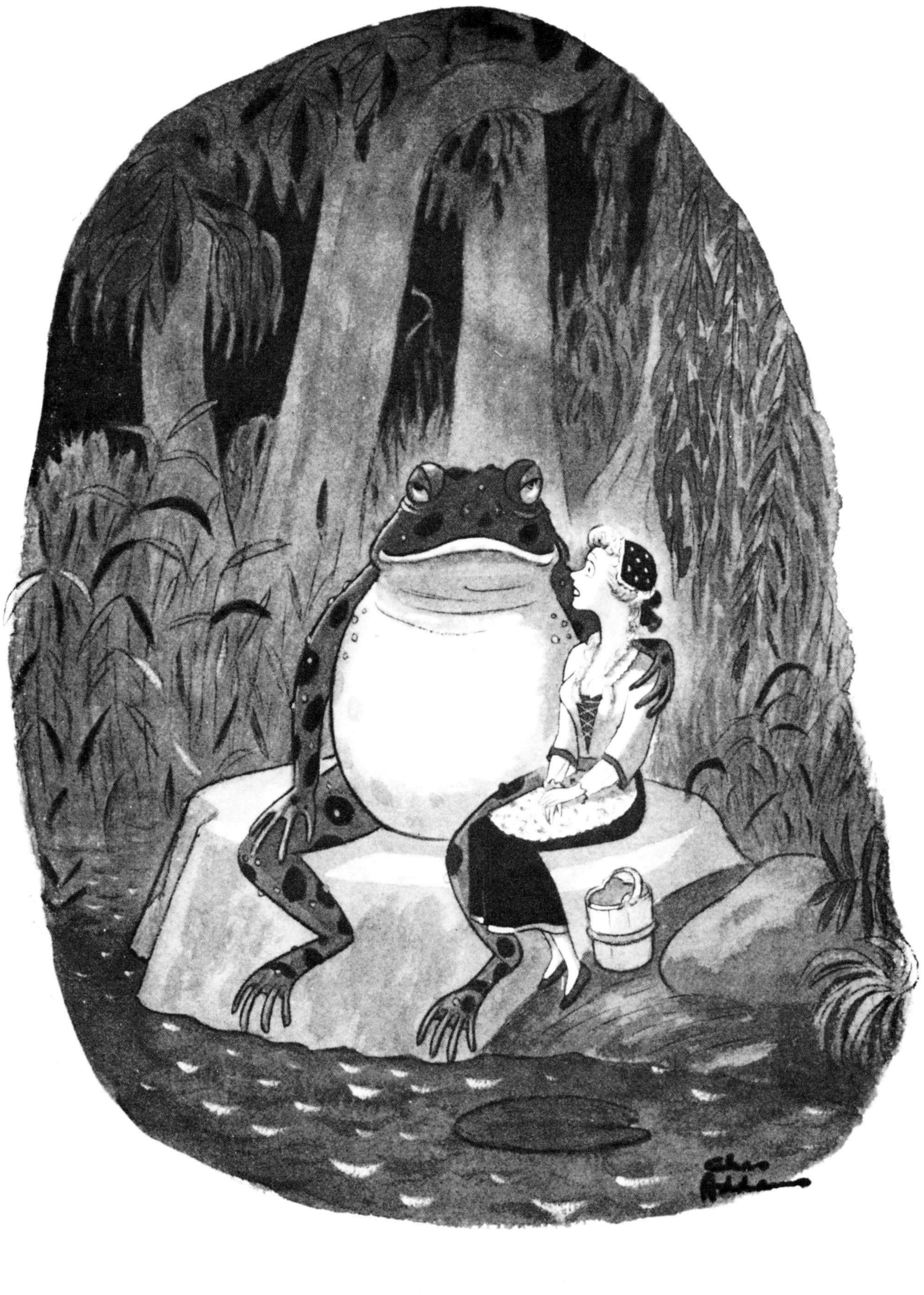
Chas Addams

"But how do I know you're an enchanted prince?"

"Sorry, folks, we quit at five."

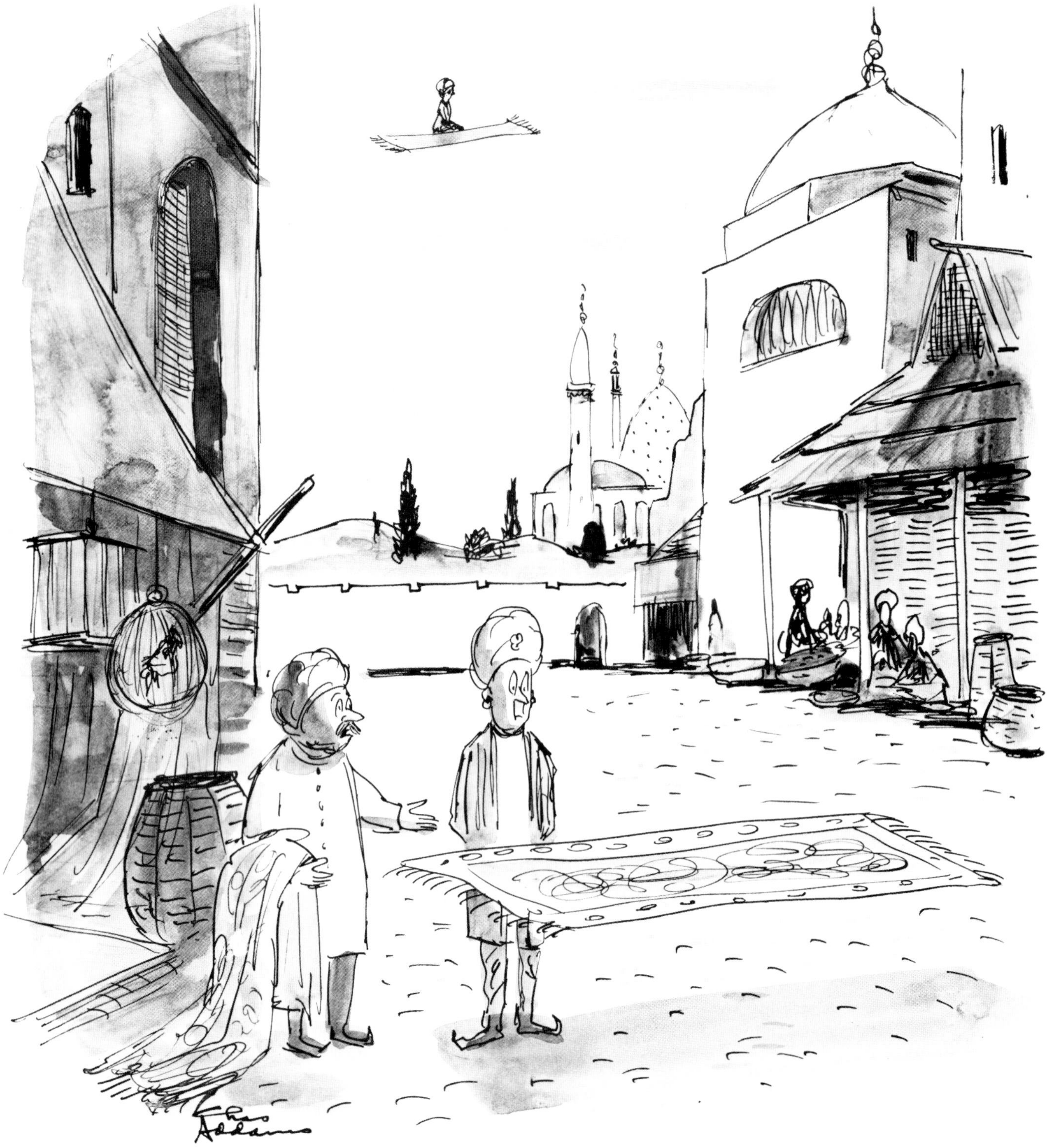
Chas Addams

"Now, this one was owned by an elderly gentleman with acrophobia."

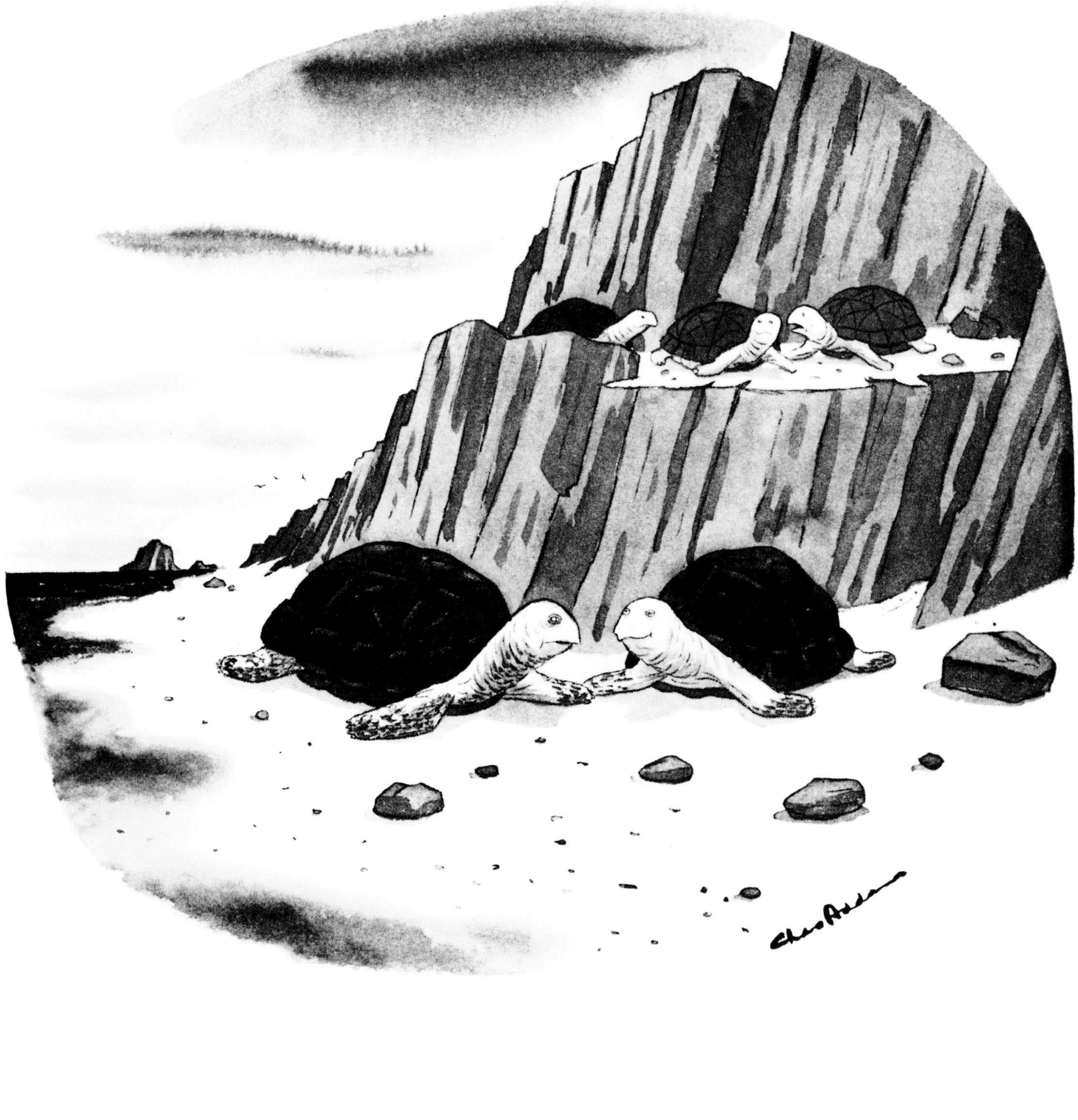
Chas Addams

"The difference may not seem so great right now, but when he's a hundred and fifty, she'll only be ninety."

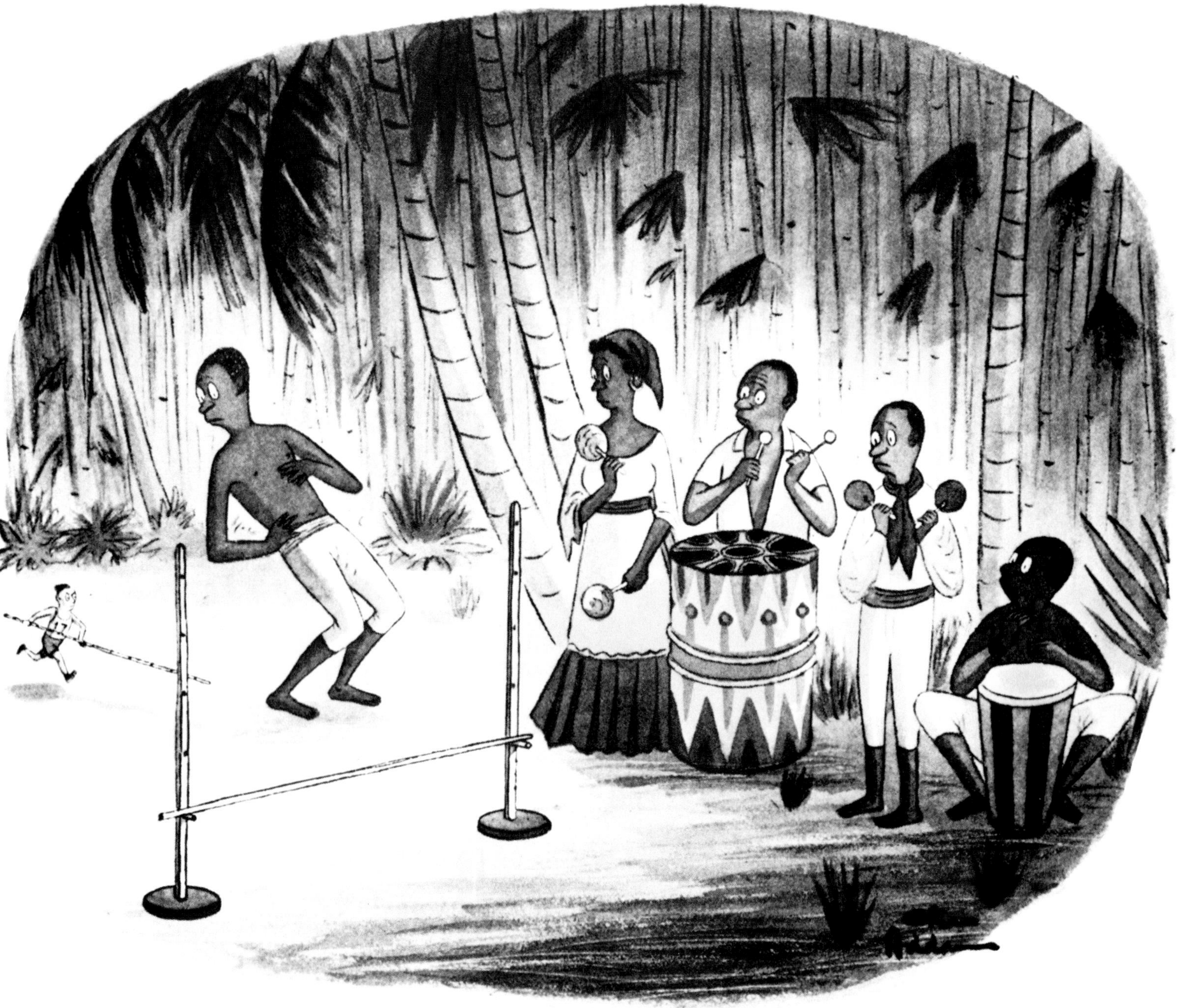

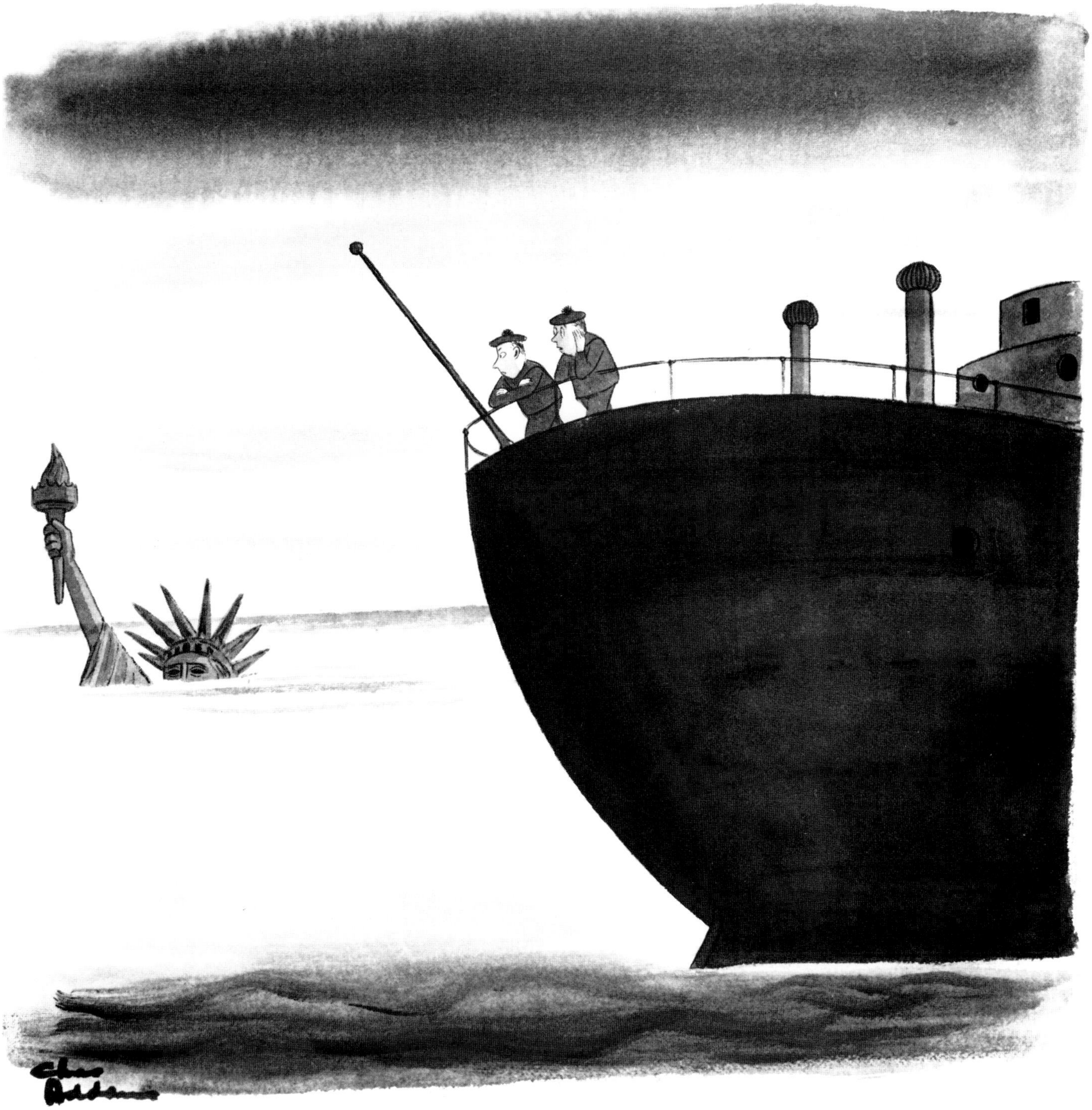

"High tide, I see."

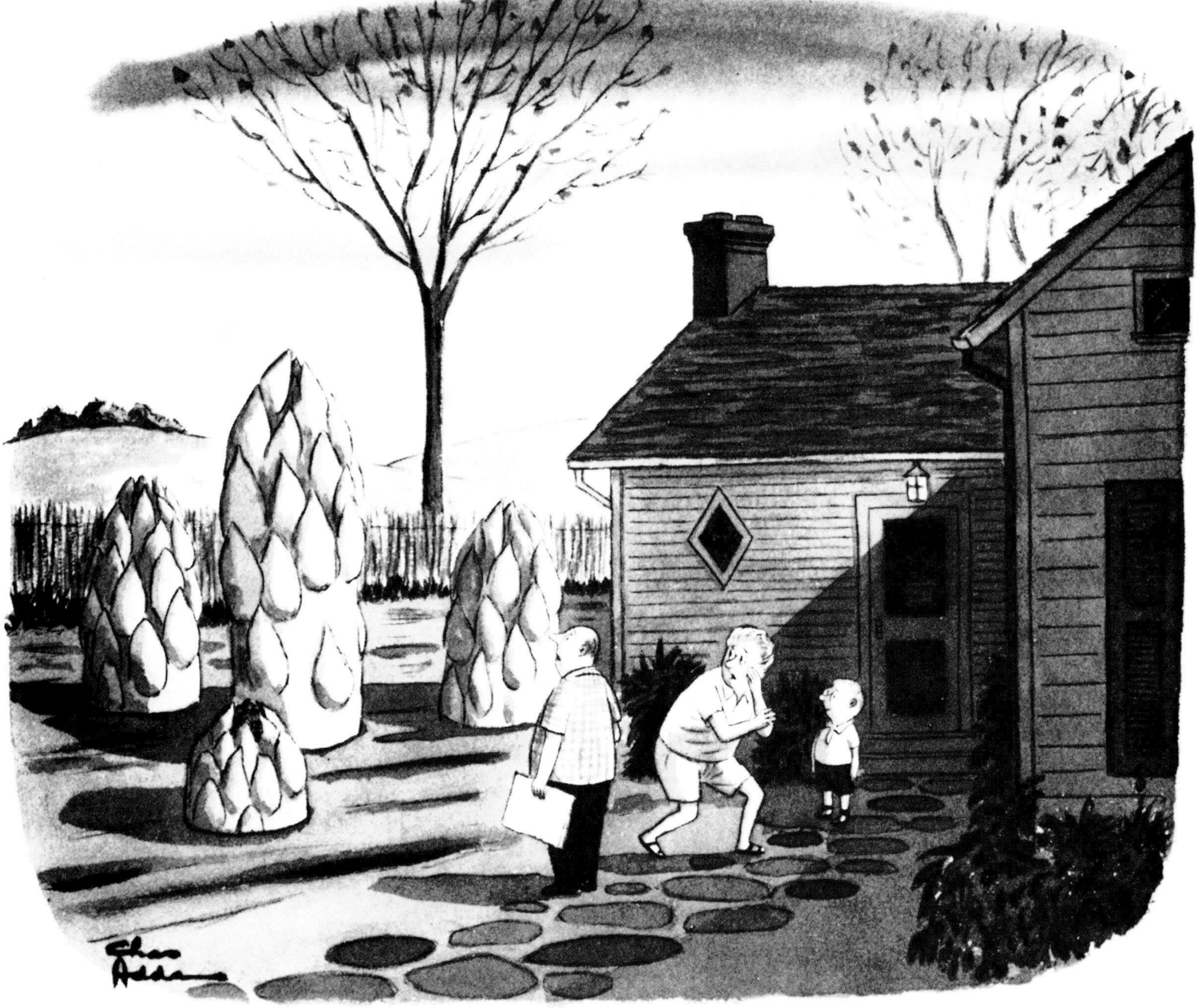

"You telephone 'Better Homes & Gardens.' I'll start making the hollandaise."

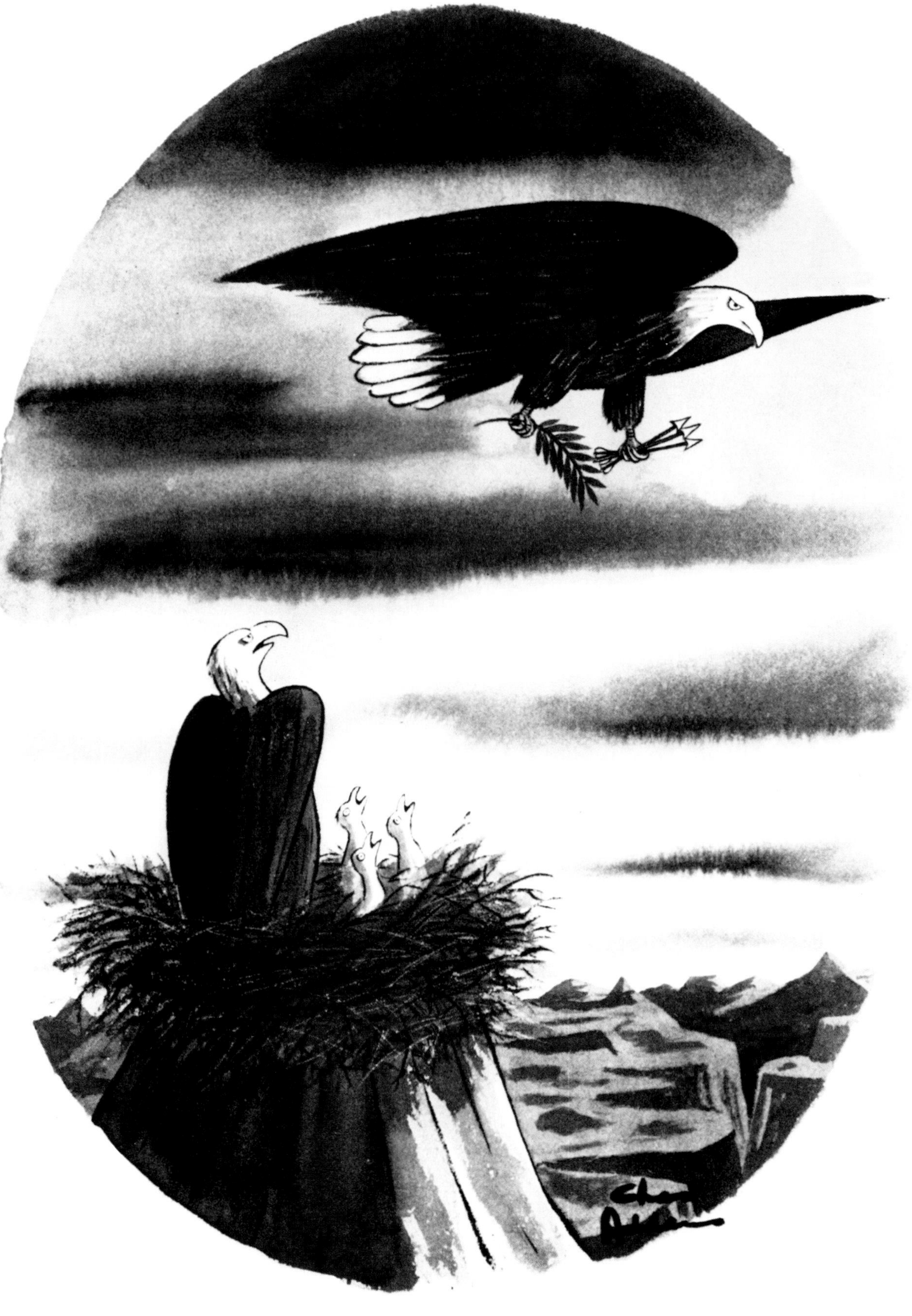

"All your father can think of these days is politics."

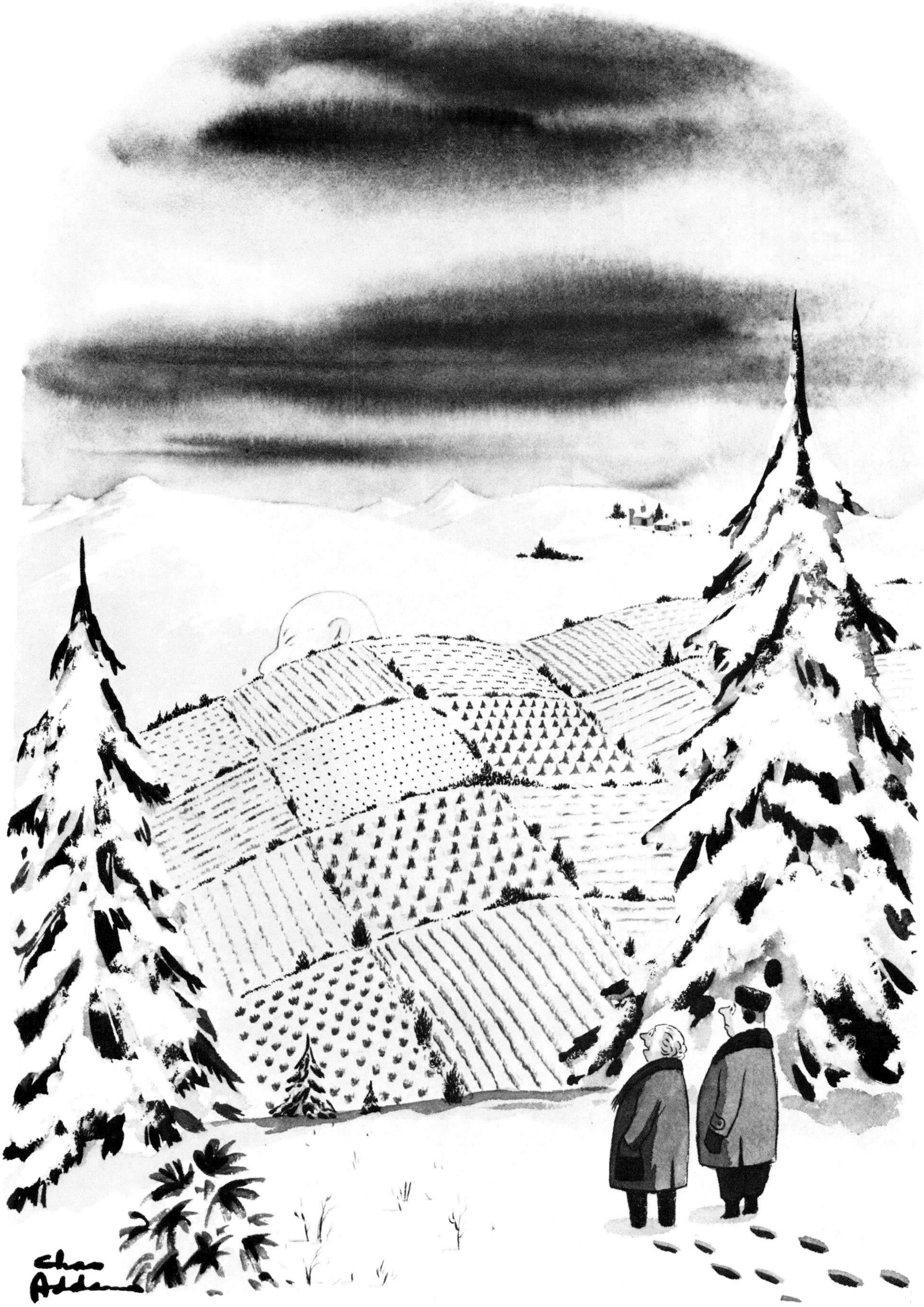

"Reminds one of a patchwork quilt, doesn't it?"

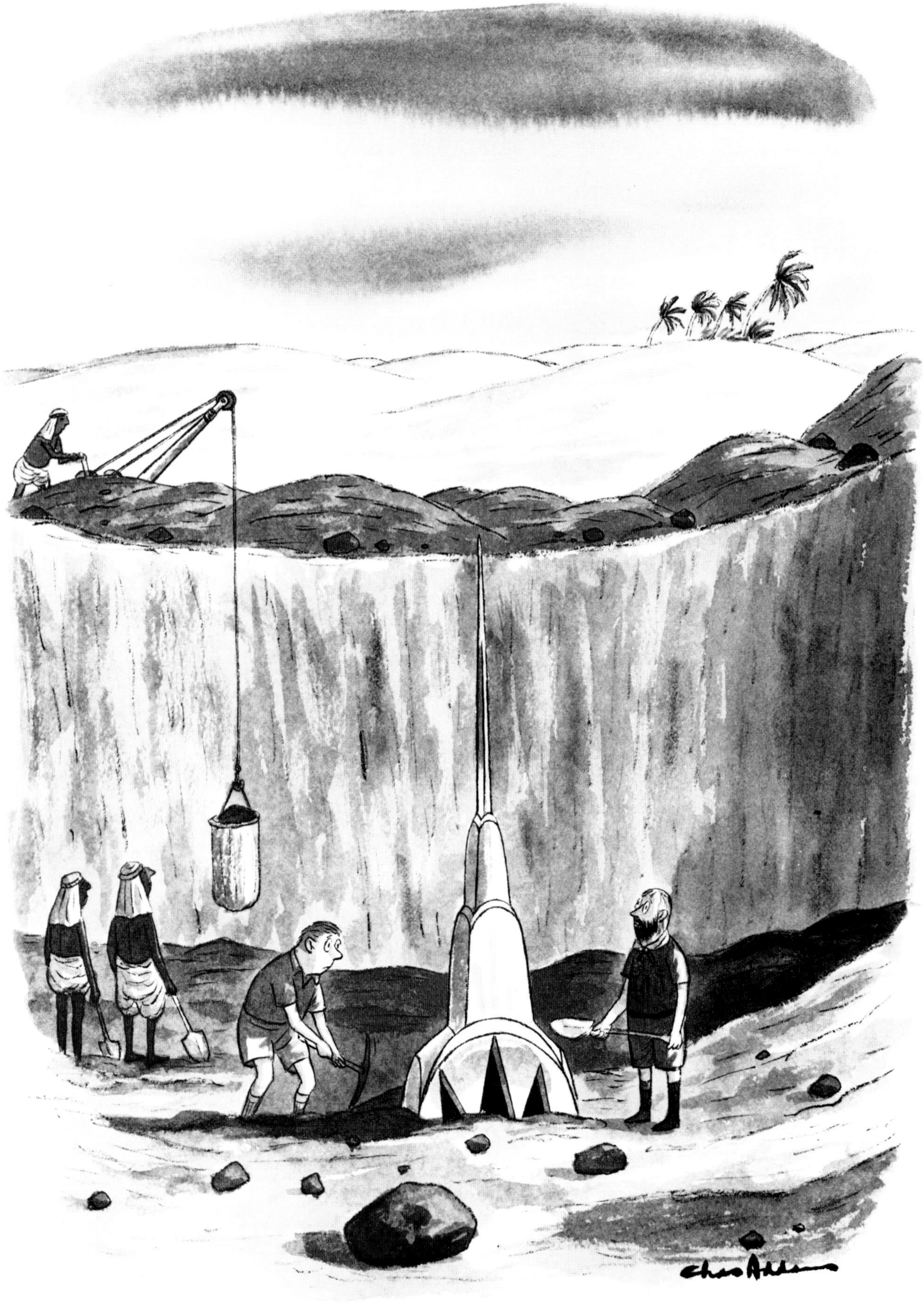
Chas Addams

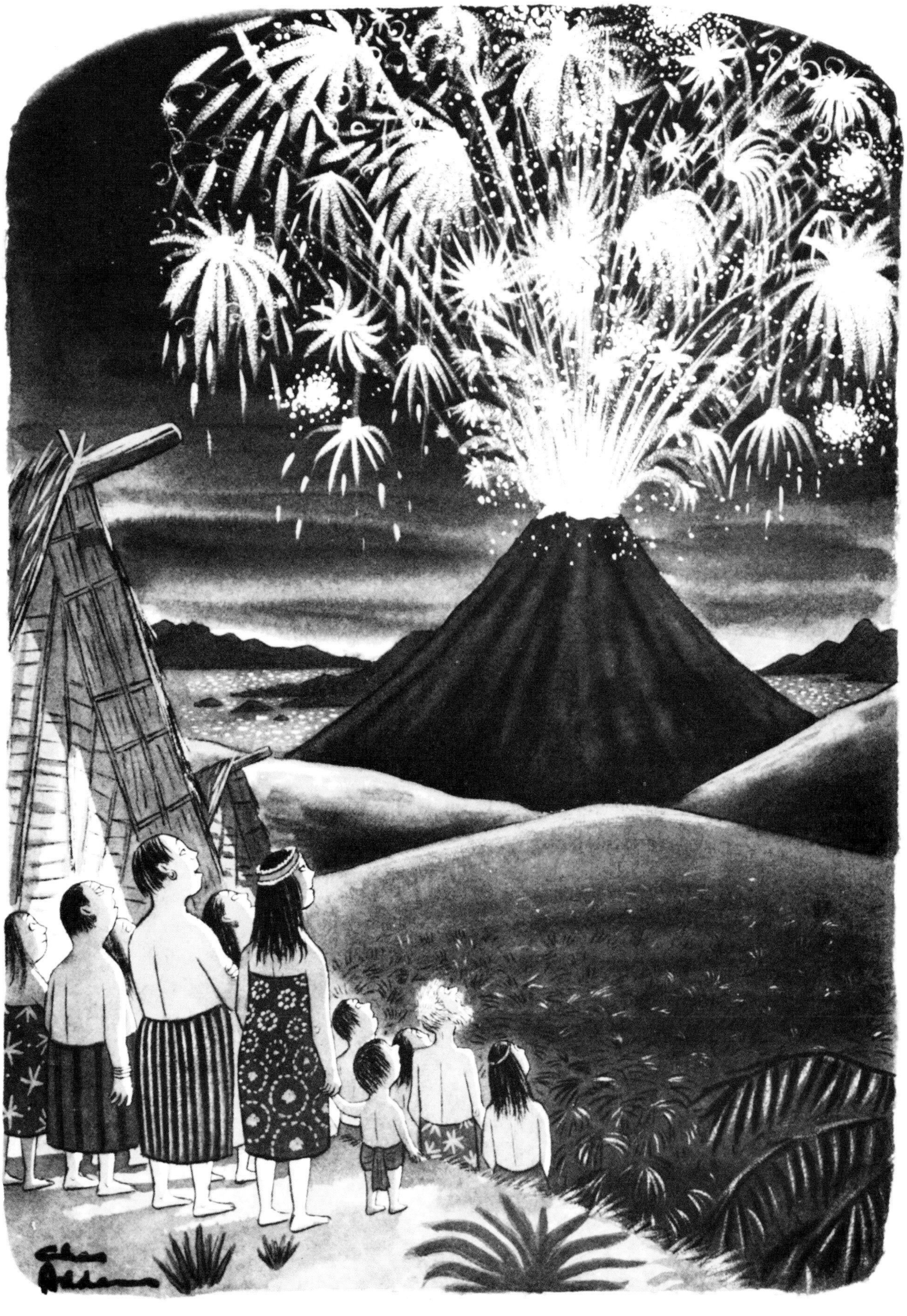

"Whatever the gods are, they aren't angry."

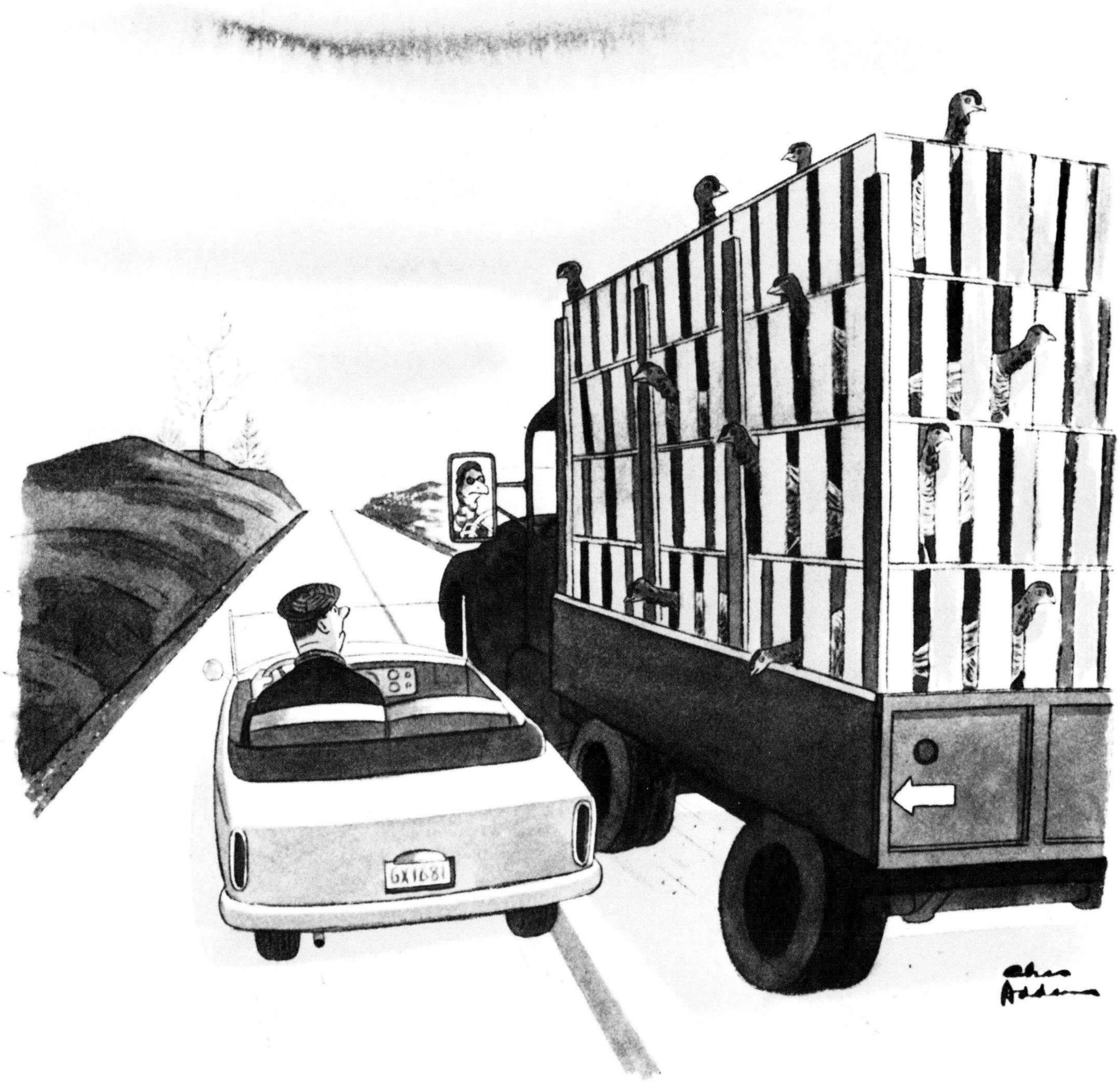
GX1681
Chas Addams

"I've heard that outside of working hours he's really a rather decent sort."

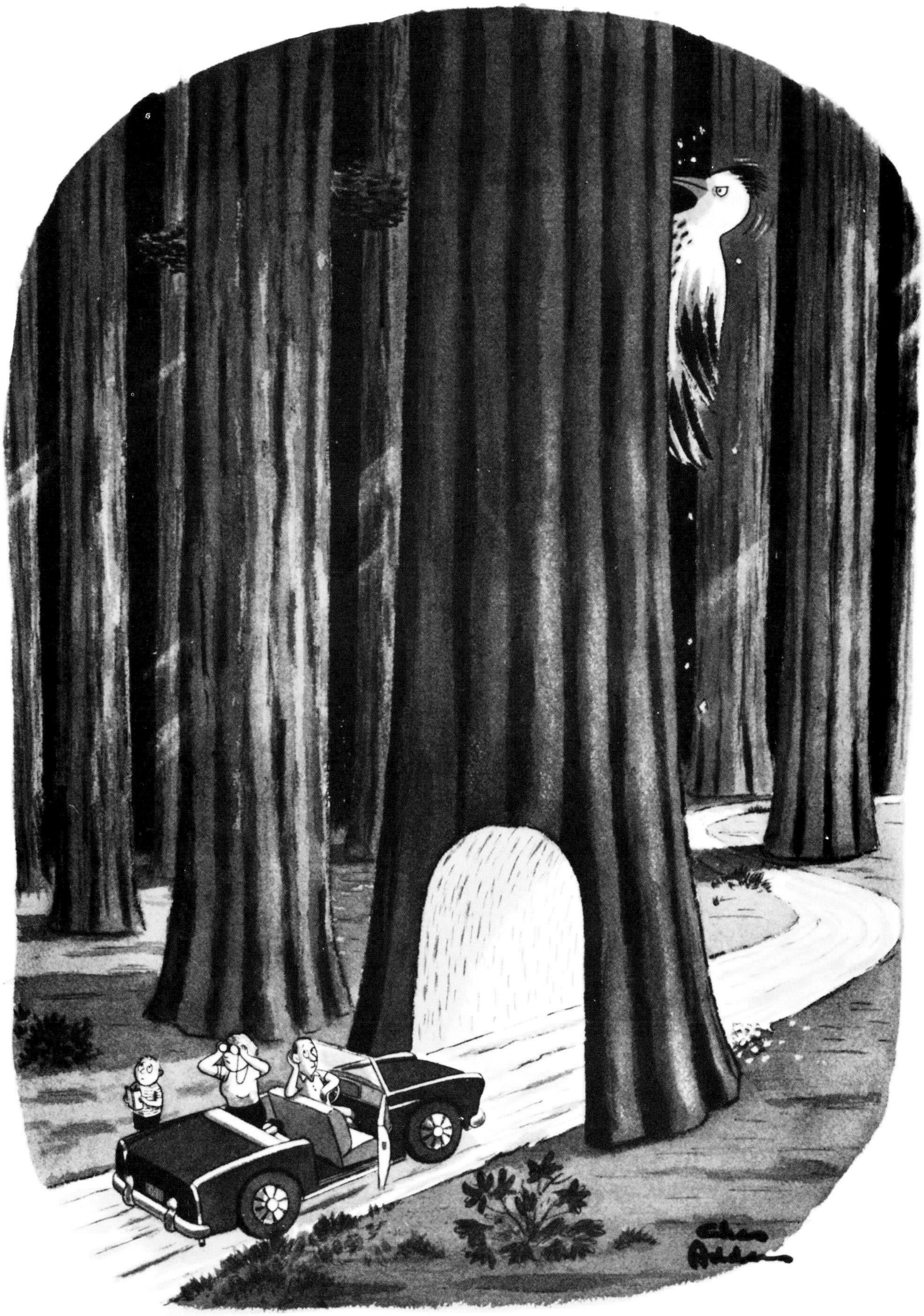
Chas Addams

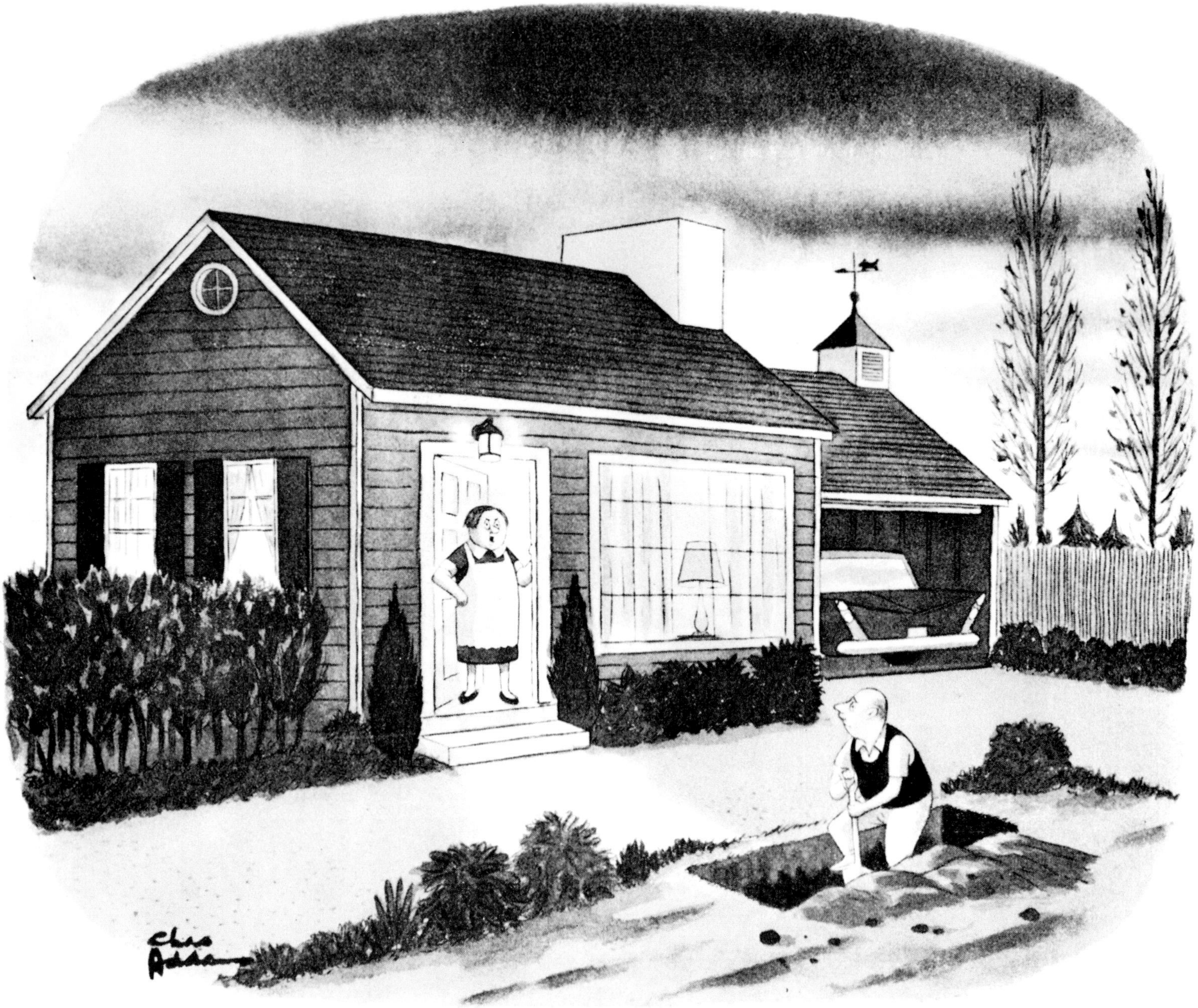

"Wallace, isn't that already too deep for glads?"

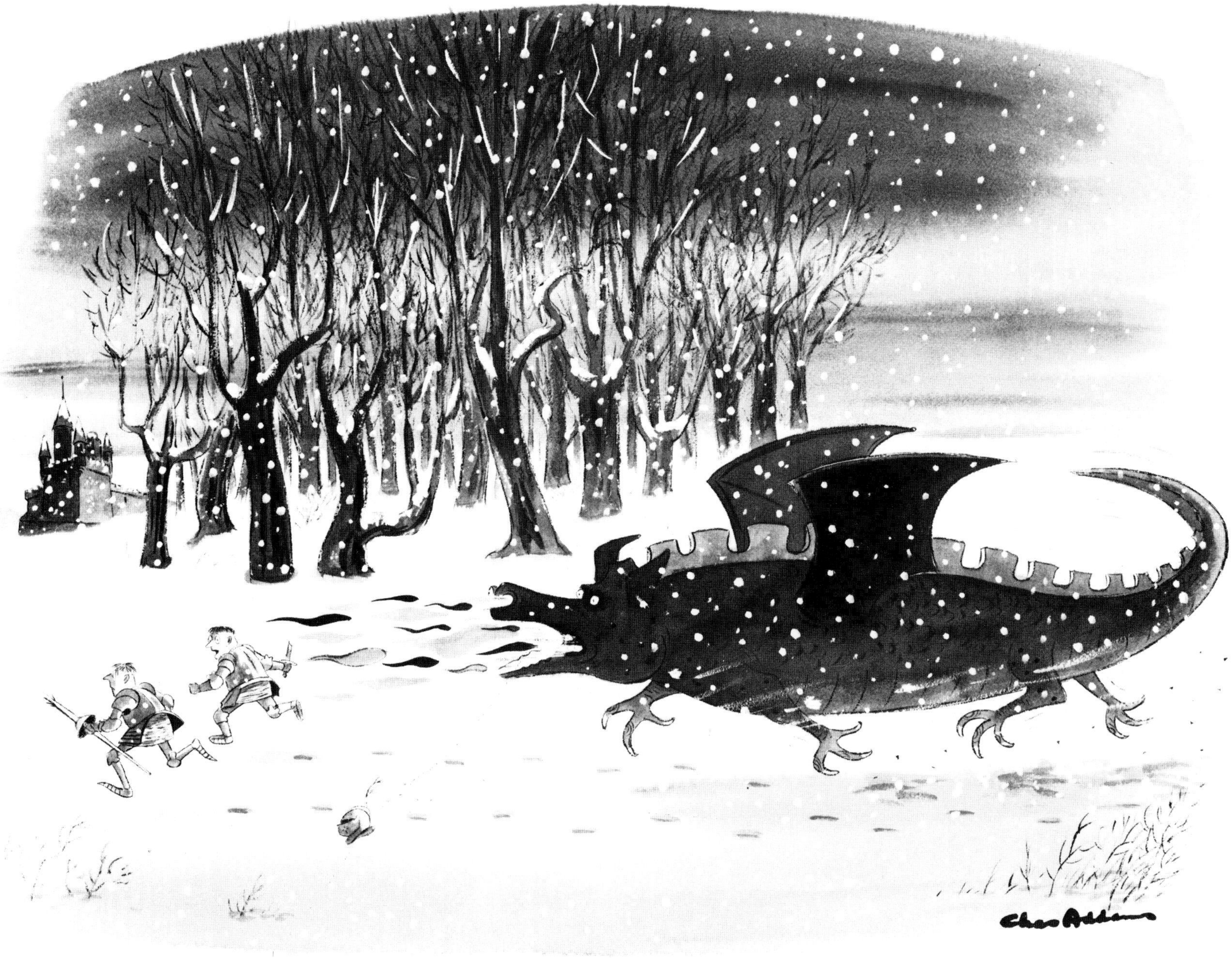
Chas Addams

"Feels good, though, doesn't it?"

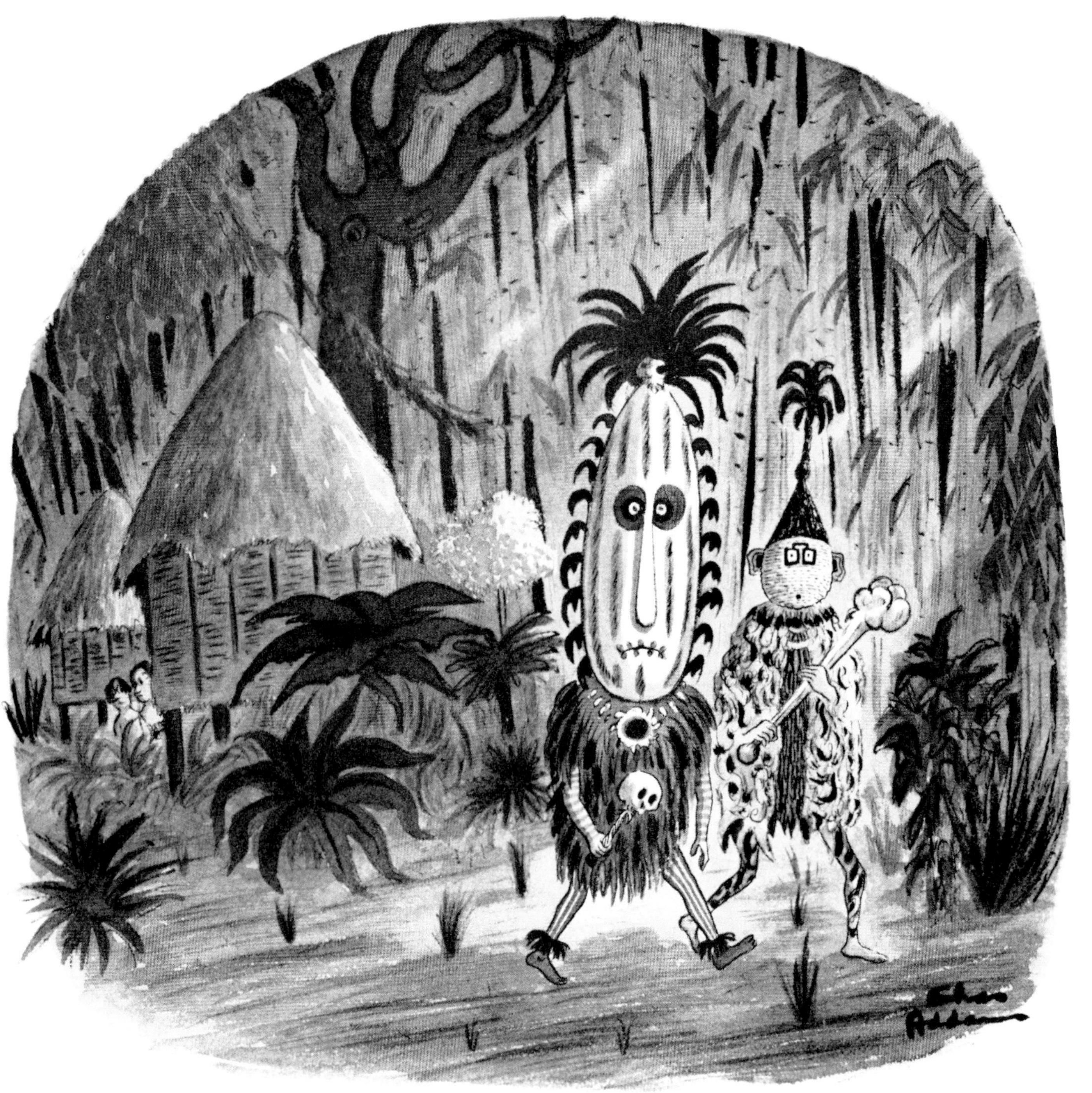

"I danced the best I could, but what the guy really has is an iron deficiency."

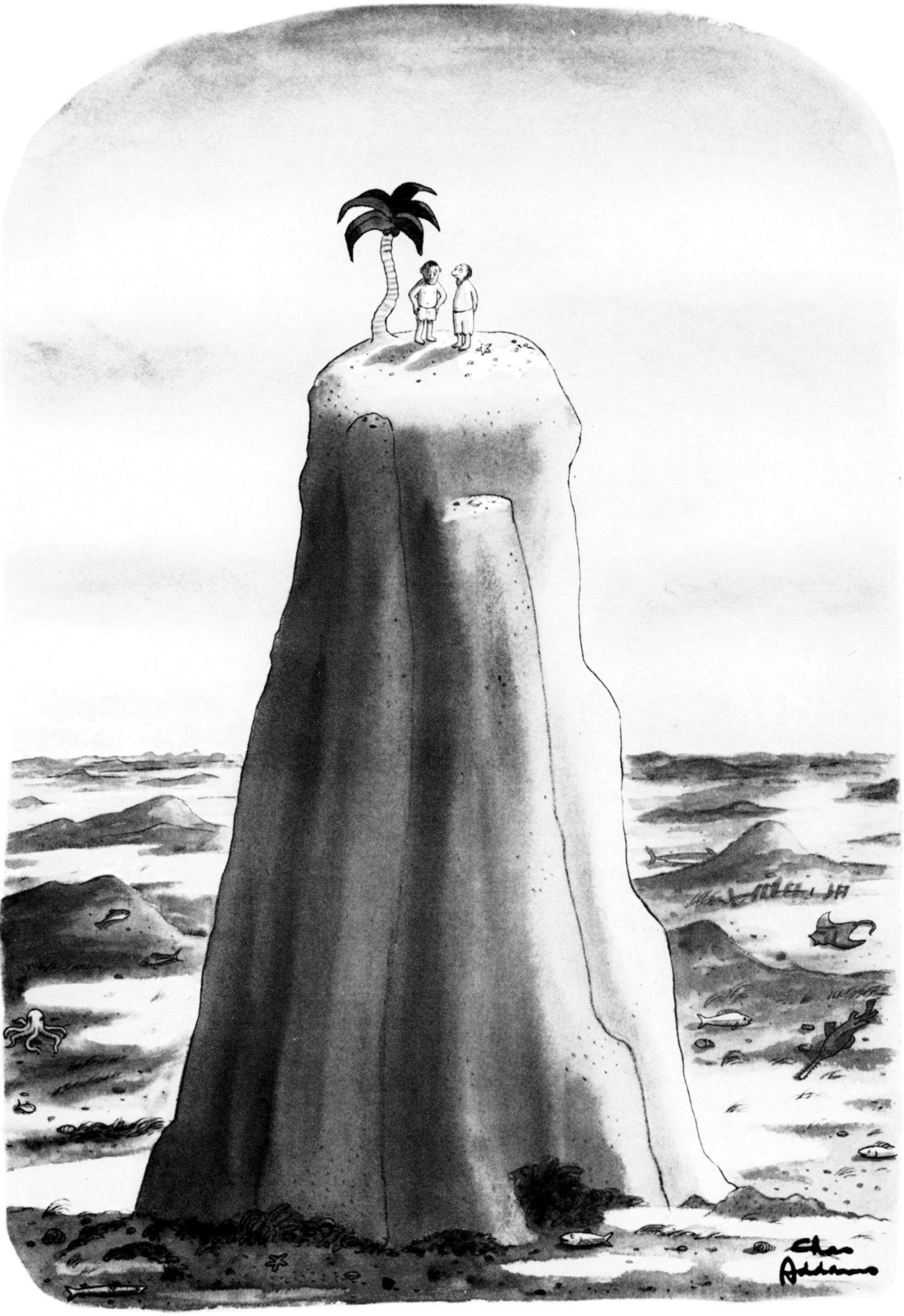
Chas Addams

"I don't see that our situation is especially improved."

"Why can't you be more like Oedipus?"

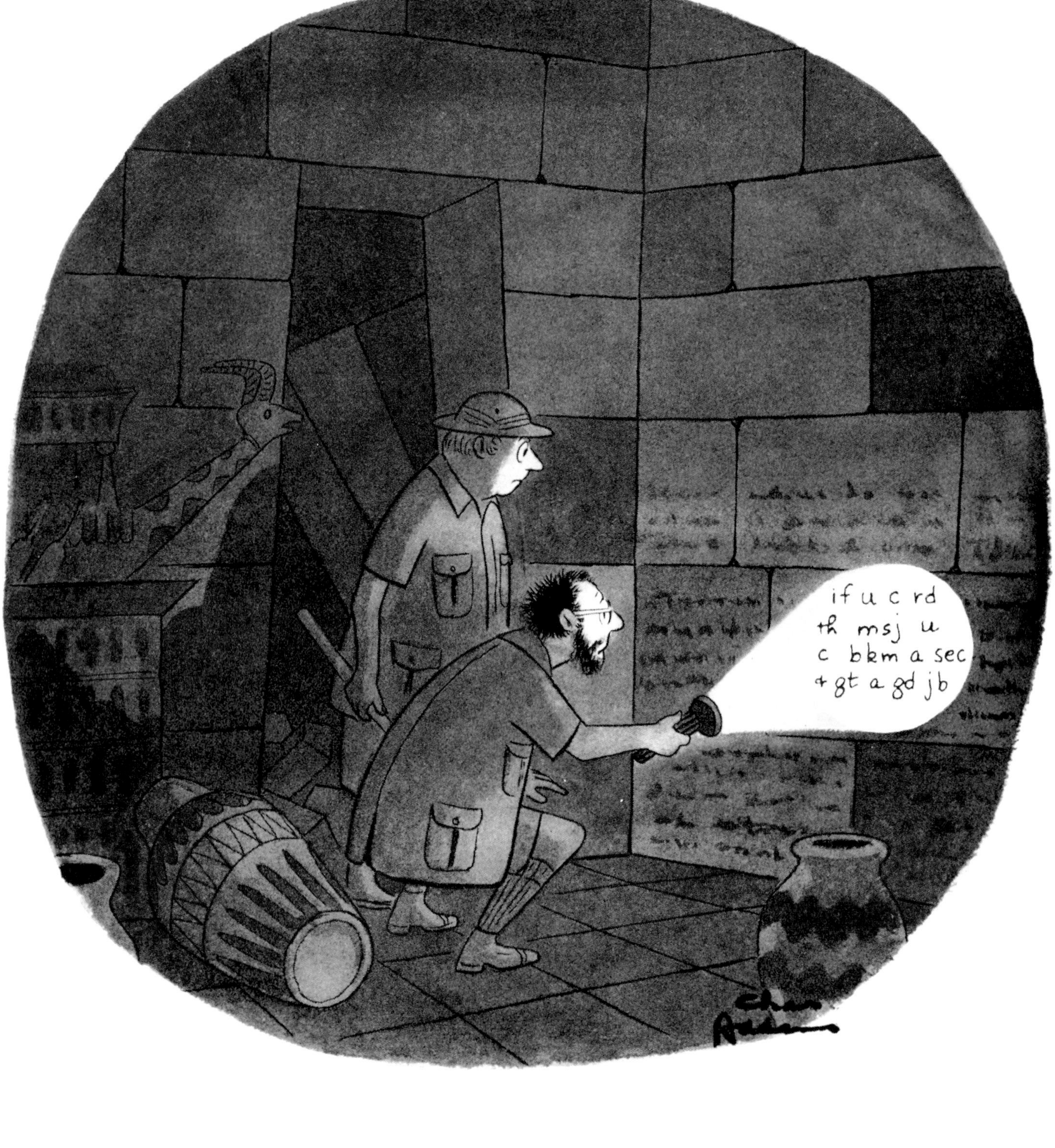
if u c rd
th msj u
c bkm a sec
+ gt a gd jb

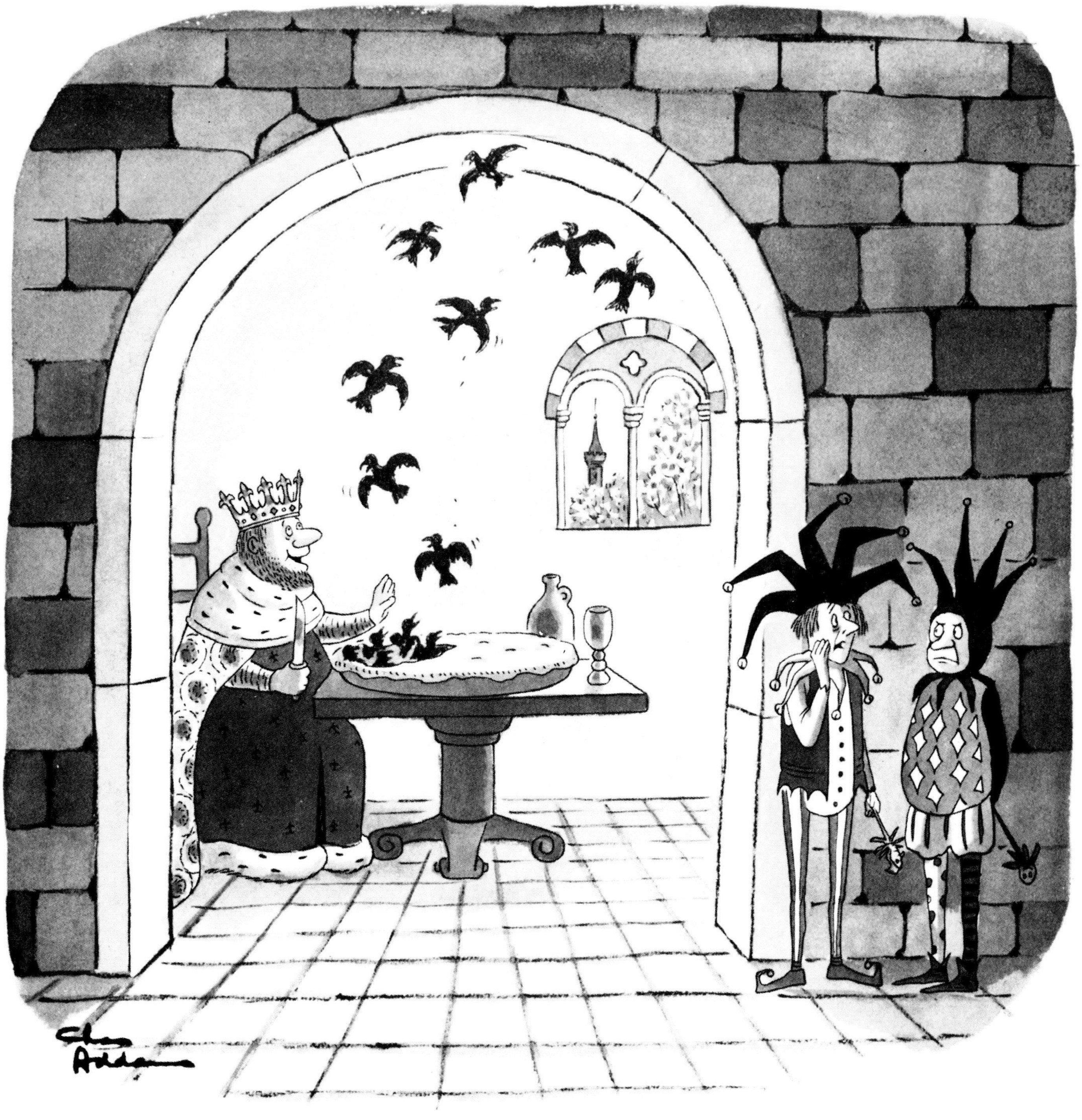

"It's going to be tough to top that."

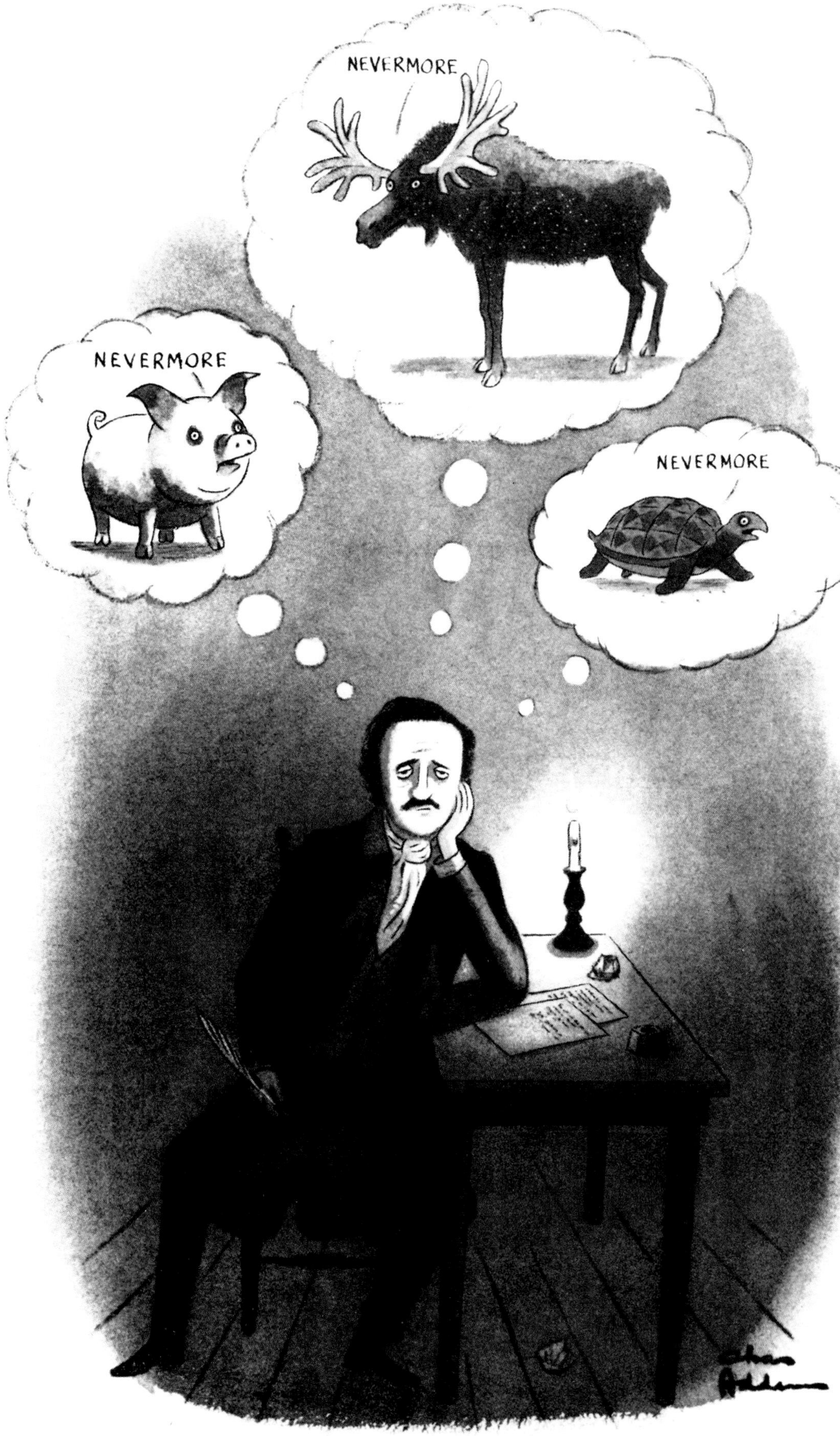
NEVERMORE
NEVERMORE
NEVERMORE

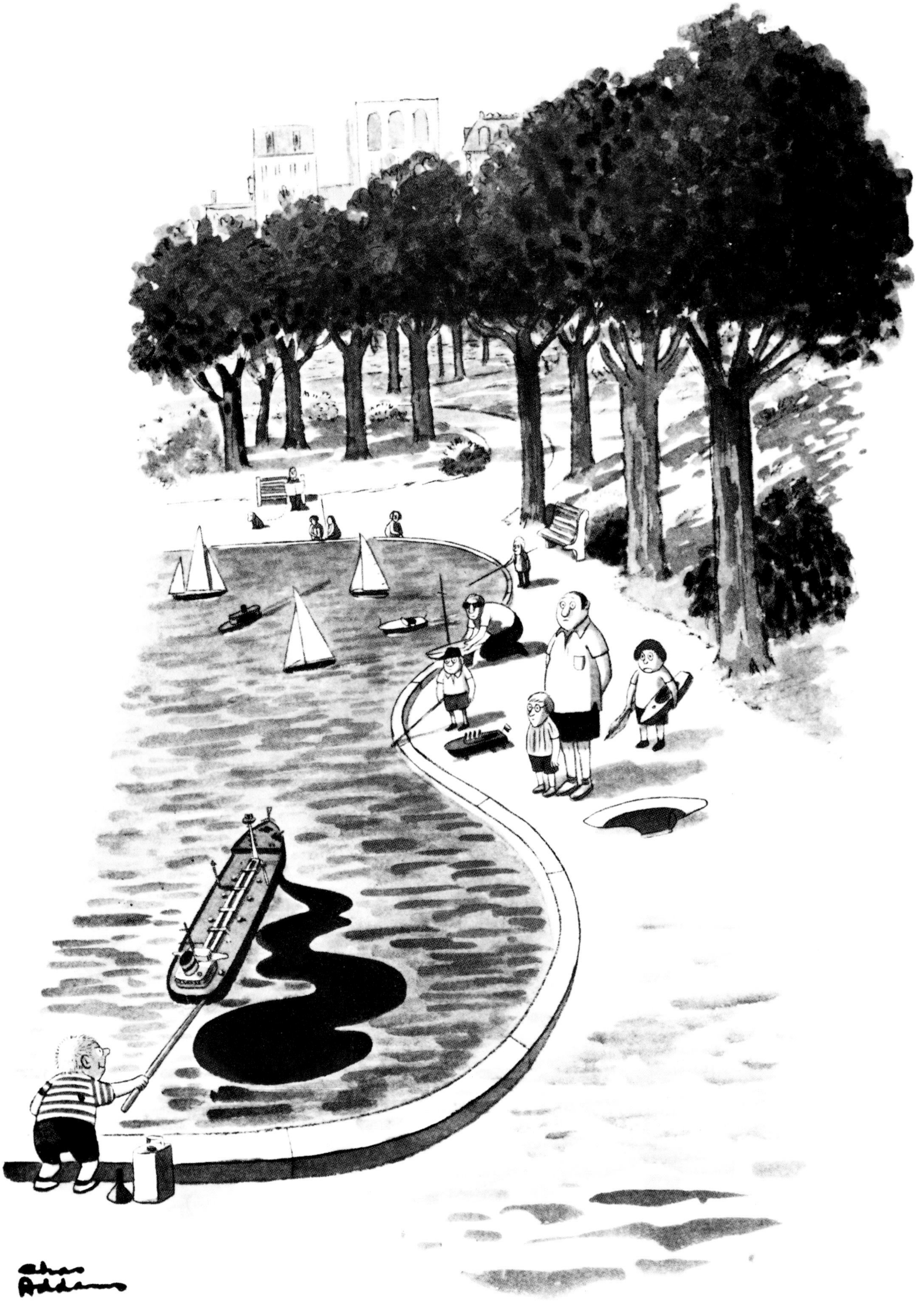

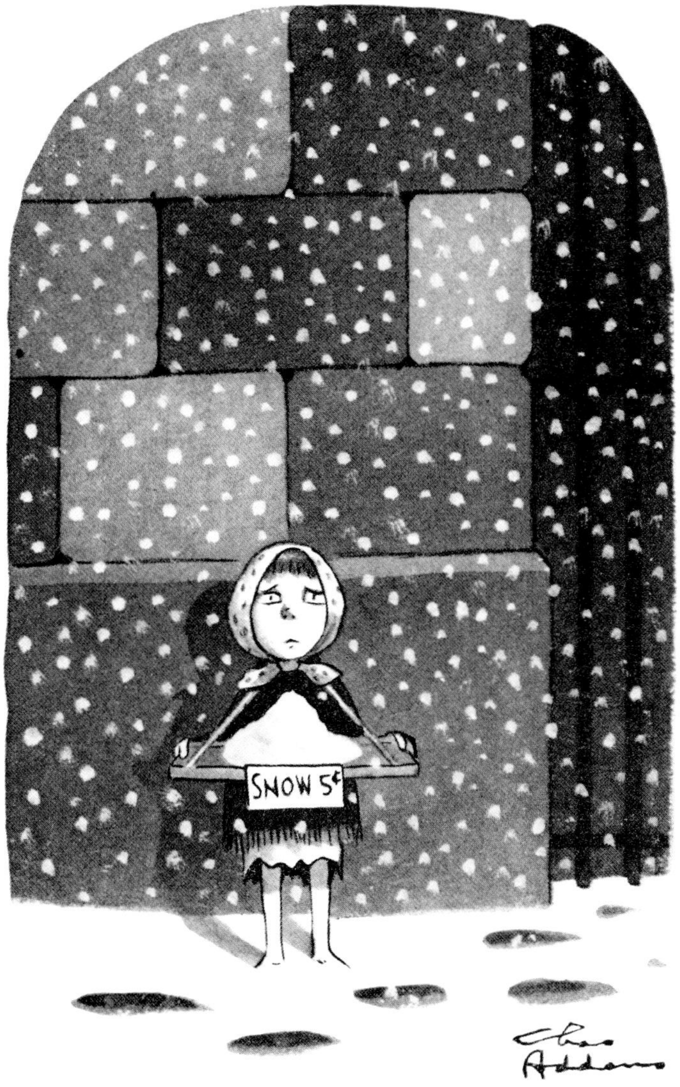
SNOW 5¢
Chas Addams

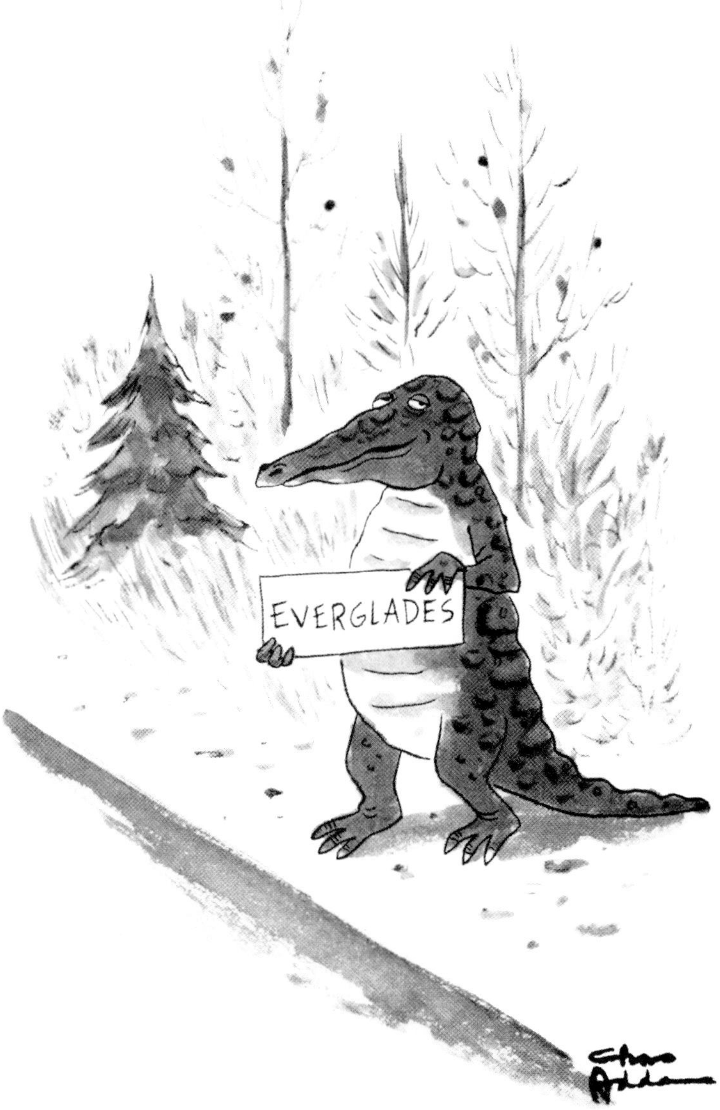
EVERGLADES
Chas Addams

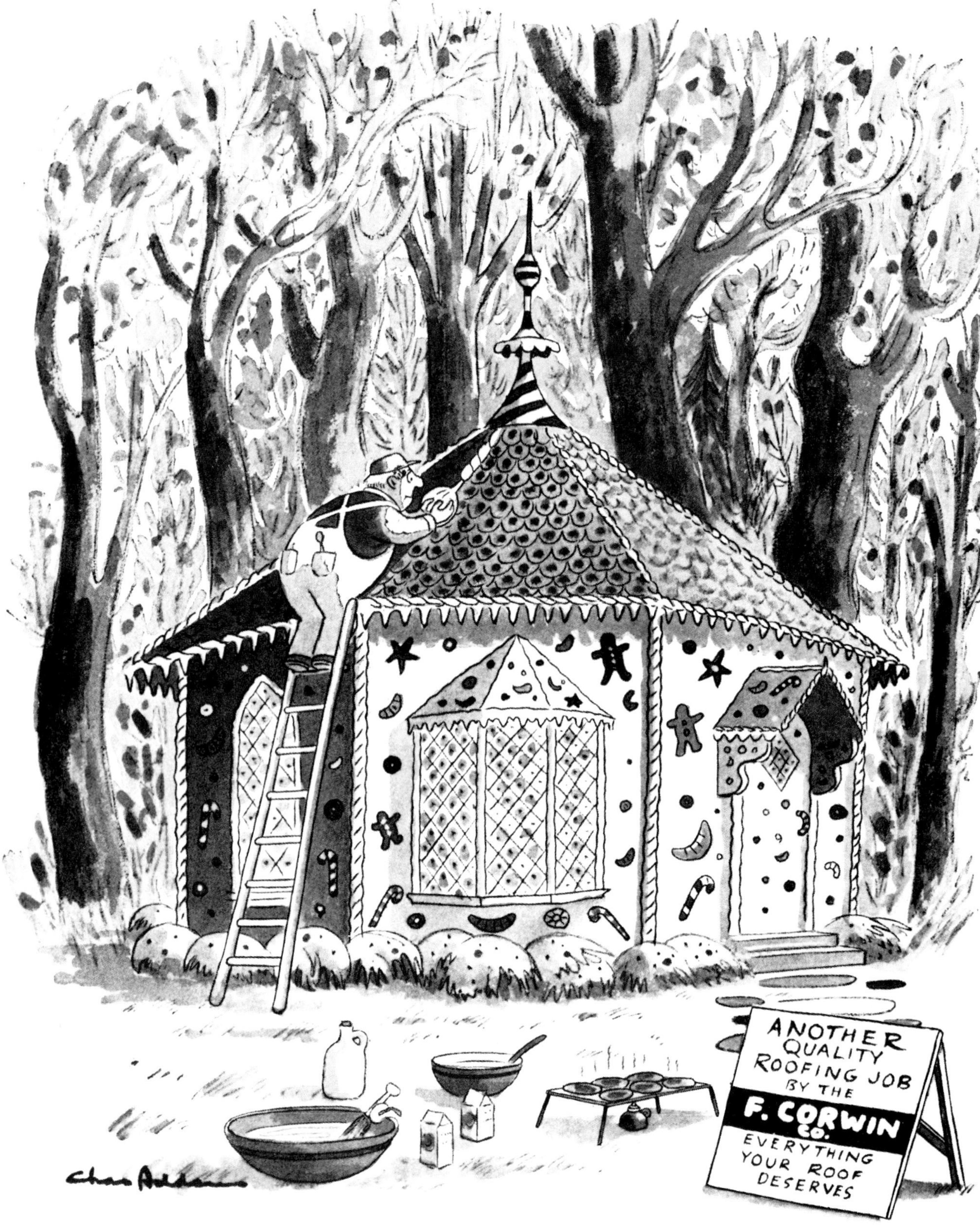
ANOTHER QUALITY ROOFING JOB BY THE
F. CORWIN CO.
EVERYTHING YOUR ROOF DESERVES

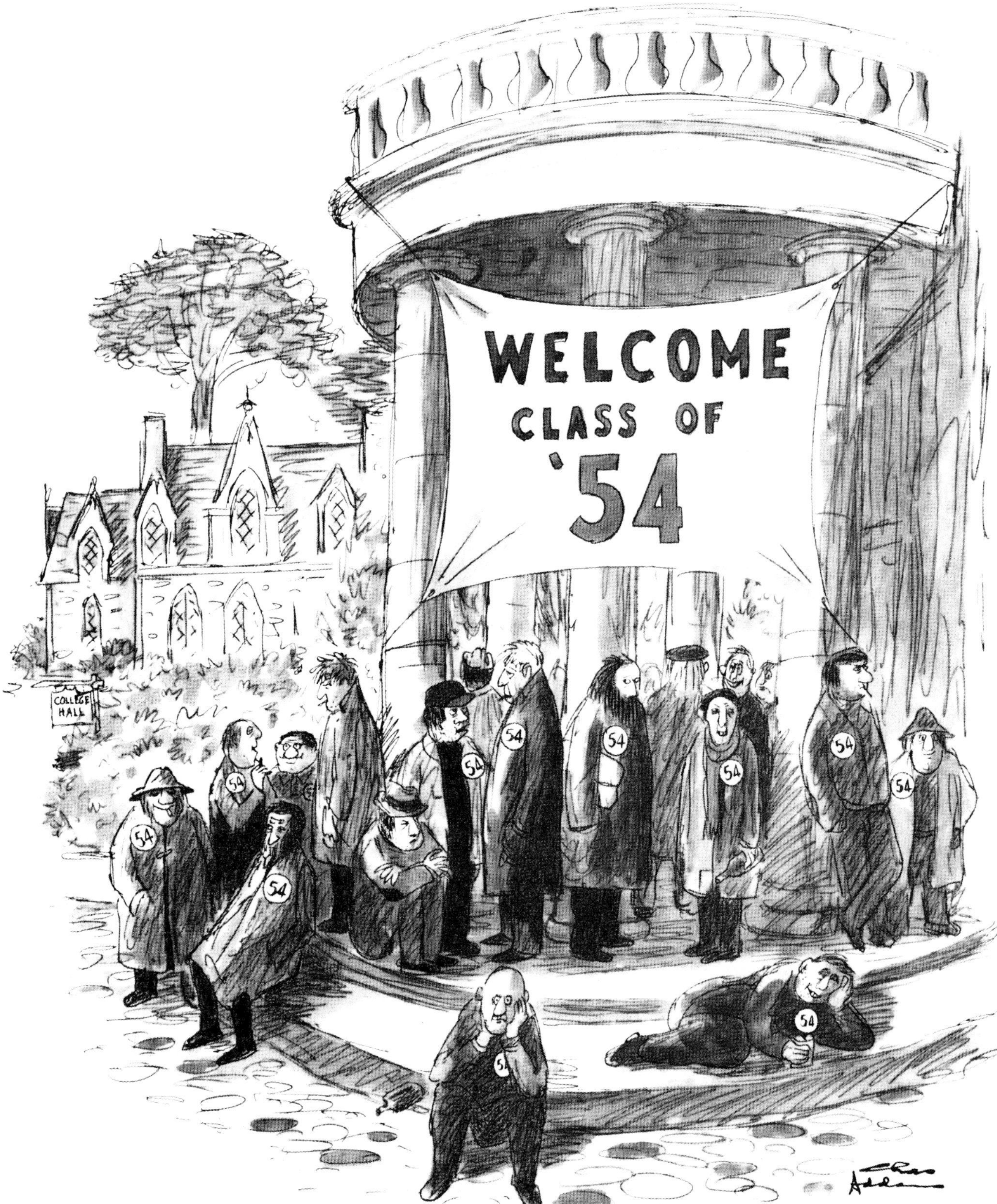
WELCOME
CLASS OF
'54
COLLEGE
HALL

"I thought it was me, but maybe the school's no damn good."

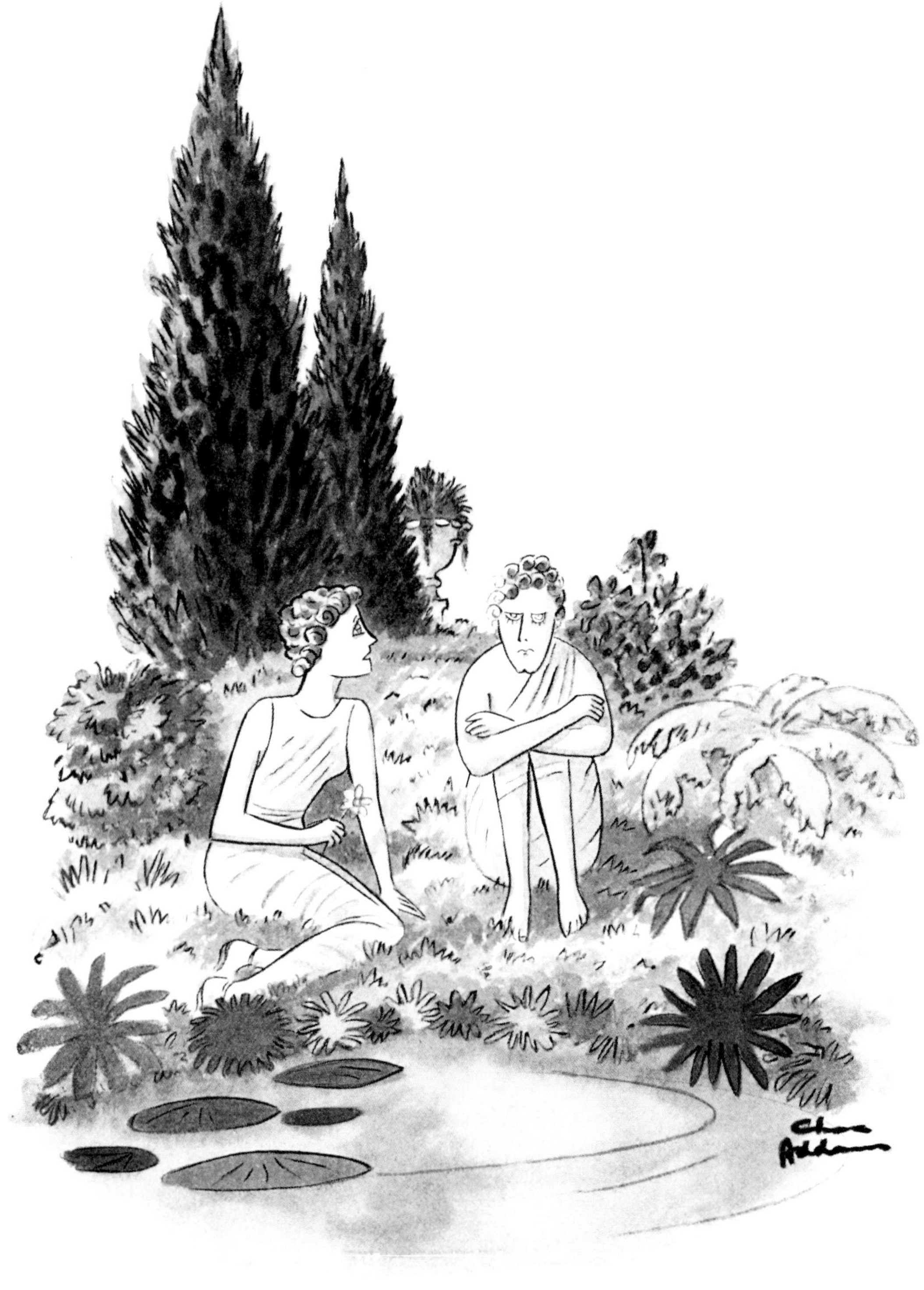
Chas Addams

"Is there someone else, Narcissus?"

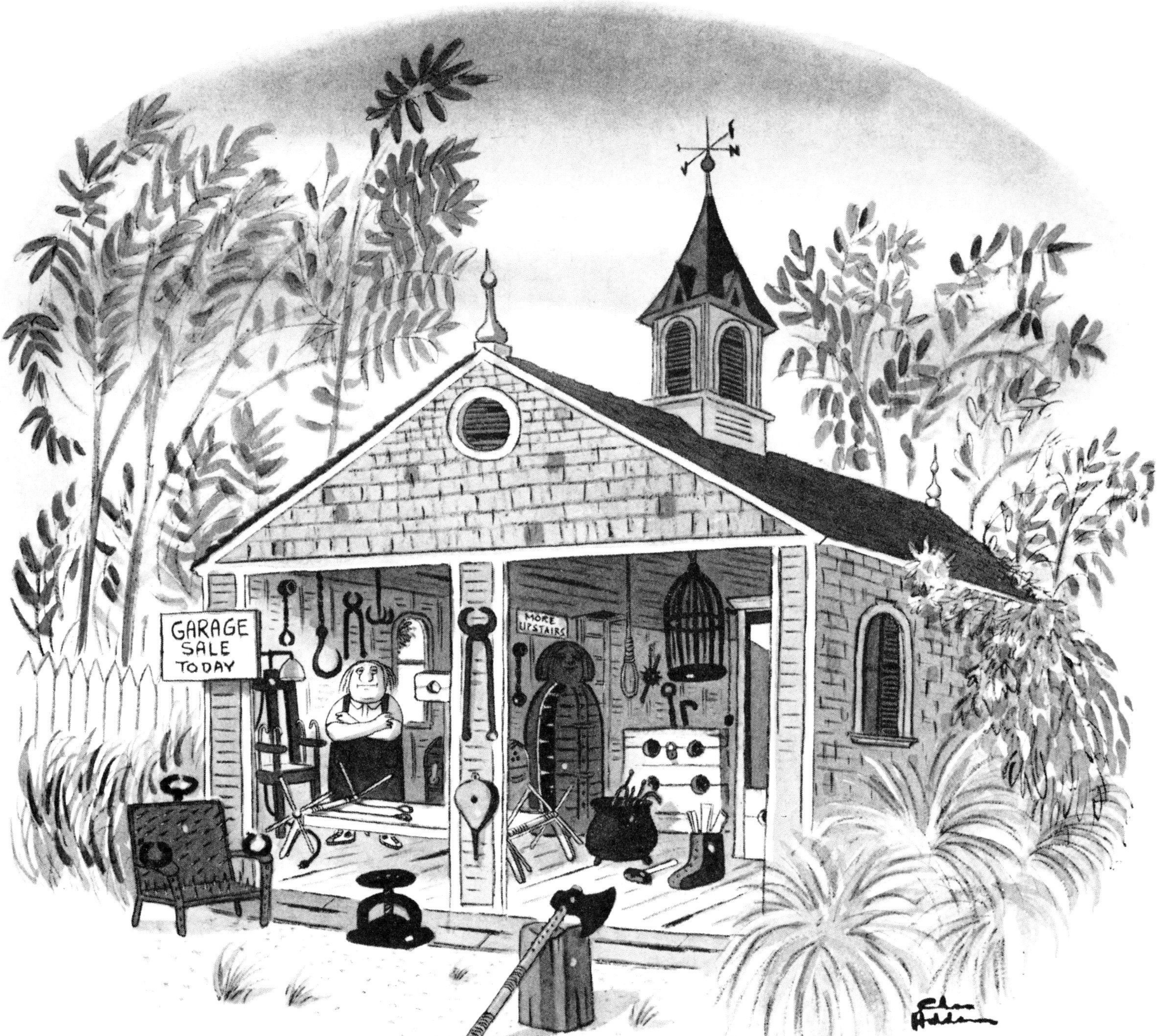
GARAGE SALE TODAY
MORE UPSTAIRS

"When I said you were allowed one phone call, I did not
mean _another_ obscene one."

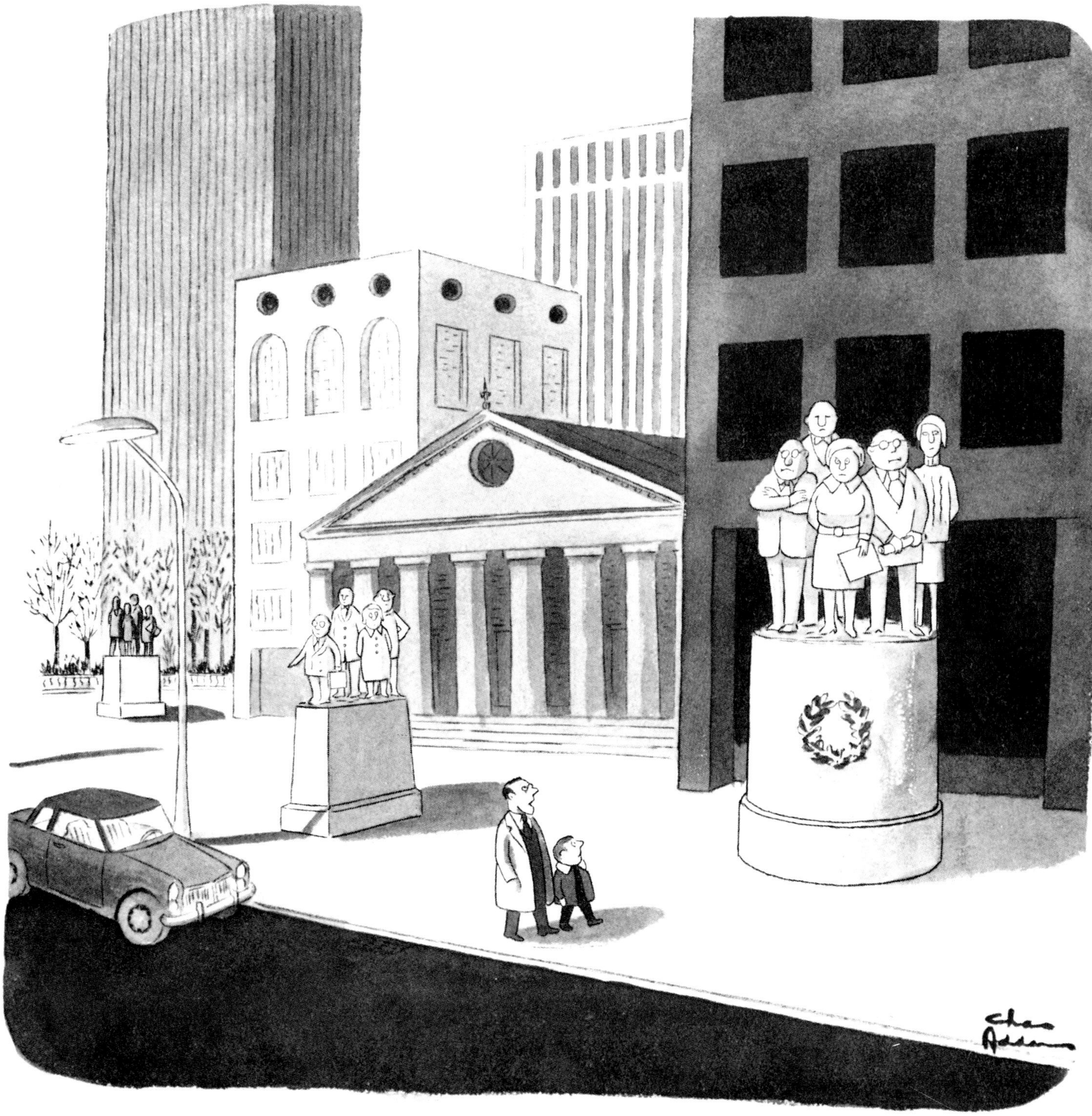
Chas Addams

"There are no great men, my boy—only great committees."

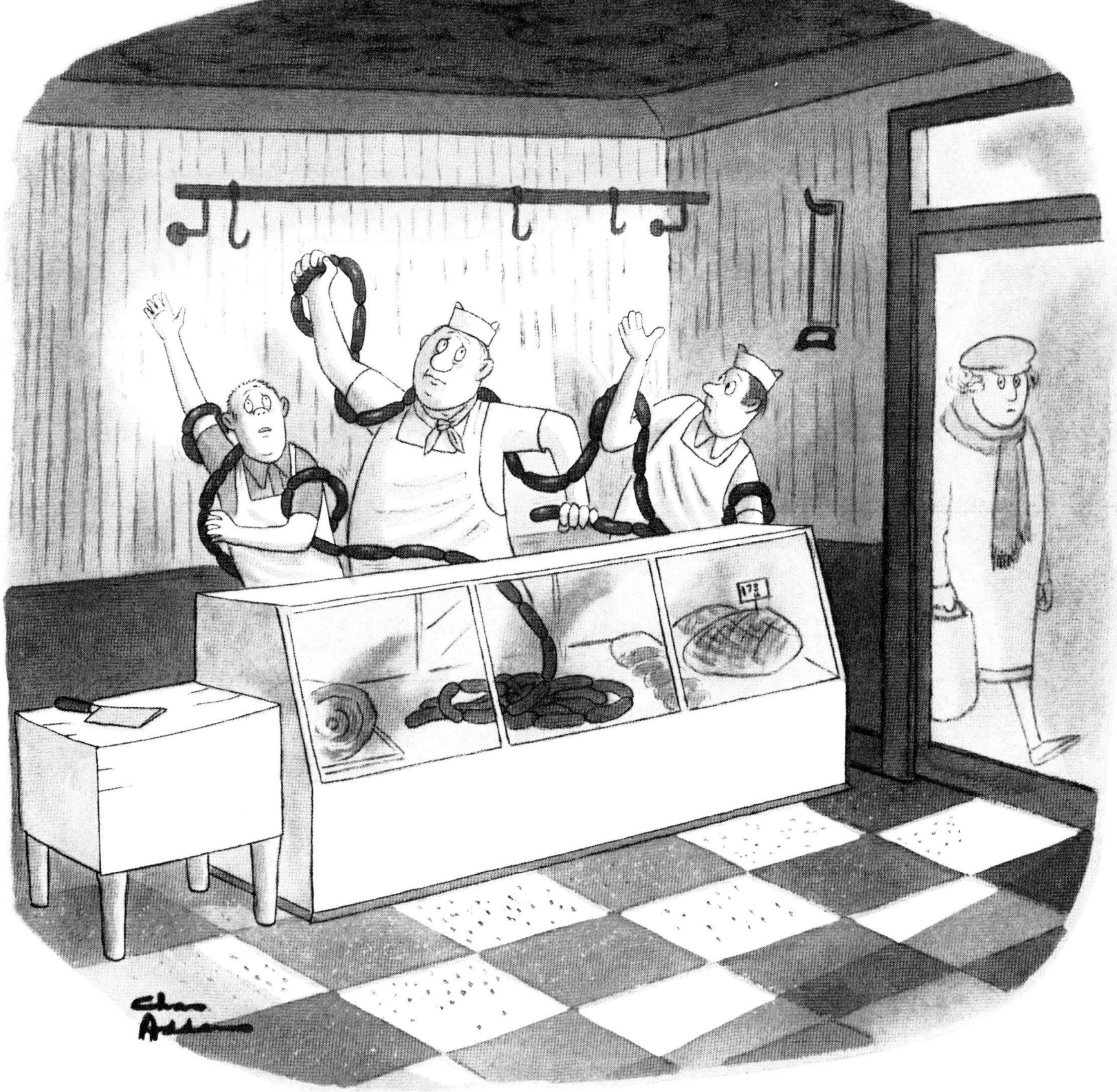
Chas Addams

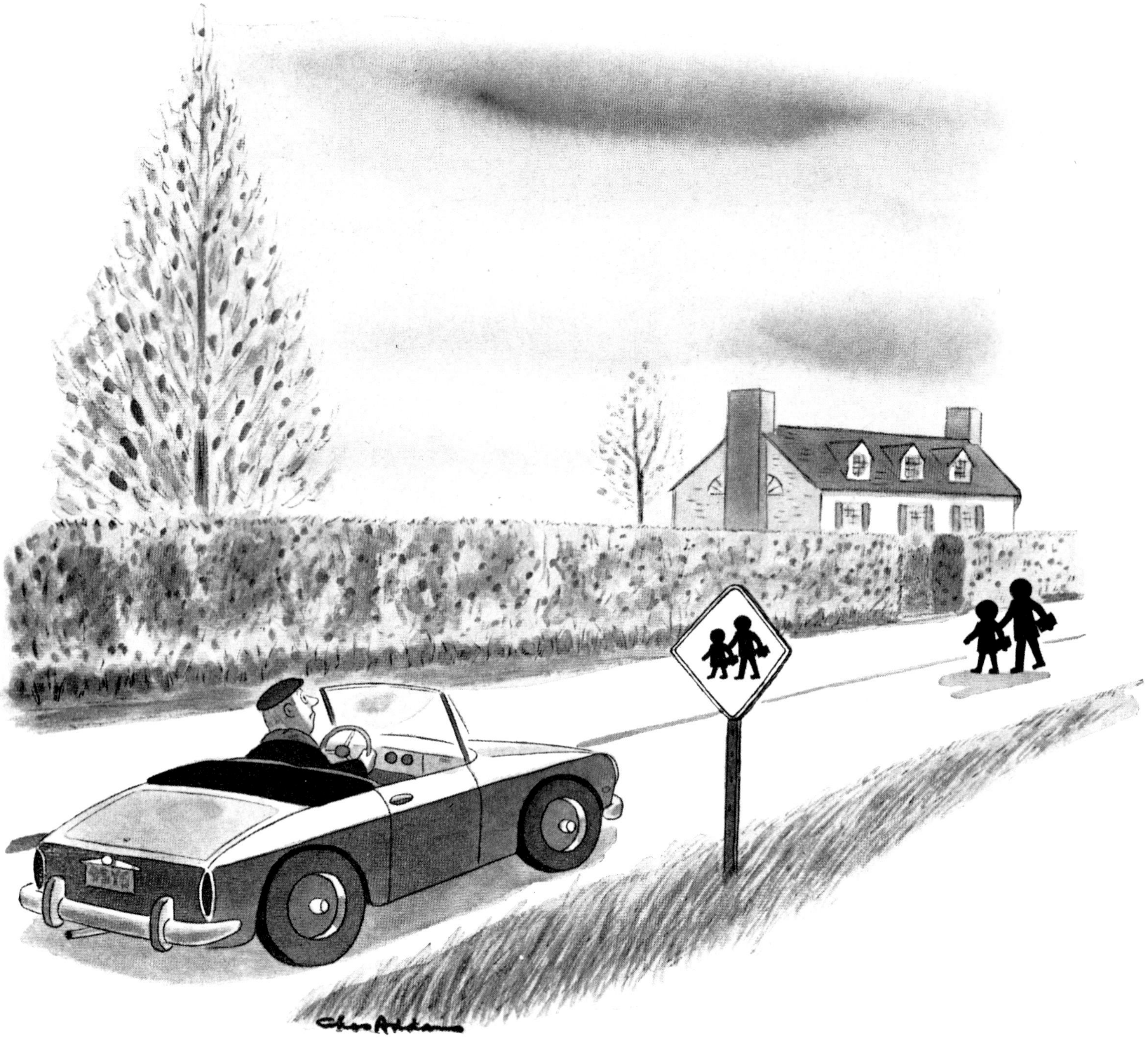

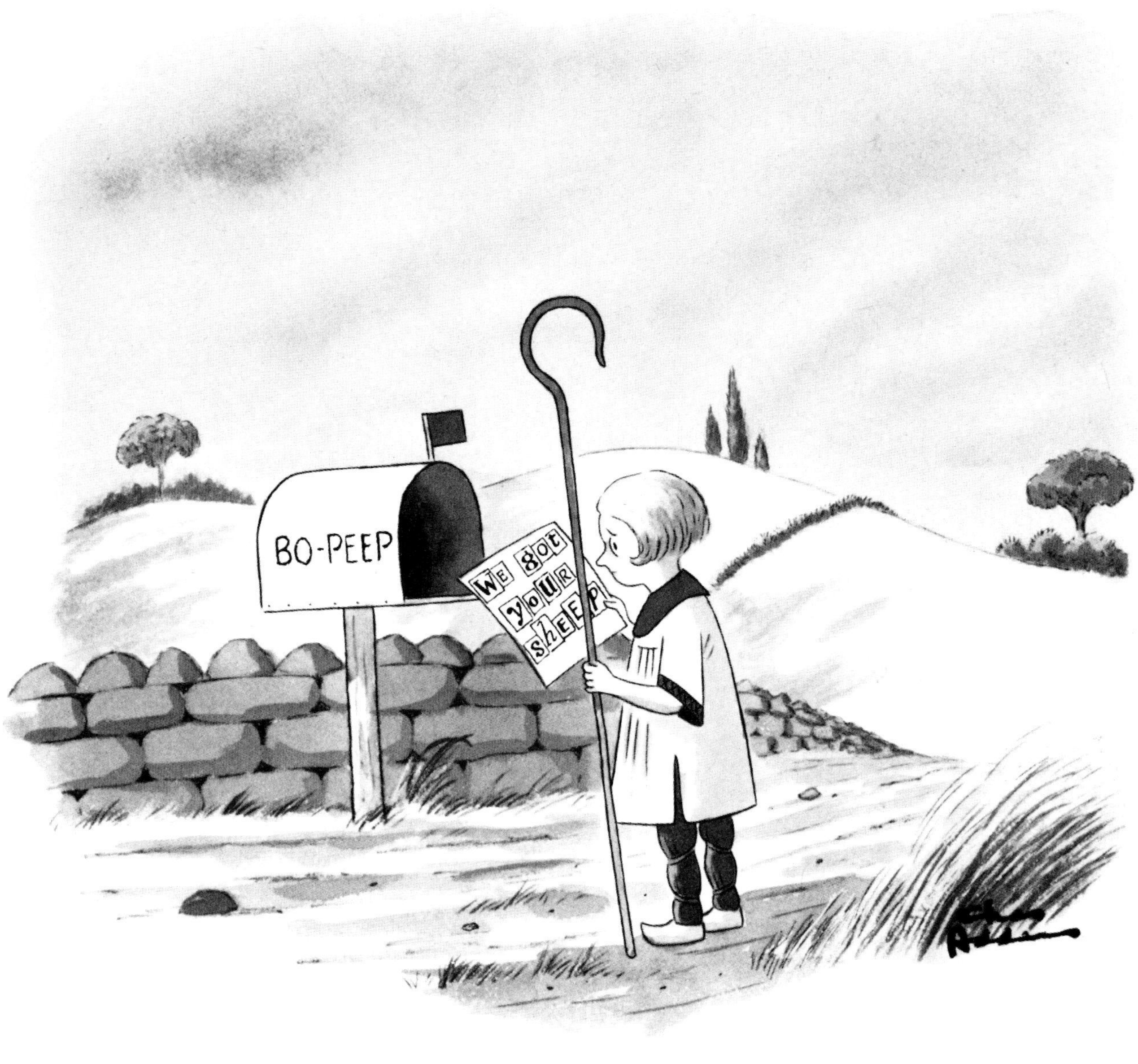
BO-PEEP
We got your sheep

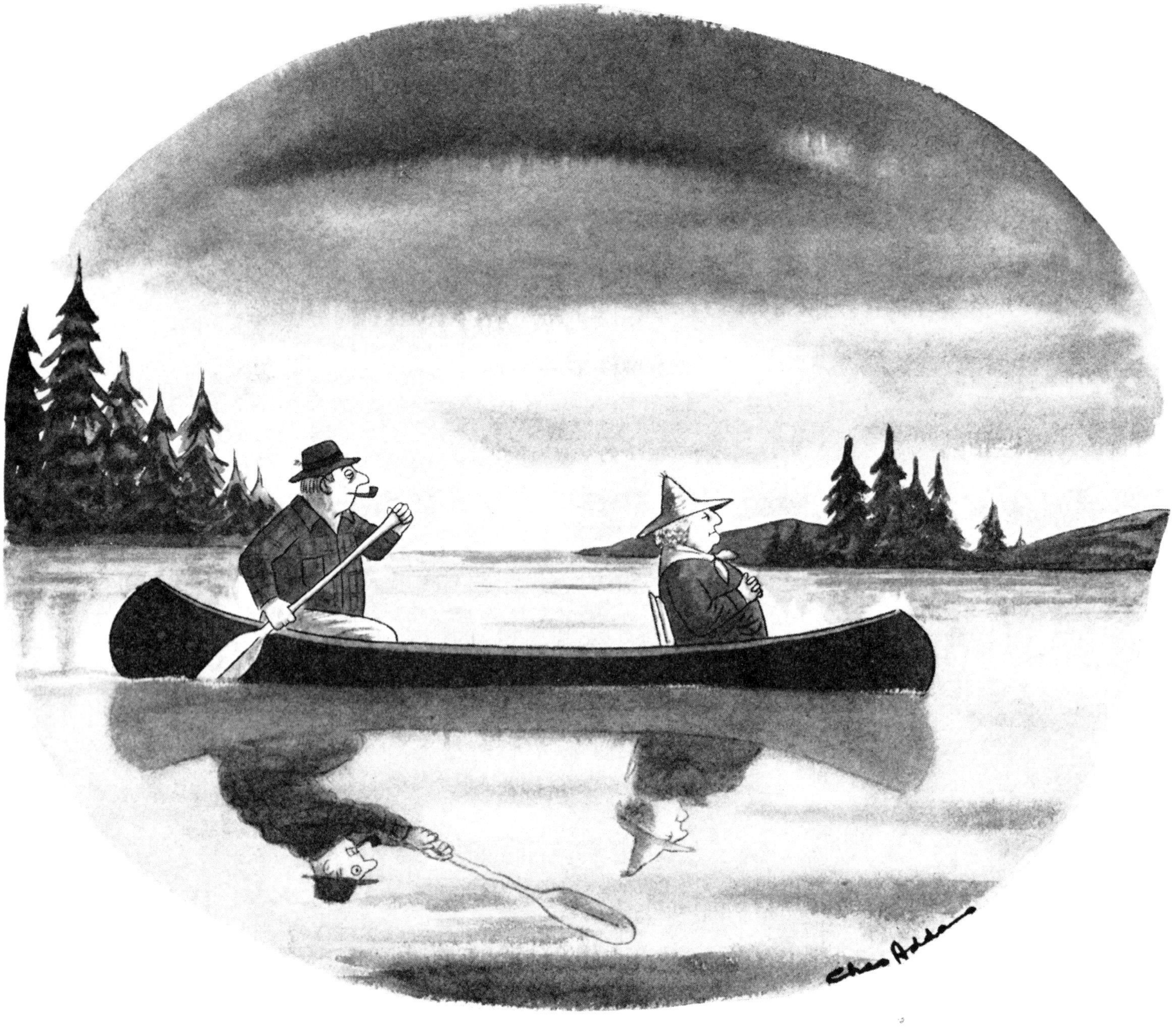
Chas Addams

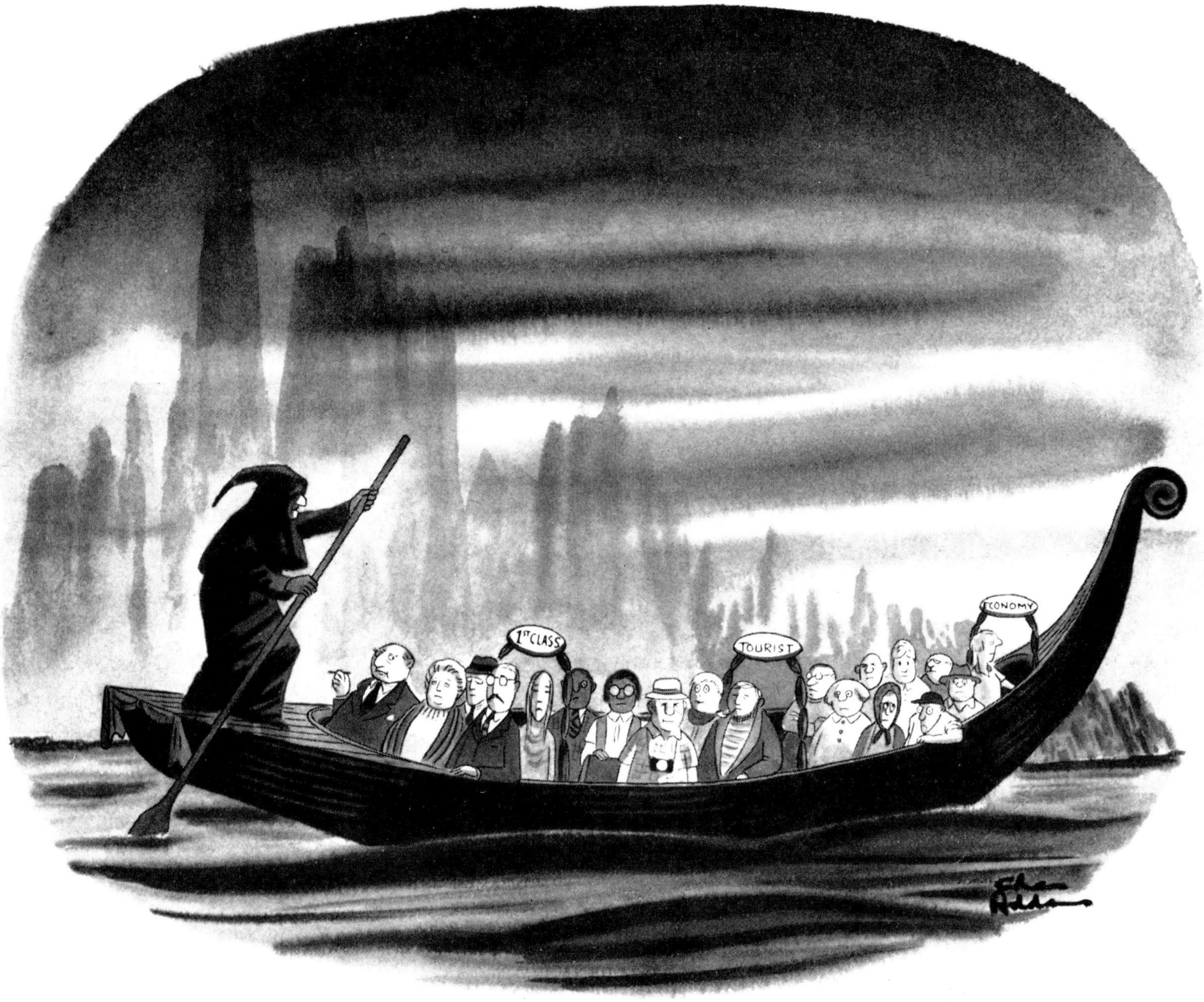
1ST CLASS
TOURIST
ECONOMY

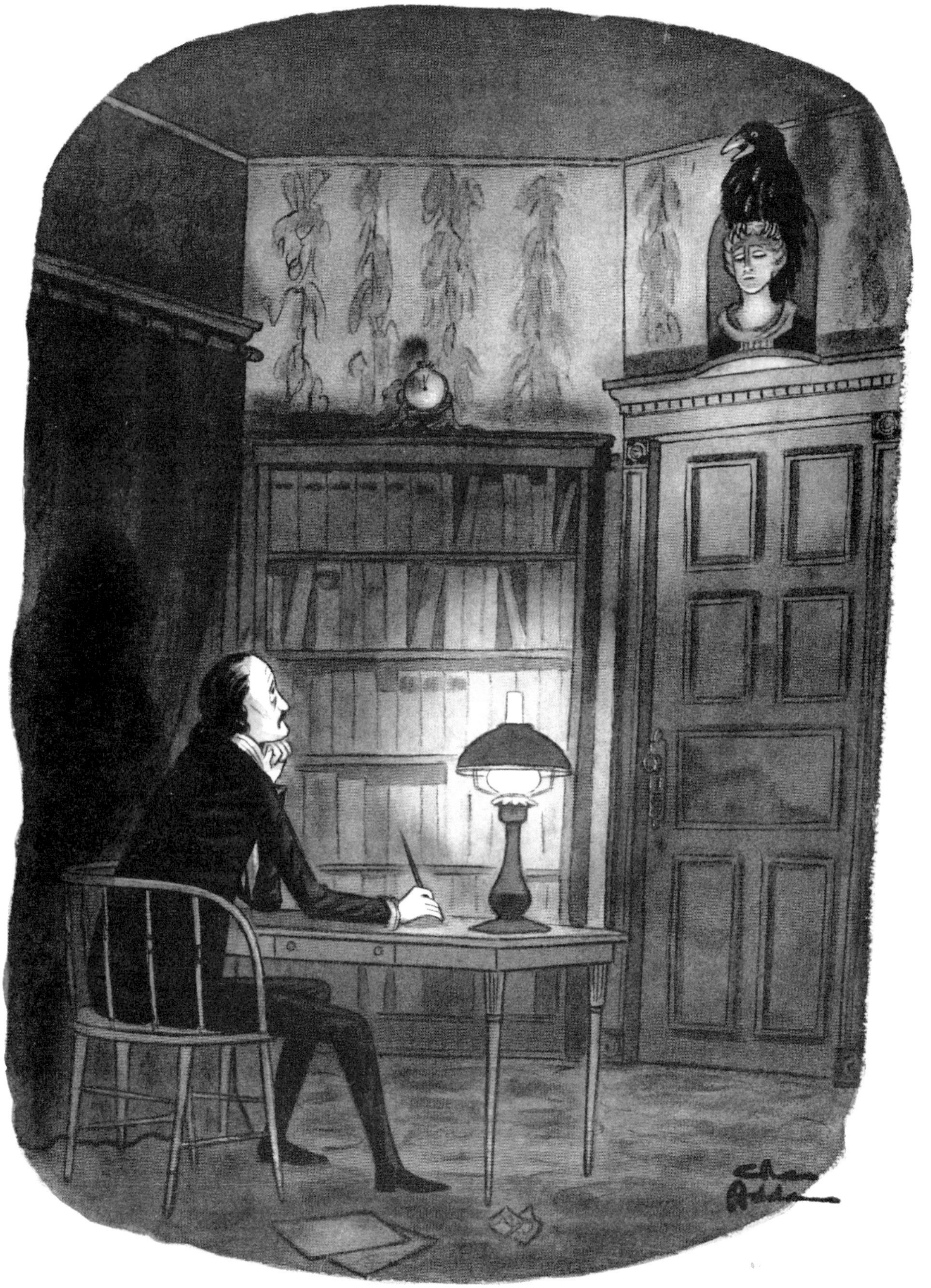

"Occasionally."

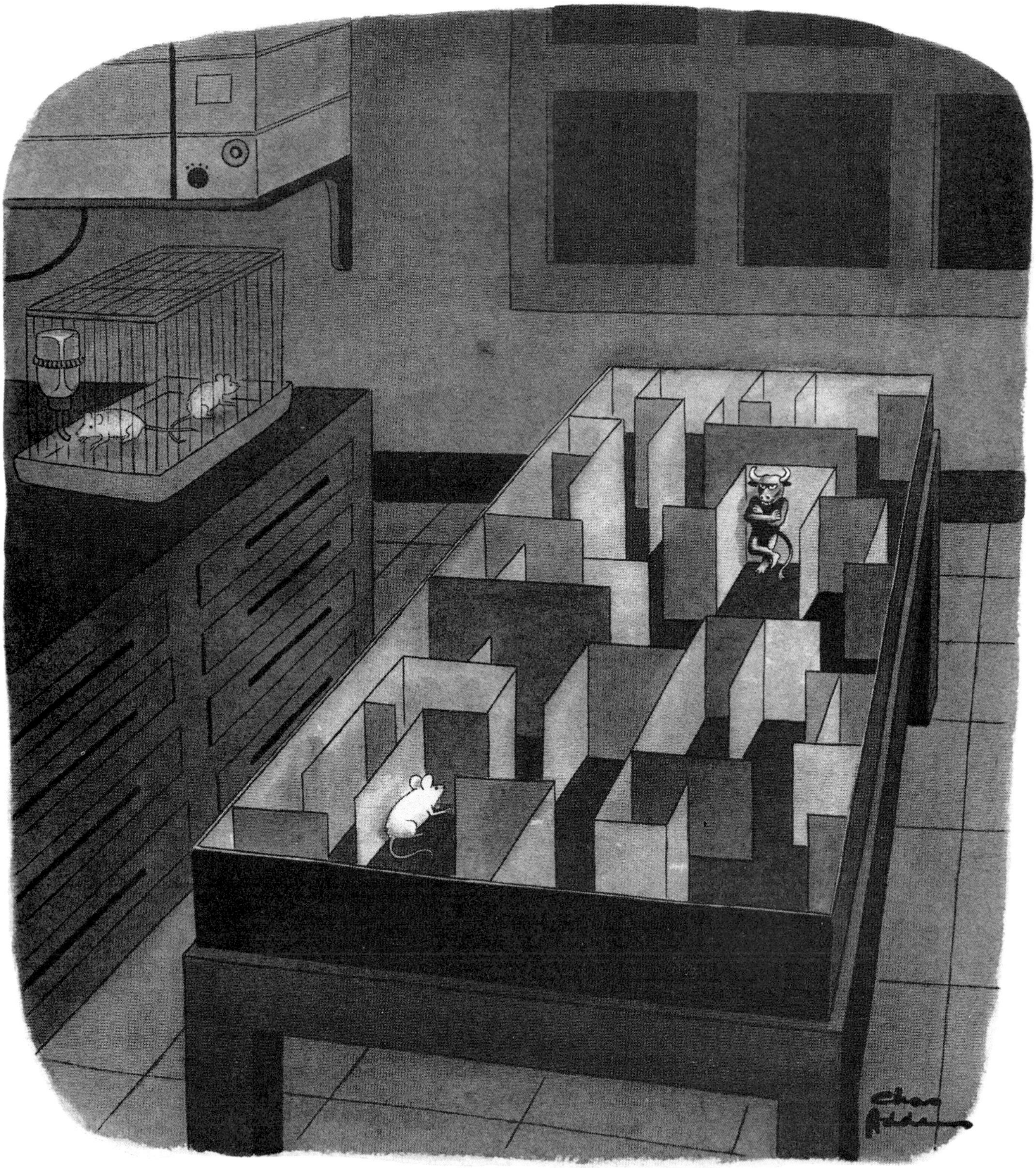

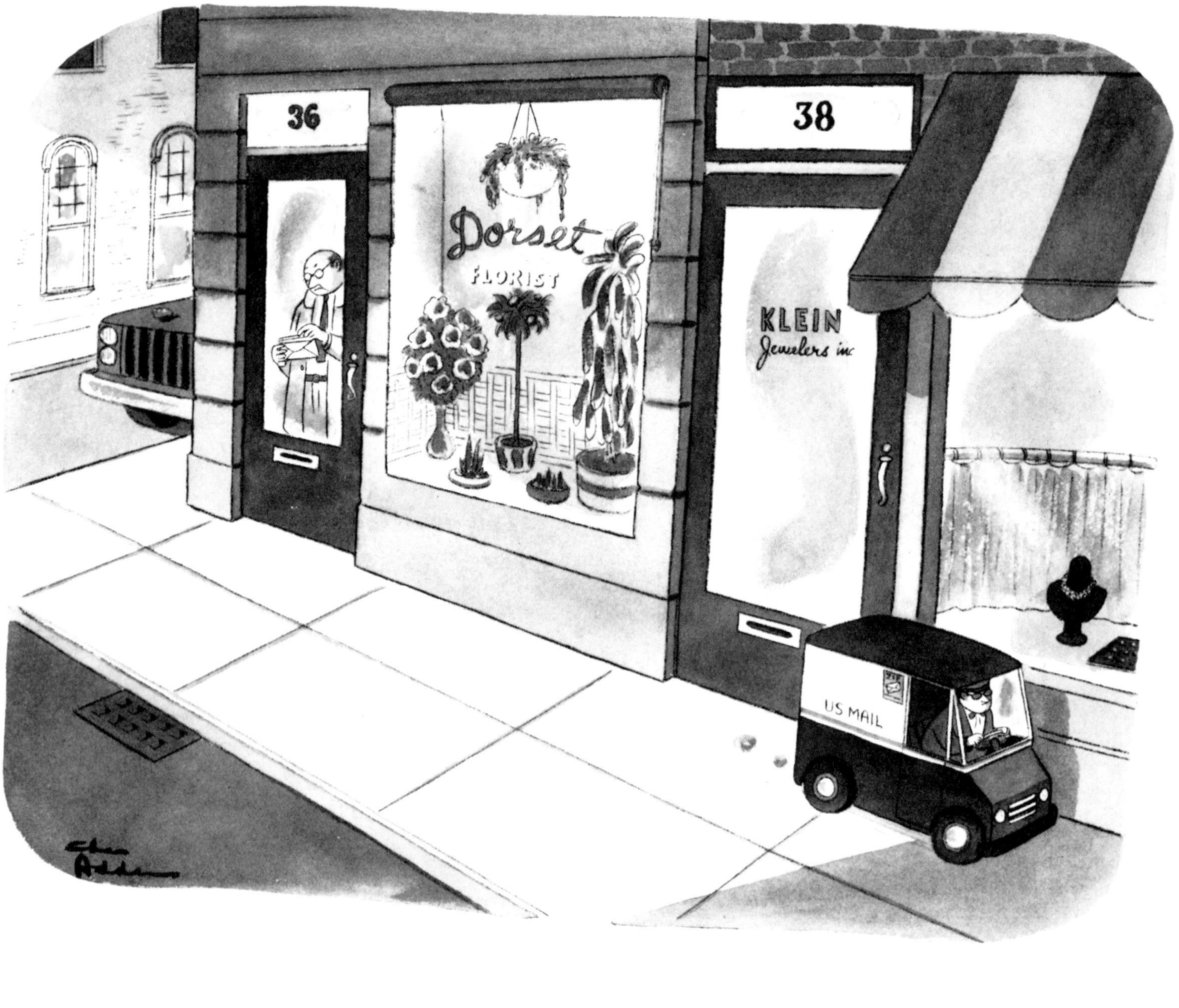
36
Dorset
FLORIST
38
KLEIN
Jewelers inc
US MAIL

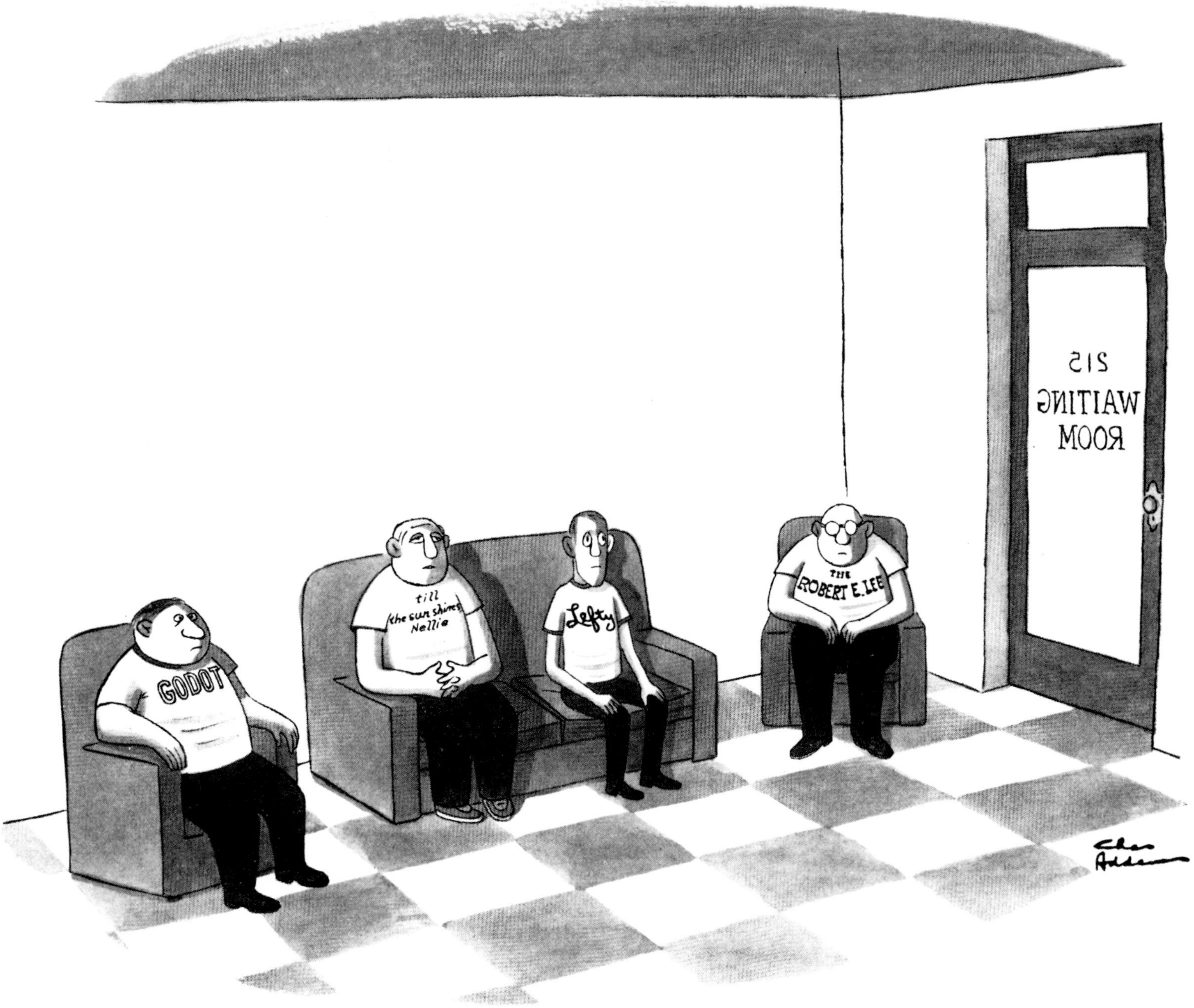
215
WAITING
ROOM
GODOT
till
the sun shines
Nellie
Lefty
THE
ROBERT E. LEE
Chas
Addams

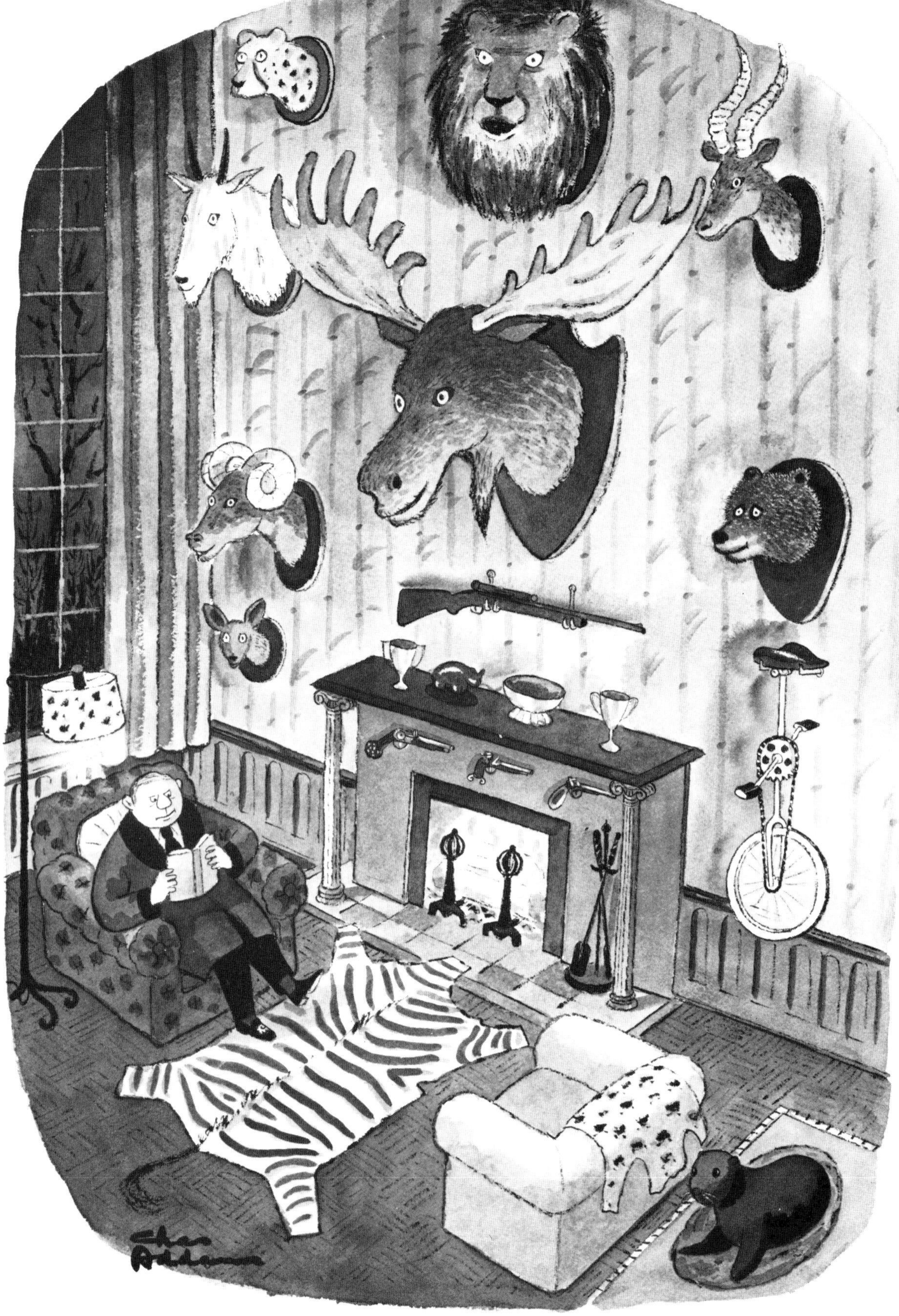
Chas Addams

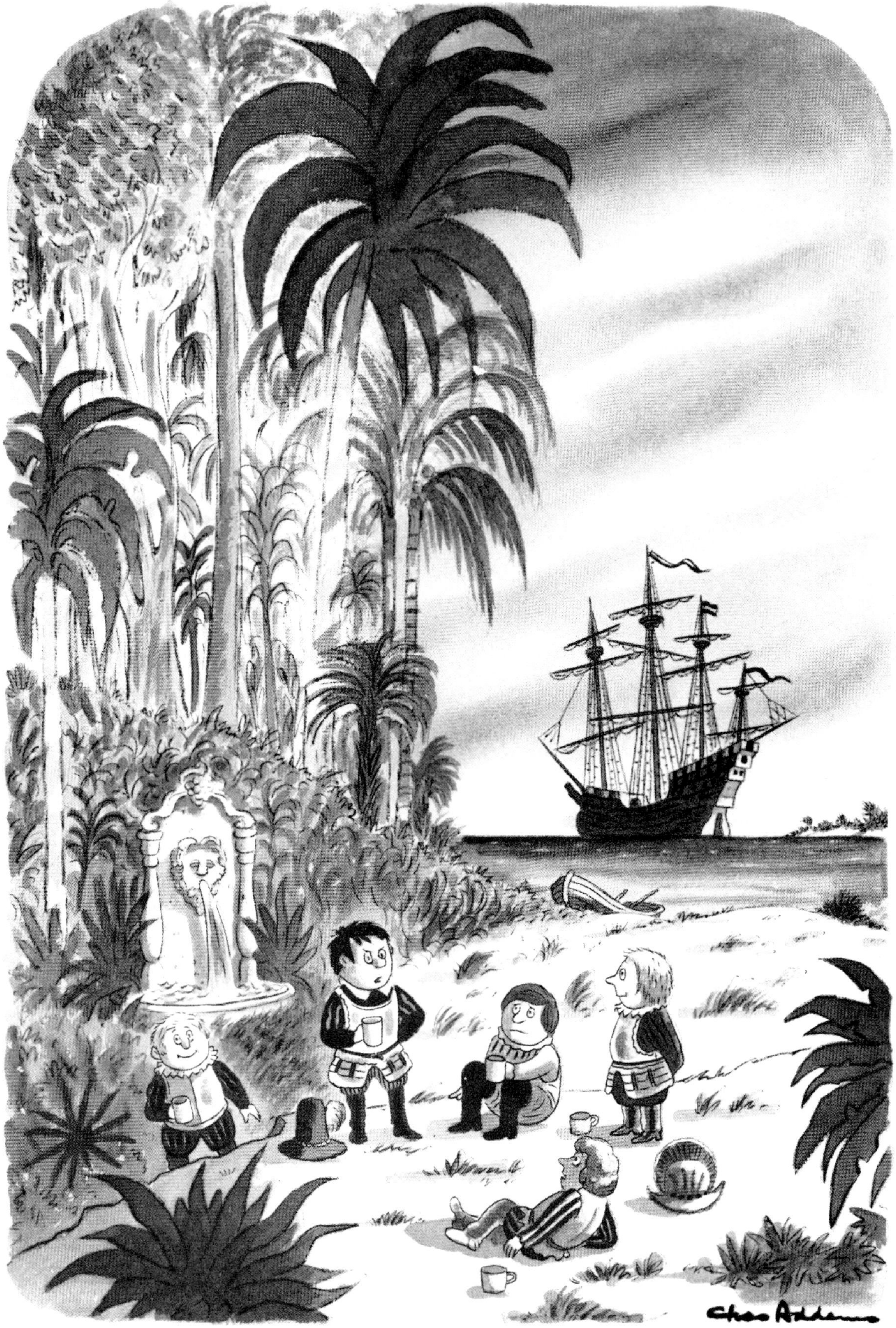
Chas Addams

"So we've discovered the Fountain of Youth. Who's going to sail the old tub back?"

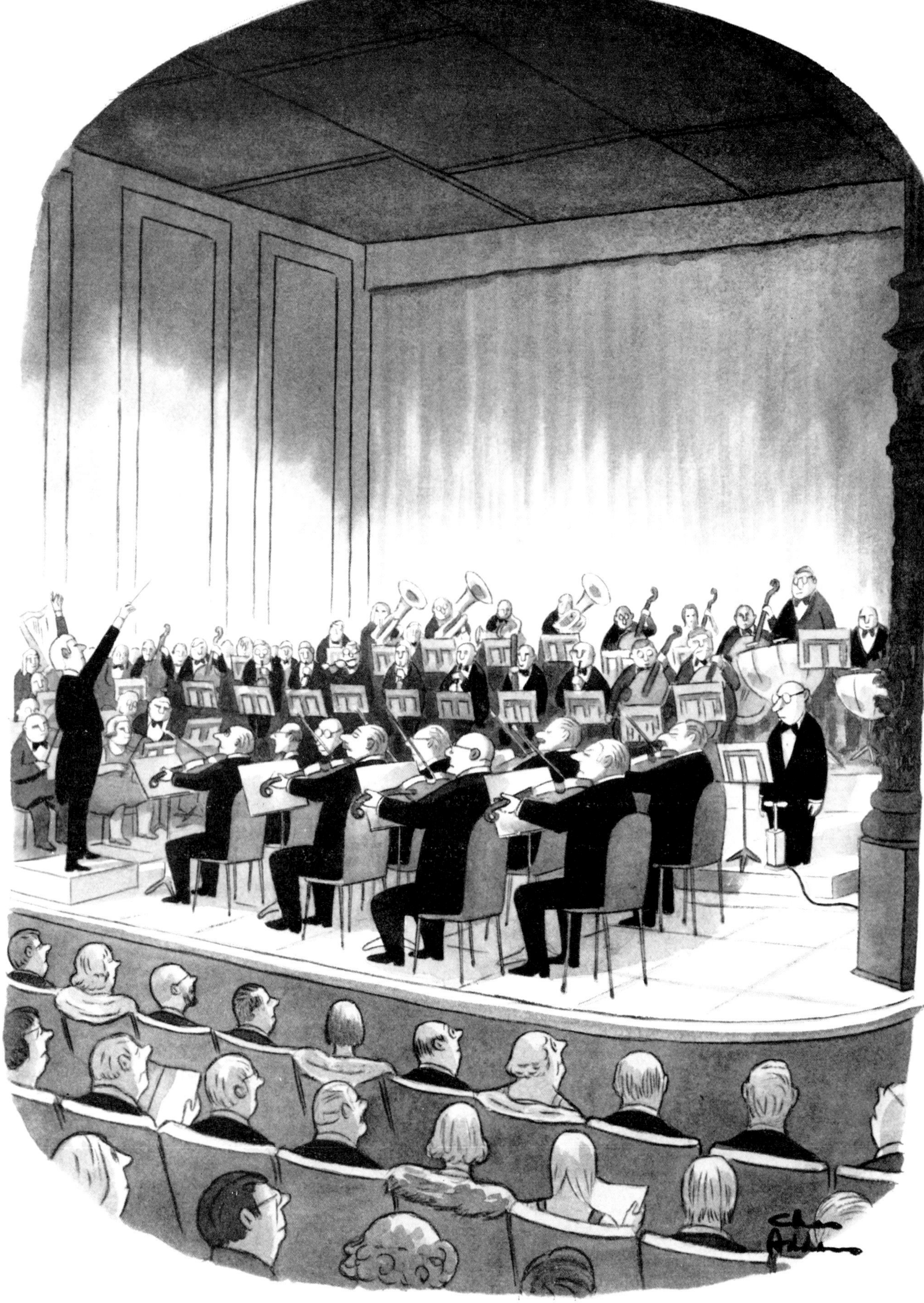

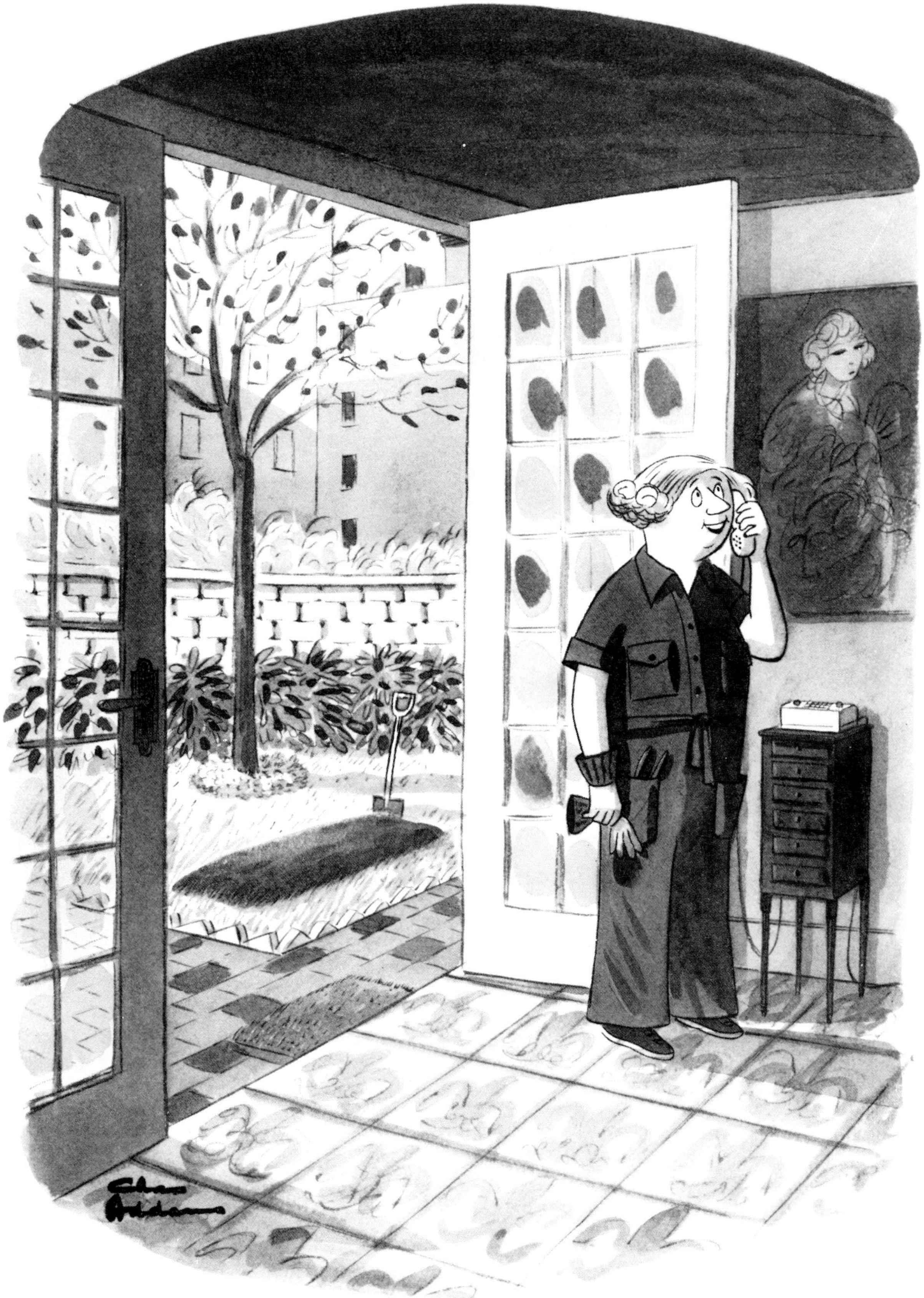
Chas Addams

"He's in the garden."

"Why can't we go to the mountains this year?"

"I'm sorry, Travers, but I'm going to have to let you go."

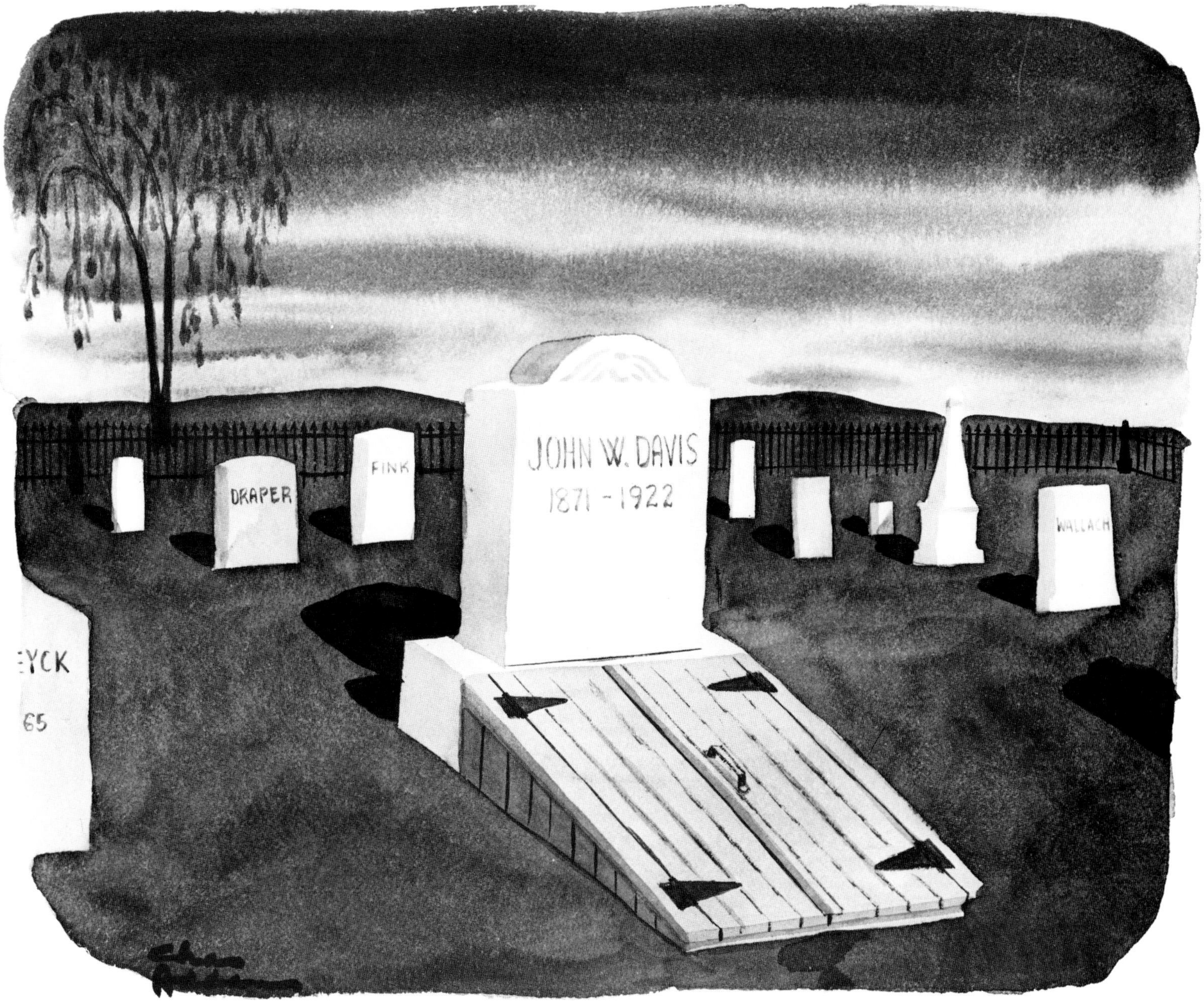
JOHN W. DAVIS
1871 - 1922
DRAPER
FINK
WALLACH
EYCK
65

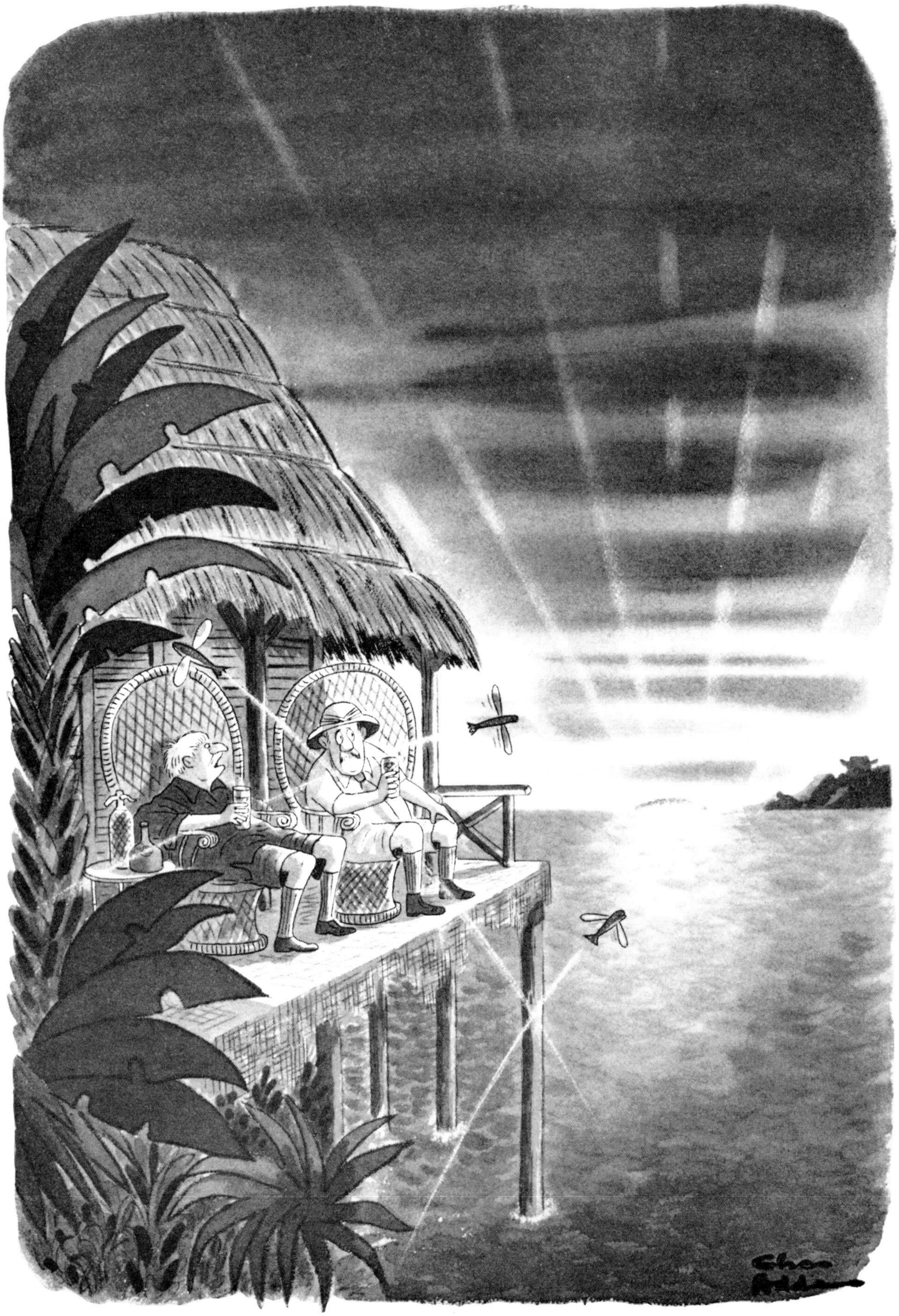

"One gets used to the flying fishes, but that bloody dawn coming up like thunder is driving me crackers."

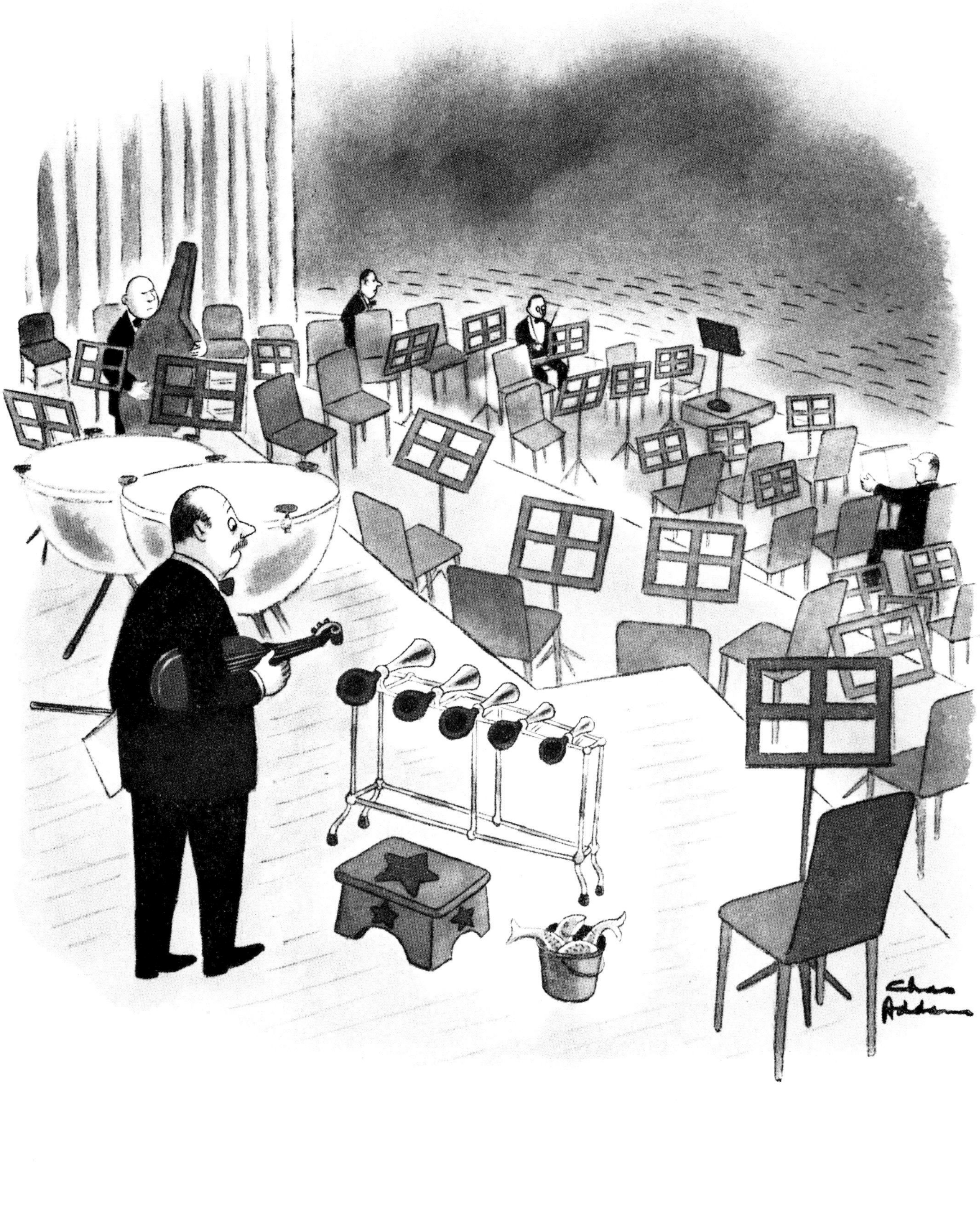
Chas Addams

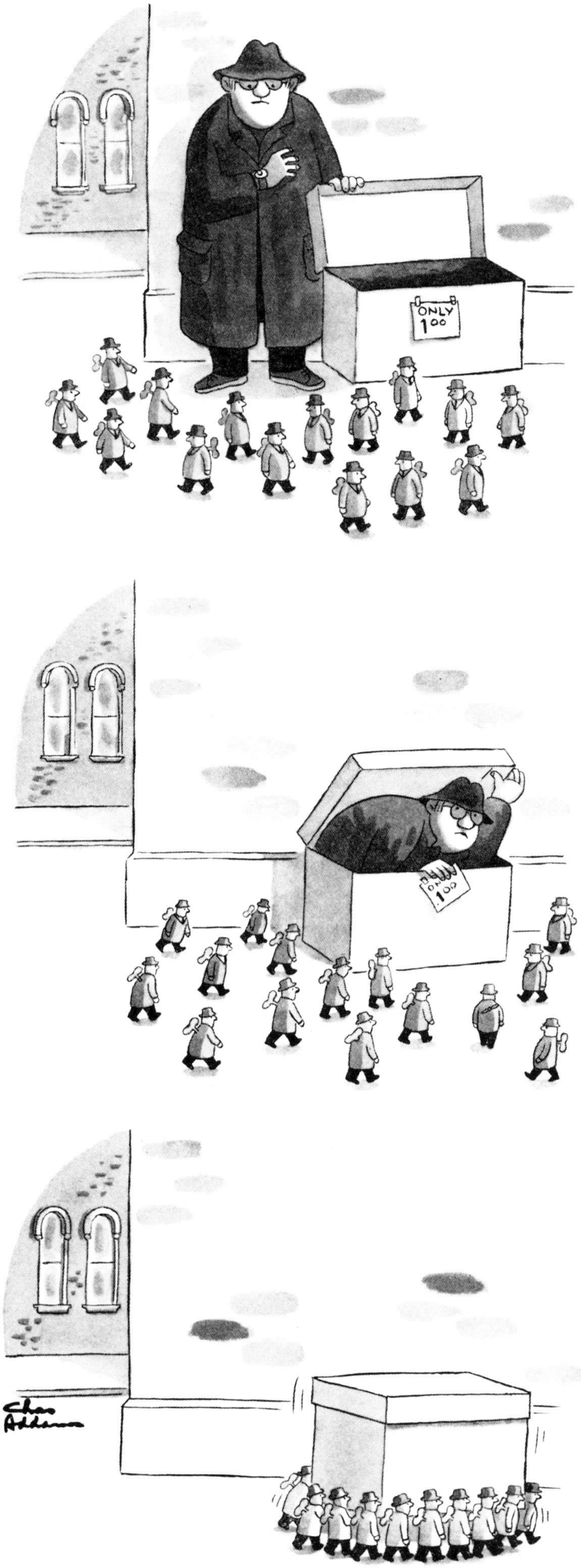
ONLY 1 00
Chas Addams

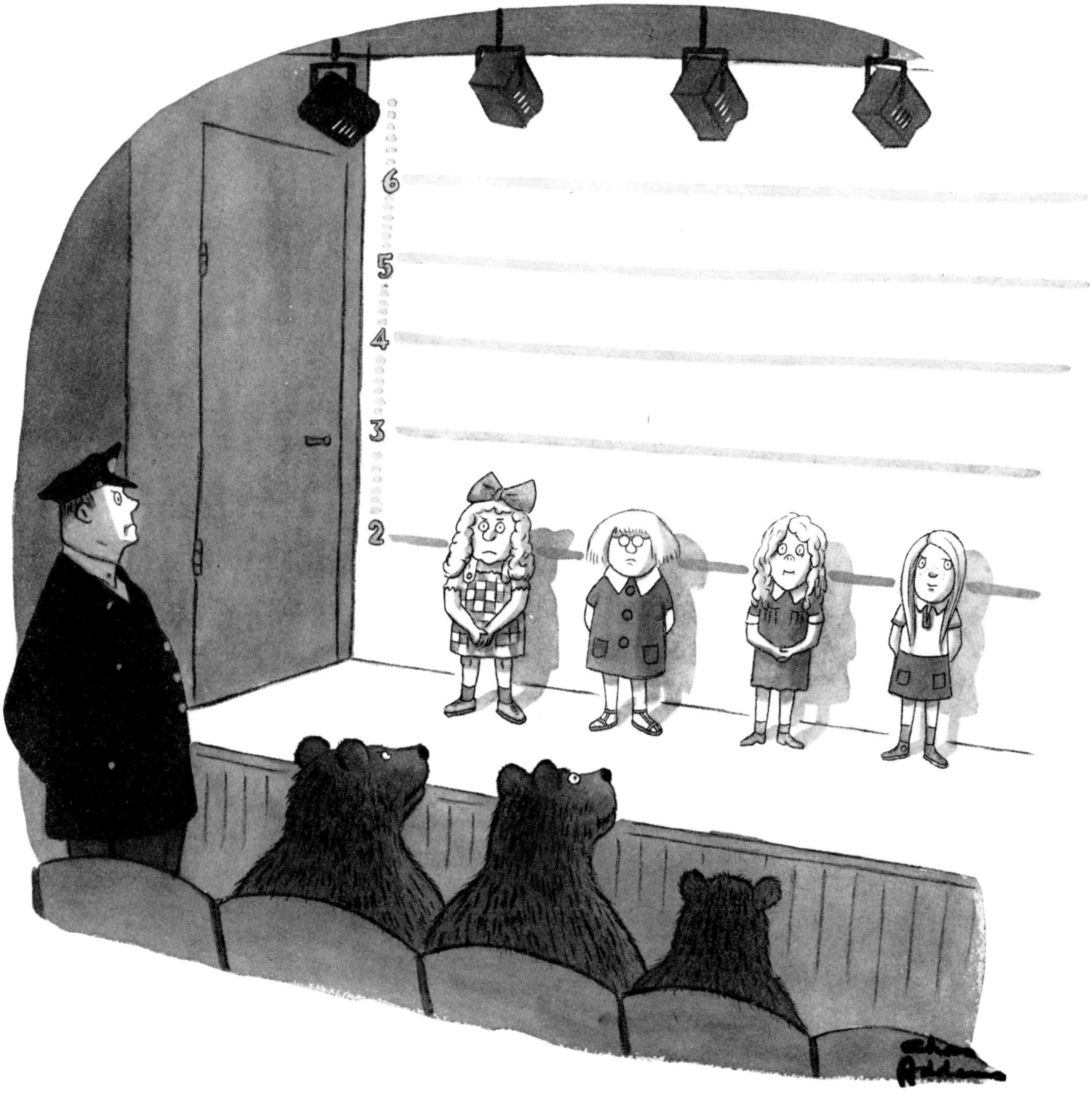
6
5
4
3
2

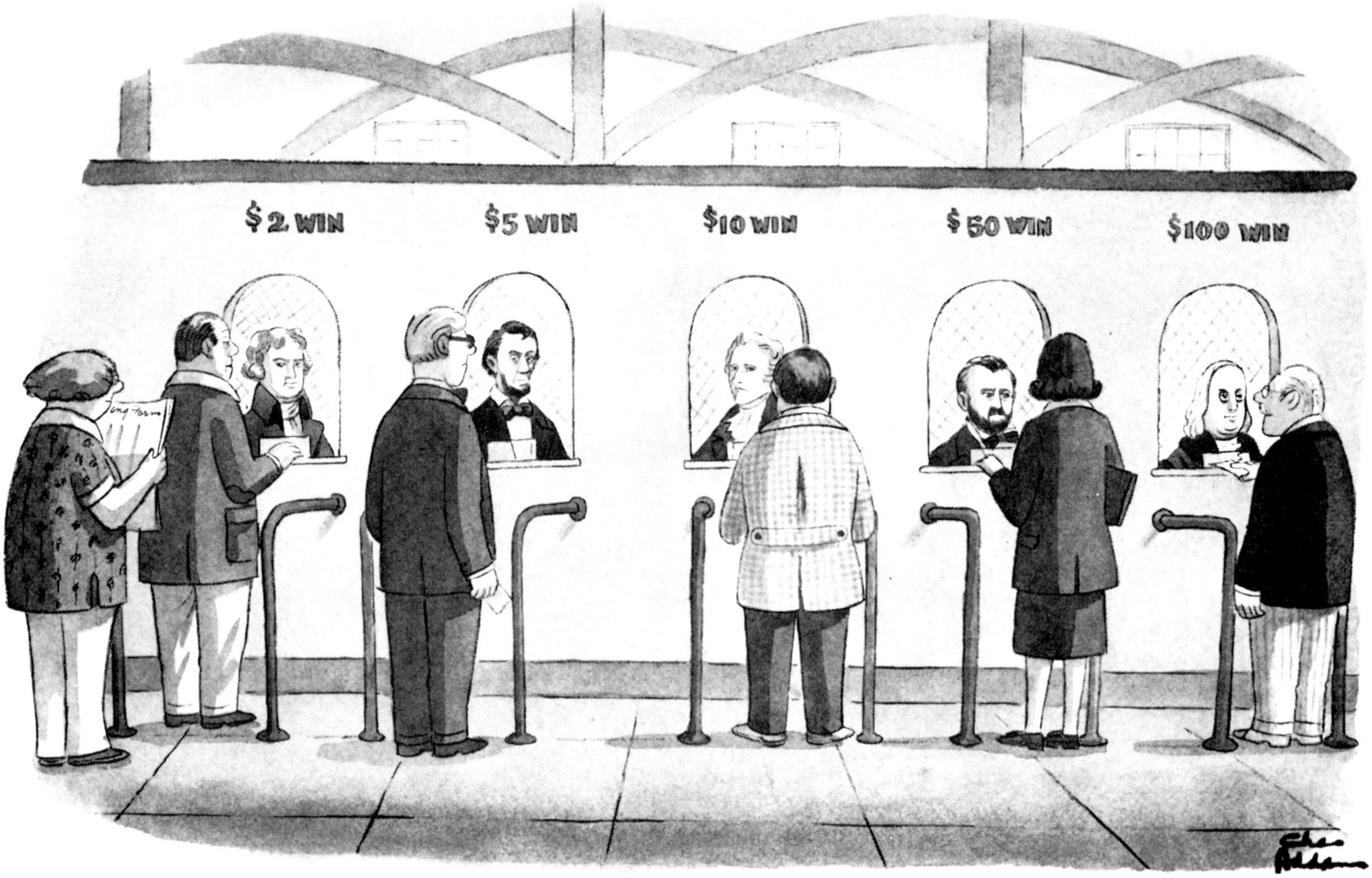
$2 WIN
$5 WIN
$10 WIN
$50 WIN
$100 WIN

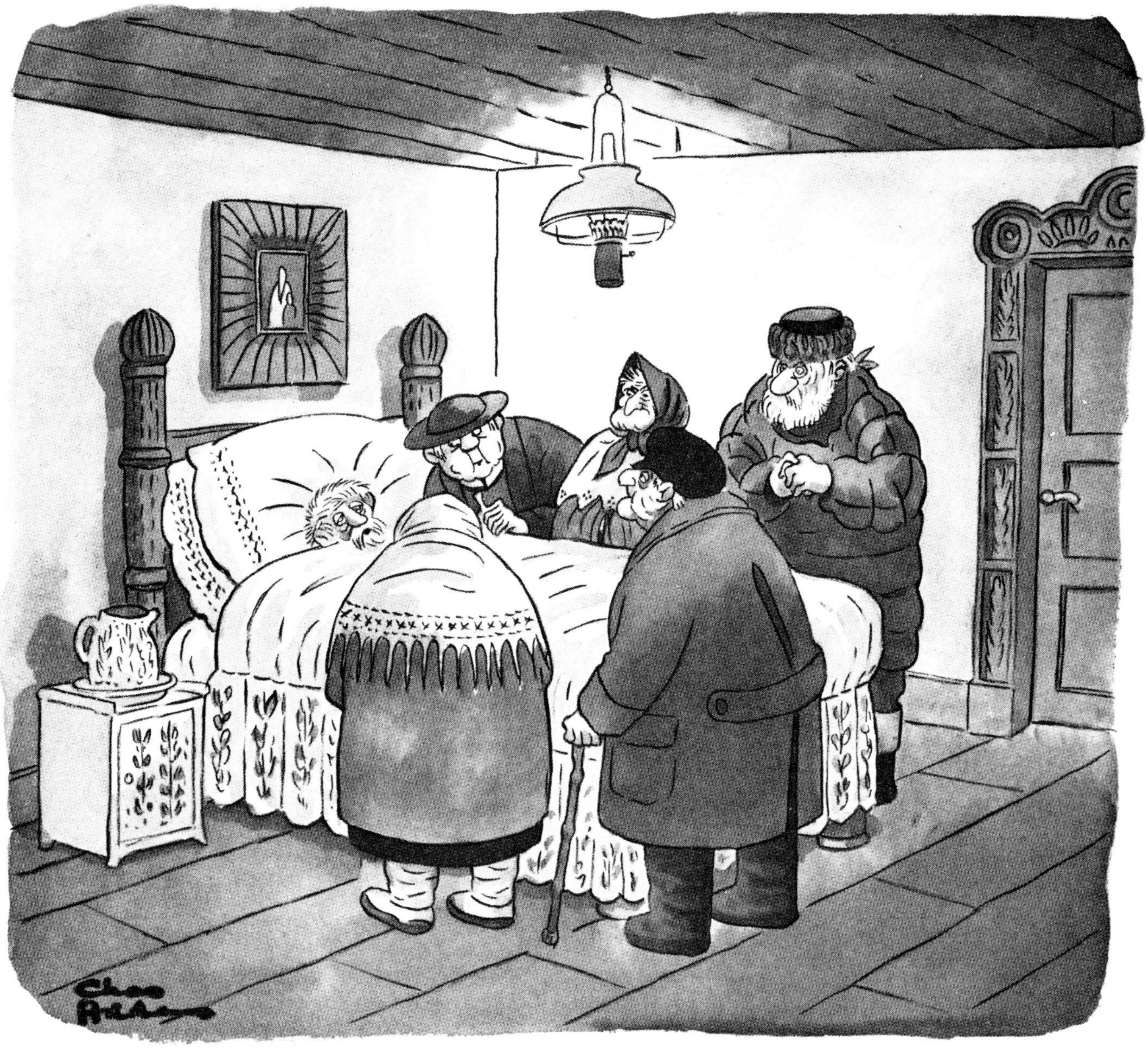
Chas Addams

"To . . . hell . . . with . . . yogurt."

"I think you know everybody."

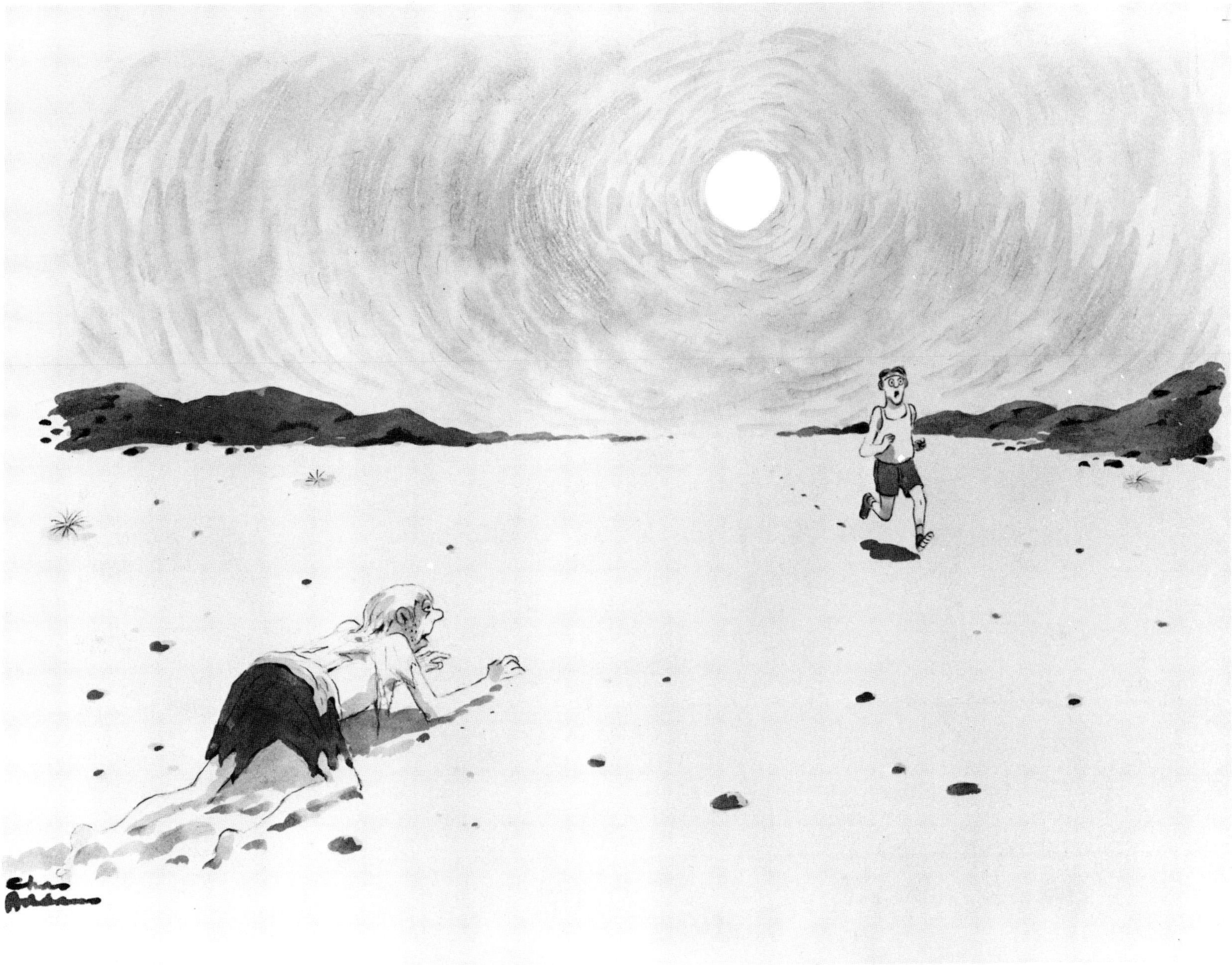
Chas Addams

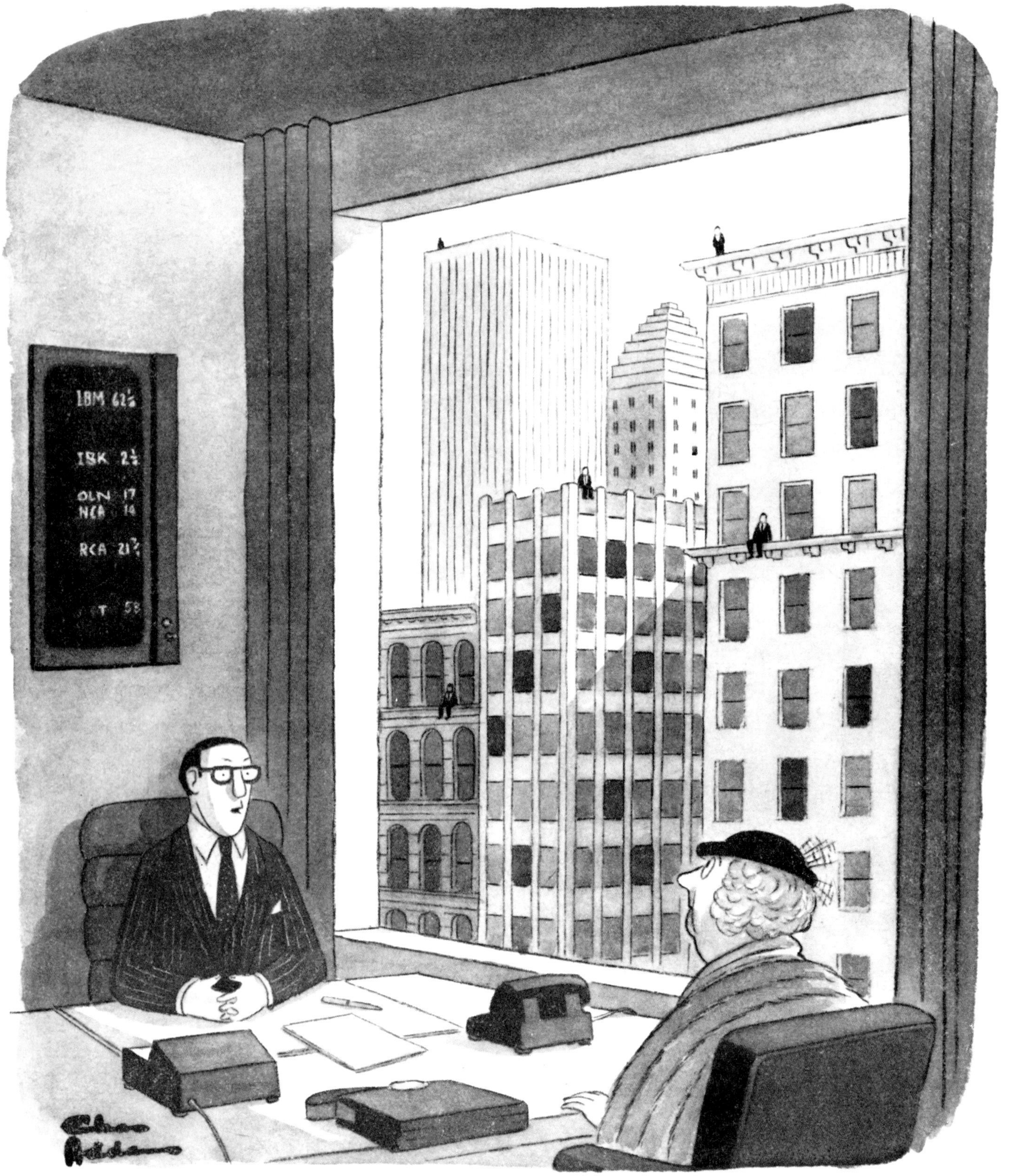
IBM 62½
IBK 2½
OLN 17
NCA 14
RCA 21⅞
58
Chas Addams

"There's no cause for panic, Mrs. Munson, but, frankly, there are certain indicators that cannot be ignored."

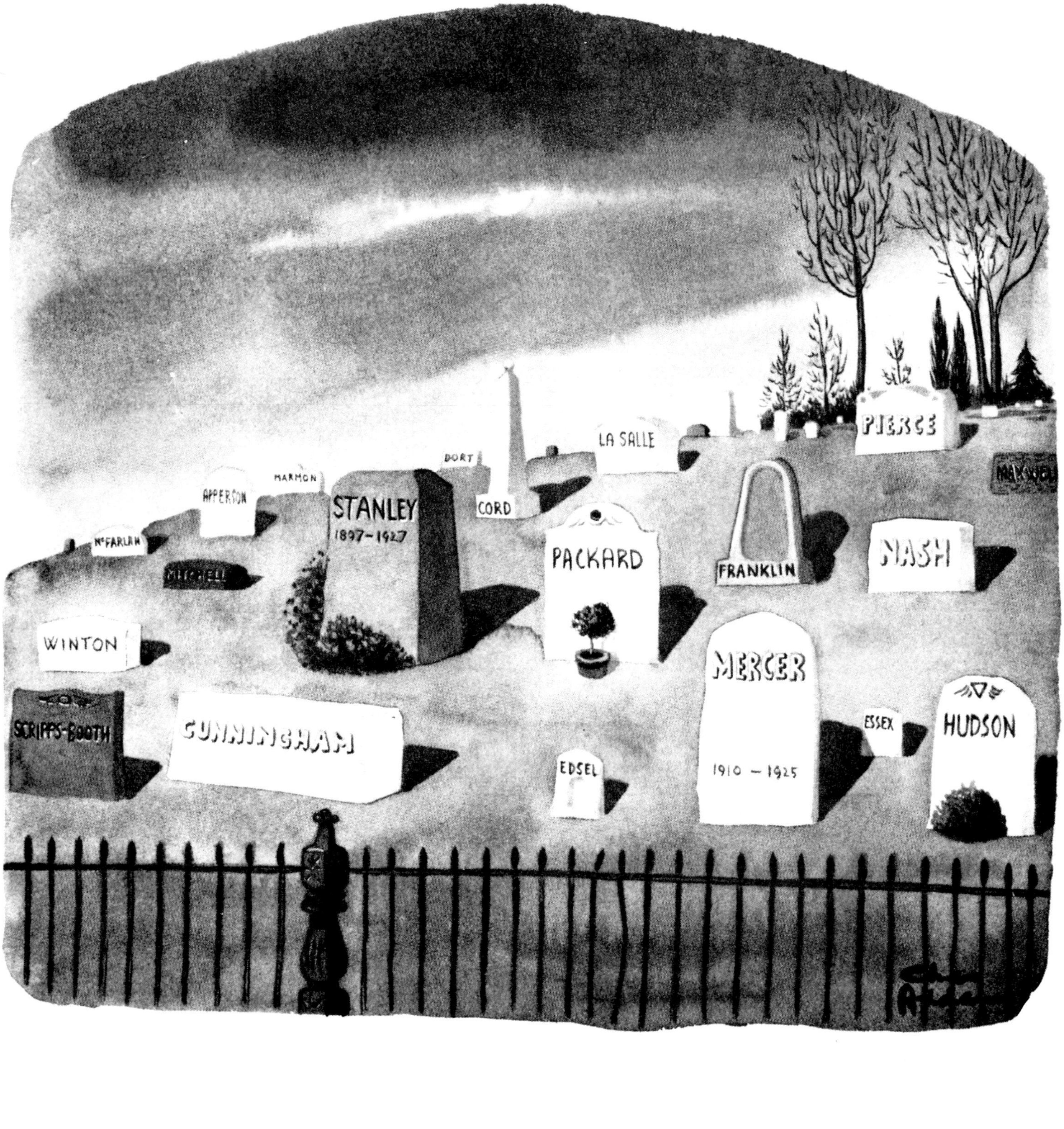
PIERCE
LA SALLE
DORT
HARMON
APPERSON
STANLEY
1897–1927
CORD
McFARLAN
MITCHELL
PACKARD
FRANKLIN
NASH
MAXWELL
WINTON
MERCER
1910 – 1925
SCRIPPS-BOOTH
CUNNINGHAM
EDSEL
ESSEX
HUDSON

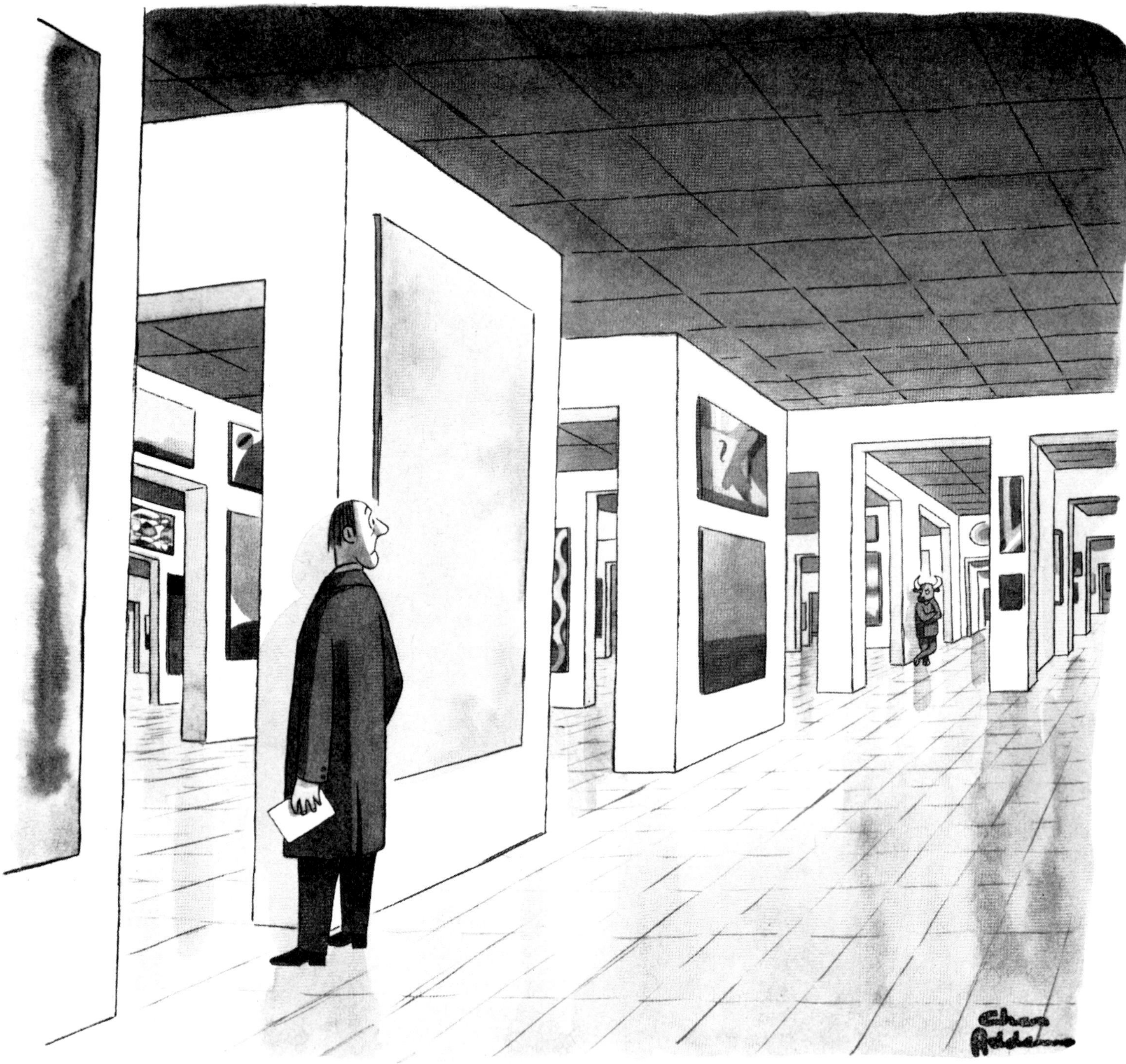

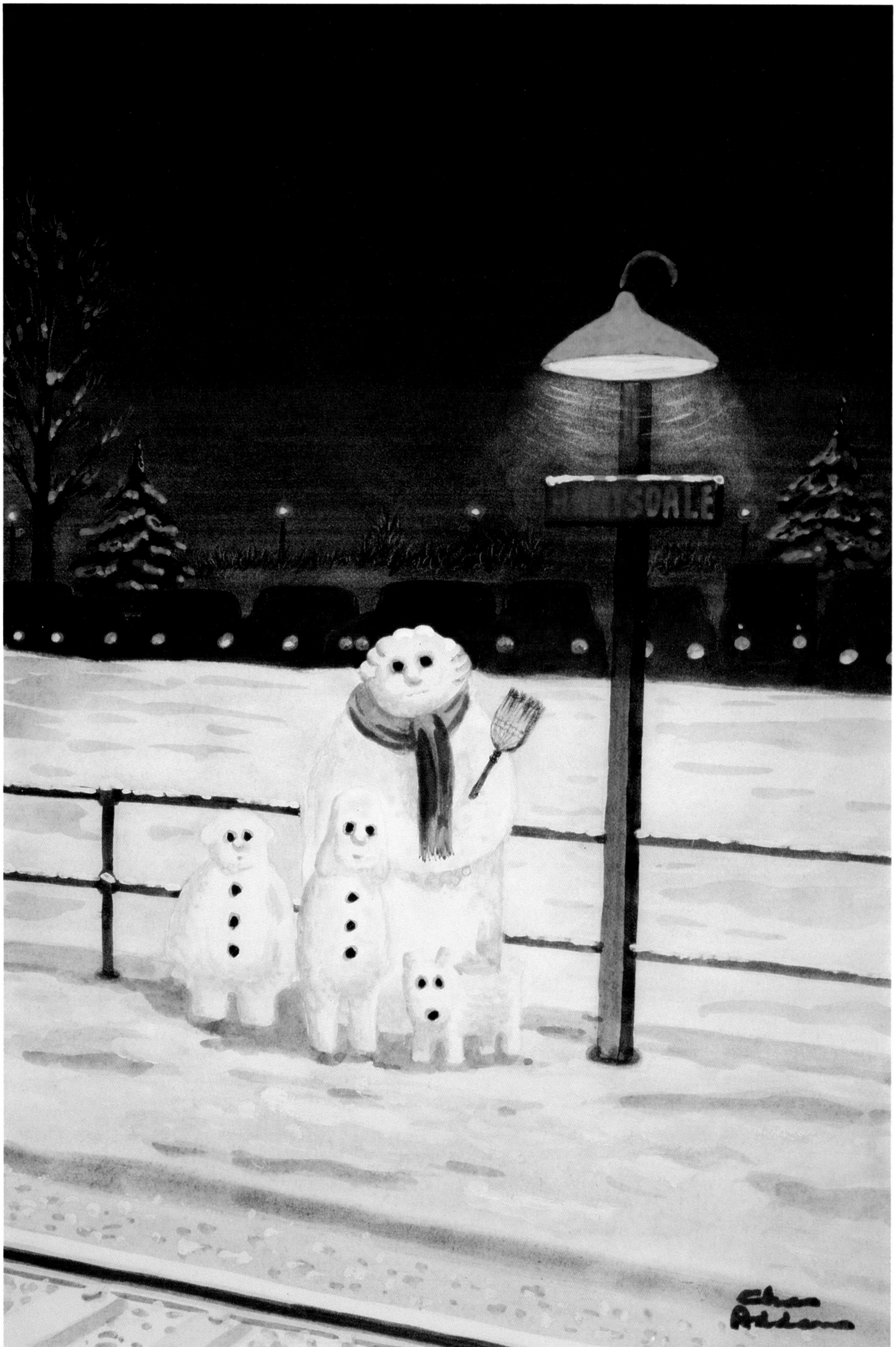

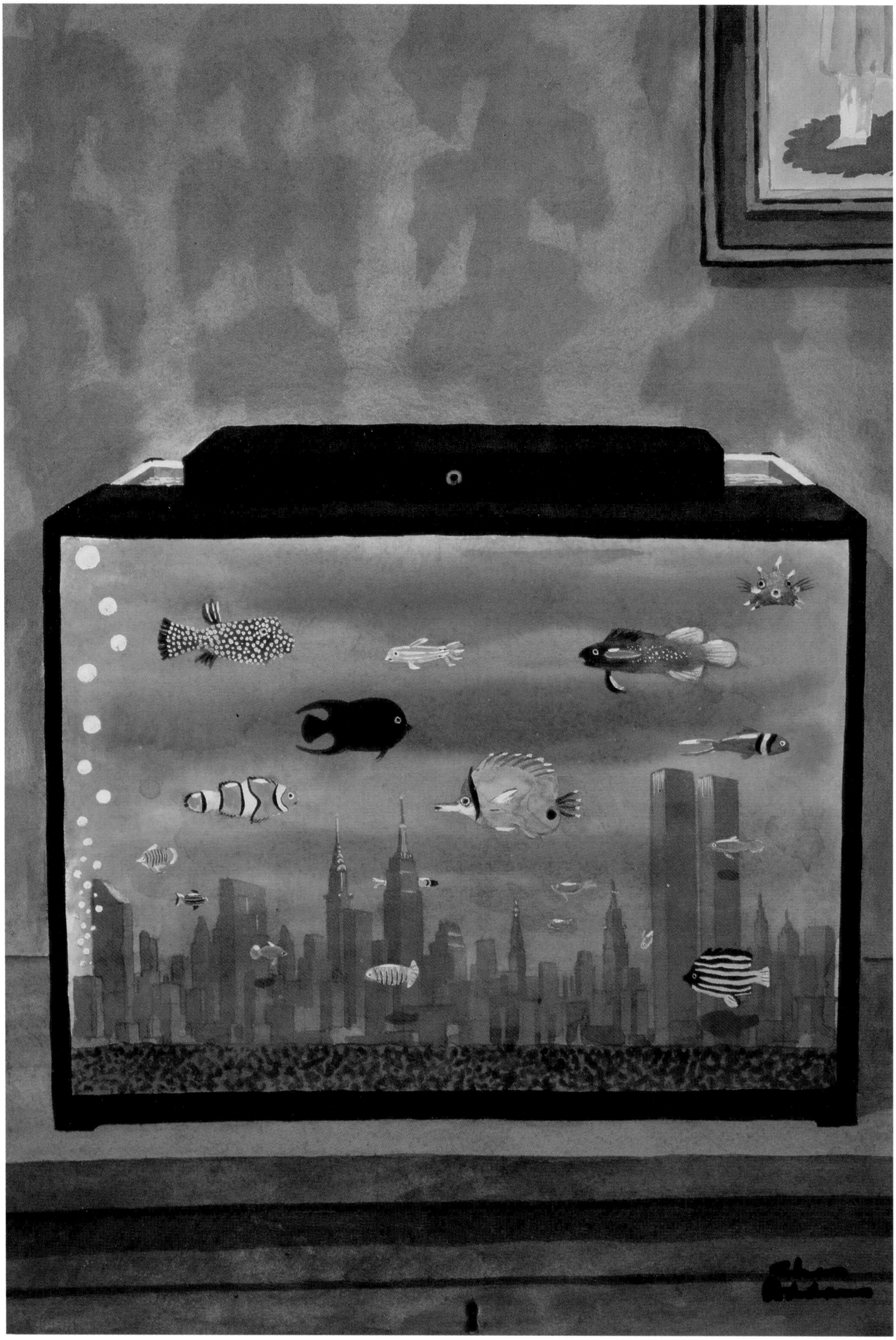

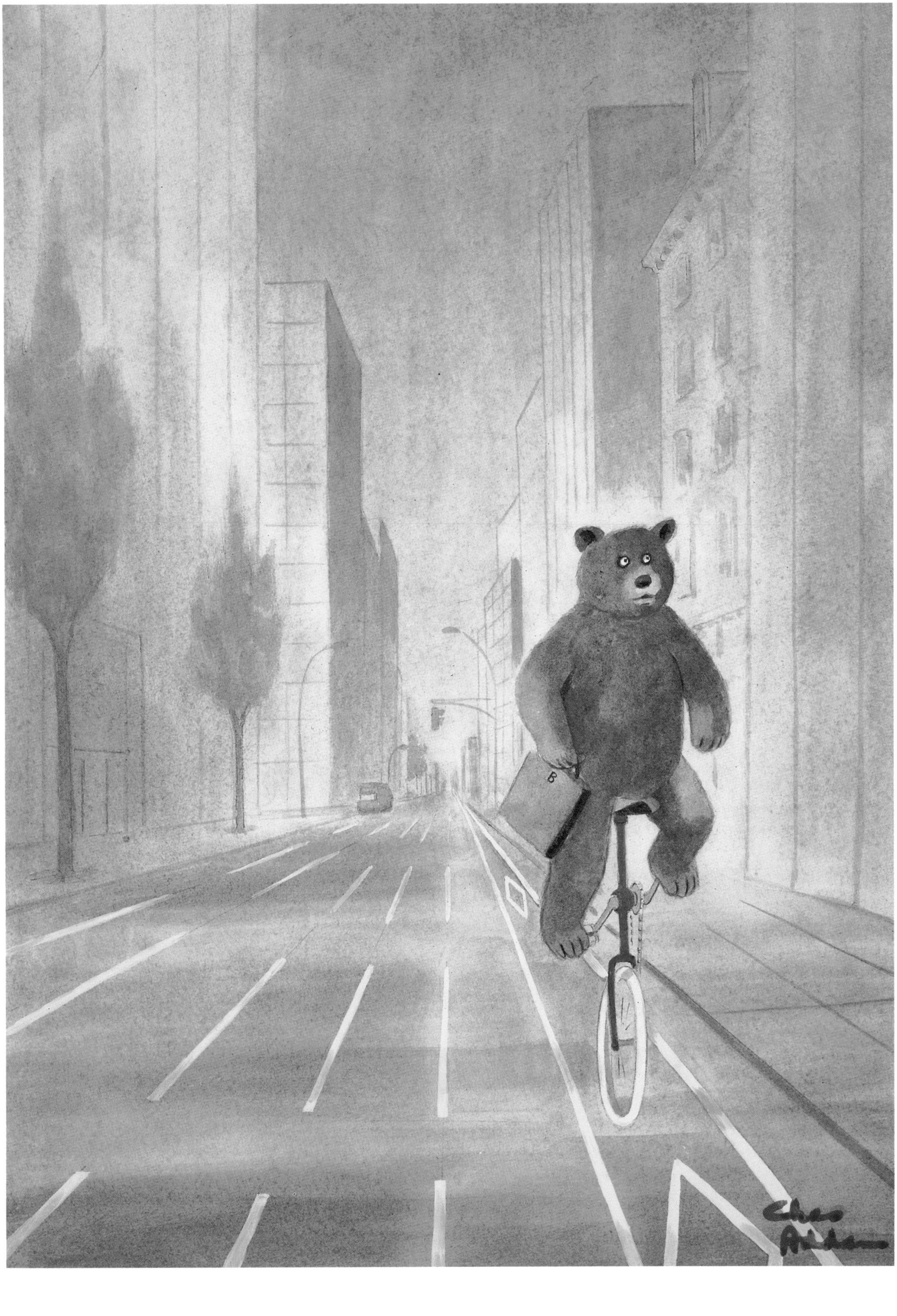
B
Chas Addams

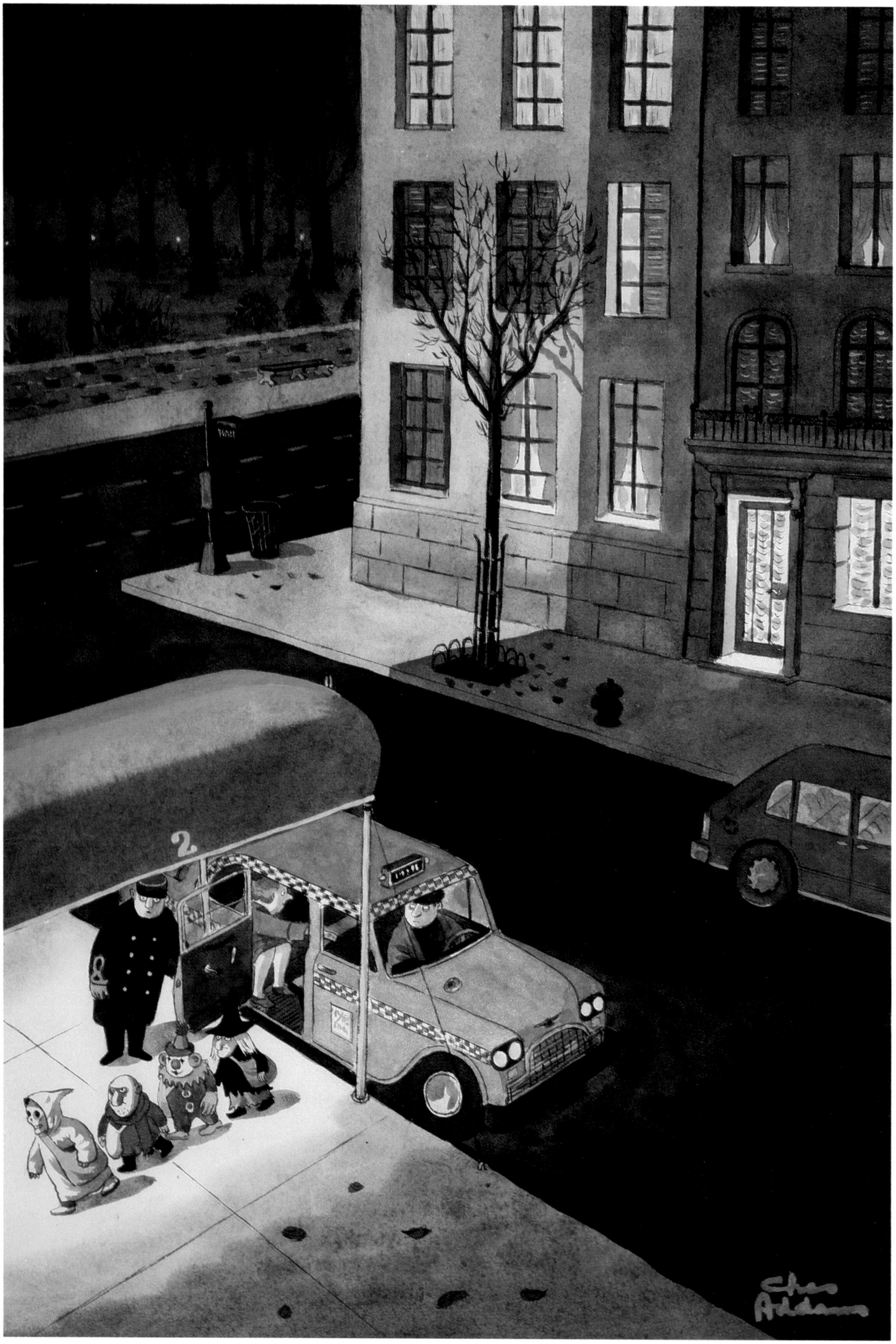
2
Chas Addams

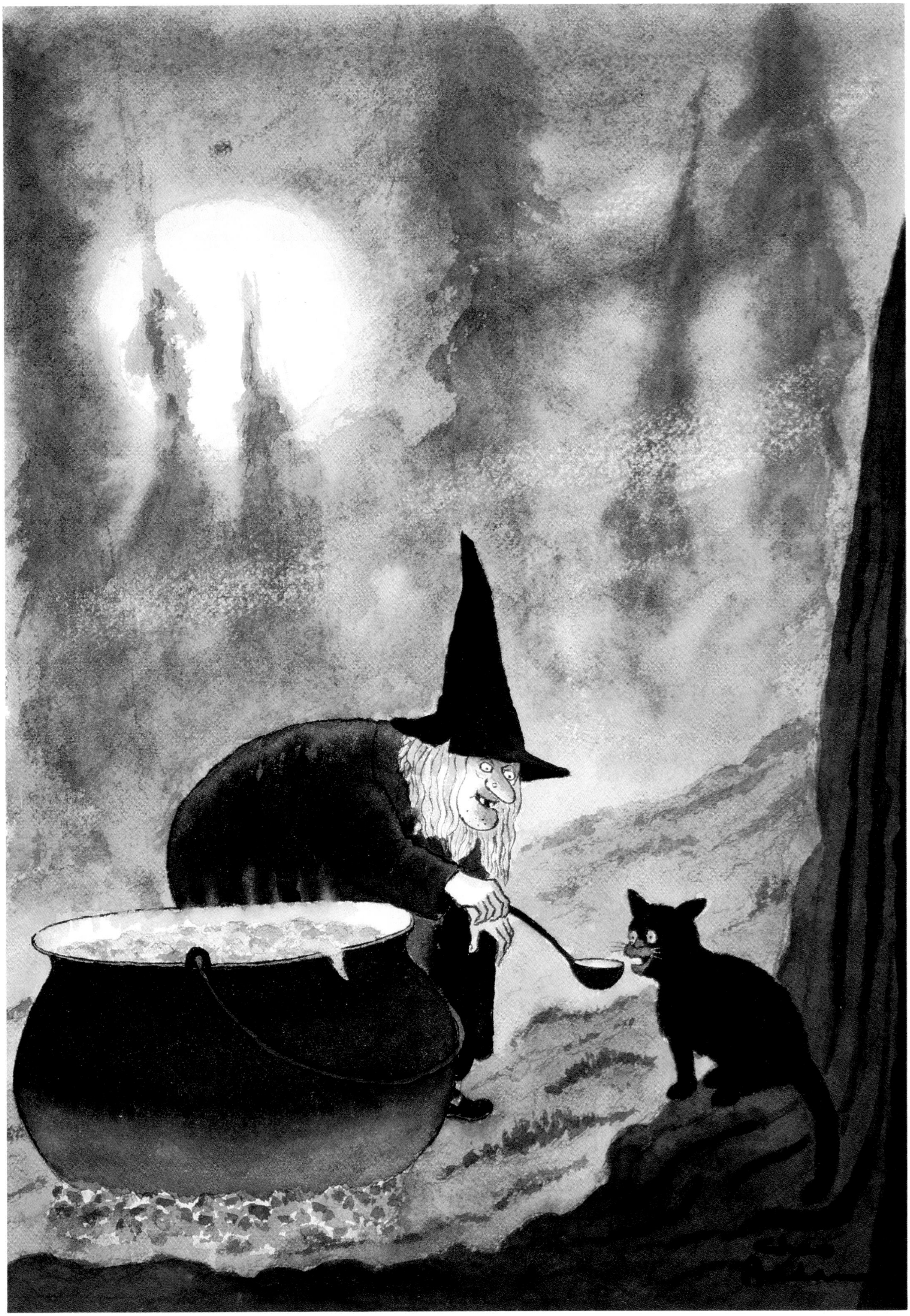

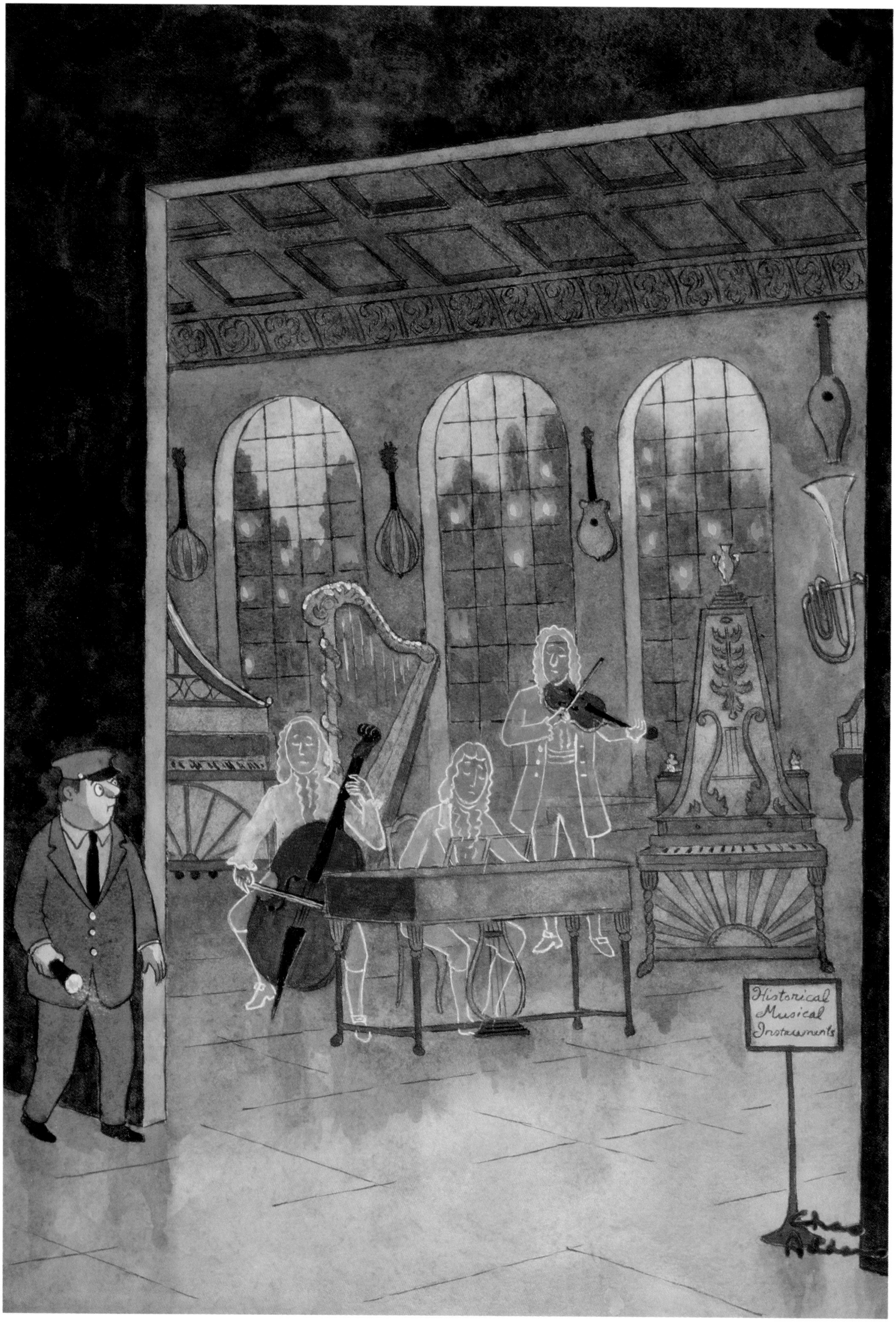
Historical
Musical
Instruments

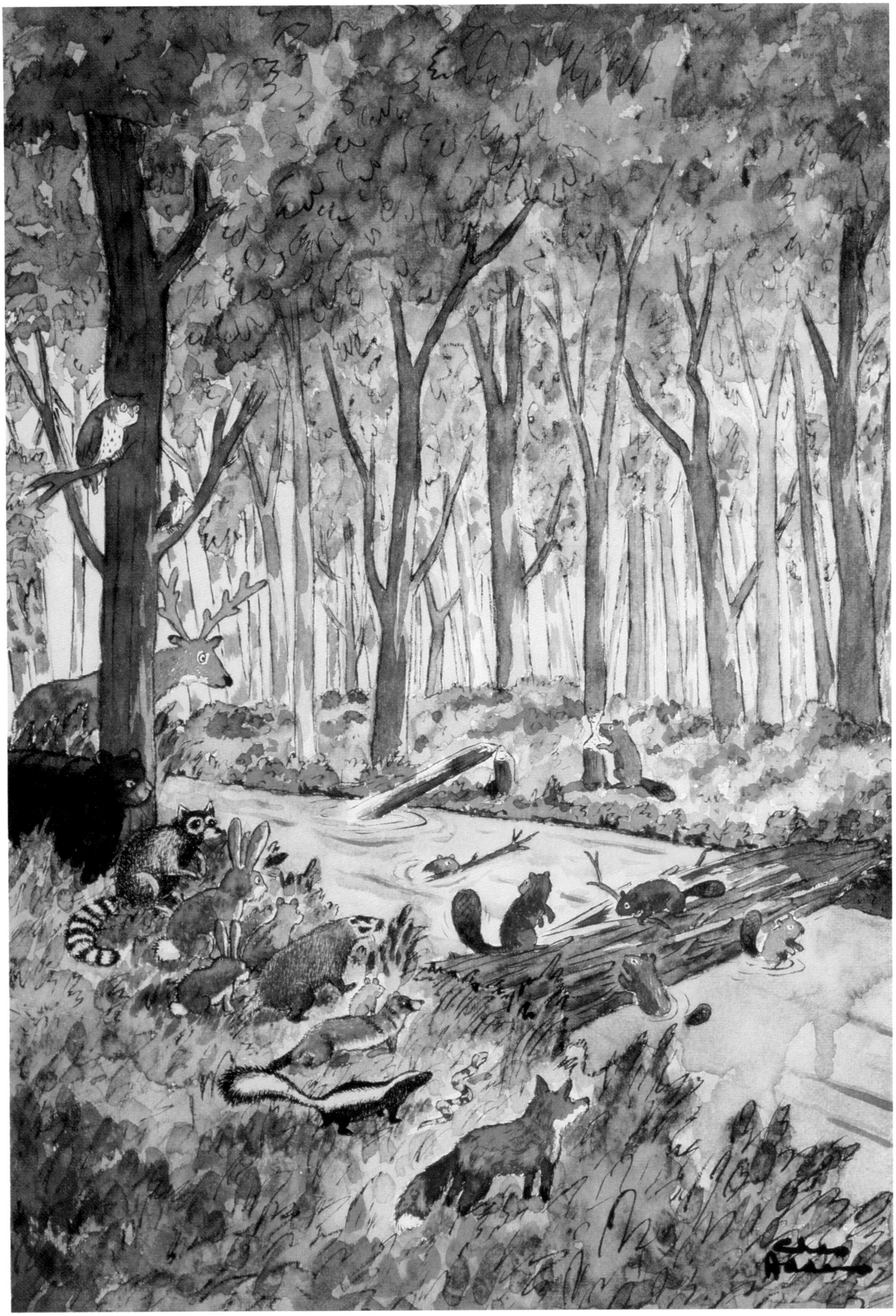

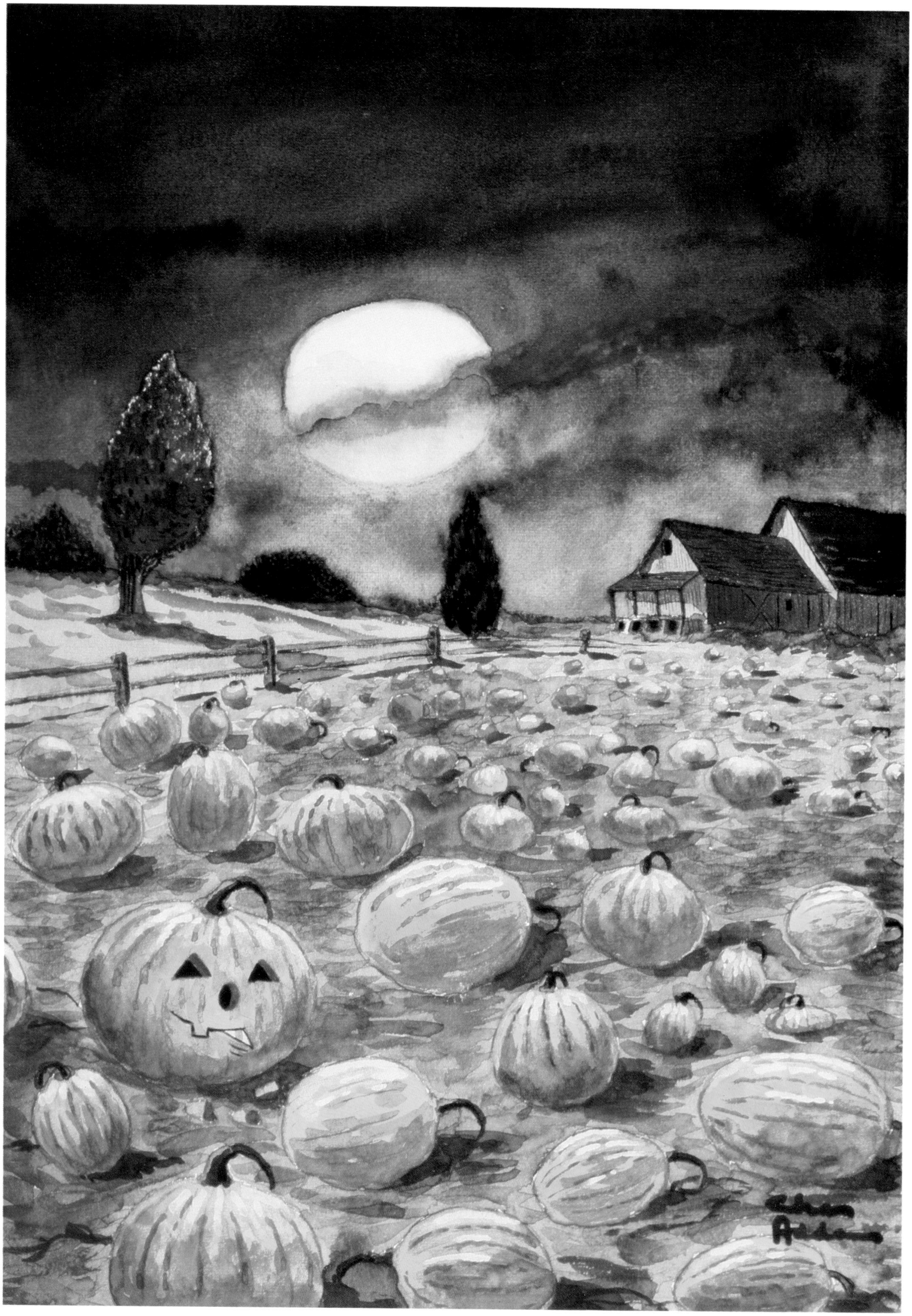

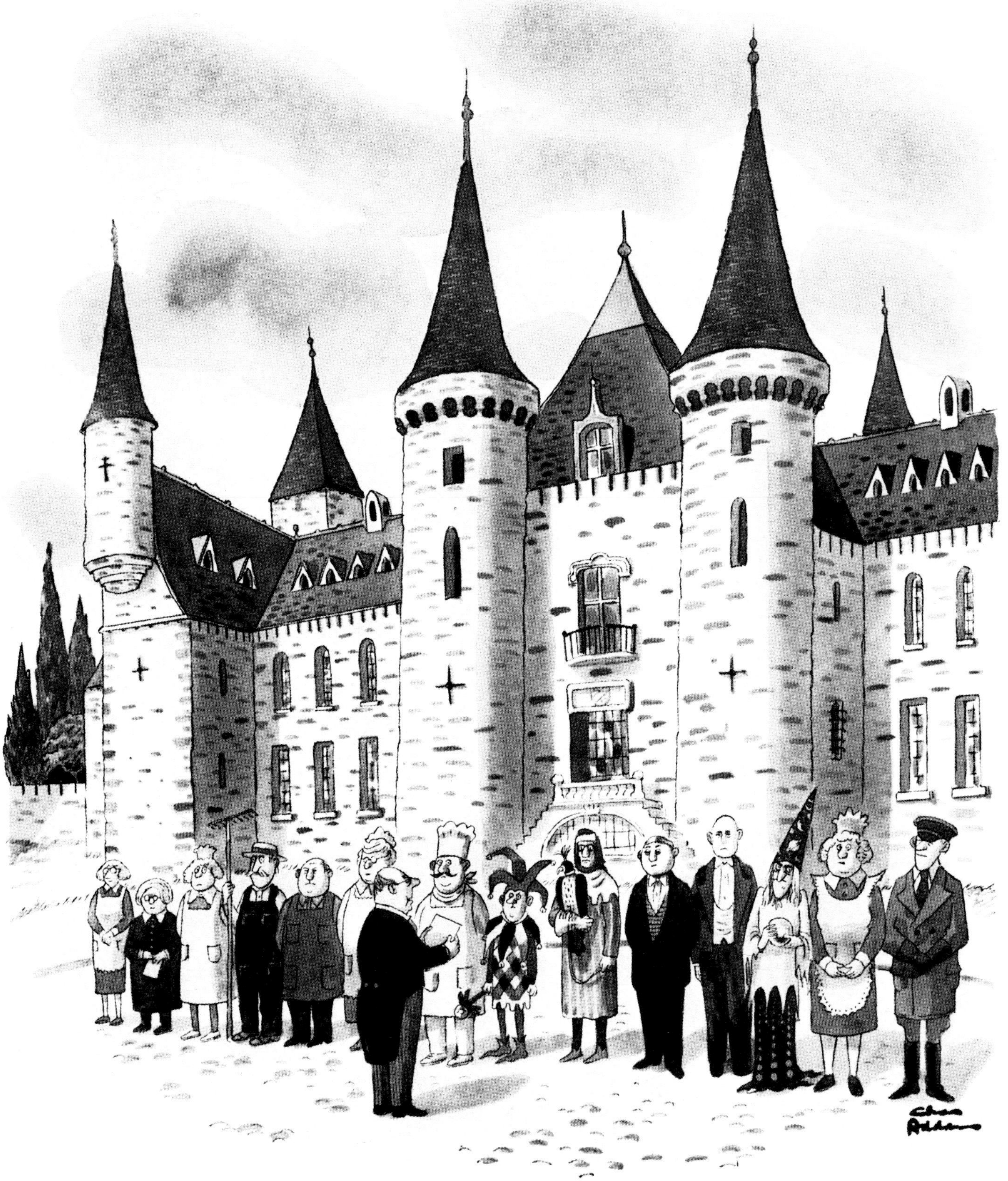

"Inflationary pressures oblige us to reduce expenditures. Therefore, the following three staff members shall be dismissed."

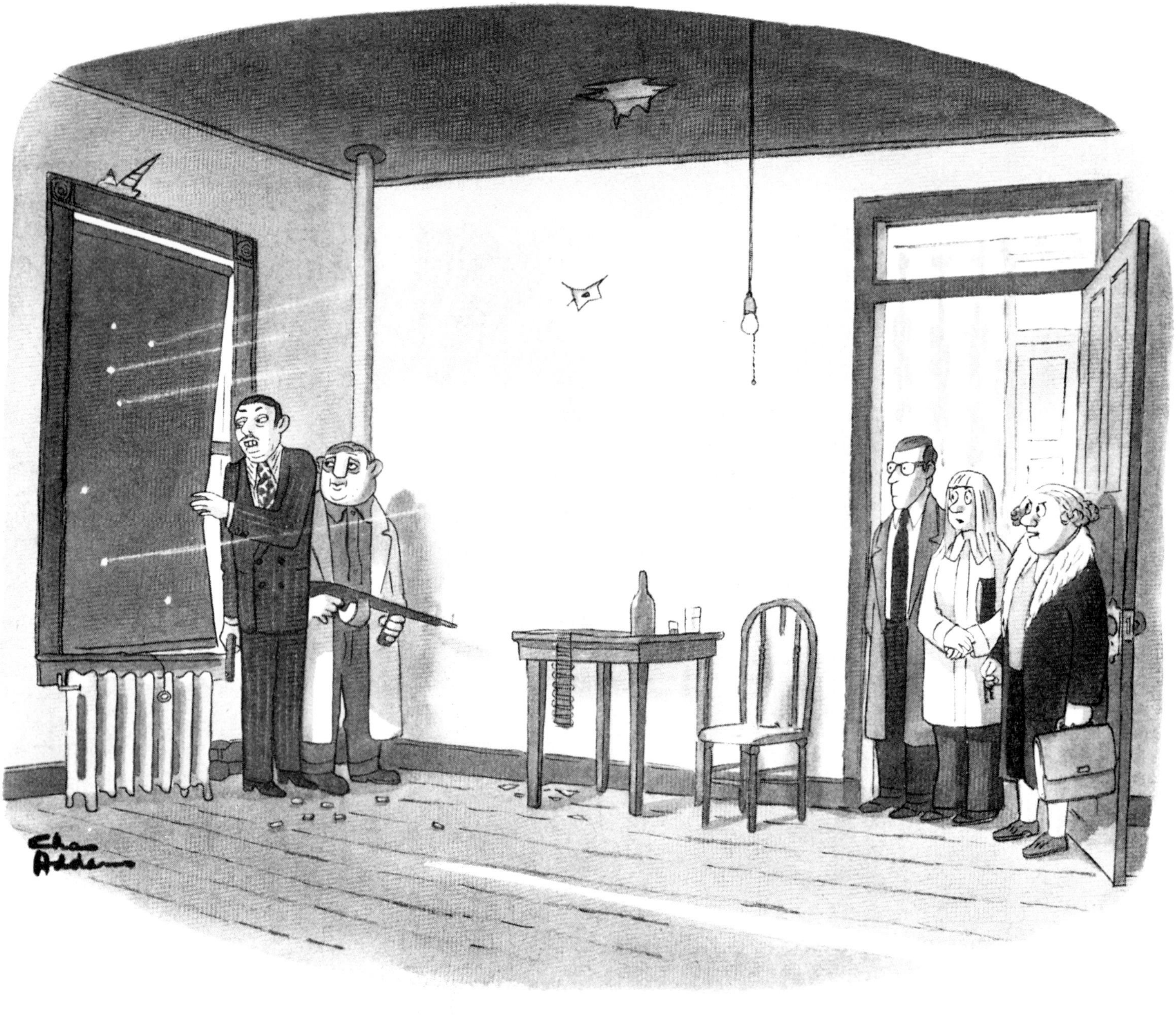
Chas Addams

"Don't worry. They'll be out by the tenth."

"I just got tired of the same old hat."

"The usual."

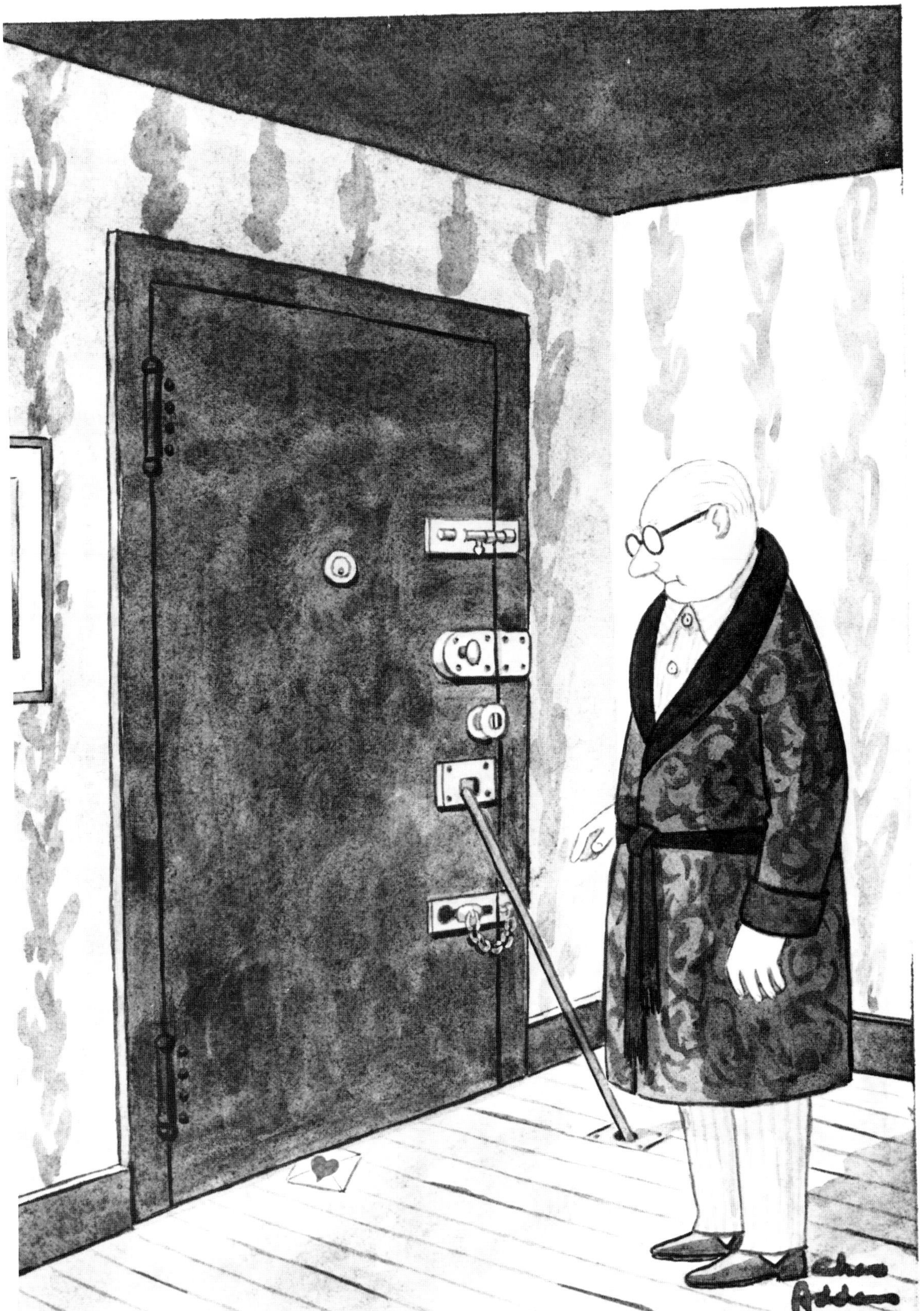
Chas Addams

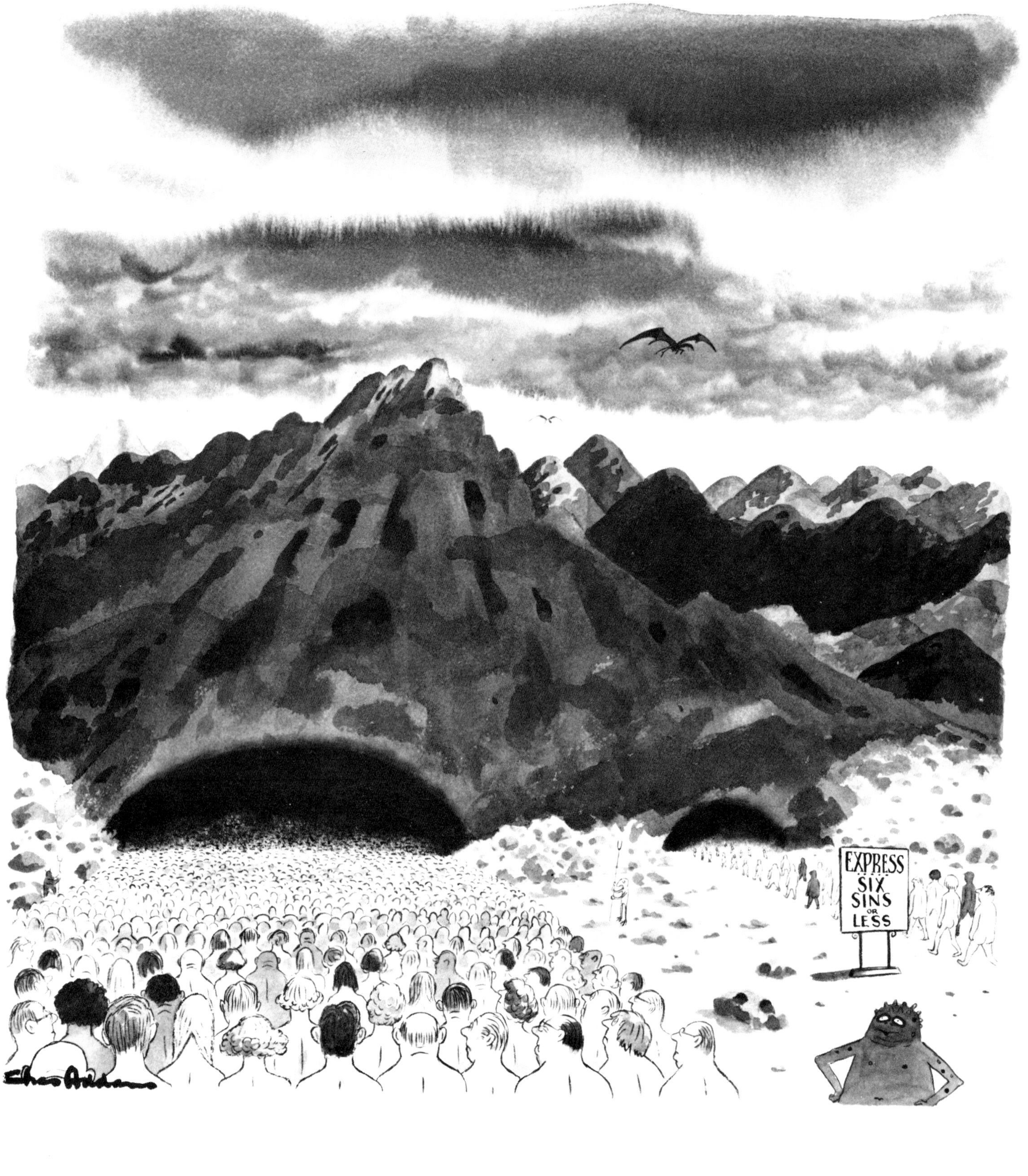
EXPRESS
SIX
SINS
OR
LESS
Chas Addams

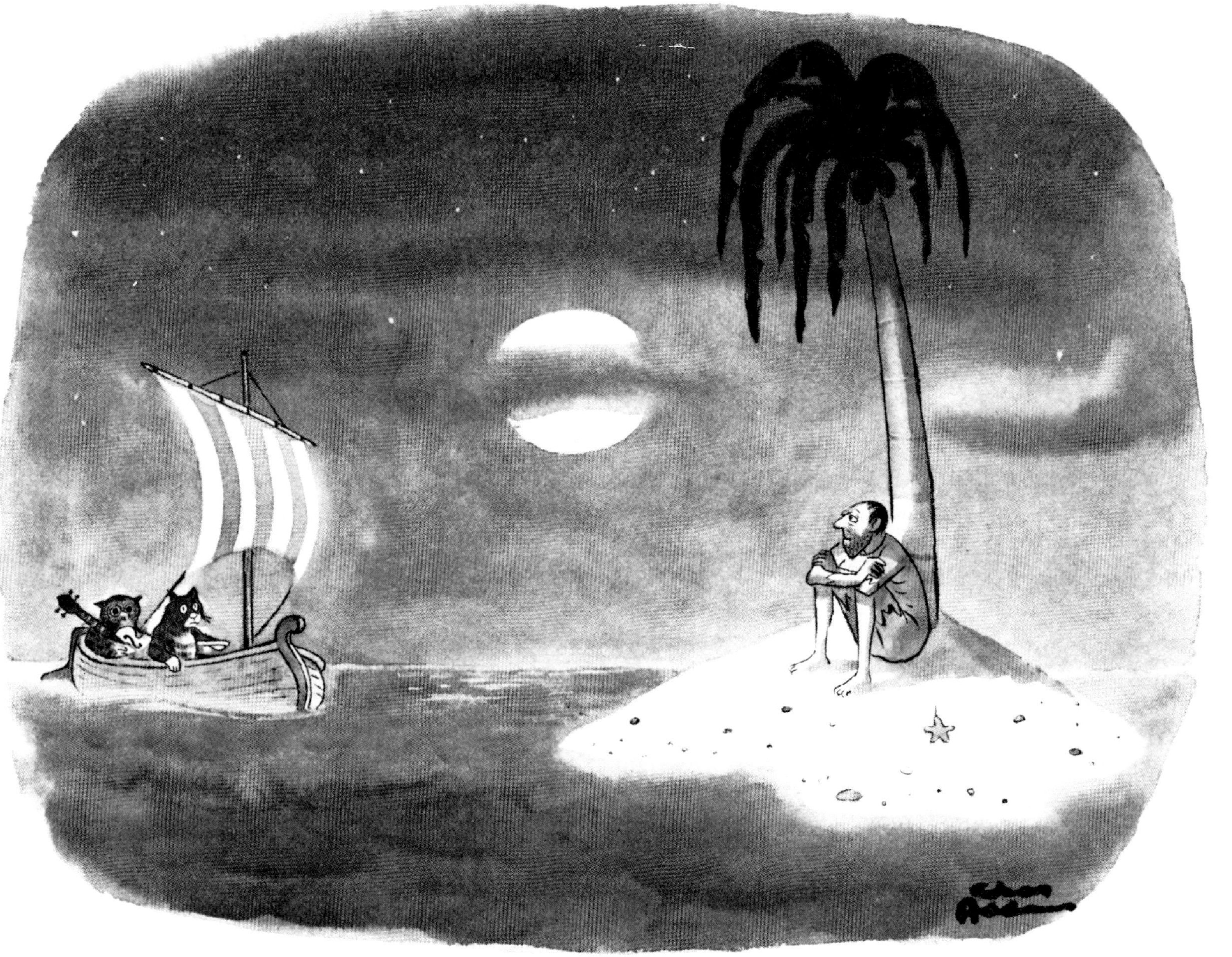

"You know something? You're very tough to shop for."

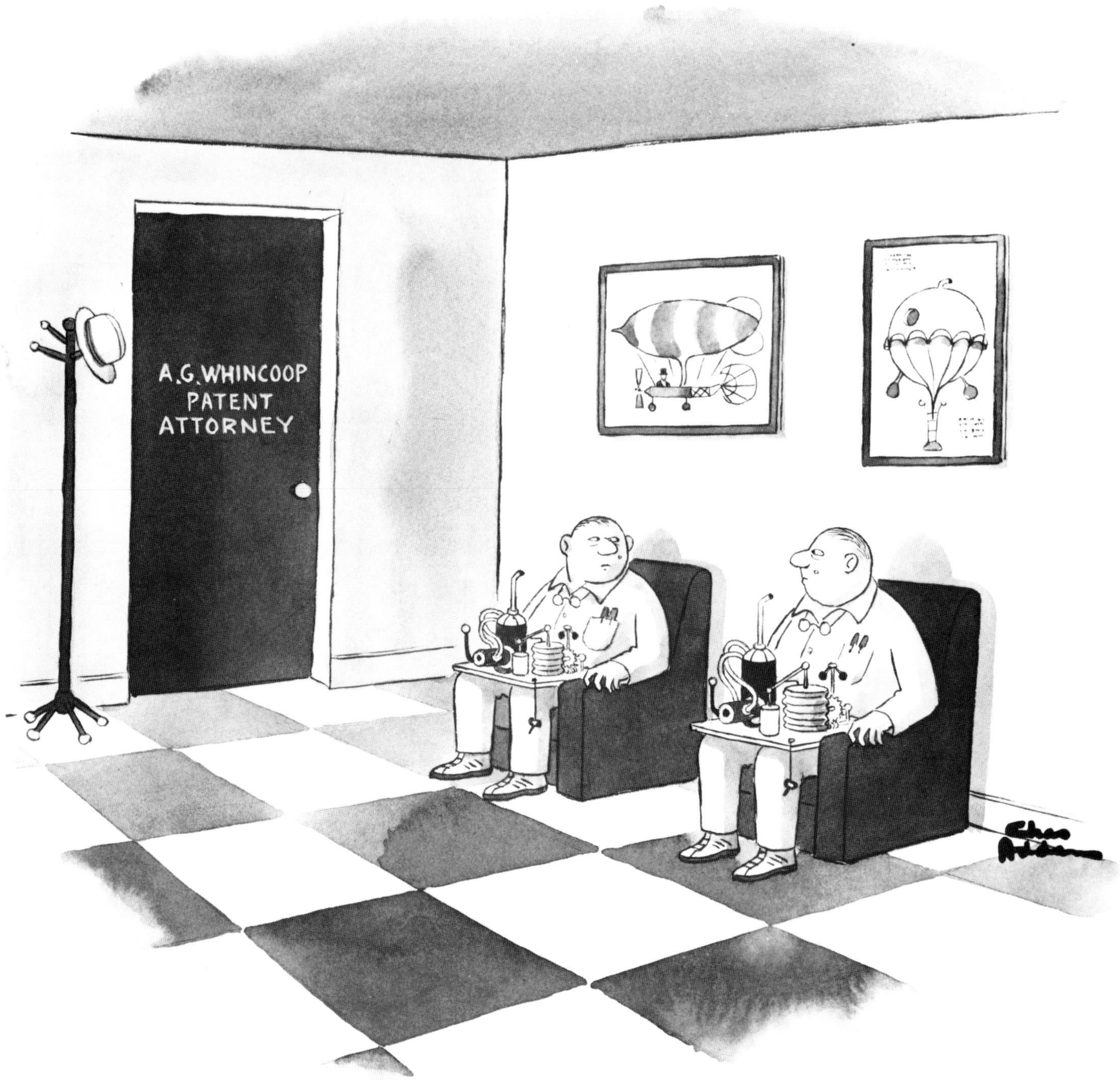
A.G. WHINCOOP
PATENT
ATTORNEY

Separated at birth, the Mallifert twins meet accidentally.

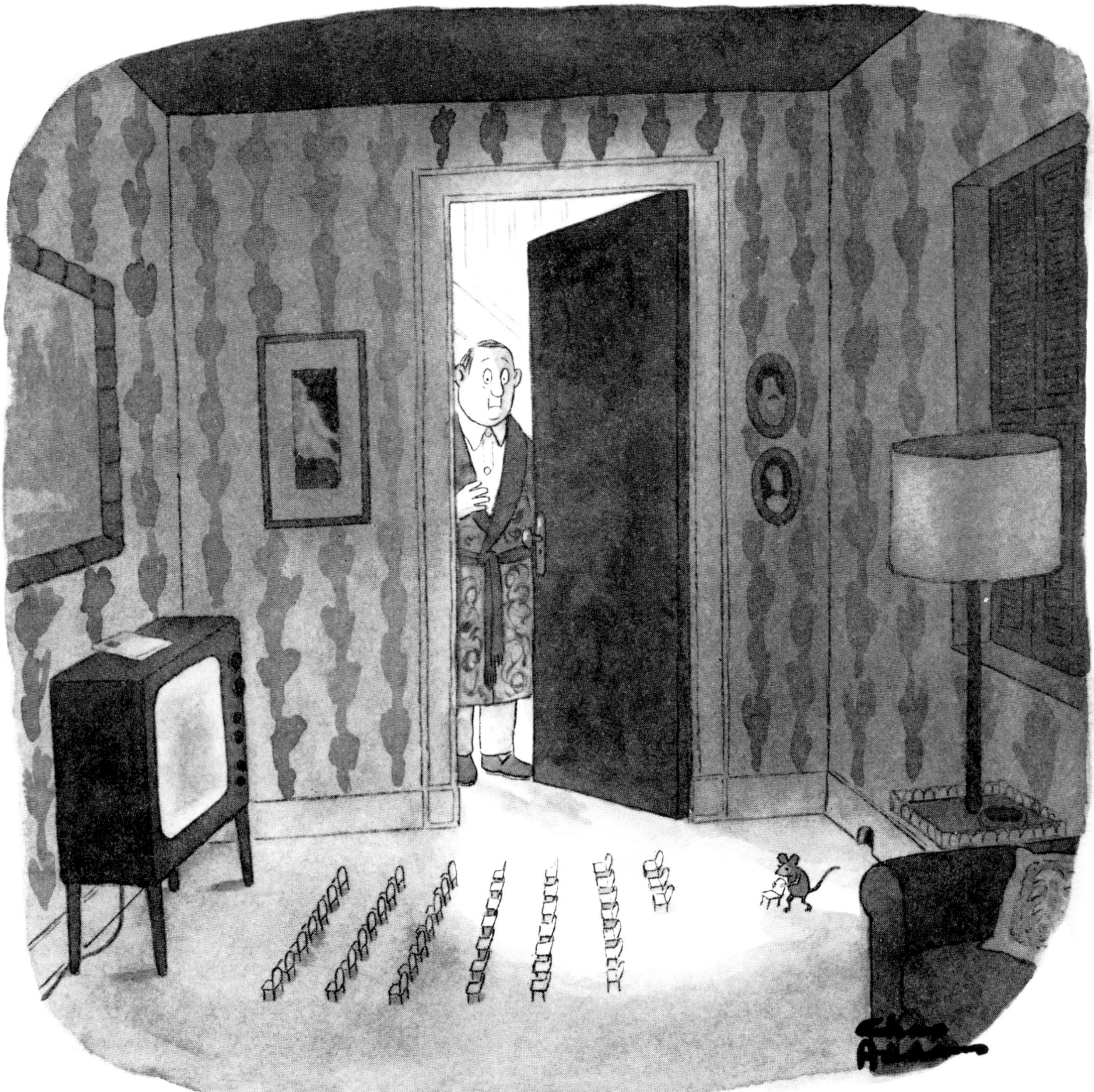

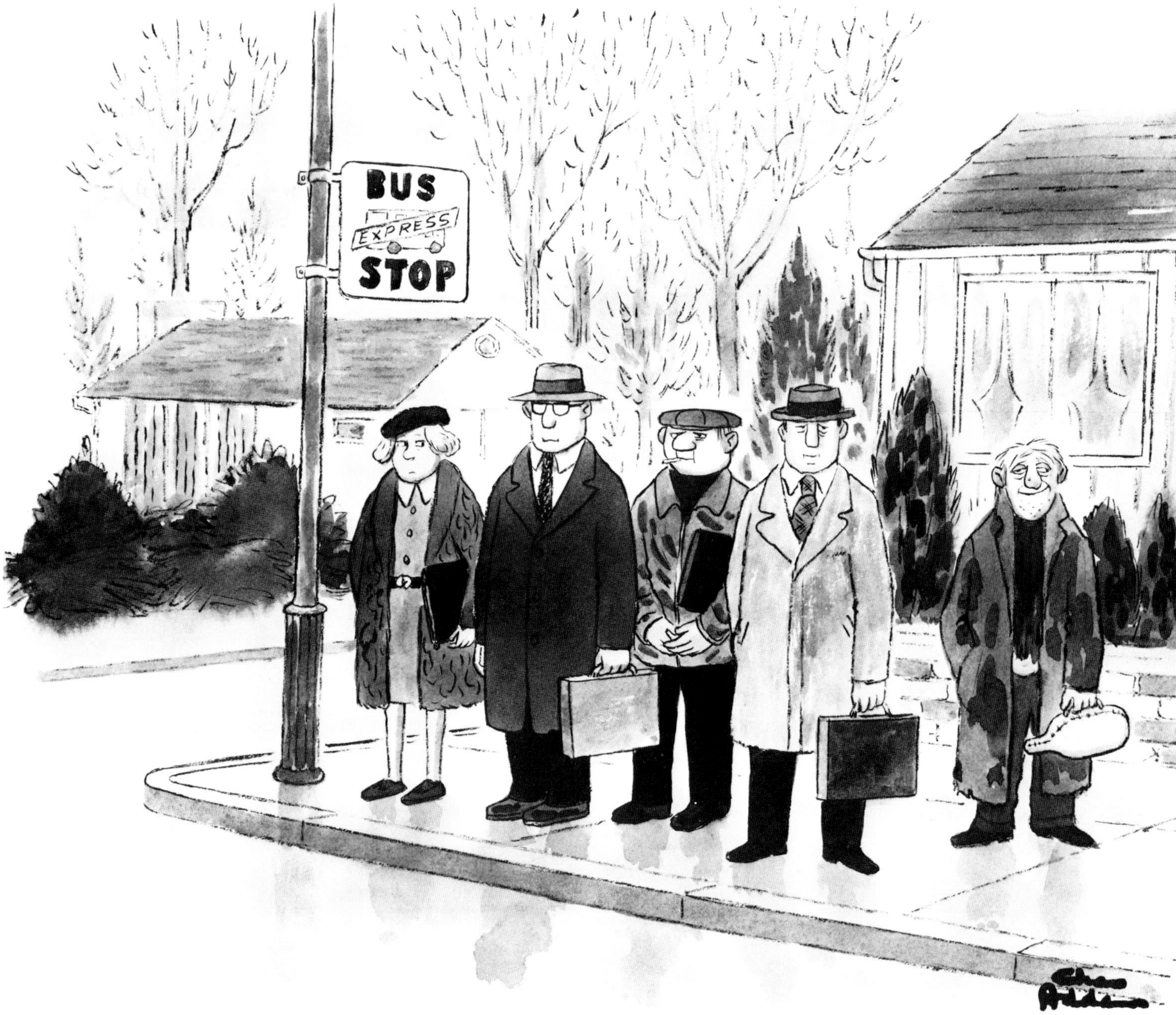
BUS
EXPRESS
STOP

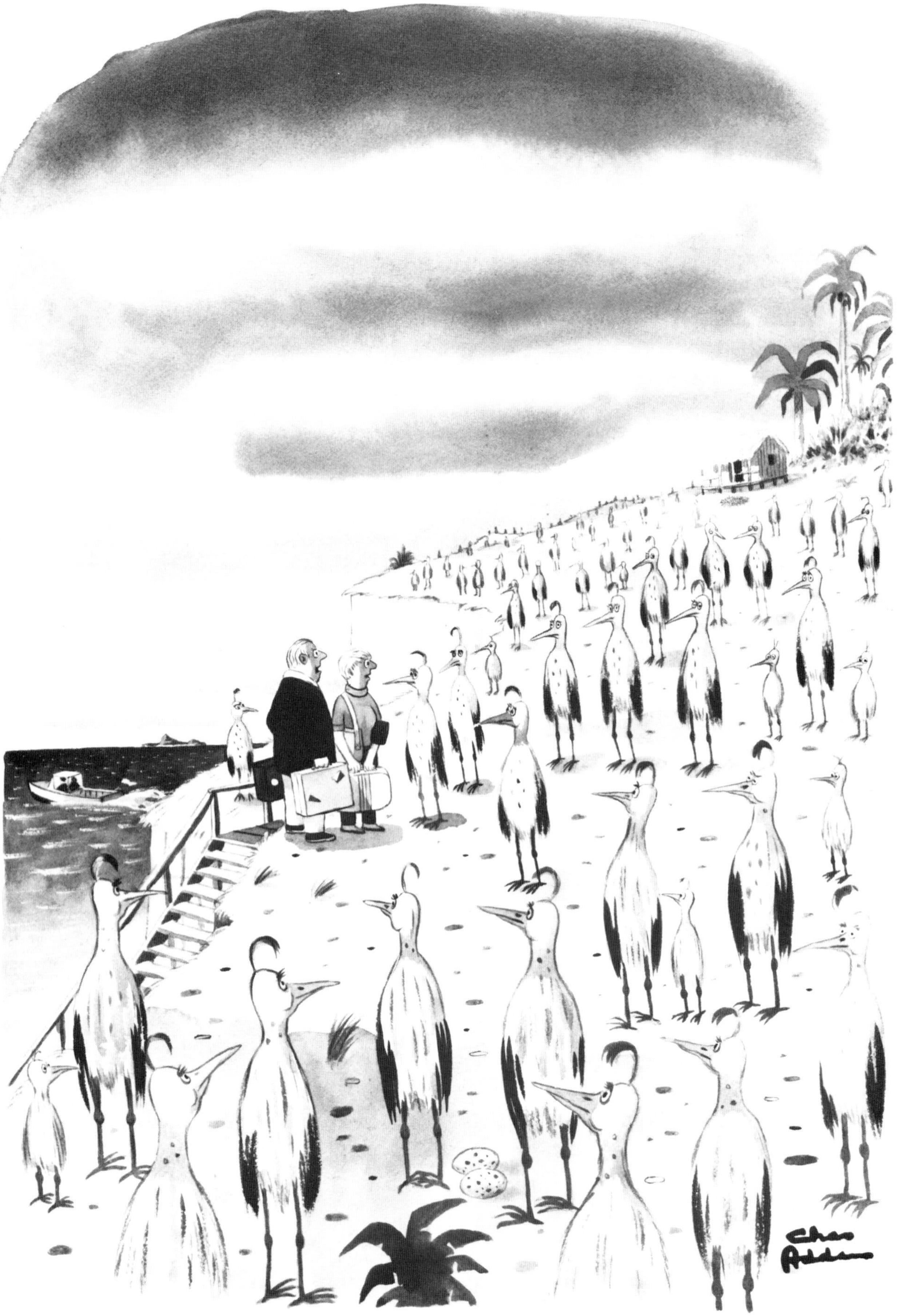
Chas Addams

"Well, you wanted a place with more birds than people."

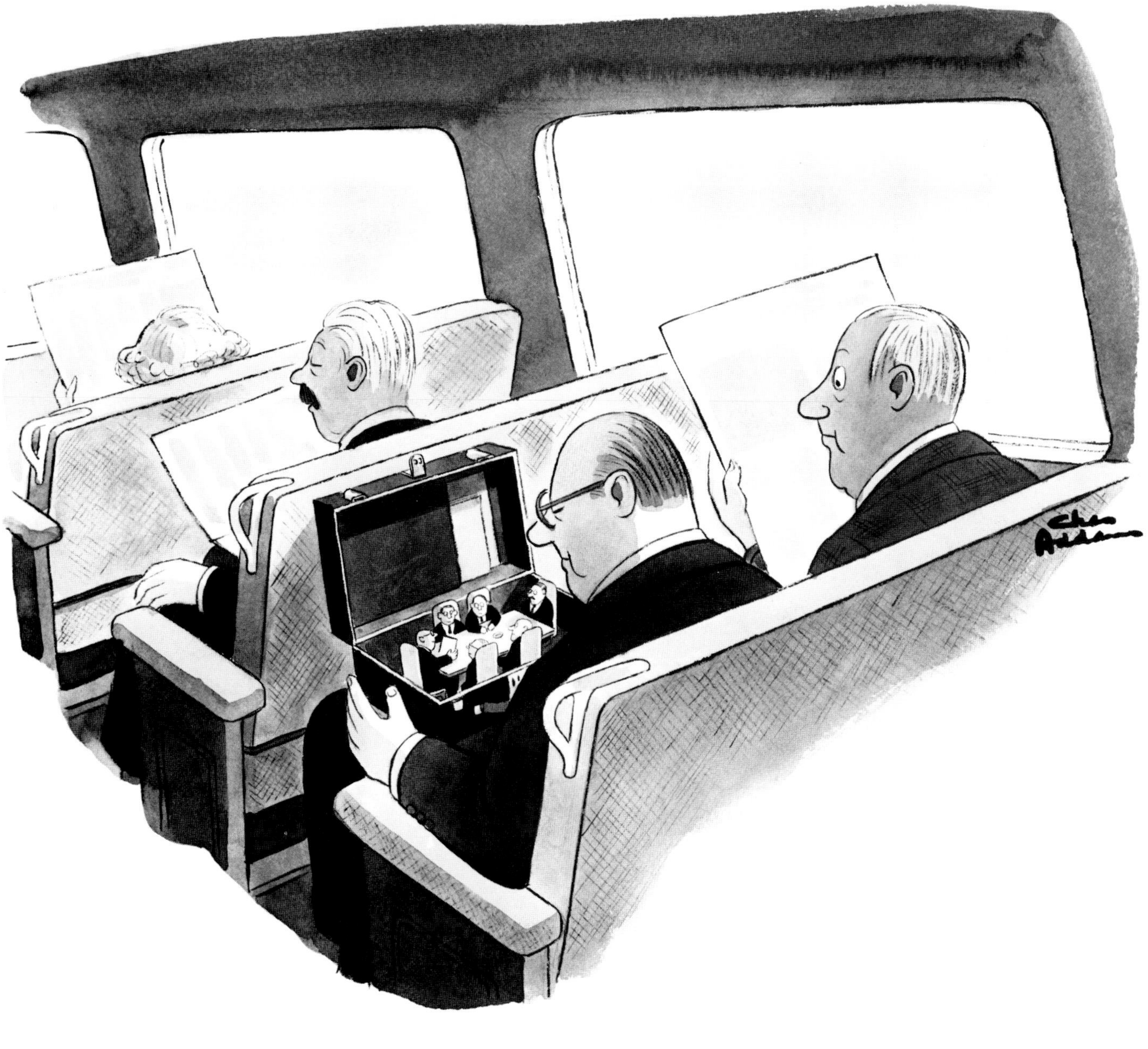
Chas Addams

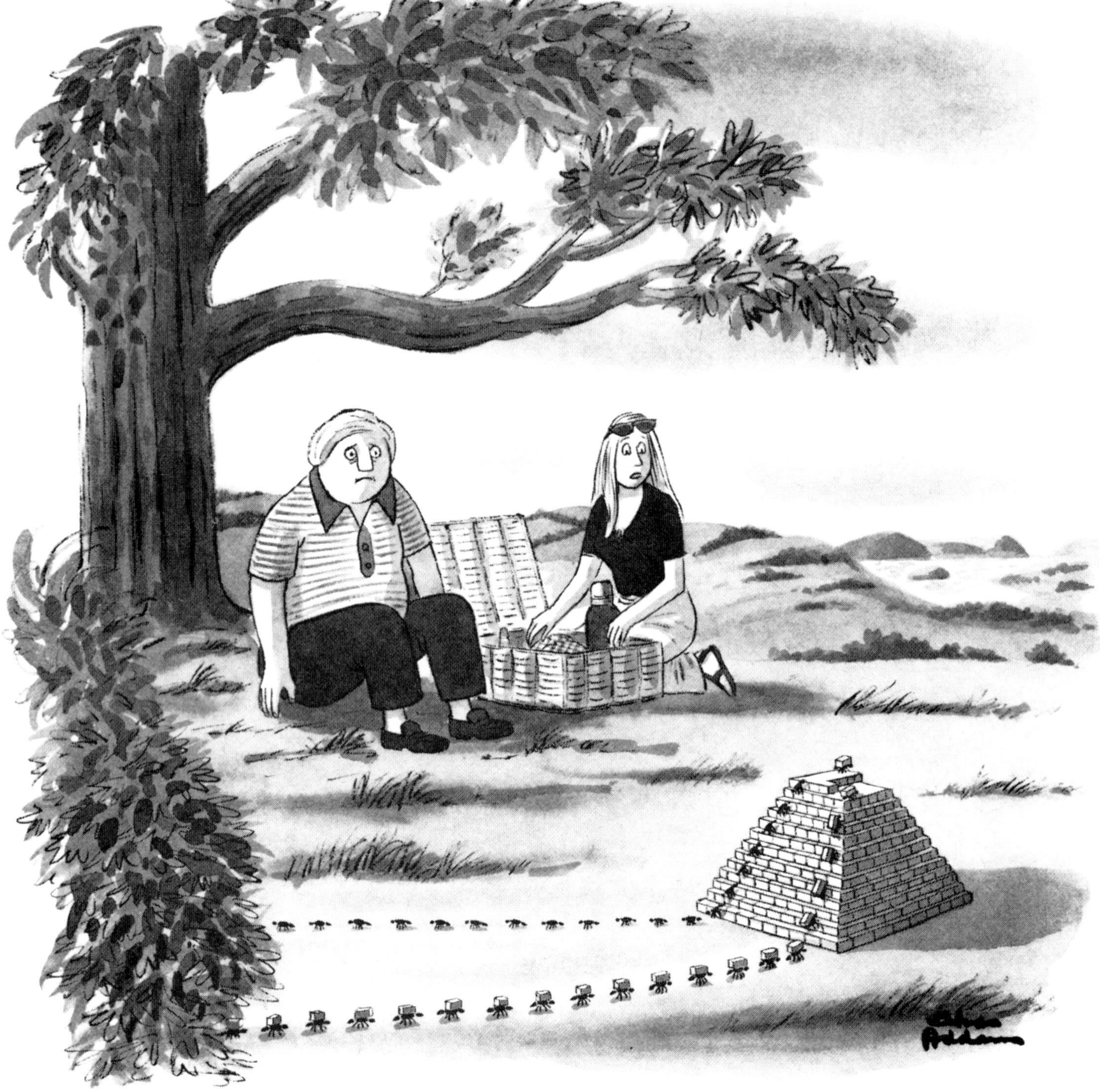

"At least they're not bothering us."

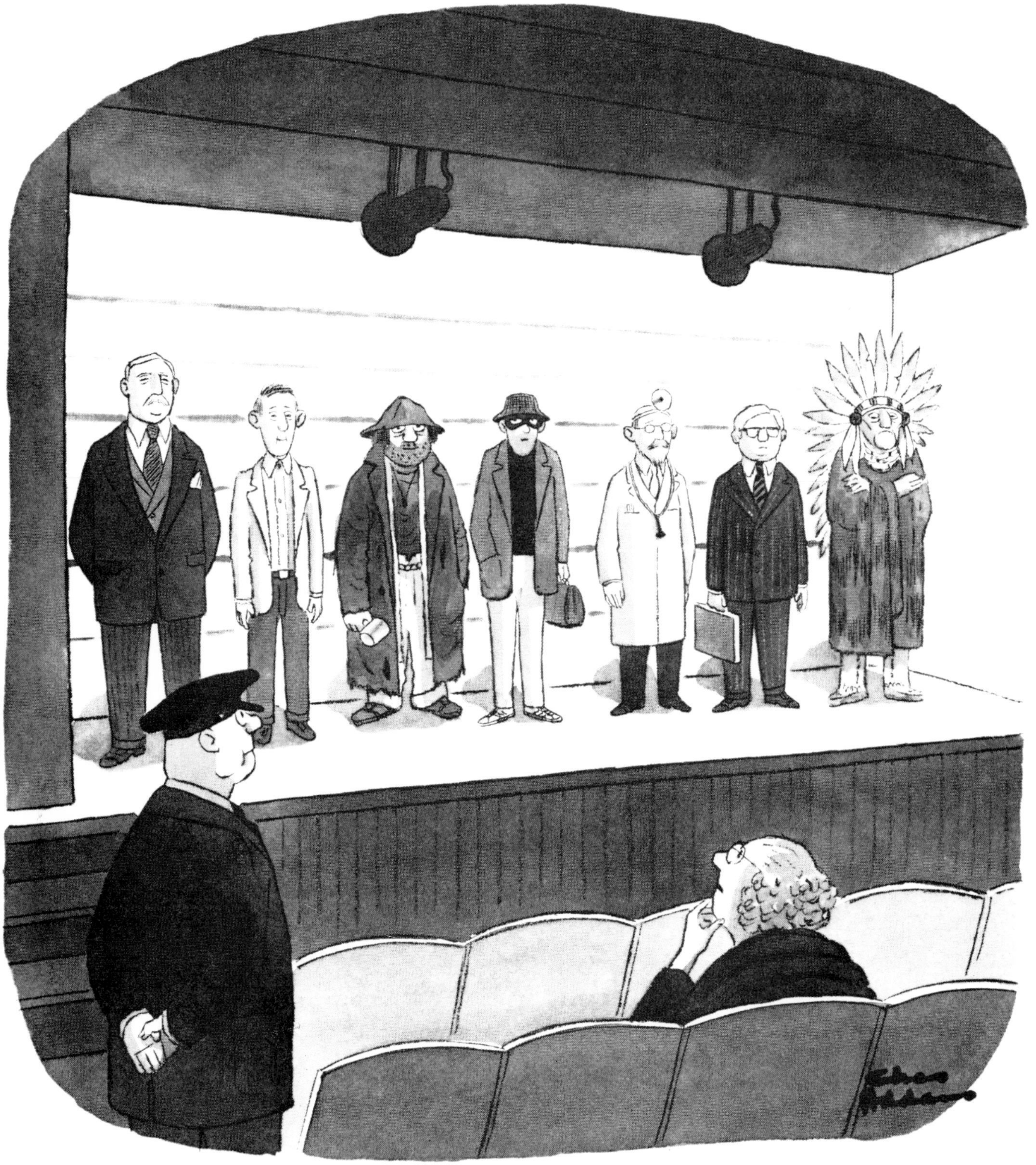
Chas Addams

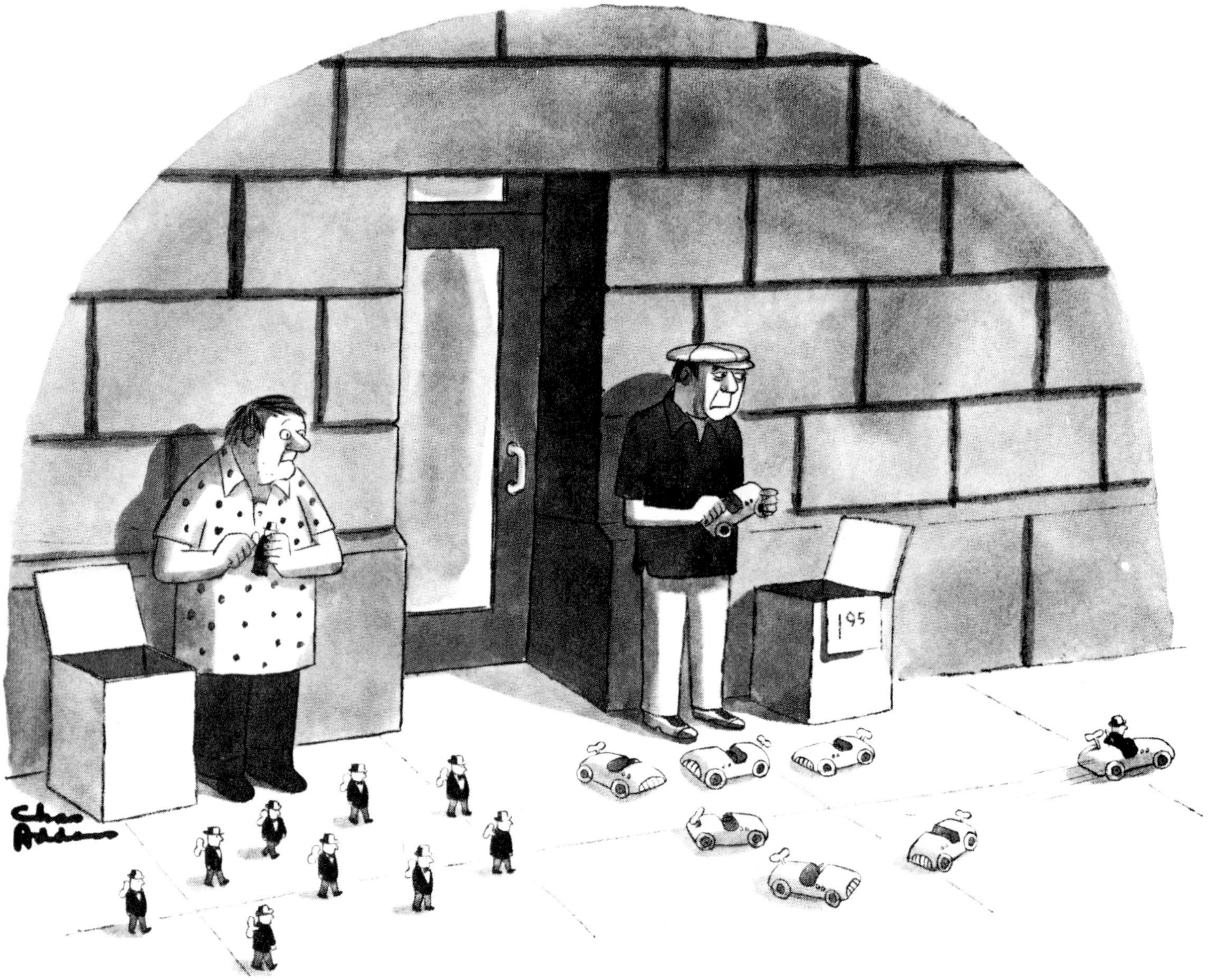
Chas Addams
1.95

*"Would you say Attila is doing an excellent job, a good job,
a fair job, or a poor job?"*

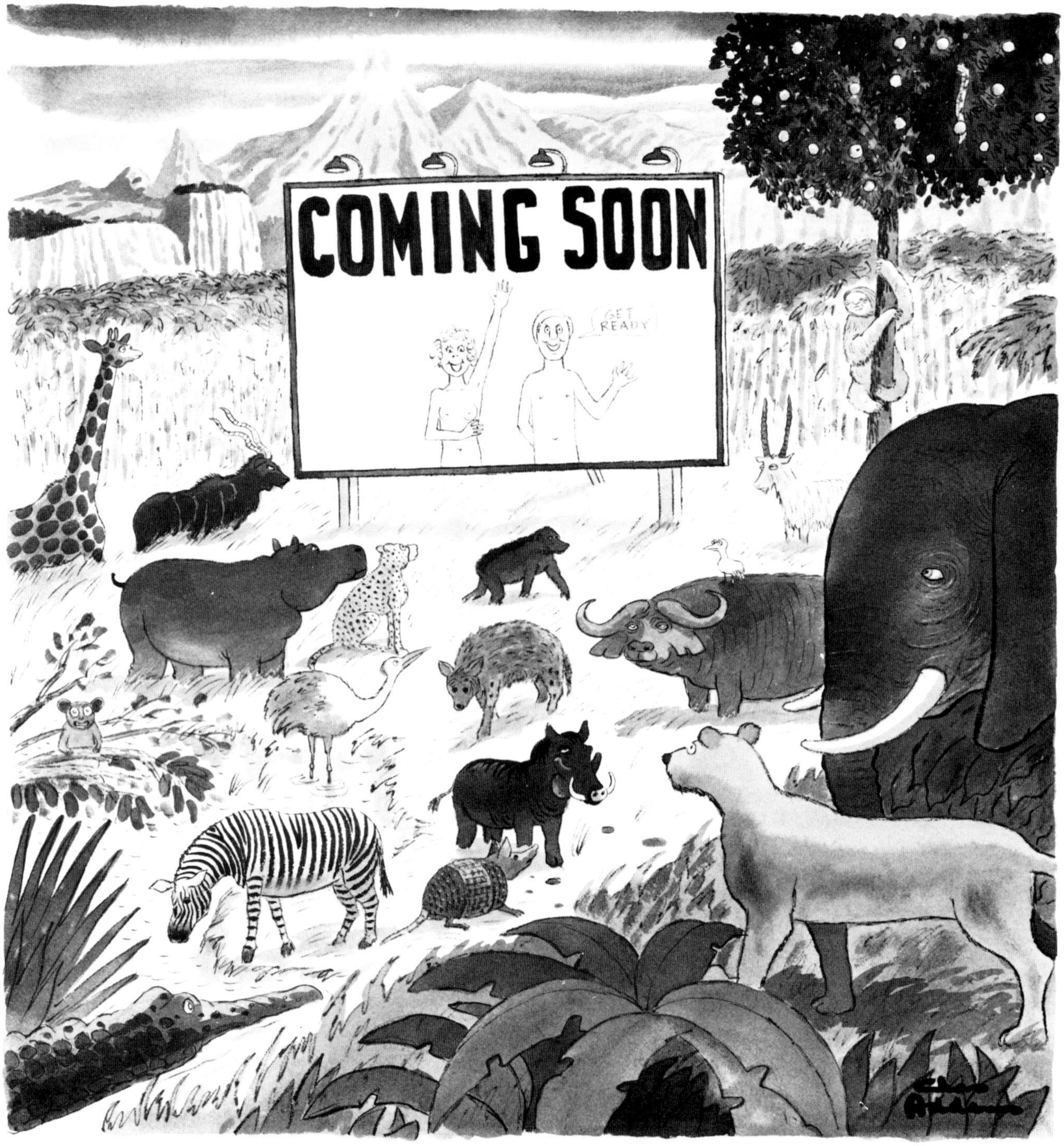
COMING SOON
GET READY

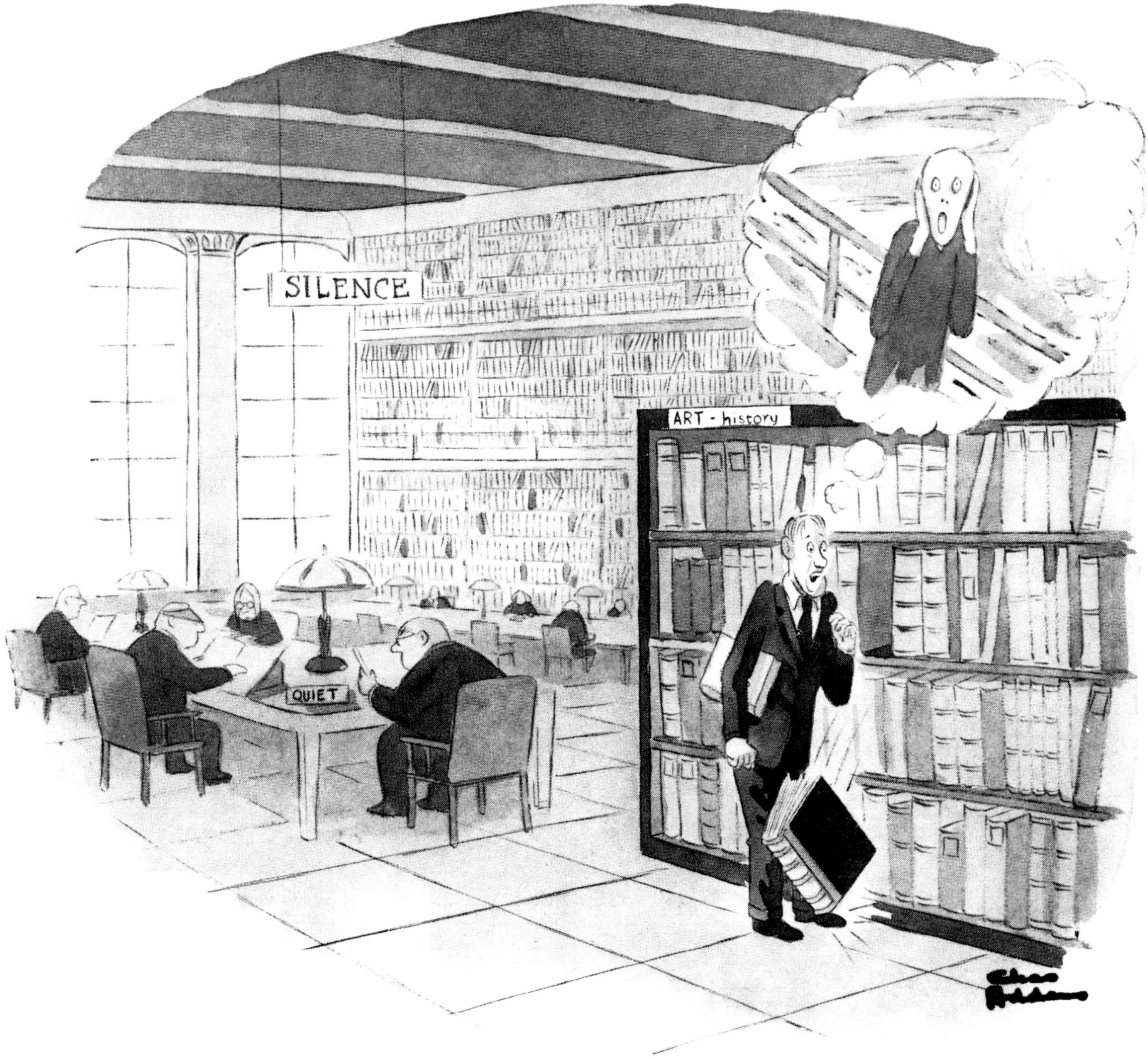
SILENCE
ART - history
QUIET

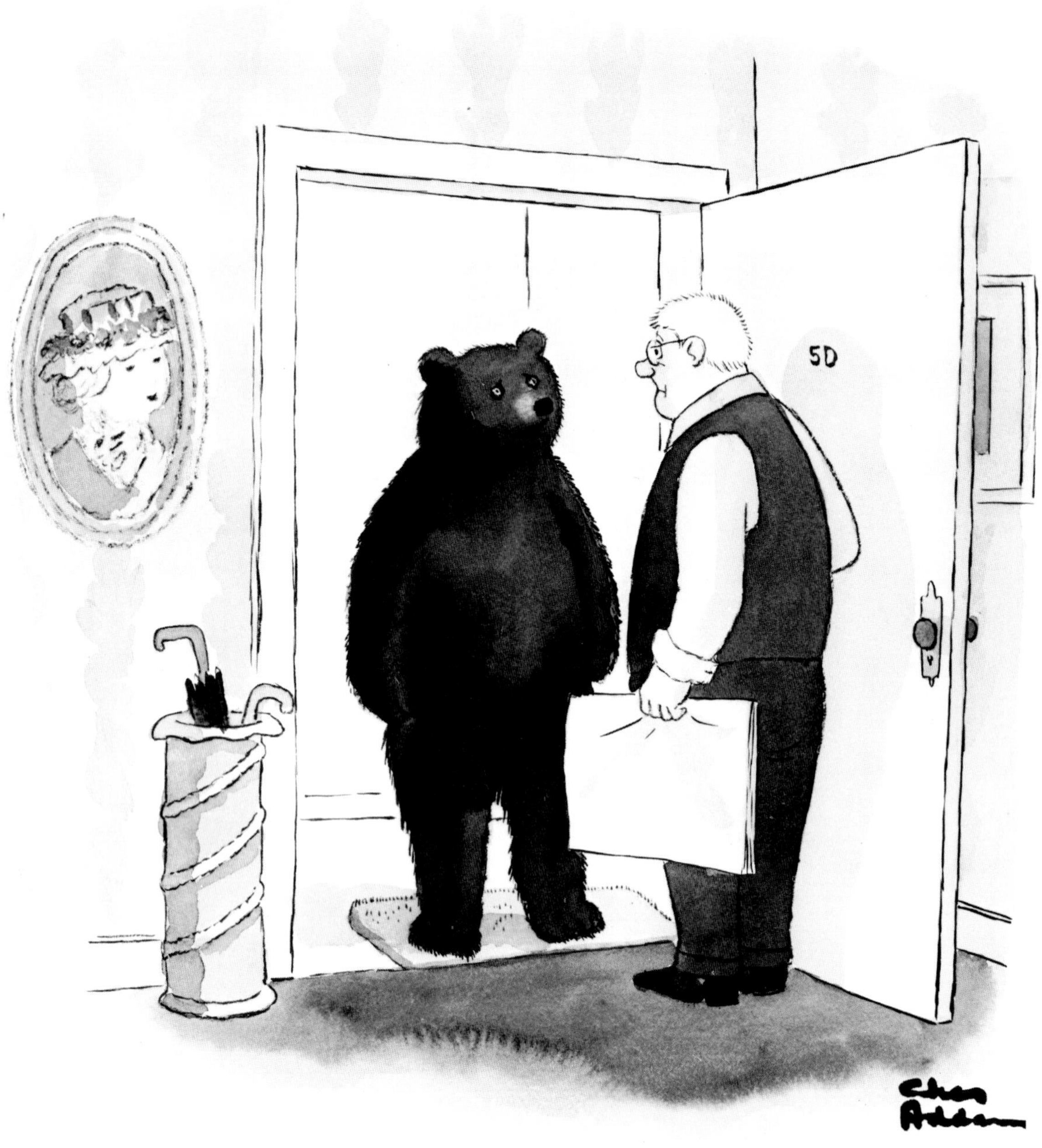
5D
Chas Addams

"You advertised a winter rental?"

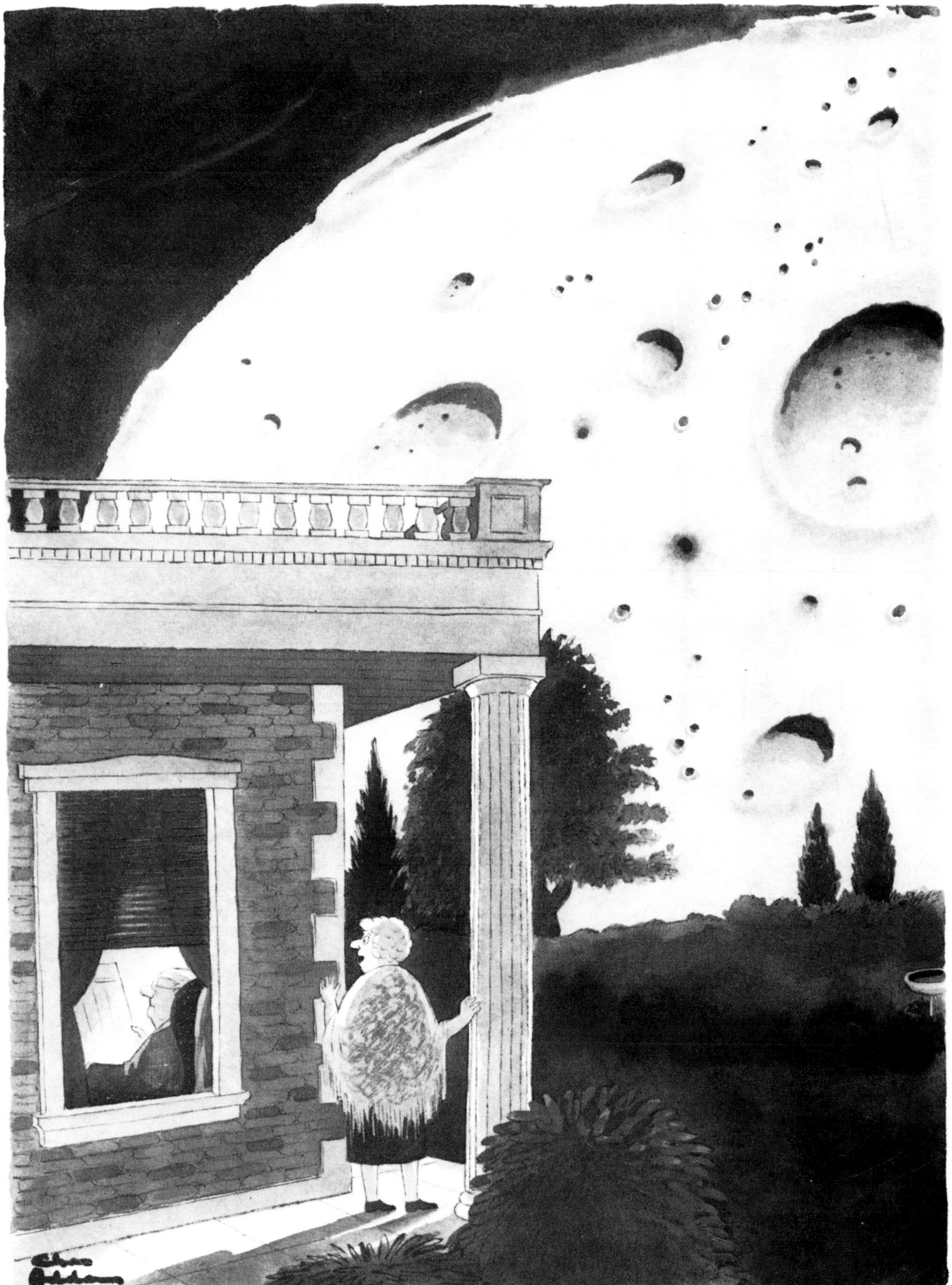

"Maynard, I do think that just this once you should come out and see the moon!"

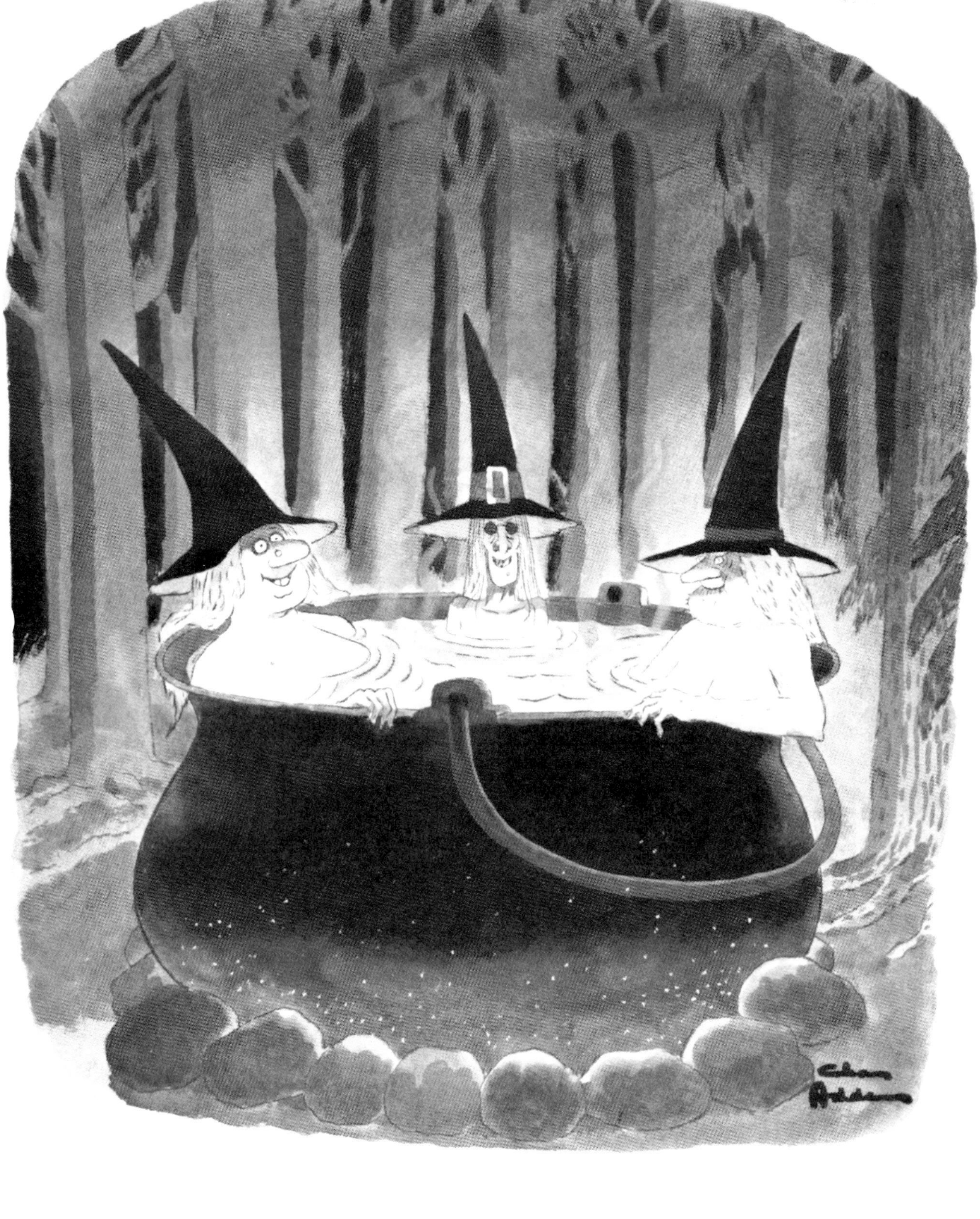
Chas Addams

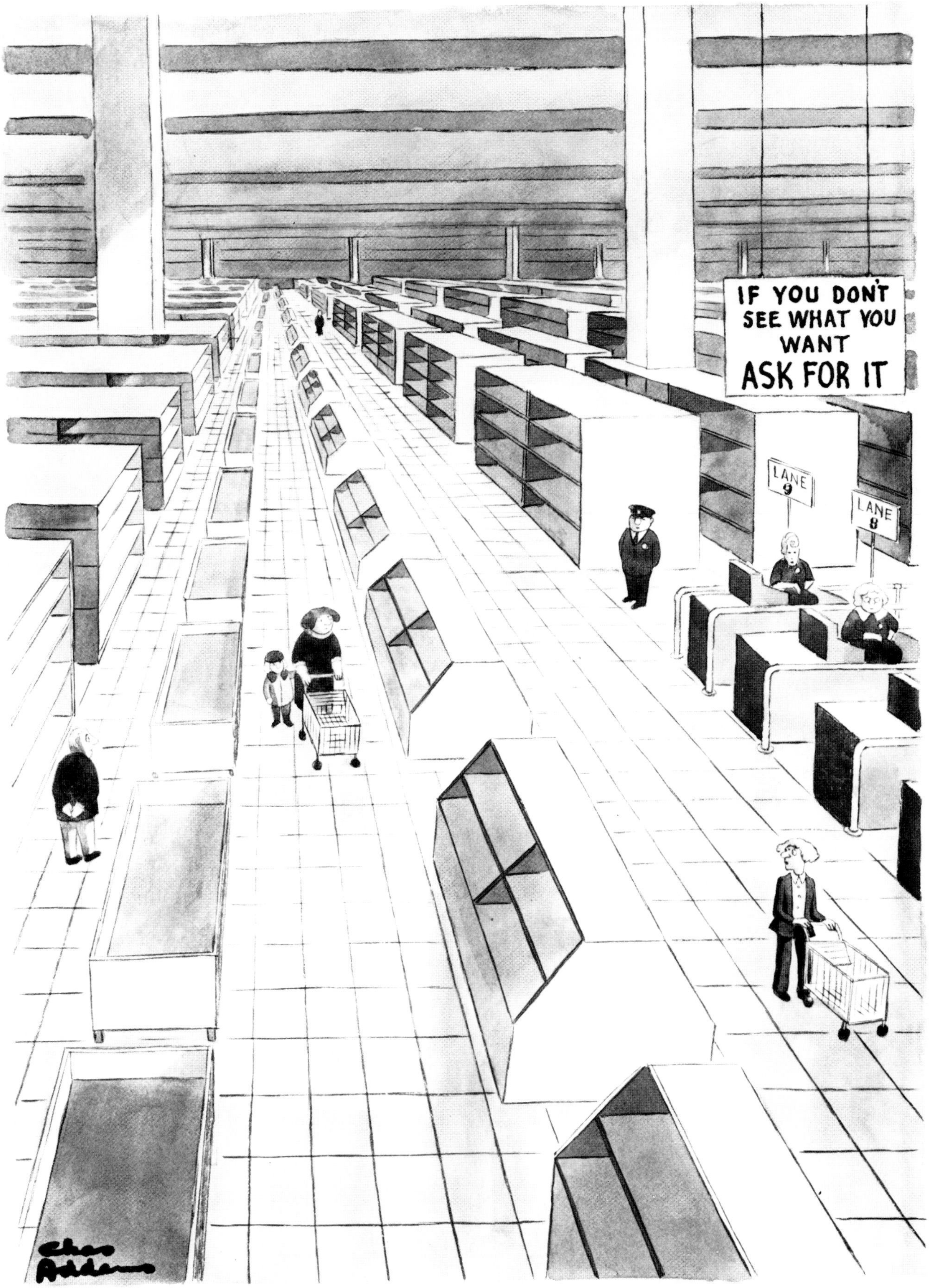
IF YOU DON'T
SEE WHAT YOU
WANT
ASK FOR IT
LANE 9
LANE 8
Chas Addams

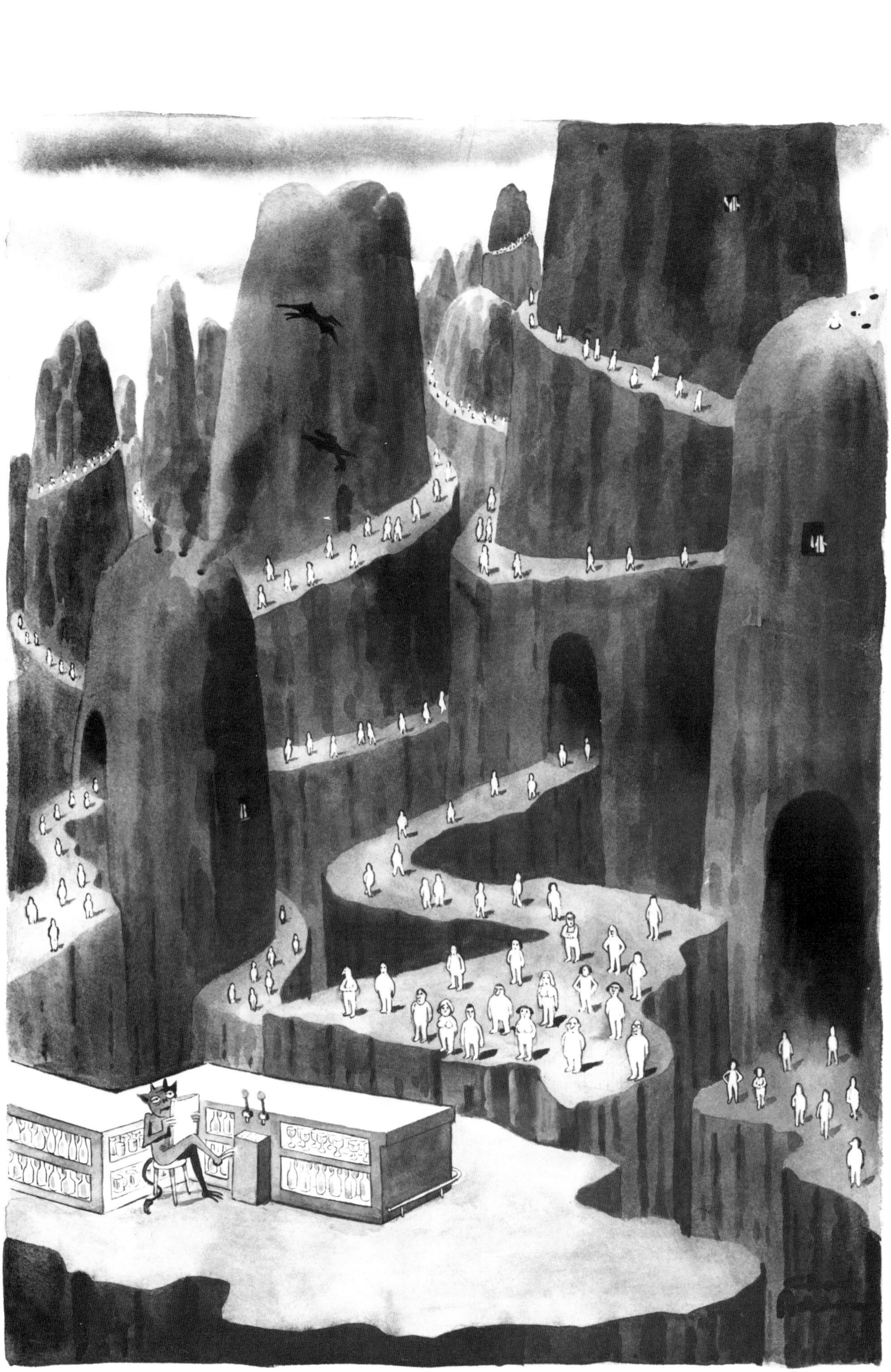

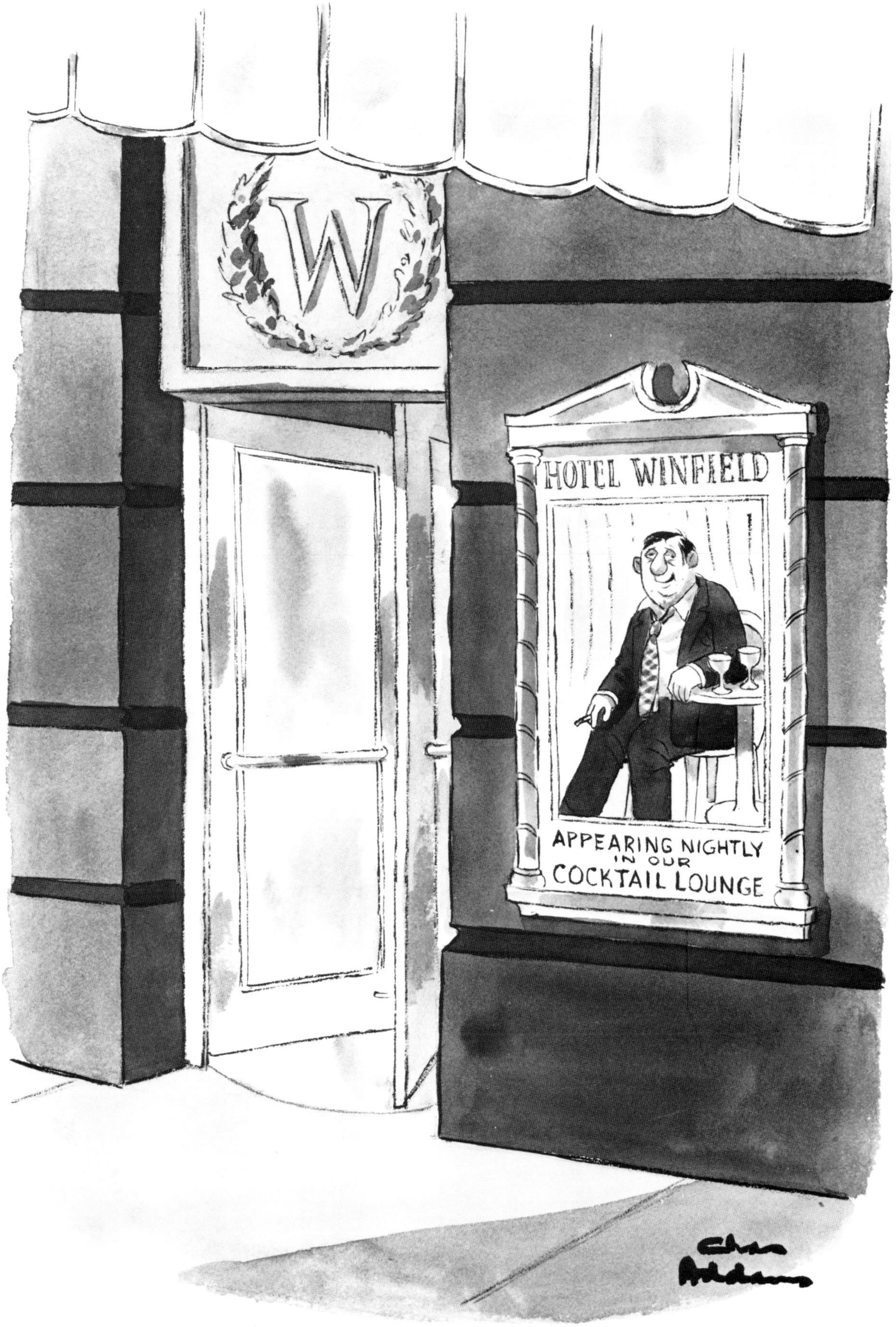
W
HOTEL WINFIELD
APPEARING NIGHTLY IN OUR
COCKTAIL LOUNGE
Chas Addams

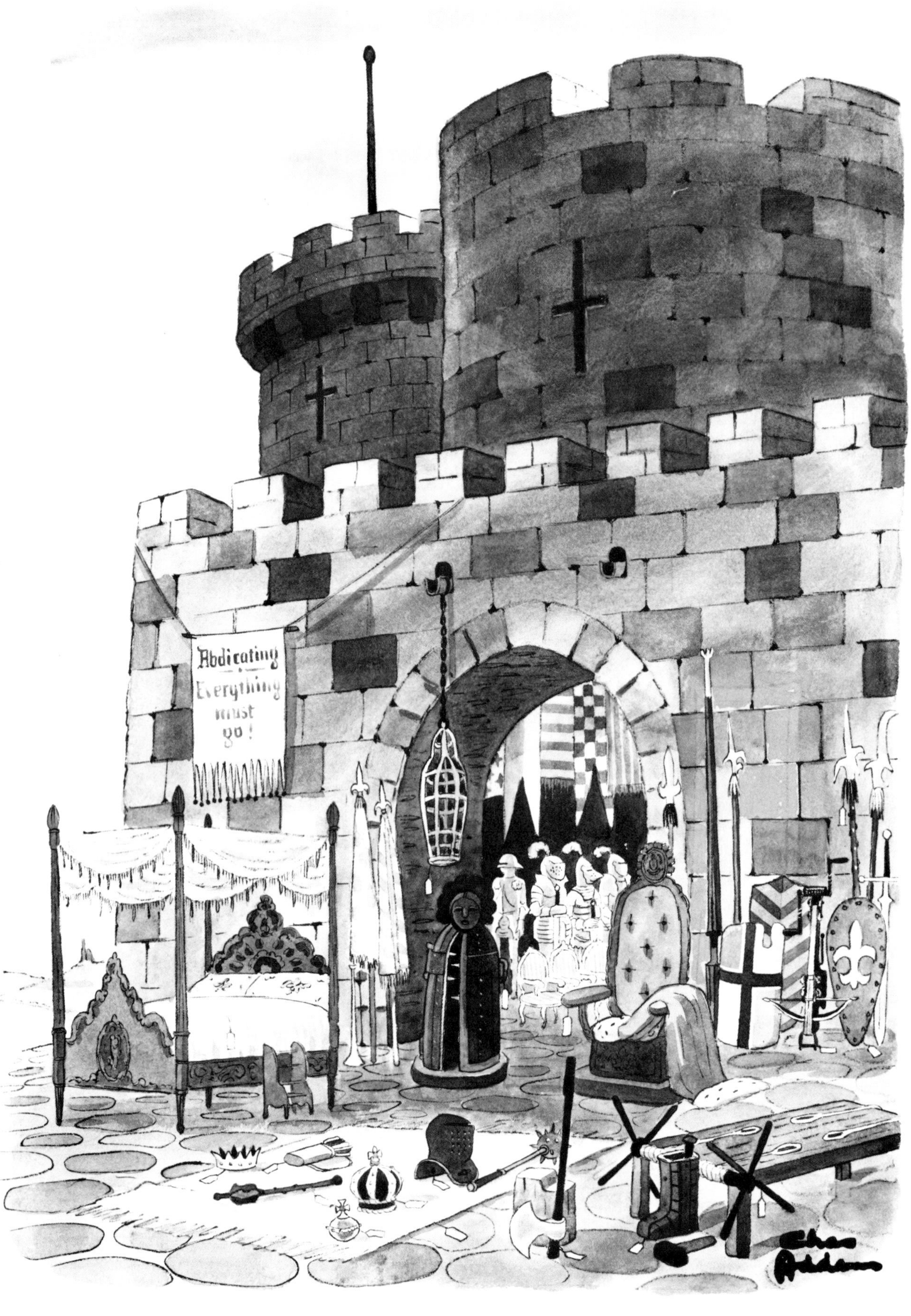
Abdicating
Everything must go!

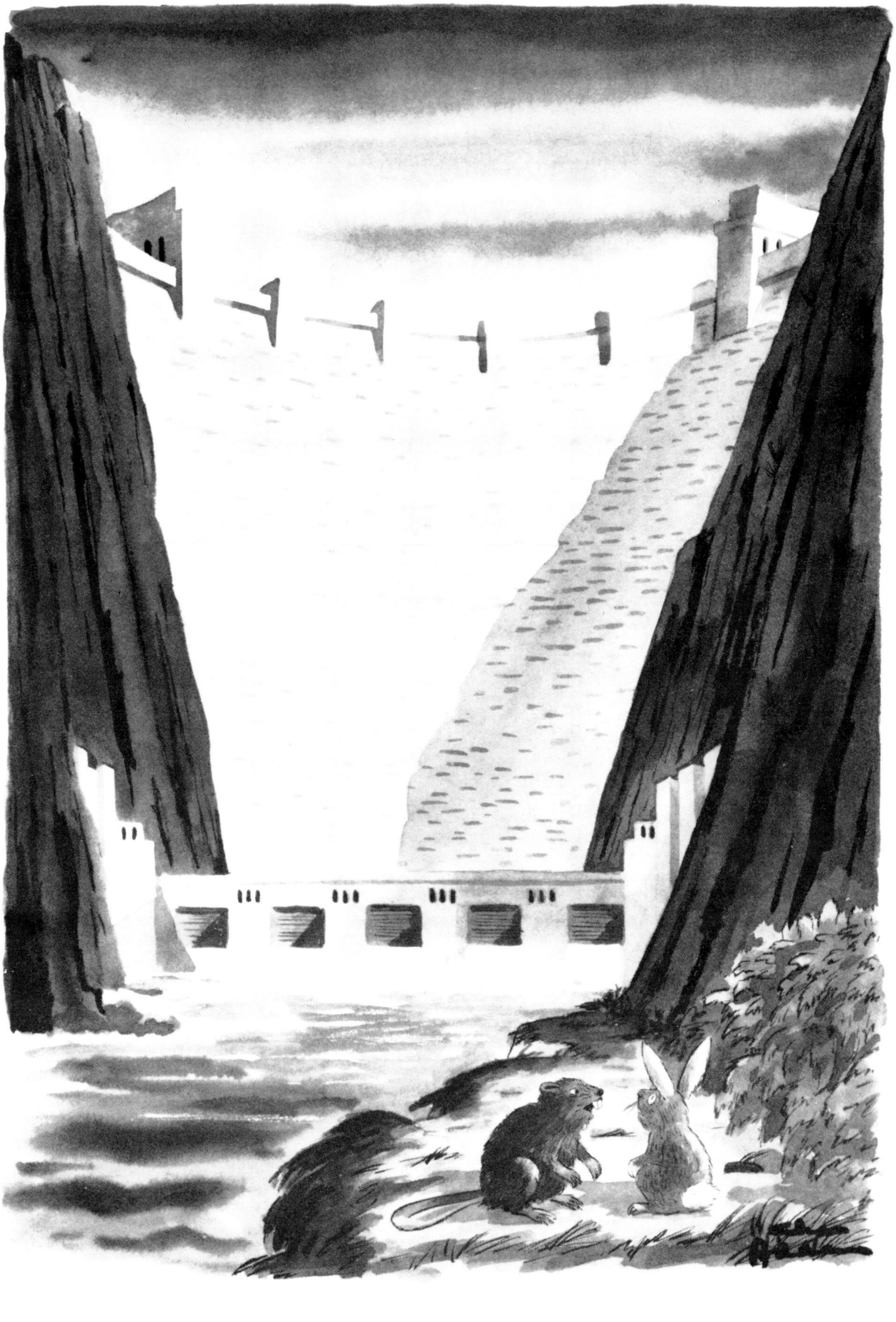

"I didn't actually build it, but it was based on my idea."

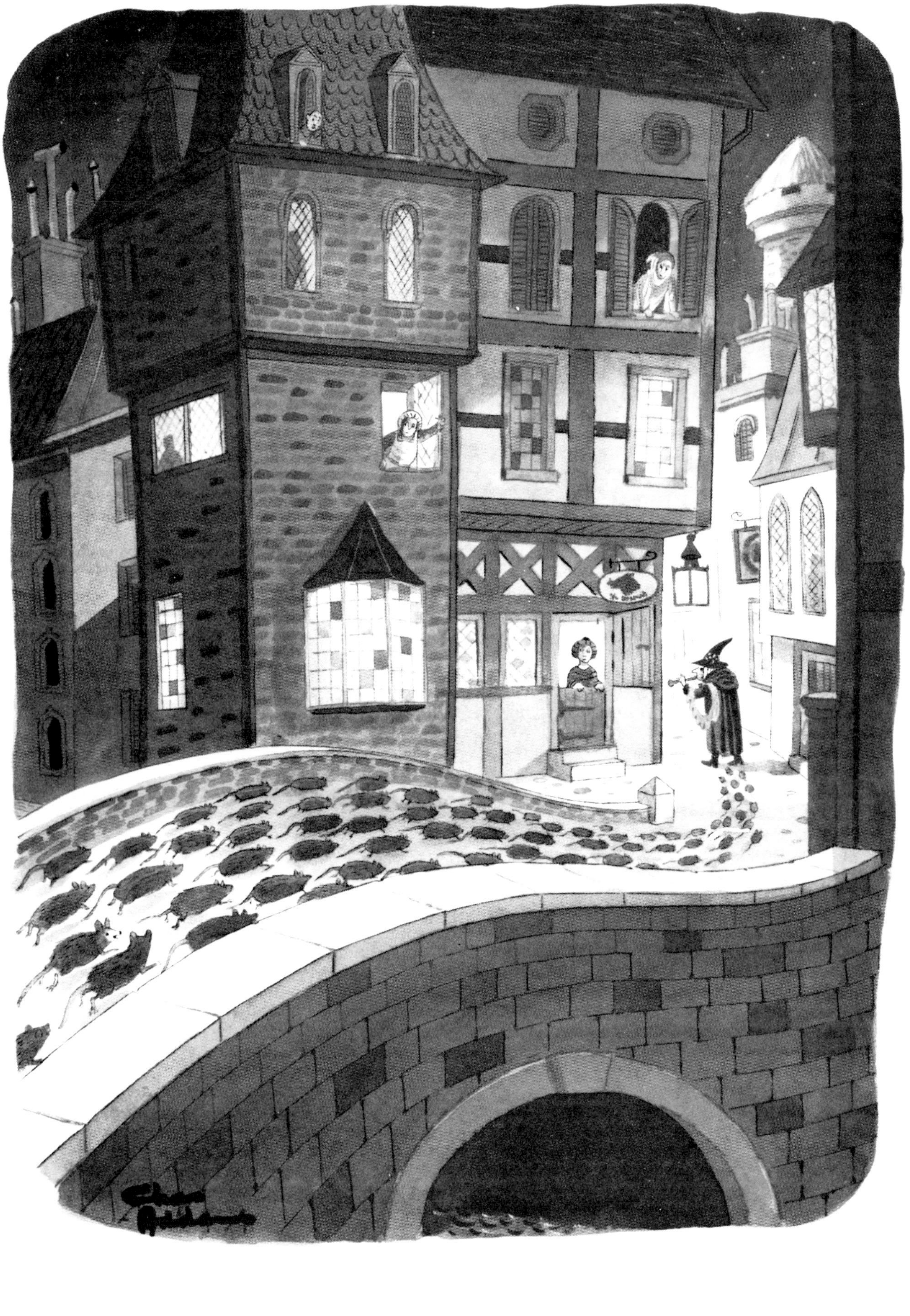

"Whoever he is, he's got charisma."

"You've changed, Irma. You used to love Sousa marches."

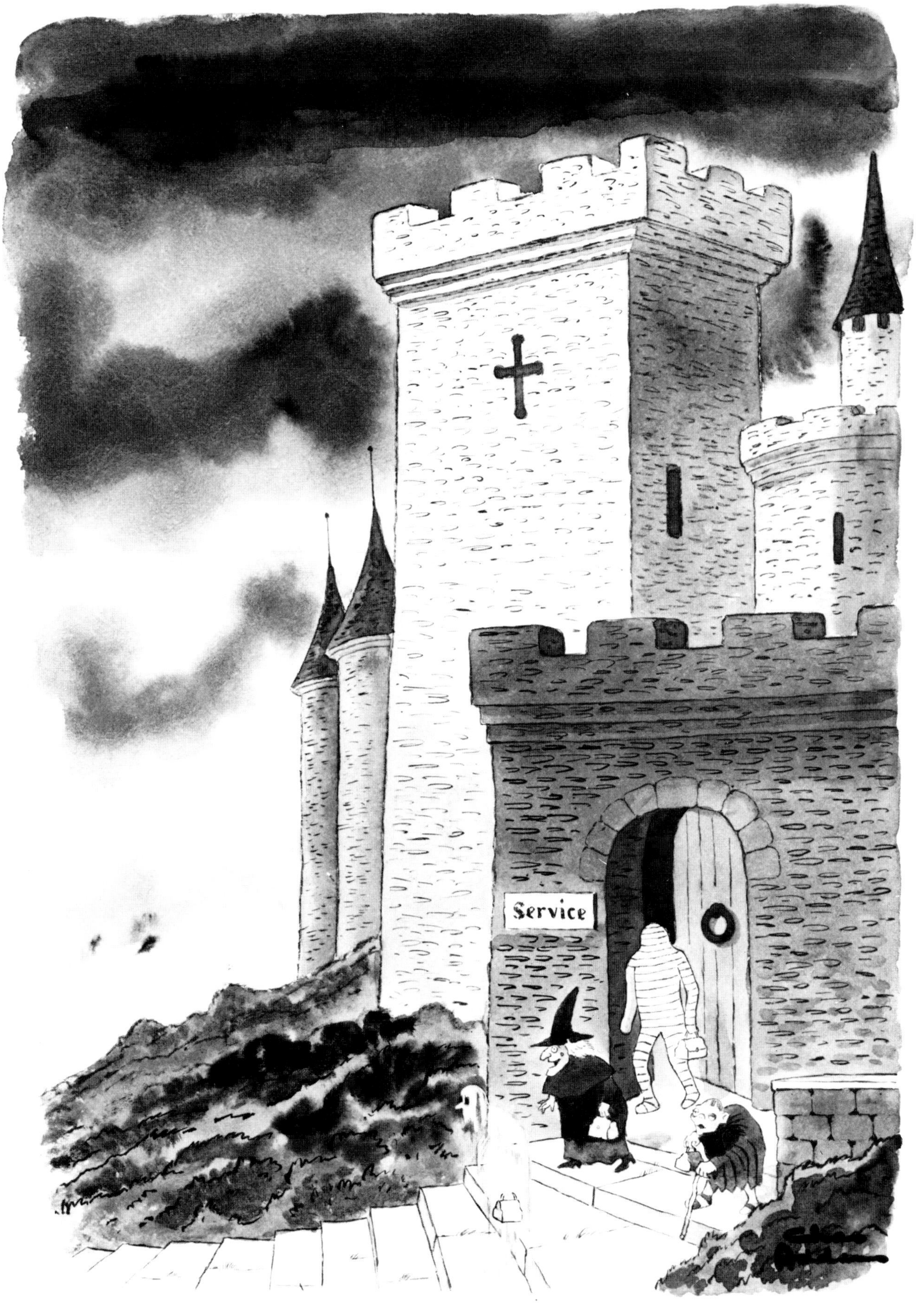
Service

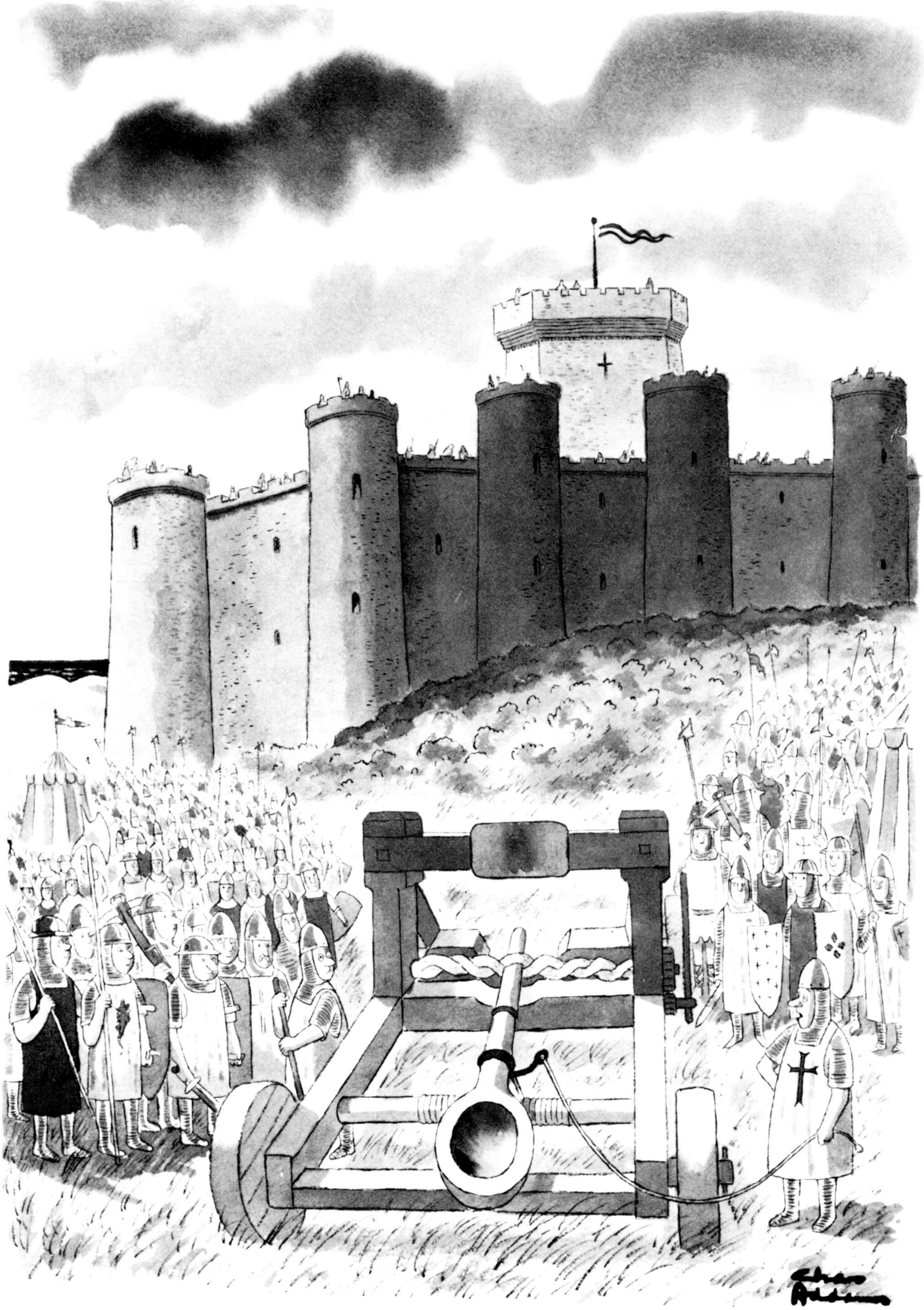

"You mean no one remembered to bring a rock?"

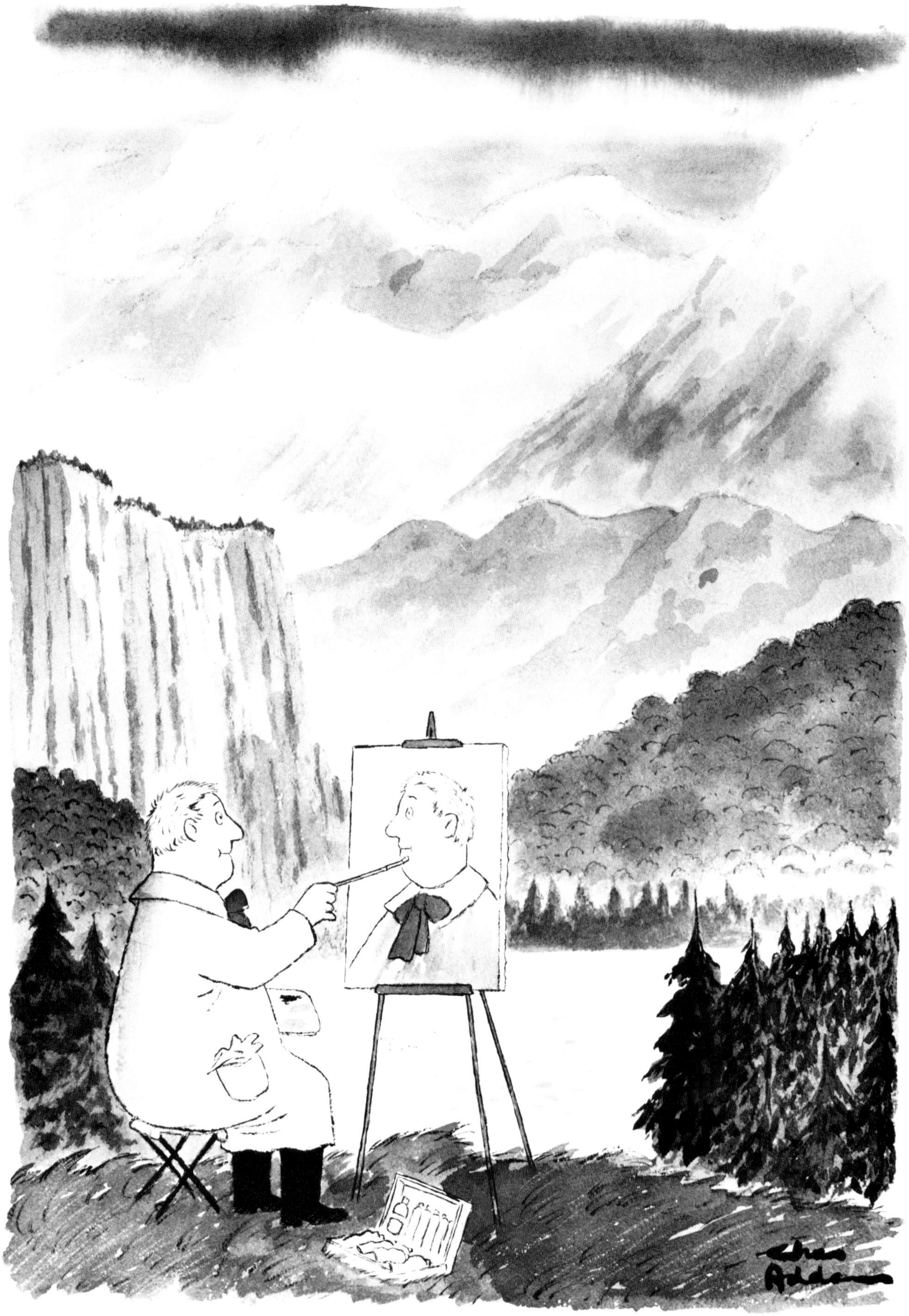
Chas Addams

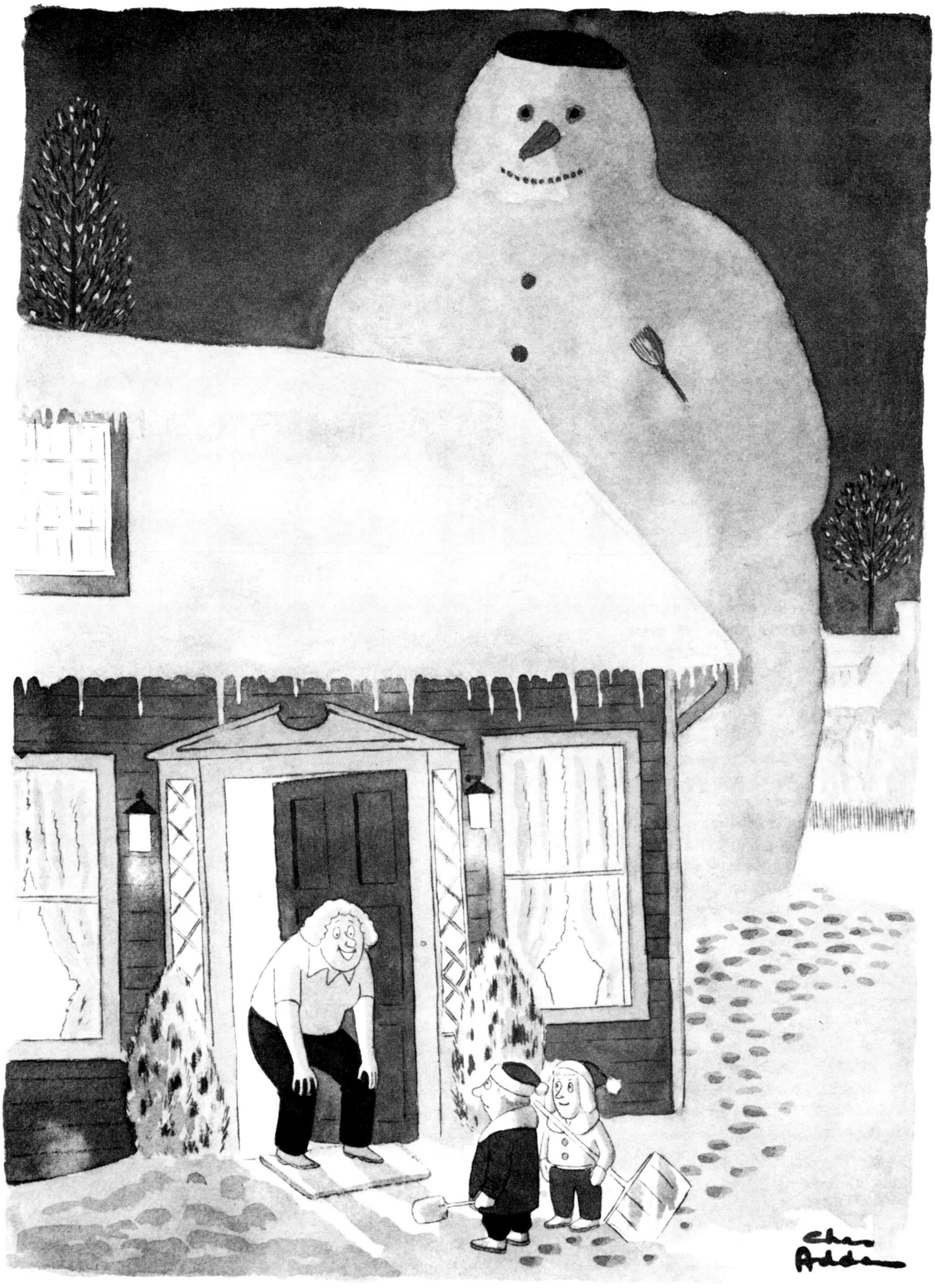

"Well, now, what have you two been doing all day?"

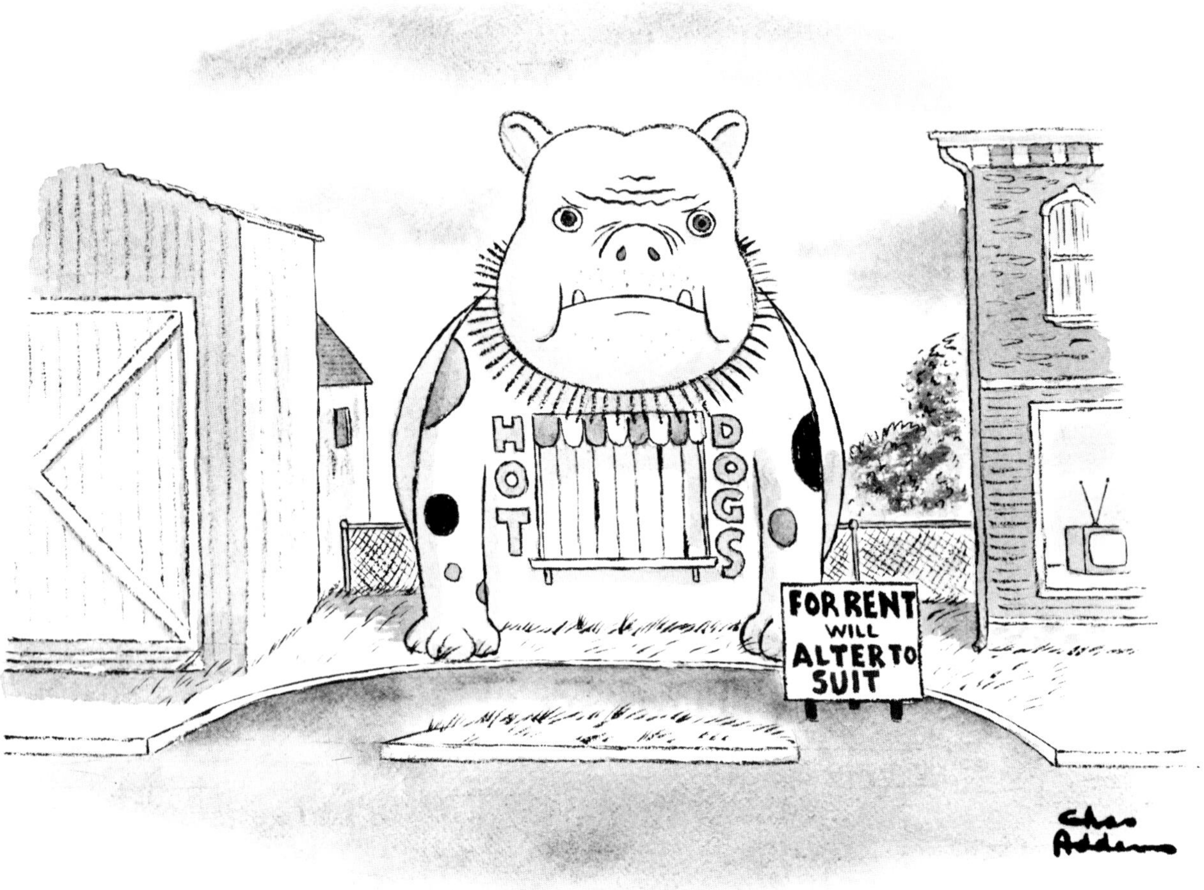
HOT
DOGS
FOR RENT
WILL
ALTER TO
SUIT
Chas Addams

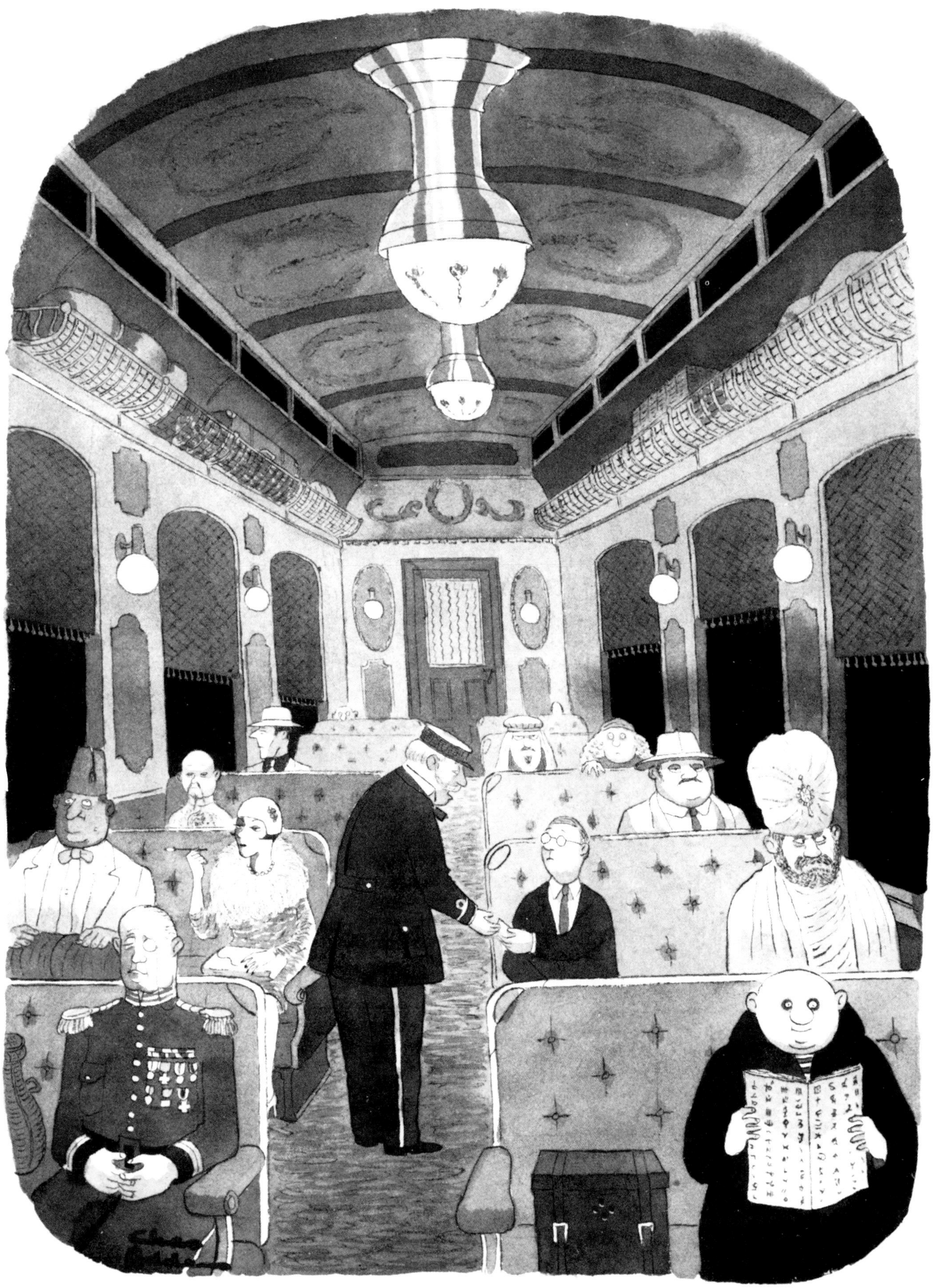

"No, this is not the 12:38 to Bridgeport."

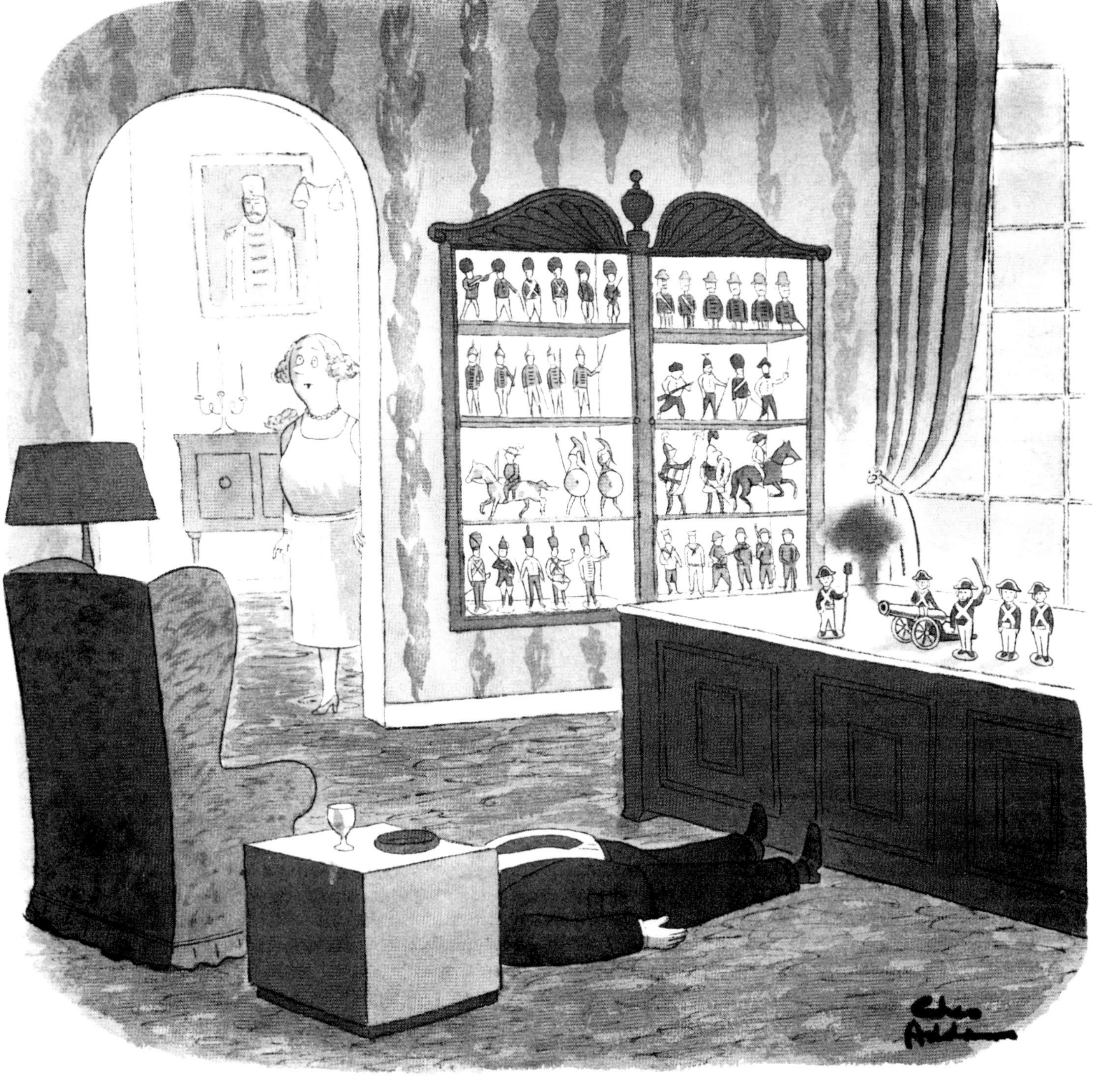

"Dinnertime, Webster."

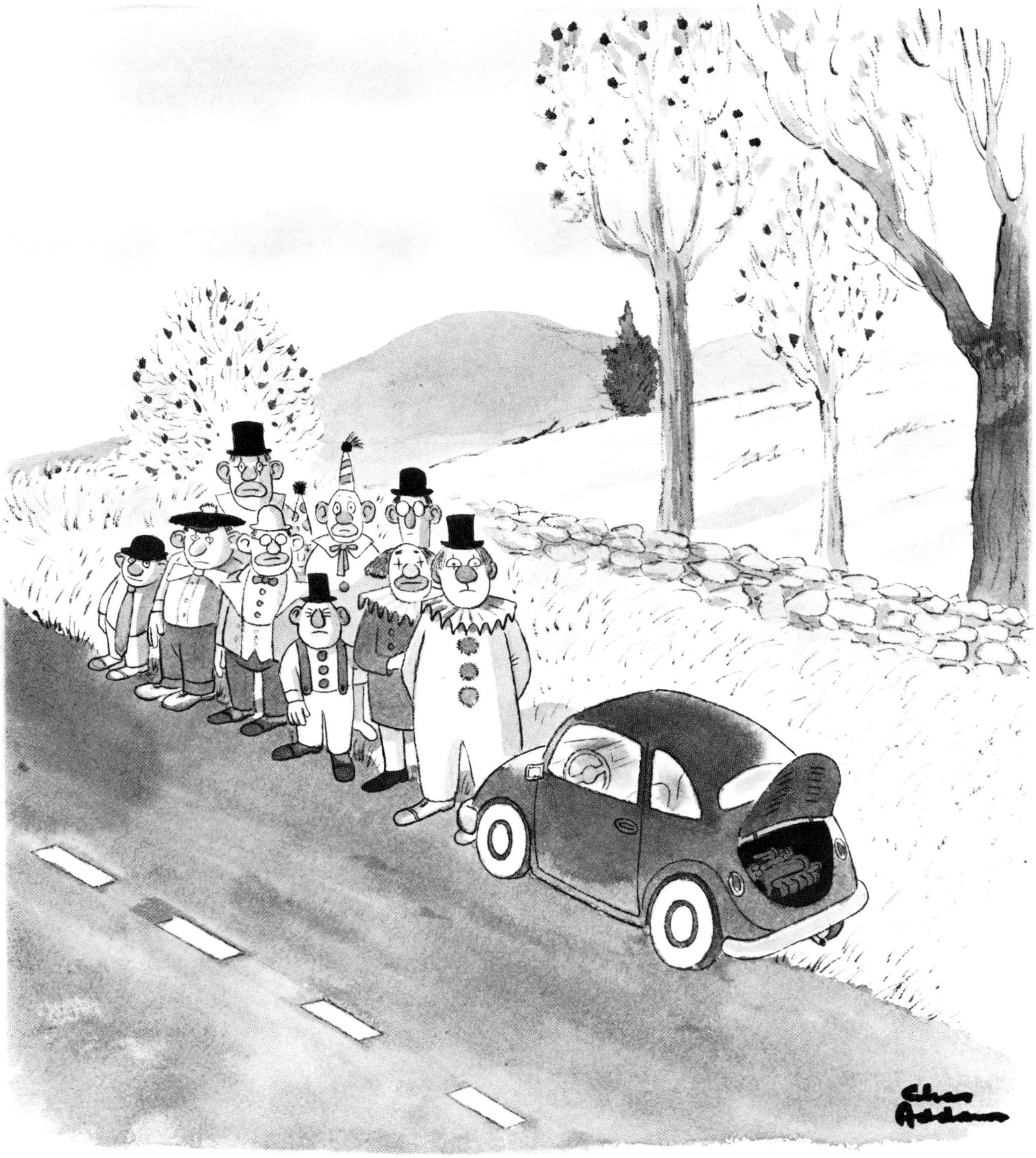
Chas Addams

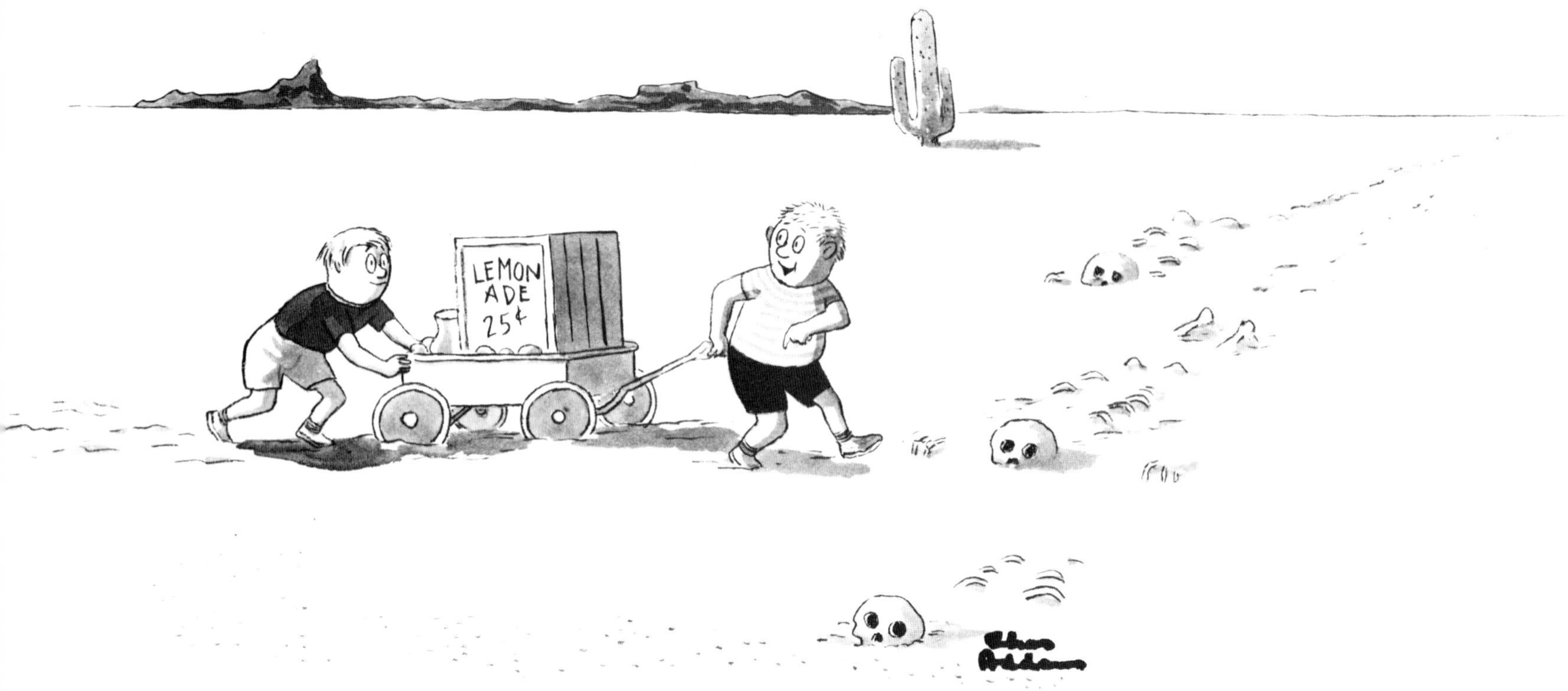
LEMON
ADE
25¢

"This looks like a good spot."

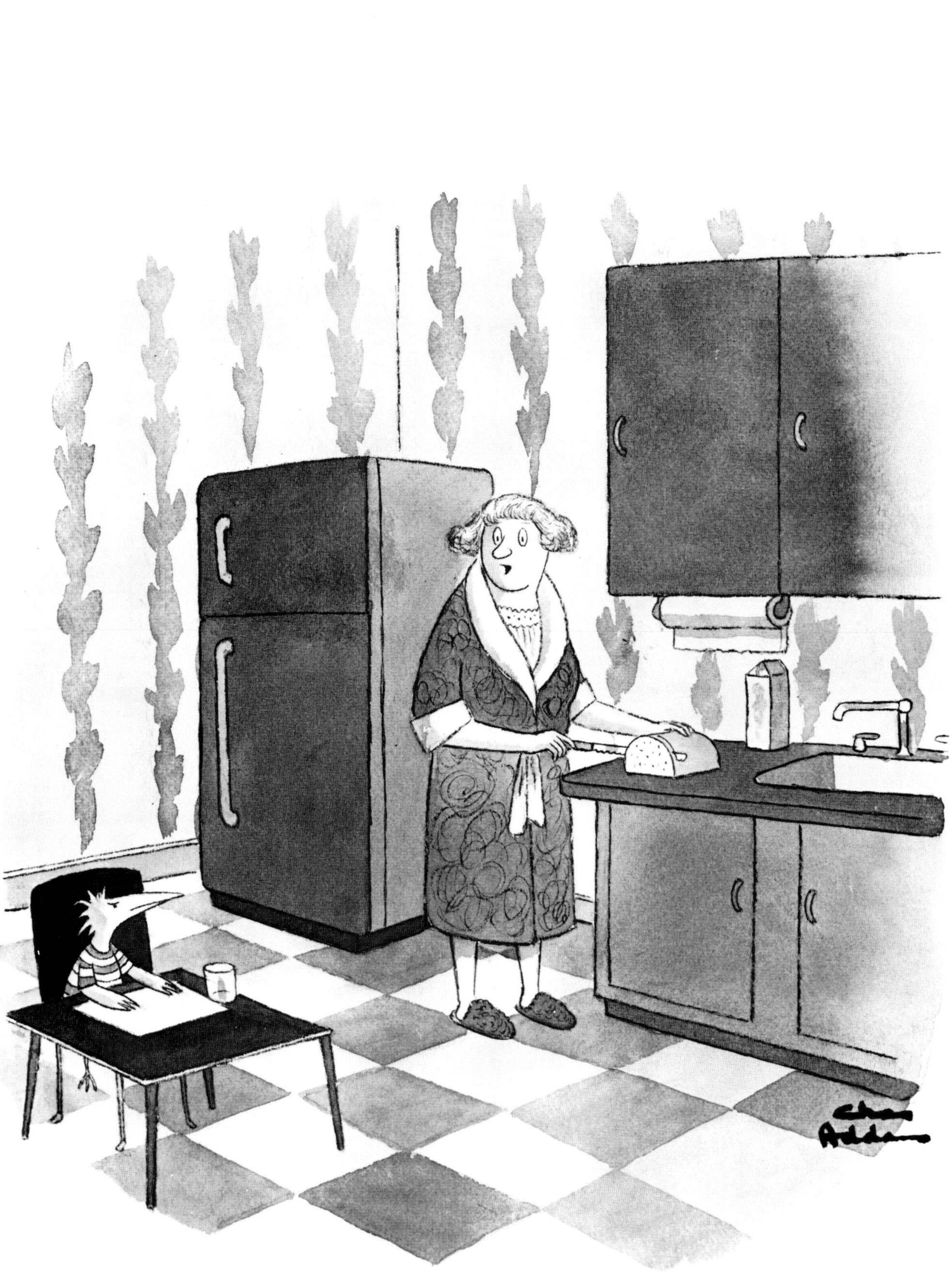
Chas Addams

"I'm telling you the truth, sweetie—the stork brought you."

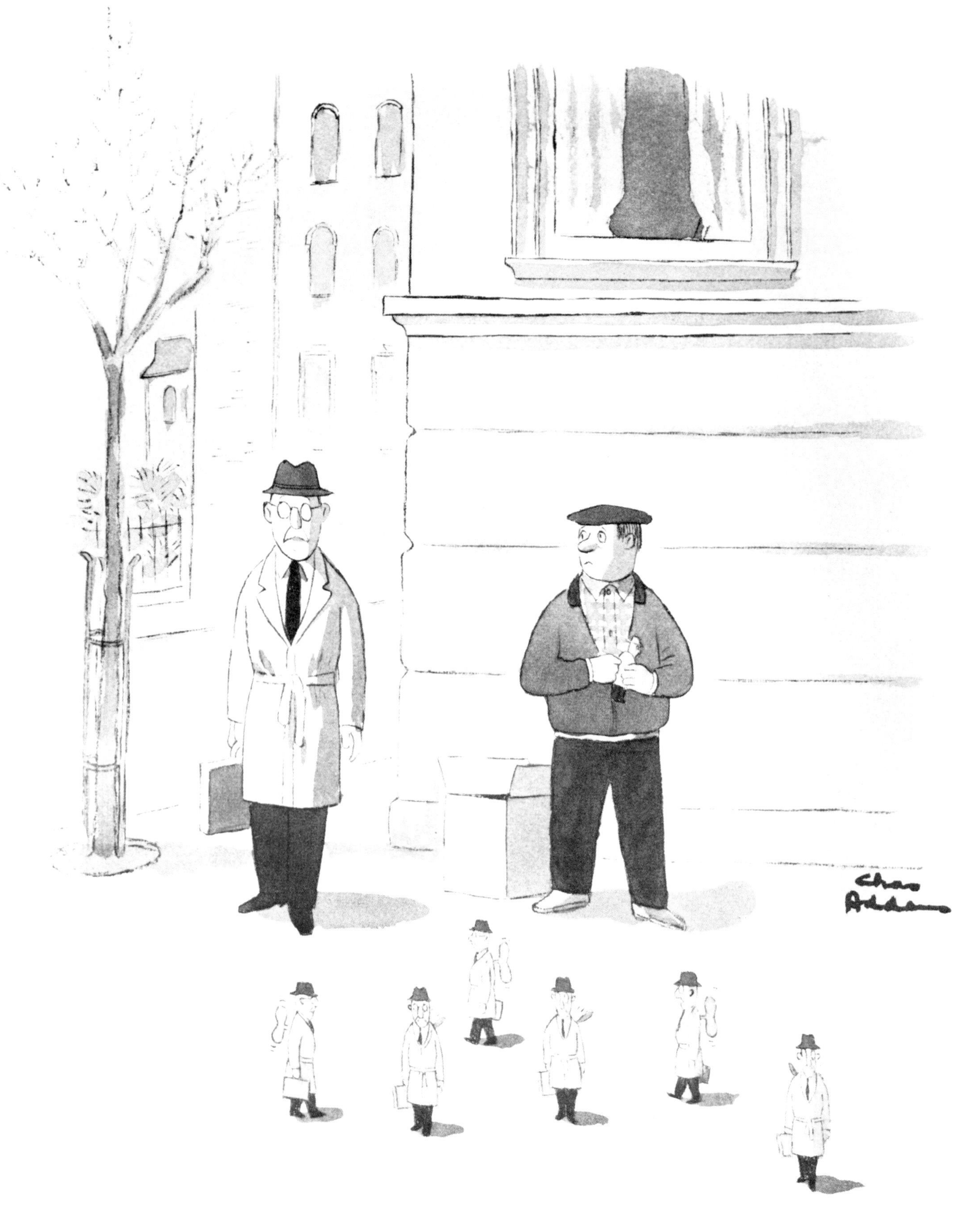
Chas Addams

"A penny for your thoughts."

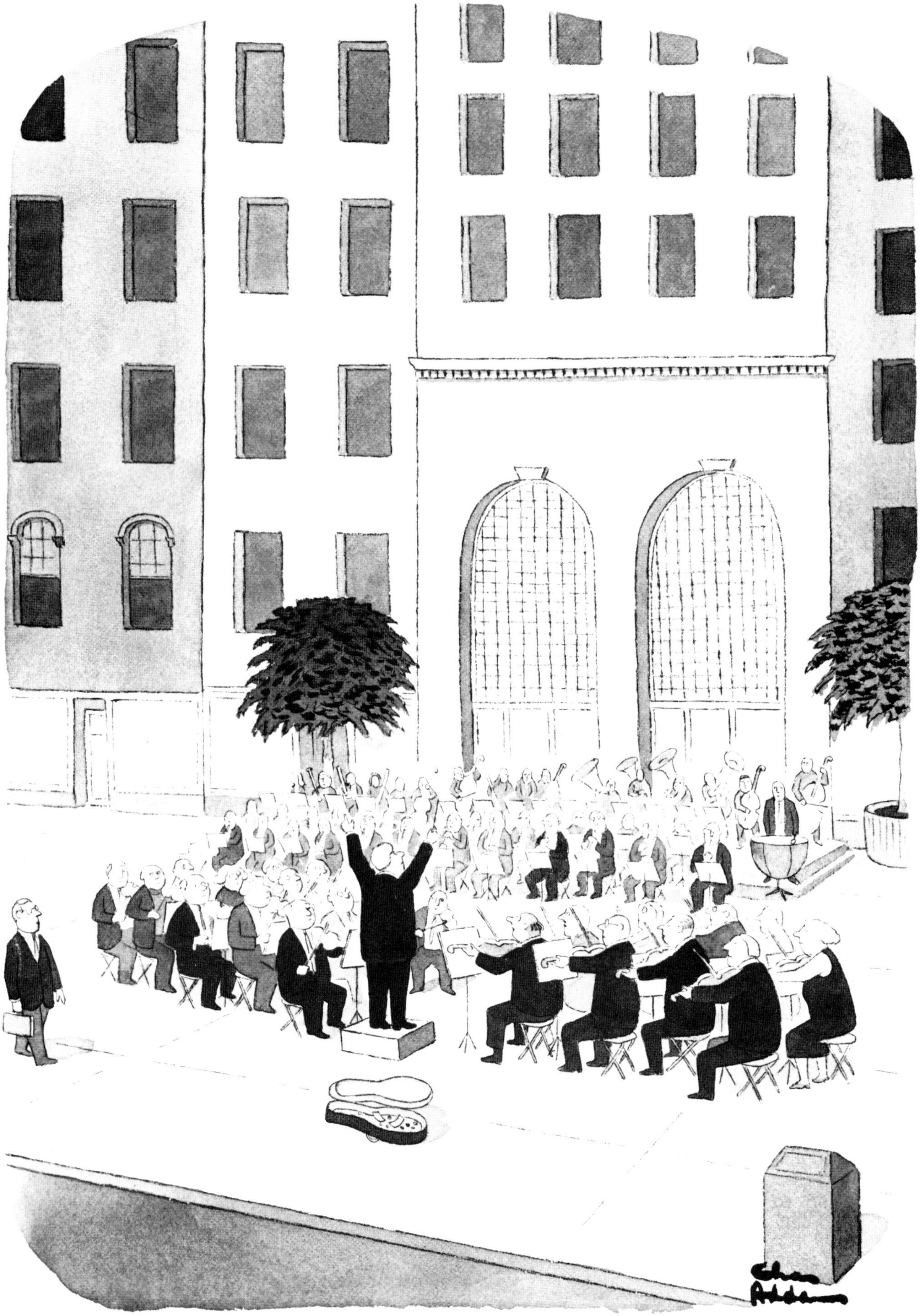

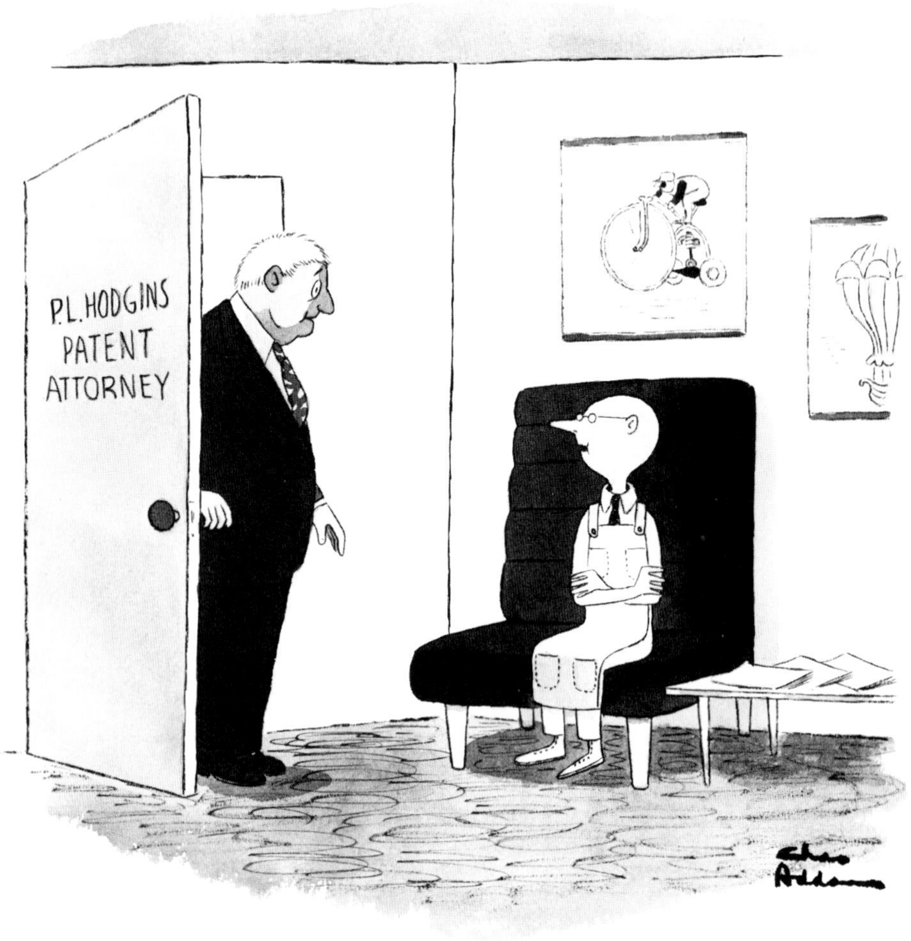
P.L. HODGINS
PATENT
ATTORNEY

"I'm the invention. The inventor should be along any moment now."

291

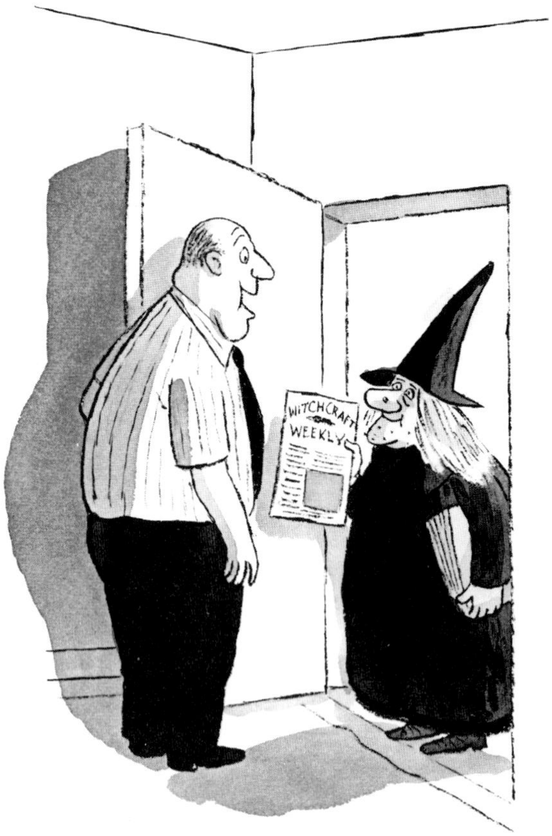

WITCHCRAFT
WEEKLY

"'Witchcraft Weekly'! You've got to be . . .

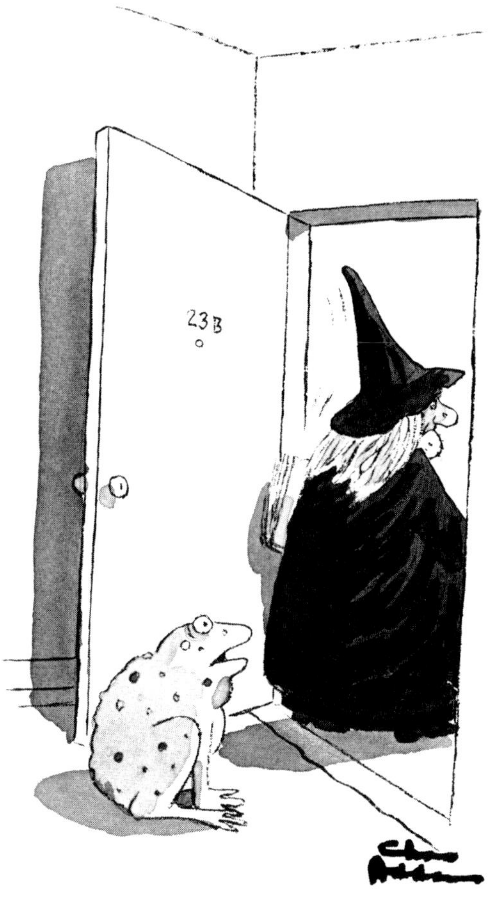

23B

. . . kidding."

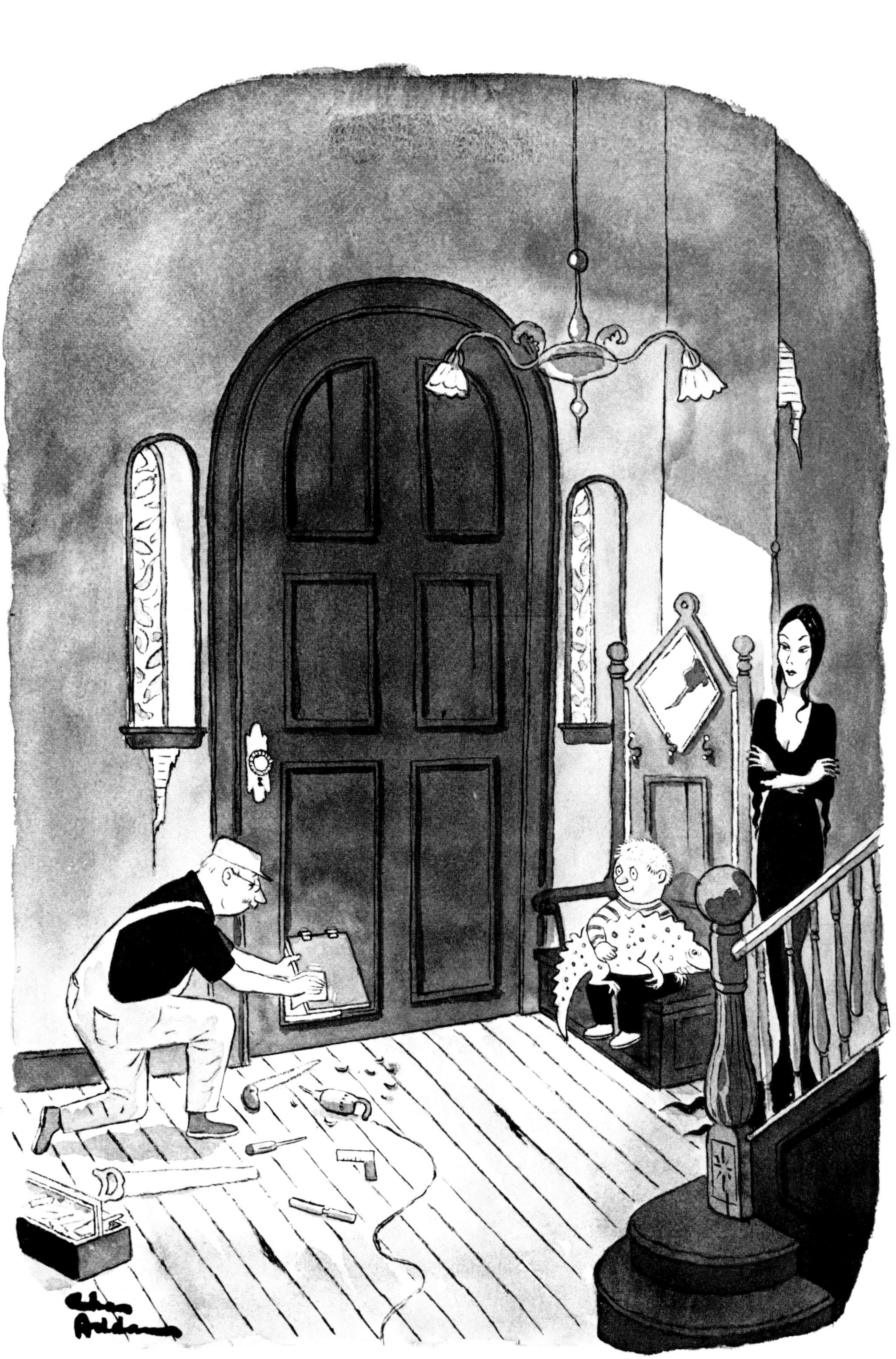

"Please, let's not talk about your day."

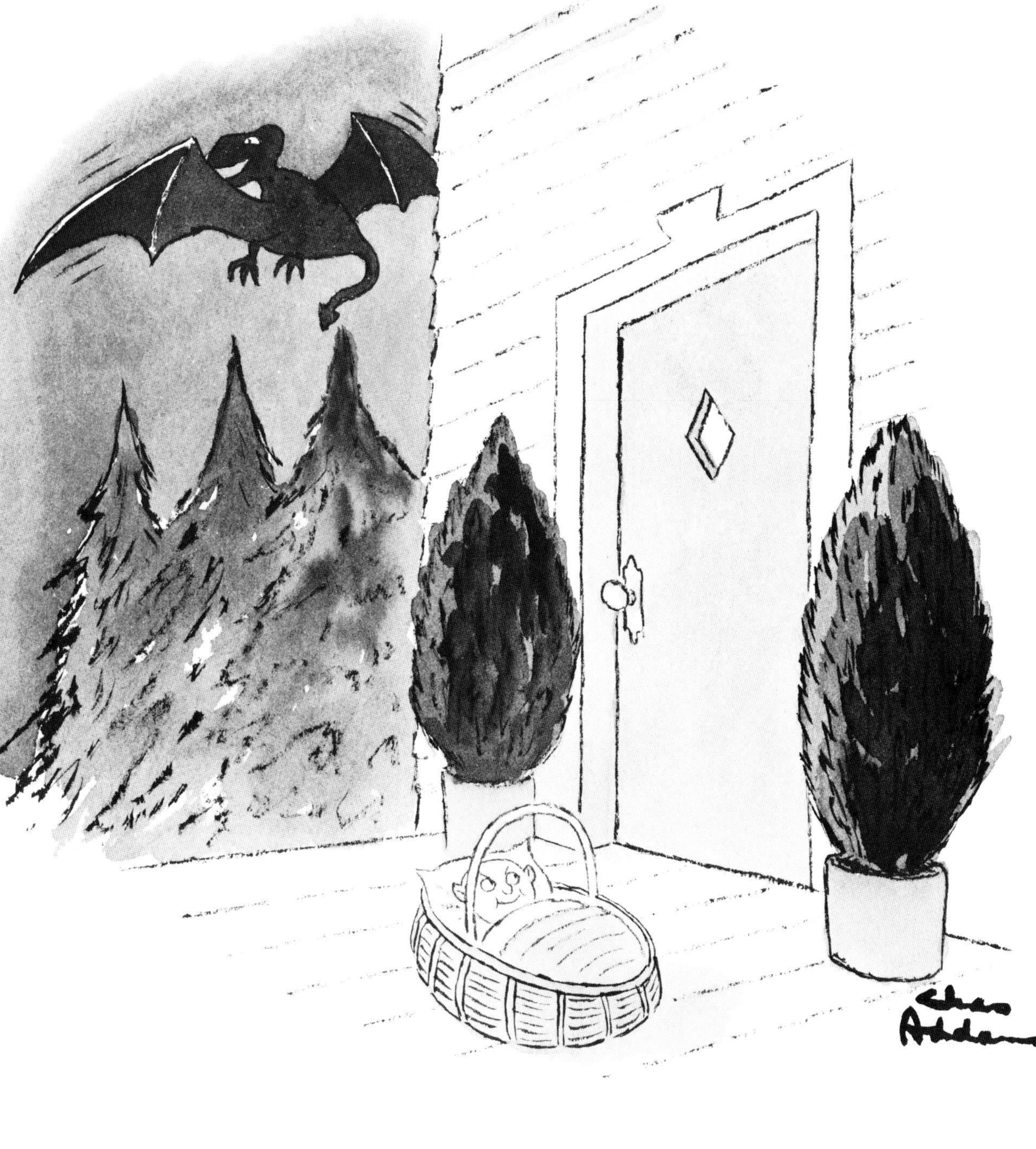
Chas Addams

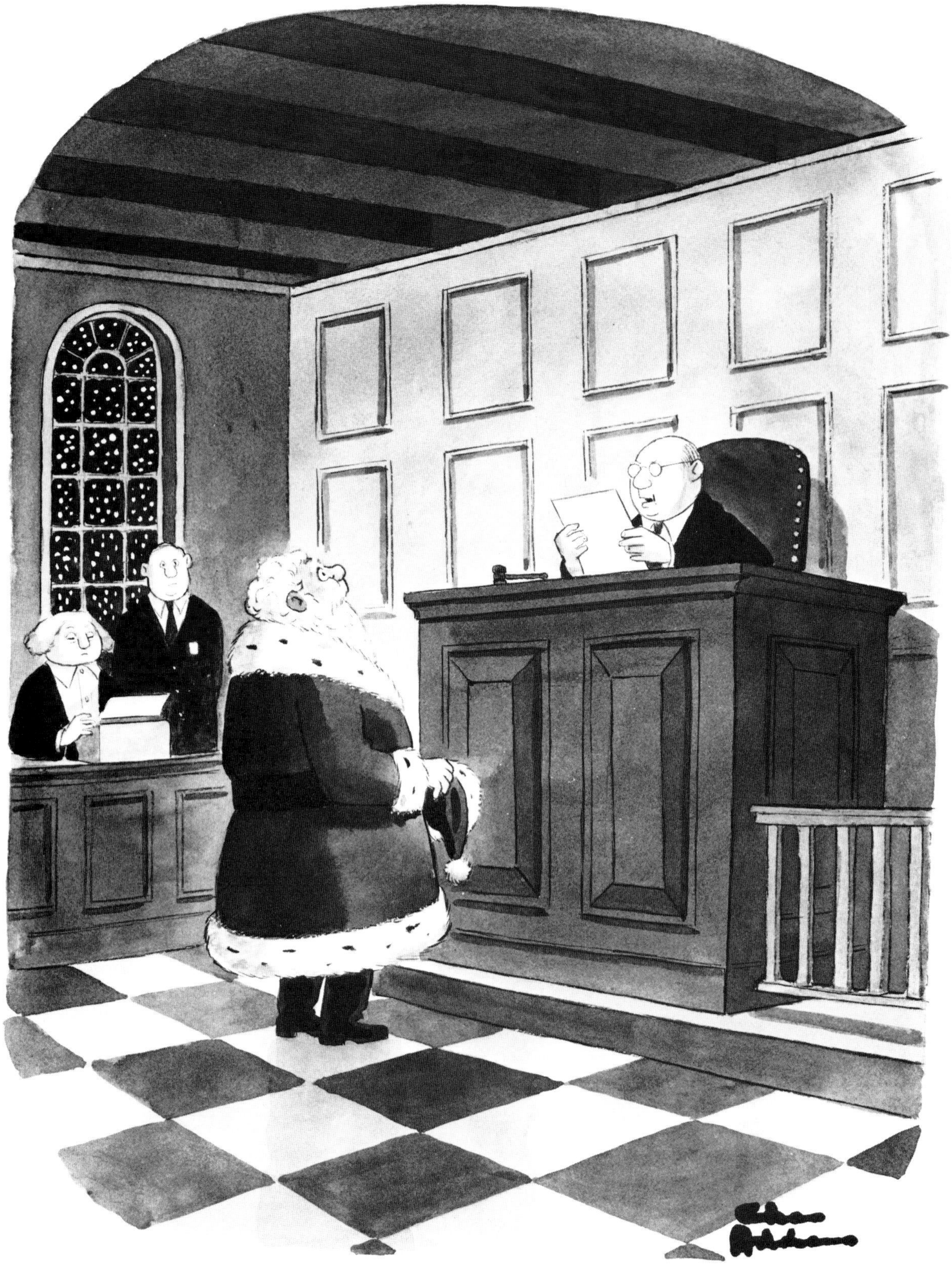

". . . flying low over housetops, landing on a roof, illegal entry into a residence via chimney, operating a sleigh without a license, keeping wild reindeer confined in harness, and creating a disturbance with loud laughter."

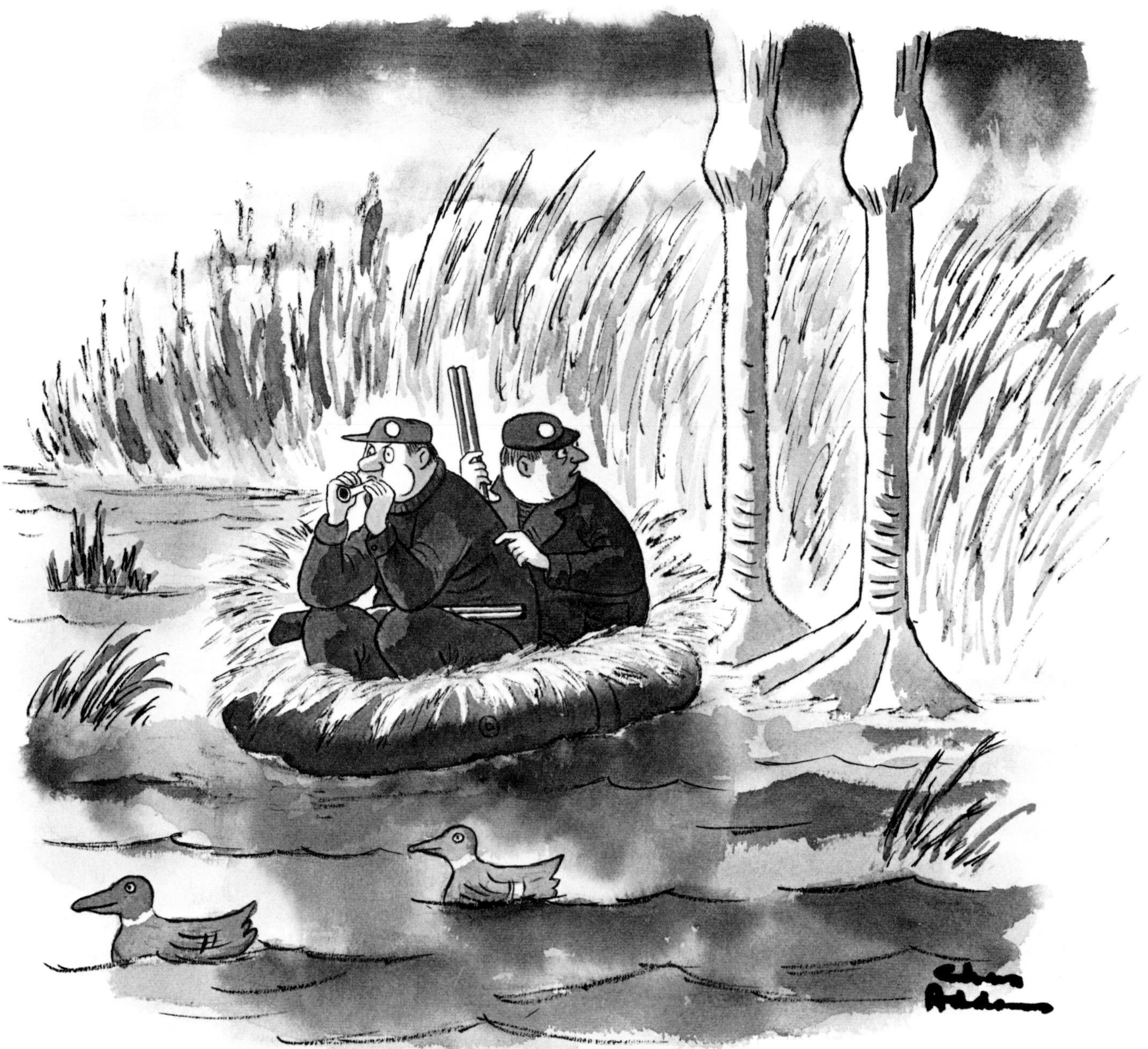
Chas Addams

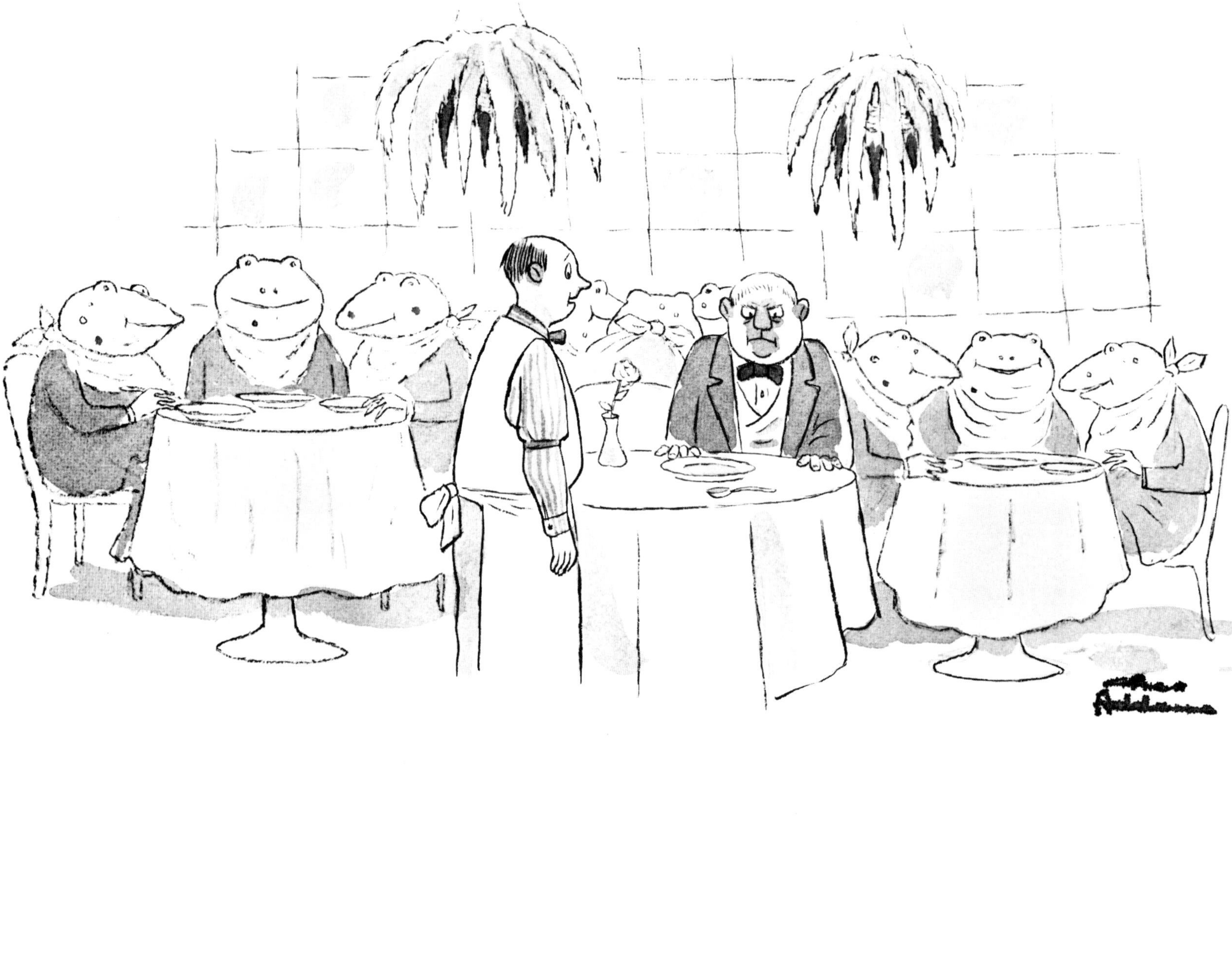

"Nobody else has complained about flies in the soup."

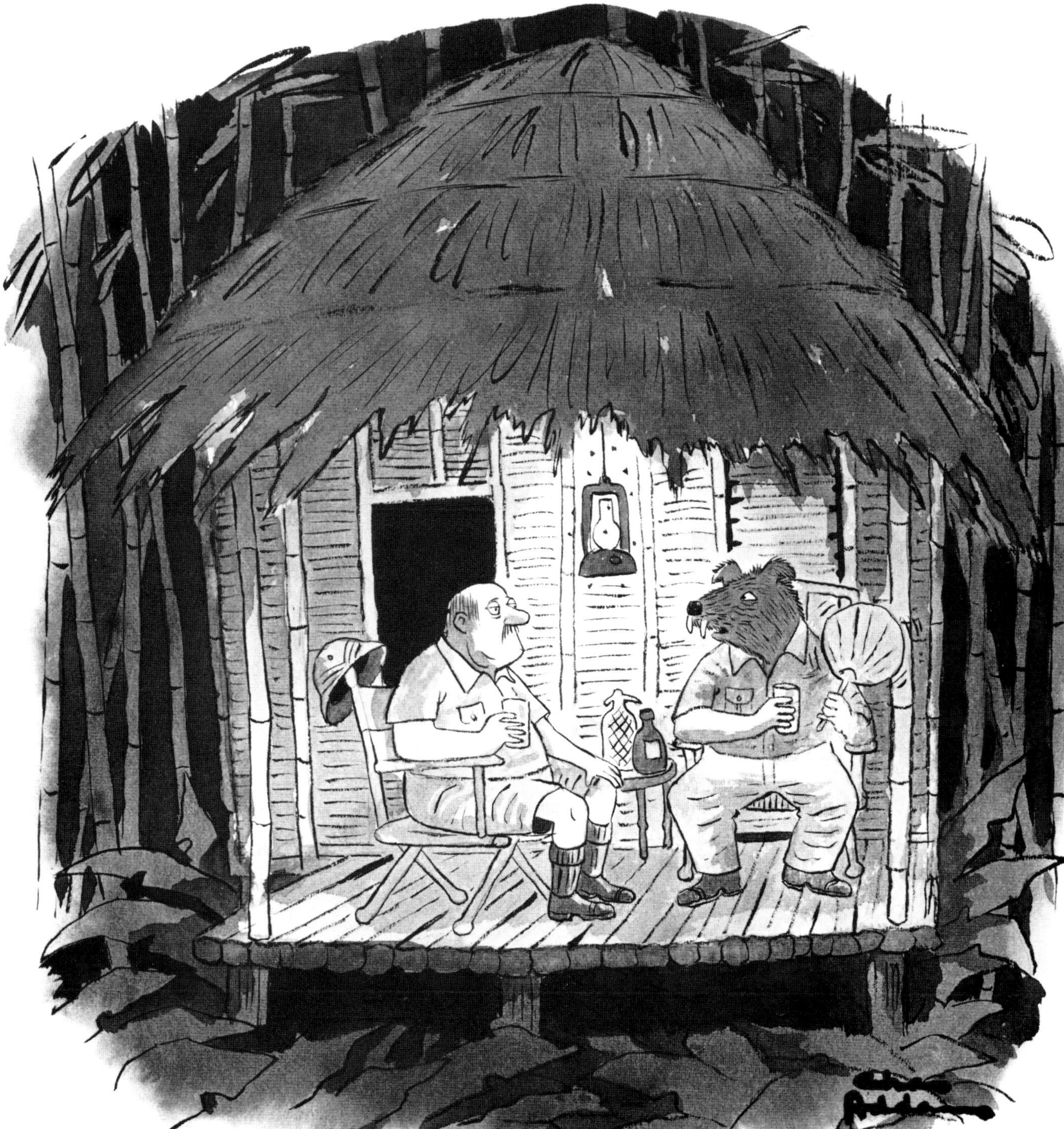

"I learned one thing from the experience. Never call a witch doctor a clever illusionist."

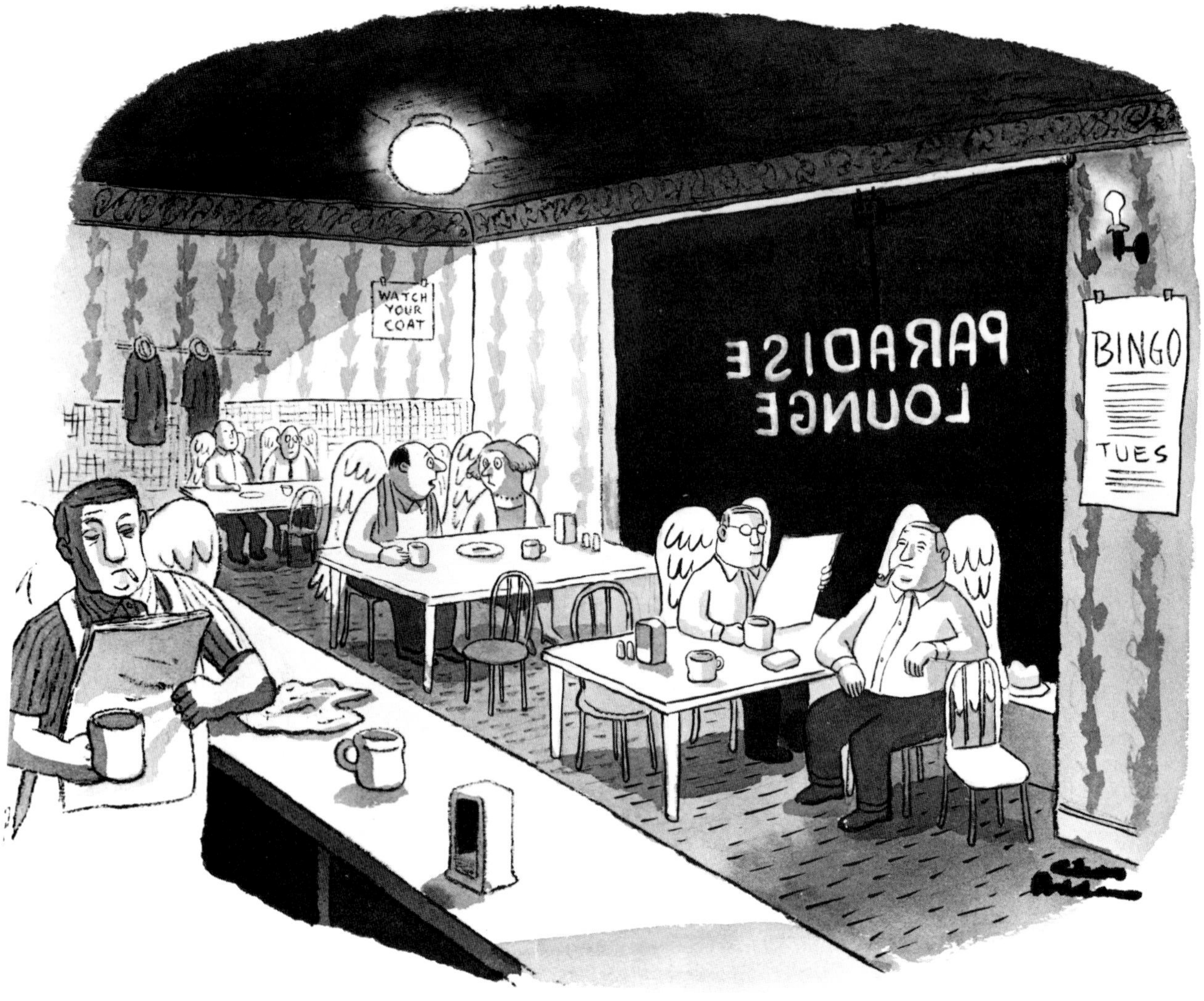
WATCH YOUR COAT
PARADISE LOUNGE
BINGO
TUES

"It's O.K., I guess, but somehow I expected more."

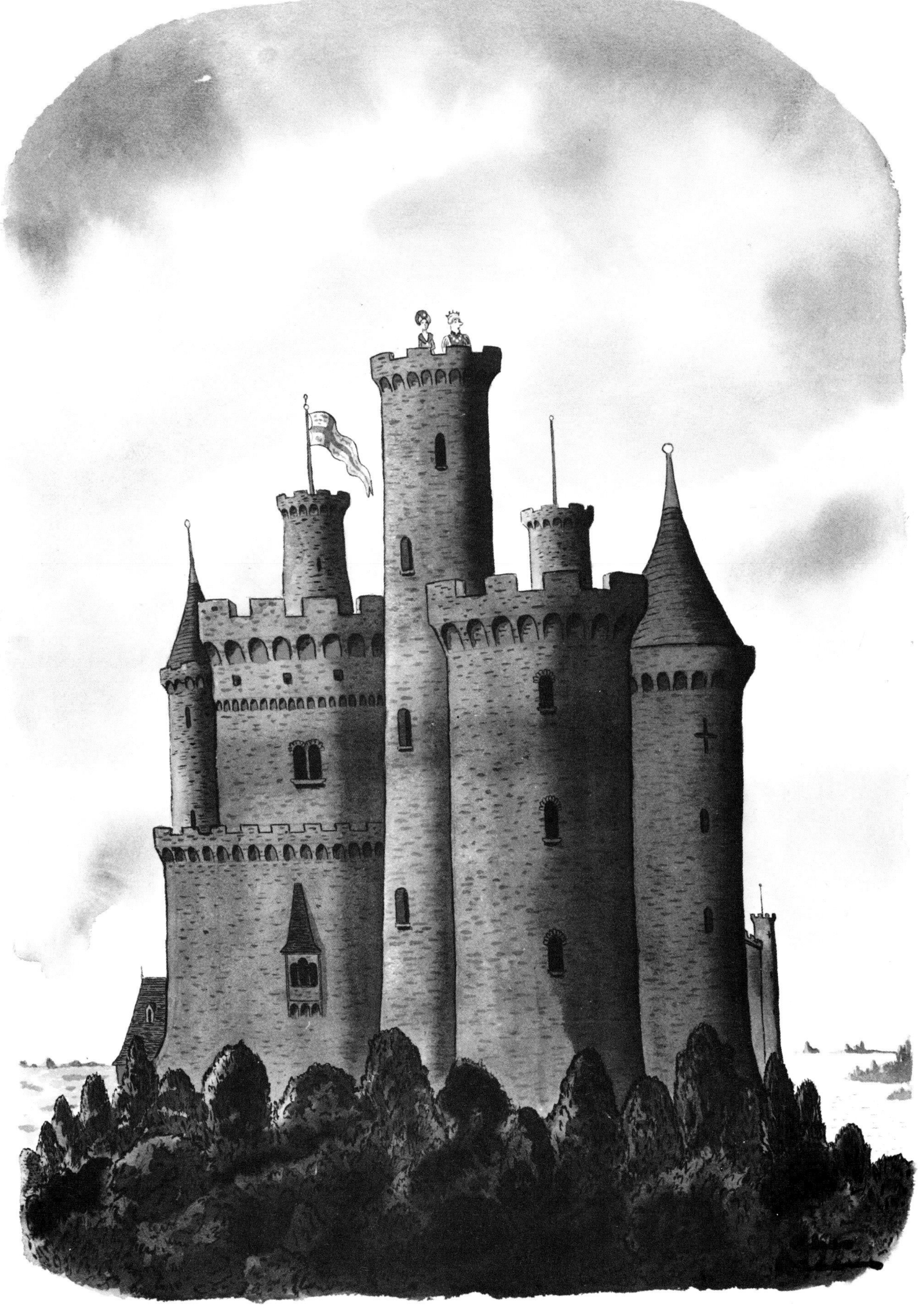

"To think we went to all that trouble and not a single foe showed up."

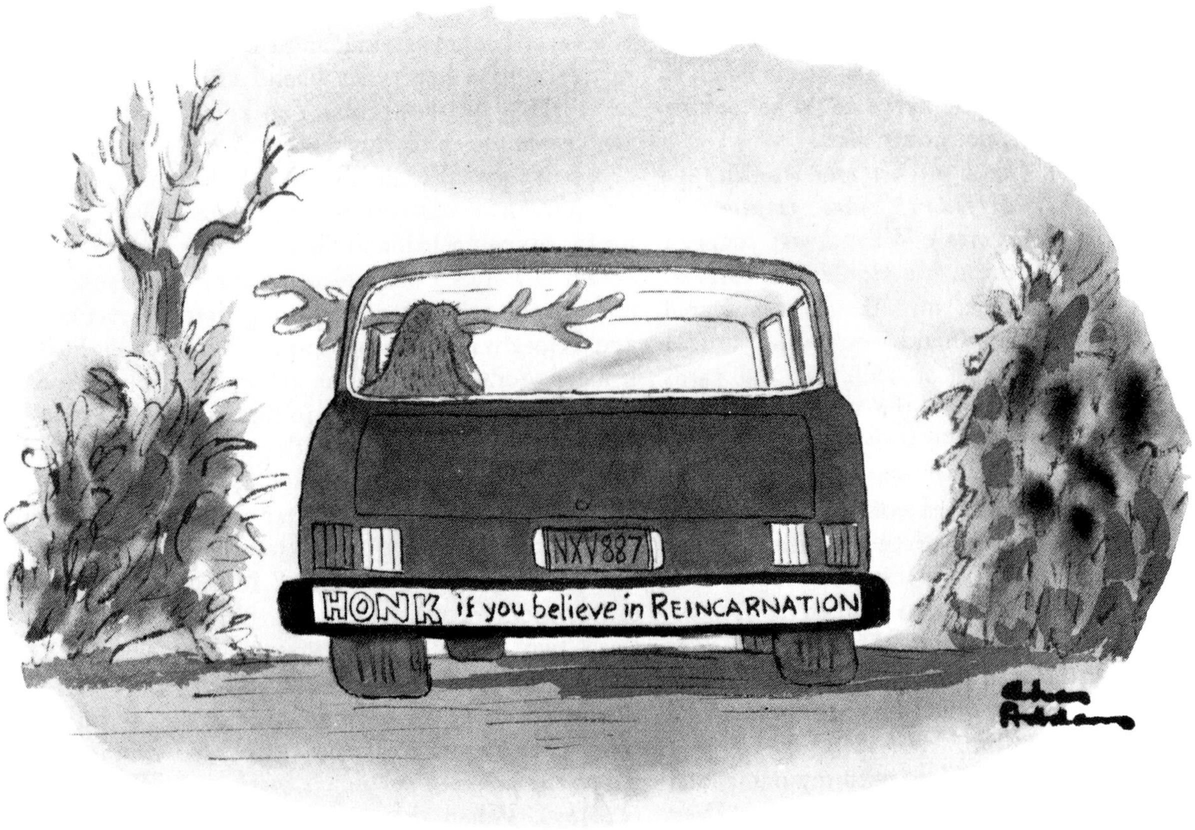
NXV887
HONK if you believe in REINCARNATION

Illustrations

Unless otherwise specified, the drawings were first published in *The New Yorker*.

76 January 10, 1948
77 December 27, 1947
78 January 31, 1948
79 February 8, 1947
80 March 27, 1948
81 May 29, 1948
82 August 28, 1948
83 June 26, 1948
84 November 20, 1948
85 January 22, 1949
86 January 29, 1949
87 March 12, 1949
88 May 14, 1949
89 April 16, 1949
90 June 11, 1949
91 August 27, 1949
92 September 24, 1949
93 December 23, 1949
94 December 10, 1949
95 December 24, 1949
96 March 4, 1950
97 February 25, 1950
98 May 13, 1950
99 July 15, 1950
100 June 24, 1950
101 April 22, 1950
102 July 1, 1950
103 August 19, 1950
104 January 6, 1951
105 December 2, 1950
106 February 3, 1951
107 February 17, 1951
108 March 10, 1951
109 July 28, 1951
110 April 28, 1951
111 September 29, 1951
112 March 1, 1952
113 January 19, 1952
114 April 12, 1952
115 May 3, 1952
116 June 7, 1952
117 November 22, 1952
118 December 13, 1952
119 November 1, 1952
120 December 27, 1952
121 April 18, 1953

122 May 16, 1953
123 June 13, 1953
124 May 2, 1953
125 March 20, 1954
126 January 16, 1954
127 July 10, 1954
128 May 29, 1954
129 August 21, 1954
130 October 16, 1954
131 September 4, 1954
132 November 6, 1954
133 January 8, 1955
134 February 17, 1955
135 April 2, 1955
136 October 8, 1955
137 June 18, 1955
138 McClure Syndicate,
     December 4, 1955
139 McClure Syndicate,
     October 9, 1955
140 February 25, 1956
141 January 28, 1956
142 February 18, 1956
143 February 18, 1956
144 March 10, 1956
145 April 21, 1956
146 *Monster Rally*, 1950
147 March 24, 1956
148 McClure Syndicate,
     1956
149 May 14, 1955
150 October 20, 1956
151 November 10, 1956
152 McClure Syndicate,
     December 23, 1956
153 McClure Syndicate,
     November 11, 1956
154 February 2, 1957
     (cover)
155 July 17, 1954 (cover)
156 February 9, 1957
157 December 15, 1956
158 February 23, 1957
159 May 25, 1957
160 April 27, 1957
161 November 1, 1958

162 September 7, 1957
163 July 27, 1957
164 February 22, 1958
165 February 8, 1958
166 August 9, 1958
167 May 10, 1958
168 May 17, 1958
169 November 22, 1958
170 April 18, 1959
171 January 3, 1959
172 May 9, 1959
173 March 14, 1959
174 June 27, 1959
175 October 17, 1959
176 *The Groaning Board*,
     1964
177 November 21, 1959
178 April 30, 1960
179 December 19, 1959
180 October 29, 1960
181 November 25, 1961
182 January 28, 1961
183 November 24, 1962
184 February 23, 1963
185 *My Crowd*, 1970
186 December 14, 1963
187 May 25, 1963
188 April 25, 1964
189 December 30, 1967
190 February 20, 1965
191 June 13, 1964
192 December 7, 1968
193 November 7, 1964
194 October 11, 1969
195 October 7, 1967
196 April 27, 1963
197 February 27, 1965
198 November 13, 1971
199 August 29, 1970
200 March 11, 1972
201 April 15, 1972
202 April 21, 1973
203 December 23, 1972
204 July 2, 1973
205 October 29, 1973
206 July 8, 1974

Covers for *The New Yorker*

Following page 82

Following page 162

Following page 242

A NOTE ON THE TYPE

This book was set in a typeface called Méridien, a classic roman designed by
Adrian Frutiger for the French type foundry Deberny et Peignot in 1957.
Adrian Frutiger was born in Interlaken, Switzerland, in 1928, and studied
type design there and at the Kunstgewerbeschule in Zurich. In 1953 he
moved to Paris, where he joined Deberny et Peignot as a member of the
design staff. Méridien, as well as his other typeface of world renown,
Univers, was created for the Lumitype photo-set machine.

Composed by The Sarabande Press, New York, New York

Printed and bound by Arcata Graphics, Kingsport, Tennessee

Designed by Iris Weinstein